ISBN 978-0-282-59578-4
PIBN 10858311

Forgotten Books is a registered trademark of FB &c Ltd.
Copyright © 2018 FB &c Ltd.
FB &c Ltd, Dalton House, 60 Windsor Avenue, London, SW19 2RR.
Company number 08720141. Registered in England and Wales.

For support please visit www.forgottenbooks.com

1 MONTH OF
FREE
READING

at
www.ForgottenBooks.com

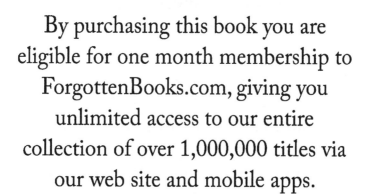

By purchasing this book you are
eligible for one month membership to
ForgottenBooks.com, giving you
unlimited access to our entire
collection of over 1,000,000 titles via
our web site and mobile apps.

To claim your free month visit:
www.forgottenbooks.com/free858311

English
Français
Deutsche
Italiano
Español
Português

www.forgottenbooks.com

Mythology Photography **Fiction**
Fishing Christianity **Art** Cooking
Essays Buddhism Freemasonry
Medicine **Biology** Music **Ancient**
Egypt Evolution Carpentry Physics
Dance Geology **Mathematics** Fitness
Shakespeare **Folklore** Yoga Marketing
Confidence Immortality Biographies
Poetry **Psychology** Witchcraft
Electronics Chemistry History **Law**
Accounting **Philosophy** Anthropology
Alchemy Drama Quantum Mechanics
Atheism Sexual Health **Ancient History**
Entrepreneurship Languages Sport
Paleontology Needlework Islam
Metaphysics Investment Archaeology
Parenting Statistics Criminology
Motivational

UNITED STATES OF AMERICA,

STATE DEPARTMENT,

INTERNATIONAL MARINE CONFERENCE.

Washington, D.C. 1889

Vol 3

1889.

REPORTS OF COMMITTEES

AND

REPORT OF UNITED STATES DELEGATES TO
SECRETARY OF STATE.

WASHINGTON:
GOVERNMENT PRINTING OFFICE.
1890.

CONTENTS.

M201515

OF

SUBJECTS TO BE CONSIDERED BY THE INTERNATIONAL MARINE CONFERENCE.

[Framed by the American Delegates in accordance with instructions from the Department of State, March, 1889.]

GENERAL DIVISION 1.

Marine signals or other means of plainly indicating the direction in which vessels are moving in fog, mist, falling snow, and thick weather, and at night.

RULES FOR THE PREVENTION OF COLLISIONS AND RULES OF THE ROAD.

1. Visibility, number, and position of lights to be carried by vessels.
    (*a*) Steamers under way.
    (*b*) Steamers towing.
    (*c*) Vessels under way, but not under command, including steamers laying cable.
    (*d*) Sailing vessels under way.
    (*e*) Sailing vessels towing.
    (*f*) Vessels at anchor.
    (*g*) Pilot vessels.
    (*h*) Fishing vessels.
2. Sound-signals; their character, number, range and position of instruments.
    (*a*) For use in fog, mist, falling snow, and thick weather, as position signals.
       For steamers under way.
       For steamers towing.
       For sailing vessels under way.
       For sailing vessels towing.
          (These signals to show the approximate course steered if possible.)
       For vessels at anchor.
       For vessels under way, but not under command, including steamers laying cable.

2. Sound-signals; their character, number, range and position of instruments—Continued.
  (b) For use in all weathers as helm signals only.
      For steamers meeting or crossing.
      For steamers overtaking.
      For steamers backing.
  (c) Whether helm signals shall be made compulsory or remain optional.
3. Steering and sailing rules.
  (a) Sailing vessels meeting, crossing, overtaking, or being overtaken by each other.
  (b) Steamers meeting, crossing, overtaking, or being overtaken by each other.
  (c) Sailing vessels, meeting, crossing, overtaking, or being overtaken by steamers.
  (d) Steamers meeting, crossing, overtaking, or being overtaken by sailing vessels.
  (e) Special rules for channels and tide-ways, where no local rules exist.
  (f) Conflict of international and local rules.
  (g) Uniform system of commands to the helm.
  (h) Speed of vessels in thick weather.

GENERAL DIVISION 2.

Regulations to determine the sea-worthiness of vessels.

(a) Construction of vessels.
(b) Equipment of vessels.
(c) Discipline of crew.
(d) Sufficiency of crew.
(e) Inspection of vessels.
(f) Uniform certificates of inspection.

GENERAL DIVISION 3.

Draft to which vessels should be restricted when loaded.

Uniform maximum load mark.

GENERAL DIVISION 4.

Uniform regulations regarding the designating and marking of vessels.

(a) Position of name on vessel.
(b) Position of name of port of registry on vessels.
(c) Size of lettering.
(d) Uniform system of draft marks.

GENERAL DIVISION 5.

Saving life and property from shipwreck.

1. Saving of life and property from shipwreck at sea.
    - (a) Duties of vessels after collision.
    - (b) Apparatus for life-saving to be carried on board ship. (Life-boats, life-preservers, life-rafts, pumps, and fire-extinguishing apparatus.)
    - (c) The use of oil and the necessary apparatus for its use.
    - (d) Uniform inspections as to (b) and (c).
2. Saving of life and property from shipwreck by operations from shore.
    - (a) Organization of, and methods employed by, life-saving institutions.
    - (b) The employment of drilled and disciplined crews at life-saving stations.
    - (c) The maintenance of patrol upon dangerous coasts by night, and during thick weather by day, for warning off vessels standing into danger and for the early discovery of wrecks.
    - (d) Uniform means of transmitting information between stranded vessels and the shore.
    - (e) Life-boats, life-saving apparatus, and appliances.
3. Official inquiries into causes and circumstances of shipwrecks and other casualties.

GENERAL DIVISION 6.

Necessary qualifications for officers and seamen, including tests for sight and color blindness.

- (a) A uniform system of examination for the different grades.
- (b) Uniform tests for visual power and color blindness.
- (c) General knowledge of methods employed at life-saving stations.
- (d) Uniform certificates of qualification.

GENERAL DIVISION 7.

Lanes for steamers on frequented routes.

- (a) With regard to the avoidance of steamer collisions.
- (b) With regard to the safety of fishermen.

GENERAL DIVISION 8.

Night signals for communicating information at sea.

- (a) A code to be used in connection with the International Code Signal book.
- (b) Or a supplementary code of limited scope to convey information of special importance to passing vessels.
- (c) Distress signals.

GENERAL DIVISION 9.

Warnings of approaching storms.

(*a*) The transmission of warnings.
(*b*) The uniformity of signals employed.

GENERAL DIVISION 10.

Reporting, marking, and removing dangerous wrecks or obstructions to navigation.

(*a*) A uniform method of reporting and marking dangerous wrecks and derelicts.
(*b*) The division of the labor, cost, and responsibility among the several maritime nations, either by geographical apportionment or otherwise:
Of the removal of dangerous derelicts;
And of searching for doubtful dangers with a view of removing them from the charts.

GENERAL DIVISION 11.

Notice of dangers to navigation.

NOTICE OF CHANGES IN LIGHTS, BUOYS, AND OTHER DAY AND NIGHT MARKS.

(*a*) A uniform method of taking bearings, of designating them (whether true or magnetic), and of reporting them.
(*b*) A uniform method of reporting, indicating, and exchanging information by the several maritime nations—to include the form of notices to mariners.
(*o*) A uniform method of distributing this information.

GENERAL DIVISION 12.

A uniform system of buoys and beacons.

(*a*) Uniformity in color of buoys.
(*b*) Uniformity in numbering of buoys.

GENERAL DIVISION 13.

The establishment of a permanent international maritime commission.

(*a*) The composition of the commission.
(*b*) Its powers and authority.

Proposed grouping of subjects for consideration by committees of the international marine conference.

1. Rules of the road and signals—General Divisions 1 and 8.
2. Saving of life and property from shipwreck by operations from shore—General Division 5, Subdivision No. 2.

3. Construction and equipment of vessels, and saving of life and property from shipwreck at sea—General Divisions 2, 3, and 4, and Sub division No. 1 of 5.

4. Qualifications of officers and seamen—General Division 6.

5. Steam lanes—General Division 7.

6. Official inquiries into shipwrecks and other casualties—General Division 5, Subdivision No. 3.

7. Transmission of warnings and information, buoys, etc.—General Divisions 9, 10, 11, and 12.

8. Permanent Maritime Commission—General Division 13.

All of which is respectfully submitted.

S. R. FRANKLIN,
Rear-Admiral.
W. T. SAMPSON,
Commander, United States Navy.
S. I. KIMBALL,
General Superintendent Life-Saving Service.
JAS. W. NORCROSS,
Master Mariner.
JOHN W. SHACKFORD,
Master, Merchant Marine.
WILLIAM W. GOODRICH,
Counsellor at Law.

———

DEPARTMENT OF STATE,
INTERNATIONAL MARINE CONFERENCE,
Washington, April 3, 1889.

SIR: I have the honor to inform you that, in conformity with the instructions of the State Department of February 27, 1889, the Delegates on the part of the United States to the International Marine Conference met on Monday, 25th ultimo, organized, and proceeded to the consideration of a detailed programme of the subjects to be considered by the International Conference for transmission to the several powers.

This programme was completed on the 30th ultimo, and is herewith inclosed.

The correspondence between the State Department and the British Government on this subject was examined, and in conformity with the intentions of our Government therein expressed, a consideration of the "International Code of Flag Signals" was excluded from the programme and a consideration of the "load line" was included. With this exception and this addition, the entire subject-matter of the act of Congress of July 9, 1888, was arranged in general divisions, following as nearly as possible the precise language of the act. These general divisions were then carefully considered and each was arranged under subdivisions and subheads.

It is believed that this arrangement in detail is sufficiently broad to include all matters bearing directly upon the principal topics, and care has been taken at the same time to avoid extending the field of deliberations of the Conference beyond the limits indicated in the act of Congress and its interpretation by the State Department.

Very respectfully,

S. R. FRANKLIN,
Rear-Admiral, U. S. Navy,
President of the Board of American Delegates.

Hon. JAMES G. BLAINE,
Secretary of State.

LIST OF COMMITTEES

WITH

RESOLUTIONS UNDER WHICH APPOINTED.

COMMITTEE ON INTERNATIONAL RULES OF THE ROAD.

Resolved, That a committee of three be appointed to prepare the material for printing the International Rules of the Road in accordance with the resolution submitted on Thursday, the 17th, together with any other memoranda of changes in the law of other powers than the United States.

COMMITTEE.

Germany . . . . Dr. F. SIEVEKING.
Siam . . . . Mr. FREDERICK W. VERNEY.
Japan . . . . SHIUZO TSUKAHARA.
Secretary, WM. TRUXTON,
Ensign, U. S. N.

COMMITTEE ON COLLOCATION OF THE RULES.

Resolved, That a Committee on Collocation of Rules, to consist of seven persons, be appointed by the President.

MOTION.

Mr. GOODRICH (United States). That the several committees be increased, each by two, and that the Committee on Collocation also be increased by two members.

COMMITTEE.

Austria-Hungary . . . . Admiral DE SPAUN.
France . . . . Captain LANNELUC.
Germany . . . . Dr. SIEVEKING.
Great Britain . . . . . . Mr. HALL.
Japan . . . . Lieutenant BABA.
Mexico . . . . Commodore MONASTERIO.
Norway . . . . Captain SALVESEN.
Russia . . . . Admiral KAZNAKOFF.
United States . . . . . . Mr. GOODRICH.
Secretary, Mr. WALTER BLAESS.

COMMITTEES ON LIGHTS AND SOUND SIGNALS.

Resolved, That the Chair appoint two committees, each to consist of seven Delegates, to be known as the Committee on Lights and the Committee on Sound Signals, whose present duty it shall be to examine and report to the Conference the literature on these two subjects which is in the possession of the Conference.

COMMITTEE ON LIGHTS.

France	Captain RICHARD.
Germany	Captain MENSING.
Great Britain	Captain WYATT.
Russia	Admiral KAZNAKOFF.
Spain	Lieut. DON BALDOMERO VEGA.
Sweden	Captain MALMBERG.
United States	Captain NORCROSS.

Secretary, Mr. WALTER BLAESS.

COMMITTEE ON SOUND SIGNALS.

Austria-Hungary	Admiral DE SPAUN.
Denmark	Mr. SCHNEIDER.
Great Britain	Admiral NARES.
Italy	Captain SETTEMBRINI.
Norway	Captain SALVESEN.
The Netherlands	Captain VAN STEYN.
United States	Captain SHACKFORD.

Secretary, Mr. SPRING RICE.

Resolved, That the former Committee on Sound Signals consider and report the specific cases in which new fog signals should be adopted, and to report specific signals for such cases.

MOTION.

MR. HALL (Great Britain). Mr. President, I now move *pro forma* that the Committee on Lights be requested to give the Conference its views on the matter referred to in the interlocutory report of the Collocation Committee.

COMMITTEE ON SYSTEMS AND DEVICES.

Resolved, That a committee, to be known as the Committee on Systems and Devices, shall be appointed by the president, and that it shall be the duty of the committee to examine and report upon any system or device connected with the business of the Conference, of which a written description, illustrated by plans whenever necessary, is furnished, and that only such as are favorably reported by the committee shall appear before the Conference.

COMMITTEE.

Belgium . . . . Mr. THO. VERBRUGGHE.
France . . . . Mr. H. VETILLART.
Great Britain . . . . Admiral N. BOWDEN-SMITH.
Mexico . . . . Commodore A. O. MONASTERIO.
United States . . . . . . Mr. S. I. KIMBALL.

Secretary, RIDGELY HUNT,
Lieut., U. S. N.

COMMITTEE ON LIGHTS FOR SMALL CRAFT.

Resolved, That a committee of nine be appointed, to consider and report on the lights to be carried or shown on small vessels, pilot vessels, and fishing-vessels.

COMMITTEE.

Belgium . . . . Mr. VERBRUGGHE.
China . . . . Capt. A. M. BISBEE.
Denmark . . . . Mr. SCHNEIDER.
France . . . . Captain LANNELUC.
Germany . . . . Capt. CHRISTIAN DONNER.
Great Britain . . . . . . Mr. GRAY.
Japan . . . . Lieutenant BABA.
The Netherlands. . . . . Captain HUBERT.
United States . . . . . . Captain NORCROSS.

Secretary, Mr. SPRING RICE.

COMMITTEE ON UNIFORM LOAD MARK.

Resolved, That the Chair appoint a committee of seven upon the subject of a uniform load-mark, General Division 3 of the programme.

MOTION.

Mr. GOODRICH (United States). That the several committees be increased each by two, and that the Committee on Collocation also be increased by two members.

COMMITTEE.

Brazil . . . . Capt. J. CORDOVIL MAURITY.
Chili . . . . Lieutenant BEAUGENCY.
China . . . . Lieutenant CHIA NI HSI.
Great Britain . . . . . . Mr. GRAY.
France . . . . Captain RICHARD.
Germany . . . . Dr. SIEVEKING.
Italy . . . . Captain SETTEMBRINI.
The Netherlands . . . . . Captain HUBERT.
United States . . . . . . Mr. GRISCOM.

Secretary, Mr. WALTER BLAESS.

GENERAL DIVISION 3.

Draft to which vessels should be restricted when loaded.

Uniform maximum load-mark.

COMMITTEE ON LIFE-SAVING SYSTEMS AND DEVICES.

Resolved, That a committee of seven, to be known as the Committee on Life-Saving Systems and Devices, shall be appointed by the President; that it shall be the duty of the committee to examine any system or device connected with the saving of life and property from shipwreck presented on or before the 12th inst., of which a written description, illustrated by plans when necessary, shall be furnished, and that only such matters as are favorably reported by the committee shall be brought before the Conference; that the committee shall submit a report when General Division 5 of the programme shall be reached for consideration.

MOTION.

Mr. GOODRICH (United States). That the several committees be increased each by two, and that the Committee on Collocation also be increased by two members.

COMMITTEE.

Belgium	Mr. VERBRUGGHE.
China	Captain BISBEE.
Chili	Rear-Admiral VIEL.
France	Captain RICHARD.
Germany	Consul General FEIGEL.
Great Britain	Captain WYATT.
Spain	Lieut. SEOANE.
The Netherlands	Captain VAN STEYN.
United States	Mr. KIMBALL.

Secretary, W. L. HOWARD,
Ensign, U. S. N.

Resolved, That the President appoint committees on the several general divisions of the programme, except General Divisions 3 and 5.

MOTION.

Mr. GOODRICH (United States). That the several committees be increased each by two, and that the Committee on Collocation also be increased by two members.

The following are the committees appointed in accordance with the above resolution and motion:

Committee No. 1.

To examine and report upon the subjects contained in General Divisions 2, 4, and 6 of the programme proposed by the United States delegates.

Brazil . . . . Capt. SALDANHA DA GAMA.
China . . . . Com'r CHEN NGEN TAO.
Costa Rica . . . . Don MANUEL ARAGON.
France . . . . Captain LANNELUC.
Germany . . . . Captain DONNER.
Great Britain . . . . . . Mr. GRAY.
Italy . . . . Captain SETTEMBRINI.
Norway . . . . Captain SALVESEN.
United States . . . . . . Captain SAMPSON.
Secretary, E. D. BOSTICK,
Lieut., U. S. N.

GENERAL DIVISION 2.

Regulations to determine the seaworthiness of vessels.

(a) Construction of vessels.
(b) Equipment of vessels.
(c) Discipline of crew.
(d) Sufficiency of crew.
(e) Inspection of vessels.
(f) Uniform certificates of inspection.

GENERAL DIVISION 4.

Uniform regulations regarding the designating and marking of vessels.

(a) Position of name on vessels.
(b) Position of name of port of registry on vessels.
(c) Size of lettering.
(d) Uniform system of draft marks.

GENERAL DIVISION 6.

Necessary qualifications for officers and seamen, including tests for sight and color blindness.

(a) A uniform system of examination for the different grades.
(b) Uniform tests for visual power and color blindness.
(c) Uniform certificates of qualification.

Committee No. 2.

To consider and report upon General Divisions 7 and 8:

Denmark . . . . Mr. GARDE.
France . . . . Captain LANNELUC.
Germany . . . . Captain DONNER.
Great Britain . . . . . . Admiral BOWDEN-SMITH.
Hawaii . . . . Mr. H. A. P. CARTER.
Portugal . . . . Mr. SOUZA ROZA.
Sweden . . . . Captain MALMBERG.
The Netherlands . . . . . Captain HUBERT.
United States . . . . . . Captain SHACKFORD.

Secretary, J. T. NEWTON,
Lieut., U. S. N.

GENERAL DIVISION 7.

Lanes for steamers on frequented routes.

(*a*) With regard to the avoidance of steamer collisions.
(*b*) With regard to the safety of fishermen.

GENERAL DIVISION 8.

Night signals for communicating information at sea.

(*a*) A code to be used in connection with the International Code
Signal book.
(*b*) Or a supplementary code of limited scope to convey information
of special importance to passing vessels.
(*c*) Distress signals.

Committee No. 3.

To consider and report upon General Divisions 9, 10, 11, and 12.

Austria-Hungary . . Lieut. SANCHEZ.
China . . . . Captain BISBEE.
France . . . . . . Mr. RIBIÈRE.
Germany . . . . . Captain MENSING.
Great Britain . . . . Admiral NARES.
Norway . . . . . . Mr. FLOOD.
Siam . . . . Mr. VERNEY.
Uruguay . . . . . Dr. ALBERTO NIN.
United States . . . . Captain SAMPSON.

Secretary, F. E. BEATTY,
Lieut., U. S. N.

GENERAL DIVISION 9.

Warnings of approaching storms.

(*a*) The transmission of warnings.
(*b*) The uniformity of signals employed.

GENERAL DIVISION 10.

Reporting, marking, and removing dangerous wrecks or obstructions to navigation.

(*a*) A uniform method of reporting and marking dangerous wrecks and derelicts.

(*b*) The division of labor, cost, and responsibity among the several maritime nations, either by geographical apportionment or otherwise— Of the removal of dangerous derelicts.

And of searching for doubtful dangers with a view of removing them from the charts.

GENERAL DIVISION 11.

Notice of dangers to navigation.

NOTICE OF CHANGES IN LIGHTS, BUOYS, AND OTHER DAY AND NIGHT MARKS.

GENERAL DIVISION 12.

A uniform system of buoys and beacons.

(*a*) Uniformity in color of buoys.
(*b*) Uniformity in numbering of buoys.

Committee No. 4.

To consider and report upon General Division 13:

Belgium	Mr. VERBRUGGHE.
Chili	Admiral VIEL.
Denmark	Mr. SCHNEIDER.
France	Captain RICHARD.
Germany	Dr. SIEVEKING.
Great Britain	Mr. HALL.
Guatemala	Mr. FERNANDO CRUZ.
Sweden	Captain MALMBERG.
United States	Mr. GRISCOM.

Secretary, Mr. SPRING RICE.

GENERAL DIVISION 13.

The establishment of a permanent maritime commission.

(*a*) The composition of the commission.
(*b*) Its powers and authority.

REPORT OF THE COMMITTEE ON INTERNATIOANL RULES OF THE ROAD.

RESOLUTION.

Resolved, That a committee of three be appointed to prepare the material for printing the International Rules of the Road in accordance with the resolution submitted on Thursday, the 17th, together with any other memoranda of changes in the law of other powers than the United States.

COMMITTEE.

Germany . . . . Dr. F. SIEVEKING.
Siam . . . . Mr. FREDERICK W. VERNEY.
Japan . . . . SHIUZO TSUKAHARA.

Your committee, in presenting the following report, desire to inform the Conference that they have not been furnished with the regulations for preventing collisions at sea in use by the following powers:

China,	Nicaragua,
Costa Rica,	Russia,
Guatemala,	Spain,
Hawaii,	Uruguay,
Honduras,	Venezuela.

In the event of these being forthcoming, the committee are ready to compare them with those of Great Britain in the form of a supplementary report.

F. SIEVEKING, DR.,
Chairman of the Committee.

OCTOBER 28, 1889.

PREAMBLES.

GREAT BRITAIN:

At the Court at Osborne House, Isle of Wight, the 11th day of August, 1884.

Present: The Queen's Most Excellent Majesty in council.

Whereas by Order in Council made in pursuance of the Merchant Shipping Act Amendment Act, 1862, and dated the fourteenth day of August, one thousand eight hundred and seventy-nine, Her Majesty, on the joint recommendation of the Admiralty and the Board of Trade, was pleased to direct that, on and after the first day of September, one thousand eight hundred and eighty, the Regulations for preventing Collisions at Sea contained in an Order in Council, dated the ninth of January, one thousand eight hundred and sixty-three, and the additions by an Order in Council dated the thirtieth day of June, one thousand eight hundred and sixty-eight, made thereto, should be annulled, and that there should be substituted therefor the new Regulations contained in the First Schedule to the said first-named Order in Council, and that the same should, from and after the first day of September, one thousand eight hundred and eighty, apply to Ships of the Countries mentioned in the said Second Schedule thereto, whether within British Jurisdiction or not;

And whereas by the Orders in Council dated respectively the twenty-fourth day of March, one thousand eight hundred and eighty, the twenty-sixth day of August, one thousand eight hundred and eighty-one, the eighteenth day of August, one thousand eight hundred and eighty-two, the twenty-third day of August, one thousand eight hundred and eighty-three, and the second day of February, one thousand eight hundred and eighty-four, Her Majesty was pleased to direct that the operation of the Article numbered 10, of the new Regulations, contained in the First Schedule of the said Order in Council of the fourteenth day of August, one thousand eight hundred and seventy-nine, should be suspended from time to time;

And whereas the Admiralty and the Board of Trade have jointly recommended to Her Majesty that, so far as regards British Ships and Boats, the Regulations hereinafter set forth shall be substituted for the Regulations contained in the First Schedule to the said Order in Council of the fourteenth day of August, one thousand eight hundred and seventy-nine:

Now, therefore, Her Majesty, by virtue of the powers vested in Her by the said recited Act, and by and with the advice of Her Privy Council, is pleased to direct that, on and after the first day of September, one thousand eight hundred and eighty-four, the Regulations contained in the Schedule hereto shall, so far as regards British Ships and Boats, be substituted for the Regulations contained in the First Schedule to the said Order in Council of the fourteenth day of August, one thousand eight hundred and seventy-nine.

C. L. PEEL.

UNITED STATES:

AN ACT to adopt the "Revised International Regulations for Preventing Collisions at Sea."

Be it enacted by the Senate and House of Representatives of the United States of America in Congress assembled, That the following " Revised International Rules and Regulations for Preventing Collisions at

Sea" shall be followed in the navigation of all public and private vessels of the United States upon the high seas and in all coast waters of the United States, except such as are otherwise provided for, namely:

BELGIUM:

1ᵉʳ août 1880. Arrêté royal portant un nouveau règlement des feux et signaux en temps de brume pour prévenir les abordages.

LÉOPOLD II, etc., etc.

Nous avons arrêté et arrêtons—

ART. 1ᵉʳ. A dater du 1ᵉʳ septembre 1880, les bâtiments de la marine de l'État, ainsi que les navires nationaux du commerce, seront assujettis aux prescriptions ci-après qui ont pour objet de prévenir les abordages.

DENMARK:

[Translation.]

We, Christian IXth, etc., order that the following rules for preventing collisions be observed by masters of steam-ships and sailing-ships. Royal Order, 18th February, 1887.

FRANCE:

LE PRÉSIDENT DE LA RÉPUBLIQUE FRANÇAIS DÉCRÈTE:

Art. 1ᵉʳ. A dater du 1ᵉʳ septembre 1884, les bâtiments de la marine nationale, ainsi que les navires du commerce français, ont à se conformer au règlement ayant pour objet de prévenir les abordages, annexé au présent décret.

(No. 1355.) Verordnung zur Verhütung des Zusammenstoßens der Schiffe auf See. Vom 7. Januar 1880.

Wir Wilhelm, von Gottes Gnaden Deutscher Kaiser, König von Preußen u. s. w.

verordnen im Namen des Reichs, auf Grund des §. 145 des Strafgesetzbuchs (Reichs-Gesetzbl. 1876 S. 40) zur Verhütung des Zusammenstoßens der Schiffe auf See, unter Aufhebung der Verordnung vom 23. Dezember 1871 (Reichs-Gesetzbl. S. 475), was folgt:

Jeder Schiffsführer hat auf See und auf den mit der See im Zusammenhange stehenden, von Seeschiffen befahrenen Gewässern die nachstehenden Vorschriften zu befolgen, auch dafür zu sorgen, daß die zur Ausführung derselben erforderlichen Signalapparate vollständig und in brauchbarem Zustande auf seinem Schiffe vorhanden sind.

JAPAN:

Notification No. 35 of Daijkwan, 16th day, 7th month, 13th year of Meiji, 1880.

The following regulations for prevention of collisions at sea shall come into operation on and after the 1st day of the 9th month of the present year, and the existing regulations (Notification No. 5 of

Daijkwan, of the 7th year of Meiji, 1874) shall be, on and after that date, hereby annulled.

(Signed) TARNHETO SHEIMO SA DAIJON.

NORWAY:

[Translation.]

Regulations for preventing collisions between vessels.
Royal Order, 28th January, 1885.

On board all Norwegian vessels the following rules for preventing collisions shall be observed:

SIAM:

Rules and regulations for steam-ships and sailing vessels.

Chow Prayah Bhanuwmgse Mahah Kosa Tibodee t'ee Praklang, Minister for Foreign Affairs, having received a command from His Majesty, the King of Siam, that inasmuch as Siamese steam-ships and sailing vessels trading to foreign ports, and foreign vessels which come for purposes of trade to Bangkok and the coast of Siam, are much more numerous than formerly, and inasmuch as accidents, from collisions between such steam-ships and sailing vessels, sometimes occur at sea in Siamese waters and in the rivers, giving rise to lawsuits difficult of decision, for the reason that there are as yet no laws for large steam-ships and sailing vessels; therefore His Majesty has thought fit that regulations should be made, supplementary to the harbor laws, in order that when lawsuits shall arise they may be decided with ease. It has pleased His Majesty, therefore, to command that a code of laws be enacted like the rules in force in Europe, which may be used by Siamese and European vessels.

GREAT BRITAIN:

"ARTICLE 1. In the following rules every steam-ship which is under sail and not under steam is to be considered a sailing-ship, and every steam-ship which is under steam, whether under sail or not, is to be considered a ship under steam."

UNITED STATES:
Identical.

AUSTRIA-HUNGARY:
Identical.

BELGIUM:
Identical.

CHILI:
Identical.

DENMARK:
Identical.

FRANCE.:
Identical.

GERMANY:
Identical.
ITALY:
Identical.
JAPAN:
Identical.
MEXICO:
Identical.
NORWAY:
Identical, only instead of " steam-ship" substitute the words
" steam-vessel" (Dampfartoi), and instead of sailing-ship the words
" sailing-vessel" (seilfartoi).
SIAM:
Identical.
SWEDEN:
Identical, only instead of " steam-ship" substitute the word
" steam-vessel" (angfartyg), and instead of " sailing-ship" the word
" sailing-vessel" (segelfartyg.)
The NETHERLANDS: .
Identical.

GREAT BRITAIN:
ARTICLE 2. The lights mentioned in the following articles num-
bered three, four, five, six, seven, eight, nine, ten, and eleven, and no
others, shall be carried in all weathers, from sunset to sunrise.
UNITED STATES:
Identical.
AUSTRIA-HUNGARY:
Identical, with the exception of the words " nine, ten, and eleven,"
for which the words " nine and ten" are substituted.
BELGIUM:
Identical, with the exception of the words " and no others," for
which the following paragraph is substituted:
"Aucun autre feu ne pourra paraître à l'extérieur du navire."
CHILI:
Identical.
DENMARK:
Identical.
FRANCE:
Identical, with the exception of the words " and no others," for
which the following paragraph is substituted:
"Aucun autre feu ne devra paraître à l'extérieur du navire."
GERMANY:
Identical, with the exception that the words " numbered " to "11,"
inclusive, are omitted.
ITALY:
Identical.

JAPAN:
Identical.
MEXICO:
Identical, with the exception that the words "numbered" to "11," inclusive, are omitted.
NORWAY:
Identical.
SIAM:
Identical.
SWEDEN:
Identical.
The NETHERLANDS:
Identical.

GREAT BRITAIN:
ARTICLE 3. A sea-going steam-ship, when under way, shall carry—

(a) On or in front of the foremast, at a height above the hull of not less than 20 feet, and if the breadth of the ship exceeds 20 feet, then at a height above the hull not less than such breadth, a bright white light, so constructed as to show an uniform and unbroken light over an arc of the horizon of 20 points of the compass, so fixed as to throw the light 10 points on each side of the ship, namely, from right ahead to 2 points abaft the beam on either side, and of such a character as to be visible on a dark night, with a clear atmosphere, at a distance of at least 5 miles.

(b) On the starboard side a green light, so constructed as to show an uniform and unbroken light over au arc of the horizon of 10 points of the compass, so fixed as to throw the light from right ahead to 2 points abaft the beam on the starboard side, and of such a character as to be visible on a dark night, with a clear atmosphere, at a distance of at least 2 miles.

(c) On the port side a red light, so constructed as to show an uniform and unbroken light over an arc of the horizon of 10 points of the compass, so fixed as to throw the light from right ahead to 2 points abaft the beam on the port side, and of such a character as to be visible on a dark night, with a clear atmosphere, at a distance of at least 2 miles.

(d) The said green and red side-lights shall be fitted with inboard screens projecting at least 3 feet forward from the light, so as to prevent these lights from being seen across the bow.
UNITED STATES:
Identical.
AUSTRIA-HUNGARY:
Identical, with the following exceptions:
1. The word "sea-going," in line one, is omitted.

AUSTRIA-HUNGARY—Continued.

    2. Subsection "*a*." Substitute for the words "twenty feet" "six meters," and in subsection "*d*," for the words "three feet" "ninety centimeters."

BELGIUM:

    Identical, with the following exceptions:

    1. Subsections "*a*" and "*d*." Substitute for the words "twenty feet" and "three feet" the words "six metres" and "ninety-one centimeters," respectively; and

    2. Subsections *a*, *b*, and *c*. Substitute for the words "with a clear atmosphere" the words "sans brume, pluie, brouillard ou neige."

CHILI:

    Identical, with the following exceptions:

    1. Subsection *a*. Instead of the words "on or in front of the foremast" to the words "such breadth," inclusive, substitute the words (translation), "on the top of the foremast, or at least at the same height and in front of it."

    2. Subsection *d*. Instead of the words "three feet" substitute the words "ninety centimeters."

DENMARK:

    Identical, with the following exceptions:

    In line 1, omit the word "sea-going."

FRANCE:

    Identical, with the following exceptions:

    Subsections "*a*" and "*d*." Instead of the words "twenty feet" and "three feet" substitute the words "six meters" and "ninety-one centimeters," respectively.

GERMANY:

    Identical, with the following exceptions:

    1. In line 1 the word "sea-going" is omitted.

    2. Subsections *a* and *d*. Instead of the words "twenty feet" and "three feet" substitute the words "six meters" and "ninety-one centimeters," respectively.

ITALY:

    Identical, with the following exceptions:

    1. In line 1 the word "sea-going" is omitted.

    2. Subsections *a* and *d*. Instead of the words "twenty feet" and "three feet" substitute the words "six meters" and "ninety centimeters," respectively.

JAPAN:

    Identical.

MEXICO:

    Identical, with the following exceptions:

    1. In line 1 the word "sea-going" is omitted.

    2. Subsection *a* and *d*. Instead of the words "twenty feet" and "three feet" substitute the words "six meters" and "ninety centimeters," respectively.

NORWAY:

Identical, with the following exceptions:

1. In line 1, instead of the words "a sea-going steam-ship" substitute "a steam-vessel."

2. Subsections "a" and "d." Instead of the words "twenty feet" and "three feet" substitute the words "six meters" and "ninety-two centimeters," respectively.

SIAM:

Identical.

SWEDEN:

Identical, with the following exceptions:

1. In line one, instead of the words "a sea-going steam-ship," substitute "a steam-vessel."

2. Subsections "a" and "d." Instead of the words "twenty feet" and "three feet," substitute the words "six meters" and "ninety-one centimeters," respectively.

THE NETHERLANDS:

Identical, with the following exceptions:

1. In line one, instead of the words "a sea-going steam-ship when under way," substitute the words "een zeestoomschip onder stoom."

2. Subsections "a" and "d." Instead of the words "twenty feet" and "three feet," substitute the words "six meters" and "nine decimeters," respectively.

GREAT BRITAIN:

ARTICLE 4. A steam-ship when towing another ship shall, in addition to her side-lights, carry two bright white lights in a vertical line, one over the other, not less than three feet apart, so as to distinguish her from other steam-ships. Each of these lights shall be of the same construction and character, and shall be carried in the same position, as the white light which other steam-ships are required to carry.

UNITED STATES:

Identical.

AUSTRIA-HUNGARY:

Identical, with the following exception:

Instead of the words "three feet," substitute the words "one meter."

BELGIUM:

Identical, with the following exception:

Instead of the words "three feet," substitute the words "ninety-one centimeters."

CHILI:

Identical, with the following exception:

Instead of the words "three feet," substitute the words "ninety centimeters."

DENMARK:

Identical.

FRANCE:
    Identical, with the following exception :
    Instead of the words "three feet," substitute the words "ninety-one centimeters."
GERMANY:
    Identical, with the following exception:
    Instead of the words "three feet," substitute the words "one meter."
ITALY:
    Identical, with the following exception:
    Instead of the words "three feet," substitute the words "one meter."
JAPAN:
    Identical.
MEXICO:
    Identical, with the exception that the words "not less than three feet apart" are omitted.
NORWAY:
    Identical, with the following exception :
    Instead of the words "three feet" substitute the words "one meter."
SIAM:
    Identical.
SWEDEN:
    Identical, with the following exception:
    Instead of the words "three feet" substitute the words "one meter."
THE NETHERLANDS:
    Identical, with the following exception:
    Instead of the words "three feet" substitute the words "nine decimeters."

GREAT BRITAIN:
    ARTICLE 5. (a) A ship, whether a steam-ship or a sailing ship, which from any accident is not under command, shall at night carry, in the same position as the white light which steam-ships are required to carry, and if a steam-ship, in place of that light, three red lights in globular lanterns, each not less than 10 inches in diameter, in a vertical line, one over the other, not less than 3 feet apart, and of such a character as to be visible on a dark night, with a clear atmosphere, at a distance of at least 2 miles, and shall by day carry in a vertical line, one over the other, not less than 3 feet apart, in front of but not lower than her foremast-head, three black balls or shapes, each 2 feet in diameter.
    (b) A ship, whether a steam-ship or a sailing ship, employed in laying or in picking up a telegraph cable, shall at night carry, in the same position as the white light which steam-ships are required to carry, and if a steam-ship, in place of that light, three lights in globular lanterns, each not less than 10 inches in diameter, in a vertical

GREAT BRITAIN—Continued.

line, over one another, not less than 6 feet apart. The highest and lowest of these lights shall be red, and the middle light shall be white, and they shall be of such a character that the red lights shall be visible at the same distance as the white light. By day she shall carry, in a vertical line, one over the other, not less than 6 feet apart, in front of but not lower than her foremast-head, three shapes not less than 2 feet in diameter, of which the top and bottom shall be globular in shape and red in color, and the middle one diamond in shape and white.

(c) The ships referred to in this article when not making any way through the water shall not carry the side-lights, but when making way shall carry them.

(d) The lights and shapes required to be shown by this article are to be taken by other ships as signals that the ship showing them is not under command, and can not therefore get out of the way. The signals to be made by ships in distress and requiring assistance are contained in article twenty-seven.

UNITED STATES:

Identical.

AUSTRIA-HUNGARY:

[Translation.]

A ship, whether a steam-ship or a sailing ship, employed in laying or picking up a telegraph cable, and also a ship which, from any accident, is not under command, shall by day carry in front of, but not lower than her foremast-head, three dark balls, or other signal shapes, not less than 65 centimeters in diameter in a vertical line, one over the other, not less than 1 meter apart.

Such ships shall, at night, carry in the same position as the white light which steam-ships are required to carry, and, if a steam-ship, in place of that light three red lights in globular lanterns, each not less than 25 centimeters in diameter, in a vertical line, one over the other, not less than 1 meter apart.

These signal shapes and lights are to be taken by other ships as signals that the ship showing them is not under command, and can not, therefore, get out of the way.

The aforesaid ships, when not making any way, shall not carry the side lights, but when making way shall carry them.

BELGIUM:

Tout navire à voiles ou à vapeur employé, soit à poser, soit à relever un câble télégraphique, tout navire qui, par une cause accidentelle, n'est pas libre de ses mouvements, doit, si c'est le jour, porter en avant de la tête du mât de misaine, et pas plus bas que cette tête de mât, trois boules noires de 0ᵐ,61 de diamètre chacune, placées verticalement l'une au-dessus de l'autre à une distance d'au moins 0ᵐ,91; si c'est pendant la nuit, il doit mettre à la place assignée au

BELGIUM—Continued.

feu blanc brillant que les bâtiments à vapeur sont tenus d'avoir en avant du mât de misaine, trois feux rouges placés dans des lanternes sphériques d'au moins 0ᵐ,25 de diamètre et disposées verticalement à une distance l'une de l'autre d'au moins 0ᵐ,91.

Ces boules ou ces lanternes servent à avertir les autres navires qui approchent que celui qui les porte n'est pas manœuvrable et par suite ne peut se garer.

Les navires ci-dessus ne doivent pas avoir les feux de côté allumés lorsqu'ils n'ont aucun sillage. Ils doivent, au contraire, les tenir allumés s'ils sont en marche soit à la voile, soit à la vapeur.

CHILI:

[Translation.]

The signals indicated in this article are special signals, and are only carried by the ships which are defined as follows:

1. The steamers employed in laying or taking up submarine telegraph cables.

2. The steamers which, from any accident, are not under command.

These ships shall carry by day in front of the foremast, at a height not exceeding the top of the foremast, three globular shapes of black color, each 60 centimeters in diameter, in a vertical line, and not less than 90 centimeters apart.

At night the same vessels shall, instead of the mast-head light, carry three red lights in globular lanterns, each not less than 25 centimeters in diameter, in a vertical line, and not less than 90 centimeters apart.

The aforesaid shapes and lights indicate that the ships showing them are not under command and can not manœuvre.

The ships referred to in this article, when not making any way through the water, shall not carry any side lights, but when making way shall carry them.

DENMARK:

Identical, with the following exception:

Subsection d. The words beginning "The signals," to the end of the subsection are omitted.

FRANCE:

Identical, with the following exceptions:

Subsections a and b. Instead of the words "ten inches" substitute the words "twenty-five centimeters," and instead of the words "two feet," substitute the words "sixty-one centimeters."

Subsection a. Instead of the words "three feet" substitute the words "ninety-one centimeters."

Subsection b. Instead of the words "six feet" substitute the words "one meter, eighty-two centimeters."

Subsection a. After the words "three black balls," the words "or shapes" are omitted.

GERMANY :

[Translation.]

A ship, whether a steam-ship or a sailing ship, employed in laying or picking up a telegraph cable, and also a ship which, from any accident, is not under command, shall by day carry in front of, but not lower than her foremast-head, three dark balls, or other signal shapes, of 65 centimeters in diameter in a vertical line, one over the other, not less than 1 meter apart.

Such ships shall, at night, carry in the same position as the white light which steam-ships are required to carry, and, if a steam-ship, in place of that light three red lights in globular lanterns, each not less than 25 centimeters in diameter, in a vertical line one over the other, not less than 1 meter apart.

These signal shapes and lights are to be taken by other ships as signals that the ship showing them is not under command, and can not, therefore, get out of the way.

The aforesaid ships, when not making any way, shall not carry the side lights, but when making way shall carry them.

ITALY :

Identical, with the following exceptions :

Subsections *a* and *b*. Instead of the words "10 inches" and "two feet" substitute the words "twenty-five centimeters" and "sixty-five centimeters."

Subsection *a*. Instead of the words "three feet" substitute the words "one meter."

Subsection *b*. Instead of the words "six feet" substitute the words "one meter."

JAPAN :

Identical.

MEXICO :

This article is omitted entirely. (See note at the end.)

NORWAY :

Identical, with the following exceptions :

Subsections *a* and *b*. Instead of the words "ten inches" substitute the words "twenty-five centimeters," and instead of the words "two feet" substitute the words "sixty centimeters."

Subsection *a*. Instead of the words "three feet" substitute the words "one meter."

Subsection *b*. Instead of the words "six feet" substitute the words "one meter, eighty centimeters."

SIAM :

Omitted. (See note at end.)

SWEDEN :

Identical, with the following exceptions :

Subsections *a* and *b*. Instead of the words "ten inches" substitute the words "twenty-five centimeters," and instead of the words "two feet" substitute the words "sixty centimeters."

SWEDEN—Continued.

Subsection *a*. Instead of the words "three feet" substitute the words "one meter."

Subsection *b*. Instead of the words "six feet" substitute the words "one meter, eighty centimeters."

THE NETHERLANDS:

Identical, with the following exceptions:

Subsections *a* and *b*. Instead of the words "ten inches" substitute the words "two and one-half decimeters," and instead of the words "two feet" substitute the words "six decimeters."

Subsection *a*. Instead of the words "three feet" substitute the words "nine decimeters."

Subsection *b*. Instead of the words "six feet" substitute the words "one meter, eight decimeters."

Subsection *d*. Instead of the words "contained in Article 27" substitute the words "contained in our decree of October 10, 1875."

GREAT BRITAIN:

ARTICLE 6. A sailing ship under way or being towed shall carry the same lights as are provided by Article 3 for a steam-ship under way, with the exception of the white light, which she shall never carry.

UNITED STATES:

Identical.

AUSTRIA-HUNGARY:

Identical.

BELGIUM:

Identical.

CHILI:

Identical.

DENMARK:

Identical.

GERMANY:

Identical.

ITALY:

Identical.

JAPAN:

Identical.

MEXICO:

Identical.

NORWAY:

Identical.

SIAM:

Identical.

SWEDEN:

Identical.

THE NETHERLANDS:

Identical.

GREAT BRITAIN:

ARTICLE 7. Whenever, as in the case of small vessels during bad weather, the green and red side lights can not be fixed, these lights shall be kept on deck, on their respective sides of the vessel ready for use, and shall, on the approach of or to other vessels, be exhibited on their respective sides in sufficient time to prevent collision, in such manner as to make them most visible, and so that the green light shall not be seen on the port side nor the red light on the starboard side. To make the use of these portable lights more certain and easy, the lanterns containing them shall each be painted outside with the color of the light they respectively contain, and shall be provided with proper screens.

UNITED STATES:

Identical.

AUSTRIA–HUNGARY:

Identical.

BELGIUM:

Identical.

CHILI:

Identical.

DENMARK:

Identical.

FRANCE:

Identical.

GERMANY:

Identical.

ITALY:

Identical.

JAPAN:

Identical.

MEXICO:

Identical.

NORWAY:

Identical.

SIAM:

Identical.

SWEDEN:

Identical.

THE NETHERLANDS:

Identical.

GREAT BRITAIN:

ARTICLE 8. A ship, whether a steam-ship or a sailing ship, when at anchor, shall carry, where it can best be seen, but at a height not exceeding 20 feet above the hull, a white light, in a globular lantern of not less than 8 inches in diameter, and so constructed as to show a clear, uniform, and unbroken light, visible all round the horizon at a distance of at least 1 mile.

UNITED STATES:
  Identical.
AUSTRIA-HUNGARY:
  Identical, with the following exceptions:
  Instead of the words "twenty feet" substitute the words "six meters;" and instead of the words "eight inches" substitute the words "twenty centimeters."
BELGIUM:
  Identical, with the following exceptions:
  Instead of the words "twenty feet" substitute the words "six meters." Instead of the words "eight inches" substitute the words "twenty centimeters."
  N. B.—The words "when at anchor" are translated "lorsqu'il est au mouillage."
CHILI:
  Identical, with the following exceptions:
  1. Instead of the words "when at anchor" substitute the words "when at anchor in a roadstead, channel, or fair-way."
  2. Instead of the words "twenty feet" substitute the words "six meters."
  3. The words "in a globular lantern of not less than 8 inches in diameter" are omitted.
DENMARK:
  Identical.
FRANCE:
  Identical, with the following exceptions:
  Instead of the words "twenty feet" substitute the words "six meters," and instead of the words "eight inches" substitute the words "twenty centimeters."
  N. B.—The words "when at anchor" are translated "lorsqu'il est au mouillage."
GERMANY:
  Identical, with the following exceptions:
  Instead of the words "twenty feet" substitute the words "six meters," and instead of the words "eight inches" substitute the words "twenty centimeters."
ITALY:
  Identical, with the following exceptions:
  Instead of the words "twenty feet" substitute the words "six meters," and instead of the words "eight inches" substitute the words "twenty centimeters."
JAPAN:
  Identical.
MEXICO:
  (See note at the end.)

NORWAY:

Identical, with the following exceptions:

Instead of the words "twenty feet" substitute the words "six meters," and instead of the words "eight inches" substitute the words "twenty centimeters."

SIAM:

Identical, with the following exceptions:

Instead of the words "twenty feet" substitute the words "six meters," and instead of the words "eight inches" substitute the words "twenty centimeters."

SWEDEN:

Identical, with the following exception:

Instead of the words "twenty feet" substitute the words "six meters," and instead of the words "eight inches" substitute the words "twenty centimeters."

THE NETHERLANDS:

Identical, with the following exceptions:

Instead of the words "twenty feet" substitute the words "six meters," and instead of the words "eight inches" substitute the words "twenty centimeters."

GREAT BRITAIN:

ARTICLE 9. A pilot vessel, when engaged on her station on pilotage duty, shall not carry the lights required for other vessels, but shall carry a white light at the mast-head, visible all round the horizon, and shall also exhibit a flare-up light or flare-up lights at short intervals, which shall never exceed fifteen minutes. A pilot vessel, when not engaged on her station on pilotage duty, shall carry lights similar to those of other ships.

UNITED STATES:

Identical.

AUSTRIA-HUNGARY:

Identical.

BELGIUM:

Identical.

DENMARK:

Identical, with the following exceptions:

In the last paragraph, instead of the words "a pilot vessel" down to the words "other ships," inclusive, substitute the following words:

[Translation.]

"Open pilot vessels, however, are not required to carry the light at the mast-head, but, on approaching another ship, or being approached by another ship, they shall show it in time to prevent a collision. A pilot vessel, when not engaged on her station on pilotage duty, shall, if decked, carry lights similar to those of other vessels; and, if open, carry lights similar to those of other open boats."

S. Ex. 53, pt. 3——3

FRANCE:
 Identical.
GERMANY:
 Identical.
ITALY:
 Identical, with the exception that the pilotage station is not specially mentioned in the first paragraph.
JAPAN:
 Identical.
MEXICO:
 (See note at the end.)
NORWAY:

[Translation. As now altered by royal order 23d April, 1887.]

 A pilot vessel, when on pilotage duty, shall not carry the lights required for other vessels, but shall at least every fifteen minutes show one or more flare-up lights, and besides, have at hand a lantern lit ready for use, of such a character as to show a clear white light all round the horizon, which, on approaching to or being approached by other vessels, shall be exhibited in sufficient time to prevent collision.

 A pilot vessel, when not on pilotage duty, shall, if a decked vessel, carry lights similar to those of other vessels, and if an open boat, similar to those of open boats.

SIAM:
 (See note at the end.)
SWEDEN:
 Identical.
THE NETHERLANDS.
 Identical.

GREAT BRITAIN:

 ARTICLE 10. Open boats and fishing vessels of less than 20 tons net registered tonnage, when under way and not when having their nets, trawls, dredges, or lines in the water, shall not be obliged to carry the colored side-lights; but every such boat and vessel shall in lieu thereof have ready at hand a lantern with a green glass on the one side and a red glass on the other side, and on approaching to or being approached by another vessel such lantern shall be exhibited in sufficient time to prevent collision, so that the green light shall not be seen on the port side nor the red light on the starboard side.

 The following portion of this article applies only to fishing vessels and boats when in the sea off the coast of Europe lying north of Cape Finisterre:

 (a) All fishing vessels and fishing boats of 20 tons net registered tonnage or upward, when under way and when not having their nets,

GREAT BRITAIN—Continued.

trawls, dredges, or lines in the water, shall carry and show the same lights as other vessels under way.

(b) All vessels when engaged in fishing with drift-nets shall exhibit two white lights from any part of the vessel where they can be best seen. Such lights shall be placed so that the vertical distance between them shall be not less than 6 feet and not more than 10 feet, and so that the horizontal distance between them, measured in a line with the keel of the vessel, shall be not less than 5 feet and not more than 10 feet. The lower of these two lights shall be the more forward, and both of them shall be of such a character and contained in lanterns of such construction as to show all round the horizon, on a dark night, with a clear atmosphere, for a distance of not less than 3 miles.

(c) All vessels when trawling, dredging, or fishing with any kind of drag-nets shall exhibit, from some part of the vessel where they can be best seen, two lights. One of these lights shall be red and the other shall be white. The red light shall be above the white light, and shall be at a vertical distance from it of not less than 6 feet and not more than 12 feet; and the horizontal distance between them, if any, shall not be more than 10 feet. These two lights shall be of such a character and contained in lanterns of such construction as to be visible all round the horizon, on a dark night, with a clear atmosphere, the white light to a distance of not less than 3 miles and the red light of not less than 2 miles.

(d) A vessel employed in line-fishing, with her lines out, shall carry the same lights as a vessel when engaged in fishing with drift-nets.

(e) If a vessel when fishing with a trawl, dredge, or any kind of drag-net, becomes stationary in consequence of her gear getting fast to a rock or other obstruction, she shall show the light and make the fog-signal for a vessel at anchor.

(f) Fishing vessels and open boats may at any time use a flare-up in addition to the lights which they are by this article required to carry and show. All flare-up lights exhibited by a vessel when trawling, dredging, or fishing with any kind of drag-net shall be shown at the afterpart of the vessel, excepting that if the vessel is hanging by the stern to her trawl, dredge, or drag-net they shall be exhibited from the bow.

(g) Every fishing vessel and every open boat when at anchor between sunset and sunrise shall exhibit a white light, visible all round the horizon, at a distance of at least 1 mile.

(h) In a fog a drift-net vessel attached to her nets, and a vessel when trawling, dredging, or fishing with any kind of a drag-net, and a vessel employed in line-fishing with her lines out, shall, at intervals of not more than two minutes, make a blast with her fog-horn and ring her bell alternately.

UNITED STATES:
Identical.

AUSTRIA-HUNGARY:

Open fishing-vessels, and other open boats are not required to carry side-lights like other ships, but, if they are not in possession of such lights, they shall carry a lantern with a green glass on the one side and a red glass on the other side. On approaching to, or being approached by, another ship, such lantern shall be exhibited in sufficient time to prevent collision, so that the green light shall not be seen on the port side nor the red light on the starboard side.

These vessels, if at anchor, or fast to their nets, and therefore not making way through the water, shall show a bright white light. They are allowed besides, if they think it advisable, to show flare-up lights from time to time.

BELGIUM:

a. Les bateaux de pêche non pontés et tout autres bateaux non pontés ne sont pas forcés, lorsqu'ils sont en marche, de porter les feux de côte obligatoires pour les autres navires ; mais s'ils ne les ont pas, ils doivent avoir à la place une lanterne toute prête et munie sur un des côtés d'un verre vert, et sur l'autre d'un verre rouge, et s'ils approchent d'un navire ou s'ils en voient approcher un, ils doivent montrer la lanterne assez à temps pour éviter un abordage, en la tenant de manière que la lumière verte ne soit vue qu'à tribord et la lumière rouge à bâbord.

b. Tout bâtiment de pêche ou tout bateau non ponté doit montrer un feu blanc brillant quand il est au mouillage.

c. Tout bâtiment de pêche occupé à la pêche au filets traînants portera à l'un de ses mâts deux feux rouges placés verticalement l'un au-dessus de l'autre, à une distance d'au moins 0ᵐ91.

d. Tout bateau pêchant à la drague portera à l'un de ses mâts deux feux placés verticalement à la distance d'au moins 0ᵐ91 l'un au-dessus de l'autre, le feu supérieur étant rouge et le feu inférieur vert; en outre, il aura les deux feux de côté réglementaires pour les autres bâtiments, ou, s'il ne peut pas les porter, il aura tout prêts et à la main les feux colorés prévus par l'article 7, ou enfin une lanterne avec un verre rouge et un verre vert comme il est dit au paragraphe *a* de cet article 10.

e. Les bâtiments de pêche, ainsi que les bateaux non pontés, pourront, en outre, s'ils le désirent, se servir d'un feu à éclats alternativement montré et caché.

f. Tous les feux exigés par cet article, à l'exception des feux de côté, doivent être contenus dans des lanternes sphériques, de manière que la lumière soit visible sans interruption sur tout l'horizon.

CHILI:

a. Open fishing boats and other open boats are not required to carry the side lights prescribed for other vessels, but if they do not carry

CHILI—Continued.

such lights they shall use a lantern with a green glass on the one side and a red glass on the other side, so that on approaching to or being approached by another vessel, they may exhibit a light in sufficient time to prevent a collision, taking care always that the green light can not be seen on the port side nor the red light on the starboard side.

b. Fishing boats or other open boats, when at anchor, shall carry a white light.

c. Boats fishing with drift nets or floating nets shall carry two colored lights in a vertical line and 90 centimeters apart.

d. Vessels engaged in fishing with ground nets or drag nets shall carry at one of their masts two lights in a vertical line, the upper red and the lower green. Besides these, they shall be provided with the side lights, or, in case they have no side lights, with the lights prescribed by Article 7, and if they have no such lights, they shall use the light referred to in subsection *a* of this article.

e. The vessels referred to in this article may use an additional white light, and exhibit the same at intervals as often as necessary.

DENMARK:

[Translation.]

Open fishing boats, as well as other open boats, whether under sail or rowing, are not required to carry the side lights prescribed for other vessels; but, if they do not carry them, they shall, instead of them, have ready at hand a lantern with a green glass on the one side and a red glass on the other side. The lantern shall be exhibited in time to prevent a collision, so that the green light shall not be seen on the port side, nor the red light on the starboard side.

All sorts of fishing boats, as well as open boats, when engaged in fishing, or when lying at anchor, shall show a clear white light from sunset to sunrise, from any part of the vessel where it can best be seen, visible all round the horizon at a distance of at least 1 mile. These vessels may also, if they think it advisable, show flare-up lights from time to time. Vessels engaged in fishing with trawls, ground nets, or any sort of drag nets, shall, in such a case, show red flare up lights. In thick weather the aforesaid vessels shall indicate their presence by blowing their fog-horn at least every two minutes. Sailing fishing boats, as well as other sailing or rowing boats, of 4 tons net register or less, are not required to show the aforesaid lights.

FRANCE:

Identical, with the following exceptions:

Subsection *b.* Instead of the words " six feet," " ten feet," and " five feet," substitute the words " one meter, eighty centimeters," " three meters," and " one meter fifty centimeters," respectively.

GERMANY:

[Translation.]

Open fishing boats and other open boats are only required to show a bright white light. In addition they may use a flare-up light.

ITALY:

Identical from the beginning of the article down to the words "on the starboard side," inclusive.

Instead of the words beginning "The following portion" down to the end of the article, substitute the following:

[Translation.]

Fishing boats, and open boats, when at anchor, shall from sunset to sunrise exhibit a white light visible all round the horizon at a distance of at least 1 mile.

Fishing boats having their nets in the water shall, in addition to the aforesaid lights, show another white light, at short intervals, at a place where it can not be mistaken for the light prescribed for pilot-vessels in Article 9. In fog every fishing boat which has its nets or lines in the water shall, at intervals of not less than two minutes, blow the fog-horn or ring the bell alternately.

JAPAN:

Open fishing boats, and other open boats, shall not be required to carry the side lights required for other vessels; but shall, if they do not carry such lights, carry a lantern having a green slide on the one side and a red slide on the other side; and on the approach of or to other vessels such lantern shall be exhibited in sufficient time to prevent collision, so that the green light shall not be seen on the port side nor the red light on the' starboard side.

Fishing vessels and open boats, when at anchor or attached to their nets, shall exhibit a bright white light.

Fishing vessels and open boats shall use a flare-up if considered expedient. They shall not be prevented from using a fog-horn by day or night.

MEXICO:

[Translation.]

Open fishing boats and other open boats are not required to carry the side lights prescribed for other vessels; but if they do not carry such lights they shall use a lantern with a green glass on the one side and a red glass on the other side, so that, on approaching a vessel, they may exhibit this light in time to prevent a collision, taking care always that the green light shall not be seen on the port side nor the red light on the starboard side.

MEXICO—Continued.

Open fishing boats, and other open boats, when at anchor, or when engaged in fishing, and not making way through the water, shall exhibit a white light.

These boats may, if they think it advisable, show an additional light at short intervals.

NORWAY:

Identical, with the following exceptions:

(1) Subsection *b*. Instead of the words "six feet," "ten feet," and "five feet" substitute the words "one meter eighty centimeters," "three meters," and "one meter fifty centimeters," respectively.

(2) A note is added as follows:

[Translation.]

Rules *b*, *c*, *d*, and *g* do not apply to open boats. As regards open fishing boats and other open boats, whether under sail or propelled by oars, in Norwegian inland waters connected with the sea, see section 28.

Section 28 is as follows:

[Translation.]

Open fishing-boats and other open boats, whether under sail or propelled by oars, in Norwegian inland waters connected with the sea, are not required to show any signal. They shall, however show due attention, and shall take every precaution to prevent a collision.

SIAM:

Open fishing-boats and other open boats shall not be required to carry the side-lights required for other vessels, but shall, if they do not carry such lights, carry a lantern having a green slide on the one side and a red slide on the other side, and on the approach of or to other vessels such lantern shall be exhibited in sufficient time to prevent collision, so that the green light shall not be seen on the port side nor the red light on the starboard side.

Fishing-vessels and open boats when at anchor, or attached to their nets and stationary, shall exhibit a bright white light.

Fishing-vessels and open boats shall, however, not be prevented from using a flare-up in addition, if considered expedient.

SWEDEN:

Identical, with the following exceptions:

Subsection *b*. Instead of the words "six feet," "five feet," and "ten feet," insert the words "one meter, eighty centimeters," "one meter, fifty centimeters," and "three meters," respectively.

THE NETHERLANDS:

[Translation.]

Open boats, whether fishing-vessels or others, are not required to carry the side-lights required by sea-going ships; but if they do not

THE NETHERLANDS—Continued.

carry these lights they must be provided with a lantern with a green glass on the one side and a red glass on the other side. This lantern shall be exhibited in sufficient time to prevent collision, so that the green light shall not be seen on the port side nor the red light on the starboard side. Fishing-vessels and open boats, when lying at anchor or attached to their nets, shall exhibit a bright white light. In addition, they may, from time to time, show a flare-up light, if they think it advisable.

GREAT BRITAIN:

ARTICLE 11. A ship which is being overtaken by another shall show from her stern to such last-mentioned ship a white light or a flare-up light.

' UNITED STATES:

Identical.

AUSTRIA-HUNGARY:

Identical.

BELGIUM:

Identical.

CHILI:

Identical.

DENMARK:

Identical.

FRANCE:

Identical.

GERMANY:

Identical.

ITALY:

Identical.

JAPAN:

Identical.

MEXICO:

See note at end.

NORWAY:

Identical.

SIAM:

See note at end.

SWEDEN:

Identical.

THE NETHERLANDS:

Identical.

GREAT BRITAIN:

ARTICLE 12. A steam-ship shall be provided with a steam-whistle or other efficient steam-sound signal, so placed that the sound may not be intercepted by any obstructions, and with an efficient fog-

GREAT BRITAIN—Continued.

horn, to be sounded by a bellows or other mechanical means, and also with an efficient bell. A sailing ship shall be provided with a similar fog-horn and bell.

In fog, mist, or falling snow, whether by day or night, the signals described in this article shall be used as follows; that is to say:

(*a*) A steam-ship under way shall make with her steam whistle or other steam-sound signal, at intervals of not more than two minutes, a prolonged blast.

(*b*) A sailing ship under way shall make with her fog-horn, at intervals of not more than two minutes, when on the starboard tack one blast, when on the port tack two blasts in succession, and when with the wind abaft the beam three blasts in succession.

(*c*) A steam-ship and a sailing ship when not under way shall, at intervals of not more than two minutes, ring the bell.

UNITED STATES:

. Identical.

AUSTRIA-HUNGARY:

Identical.

BELGIUM:

Identical.

CHILI:

Identical, with the following exception:

The words in the first paragraph, "a sailing ship shall be provided with a similar fog-horn and bell," are omitted.

DENMARK:

Identical, with the following exception:

The words (translation) "sailing and rowing vessels of four tons net register, or less, are not required to make the aforesaid sound signals" are added at the end of the article.

FRANCE:

Identical.

GERMANY:

Identical.

ITALY:

Identical.

JAPAN:

Identical.

MEXICO:

See note at end.

NORWAY:

Identical.

SIAM:

See note at end.

SWEDEN:

Identical.

THE NETHERLANDS:
  Identical.

GREAT BRITAIN:
  ARTICLE 13. Every ship, whether a sailing ship or a steam-ship,
shall in a fog, mist, or falling snow, go at a moderate speed.

UNITED STATES:
  Identical.

AUSTRIA-HUNGARY:
  Identical.

BELGIUM:
  Identical :

CHILI:
  Identical, with the following exception :
  Instead of words " go at a moderate speed," substitute the words
(translation) "slacken her speed."

DENMARK:
  Identical.

FRANCE:
  Identical.

GERMANY:
  Identical.

ITALY:
  Identical.

JAPAN:
  Identical.

MEXICO:
  (See note at end.)

NORWAY:
  Identical.

SIAM:
  See note at end.

SWEDEN:
  Identical.

THE NETHERLANDS:
  Identical.

GREAT BRITAIN:
  ARTICLE 14. When two sailing ships are approaching one another
so as to involve risk of collision, one of them shall keep out of the
way of the other as follows, namely :
  (a.) A ship which is running free shall keep out of the way of a ship
which is close-hauled.
  (b.) A ship which is close-hauled on the port tack shall keep out
of the way of a ship which is close-hauled on the starboard tack.
  (c.) When both are running free, with the wind on different sides,
the ship which has the wind on the port side shall keep out of the way
of the other.

GREAT BRITAIN—Continued.

(*d*.) When both are running free, with the wind on the same side, the ship which is to winwdard shall keep out of the way of the ship which is to leeward.

(*e*.) A ship which has the wind aft shall keep out of the way of the other ship.

UNITED STATES:
Identical.

AUSTRIA-HUNGARY:
Identical.

BELGIUM:
Identical.

CHILI:
Identical.

DENMARK:
Identical.

FRANCE:
Identical.

GERMANY:
Identical.

ITALY:
Identical.

JAPAN:
Identical.

MEXICO:
See note at end.

NORWAY:
Identical.

SIAM:
(See note at end.)

SWEDEN:
Identical.

THE NETHERLANDS:
Identical.

GREAT BRITAIN:

ARTICLE 15. If two ships under steam are meeting end on, or nearly end on, so as to involve risk of collision, each shall alter her course to starboard, so that each may pass on the port side of the other. This article only applies to cases where ships are meeting end on, or nearly end on, in such a manner as to involve risk of collision, and does not apply to two ships which must, if both keep on their respective courses, pass clear of each other. The only cases to which it does apply are when each of the two ships is end on, or nearly end on, to the other; in other words, to cases in which by day each ship sees the masts of the other in a line, or nearly in a line, with her own,

GREAT BRITAIN—Continued.

and by night to cases in which each ship is in such a position as to see both the side-lights of the other. It does not apply by day to cases in which a ship sees another ahead crossing her own course, or by night to cases where the red light of one ship is opposed to the red light of the other, or where the green light of one ship is opposed to the green light of the other, or where a red light without a green light, or a green light without a red light, is seen ahead, or where both green and red lights are seen anywhere but ahead.

UNITED STATES:

Identical.

AUSTRIA-HUNGARY:

Identical.

BELGIUM:

Identical.

CHILI:

Identical, with the following exceptions:

Instead of the words "the only cases to which it does apply" down to the end of the article substitute the following:

[Translation.]

It is to be understood that ships are "end on," or "nearly end on," if, by day, one ship sees the masts of the other in a line with her own or less than 2½ points out of that line; and, by night, if one ship is in such a position as to divide the two side lights of the other ship by her stem.

DENMARK:

Identical.

FRANCE:

Identical.

GERMANY:

Identical.

ITALY:

Identical, with the following exception:

The words commencing "This article only applies to cases where ships are meeting end on" down to the end of the article are omitted.

JAPAN:

Identical.

MEXICO:

Identical, with the following exception:

The words commencing "This article only applies to cases where ships are meeting end on" down to the end of the article are omitted.

NORWAY:

Identical.

SIAM:

Identical (see Article 20 of the Siamese Rules).

SWEDEN :
　　Identical.
THE NETHERLANDS:
　　Identical.

GREAT BRITAIN :
　　ARTICLE 16. If two ships under steam are crossing so as to involve risk of collision the ship which has the other on her own starboard side shall keep out of the way of the other.
UNITED STATES:
　　Identical.
AUSTRIA-HUNGARY :
　　Identical.
BELGIUM :
　　Identical.
CHILI:
　　Identical.
DENMARK :
　　Identical.
FRANCE :
　　Identical.
GERMANY :
　　Identical.
ITALY :
　　Identical.
JAPAN:
　　Identical.
MEXICO :
　　Identical.
NORWAY.
　　Identical.
SIAM :
　　Identical.
SWEDEN:
　　Identical.
THE NETHERLANDS :
　　Identical.

GREAT BRITAIN :
　　ARTICLE 17. If two ships, one of which is a sailing ship and the other a steam-ship, are proceeding in such directions as to involve risk of collision, the steam-ship shall keep out of the way of the sailing ship.
UNITED STATES:
　　Identical.
AUSTRIA-HUNGARY :
　　Identical.

BELGIUM:
Identical.
CHILI:
Identical.
DENMARK:
Identical.
FRANCE:
Identical.
GERMANY:
Identical.
ITALY:
Identical.
JAPAN:
Identical.
MEXICO:
Identical.
NORWAY:
Identical.
SIAM:
Identical.
SWEDEN:
Identical.
THE NETHERLANDS:
Identical.

GREAT BRITAIN:
ARTICLE 18. Every steam-ship when approaching another ship so as to involve risk of collision shall slacken her speed, or stop and reverse, if necessary.
UNITED STATES:
Identical.
AUSTRIA-HUNGARY:
Identical, with the following exception:
Instead of the words "shall slacken her speed, or stop and reverse, if necessary," substitute the words (translation) shall slacken her speed, or, if necessary, stop and reverse."
BELGIUM:
Identical, with the following exception:
Instead of the words "shall slacken her speed, or stop and reverse, if necessary," substitute the words "doit diminuer de vitesse, ou stopper et même marcher en arrière, si cela est nécessaire."
CHILI:
Identical, with the following exception:
Instead of the words "shall slacken her speed," etc., substitute the words (translation) "shall slacken her speed, and, if necessary, stop and reverse."
DENMARK:
Identical.

FRANCE:
  Identical, with the following exception :
  Instead of the words "shall slacken her speed," etc., substitute the
words " doit diminuer de vitesse,ou stopper et même marcher en arri-
ère, si cela est nécessaire."
GERMANY :
  Identical, with the following exception :
  Instead of the words "shall slacken her speed," etc., substitute the
words (translation) " shall slacken her speed,or, if necessary, stop and
reverse."
ITALY :
  Identical.
JAPAN:
  Identical.
MEXICO :
  (See note at end.)
NORWAY :
  Identical, with the following exception
  Instead of the words " shall slacken her speed," etc., substitute the
words (translation) "shall slacken her speed, or, if necessary, stop
and reverse."
SIAM :
  Identical, with the following exception :
  Instead of the words " shall slacken her speed," etc., substitute the
words " shall slacken her speed, or, if necessary, stop and reverse."
SWEDEN :
  Identical, with the following exception :
  Instead of the words "shall slacken her speed," etc., substitute the
words (translation) "shall slacken her speed, or, if necessary, stop
and reverse."
THE NETHERLANDS :
  Identical, with the following exception :
  Instead of the words " shall slacken her speed," etc., substitute the
words (translation) "shall slacken her speed, or, if necessary, stop
and reverse. "

GREAT BRITAIN :
  ARTICLE 19. In taking any course authorized or required by these
regulations, a steam-ship under way may indicate that course to
any other ship which she has in sight by the following signals on her
steam-whistle, namely :
  One short blast to mean " I am directing my course to starboard."
  Two short blasts to mean " I am directing my course to port."
  Three short blasts to mean " I am going full speed astern."
  The use of these signals is optional, but if they are used the course
of the ship must be in accordance with the signal made.

UNITED STATES:
　　Identical.
AUSTRIA-HUNGARY:
　　Identical.
BELGIUM:
　　Identical.
CHILI:
　　This article is identical in meaning, although not in form, with
that of Great Britain.
DENMARK:
　　Identical.
FRANCE:
　　Identical.
GERMANY:
　　Identical.
ITALY:
　　Identical, with the following exception:
　　Omit the words in the last paragraph "but if they are used" to
the end of the article.
JAPAN:
　　Identical.
MEXICO:
　　(See note at end.)
NORWAY:
　　Identical.
SIAM:
　　(See note at end.)
SWEDEN:
　　Identical.
THE NETHERLANDS:
　　Identical

GREAT BRITAIN:
　　ARTICLE 20. Notwithstanding anything contained in any preceding
article, every ship, whether a sailing-ship or a steam-ship, overtaking
any other shall keep out of the way of the overtaken ship.
UNITED STATES:
　　Identical.
AUSTRIA-HUNGARY:
　　This article intended to be identical with that of Great Britain,
but the word "notwithstanding" is translated by "unbeschadet"
instead of by "ohne rucksicht auf" (the word used by Germany in
the same article.)
BELGIUM:
　　Identical.

CHILI:

This article is as follows:

(Translation.) " Every ship overtaking any other shall keep out of the way of the latter."

DENMARK:

Identical.

FRANCE:

Identical.

GERMANY:

Identical.

ITALY:

Identical.

JAPAN:

Identical.

MEXICO:

Identical.

NORWAY:

Identical.

SIAM:

Identical.

SWEDEN:

Identical.

THE NETHERLANDS:

Identical.

GREAT BRITAIN:

ARTICLE 21. In narrow channels every steamship shall, when it is safe and practicable, keep to that side of the fairway or mid-channel which lies on the starboard side of such ship.

UNITED STATES:

Identical.

AUSTRIA-HUNGARY:

Identical.

BELGIUM:

Identical.

CHILI:

Identical.

DENMARK:

Identical.

FRANCE:

Identical.

GERMANY:

Identical.

ITALY:

Identical.

JAPAN:

Identical.

MEXICO:
See note at end.
NORWAY:
Identical.
SIAM:
See note at end.
SWEDEN:
Identical.
THE NETHERLANDS:
Identical.

GREAT BRITAIN:
ARTICLE 22. Where by the above rules one of two ships is to keep
out of the way the other shall keep her course.
UNITED STATES:
Identical.
AUSTRIA-HUNGARY:
Identical.
BELGIUM:
Identical.
CHILI:
Identical.
DENMARK:
Identical.
FRANCE:
Identical.
GERMANY:
Identical.
ITALY:
Identical.
JAPAN:
Identical.
MEXICO:
Probably intended to be identical.
NORWAY:
Identical.
SIAM:
Identical.
SWEDEN:
Identical.
THE NETHERLANDS:
Identical.

GREAT BRITAIN:
ARTICLE 23. In obeying and construing these rules due regard
shall be had to all dangers of navigation, and to any special circumstances which may render a departure from the above rules necessary
in order to avoid immediate danger.

UNITED STATES:
 Identical.
AUSTRIA-HUNGARY:
 Identical.
BELGIUM:
 Identical.
CHILI:
 Identical.
DENMARK:
 Identical.
FRANCE:
 Identical.
GERMANY:
 Identical.
ITALY:
 Identical.
JAPAN:
 Identical.
MEXICO:
 Identical.
NORWAY:
 Identical.
SIAM:
 Identical
SWEDEN:
 Identical.
THE NETHERLANDS:
 Identical.

GREAT BRITAIN:
 ARTICLE 24. Nothing in these rules shall exonerate any ship, or
the owner, or master, or crew thereof, from the consequences of any
neglect to carry lights or signals, or of any neglect to keep a proper
lookout, or of the neglect of any precaution which may be required
by the ordinary practice of seamen or by the special circumstances of
the case.
UNITED STATES:
 Identical.
AUSTRIA-HUNGARY:
 Identical.
BELGIUM:
 Identical.
CHILI:
 Identical.
DENMARK:
 Identical.

FRANCE:
    Identical.
GERMANY:
    Identical.
ITALY:
    Identical.
JAPAN:
    Identical.
MEXICO: ·
    Identical.
NORWAY:
    Identical.
SIAM:
    Identical.
SWEDEN:
    Identical.
THE NETHERLANDS:
    Identical.

GREAT BRITAIN:
    ARTICLE 25. Nothing in these rules shall interfere with the opera-
tion of a special rule, duly made by local authority, relative to the
navigation of any harbor, river, or inland navigation.
UNITED STATES:
    Identical.
AUSTRIA-HUNGARY:
    Identical.
BELGIUM:
    Identical.
CHILI:
    This article omitted.
DENMARK:
    Identical.
FRANCE:
    Identical.
GERMANY:
    Identical.
ITALY:
    Identical.
JAPAN:
    Identical.
MEXICO:
    This article omitted.
NORWAY:
    Identical.
SIAM:
    This article omitted, but see preamble to the Siamese rules.

SWEDEN:
Identical.
THE NETHERLANDS:
Identical.

GREAT BRITAIN:
ARTICLE 26. Nothing in these rules shall interfere with the operation of any special rules made by the Government of any nation with respect to additional station and signal lights for two or more ships of war or for ships sailing under convoy.
UNITED STATES:
Identical.
AUSTRIA-HUNGARY:
Identical, except that the word "additional," before the words "station and signal lights," is omitted.
BELGIUM:
Identical.
CHILI:
This article is omitted.
DENMARK:
Identical, except that the word "additional," before the words "station and signal lights," is omitted.
FRANCE:
Identical.
GERMANY:
Identical.
ITALY:
This article omitted.
JAPAN:
Identical.
MEXICO:
This article omitted.
NORWAY:
Identical.
SIAM:
This article omitted.
SWEDEN:
Identical.
THE NETHERLANDS:
Identical.

GREAT BRITAIN:
ARTICLE 27. When a ship is in distress and requires assistance from other ships or from the shore, the following shall be the signals to be used or displayed by her, either together or separately, that is to say:
In the daytime—
First. A gun fired at intervals of about a minute.

GREAT BRITAIN—continued.

Second. The international code signal of distress indicated by N. O.

Third. The distant signal, consisting of a square flag, having either above or below it a ball, or anything resembling a ball.

At night—

First. A gun fired at intervals of about a minute.

Second. Flames on the ship (as from a burning tar-barrel, oil-barrel, and so forth).

Third. Rockets or shells, throwing stars of any color or description, fired one at a time, at short intervals.

UNITED STATES :
Identical.

AUSTRIA-HUNGARY :*

BELGIUM :*

CHILI:*

DENMARK :*

FRANCE :
Identical.

GERMANY:
Identical.   Given by the imperial decree of August 14, 1876.

ITALY :*

JAPAN :
Identical.

MEXICO:*

NORWAY:
Identical.

SIAM :*

SWEDEN :
Identical.

THE NETHERLANDS:
Identical.   Given by the royal order of October 10, 1875.

---

* Some powers have not considered this article which provides signals for ships in distress as proper to be inserted in regulations for preventing collisions at sea, and have therefore omitted it.

NOTE.—In the case of Mexico and Siam the rules furnished to the Conference are dated prior to 1884, and it is not known whether these countries have adopted the changes introduced in 1884, and subsequently, into the rules of other countries. It has, therefore, not always been possible, in the case of Mexico and Siam, to apply the same method of comparison with the rules of Great Britain, as has been applied with regard to other countries.

FINAL REPORT OF THE COMMITTEE ON COLLOCATION OF THE RULES.

RESOLUTION.

Resolved, That a Committee on Collocation of Rules, to consist of seven persons, be appointed by the President.

MOTION.

Mr. GOODRICH (United States). That the several committees be increased each by two, and that the Committee on Collocation also be increased by two members.

COMMITTEE.

Austria-Hungary	Admiral DE SPAUN.
France	Captain LANNELUC.
Germany	Dr. SIEVEKING.
Great Britain	Mr. HALL.
Japan	Lieutenant BABA.
Mexico	Commodore MONASTERIO.
Norway	Captain SALVESEN.
Russia	Admiral KAZNAKOFF.
United States	Mr. GOODRICH.

REPORT.

To Rear-Admiral SAMUEL R. FRANKLIN, U. S. Navy,
President of the International Marine Conference, etc.:

Washington.

SIR: In compliance with the resolution passed by the Conference on 20th instant, your committee have completed their former report by embodying into the regulations and notes the changes and additions recently adopted by the Conference.

The final regulations and notes, as revised by your committee are hereto annexed in Appendices A and B, respectively.

We have the honor to be, sir, your most obedient servants,

WM. W. GOODRICH, *Chairman,*
United States.
Rear-Admiral DE SPAUN,
Austria-Hungary.
Dr. SIEVEKING,
Germany.
CHARLES HALL,
Great Britain.
S. TSUKAHARA,
Japan.
Commodore MONASTERIO,
Mexico.
Captain SALVESEN,
Norway.
Vice-Admiral KAZNAKOFF,
Russia.

APPENDIX A.

REGULATIONS FOR PREVENTING COLLISIONS AT SEA.

PRELIMINARY.

These rules shall be followed by all vessels upon the high seas and in all waters connected therewith, navigable by sea-going vessels.

In the following rules every steam vessel which is under sail and not under steam is to be considered a sailing vessel, and every vessel under steam, whether under sail or not, is to be considered a steam-vessel.

The word "*steam-vessel*" shall include any vessel propelled by machinery.

A vessel is "*under way*" within the meaning of these rules, when she is not at anchor, or made fast to the shore, or aground.

RULES CONCERNING LIGHTS, ETC.

The word "*visible*" in these rules when applied to lights shall mean visible on a dark night with a clear atmosphere.

ARTICLE 1. The rules concerning lights shall be complied with in all weathers from sunset to sunrise, and during such time no other lights which may be mistaken for the prescribed lights shall be exhibited.

ART. 2. A steam-vessel when under way shall carry—

(a) On or in front of the foremast, or if a vessel without a foremast then in the fore part of the vessel, at a height above the hull of not less than 20 feet, and if the breadth of the vessel exceeds 20 feet, then at a height above the hull not less than such breadth, so however, that the light need not be carried at a greater height above the hull than 40 feet, a bright white light, so constructed as to show an unbroken light over an arc of the horizon of 20 points of the compass, so fixed as to throw the light 10 points on each side of the vessel, viz., from right ahead to 2 points abaft the beam on either side, and of such a character as to be visible at a distance of at least 5 miles.

(b) On the starboard side a green light so constructed as to show an unbroken light over an arc of the horizon of 10 points of the compass, so fixed as to throw the light from right ahead to 2 points abaft the beam on the starboard side, and of such a character as to be visible at a distance of at least 2 miles.

(c) On the port side a red light so constructed as to show an unbroken light over an arc of the horizon of 10 points of the compass, so fixed as to throw the light from right ahead to 2 points abaft the beam on the port side, and of such a character as to be visible at a distance of at least 2 miles.

(d) The said green and red side-lights shall be fitted with inboard screens projecting at least 3 feet forward from the light so as to prevent these lights from being seen across the bow.

(e) A steam-vessel when under way may carry an additional white light similar in construction to the light mentioned in subdivision (a). These two lights shall be so placed in line with the keel that one shall be at least 15 feet higher than the other, and in such a position with reference to each other that the lower light shall be forward of the upper one. The vertical distance between these lights shall be less than the horizontal distance.

ART. 3. A steam-vessel when towing another vessel shall, in addition to her side-lights, carry two bright white lights in a vertical line one over the other, not less than 6 feet apart, and when towing more than one vessel shall carry an additional bright white light 6 feet above or below such lights, if the length of the tow measuring from the stern of the towing vessel to the stern of the last vessel towed exceeds 600 feet. Each of these lights shall be of the same construction and character, and shall be carried in the same position as the white light mentioned in article 2 (a), excepting the additional light, which may be carried at a height of not less than 14 feet above the hull.

Such steam-vessel may carry a small white light abaft the funnel or aftermast for the vessel towed to steer by, but such light shall not be visible forward of the beam.

ART. 4. (a) A vessel which from any accident is not under command shall carry at the same height as the white light mentioned in article 2 (a), where they can best be seen, and if a steam-vessel in lieu of that light, two red lights, in a vertical line one over the other, not less than 6 feet apart, and of such a character as to be visible all around the horizon at a distance of at least 2 miles; and shall by day carry in a vertical line one over the other, not less than 6 feet apart, where they can best be seen, two black balls or shapes, each 2 feet in diameter.

(b) A vessel employed in laying or in picking up a telegraph cable shall carry in the same position as the white light mentioned in article 2 (a), and if a steam-vessel in lieu of that light, three lights in a vertical line one over the other, not less than 6 feet apart. The highest and lowest of these lights shall be red, and the middle light shall be white, and they shall be of such a character as to be visible all around the horizon, at a distance of at least 2 miles. By day she shall carry in a vertical line one over the other, not less than 6 feet apart, where they can best be seen, three shapes not less than 2 feet in diameter, of which the highest and the lowest shall be globular in shape and red in color, and the middle one diamond in shape and white.

(c) The vessels referred to in this article, when not making way through the water, shall not carry the side-lights, but when making way shall carry them.

(d) The lights and shapes required to be shown by this article are to be taken by other vessels as signals that the vessel showing them is not under command and can not therefore get out of the way.

These signals are not signals of vessels in distress and requiring assistance. Such signals are contained in article 31.

ART. 5. A sailing vessel under way, and any vessel being towed, shall carry the same lights as are prescribed by article 2 for a steam-vessel under way, with the exception of the white lights mentioned therein, which they shall never carry.

ART. 6. Whenever, as in the case of small vessels under way during bad weather, the green and red side-lights can not be fixed, these lights shall be kept at hand, lighted and ready for use; and shall on the approach of or to other vessels, be exhibited on their respective sides in sufficient time to prevent collision, in such manner as to make them most visible, and so that the green light shall not be seen on the port side nor the red light on the starboard side, nor if practicable more than 2 points abaft the beam on their respective sides.

To make the use of these portable lights more certain and easy, the lanterns containing them shall each be painted outside with the color of the light they respectively contain, and shall be provided with proper screens.

ART. 7. Steam-vessels of less than 40, and vessels under oars or sails, of less than 20 tons, gross tonnage, respectively, when under way, shall not be obliged to carry the lights mentioned in article 2 (a) (b) and (c), but if they do not carry them they shall be provided with the following lights:

1. Steam-vessels of less than 40 tons shall carry:

    (a) In the fore part of the vessel, or on or in front of the funnel, where it can best be seen, and at a height above the gunwale of not less than 9 feet, a bright white light constructed and fixed as prescribed in article 2 (a), and of such a character as to be visible at a distance of at least 2 miles.

    (b) Green and red side-lights, constructed and fixed as prescribed in article 2 (b) and (c), and of such a character as to be visible at a distance of at least 1 mile, or a combined lantern showing a green light and a red light from right ahead to 2 points abaft the beam on their respective sides. Such lantern shall be carried not less than 3 feet below the white light.

2. Small steam-boats, such as are carried by sea-going vessels, may carry the white light at a less height than 9 feet above the gunwale, but it shall be carried above the combined lantern, mentioned in subdivision 1 (b).

3. Vessels under oars or sails, of less than 20 tons, shall have ready at hand a lantern with a green glass on one side and a red glass on the other, which, on the approach of or to other vessels, shall be exhibited in sufficient time to prevent collision, so that the green light shall not be seen on the port side nor the red light on the starboard side.

The vessels referred to in this article shall not be obliged to carry the lights prescribed by article 4 (*a*), and article 11, last paragraph.

ART. 8. Pilot vessels when engaged on their station on pilotage duty, shall not show the lights required for other vessels, but shall carry a white light at the masthead, visible all around the horizon, and shall also exhibit a flare-up light or flare-up lights at short intervals, which shall never exceed fifteen minutes.

On the near approach of or to other vessels they shall have their side-lights lighted, ready for use, and shall flash or show them at short intervals, to indicate the direction in which they are heading, but the green light shall not be shown on the port side, nor the red light on the starboard side.

A pilot-vessel of such a class as to be obliged to go alongside of a vessel to put a pilot on board, may show the white light instead of carrying it at the masthead, and may, instead of the colored lights above mentioned, have at hand ready for use a lantern with a green glass on the one side and a red glass on the other, to be used as prescribed above.

Pilot-vessels when not engaged on their station on pilotage duty, shall carry lights similar to those of other vessels of their tonnage.

ART. 9. Fishing vessels and fishing boats when under way, and when not required by this article to carry or show the lights therein named, shall carry or show the lights prescribed for vessels of their tonnage under way.

(*a*) Vessels and boats when fishing with drift-nets shall exhibit two white lights from any part of the vessel where they can best be seen. Such lights shall be placed so that the vertical distance between them shall be not less than 6 feet and not more than 10 feet, and so that the horizontal distance between them, measured in a line with the keel, shall be not less than 5 feet and not more than 10 feet. The lower of these two lights shall be the more forward, and both of them shall be of such a character as to show all around the horizon, and to be visible at a distance of not less than 3 miles.

(*b*) Vessels when engaged in trawling, by which is meant the dragging of an apparatus along the bottom of the sea—

1. If steam-vessels, shall carry in the same position as the white light mentioned in article 2 (*a*), a tricolored lantern so constructed and fixed as to show a white light from right ahead to 2 points on each bow, and a green light and a red light over an arc of the horizon from 2 points on either bow to 2 points abaft the beam on the starboard and port side respectively; and not less than 6 nor more than 12 feet below the tricolored lantern, a white light in a lantern, so constructed as to show a clear uniform and unbroken light all around the horizon.

2. If sailing vessels of 7 tons gross tonnage and upwards, shal carry a white light in a lantern, so constructed as to show a clear, uniform, and unbroken light all around the horizon, and shall also be provided with a sufficient supply of red pyrotechnic lights, which shall each burn for at least 30 seconds, and shall be shown on the approach of or to other vessels in sufficient time to prevent collision.

In the Mediterranean Sea, the vessels referred to in subdivision (b) 2 may use a flare-up light in lieu of a pyrotechnic light.

All lights mentioned in subdivision b (1) and (2) shall be visible at a distance of at least 2 miles.

3. If sailing vessels of less than 7 tons gross tonnage, shall not be obliged to carry the white light mentioned in subdivision b (2) of this article, but if they do not carry such light they shall have at hand, ready for use, a lantern showing a bright white light, which shall, on the approach of or to other vessels be exhibited where it can best be seen, in sufficient time to prevent collision; and they shall also show a red pyrotechnic light, as prescribed in subdivision b (2), or in lieu thereof a flare-up light.

(c) Vessels and boats when line-fishing with their lines out and attached to their lines, and when not at anchor or stationary, shall carry the same lights as vessels fishing with drift-nets.

(d) Fishing vessels and fishing boats may at any time use a flare-up light in addition to the lights which they are by this article required to carry and show. All flare-up lights exhibited by a vessel when trawling or fishing with any kind of drag-net shall be shown at the after part of the vessel, excepting that, if the vessel is hanging by the stern to her fishing-gear, they. shall be exhibited from the bow.

(e) Every fishing-vessel and every boat when at anchor shall exhibit a white light visible all around the horizon at a distance of at least 1 mile.

(f) If a vessel or boat, when fishing, becomes stationary in consequence of her gear getting fast to a rock or other obstruction; she shall show the light and make the fog-signal pre. scribed for a vessel at anchor, respectively. (See article 15 (d) (e) and last paragraph.)

(g) In fog, mist, falling snow, or heavy rain-storms, drift-net vessels attached to their nets, and vessels when trawling, dredging, or fishing with any kind of drag-net, and vessels line-fishing with their lines out, shall, if of 20 tons gross tonnage or upwards, respectively, at intervals of not more than 1 minute, make a blast; if steam-vessels with the whistle or siren, and if sailing vessels with the fog-horn, each blast to be followed by ringing the bell.

(*h*) Sailing vessels or boats fishing with nets or lines or trawls, when under way, shall in day-time indicate their occupation to an approaching vessel by displaying a basket or other efficient signal, where it can best be seen.

The vessels referred to in this article shall not be obliged to carry the lights prescribed by article 4 (*a*), and article 11, last paragraph.

ART. 10. A vessel which is being overtaken by another shall show from her stern to such last-mentioned vessel a white light or a flare-up light.

The white light required to be shown by this article may be fixed and carried in a lantern, but in such case the lantern shall be so constructed, fitted, and screened that it shall throw an unbroken light over an arc of the horizon of 12 points of the compass, viz, for 6 points from right aft on each side of the vessel, so as to be visible at a distance of at least 1 mile. Such light shall be carried as nearly as practicable on the same level as the side lights.

ART. 11. A vessel under 150 fee t in length, when at anchor, shal carry forward, where it can best be seen, but at a height not exceeding 20 feet above the hull, a white light in a lantern so constructed as to show a clear, uniform, and unbroken light, visible all around the horizon at a distance of at least 1 mile.

A vessel of 150 feet or upwards in length, when at anchor, shall carry in the forward part of the vessel, at a height of not less than 20 and not exceeding 40 feet above the hull, one such light, and at or near the stern of the vessel, and at such a height that it shall be not less than 15 feet lower than the forward light, another such light.

The length of a vessel shall be deemed to be the length appearing in her certificate of registry.

A vessel aground in or near a fair-way shall carry the above light or lights and the two red lights prescribed by article 4 (*a*).

ART. 12. Every vessel may, if necessary in order to attract attention, in addition to the lights which she is by these rules required to carry, show a flare-up light or use any detonating signal that can not be mis-taken for a distress signal.

ART. 13. Nothing in these rules shall interfere with the operation of any special rules made by the Government of any nation, with respect to additional station and signal-lights for two or more ships of war or for vessels sailing under convoy, or with the exhibition of recognition signals adopted by ship-owners, which have been authorized by their respective Governments and duly registered and published.

ART. 14. A steam-vessel proceeding under sail only, but having her funnel up, shall carry in day-time, forward, where it can best be seen, one black ball or shape 2 feet in diameter.

SOUND SIGNALS FOR FOG, ETC.

ART. 15. All signals prescribed by this article for vessels under way shall be given:

1. By "*steam-vessels*" on the whistle or siren.
2. By "*sailing-vessels and vessels towed*" on the fog-horn.

The words "*prolonged blast*" used in this article shall mean a blast of from four to six seconds duration.

A steam-vessel shall be provided with an efficient whistle or siren, sounded by steam or some substitute for steam, so placed that the sound may not be intercepted by any obstruction, and with an efficient fog-horn, to be sounded by mechanical means, and also with an efficient bell.* A sailing vessel of 20 tons gross tonnage or upwards shall be provided with a similar fog-horn and bell.

In fog, mist, falling snow, or heavy rain-storms, whether by day or night, the signals described in this article shall be used as follows, viz:

(a) A steam-vessel having way upon her shall sound, at intervals of not more than two minutes, a prolonged blast.

(b) A steam-vessel under way, but stopped and having no way upon her, shall sound, at intervals of not more than two minutes, two prolonged blasts, with an interval of about one second between them.

(c) A sailing-vessel under way shall sound, at intervals of not more than one minute, when on the starboard tack one blast, when on the port tack two blasts in succession, and when with the wind abaft the beam three blasts in succession.

(d) A vessel, when at anchor, shall, at intervals of not more than one minute, ring the bell rapidly for about five seconds.

(e) A vessel, at anchor at sea, when not in ordinary anchorage ground and when in such a position as to be an obstruction to vessels under way, shall sound, if a steam-vessel, at intervals of not more than two minutes, two prolonged blasts with her whistle or siren, followed by ringing her bell; or, if a sailing vessel, at intervals of not more than one minute, two blasts with her fog-horn, followed by ringing her bell.

(f) A vessel, when towing, shall, instead of the signals prescribed in subdivisions (a) and (c) of this article, at intervals of not more than two minutes, sound three blasts in succession, viz, one prolonged blast followed by two short blasts. A vessel towed may give this signal and she shall not give any other.

---

*NOTE.—In all cases where the Rules require a bell to be used a drum may be substituted on board Turkish vessels, or a gong where such articles are used on board small sea-going vessels.

(*g*) A steam-vessel, wishing to indicate to another "The way is off my vessel, you may feel your way past me," may sound three blasts in succession, viz, short, long, short, with intervals of about one second between them.

(*h*) A vessel employed in laying or in picking up a telegraph cable shall, on hearing the fog-signal of an approaching vessel, sound in answer three prolonged blasts in succession.

(*i*) A vessel under way, which is unable to get out of the way of an approaching vessel through being not under command, or unable to maneuver as required by these Rules, shall, on hearing the fog-signal of an approaching vessel, sound in answer four short blasts in succession.

Sailing-vessels and boats of less than 20 tons gross tonnage shall not be obliged to give the above-mentioned signals, but if they do not, they shall make some other efficient sound-signal at intervals of not more than one minute.

SPEED OF SHIPS TO BE MODERATE IN FOG, ETC.

ART. 16. Every vessel shall, in a fog, mist, falling snow, or heavy rain-storm, go at a moderate speed, having careful regard to the existing circumstances and conditions.

A steam-vessel hearing, apparently forward of her beam, the fog-signal of a vessel the position of which is not ascertained, shall, so far as the circumstances of the case admit, stop her engines, and then navigate with caution until danger of collision is over.

STEERING AND SAILING RULES.

PRELIMINARY—RISK OF COLLISION.

Risk of collision can, when circumstances permit, be ascertained by carefully watching the compass bearing of an approaching vessel. If the bearing does not appreciably change, such risk should be deemed to exist.

ART. 17. When two sailing vessels are approaching one another, so as to involve risk of collision, one of them shall keep out of the way of the other, as follows, viz:

(*a*) A vessel which is running free shall keep out of the way of a vessel which is close-hauled.

(*b*) A vessel which is close-hauled on the port tack shall keep out the way of a vessel which is close-hauled on the starboard tack.

(*c*) When both are running free, with the wind on different sides, the vessel which has the wind on the port side shall keep out of the way of the other.

(*d*) When both are running free, with the wind on the same side, the vessel which is to windward shall keep out of the way of the vessel which is to leeward.

(*e*) A vessel which has the wind aft shall keep out of the way of the other vessel.

ART. 18. When two steam-vessels are meeting end on, or nearly end on, so as to involve risk of collision, each shall alter her course to starboard, so that each may pass on the port side of the other.

This article only applies to cases where vessels are meeting end on, or nearly end on, in such a manner as to involve risk of collision, and does not apply to two vessels which must, if both keep on their respective courses, pass clear of each other.

The only cases to which it does apply are, when each of the two vessels is end on, or nearly end on, to the other; in other words, to cases in which, by day, each vessel sees the masts of the other in a line, or nearly in a line, with her own; and by night, to cases in which each vessel is in such a position as to see both the side-lights of the other.

It does not apply, by day, to cases in which a vessel sees another ahead crossing her own course; or by night, to cases where the red light of one vessel is opposed to the red light of the other, or where the green light of one vessel is opposed to the green light of the other, or where a red light without a green light, or a green light without a red light, is seen ahead, or where both green and red lights are seen anywhere but ahead.

ART. 19. When two steam-vessels are crossing, so as to involve risk of collision, the vessel which has the other on her own starboard side shall keep out of the way of the other.

ART. 20. When a steam-vessel and a sailing vessel are proceeding in such directions as to involve risk of collision, the steam-vessel shall keep out of the way of the sailing vessel.

ART. 21. Where by any of these rules one of two vessels is to keep out of the way, the other shall keep her course and speed.

ART. 22. Every vessel which is directed by these rules to keep out of the way of another vessel, shall, if the circumstances of the case admit, avoid crossing ahead of the other.

ART. 23. Every steam-vessel which is directed by these rules to keep out of the way of another vessel shall, on approaching her, if necessary, slacken her speed or stop or reverse.

ART. 24. Notwithstanding anything contained in these rules, every vessel, overtaking any other, shall keep out of the way of the overtaken vessel.

Every vessel coming up with another vessel from any direction more than two points abaft her beam, *i. e.*, in such a position, with reference to the vessel which she is overtaking that at night she would be unable to see either of that vessel's side-lights, shall be deemed to be an overtaking vessel; and no subsequent alteration of the bearing between the two vessels shall make the overtaking vessel a crossing vessel within the meaning of these rules, or relieve her of the duty of keeping clear of the overtaken vessel until she is finally past and clear.

As by day the overtaking vessel can not always know with certainty whether she is forward of or abaft this direction from the other vessel, she should, if in doubt, assume that she is an overtaking vessel and keep out of the way.

ART. 25. In narrow channels every steam-vessel shall, when it is safe and practicable, keep to that side of the fair-way or mid-channel which lies on the starboard side of such vessel.

ART. 26. Sailing vessels under way shall keep out of the way of sailing vessels or boats fishing with nets, or lines, or trawls. This rule shall not give to any vessel or boat engaged in fishing the right of obstructing a fair-way used by vessels other than fishing-vessels or boats.

ART. 27. In obeying and construing these rules due regard shall be had to all dangers of navigation and collision, and to any special circumstances which may render a departure from the above rules necessary in order to avoid immediate danger.

SOUND-SIGNALS FOR VESSELS IN SIGHT OF ONE ANOTHER.

ART. 28. The words "*short-blast*" used in this article shall mean a blast of about one second's duration.

When vessels are in sight of one another, a steam-vessel under way, in taking any course authorized or required by these rules, shall indicate that course by the following signals on her whistle or siren, viz:

One short blast to mean, "I am directing my course to starboard."

Two short blasts to mean, "I am directing my course to port."

Three short blasts to mean, "My engines are going full speed astern."

NO VESSEL, UNDER ANY CIRCUMSTANCES, TO NEGLECT PROPER PRE-CAUTIONS.

ART. 29. Nothing in these rules shall exonerate any vessel, or the owner, or master, or crew thereof, from the consequences of any neglect to carry lights or signals, or of any neglect to keep a proper look-out, or of the neglect of any precaution which may be required by the ordinary practice of seamen, or by the special circumstances of the case.

RESERVATION OF RULES FOR HARBORS AND INLAND NAVIGATION.

ART. 30. Nothing in these rules shall interfere with the operation of a special rule, duly made by local authority, relative to the navigation of any harbor, river, or inland waters.

DISTRESS SIGNALS.

ART. 31. When a vessel is in distress and requires assistance from other vessels or from the shore, the following shall be the signals to be used or displayed by her, either together or separately, viz:

In the day-time—

1. A gun fired at intervals of about a minute;
2. The International Code signal of distress indicated by N. C.;
3. The distant signal, consisting of a square flag, having either above or below it a ball or anything resembling a ball;
4. Rockets or shells as prescribed below for use at night;
5. A continuous sounding with any fog-signal apparatus.

At night—

1. A gun fired at intervals of about a minute;
2. Flames on the vessel (as from a burning tar-barrel, oil-barrel, etc.);
3. Rockets or shells, bursting in the air with a loud report and throwing stars of any color or description, fired one at a time at short intervals.
4. A continuous sounding with any fog-signal apparatus.

APPENDIX B.

The following resolutions have been approved of by the Conference and are recommended to the attention of the powers represented thereat:

1. The power of all lights should be expressed by referring them all to one standard, by which the light issuing from the lantern should be measured.

2. The minimum power only of each light should be definitely fixed, leaving it to the judgment of the parties responsible for fitting out the vessels with proper lanterns to employ lamps of this or greater power.

3. The use of incandescent lamps should be permitted; the use of arc lights at present should be excluded for all purposes other than signaling and searching.

4. Each lantern should be so constructed that the minimum power of light can be found at every point where the light is to be visible after the lamp has been fitted with proper screens.

5. The lantern should be so constructed as to insure the light having at least the required minimum power in the ideal line connecting the lantern with the horizon, even though the vessel be heeled one way or the other 10 degrees.

6. The color of the glasses by which the coloring of the light is to be produced should be so chosen that, if possible, the red light shall have no admixture of green, nor the green light of red rays, and that both colors can be readily and unmistakably distinguished.

7. No detailed description should be internationally adopted for the construction of the lamp or lantern, so that a fair chance may be given to inventors to produce serviceable articles.

8. The side lights should be so screened as to prevent the most con-vergent rays of the lights being seen across the bows more than half a point.

9. The side lights should be placed in steam-vessels not forward of the mast head light.

10. To meet the number of complaints as to the absence of proper lights on sailing vessels the attention of the powers is called to the bet-ter enforcement of the regulations in that behalf.

11. All steam-whistles, sirens, fog-horns, and bells should be thor-oughly tested as to their efficiency, and should be capable of being heard at a stated minimum distance, and should be so regulated that the tones of whistles and sirens should be as distinct as possible from the sound of fog-horns.

12. Steam-vessels should be provided, if possible, with means of blow-ing off surplus steam when the engines are stopped, in such a manner as to occasion as little noise as possible.

13. In clear weather at sea no vessel should attempt to cross the bows of the leaders of any squadron of three or more ships of war in regular formation, nor unnecessarily to pass through the lines of such squadron.

14. In every case of collision between two vessels it should be the duty of the master or person in charge of each vessel, if and so far as he can do so without serious danger to his own vessel, crew, and pas-sengers (if any), to stay by the other vessel until he has ascertained that she has no need of further assistance, and to render to the other vessel, her master, crew, and passengers (if any), such assistance as may be practicable and as may be necessary in order to save them from any danger caused by the collision, and also to give to the master or per-son in charge of the other vessel the name of his own vessel and her port of registry, or the port or place to which she belongs, and also the name of the ports and places from which and to which she is bound.

REPORT OF THE COMMITTEE ON LIGHTS.

[Accompanied by an appendix and three plates.]

RESOLUTION.

Resolved, That the Chair appoint two committees, each to consist of seven delegates, to be known as the Committee on Lights and the Committee on Sound Signals, whose present duty it shall be to examine and report to the Conference the literature on these two subjects which is in the possession of the Conference.

COMMITTEE.

France, ...	Captain RICHARD.
Germany, ...	Captain MENSING.
Great Britain, . . .	Captain WYATT.
Russia, ...	Admiral KAZNAKOFF.
Spain, ...	Lieut. DON BALDOMERO VEGA.
Sweden, ...	Captain MALMBERG.
United States, . . .	Captain NORCROSS.

WASHINGTON, *November* 4, 1889.

To Rear-Admiral S. R. FRANKLIN, U. S. Navy,

President of the International Marine Conference, etc. :

SIR : The Committee on Lights, pursuant to the resolution adopted by the International Marine Conference on the 17th ultimo, instructing the said committee to examine and report on the literature on lights in possession of this Conference, have agreed upon a report, which they have the honor to respectfully submit:

The literature submitted to the consideration of the Conference consists of papers, most of which offer certain distinct proposals. All these bear witness of the great interest the work of the Conference has excited, and a number of them show evident marks of the deep thought and great ingenuity brought to bear on the subject by the authors. Nevertheless, the committee have not thought it advisable to single out any special system for adoption, but content themselves with reporting in general terms upon such as are typical of their class. The committee, however, take this opportunity to express their sense of appreciation of the interest taken in the work, the sincerity of effort, and the ingenuity of which nearly every proposal bears evidence.

68

Before entering into a more detailed discussion of the proposals submitted to the Conference regarding lights the committee feel it their duty to say that it is absolutely necessary to be as conservative in regard to the existing rules concerning lights as possible. It has to be borne in mind that these rules, after being nearly forty years in force, have become as familiar to every seaman as if they were cast in iron letters and so impressed on their minds. Every change, therefore, has to be considered most seriously before its adoption, and this should be done only when considered absolutely necessary. Otherwise such an adoption may lead to confusion, and this probably would beget serious danger to life and property at sea, for the better protection of which this Conference is assembled.

Bearing this in mind, the committee beg leave to state that, although they have no direct evidence of the insufficiency of the present system of lights, they nevertheless are of the opinion that the regulations actually in force are insufficient to make the presence of a sailing vessel known to a fast steamer approaching her, soon enough to give the latter ample time to keep out of the way.

For, if a steam-vessel has to keep out of the way of a sailing vessel, then it is clearly the duty of the latter to make her presence known soon enough to make it possible for the steam-vessel to comply with the regulations.

In this respect the side lights at present shown by sailing vessels (Articles 6 and 7) and the white or the flare-up lights exhibited astern (Article 11) are not satisfactory. It is considered, therefore, desirable that some plan be found by which the presence of a sailing-vessel should be indicated at a greater distance than under the present regulations.

The proposals which have been submitted to the consideration of this committee aim to supply this want :

A. By introducing a white light to be carried a considerable distance above the side lights and to be visible at a greater distance than these, say 4 or 5 miles.

B. By increasing the power of the side lights.

Both these systems would increase the cost of fitting out vessels—a matter worth consideration.

(A) The introduction of a white light, such as is carried by steamers under way, according to the present rules, would, in the opinion of the committee, indicate the whereabouts of a sailing vessel in a simple and efficient way, and at such a distance that even the fastest steamers would have ample time for maneuvering in order to keep clear.

But the white light on sailing vessels would complicate the system of carrying lights on *all* classes of ships, since it would, as a matter of course, necessitate an increased number of lights to be carried by steamers also.

The adoption of such a light would moreover give to a sailing vessel in the future the same system of lights carried at present by a steam-vessel. This would bring about a radical change in the regulations, which should, if possible, be avoided.

The committee are fully aware also of the difficulty of placing a white light on board of a sailing vessel in such a manner as never to be obscured by the sails, particularly the head-sails.

There seem to be but the following places in which these lights might be carried:

(1) On the end of the bowsprit.

(2) Under the foretop.

(3) Under the foretopmast cross-trees.

(4) At the truck of a mast.

But none of these positions can be especially recommended to the consideration of the Conference.

(B) It appears very difficult, if at all possible, to increase the power of a ship's side lights from the present range of 2 miles to that of 3, as proposed, without at the same time increasing the size of the lantern in a manner which would make it too cumbersome and expensive for use on board ship where the conditions are such as to make the construction of lanterns particularly difficult. The range of a light increases only in the ratio of the square root of its power, and it would be necessary to increase the latter in the ratio of 4 to 9 or 1 to 2.25 in order to get the desired range mentioned above.

The committee had no exact data before them on which they could safely base a more detailed investigation of this important and difficult question, and they therefore took the liberty to suggest that a number of experiments be carried out by the Light-House Board of the United States in order to furnish the material necessary for further discussion.

Probably the construction of a more powerful light would necessitate the use of a wick of much larger diameter than that used at present, if not of a second wick, and this addition would again make it much more difficult to screen the lights properly. An electric light, on account of its smaller diameter, could no doubt be more easily arranged in such a manner as to meet the difficulty, but, in the opinion of the committee, such a light can not be made compulsory at the present day.

The committee, therefore come to the conclusion that though they can not but consider an increase in the power of the side lights most desirable, they do not find themselves at the present moment in a position to recommend any means by the adoption of which the desired end could with certainty be attained. This, however, may, as they hope, result from the experiments now undertaken by the Light-House Board of the United States.

Résumé : The committee, while fully aware of the great desirability of making the presence of a sailing vessel known at a greater distance than at present, are unable to recommend any of the systems submitted to their consideration as being free from all reasonable objections.

Much of the uncertainty at present felt on this account could, however, be avoided were the regulations properly enforced. And since among the papers submitted there are many complaints of the absence of proper lights on board sailing vessels, they believe that the attention of the different Governments should be called to the necessity of better enforcing the regulations in 'the future.

MEANS PROPOSED TO BETTER INDICATE THE COURSE OF A SHIP.

Among other proposals submitted to the Conference, those which aim at a better indication of the direction of a ship's keel are the most important. They may be classed as follows:

A. Those in which range-lights are made use of, *i. e.*, lights placed at a considerable horizontal distance from each other, and placed in the same vertical plane with the keel.

B. Those in which two or more side-lights are used on the same side of the ship.

C. Those in which it is proposed to give to the side-lights a certain relative position in regard to the white masthead-light of a steam-vessel.

A.—SYSTEMS IN WHICH RANGE-LIGHTS ARE MADE USE OF.

Range-lights were proposed a long time ago. They have been in use on board vessels navigating the inland waters of the United States of America for a considerable period, and have been made compulsory for such vessels by the rules approved by the Secretary of the Treasury, Circular No. 14, of March 1, 1883, rule 7.

The claim of originality for any of the systems submitted to the Conference can for this reason be entertained only in so far as the original system has been changed in one way or the other.

A list of the systems proposed will be found in Appendix A.

The committee regret that they could not report on other proposals regarding such lights, which have been made in different countries during a considerable number of years, and they beg to state that in their opinion a number of these are not inferior to many of the systems under discussion.

The system proposed by Lieut. F. F. Fletcher, U. S. Navy, has been explained to the committee by Commander Chadwick, U. S. Navy, whose "Report of trials on running-lights and sound-signals" by the United States war vessels *Yorktown*, *Despatch*, and *Triana*, has been officially brought to the notice of the Conference. This report speaks favorably of that system, and the committee have selected it therefore as a *representative* one of this class, and one well suited to be commented upon.

This has been done in order to be able to discuss the important question before us more in detail than would have been possible if only general principles were discussed.

The committee beg to state that the comments made regarding this system may be applied to nearly all other systems proposed, bearing in mind, however, that changes in particulars may influence the result to which we have come, but only in an unimportant degree.

The light-system of Lieutenant Fletcher consists in making use of a range of three lights, which have been placed as follows:

Forward of the foremast, at a distance apart not less than the beam of the ship, two bright white range-lights of the same character as the present masthead-light, visible from ahead to two points abaft the beam on either side. These lights shall be in the vertical plane of the keel, with the lower one so placed forward of the upper one that an imaginary line through them will make an angle of 55 degrees with the vertical. The third light is placed near the stern on the taffrail and screened so as to throw a light from right astern to two points forward of the beam.

When right ahead of a steam-ship an imaginary line through her two range-lights will appear vertical if the ship be on an even keel.

On the starboard bow of a steam-ship an imaginary line through her two range-lights will appear inclined from the vertical to the right, and on the port bow to the left from the vertical.

When more than four points on the bow of a steam-ship her range-lights will appear inclined more than 45 degrees, and at six points her stern-light is visible.

If we imagine that an observer is stationed at a great distance and a ship, lighted in the proposed manner, turned around the perpendicular through her middle range-light, then it will be seen that the horizontal distance between the masthead-light and the forward range-light does not increase in the same ratio as the angle between the visual line of the observer and the keel of the ship, but only in the ratio of the sines of this angle. (See Fig. 1, in which the distance of the observer is assumed to be indefinite, and, in consequence, the visual lines parallel to each other.)

By a glance at the accompanying diagram (Fig. 1) it is easily seen that the lights at an angle of six points appear at the same distance as at an angle of ten points. The same is true with regard to the angles of seven and nine points, and others which may be symmetrically placed to the line, Ll_8, up to two points of this line.

The horizontal distance at which the two forward range-lights at different angles appear has been calculated, and will be found in column b of the following table for a perpendicular distance between the lights of 21.2 feet, which makes the horizontal distance between the lights for an angle of 55 degrees = 30 feet.

a	b	c	d
If the angle of keel of ship and visual line of observer is—	Then the horizontal distance between 2 forward range lights will be—	If $2\frac{1}{2}^{o}$ be a unit, and it is assumed that each unit corresponds with one point, then for other points the distance is—	Difference between columns b and c.
	Feet.		
1 point	5. 9	5. 3	—0. 6
2 points	11. 5	10. 6	—0. 9
3 points	16. 7	15. 9	—0. 8
4 points	21. 2	21. 2	+ or —0. 0
5 points	24. 9	....	....
6 points	27. 7	....	....
7 points	29. 4	....	....
8 points	30. 0	....	....
9 points	29. 4	....	....
10 points	27. 7	....	....

We see from column b that the horizontal distance under which the two range-lights are seen, after the ship has turned four points, has become 21.2 feet, and at this point is equal to the perpendicular distance between the lights; the triangle formed by the horizontal line through the forward range-light, the perpendicular through the foremasthead-light, and the line connecting the lights, has become equilateral, both angles at the connecting line (Ll_4 Fig. 2, being 45°).

Now, order a look-out to watch carefully, and give him the following instructions: That when he sees the two white lights, one below the other, the ship which shows them is heading directly for him; that if a plumb line from the masthead-light appears to be separated from the forward light one-quarter of that distance, her course makes an angle of two points; and that if the distance is equal to three-quarters, or equal to the whole of the perpendicular, then that ship's course will be three or four points inclined to his eye-line.

Such instruction may be understood by a sailor and may not. But if he should understand it and is accustomed to judge distances somewhat correctly, he will be able to determine the other ship's course pretty accurately, for, as column d shows, there is only a small difference between columns b and c, and it appears probable that, as Commander Chadwick found to be the case during the trials he made, an ordinary sailor may very well judge by this method whether a ship's course is inclined to his eye-line one, two, three or four points, without probably making a greater mistake than half a point. (*See* report, page 7, ¶ 4.)

In Sector B, Fig. 3 (that is, from four to six points), it would become more difficult to judge the course correctly; because here the horizontal alteration of distances between the lights becomes much smaller for the same alteration of the course of the ship, but the error will probably not become more than one point. At six points the after range-light would come in view, but it will probably not be possible to estimate the bearing in sector C more closely than to say, that an observer is "abeam" of the other vessel. Errors up to two points may, on this account, be expected.

Further aft than ten points from right ahead, both the forward range-lights, as well as the side-lights, will be shut in, and by the stern-light alone it will only be possible to say that an observer is within six points on either quarter.

The advantages of Lieutenant Fletcher's system of range-lights, and all others similar to this, consist, therefore, in that it affords the means by which the course of a ship can be found by simple observation and comparison alone, by an observer stationed in a sector from right ahead to six points on either side (Sectors A and B, Fig. 3), with tolerable accuracy, say within one point, provided, however, that the ship observed has no perceptible heel.

If this should be the case, then the indication of the course will become less correct, and be changed in a ratio of about three-quarters of the amount of heel. This will be seen by reference to Fig. 4, in which S is the ship seen by an observer stationed right ahead; L and l the two range-lights and a the angle of heel. The two lights appear not in a vertical line, one below the other, but inclined, and the lower light to the right of the perpendicular through L, at a distance $ll_x = Ll \sin a$.

If we assume, as before, $Ll = 21.2$ feet, and $a = 12°$, then ll_x is $= 4.4$ feet; if we compare this with the table page 73, column b, we find that this would correspond to a change of course of about three-quarters of a point (more exactly: $8.5°$), and that the observations of the ship's lanterns lead in this case to an error of this amount, whereas if the ship had been on an even keel the indication of the ship's course would have been more correct in this position than in any other.

True, in the present case, the side-lights would have been visible and could have been used to correct this error.

But this could *not* have been done if the ship's head had been turned from one to two points, where the error would have been about the same.

From the foregoing it follows that the use of range-lights on the high seas does not offer the same advantages as have been found to be derived from it by vessels navigating inland waters, and this should not be lost sight of in coming to a conclusion regarding the introduction of such a system.

A practical difficulty will also be found in the placing of the forward range-light according to the demands of this system. For if a ship's foremast is placed 60 feet from the bow, and the foremasthead-light at a height of 30 feet above the hull, the forward range-light, with a minimum vertical distance of 15 feet, would be placed 15 feet above the hull and 34 from the bow; that is, in a place where it is presumably difficult to keep it, if a fast steam-ship is going at full speed against a head sea.

If such a ship be provided with a turtle deck it would probably be difficult to hoist or lower the lantern without slackening the speed and to control the burning of the light.

It has also to be kept in view that a white light, accidentally shown somewhere about the stern, for instance, a bright binnacle light, could be mistaken for the stern-light, and thus lead to the belief that the observer is abeam of a vessel, when he is actually in a sector within six points from ahead.

It has to be remembered, too, that what a seaman especially wants to find out when he watches another ship is whether she is proceeding in such a manner as to involve risk of collision.

But the knowledge of the course of the ship alone is not sufficient to determine this. It would remain necessary to watch the compass-bearing of the ship in sight, whether she be fitted with range-lights or not.

The greatest advantage of the above system, in the opinion of the committee, is that a small change in the course of a steamer approaching end on, or nearly so, is at once and unmistakably indicated.

Lieutenant Fletcher also proposes that the foremast-light be occulted every half minute for steamers going at a greater speed than 13 knots.

This proposition can not be recommended by the committee, as the construction of such a lantern is too complicated. It would, moreover, give only a very approximate idea of the speed of steam-ships, as these are known to proceed at the present day at any speed up to 20 knots and more.

Conclusions.—Range-lights, if properly placed and fitted, indicate, under certain circumstances, a ship's course in a more accurate way than at present. This is of some advantage, and therefore, in the opinion of the committee, the *optional* introduction of some such system may be proposed for the favorable consideration of the Conference, adding, however, that no definite system should be decided upon for adoption before this subject has been more fully studied, and before a larger number of experiments under different circumstances have been carried out.

B.—SYSTEM IN WHICH TWO OR MORE SIDE LIGHTS ARE EMPLOYED ON THE SAME SIDE.

There are certain general objections to the introduction of a system which, in some cases, would require double the number of lanterns carried at present, and more, and it is considered advisable to state these before going into further particulars.

(1) It has been found very difficult to compel certain classes of ships to carry the lights prescribed for them by the regulations actually in force. It has to be expected that had they to carry double the number of lanterns there would result presumably still more cases of non-compliance with the law.

(2) The care of a larger number of lanterns would require more men than could be spared for such service on board of small vessels.

(3) The cost of the outfit of every vessel, and the cost of providing the illuminant would be considerably increased. This would probably not affect the owners of large steam-ships, but would not easily be borne by the man who owns only a portion of a small sailing vessel.

Of the proposals submitted a number were so definite that diagrams showing the number and arrangement of lights proposed could be drawn (see Figs. 5 to 12).

In these A is to be the sector in which two colored side lights are visible; B the sector in which one colored side light; C the sector in which only the white stern light (Article 11) or a white side light (Fig. 12) is visible.

It will be seen by reference to the figures that an observer has only to count the number of side lights visible from his position in order to know in which of the sectors A, B, or C he is. It is evident then that the course of a vessel by the adoption of any one of the proposals submitted could only be ascertained very approximately, and this advantage does not seem to the committee important enough to warrant the recommendation of any of the proposals submitted to the favorable consideration of the Conference.

It is true, that by placing the lights on each side at a certain defined distance from each other, it would be possible to estimate the course of a vessel more approximately than at present, at least when two lights are seen.

Practically it would be most difficult to comply with such a proposition, and it therefore can not be recommended. In addition to this it ought to be stated that, as far as known to the committee, only a few experiments have been made with systems employing double side lights at sea. The Royal Spanish Navy has tried it already in a squadron, and has found that the advantage gained by double side lights were not so great as to recommend their adoption. Neither have they given satisfaction to the officer in charge of the trials made in the United States (Report on trials quoted above, p. 7, ¶ 4), and some of the advantages claimed for these systems remain to be proved before they can be considered as having more than theoretical value.

C.—SYSTEMS IN WHICH THE DIRECTION OF A STEAM-VESSEL IS SHOWN BY PLACING THE SIDE LIGHTS IN A CERTAIN POSITION RELATIVE TO THE MAST-HEAD LIGHT.

It is evident that if the side lights of all steam-vessels were so placed that a vertical plane through the line drawn from them to the mast-head light would form a certain known angle with the keel, it would be possible to estimate the direction in which a ship is heading more approximately than at present.

If, for instance, a ship had her lights so placed that the vertical plane through the line connecting the foremast-head light with the side lights would form an angle of 45° with the keel, counting from right ahead, then an observer on the starboard side of such a vessel would know that if the lights were visible one below the other that the course of the ship he sees was inclined four points to his eye-line; that if he saw the green light to the left of the foremast light he would be in the sector between this line and the bow, and if he saw the green light to the right of the foremast light that then he would be in the sector aft of the four points line.

By noticing whether the horizontal distance between the two lights was larger or smaller he would get another indication, and an observer would, therefore, be able to judge the course of a ship sighted pretty closely, say, within one or two points.

Unfortunately it is, in the committee's opinion, practically impossible to assign to the side lights a certain fixed position in regard to the foremast light, particularly if this position should be chosen *forward* of the mast, by which, no doubt, the greatest advantage could be gained. But we think that at least some advantage might be gained by placing the side lights *abaft* the mast, at as nearly a certain fixed angle as circumstances will permit. Such a change could be made, probably, without incurring great expense, and we wish to propose to the Conference the adoption of a rule according to which steamers would have to carry their side lights *abaft* the foremast light, the connecting line forming an angle of six points with the keel, or as nearly so as possible.

Besides these proposals there were a number of other propositions to better indicate a ship's course, submitted to the consideration of the Conference, which, though they may possess considerable merit, could not be commented upon according to the resolution of the Conference, under date of October 21, by which it was resolved that no change should be made in the use of the present mast-head light and colored side lights. On that account proposals that made use of multi-colored mast-head lights, white side lights, etc., could not be considered.

STERN LIGHTS.

Amongst the literature placed before us there are some papers proposing a stern light fixed near the stern on the taffrail or thereabout. Such an arrangement would possess some advantages and would make it less necessary to look out astern for overtaking ships in order to show them the white light required by Article 11.

It would be impossible for small vessels to carry it in this position in bad weather, and therefore it can not be recommended that a white light, fixed at the stern, be made *compulsory* for all vessels, large and small, but there seems to be nothing in the way of *permitting* all vessels to show a white light from the stern permanently.

In the case that the Conference should adopt this proposition it would be well to have such lights screened so as to be visible at a certain angle only. This, under certain circumstances, would serve as an additional means to determine the course of a ship.

The committee do not believe that any bad result would come from having the stern light and side light visible at the same time, as they would, under the circumstances, not be seen except at a considerable distance apart, and we, therefore, recommend that if such lights should be permitted, they be fixed so as to be visible from astern to abeam on either side.

TWO LIGHTS AS ANCHOR LIGHTS.

There is a proposition before the committee by which it is prescribed that two anchor lights—one at the bow, one at the stern—should be made compulsory for large steam-vessels. In such vessels it is impossible to place a white light in such a manner as to be visible all around the horizon (Article 8) on account of the funnels. It is, therefore, in the opinion of the committee, advisable to make a second white anchor-light compulsory for all large steam-vessels. Perhaps it would be well to draw the line in such a manner that all steam-vessels which, as a class, have funnels higher than 20 feet above the hull—this being the maximum height at which anchor lights can be carried (Article 8)— should have to carry two lanterns.

Among the suggestions submitted to the Conference there are a number which are not definite enough to be commented upon, but which have suggested some resolutions, which are appended, and are herewith submitted to the Conference.

1. That in the opinion of the committee the power of all running and anchor lights should be expressed by referring them all to one standard by which the light issuing from the lantern should be measured.

2. That the minimum power only of each such light should be definitely fixed, leaving it to the judgment of the parties responsible for fitting out the ship with proper lanterns to employ lamps of this or of higher power.

3. That the use of electric incandescent lamps is to be permitted; that the use of the arc light, however, is to be, at least for the present, excluded for all purposes other than signaling and searching.

4. That each lantern must be so constructed that the minimum power of light is to be found at every point where the light is to be visible, after the lamp has been fitted with proper screens.

5. That the lanterns shall be so constructed as to insure the light having at least the required minimum power in the ideal line connecting the lantern with the horizon, even though the ship be heeled one way or the other 12 degrees.

6. That the color of the glasses by which the coloring of the light is to be produced be so chosen that the lights retain their distinctive color even in a fog.

PLATE I.

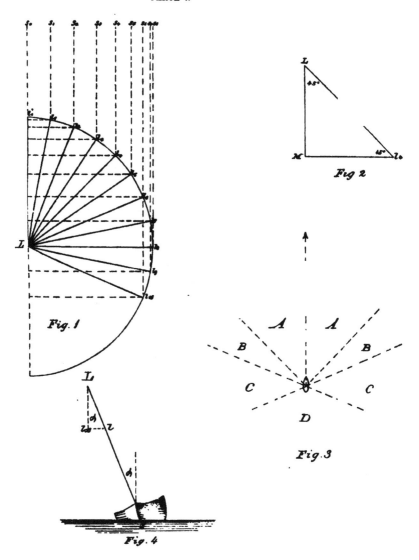

Fig. 1

Fig. 2

Fig. 3

Fig. 4

$S_0 \ldots S_9$. Lines of Vision.
L. Foremast-Light.
$l_0 \ldots l_{10}$. Forward Range Light, when the ship is turned o to 10 points.

PLATE II.

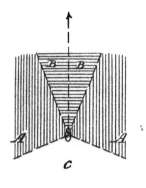

Fig. 5

System. G. T. Parry

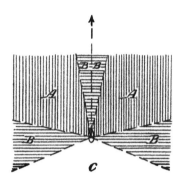

Fig. 6

System. Capt. Manzanos

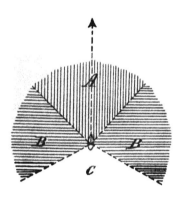

Fig. 7

System. Bainbridge-Hoff

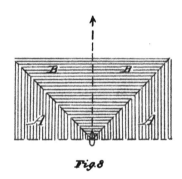

Fig. 8

System. Littrow

B, sector in which one side-light is shown, shaded thus ≡≡≡

A, sector in which two side-lights are shown, shaded thus ‖‖‖

C, sector in which one white light is shown, not shaded.

PLATE III

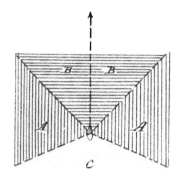

Fig. 9

System - Lagerwall

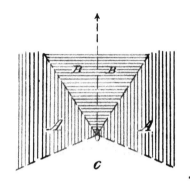

Fig. 10

System tried onboard U S S Yorktown

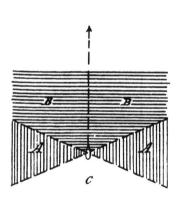

Fig. 11

System - D. Jose' R. Giralt

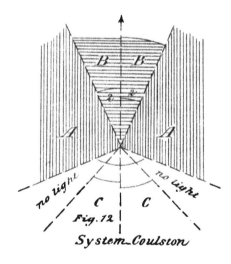

Fig. 12

System Coulston

7. That no detailed description should be internationally adopted for the construction of the lamp or lantern, so that a fair chance be given inventors to produce serviceable articles.

We have the honor to be, sir, your obedient servants,

Vice-Admiral N. KAZNAKOFF, *Chairman,*

Delegate for Russia.

E. RICHARD,

Delegate for France.

B. VEGA DE SEOANE,

Delegate for Spain.

JAS. W. NORCROSS,

Delegate for the United States.

HENRY WYATT,

Delegate for Great Britain.

F. MALMBERG,

Delegate for Sweden.

A. MENSING,

Delegate for Germany.

APPENDIX A.

	Names of persons having proposed distinct systems of range lights or names of systems.	Short indication of measures proposed.
1	M. A. Hautreux, lieutenant de vaisseau, and M. Launeluc, capitaine au long cours.	All sailing and steam-vessels to carry a white light at the foremast and side lights. The steam-vessels to show, besides these, a white light in front of mast-head light. The line connecting these two to be 45 degrees with the vertical. All lights for steam-ships to be electric. The foremast-light to be scintillating for steam-ships of over 12 knots speed.
2	F. F. Fletcher, lieutenant, U. S. Navy.	Forward of the foremast, at a distance apart not less than the beam of the ship, two bright white range lights of the same character as the present mast-head light, visible from ahead to two points abaft each beam. These lights shall be in the vertical plane of the keel, with the lower one so placed forward of the upper one that an imaginary line through them will make an angle of 55 degrees with the vertical.
3	Modified Fletcher System	Forward range lights as in system No. 2; a white light to show all round the horizon, and at the same height as the forward upper range light, to be placed as far aft as possible, in lieu of the light at stern.
4	United States Inland Range System.	With present system of mast-head light and side lights an after range light is employed, visible around the horizon, and placed at twice the height of the forward mast-head light, if possible.
5	M. L. Wood, lieutenant, U. S. Navy.	Side lights, as at present used, both for sailing and steam-vessels: (1) a white top light under the foretop; (2) a white peak light, visible all around the horizon on a monkey gaff. In addition to these, steamers have to carry a red top light, 3 feet below the white top light, and a white bow light with a reflector, in a funnel shaped screen box, visible from the bow four points on either side.
6	John M. Hudson, captain of the ship *Red, White, Blue.*	All steam-vessels to be fitted with mast-head light and side lights, as at present, and to carry a central range of two white lights besides; the stern light to be placed near the flag-staff aft; the front light to be placed not more than 80 or 100 feet in front of this.
7	George P. Blow, ensign, U. S. Navy.	Sailing vessels and steam-vessels to be fitted with two range lights. The front light to show green on the starboard and red on the port side, visible from right ahead to two points abaft the beam on either side. The after light to be a light or combination of two lights, visible all around the horizon, proposed to denote the speed of steamers and the rig of sailing vessels. No side light and no stern light to be used with this system.

ADDITIONAL REPORT OF THE COMMITTEE ON LIGHTS.

WASHINGTON, *December* 12, 1889.

To Rear-Admiral S. R. FRANKLIN, *U. S. Navy,*
  President of the International Marine Conference, etc.:

SIR: In accordance with the resolution passed by the .Conference on the 9th instant, your committee have again considered the question whether it would be advisable to assign a certain position to the side lights, as has been done by extra amendment No. 41 to Article 3, which has led to the rule adopted by the Conference, viz:

"The said green and red side lights to be placed in steam-vessels not forward of the mast-head light and in sailing vessels as near abreast the foremast as practicable."

Doubts have been raised by the Collocation Committee on the advisability of this rule on the ground that it involves a radical change and leads to great expense by compelling a very material alteration of the present construction of many ships, consequences which are said to outweigh the slight advantage of the introduction of the rule in question.

Your committee, after having most carefully considered the subject, are unanimous in reporting that in their opinion the rule passed by the Conference ought to be maintained.

In the report dated November 4, 1889, the reasons have been given why in principle it would be advisable to have the side lights of all steam-vessels so placed that a vertical plane through the line drawn from them to the mast-head light would form a certain known angle with the keel. It has at the same time been acknowledged to be practically impossible to give the side lights a certain fixed position in regard to the foremast light, but it has been thought practicable and therefore has been recommended to introduce a rule by which steamers are compelled to carry the side lights abaft the foremast light, the connecting line forming an angle of six points with the keel, or as nearly so as possible.

The considerations which have led to this recommendation appear to your committee to be sound, and whilst confirming what has been said in the former report we beg to add the following remarks:

The rule as adopted by the Conference does not, it is true, go quite so far in assigning to the side lights a certain fixed position with regard to the mast-head lights as the recommendation contained in our report of the 4th of November. Nevertheless, by preventing steam-vessels from carrying the side lights forward of the mast-head light, it will serve to give more certainty to the respective position of the regulation lights, and thus, in our opinion, will mark a decided improvement of the means of ascertaining the course of an approaching steamer, which improvement will gradually be increased when experience shows the advantages of the system.

On the other hand, the difficulties connected with the introduction of the rule appear to be not at all insurmountable. Many ships are even now constructed so as not to require any changes in consequence of the adoption of this rule. Others might easily comply with the rule by changing the position of the mast-head light in placing it more forward of the foremast. And even if the position of the side lights should have to be altered, this could in most cases be done without incurring too heavy expense.

We therefore recommend to let the rule stand as it is, provided, however, that the rule be adopted universally. Having regard to the difficulties which some ship-owners may justly feel if they had to comply with the new rule at once, your committee think that sufficient time should be allowed for the effecting of the changes necessitated by the rule, so as to enable ship-owners to carry out these changes under the most convenient conditions. Vessels now in course of construction will, of course, be able to adopt the new principle at once.

As regards sailing vessels, the committee do not consider it necessary to adopt the above-mentioned rule.

We have the honor to be, sir, your most obedient servants,

Vice-Admiral N. KAZNAKOFF,
Chairman, Russia.
E. RICHARD,
France.
B. VEGA DE SEOANE,
Spain.
JAS. W. NORCROSS,
United States.
HENRY WYATT,
Great Britain.
F. MALMBERG,
Sweden.
A. MENSING,
Germany.

S. Ex. 53, pt. 3——6

REPORT OF THE COMMITTEE ON SOUND-SIGNALS.

Resolved, That the Chair appoint two committees, each to consist of seven delegates, to be known as the Committee on Lights and the Committee on Sound-Signals, whose present duty it shall be to examine and report to the Conference the literature on these two subjects which is in the possession of the Conference.

COMMITTEE:

Austria-Hungary	Admiral DE SPAUN.
Denmark	Mr. SCHNEIDER.
Great Britain	Admiral NARES.
Italy	Captain SETTEMBRINI.
Norway	Captain SALVESEN.
The Netherlands	Captain VAN STEYN.
United States	Captain SHACKFORD.

WASHINGTON, *October* 31, 1889.

Rear-Admiral S. R. FRANKLIN, U. S. Navy,
  President International Marine Conference:

SIR: Since our first meeting, on the 23d instant, we have examined the numerous proposals that have been placed before the Conference and submitted to us, for indicating in fog, mist, or falling snow the direction in which a vessel is proceeding by means of sound-signals, in agreement with the course steered, the sounds or characters being made by one or more steam-whistles or fog-horns, and varying in number, length of note, or pitch of tone, to distinguish the course of a vessel.

We have also had before us a memorandum prepared by the Com-

mittee of the Second Northern Maritime Conference, held at Copenhagen, dated 1888. It is there stated that—

"The sound-signals in *fog, mist, or falling snow*, according to Article ·
12, are commonly regarded as insufficient, as hereby only is prescribed
'that a steam-ship under way shall make with her steam-whistle, or
other steam sound-signal, at intervals of not more than two minutes, a
prolonged blast,' as by this means only the very incomplete information
is obtained that a steamer is within the range of hearing. Proposals
to the remedy thereof exist in a considerable number, partly as to
sound-signals indicating alterations of a ship's course and partly as to
indicating the courses of a ship. Fog sound-signals for maneuvering
seem to have gained only a few adherents, as they generally are considered to be more misleading than leading in crowded fair-ways. On
the contrary, a steam-whistle system for 'compass course-signals' is
commonly considered as practical and useful.

"The objections to a compass course-signal system seem to be derived from a fear, partly that such combined signals might easily be
misunderstood, and thereby do more harm than good, and partly on
account of the difficulty of deciding with certainty the exact direction
in which the signals are heard. Nevertheless, as far as we can judge,
it seems that if the 'whistling' which now only signifies 'here is a
steamer' was arranged in such a manner that it did signify 'here is a
steamer steering a certain course,' that this could not make the situation worse, but rather serve to better it. Adherents and non-adherents
to such a system do, however, agree that neither the steam-whistle nor
the fog-horn are, as a rule, of sufficient efficiency, and that this matter,
therefore, ought to be regulated by international agreements."

We have also considered (1) the replies to a circular sent out by the
United States Hydrographic Office to the branch offices, asking for the
opinion of practical men on the subjects referred to in the programme
of the Conference, an epitome of which replies so far as they relate to
the subjects on which we are to report we have prepared and have annexed (Appendix A); (2) the opinions expressed, in reply to a circular
letter sent out by Captain Shackford, by a number of experienced seamen employed in navigating vessels in American waters and in the
Atlantic, the majority of whom express themselves against the introduction of course-indicating sound-signals; and (3) a memorandum
(Appendix B) on the use of such signals, prepared lately by the British
Board of Trade, which discusses the whole subject and contains the
opinions of the most experienced British shipmasters, a very large proportion of whom are against the introduction of such signals.

We have further considered certain proposals for the introduction of
a general system of sound-signals for use in all weathers; for the
adoption of a few sound-signals of an urgent or specially important nature, and for the adoption of sound-signals to denote any movement of
helm.

The present authorized compulsory signals made by a moving vessel at sea, in fog, mist, or falling snow, are a prolonged blast on the steam-whistle of a steam-ship, or one, two, or three blasts on the fog-horn of a sailing vessel.

We are informed and believe that the custom of careful seamen, when navigating steam-ships in fog by means of these signals, coupled with the injunction to proceed at a moderate speed under Article 13 of the International Regulations, is, immediately the fog-signal of another ship *not in sight* is heard, apparently approaching from any direction before the beam, to reduce speed in agreement with the density of the atmosphere, and if necessary to stop and remain stopped until the other ship is located with as much accuracy as possible, then to proceed cautiously until all danger of collision has ceased to exist.

The principal difficulty in making use of a practical system of sound-signaling in foggy weather is in *taking in* the signal correctly, not in making it.

Until seamen are able to localize a sound with as great precision as they can the position of a light or object seen visually the results to the mercantile marine from the adoption of a system of course-indicating fog-signals are, in the opinion of the committee, of doubtful advantage. The chief use would appear to be to give facilities to approaching vessels, when not in sight of one another, and therefore when not certain of one another's position, to continue their respective courses without having first localized the direction and distance of the neighboring ship, and for the two vessels to try to pass close to each other without taking the precaution of first reducing, or, if necessary, stopping their way through the water.

It is for the Conference to decide on the vital question whether to permit the use of such signals in the mercantile marine or not. But the committee submit that increased danger might probably result—owing to the inability of the large majority of men to localize sound with sufficient accuracy—if those in charge of steam-ships are encouraged to navigate their vessels past others not in sight in a less cautious manner than they do at present.

The committee are of the opinion that, however simple an adopted system of course-indicating sound-signals may be, and however distinct in character the symbols chosen are from the signals now authorized and used, if vessels were navigated in dependence on them, when neither can see the other, there would be a danger of the officer in charge reading the signal incorrectly; or, if read correctly, of interpreting it wrongly.

Further, if such signals were in use in crowded waters, we apprehend that danger would result from the uncertainty and confusion produced by the multiplicity of signals, and from a feeling of false security that would be created in the minds of many,

The committee would invite the consideration of the Conference to the following points:

(1) We are of the opinion that many of the steam-whistles, and the fog-horns and bells now in general use can not be heard a sufficient distance; we therefore recommend the use of instruments giving a louder sound; and we consider it desirable that the sounds given by steam-whistles and fog-horns should be regulated so that the tones of the steamer's fog-whistle should be as distinct as possible from the sound of the sailing vessel's fog-horn.

(2) As a vessel at anchor in a fog, etc., in a fair-way at sea, is in a more dangerous position, particularly while swinging round broadside to the main line of route with a change of tide, than if under way and sounding the authorized fog-horn, we would suggest that such a vessel should be compelled to use a more efficient sound-signal than the bell at present authorized.

(3) As in a fog, etc., a tug towing another vessel forms an exceptional danger, we would suggest that the tug and the one or more vessels towed should be compelled to sound a special fog-signal.

(4) We would suggest that a vessel "not under command" should be compelled to sound a special fog-signal.

(5) We invite attention to the desirability of not fixing the duration of the steam-ship's prolonged blast warning signal under Article 12 of the regulations at any minimum until exhaustive experiments have shown that the efficiency of the signal is not reduced thereby. On this subject we attach some remarks on experiments made by M. Lefèbre in Holland (Appendix C).

(6) As regards the adoption of a general system of sound-signals, we learn by a return prepared by the British Board of Trade (copy of which is attached, Appendix D), that the majority of ship-owners and master mariners are of opinion that there is at present no demand or necessity for such a system in the mercantile marine. Apart from the question as to war necessities, we concur in this opinion. But we would recommend the Conference to consider the desirability of introducing a few urgent and important sound-signals, particularly one to denote that, when two neighboring ships are stopped in a thick fog, one vessel making the signal will remain stopped while the other is carefully feeling her way past her.

(7) As regards helm-signals by sound, we are of opinion that it is not desirable to alter the present universally-adopted signals.

(8) We consider it worthy the attention of the Conference whether the custom followed at present by careful seamen of slowing or stopping on hearing the fog-signal of another ship not in sight, unless certain of her bearing and distance, could be made compulsory by a regulation so worded as not to relieve those in charge from full responsibility.

(9) As a relatively important matter, we would direct the attention of the Conference to the desirability of steam-ships being provided with means of blowing off the surplus steam when the engines are stopped in such a manner as to occasion as little noise as possible.

SPAUN,
Delegate for the Austro-Hungarian Government
AUG. SCHNEIDER,
Delegate for Denmark.
G. S. NARES,
Chairman of Committee, Delegate for Great Britain.
R. SETTEMBRINI,
Delegate for Italy.
T. SALVESON,
Delegate for Norway.
VAN STEYN,
Delegate for The Netherlands.
J. W. SHACKFORD,
Delegate for the United States.

APPENDIX A.

CIRCULAR TO BRANCH HYDROGRAPHIC OFFICES.

HYDROGRAPHIC OFFICE, NAVY DEPARTMENT,
Washington, D. C., May 3, 1889.

SIR: A copy of the programme of subjects to be considered by the International Marine Conference has been forwarded to you to-day. It is the desire of the chief of the Bureau of Navigation for you to discuss this matter thoroughly with all those who are interested and competent to judge, and to make a report in detail to this office. The object of this is to formulate practical views for the use of our commissioners on all or any of the subjects referred to, or on any others that may have been omitted. This matter must be taken up at once, although sufficient time will be allowed to do the subject that justice which its magnitude and importance demand.

Attention is called to the April number of the North American Review, containing articles bearing on this subject.

Very respectfully,

G. L. DYER,
Hydrographer.

SUMMARY OF OPINIONS AS TO FOG-SIGNALS, ETC.

Branch Hydrographic Office, New York, August 13.—Doubt as to what quality of whistle is most audible, also as to course-indicating signals; it would seem that, as they are simpler than bugles, sailors could learn former as easily as cavalry horses learn latter. Suggests *speed* to be limited to 6 knots an hour. Experiments should be made as to penetrating power of signals, and a code of compass-signals made. Incloses codes of maneuvering signals and compass course-signals.

Branch Hydrographic Office, Norfolk, Va.—Fog-signals should not imply how the vessel is heading as regards the wind. All vessels should slow in a fog—speed not to exceed 5 or 6 knots an hour. Helm-signals should be made in clear and foggy weather. Systems adopted should be simple and international and enforced by law.

Branch Hydrographic Office, Boston, Mass., September 19—*Fog-signals:* No complication whatever should be attempted. Many authorities in favor of *course-signals*—not more than eight points of compass. Advise Morse system, also, signals for vessels towing, not under command, and anchoring. *Helm-signals*, especially during foggy weather, are unnecessary complications, at least in open sea; necessary in narrow inland waters. Should be uniform for all nations. Regulation for *moderate* speed in fog should be amended to *slow* speed, *i. e.*, not more than half speed.

Merchants' Exchange, San Francisco, September 30.—In favor of sound-signals. Incloses code, depending on number of sounds.

Branch Hydrographic Office, Baltimore, Md., September 26.—Any code of course sound-signals should be of simplest kind, have few elements, and only attempt to indicate four compass points. Helm-signals should be compulsory. *Speed in fog* should be lowest speed at which vessel readily answers helm.

W. R. Mayo to Secretary Chamber of Commerce.—Has seen various methods proposed for indicating the direction a vessel may be heading in a fog, etc., but believes that all of them are so complicated as to be useless, and they may therefore do harm. The present sound-signals for fog are good, and if steamers approaching each other in a fog would adopt the precaution of slowing down close and *feeling* their way by each other no trouble would occur. The great requisite, in fog and other thick weather, is not more signaling from steam-whistles, but greater precaution on the part of ship-masters.

R. H. Hughes, master steam-ship Nova Scotian.—Suggests a sound-signal for vessels not under command or laying a telegraph cable. Fishing vessels at anchor to sound an automatic whistle. Present helm-signals should be made compulsory.

Paul Brown, master steam-ship Victor.—Suggests sound-signals for a compass direction. Signals should be sounded by minutes. Helm-signals should be made compulsory. Suggests a sound-signal for vessels not under command.

Opinions of various experienced mariners and other practical men obtained by Sergeant Paul Daniels.—Course-direction signals not practicable. Present rules are generally satisfactory if properly carried out. Present helm-signals should be made compulsory. Fog-signals should be sounded every thirty seconds. Sound-signals should be adopted to denote a vessel not under command, a vessel towing, and a vessel laying or taking up a telegraph cable. The speed of vessels approaching the coast in thick weather should be reduced to at least one-half speed, say 6 or 7 knots.

Mr. R. B. Forbes.—Proposes direction-signals for eastward and westward bound vessels. Thinks it undesirable to establish signals for every course steered. Speed need not be reduced in thick weather.

D. A. Nash, personal opinion to Ensign Blow.—Proposes direction-signals for eight points. The signals should be repeated, as one signal is often imperfectly heard.

North German Lloyds' New York agent to Ensign Blow.—No remarks on fog-signals.

H. G. Johnson, master, to officer in charge of Hydrographic Office, New York.—Present regulations are all that is necessary. The rules are very good and such as are in familiar use by navigators.

Steam-ship Pennland to Ensign Blow.—Course-signals for steam-vessels would be advantageous. Present regulations for sailing vessels are all that are necessary. Fog-signals should be sounded at least every minute. Present helm-signals should be made compulsory.

R. H. Hughes, master.—Present helm fog-signals should be made compulsory. Fishing vessels at anchor should sound an automatic whistle.

OPINIONS ON FOG-SIGNALS COLLECTED AT BRANCH HYDROGRAPHIC OFFICE IN NEW YORK, FROM CAPTAINS OF STEAM AND SAILING VESSELS AND SHIPPING MEN GENERALLY.

Captain Burn, of steam-ship *El Dorado*, believes that the present rules of the road are sufficient. Thinks steamers should be fitted with very powerful whistles. Recommends steam siren with parabolic reflector. In fog, both vessels should stop on hearing signals, and feel their way past each other.

Captain Mason (steam-ship *Chalmette*), Captain Higgins (steam-ship *Excelsior*), and Captain Burdick (superintendent of American pier). All agree in the following opinion : That the present rules are sufficient if enforced. The simpler they are, the better.

Captain Murray of (steam-ship *Alaska*). Is satisfied with the present rules. Not in favor of any code of course-signals. Present helm signals should be compulsory.

Mr. Reiley (chief officer steam-ship *Lampasas*). Is satisfied with present rules.

Mr. Dennett (steam-ship *State of Texas*). Is satisfied with present rules.

Captain Rogers (bark *Siddarthe*). Satisfied with present fog-signals.

Captain Stevens (steam-ship *Manhattan*). Is against any complicated code.

Mr. Russell (chief officer steam-ship *City of Atlanta*). Rules of the road good enough as they are.

Captain Risk (steam-ship *Comal*). Advocates uniform size, power, and position of whistles.

Captain Fearon (steam-ship *Dawpool*). Advocates uniformity in instruments to be worked by compressed air.

Aaron Vanderbilt (J. E. Ward & Co.) Advocates single and efficient code of signals (1 to 4 blasts); compass-course signals, uniform pattern of whistles; increased power and range.

Captain Wilkinson (steam-ship *Denholm*). Fog-horns on sailing vessels useless. Steam-whistle should be placed as high as possible, so that sound can pass over smoke-stack, etc.

Mr. Jones (chief officer *Basil*). Thinks present rules sufficient if properly observed.

Captain Bolger (steam-ship *Nueces*) and Captain William (schooner *Stella H. Kenyon*). Satisfied with rules if enforced.

Captain Stevenson (steam-ship *Seneca*) and Captain Lewis (steam-ship *Rio Grande*). Agree with above.

Captain Hansen (steam-ship *City of Atlanta*). Satisfied with rules; thinks that there should be a signal whistle to designate a vessel stopped at sea—not necessarily disabled, but drifting and not making headway.

Mr. Millard (chief officer *Truro City*). Satisfied with rules if enforced.

Captain Homer (steam-ship *Lucy C. Miller*). Agrees with above.

Pilot Joseph Nelson (pilot-boat *Stafford*). Does not believe in any possible code of signals to determine course in fog.

Mr. T. S. Negus (chairman New York Board of Pilots) says that he has seen numbers of sound-signals suggested. They are inadmissible; too complicated.

Capt. Ambrose Snow (president N. Y. Board of Pilot Commissioners). The best rule for preventing collisions in fog would be to require vessels to move slowly or anchor, if possible, and to come to a full stop on hearing signal.

Captain Grant (steam-ship *Pennland*). Fog-horns used by sailing vessels useless. All vessels should have whistles of greater power. In fog, vessels should stop at once on hearing signal.

Captain Gioccoechia (steam-ship *Gaditano*) thinks four compass courses should be signaled. Does not think any code depending on number of blasts advisable; recommends tones; whistles should be placed both forward on forecastle and aft, and should be blown simultaneously.

Mr. John R. Hughes (inventor of code of fog-signals) believes that some system of compass courses is essential. Thinks helm-signals should be retained only in case two vessels are in sight. No system depending directly on number or length of blasts practicable. Each vessel should carry in fog, as high up as possible, a large metal spherical cage or bell, which could be easily seen above fog in day-time.

Captain Kennedy (formerly steam-ship *Germanic*). Fog-horns on sailing vessels no use. For steamers, believes code of signals could be used, giving eight compass courses. Code to be simple; short and long blasts; deep and shrill whistles.

Captain J. McCarthy (pilot-boat *J. F. Loabat*) thinks some code for compass signals should be obligatory; it should be simple; two whistles of distinct tone; one to be blown until whistle of another vessel is heard and located. Slowing down in a fog "a mere farce."

Lieutenant Smythe (revenue steam-ship *Washington*). Code of compass course-signals recommended; eight points.

Captain Clampett (Delaware River pilot). Shrill whistle can be heard twice as far as deep whistles.

Captain Moody (steam-ship *State of Georgia*). Hoarse whistle can be distinguished better than shrill.

W. C. Almy, steamer Old Point Comfort, to branch Hydrographic Office, Va.—Advocates four *compass course-signals* in fog; long and short blasts.

W. Whittle, steamer Georgia.—Advocates helm-signals in fog, which should be compulsory. *Speed in fog.* No vessel should go at a speed greater than that at which she can hear the signal of another at a distance sufficient to stop; vessel in doubt should stop at once.

Branch Hydrographic Office, Philadelphia, Pa.—Steamers should carry two whistles. Is in favor of a code of compass course-signals; not more than 3 notes in any one compass-signal. Eight compass courses. Helm-signals, in all weather, should be compulsory.

Branch Hydrographic Office, Portland, Oreg.—In favor of a code of compass course-signals, four points. Helm-signals should be compulsory.

W. R. Mayo, U. S. customs, to chamber of commerce, Va.—Compass course-signals in fog inadmissible. Helm-signals good, if steamers approaching adopt precaution of slowing down and feeling their way past each other.

Opinions collected by branch Hydrographic Office, N. Y.—Against course-signals. Helm-signals should be compulsory. Advises a number of successive whistles to call attention of vessel or steamer ahead to that overtaking it. Sailing vessel running with free wind must conform to signals of steamers. Speed in foggy weather can not be accurately determined in miles; sailing vessels should be obliged to obey rule.

Providence and Stonington Steamship Company.—Advises one long blast of whistle, eight seconds' duration, at intervals of thirty seconds. As position signal in fog, recommends automatic machine; also compass course-signals showing 8 points. Steamers towing should have a distinctive signal. All fog-horns should be inspected. Signals on horns of sailing vessels should be on the same principle as steamers' whistles; no use to indicate tack. Against a new code of signals, if it is at cost of simplicity. Bells should be regulated by law. Considers present arrangements as to helm-signals in United States waters good. Signal for stopping should be regulated; it should be specified whether "I am stopping" refers to vessel or engine. Helm-signals should be compulsory in all conditions of the atmosphere. Speed in fog should be rapid, provided ships stop or slow immediately on hearing another vessel's fog-signal.

OPINIONS SENT TO ENSIGN BLOW.

Lieut. H. Barroll, U. S. Navy, recommends slowing down in fog. Unqualified objection to any additional fog-signal.

Captain Yates, U. S. Navy, recommends two whistles and eight compass course-signals by long and short blasts. In favor of helm-signals.

Commander Cooper, U. S. Navy, agrees with Captain Yates.

Captain Bachelder, U. S. Navy, agrees.

Captain Wise, U. S. Navy. Compass course signals could not be used on merchant vessels.

J. L. Moffat, M. D , recommends only distress signal.

A. P. Cooke, U. S. Navy. Mr. Blow's system of signals too elaborate.

C. A. Adams, U. S. Navy, agrees with Mr. Blow's code.

J. A. Clampitt also agrees.

Mr. J. Bryde (master-mariner) approves of Mr. Blow's system, if only used for the four quadrants.

Captain G. Moodie (steam-ship *State of Georgia*). In favor of code.

H. P. McIntosh, U. S. Navy. Against long and short blasts.

Captain Laub (*Thingvalla*). Advocates stopping when whistle is heard. Wants signal for vessel that is to keep her course.

Capt. J. McKee (*Yemassee*). In favor of running slow in fog.

E. Kemble (steam-ship *Iroquois*). Sailing vessels should have better horns. In favor of compass course signals to indicate eight courses.

CLYDE'S COASTWISE AND WEST INDIA STEAM LINES (WILLIAM P. CLYDE & CO.).

H. A. Bearse, steam-ship Cherokee.—Sound-signals for sailing vessels should be better; for steamers are good; in favor of *four* compass course signals by short and long blasts. In fog or thick weather half rate of speed, so as to have full control of the vessel.

Capt. S. C. Platt, steam-ship Seminole.—On examination of the code of fog-signals of Mr. J. R. Hughes he would call it impracticable. Whistles should be made much larger and sounded oftener; sailing vessels should make a louder noise at shorter intervals.

Capt. A. D. Ingram, steam-ship Benefactor.—Steamers should not be allowed to run at full speed, but should stop to locate a sound. Recommends a steam siren of uniform size, giving a sound at regular intervals, and a steam whistle for giving and answering signals within safe hearing distance, so that after hearing the siren the whistle only should indicate by the blasts if the ship is porting or starboarding. For sailing vessels recommends an automatic compressed air-horn and a large bell when at anchor.

Master-Mariner F. W. Fuler.—Only about lights.

Master-Mariner A. Schück, from Hamburg.—No observations on sound-signals.

Commander C. W. Kennedy, White Star steamer Germanic.—Eight *sound-signals* are all that is required. No systems given. *Helm signals,* now optional, should be *compulsory.* Two powerful steam whistles, *one deep, one shrill-toned,* to give these signals. Instead of the *fog-horns* for sailing vessels, recommends a *gong;* the horns only for fishing vessels. A small cannon for pilot vessels on the stations; the *gong* when off the stations.

James A. Dumont, Supervising Inspector-General.—Thinks that the intervals between sound-signals should be one and not two minutes. No course signals should be given. Ships should run slow in fog, with frequent stoppages. Bells should be rung every two minutes. Helm signals in all weather should be compulsory.

The National Board of Marine Underwriters, New York.—Recommends the siren horn for steamers; improved fog-horns worked by levers for sailing vessels. In favor of introduction of course signals for steamers and sailing vessels. Vessels should stop on becoming aware of proximity. There should be special signals for a steamer towing to designate number of vessels towed. Helm signals should be compulsory. Recommends bell or short blasts of whistle for ships not under command. In fog vessels should go full speed in open sea, but should slow down on approaching the coast.

Philadelphia Maritime Exchange.—Recommends use of whistles of regulated power. The signal code should be simple and always definite. An alarm gun or bomb should be fired when a vessel approaches from a quarter where it is impossible that a whistle can be heard.

Liverpool Humane Society.—Thinks sound-signals should be used more systematically. Recommends gong for pilot-boats. The use of gongs for lights-ships should be abandoned.

APPENDIX B.

COURSE INDICATING SIGNALS.

In order to obtain the opinion of a number of practical and experienced seamen as to the advisability of adopting some system of course or route indicating sound signals for use in fog, mist, or falling snow, the Board of Trade caused copies of the following letter, dated 11th March, 1889, and of the inclosures, Papers A, B, C, D, and E, to be sent to forty-four of the principal firms of ship-owners and to five ship-masters and seamen's societies. Each firm of owners was invited to obtain the opinions of six of their most experienced masters upon the question printed in italics at the head of the letter. An abstract of the replies received will be found at page 113.

INTERNATIONAL CODE OF SIGNALS COMMITTEE.

PROPOSALS RESPECTING COURSE INDICATING SOUND–SIGNALS.

MARINE DEPARTMENT, BOARD OF TRADE,
7, Whitehall Gardens, London, S. W., March 11, 1889.

SIR: *The question for consideration, and on which your opinion is invited, is as follows, viz: "Is it practicable, and if so, is it advisable, to introduce some system of course or route indicating sound-signals to be made by steamships under way in fog, mist, or falling snow, when neither can see the other?" And on this question I submit for your consideration and advice the following observations:*

1. The present law on the subject of " sound-signal" and " course indicating signals" is contained in Articles 12 and 19 of the International Regulations, which are as follows:

SOUND-SIGNALS FOR FOG, ETC.

"ART. 12. A steam-ship shall be provided with a steam-whistle or other efficient steam sound-signal, so placed that the sound may not be intercepted by any obstructions, and with an efficient fog-horn, to be sounded by a bellows or other mechanical means, and also with an efficient bell.* A sailing ship shall be provided with a similar fog-horn and bell.

"In fog, mist, or falling snow, whether by day or night, the signals described in this article shall be used as follows; that is to say:

" (a) A steam-ship under way shall make with her steam-whistle or other steam sound-signal, at intervals of not more than two minutes, a prolonged blast.

---

* In all cases where the Regulations require a bell to be used a drum will be substituted on board Turkish vessels.

" (b) A sailing ship under way shall make with her fog-horn, at intervals of not more than two minutes, when on the starboard tack, one blast, when on the port tack, two blasts in succession, and when with the wind abaft the beam three blasts in succession.

" (c) A steam-ship and a sailing ship, when not under way, shall, at intervals of not more than two minutes, ring the bell.

"ART. 19. In taking any course authorized or required by these Regulations, a steam-ship under way may indicate that course to any other ship which she has in sight by the following signals on her steam-whistle, viz:

" One short blast to mean 'I am directing my course to starboard.'

" Two short blasts to mean 'I am directing my course to port.'

" Three short blasts to mean 'I am going at full speed astern.'

" The use of these signals is optional, but if they are used the course of the ship must be in accordance with the signal made."

N. B.—*It is to be noted that Article 19 only applies when the vessel making the signal has the other vessel " in sight."*

Art. 13, respecting the speed of ships in fog, etc., is in the following terms:

SPEED OF SHIPS TO BE MODERATE IN FOG, ETC.

"ART. 13. Every ship, whether a sailing ship or steam-ship, shall, in a fog, mist, or falling snow, go at a moderate speed."

2. The International Code of Signals Committee recently appointed by the Board of Trade have taken steps to ascertain whether there is a general demand on the part of the mercantile marine for the establishment of some system whereby the signals in the International Code Book may be made by night as well as by day.

In the course of their interim report, dated 15th January, 1889, the committee state as follows:—

" So far as we have been able to ascertain at present there appears to be no *general* demand on the part of the mercantile marine for the establishment of a general system of night signaling. At the same time we think it advisable to adopt some plan by which a few urgent and important signals may be made by night as well as by day."

The signals selected by the committee for this purpose are as follows:

Urgent or important signals which may be made at night or during fog, either by flashes of white light or by a combination of long and short sounds on the steam-whistle, fog-horn, siren, bugle, etc. In the day-time they will be made by flags, if the weather is clear.

INSTRUCTIONS FOR THE USE OF FLASHING OR SOUND-SIGNALS.

1.

With flashing signals the lamp must always be turned toward the person addressed.

2.

To attract attention, a series of rapid short flashes or sounds should be made and continued until the person addressed gives the sign of attention by doing the same.

If, however, it is supposed that the person addressed can not reply, the signal may be made after a moderate pause, or, under certain circumstances, the communication may be made direct without preparatory signs.

3.

After making a few rapid short flashes or sounds as an acknowledgment, the receiver must watch or listen attentively until the communication is completed, when he must make the sign indicated below, showing that the message is understood.

4.

If the receiver does not understand the message, he must wait until the signal is repeated.

5.

Duration of short flashes or sounds ....1 second.
Duration of long flashes or sounds.........................3 seconds.
Interval between each flash or sound.......................1 second.
Answer, or " I understand " ...... ▬ ▬ ▬ ▬ ▬ etc.

Flags.	Signals.	Flashes or sounds.
NP	I want assistance. Please remain by me	
JK	You are standing into danger	
PG	Beware of derelict, dangerous to navigation	
QC	Have encountered ice	
PD	The way is off my ship, you may feel your way past me..................	
JB	Stop, or heave to ; I have something important to communicate	
PR	I am disabled. Communicate with me....................................	
	When a vessel is in "tow," the following flashes or sounds may be made from her to the tug or towing vessel :—	
KR	Steer more to port..	
KS	Steer more to starboard..	

The International Code of Signals Committee having thus accepted the principle that it is advisable to adopt certain few special sound-signals, the board of trade have requested the committee further to consider and report upon the following points:

" *Whether, in the interests of safety, it is desirable to establish a system of sound-signals to be used by steam-vessels during foggy weather to denote the direction in which they are proceeding.*

" *Whether, on the same grounds and for the same purposes, it is necessary to establish a system of sound signals to be used by sailing vessels under like circumstances.*

" *Whether such system should be limited to crowded waters and narrow seas near coasts, or whether it should be extended to the open seas also.*

" *If any system is deemed by the committee to be practical, what that system is.*"

These matters are accordingly receiving careful consideration, and will be referred to in the final report of the committee.

3. The present International Rules as to sound-signals are based on the assumption that *in a fog, mist, or falling snow* a vessel is to go at a moderate speed, and to blow a whistle or fog-horn as a warning that she is somewhere in the locality (Article 12), and as a caution to other vessels that may be in her neighborhood. Nothing more is intended to be conveyed by the signal sounded under the existing regulation by a steam-vessel in *thick* weather. In clear weather, as has been pointed out, a steam-ship may indicate an alteration in her course to any other ship *which she has in sight* by certain specified signals (Article 19).

4. *Sailing ships.*—A sailing ship is at present required to indicate the tack she is on with the wind forward of the beam, or if running with the wind abaft the beam to indicate the same by another distinctive signal.

5. It would therefore, as far as steam-vessels are concerned, effect fundamental alteration in the principle of the rules if a system of sound-signals were to be now adopted with the object of indicating the course of the steam-vessel making that signal in a fog, etc.

6. The many proposals which have been made to the Board of Trade from time to time regarding course indicating signals to be used by ships under way in a fog, etc., may be fairly described as of two broad classes, one class being founded on compass courses and the other on routes. The paper marked A is an attempt in the direction of indicating compass courses, and that marked B is an attempt in the direction of route courses.

Please understand that the papers A and B inclosed do not lay any claim to originality; they are rather examples of the two classes of proposals collated on the very numerous suggestions which have been made on the subject, and to which I have already referred.

7. I should also like to call your attention to the fact that in 1883 the Council of the Society of Arts appointed a committee to consider the question of collisions at sea. In addition to Sir W. Siemens (who, as chairman of the council of the society, was an *ex-officio* member) the following gentlemen composed the committee:

Sir A. Ryder (chairman), Sir Frederick Abel, Sir Frederick Bramwell, Andrew Cassels, esq., Lord Alfred S. Churchill, B. Francis Cobb, esq., Sir Edward Inglefield, Loftus Perkins, esq.

A preliminary report prepared by Admiral Ryder for submission to this committee was printed in the journal of the Society of Arts for May 2, 1884. No report signed by the members of the committee appears to have been issued.

The following extract from this preliminary report of Admiral Ryder refers specially to fog-signals and course-indicating signals:

"2. Nearly all the methods proposed assume the desirability of a code, international or not, of fog-signals, and in many of the inventions great ingenuity has been displayed. Supposing the objections to an elaborate code to be got over, there can be little doubt that several of the systems proposed would be very well adapted for the purposes required. The committee, however, after giving special attention to the question of an international code of fog-signals, have come to the conclusion that the introduction of an international code for use by merchant ships would be more likely to cause confusion or disaster than to conduce to safety; first, because the difficulty of making intelligible signals in a fog is very great; and secondly, because it is to be feared that the authorization of such a code would foster a fancied feeling of security and encourage the practice of steaming at high speed under dangerous circumstances. The committee believe that the utmost that could be done would be an indication of the direction of the ship's head as regards the vessel she is signaling to, as proposed by Mr. Rothery; and, in crowded channels, the indication by steamers of the fact that they were outward or homeward bound. At the same time the committee are fully sensible of the desirability of increasing by all possible means the power of fog-horns, and the general adoption of some form of 'siren' (an improved steam-whistle) for use on board ship."

8. Before the International Code of Signals Committee proceed to a consideration of the points referred to them I am anxious to obtain for them the opinion of a few practical persons qualified to speak with authority on the subject from the point of view of the ship-owners and officers of the Mercantile Marine.

9. Under these circumstances, I shall be much obliged if you will kindly furnish me (confidentially) with your own opinion as to the necessity or desirability of extending the present regulations, so as to in-

S. Ex. 53, pt. 3——7

clude either compulsory or optional course-indicating signals for use
in fog, mist, or falling snow when vessels under steam or sail can not
see each other.* I shall also be glad to receive the opinions of any of
your experienced masters on the same subject. If, in your opinion, it
is both practicable and advisable to establish some system of course-
indicating signals for use during fog, etc., when ships under way can
not see each other, it would further be of material assistance to the
committee if the nature of the system you prefer be indicated.

10. I can not withhold an expression of my own opinion that some of
the objections contained in the paper marked C call for the very gravest
consideration, and I feel that the committee, before recommending the
adoption of course or route-indicating signals by ships in fog, etc., will
need to be well assured that the adopting of any system would not be
the means of increasing rather than of diminishing the present risk of
collision by encouraging masters, under the false security of trusting to
the use of course or route-indicating signals, to run greater risks than
at present by not reducing speed, and by altering the ship's course in
fogs when neighboring vessels are not in sight, on the strength of sound
signals that can not be located with certainty.

11. The committee appointed to consider these questions are Col. H.
M. Hozier, Admiral Sir F. L. McClintock, F. R. S.; Sir D. Murray, Bart.;
Admiral Sir G. S. Nares, K. C. B.; Admiral N. Bowden-Smith, and
Capt. C. P. Wilson, and myself as chairman.

I am, your obedient servant,

THOMAS GRAY.

PAPER A.—*Memorandum by Admiral N. Bowden-Smith.*

SUGGESTIONS RESPECTING FOG-SIGNALS.

16, QUEEN'S GATE TERRACE, S. W.
January 5, 1889.

SIR: I send you herewith my answers to the questions relating to fog-
signals at sea, with suggestions for the consideration of the International Code Committee.

May I ask you to forward me a copy of suggestions made by other
members of the committee, that I may consider them before the next
meeting?

I have, &c.,

N. BOWDEN-SMITH.

The SECRETARY, INTERNATIONAL CODE OF SIGNALS COMMITTEE.

* NOTE.—In this connection I must ask you to bear in mind that the committee
have already tentatively recommended for adoption the signal P. D. (- —— -) to be
used by a steam-ship which can not see the other, to signify that the way is off the
steam-ship making it, and that the steam-ship hearing it may feel her way past the
steam-ship making it.—T. G.

Relating to fog-signals at sea.

Questions.	Answers.
Whether in the interests of safety it is desirable to establish a system of sound signals to be used by steam-vessels during foggy weather to denote the direction in which they are proceeding.	Yes.
Whether on the same grounds and for the same purpose it is necessary to establish a system of sound signals to be used by sailing-vessels under like circumstances.	Consider the existing fog-horn signals are sufficient.
Whether such system should be limited to crowded waters and narrow seas near coasts, or whether it should be extended to the open sea also.	It should be extended to the open sea, for though in some parts of the world vessels do not traverse the same route on their outward and homeward voyage, there are other seas on which steamers pass each other on the same track.
If any system is deemed by the committee to be practical, what that system is.	The simplest system would appear to be an arrangement of blasts on the steam-whistles as described hereafter, the bell being reserved for ships at anchor as at present.

The following proposals for denoting the approximate course of a steamer in a fog have no pretensions to originality.

They resemble many of those suggested in the abstract of fog-signals tabulated by the Marine Department of the Board of Trade, notably No. 28, by Mr. J. H. Garfit.

It is proposed to authorize eight combinations of long and short blasts, which will be readily understood by referring to the diagram.

From the north section to the SE. section the signals will commence with one long blast; from the south section to the NW. section with two long blasts.

The duration of the long blasts to be four seconds, the short blasts one second, with one second intervals; thus it will require fifteen seconds to make the longest or NW. signal.

It would not be desirable to introduce more than two long blasts on account of the length of time they occupy.

This system would seem to work well in the English Channel, where a large majority of the steamers would every two minutes be making the NE. or the SW. signal. Again, on the coast of Portugal, where fogs are very prevalent, they would be nearly all steering north or south, and sounding the corresponding signals.

With regard to vessels altering their course in a fog, they should be directed to continue making the same sounds until they had actually changed into another section; thus, if a ship has been steering N., and altered to NNE., she should continue blowing one long blast till she was steering to the eastward of NNE. It is the case that in this way two ships may for a time be steering the same course though uttering different sounds such as on a NNW. course where one vessel might be sounding one long blast and the other two long and three short; but this can not well be avoided.

The present system of all steamers sounding one prolonged blast gives no indication whatever of the direction in which they are proceeding, but the proposed scheme, though it lays down no fresh instructions as to how the officers in charge are to act, should help them to form a decision in carrying out the rule of the road.

A vessel stopped, and having no way on, to sound three long blasts every two minutes.

The long blasts in this case to be of eight seconds duration with two seconds interval.

——

PAPER B.—*Memorandum by Sir George Nares.*

PROPOSED ADOPTION OF A SYSTEM OF SOUND SIGNALS 'TO DENOTE IN FOGGY WEATHER THE DIRECTION IN WHICH A VESSEL IS PRO-CEEDING.

At present a sailing vessel's fog-signal, if she is close hauled, coupled with the known direction of the wind, gives a more or less accurate indication of the direction in which she is proceeding. The fog-signal of a sailing vessel with a fair wind and that of a steam-vessel indicates the vessel's presence alone. Even if the sound is located, it is only by the increased loudness, or a change in the direction of succeeding signals that a guess can be made as to the direction in which the vessel is proceeding.

If unconfusing and readily learnt sound-signals can be introduced, giving better information regarding the direction in which a vessel is proceeding, an officer hearing such a signal would be less embarrassed than he now is; and he would be placed in a better position for more readily adopting any further precautions that the situation required.

The adoption of additional " course" or "direction" fog-signals by vessels should in no way interfere with the present rules regarding the right of way of one vessel over another vessel.

All vessels must take the same full precautions to prevent a collision that they are required to take now.

The provision under Article 13, providing that in a fog, etc., every ship shall go at a moderate speed; and that under Article 17, providing that a steam-vessel shall keep out of the way of a sailing vessel, should in no way be relaxed or interfered with.

Article 19, regarding helm-signals, should, as at present, only apply to vessels actually in sight of one another.

The reading of another vessel's fog-signal incorrectly should in no case be accepted as any excuse in the event of a collision occurring.

New " course" signals should conflict as little as possible with the signals at present in use; and considering the crowded navigation of many districts and the additional symbols adopted, the number of sounds forming any one signal should be the fewest and simplest possible.

Compass-signals are thus precluded from consideration. For any compass system requires that the officer in charge should remember and be in the expectation of hearing at least eight different symbols; if

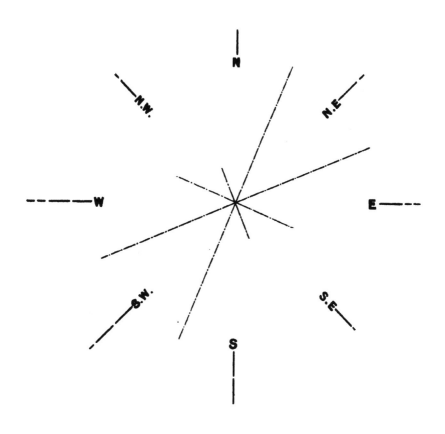

only four were used, vessels steering within 89 degrees of each other—that is, crossing each other's course almost at right angles—would be sounding the same signal.

There remains only for consideration some system similar in principle to the "route" systems suggested by Capt. Hon. F. G. Crofton, R. N., Captain Wilcox, and others.

As a modification of the various proposals, I submit for consideration the following "direct route" systems; involving two additional signals for vessels steering along a "direct route" into and out of harbor, port, or river; and two for vessels bound in one and the other direction along a "direct sea route"; four in all; leaving steam-vessels on cross ferry or "cross channel" passages to sound a modified form of the present prolonged steam blast; and all other "crossing vessels," that is, all vessels crossing a "direct sea or harbor route" at a greater angle than 45°, to use, if a steamer, the single prolonged steam blast now in use for all steam-vessels under way; if a sailing vessel, the fog-horn signals authorized at present.

These systems are distinct in themselves. The harbor, etc., system can be adopted irrespectively to the oceanic system, and *vice versa*.

If these proposed signals are adopted, although the number of sounds made by vessels will be increased, the actual number of signals heard at any one time will remain the same as at present.

By the adoption of signals made up of sounds of different character the well-known difficulty of correctly locating a signal will, I think, be lessened; certainly will not be increased.

THE "DIRECT-ROUTE" SYSTEM OF FOG-SIGNALS.

A.—Vessels proceeding, or when not at anchor wishing to proceed, along a "direct route" when entering or leaving a port, harbor, or river shall sound during fog, etc., one of two signals, according to the direction in which she is proceeding along the "direct route."

At present, in whatever direction a steam-vessel is proceeding, she sounds one prolonged steam blast to denote a steam-vessel under way. As the two simplest additional symbols I propose to add directly after the prolonged (long) steam blast one short steam blast, to indicate a steam-vessel proceeding along a "direct route" into port, etc., and two short steam blasts to indicate a steam-vessel proceeding along a "direct route" out of port, etc.; that is:

Entering port, etc., long; short. ▬▬▬ ▬

Leaving port, etc., long; short, short. ▬▬▬ ▬ ▬

Sailing vessels proceeding along a "direct route" when entering or leaving port, etc., if on the starboard or port tack to sound the present fog-signals. If with the wind abaft the beam, to sound on the fog horn instead of the present three blasts the same signals as proposed for steamers to sound with the steam blast.

B.—Vessels proceeding, or when not at anchor wishing to proceed, along a "direct route" in any sea or water where fogs are experienced, and which is specially defined as a "direct route" for sound-signal purposes during fog, shall sound during fog, etc., one of two signals, according to the direction in which she is proceeding along the "direct route."

For these vessels I propose, as the signals next simplest and distinct in character, to add directly after the prolonged steam blast, denoting a steam-vessel under way, one short and one long steam blast to indicate a vessel proceeding in one direction, and the opposite symbol or one long and one short steam blast to indicate a steam-vessel proceeding in the opposite direction; that is:

For one direction, long; short, long. ▬▬▬▬ ▬ ▬▬▬▬▬
The opposite direction, long; long, short. ▬▬▬▬ ▬▬▬▬▬ ▬

A sailing vessel proceeding along a "direct sea route" with a fair wind to sound the above on her fog-horn in lieu of the present three blasts.

A steam-vessel not at anchor, but completely stopped, to ring her bell, but only at the same time as and while sounding her "direct route" signal for the direction she wishes to take along the "direct route," or while sounding the "cross-channel" signal if wishing to cross the "direct route."

A vessel altering her course to clear another vessel in sight to sound the helm signal now allowed optionally.

C.—Steam-vessels employed on "cross-ferries" and on established "cross-channel" passages shall modify the prolonged steam blast, denoting a steam-vessel under way, so that the sound shall either commence low and be gradually raised, or commence loud and be gradually lowered.

In British waters all steam-vessels crossing a "direct sea route" on an established "cross-channel" route shall, when bound towards Great Britain, sound a prolonged steam blast, which shall commence as abruptly as possible loud, and be gradually lowered in tone; when bound from Great Britain, shall sound a prolonged steam blast, which shall commence in a low tone, and, gradually increasing in loudness, end loud as abruptly as possible.

D.—Vessels crossing a "direct harbor, etc., route" or a "direct sea route," other than those specified under C, and all vessels navigating districts not specially defined as "direct routes" for fog signal purposes, or especially exempted, to sound the signals now authorized.

If a steamer, a prolonged steam blast.

If a sailing vessel, one, two, or three blasts on the fog-horn.

As almost all "direct sea routes" in foggy districts, in both the Atlantic and Pacific Oceans, are in a direction easterly and westerly, those directions may suitably form the basis for conformity in an adopted "direct-route" system of signals.

Thus, with a very few exceptions, vessels steering an easterly course along a specified "direct sea route" sound in fog, etc—

Long; short, long. ——————   ——————

Those steering a westerly course, sound—

Long; long, short. ——————   —————— —

EXAMPLES.

Proposed "direct sea routes."

Vessels on the routes mentioned sound—

Long; short, long. ——————   — —

Vessels steering in the opposite direction sound—

Long; long, short. ——————   —————— —

North Atlantic:

Northward and northeastward ..Along east coast of North America.

Eastward ....Out of Gulf of St. Lawrence.

Eastward ....Across North Atlantic.

Southeastward....................From north of Ireland towards Liverpool.

Northeastward. ....From south of Irish Channel towards Liverpool.

Eastward ....Up English Channel.

Northward.........................From Cape St. Vincent along coast of Portugal.

Eastward ....Across Bay of Biscay.

North Sea:

Northeastward ....From English Channel to northwest European ports south of Skagerrack.

Northeastward ....From English Channel to Baltic.

Northeastward ....From Thames to Baltic.

Northeastward ....From European ports to Baltic.

Northward ....In North Sea along coast of Great Britain.

Eastward ....From an offing of 80 miles off British coast to Baltic.

Baltic:

Southerly ....In Kattegat, the Sound, and the Belts.

Northeastward ....In Baltic.

Eastward ....In Gulf of Finland.

Northeastward ....In Gulf of Bothnia.

Mediterranean, etc.:

Eastward ....Gibraltar to Cape Bon, Malta, and Egypt.

Eastward ....Gibraltar to Cape De Gata, and Cape Creux Gulf of Lyons.

Southeastward ....Offing off Gulf of Lyons to Skerki Channel.

Southeastward ....Offing off Gulf of Lyons to Bonifacio Strait.

Eastward ....Offing off Gulf of Lyons to offing in Gulf of Genoa.

Southeastward ....Offing off Gulf of Genoa to Maretimo and Malta.

Southeastward ....Offing off Gulf of Genoa to Strait of Messina and off Syracuse.

Southeastward ....In Adriatic and along west coast of Greece.

Southwestward ....From Adriatic to offing off Cape Spartivento.

Eastward ....Candia to Egypt.

Northeastward ....Cerigo to offing off Dardanelles.

Northward.........................On east side of Archipelago.

Northeastward ....On coast of Syria.

Northeastward ....On west shore of Black Sea.

Northeastward ....Offing north of Bosphorus to Krimea.

Northeastward ....Offing north of Bosphorus to Kertch Strait.

Mediterranean, etc.=Continued.

    Southeastward ....Kertch Strait to offing off Batoum.

    Eastward ....On south shore of Black Sea.

    Northeastward ....Offing north of Kertch Strait to Gulf of Azov.

North Pacific:

    Northeastward ....In China Sea.

    Northward ....In Yellow Sea.

    Northeastward ....In Japan Sea.

    Eastward ....Across North Pacific to offing off American coast.

    Southeastward and southward..Along west coast of North America.

In the Atlantic the "direct routes," as distinct from the "crossing routes," that do not trend in a direction easterly and westerly are—

(1) East coast of Ireland trending northerly and southerly.

(2) West coast of Portugal and France trending northerly and southerly.

(3) East coast of Great Britain trending northerly and southerly.

(4) The Kattegat, Sound, and Belts trending northerly and southerly.

The principle adopted for these districts is that vessels sound the signal they would sound on an extended voyage before or after passing through the districts named.

(1) Vessels steering eastward and rounding Tuskar light-house on a northerly course continue to sound the easterly "direct sea route" signal; while, as provided for under D in the specially exempted district between Rockabill light-house and the Isle of Man, they sound the present authorized signal; on passing westward of the south point of the Isle of Man they join the "direct sea route," passing through the Irish Channel, after which, if bound south along the coast of Ireland, they sound the present authorized signal until passing Rockabill, when they join the "direct route," rounding the southeast point of Ireland.

Vessels rounding the north of Ireland on an easterly course continue to sound the easterly "direct route" signal until abreast the south point of Isle of Man.

(2) Vessels steering a northerly course along the coast of Portugal sound the easterly "direct route" signal.

(3) Vessels steering a northerly course up the North Sea near the British coast sound the easterly "direct route" signal until entering the specially-exempted district of Kinnaird Head, when they would sound the present authorized signal until nearing the Pentland Firth and joining the "direct sea route," passing north of Scotland.

Vessels steering a southerly course from the east entrance to the Pentland Firth would sound the present authorized signal until off Kinnaird Head, after which they would sound the westerly "direct route" signal.

(4) Vessels entering the Baltic continue to sound the easterly "direct route" signal while passing southward through the Kattegat, the Sound, and the Belts. Vessels leaving the Baltic continue to sound the westerly "direct route" signal while passing northward through the Sound, the Belts, and the Kattegat.

" Cross channel" passages which would sound the signals defined under C.

Crossing the English Channel " direct sea route."

Crossing the St. George's and the North Irish Channel "direct sea routes."

Crossing the Bay of Biscay " direct sea routes."

Crossing between the East British ports north of London and the Baltic, while westward of an offing of 80 miles from the British coast, and crossing the North Sea " direct sea route."

Crossing the " direct sea route " between Sardinia and Italy.

Crossing the " direct sea route" in Malta Channel, and South of the Strait of Messina.

Crossing the "direct sea route" between the Bosphorus and Crimea.

Crossing the "direct sea routes" at the entrance to the Gulf of Genoa and Lyons.

Sea routes which would be specially exempted (under D.)

1. Ocean routes which cross a more frequented ocean route which has been defined as a "direct sea route"; as:

Between the Scilly Isles and ports north while crossing the Bristol Channel.

2. Vessels requiring to change from the eastward to the westward bound signal while on the same voyage, as:

The West European and Mediterranean trade while between Gibraltar and Cape St. Vincent.

Between the Archipelago and Egypt while passing Kaso Island.

3. Vessels on a "direct sea route" which would meet each other after rounding an island, as:—

The Atlantic trade with ports on the east coasts of the British islands, while navigating between stated points, as Rockabill and south end of Isle of Man; and Kinnaird Head and the Pentland Firth.

If the proposed "direct route" signals for entering and leaving ports, etc., are adopted by the local harbor authorities, they would apply specially to vessels navigating within the local limits of each port.

If the " direct sea route" is adopted by international agreement, I propose that the outer or sea limits of each local district should be for fog-signal purposes extended seaward to the line of "direct sea route" nearest to the port, etc., or to some clearly defined area in the offing of the port, etc.

Thus the "direct port, etc., route" signals would apply equally to all vessels on the landward side of a "direct sea route" that were approaching the land or steering out from the land to sea. On these vessels arriving on a " direct sea route" and steering along it they would alter their signal from "outward bound" to the "direct sea route" signal. On arriving near a "direct sea route" and crossing it, they would sound the "cross channel" signal or the present authorized signal.

For a port like Constantinople the "inward and ontward route" signals would extend to an offing southwest of the Dardanelles and to an offing north of the Bosphorus.

NEW SIGNALS PROPOSED.

Steam or fog-horn. Steam blast if a steam-vessel; fog-horn if a sailing vessel with wind abaft the beam.

—————— Vessel entering port, etc., or approaching land on a "direct route."

—————— — — Vessel leaving port, etc., or steering out from land on a "direct route."

—————— — —— Vessel steering easterly* along a "direct sea route."

—————— —— — Vessel steering westerly* along a "direct sea route."

Steam blast with bell. Steam-vessel stopped, but not at anchor.

Example.

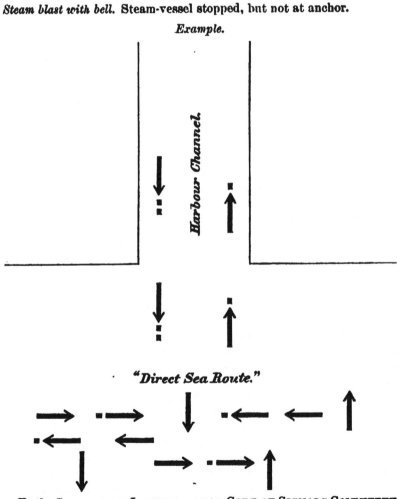

"Direct Sea Route."

To the SECRETARY, INTERNATIONAL CODE OF SIGNALS COMMITTEE.
February 14, 1889.

———————————

* Except in a few special districts.

PAPER C.—*Memorandum by Sir Digby Murray.*

FOG-SIGNALS AT SEA.

JANUARY 24, 1889.

Questions in the extended reference to the committee.	Replies.
Whether in the interests of safety it is desirable to establish a system of "sound signals" to be used by steam-vessels during foggy weather to denote the direction in which they are proceeding.	No.
Whether on the same grounds and for the same purpose it is necessary to establish a system of sound signals to be used by sailing vessels under like circumstances.	No.
Whether such system should be limited to crowded waters and narrow seas near coasts; or whether it should be extended to the open sea also.	It is less applicable to crowded waters where many steamers may be approaching one another at the same moment than it would be to the open sea.
If any system is deemed by the committee to be practical what that system is?	In my opinion no system.

REASONS.

When the late Rule of the Road Committee framed the course signals, Article 19 of the present regulations, they were most careful to impose the restriction that they should only be used by a steam-ship under way to indicate her course " to any other ship which she has *in sight.*"

This conclusion was arrived at without one single dissentient, as it was felt that to encourage the officer of any ship to alter her course in consequence of hearing a sound, the distance and direction of which was necessarily unknown to him, would be fatal to safety.

I am still of opinion that the committee in this exercised a wise discretion.

The collision which occurred between the steam-ships *Britannic* and *Celtic* on the 19th of May, 1887, was brought about by the commander and second officer of the *Britannic* thinking the fog-whistle which they heard was on their port bow and porting to avoid it, whereas the sound was really on their starboard bow, and when the *Celtic* was at last sighted it was too late to avoid collision. If both ships had kept their courses there would have been no collision.

On the 5th January, 1889, the steam-ships *Kenley* and *Pione* were approaching one another in a thick fog in the North Sea. The *Kenley* improperly ported and blew one blast of the steam-whistle before seeing the *Pione*. (It is uncertain whether the *Pione* did or did not blow two blasts and starboard, as the case has not yet been heard in the Admiralty Court.) The result was a collision, in which the *Kenley* was sunk.

In crowded waters and narrow channels it is possible, and indeed it often happens, that several steamers are approaching one another at the same time, and if, as has been suggested, all these vessels are to make distinctive signals indicating their course, or if, as has also been suggested, vessels following the direct route are to make distinctive signals in accordance with their direction, and vessels crossing the direct route are to make different signals, the position and distance of all these vessels being unknown with regard to one another, the result to my mind would be most confusing.

Let us consider with the assistance of a few diagrams the least complicated of these proposals, "The direct route system in the open sea."

↓ B 1.   ↓ B 2.   ↓ B 3.

↑ A.

A is a steam-ship bound from New York to the eastward, and consequently on a direct route and making the signal proposed for direct route vessels bound to the eastward. The officer of the watch hears a signal from another steam-ship bound in the opposite direction, which sound may be in the direction marked B 1, B 2, or B 3, or possibly much broader upon either bow, and the distance of which is unknown. What should the officer of the watch or commander of the ship do?

Undoubtedly keep his course, but get the way off his ship as quickly as possible. If the approaching steam-ship is either in the position B 1 or B 3, the two ships will both clear one another, provided that neither alter their course.

The two steamers have a beam respectively of 41 and 45 feet (the beams of the *Britannic* and *Celtic*), and the odds are very greatly against a collision stem on; but even if it does take place, the consequences are far less likely to be serious than if either vessel ported or starboarded, and in that manner exposed her broadside to the other.

Let me now suppose that this vessel bound to the eastward hears the signal of a crossing steamer, bound, say, from some one of the southern ports to Boston.

B 1.   B 2.   B 3.

←   ←   ←

→   →   →

↑ A.

If the officer of watch A could be certain the crossing steamer was in the position B 1 or B 2, and standing to the northward, he might proceed in safety, but she might be in the position B 3, or even more on his starboard bow, or if there is no difference between the signals of vessels crossing the direct route bound north and south his position would be still further complicated. His only safe procedure in any case would be to get the way off his ship. .

In my opinion, whenever the officer in charge of the deck of a steamship hears during fog the sound of another steamer's whistle, or a sailing ship's fog-horn anywhere apparently forward of abeam, he should at once get the way off his own ship, and after the way is entirely off her he should proceed with the greatest caution until he is finally past the danger, and should never, until the approaching vessel is seen, alter the helm under the impression that he can localize the direction and distance of the sound in which he is almost certain to be deceived.

If these views are accepted by the committee as correct, there remains for consideration the question as to whether any good is likely to result from having distinctive signals of any kind to indicate the course or direction in which steam-ships are proceeding during fog.

If as in crowded waters several steam-ships were approaching one another not only no good is in my opinion likely to arise, but such a system of signaling would give rise to confusion, and if the result of it was to occasion over confidence in the mind of the officers in charge, and induce them to alter the helm, it would, I think, be distinctly prejudicial to safety.

In more open water, if two steam-ships only were approaching one another at one and the same time, and the officers of both were required to first get the way off their ships, and then one ship was to remain with her engines stopped until the other had passed, as suggested by Captain Wilcox, such an arrangement would, I think, be in the direction of safety.

As, however, such conditions would only apply in a limited number of cases, and those the least dangerous, and could not with safety, in my opinion, be made generally applicable, I am not in favor of altering the present regulations in this respect.

PAPER D.—*Memorandum by Admiral Sir F. L. McClintock.*

SOUND-SIGNALS.

8, ATHERSTONE TERRACE, LONDON, S. W.,
February 21, 1889.

SIR: Having considered the four points in Lord Stanley of Preston's Minute, I have to report to the International Signals Committee as follows:

To establish a system of fog-signals to be used by steam-ships during foggy weather to denote the direction in which they are proceeding, if made compulsory, would, in my opinion, rather increase than diminish the danger of collision.

Also, I think it undesirable either to alter the established fog-signals or to add fresh ones.

But I think that the optional use of a few sound-signals might be permitted with advantage.

The use of the signal P D should, I think, be encouraged; it is not liable to be mistaken for any other existing fog-signal and it would always suggest the most prudent thing to do in a dense fog.

I think that eight course signals should be established for optional use. There are times in dense fog during still weather when ships moving slowly would be glad to use their course signal in reply to the ordinary prolonged blast.

Mr. Barker's Marine Safety Signal Code of eight compass signals (No. 9 in the abstract of fog-signals) appears to have been most carefully thought out, and it could be adopted without interfering with any of the established sound-signals; it also seems better suited than most others for ready recognition and easy remembrance; for instance, signals beginning with a long sound indicate an eastward course, with a short sound a westward course. It seems probable that two of these signals would soon grow into use in the English Channel with the outward and homeward bound ships.

F. L. McCLINTOCK.

The SECRETARY, INTERNATIONAL CODE OF SIGNALS COMMITTEE.

PAPER E.—*Memorandum by Capt. O. P. Wilson.*

MEMORANDUM ON FURTHER REFERENCE FROM THE BOARD OF TRADE
AS TO SOUND-SIGNALS.

BOARD OF TRADE SURVEYOR'S OFFICE,
ST. KATHERINE DOCK HOUSE, TOWER HILL, E.,
February 20, 1889.

SIR: I doubt if, "in the interest of safety, it is desirable to establish
a system of sound-signals to be used by steam-vessels during foggy
weather to denote the direction in which they are proceeding," on the
ground of the very great difficulty of ascertaining the bearing of one
vessel from another during foggy weather. It may thus come about
that under the supposition a vessel is in a different position from that
really occupied by her, maneuvers may be attempted which might
actually bring about the collision both are desirous by their signaling
to avoid.

On the same grounds I also doubt if it is desirable to establish a
system of sound-signals to be used by sailing vessels under like circumstances. If sailing vessels were liable to meet other sailing vessels
only during foggy weather, I should be disposed to modify these views,
but as sailing vessels are quite as likely to meet steamers as sailing
vessels, I am induced to treat them very much in the same category as
to steamers meeting.

In Article 12 of the International Rules for Preventing Collisions at
Sea, means are provided for sailing vessels to indicate approximately
the course they are steering, and there is no doubt that with them the
direction of the wind is a material assistance in arriving at an approximate estimate of what course each vessel is steering; moreover, time
in their case is not so much a factor to be considered in consequence
of foggy weather being generally accompanied by light winds or calms.

In Article 12 falling snow is referred to, when of course it is possible
a gale of wind may be blowing, but the words of the reference to us
mentions only "during foggy weather."

I see no reason to draw distinction between sound-signals being limited to crowded waters and narrow seas, or extended to open sea also.
In fact, I think that they are quite as likely to be of as much, if not
more, use in the open sea, where there is less probability of the signaling of one vessel being confounded with that of another. The main
difficulty in establishing a system of sound-signals that presents itself
to me is the liability, when a number of vessels are present, of the signals of one vessel being misinterpreted to refer to that of another.

With reference to the various systems that have been proposed from
time to time, I think they can be conveniently divided into two catego-
ries:

(1) Signals indicating the points of the compass only, and

(2) Vocabulary signals.

Signals in the first category do not, I consider, go far enough to make it worth while adopting them for the reasons given above.

The only vocabulary system with which I am acquainted, and that only very slightly, is the Morse system. The advantages attending it are apparently the ease with which it can be used for conversational purposes; secondly, its adaptability to light as well as sound, and to day as well as night, thereby doing away with the necessity of learning a second code; and, thirdly, that it would harmonize with the system in use in Her Majesty's naval and military services. The only objection to it that occurs to me is that it is somewhat complicated, and it is very questionable whether the officers of the mercantile marine would have sufficient leisure to perfect themselves in its use.

On the whole question I am against the establishment of a syste.n of sound-signals until some invention has been perfected whereby the bearing of one vessel from another during foggy weather can be correctly indicated.

In Article 19 optional sound-signals are provided for indicating the maneuver a steam-vessel is executing, but as that article has no reference to foggy weather I do not think it necessary to refer to it in detail, except to say that I have every reason to believe it is found very useful in practice.

If it is eventually decided that sound-signals are to be adopted for foggy weather it would be desirable to make them uniform with Article 19, so that the same signal might be applicable in both clear and foggy weather.

I have, etc.,

CHARLES P. WILSON.

The SECRETARY, INTERNATIONAL CODE OF SIGNALS COMMITTEE.

SOUND-SIGNALS FOR USE IN FOG.

GENERAL SUMMARY OF REPLIES.

There have been received from—

Replies.

Masters who are opposed to the introduction of any compulsory system of sound-signals 119

Owners and societies who are opposed to the introduction of any compulsory system of sound-signals 10

Masters who advocate the adoption of a few simple signals, chiefly those provided by Article 19 of the regulations for preventing collisions at sea........... 48

Owners who advocate the adoption of a few simple signals, chiefly those provided by Article 19 of the regulations for preventing collisions at sea........... 2

Masters who advocate the adoption of more complete systems of signals......... 28

Seamen's societies which advocate the adoption of more complete systems of signals 1

The chief reasons given by those who object to the introduction of any system of fog-signals are, the confusion they would cause in crowded waters, the difficulty of locating sounds in fog, the false confidence they would give to officers in charge of the vessels using them, and the considerable degree of skill and experience necessary to prevent the possibility of mistake in the event of any complex system being adopted.

Abstract of observations on the proposed introduction of a system of sound-signals for indicating the routes or courses of steam-ships in fog, mist, etc.

London and Northwestern Railway:

Dent, Admiral.—Deprecates any change, but thinks present long blast for steam-ships might be continued, followed by one short blast when vessel's head is anywhere from N. to E.; by two between E. and S.; S. and W. three; W. and N. four.

Should not steam-ships with all way off use bells?

Thinks the views of Sir George Nares and Admiral Bowden-Smith might be carried out in a simplified form.

Beaumont, J. A., and Johns, D., masters.—Think it would not be advisable.

Taylor, G.; Varian, T. J.; Haldane, A. M.; Clay, T. G.; Thomas, R.; Green, J.; Roche, J. S. N., masters.—All think the use of sound-signals would greatly increase the risk of collision in crowded channels.

Liddicoat, T., and Gordon A., masters.—Think some simple modification of the present system desirable. Captain Liddicoat approves of the system used in the United States, and Captain Gordon thinks the system suggested by the naval officers and given in the memorandum much too complicated for the merchant service.

Leyland, F., & Co.:

Hill, M., master steam-ship *Bavarian.*—Vessels approaching each other in fog should both stop, and, if necessary, use PD sound-signals until clear of each other.

McConkey, A. E., steam-ship *Persian.*—The impossibility of judging from what direction sounds proceed in dense fog would render any compulsory system worse than useless, but in light fog an optional system of eight or four point signals by combinations of long and short blasts might be useful in open water. In channel work such signals would cause confusion.

Want, W. H., steam-ship *Bostonian.*—Compass-signals would cause confusion, but would suggest the general use, in fog as well as clear weather, of the signals specified in Article 19, with one or two modifications.

S. Ex. 53, pt. 3——8

Leyland, F., & Co.—Continued.

Parry, E., steam-ship *Venetian.*—Thinks the signals under Article 19 sufficient for steamers in fog, and would make no distinction between channels and open sea.

Laurenson, C., steam-ship *Falernian.*—Would make the use of Article 19 signals compulsory in fog; any additional signals would cause confusion.

McLay, F. L., superintendent.—Approves of Admiral Bowden-Smith's suggestions *re* compass-signals.

General Steam Navigation Company:

Ellis, J., marine superintendent; Dyer, Randall, Joslin, Mallett, Botwright, Cox, Laing, Harding, Wright, masters.—Are all opposed to any system of sound-signals. Such signals can not be located in dense fog; they would cause confusion and increase danger by inducing masters to rely upon them, and thus lessen caution in other directions. The signaling appliances of all vessels should be officially inspected.

Great Eastern Railway Company:

Howard, D., marine superintendent.—Thinks the present rules sufficient; numerous sound-signals would cause confusion in narrow channels. There is room for improvement in lights and whistles, and every vessel should show a stern light.

Robinson, J. H.; Gay, W. S.; Henderson, R.; Ablett, J. (masters).—Are all opposed to any change in the present system. Shedlock, H., and Henderson, J., masters.—Are of the same opinion, but the former approves of Mr. Barker's proposal for vessels steering E. to use one long blast and those steering W. one short one, while Captain Henderson urges a more strict observance of Article 13 by sailing as well as steam vessels.

Shaw, Savill, and Albion Company:

Shaw, Savill, and Albion Company.—Any system of sound-signals will very greatly increase risk unless it is of the most simple character.

Barlow, B. J., master.—A system of course or route signals is not practicable, because it is impossible for any man to tell within several points from what direction a sound is coming in a fog, and therefore any rule to avoid a danger which you can not see, and the bearing of which is uncertain, would be most risky; would cause great confusion in crowded channels.

Burton, G., steam-ship *Coptic.*—A system of sound (course) signals would lead to confusion; suggests advisability of using Article 19 signals in fog; and the " direct sea-route " signals proposed by Sir G. Nares might be useful, and perhaps might also be adopted for entering and leaving port. Suggests use of siren for indicating vicinity, and whistle for indicating measures adopted. The horns of sailing ships should be more carefully tested than at present.

Shaw, Savill, and Albion Company—Continued.

Marine Superintendent.—Thinks steam-ship should use the fog signals prescribed by Article 12 for sailing ships, and that, for the time, they should be assumed to be sailing ships and signal according to tack and direction of wind. Proposes a number of short blasts as a signal for "engine stopped," that the term "moderate speed" should be defined as one-third the usual speed. Is strongly opposed to any complex system of sound-signals.

Southeastern Railway Company :

Commander Boxer, R. N., superintendent.—Thinks each steam-ship should carry two swiveled sirens; a high-note one on port side to indicate all northern courses, and a low bass to starboard for southern ; the various courses being indicated by the number of blasts, one to four, as per diagram, and five for going astern. Sailing vessels to use horns in same way.

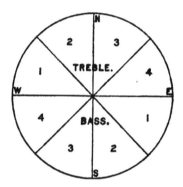

Davies, G.; Hammond F.; Kilbee, P.; Hall, J.; Hammond, J.; Harrold, H.; and Winton, O., masters.—All think there should be some system of sound-signals.

London, Brighton, and South Coast Railway Company:

Their harbor master (with many years' sea experience) thinks the present rules sufficient, and that a system of sound-signals would cause confusion.

Hemmings, H. W., master.—Thinks if the present signals were strictly used collisions would decrease. Approves of Admiral Bowden-Smith's system if it could be modified to four sounds for compass points.

Sharp, R., master.—Thinks there should be a system of long and short blast compass-signals.

Breach, C. W., master.—Thinks course or route signals would increase danger, but suggests that vessels on hearing each other might indicate their relative positions by combinations of long and short blasts, speed being reduced until vessels are clear. Approves of Morse system of sound and flash signals.

London, Brighton, and South Coast Railway Company—Continued.

Hall, J. M.; Wade, J., masters.—Are opposed to any change.

Hartfield, G., master.—Thinks two minutes between blasts in present rule too long, and that there might be a specified number of blasts for vessels approaching or leaving land.

Hinton, J., master.—Thinks two minutes between blasts too long, and that "moderate speed" should be defined.

Aubriot, A., master.—Does not approve of a system of sound-signals. Thinks term "moderate speed" too vague, and that all vessels should show stern lights. Sailing vessels are often very badly lighted.

Sylvestre, L., master.—Thinks there should be a system of sound-signals. Points out that term "moderate speed" is very indefinite.

Phelipot, L., master.—Submits similar suggestions to the foregoing.

Phelipot, A., master.—Thinks "moderate speed" should be defined, and that there should be a system of sound-signals. The lights and whistles of vessels are often inefficient at present, and require supervision.

Ismay, T. H.:

Ismay, T. H., and Hewitt, Captain, superintendent.—Additional signals would cause confusion in crowded waters, and increase danger generally by inducing undue confidence in them. All their commanders are opposed to any new system, but one of Article 19 signals might be used for denoting that way is taken off, and a similar signal for reply. Simplicity is a great object.

Maclver, H.:

Thinks the present regulations, if strictly observed, preferable to any code of signals; but Captain Barker's automatic is the best system he is acquainted with.

Great Western Railway Company :

Lecky, Captain, superintendent.—Is opposed to any change in the present simple system. The average master is unfit to work any complex method.

Davies, C., master.—Thinks the present system sufficient. Approves of the harbor signals in Paper B., but course signals generally would increase danger.

Pearn, W. L., master.—Fears that sound-signals would cause confusion, but approves generally of proposals in Paper A. Thinks Article 19 signals might be adopted for fog.

Pearn, T., master.—Thinks there should be a system for steamships, but the present signals are sufficient for sailing ships. (Submits a detailed statement of suggestions for improving the system proposed by Admiral Bowden-Smith.) The use of Article 19 signals should be made compulsory.

Shipmasters' Society:

The committee (and members in port) think any enlarged system of sound-signals would cause great confusion in crowded waters, while its use would require much practice. It is very difficult to locate sounds in fog. They think any system adopted should be universal, and should apply to sailing as well as steam vessels, and suggest merely the use of the present optional course signals in fogs, with perhaps P D added. Most masters think "moderate speed" should be defined.

McGregor, J.:

Hutton, J. S., marine superintendent.—Thinks the present sound-signals should not be altered, but that sirens are more suitable than whistles for steam-ships, the sound being more penetrating. Bells should be of good metal, and should exceed 16 inches in diameter. A system of compass signals (diagram submitted) would require 56 sounds, and the risk of the confusion would be great.

Holt, Alfred:

Has consulted other persons whom he thinks competent judges, and finds that opinion generally is against any system of sound-signals; some of them are, however, inclined to support the system proposed by Admiral Bowden-Smith. Mr. Holt is opposed to the adoption of a system.

Cayzer, Irvine & Co., M. 8,430:

Joss, J.—Is opposed to any system of sound-signals. Thinks signal whistles should be at bows to be more audible from other vessels and to avoid deafening of officers. In sailing vessels fog-horns are often inadequate and lights bad and badly placed. Thinks the questions and replies at the head of the Paper C, by Sir Digby Murray, cover the whole of the ground, and these replies he thoroughly indorses.

Philip, A. I., master.—Suggests a system of course (outward, homeward, channel, and coasting) signals, consisting of one, two, and three long blasts; but steam-ships meeting in fog should stop and feel their way cautiously.

Beer, S., master.—A compulsory system would induce recklessness and also cause confusion, but thinks the system of Admiral Bowden-Smith would often be very useful if it were made optional.

Millar, W., master.—Thinks the difficulty of locating sound in fogs would tend to make a system of signals dangerous.

——— ———, master of *Clan Graham.*—Submits a system of course-signals to be made by means of blasts upon the siren and steam-whistle.

Harrison, N., master.—His views on the matter coincide very much with those expressed by Sir D. Murray, Admiral Sir F. McClin-

Cayzer, Irvine & Co., M. 8,430—Continued.

> tock, and Captain C. P. Wilson. Is opposed to any compulsory system, but thinks Admiral Bowden-Smith's code, with certain modifications, might be made optional.
>
> Rule, W. I., master.—Thinks a few simple signals might be introduced, to be added to if found to work satisfactory.

Wilson, T., Sons, & Co :

> Rutter, J., superintendent.—Thinks a system of sound-signals would be an element of great danger.
>
> Worth, W. G., master.—Sound-signals are impracticable on account of the difficulty of locating them. The sirens now used cause confusion when near light-ships.
>
> Scarr, G., master.—A system of signals would increase danger. Present system is sufficient, but it is very desirable that all whistles should be of a uniform pattern.
>
> Wilson, R., master.—Would merely impose a system, already often used, of one blast for going ahead, two for stopped, and three going astern.
>
> Pepper, G., master.—Thinks Article 19 signals with P D added would be sufficient. Any extensive code would increase danger.
>
> Vickerman, W., master.—A system of sound-signals would increase danger, owing to the confusion that would arise in crowded channels and the difficulty of locating sounds in fog.
>
> Irvin, T. M., master.—Thinks all steam-ships should be compelled to have uniform whistles, quite distinct from the light-ship sirens they now often resemble. Nothing more than Article 19 signals is required for use in fog, and these might be adopted.

Leyland, R. W..

> Entirely agrees with Sir D. Murray's objections to sound-signals, but thinks vessels should carry lights arranged as helm indicators.
>
> Richardson, N., master.—A change in the present system would lead to danger. The horns of sailing-ships should be more powerful.

McIver, D., & Co :

> Billinge, E., master.—Whistles and horns should be more powerful than at present. Article 19 signals, with slight alterations, might be used in fog. Systems in Papers A and B are too elaborate and quite unfit for use in the merchant service.
>
> Gill, master.—Thinks it important to have a few simple signals to denote up, down, and crossing English and Irish Channels.
>
> McConochie, J., master.—Agrees with Sir D. Murray and Admiral Sir F. L. McClintock as to the undesirability of establishing a code of sound-signals. Would encourage the use of P D, but believes route-signals would only increase danger.

Guion & Co. :

Munder, G. S., master.—Sound-signals for fog are impracticable, owing to the difficulty of locating them and the confusion they would cause in crowded channels. Slow speed and caution are· necessary when two vessels hear each other, and optional use of Article 19 signals sometimes advantageous. To stop is very undesirable, as steam blows off and drowns all sound. Suggests short blasts, blown continuously, as a distress signal.

Worral, J. P., master.—Sound-signals would cause confusion. Thinks "moderate speed" (Article 13) should be defined as not exceeding 9 knots.

Cushing, J. A., master.—Course or route signals would cause confusion, but approves of American code, *i. e.*, one blast for "my course is to starboard;" two, "to port;" three, "full speed astern," with another signal for "way off" and "stopped." Whistles and horns should be increased in power, and speed reduced in fog.

Brooks, S., master.—Compass signals much too complicated; would merely have one blast for "port helm" and two for "starboard." Whistles should be required to be efficient, and "moderate speed" should not exceed 8 knots.

Rigby, C. L., master.—Entirely advocates the American system, but to render it effective some powerful, clear-sounding instrument must be approved and universally used. Simplicity is the chief point, as prompt action is so necessary.

Kiddle, Captain :

Sound-signaling impracticable on account of existing general inability to distinguish notes.

Glover Bros:

Buchanan J., master.—Would not alter the present signals, but would provide five optional ones—viz, P D and (4) north, south, east, and west—signals by combinations of long and short blasts.

Rainey, A. G., master.—Approves of Admiral Bowden-Smith's suggestions; also thinks Article 19 signals and P D might be used, but there is much difficulty in locating sounds, especially near high land, which produces echoes. High speed in fog is now a great source of danger. Would not alter sailing-ship signals.

Glover, Terrot, master.—Thinks it impossible for the average shipmaster to devote the time or acquire the prompt accuracy necessary for the successful working of a complete sound-signal system. To establish such a system would be to induce more reckless navigation, and thus increase danger.

Glover, Thomas, master.—Thinks what is chiefly required is a definite system for indicating the position of the helm by siren signals; the main cause of collision being uncertainty on this point when vessels are nearing each other.

McGregor, Son, & Co.:

Taylor, A., master.—Is strongly opposed to any alteration, both on account of the utter confusion a sound-signal system would cause in crowded channels, and the difficulty of locating sounds. Would make it criminal to exceed 4 knots in fog; the only safe course for approaching vessels in fog is to slow down and feel their way. Entirely agrees with the reasons given by Sir D. Murray for not having the present regulations altered.

Duke, W. E., master.—Would make the use of Article 19 signals, with P D added, compulsory in fog.

Peninsular and Oriental Steam Navigation Company:

Their nautical committee, composed of Lord Sudely, director, Capt. W. E. Angrove, marine superintendent, and Capt. J. E. Almond, nautical inspector, are strongly convinced that any elaborate system would increase danger, as the exactness necessary for working it is not to be found on board the lower class of merchant ships. Would simply add P D to present signals. Captain Almond calls special attention to the difficulty of locating sounds and measuring their length.

Tomlin, Barratt, Orman, Reeves, Fraser, Worcester, Stead, Adamson, Loggin, Edwardes, Stewart, Andrews, Harvey, and Angove, masters.—All oppose the introduction of any code of sound-signals, chiefly on account of the difficulty of locating sounds in fog and the risk of confusion. Attention is called to vagueness of the term "moderate speed" by Captain Loggin and Captain Fraser; and Captain Edwardes thinks if Article 19 signals were optional they might be useful when only two steamers were in proximity. Captain Orman remarks that if a vessel had sounded a compass signal and then had to alter her helm, confusion would arise, but he agrees with Sir D. Murray and Sir F. L. McClintock in recommending P D.

Wyat, Captain.—Approves of Admiral Bowden-Smith's suggestions, subject to certain modifications. Present position of whistle is a bad one, as it deafens officer on bridge; whistle should be at foremast head.

National Steam-ship Company:

Their captains do not think it practicable to introduce a system of sound-signals. What is required is to regulate the speed of steam-ships in fog; also more powerful fog-horns for sailing ships.

Watts, Ward & Co.:

Graystone, S., master.—Thinks rules for fog should allow considerable latitude, and that any code system would cause confusion in crowded waters. Signals should be more powerful.

Valder, R., master.—Thinks present signals sufficient. It is difficult to locate sound in fog, and a system useful on the ocean might be confusing on English coasts.

Watts, Ward & Co.—Continued.

Scott, M., master.—Agrees with foregoing, but suggests four long blasts to indicate " stopped," and five for reply " understood," to be used by two steam-ships when in proximity.

Cox, R. M., master.—A code would induce false confidence and cause confusion. It is difficult to locate sounds in fog, and difficult in time of anxiety, to estimate their duration.

Raeburn, J., master.—Approves of the compass signals suggested in Paper A, the port signals in Paper B, and P D signal. Any complicated system would cause confusion. All signals should produce uniform sounds. The term "moderate speed" in Article 13 is too vague.

Fenwick, J., & Son :

Sound-signals would increase danger, especially in crowded water.

Scott, W., master.—Would extend Article 12*a*, by requiring approaching steam-ship to stop and indicate their intended course.

Brown, W. B., master.—Stern lights should always be shown, and use of siren prohibited on account of its similarity to light-house signals.

Watson, J. S., Munroe, A., and Hodden, G., masters.—A system of signals would only cause confusion.

Geary, W., master.—Stern light should be made compulsory and use of siren prohibited. Whistles and horns should be of the best. Approaching steam-ships should get their way off and pass cautiously. Present rules are simple, and this is a great advantage.

London and Southwestern Railway Company :

Edom, F., Merrett, T., Mortimer, H. D., Nutbeem, G. N., Vander-plank, C., Dyer, J., Lainson, T., Gregory, W., Bishop, W., Mabb, R. C., Heathcotte, R., masters.—Are opposed to the introduction of any system, chiefly on account of the risk of confusion. Five of the foregoing advocate the P D signal, and two call attention to vagueness of term " moderate speed."

Allix, G., master.—Advocates an eight-course compass signal, also signal P D. Fog-horns should be more powerful than at present.

Kemp, F. E., master.—Would make the use of Article 19 signals compulsory in fog.

Lewis, G. H., master.—The Morse or some other suitable system should be used by steam-ships everywhere, but no change necessary for sailing ships.

Eastern Steam-ship Company :

Westray & Co.—Would introduce no change except use of P D, and two signals for "up" and "down" rivers. A sound-signal system would cause confusion, induce undue confidence, be difficult to remember, and would render the law concerning navigation very uncertain.

Eastern Steam-ship Company—Continued.

Long, D. O., Prentice, W. L., Cox, J. S., and Scott, T., masters.— Are opposed to the introduction of any systems chiefly on account of the risk of confusion. Captain Prentice approves of P D, and Captain Cox thinks whistles and horns generally should be improved. Captain Scott says the working of a system would absorb attention to a dangerous extent.

British India Steam Navigation Company :

Smith, J., master.—Approves of the eight-point course signals of Admiral Bowden-Smith. These are simple and would not cause confusion. Sees no risk of inducing overconfidence, and the difficulty sometimes experienced in locating sound is no real objection.

Avern, I., master.—Also approves of the eight-point course signals.

Hutchinson, W. E., master.—It is difficult to locate sound in fog, and additional signals would only increase risk. If any adopted they should be course indicating and very simple.

Sayers, N. E., master.—Fully agrees with Sir D. Murray that present rules should not be altered. Sound-signals would cause confusion.

Hodgkinson, G.—Thinks there should be a voluntary system for steam-ships, and approves of that of Admiral Bowden-Smith. For sailing ships a signal for indicating the direction of the wind, when abaft the beam, is all that is required.

Irish Steam-ship Association:

A system of sound-signals would increase danger.

City of Dublin Steam-Packet Company:

Kendall, T. G.; Thomas, J.; Thomson, T.; Chittick, J.; O'Neill, D., masters; and Watson, W., superintendent.—Are all opposed to the adoption of a system of sound-signals. The objections are the risk of confusion and the difficulty of locating sounds in fog. Captains Kendall and Thomas think the P D signal might be useful.

Allan Line of Steam-ships :

Dunlap, N.—Is opposed to any elaborate system of signals, but whistles, etc., should be required to be of sufficient power.

Macnicol, A., master.—Would merely adopt P D, and increase the power of horns and whistles. A signal system would cause confusion.

Hughes, R., master.—A course indicating system is impracticable, but the urgent signals on page 4 of memorandum might be adopted with a signal for reply " understood." A signal for " not moving " is also required.

Wylie, H., master.—No additional signals required, but suggests substitution of gong for the bell as being more penetrating.

Allan Line of Steam-ships—Continued.

Menzies, C. J., master.—Compass signals would cause confusion, but approves of Captain Crofton's system. Whistles should be uniform, low tone for ocean, and shrill for coast trade; one blast for one direction, and two for opposite. Two steam-ships when approaching should both slow.

Killop, D. M., master.—Endorses the opinion of Sir D. Murray and Sir F. L. McClintock, and is opposed to any system of signals; but an optional signal for up and down channel might be useful.

Stephen, J. G., master.—Sound-signals would cause confusion. Steam-ships which have had to stop in fog should sound three blasts every two minutes.

Carruthers, R., master.—Is opposed to the introduction of any system.

Moore, R. P., master.—Present system is quite sufficient, but advocates use of P D.

Richardson, W., master.—It is impossible to locate sounds in fog and any system would cause confusion. Thinks present American system might be extended by adopting three blasts for "stopped," and four for "going astern."

France, J., master.—A sound-signal system would cause great confusion and increase collisions. Present signals sufficient.

Dunlop, W., master.—Does not think any new system necessary, but approves of P D. There should be a standard minimum of power fixed for whistles.

Watts, R. S., master.—Few whistles can give sounds uniformly, and it is difficult to estimate duration or direction of sounds. Moreover, a system of signals would induce less careful navigation.

Temperley, Carter, and Darke:

Think course signals would increase danger owing to the difficulty of locating sounds in fog and the confusion that would arise in crowded waters. Moderate speed should be defined, say, five miles per hour.

Jackson. J. E., master.—Thinks a concise system by means of long and short blasts would be useful for steam-ships, but no change necessary for sailing ships. The risk of collision will not, however, be lessened unless a strict rule is made that steam-ships shall not exceed, say 6 knots in fog. Under present system masters are compelled to run at high speed, and officers generally are overworked by frequent watches. Steam-whistles should be aloft as they deafen officers on bridge and drown signals of other vessels.

Royal Mail Steam-Packet Company:

Armstrong, B. G., master.—Is opposed to any system, as it is difficult to locate sounds in fog. Slow speed and caution the best safeguards. Present horns of sailing ships are sufficient.

Royal Mail Steam-Packet Company—Continued.

Dickinson, L. R , master.—Fully agrees with the proposal of Admiral Sir F. McClintock for allowing the use of a few optional signals, and would reduce the interval for the compulsory article 12 *a* signal to one minute.

Woolward, A., master.—The variety and uncertainty of the sounds produced by whistles would make any system dangerous.

Gillies, A., master.—Course signals would be confusing and dangerous in crowded channels, but useful in the open sea. Article 12 signals should be blown once every minute, and vessels in thick fog should be compelled to stop and blow P D at one minute intervals.

Brander, J., master.—Quite agrees with Sir D. Murray and Captain Wilson that a sound-signal system would cause confusion and danger owing to the difficulty of locating sounds; and does not advocate optional signals. Vessels should be compelled to stop dead in fog, etc., only moving to avoid danger.

Gillies, W., master.—Thinks all vessels should stop in fog, moving only to avoid danger, and then sounding (steam-ship) four whistles of four seconds each, and sailing ships four similar blasts on fog-horns. But if a moderate speed in fog is allowed a system of helm and tack indicating signals might be allowed. For steam-ship, one blast, port; two blasts, starboard; three blasts, going astern; and the same for two respective tacks of sailing ships, with four blasts for no steerage way, and three for wind free.

Hall Bros.:

Steele, J. B., master.—Would make the use of Article 19 signals compulsory, but otherwise any alteration is unadvisable. Unless thoroughly understood, a sound-signal system would increase danger. Caution is the chief safeguard.

Innes, G., master.—Would only adopt P D. Any general system would cause great confusion in crowded waters. Sailing ships often proceed at an 8 to 10-knot speed in fog, and this is a great source of danger.

Aikman, J., master.—Is opposed to any system of signals on account of the difficulty of locating sounds in fog, the risk of confusion, and of inducing false confidence. Would only adopt Article 19 signals and make their use general in all waters. All whistles and horns should be inspected. The latter are often very defective.

Carpenter, I. T., master.—Agrees with Sir D. Murray's objections. Some of the systems proposed would cause great confusion, and could not be carried out with the appliances now in use. P D would be useful. Whistles and horns should be improved

Hall Bros.—Continued.

and made uniform. Calls attention to the necessity of fixing sailing routes, and to the confusion now caused by the practice of continuously showing a stern light on board steam-ships.

Hunter, T., master.—Instead of the present inefficient horns and whistles there should be carried two of each (one high and one low note), the high to be sounded for courses from south-south-west to north-northwest, and the low from north-northeast to south-southeast, and combinations of high and low for other courses.

Rogers, O., master.—The systems described in papers A and B would cause a babel of sounds in crowded waters. He would only make the use of Article 19 signals compulsory in fog, with four blasts for "stopped" added. Speed in fog should be limited to 3 knots, and sound-signals more powerful.

Satterly, I. T., master.—Steam ships should use a siren on outward and a whistle on homeward voyage. Any detailed code would be unworkable, as sounds are very imperfectly heard to windward, and if one blast of a code signal were missed a collision might result. Present sailing-ship signals are sufficient.

Smith, A. R., master.—Course or route signals would cause confusion. Present signals with P D added are sufficient.

Lowrie, W., master.—All signals should be larger and more effective, and an additional bell should be carried in the stern of vessels over 300 feet long. Reduced speed should be defined, and copies of rules, etc., *re* road and signals posted in chart rooms.

British Ship-masters' Association (Hull):

Any great alteration would cause confusion. They would simply make the use of article 19 signals compulsory in fog, with one long blast added for "going slowly ahead." Also approve of P D. Sirens should be prohibited on board steam-ships, as their use leads to confusion. All whistles should be uniform. Caution is the chief safeguard in fog.

Henderson Bros. :

Hedderwick, J., master.—Thinks an elaborate system could not be worked with certainty, as it is difficult to locate sounds, and confusion and misunderstanding would arise, whilst speed would be increased. Would merely utilize article 19 signals for fog, etc. These would in some degree conduce to safety.

Young, H., master.—Thinks article 19 signals and P D sufficient, and that any general system would cause confusion. The only safe course on hearing a steam signal ahead in fog is to stop. The interval between the blasts (article 12a) should be reduced from two minutes to thirty seconds,

Henderson Bros.—Continued.

Craig, J., master.—Sir D. Murray's paper O fully meets his views. It is difficult to locate sounds in fog, and a code of signals would cause confusion. The insufficient power of the horns of sailing ships is the greatest source of danger.

Harris, J., master.—A system of compass signals would cause confusion. The first two of article 19 signals should be made compulsory, and when two steam-ships are meeting, the first to signal "port" or "starboard" should hold the course signaled, the other being bound to steer accordingly or stop. All sailing ships should have equally powerful horns.

Wilson, J., master.—Any elaborate system would cause confusion, but article 19 signals might be used as they are at present in America. The power of whistles should be increased, some being inaudible except at short distances.

McFee, R., master.—Compass signals would cause confusion, but all steam-ships should use the siren or graduated whistle and sound a series of howls for port helm and of toots for starboard. Three long blasts to be used when overtaken or for going astern.

Scottish Ship-masters' Association:

Braes, master (State Line).—Any elaborate system would cause confusion. Would merely legalize use of article 19 signals, with P D added, in fog. Vessels approaching each other in fog should be compelled to stop and feel their way.

Lindquister, master.—All steam-ships should carry sirens and make long howls for starboard, and series of toots for port, courses in fog, with distinct three-blast signals for "going astern" and "stopped." But these signals should be optional, as their compulsory use would cause confusion in crowded channels. Is opposed to any system of course or route signals.

Renfrew, master.—Any compulsory system would increase danger. Would merely add P D and increase the power of whistles, etc.

Howling, master.—Many of the suggested systems made would lead to utter confusion. Would merely adopt (permissively) article 19 signals with P D added, and improve the power of whistles, etc.

Scottish Ship-masters' Association :

Parker, R., master.—Expresses similar views to the foregoing, except that he would adopt only the three-blast (article 19) signal and P D for fog.

White, H., master.—Would merely adopt article 19 signals and P D for use in fog. Anything more would increase danger in crowded waters.

Amalgamated British Seamen's Protection Society :

Advocate the adoption of Mr. Jeffries's eight-course signal system, consisting of combination of long and short blasts with two seconds' intervals.

Dublin Local Marine Board:

> Do not advocate any code of fog-signals, but think it would be well
> if signal could be provided to indicate which of the two meeting
> ships should stop and allow the other to proceed.

Cunard. M 15648:

> No change. Advise the adoption of signal P D. Difficult to *hear*
> fog-horns. They are not loud enough.

APPENDIX O.

*EXPERIMENTS MADE IN HOLLAND ABOUT FORCE AND DURATION OF
A SOUND-SIGNAL BY MR. LEFÈBRE.*

A steam-whistle of 2 inches in diameter requires a pressure of about
2 atmospheres in order to make the sound heard at the distance of 1
kilometer (⅕ of a knot), whereas a steam-whistle of 6 inches in diameter
with a pressure of 6 atmospheres makes its sound heard at a distance of
14 kilometers (about 7 miles). If, however, the whistle be placed in a
horizontal position within a reflector, the 2-inch whistle can be heard at
4 kilometers (2.2 miles), which is about the same as the distance at which
the side-lights throw their lights.

As a fixed reflector might be considered against the rules, the apparatus might be made to revolve. The arrangement to effect this is very
simple.

Another theory of his is that a sound wants at least from six to eight
seconds to enable it to be heard; consequently, the duration of the sound
or blast should not be fixed at a less minimum. It may be that the
meaning is, the first sound or blast ought to have this duration to well
attract the attention.

With regard to the weights in the bellows, he states that an instrument
with a pressure of 11 pounds, placed in a nearly horizontal position,
and provided with a suitable reflector, can be heard at a distance of 4
kilometers (2.2 miles), and with a pressure of 18 pounds, at a distance
of 14 kilometers (about 7 miles). In order to distinguish between steam-
ships and sailing vessels, all steam-whistles should produce the same
tone, and all fog-horns also the same tone, but a little higher. By comparing the sound heard with the sound of the instrument on board one's
own ship, it will be easy to ascertain whether a steam-ship or sailing
vessel is approaching.

In case it should be deemed advisable to distinguish between signals
from the shore or from a ship, either the ship or the shore might be required to produce a double sound simultaneously.

With a bell of 8 inches, as now generally in use, the sound travels
only as far as 600 meters (⅓ of a mile), and it requires a bell of a weight

of 80 kilogrames to transmit the sound at a distance of 1,500 meters ($\frac{5}{8}$ of a mile).

The sound of a movable bell (*i. e.*, when the tongue or clapper is fixed) travels farther than when the reverse is the case.

APPENDIX D.

ORDER OF REFERENCE TO THE COMMITTEE.

At the Council Chamber, Whitehall, this 20th day of December, 1887.
Present: The Right Hon. Lord Stanley of Preston, G. C. B., etc.
The Board of Trade are pleased to appoint the following gentlemen, viz,

Thomas Gray, esq., C. B., assistant secretary, marine department, Board of Trade (chairman);

Capt. H. M. Hozier, secretary to Lloyd's;

*Robert Jackson, esq., register-general of shipping and seamen;

Admiral Sir F. L. McClintock, F. R. S., an Elder Brother of the Trinity House;

Sir Digby Murray, Bart., one of the professional officers of the Board of Trade;

Rear-Admiral Sir George S. Nares, R. N., K. C. B., one of the professional officers of the Board of Trade;

†Captain Bowden-Smith, R. N.;

Capt. C. P. Wilson, I. N., principal officer of the Board of Trade for the London district;

to be a committee to undertake and to report upon the following matters, viz:

(1) To bring the International Signal Book up to date.

(2) To report whether the time has arrived when it may be deemed desirable to establish a system whereby the signals in the International Code Book may be made by night as well as by day.

(3) To report whether there is a general demand on the part of the mercantile marine for such a system, and, if so, what system should be adopted.

(4) To report (if a system whereby the signals in the International Code Book could be made at night were established) whether any danger is likely to arise therefrom owing to the inducement it might afford to ships to approach one another closely at night for the purpose of signaling.

(5) To report whether there ought to be any, and, if so, what restrictions on the use of night signals, especially in crowded waters, as, for instance, the English and Irish Channels.

----

* Since resigned.   † Now Rear-Admiral.

(6) If the committee do not recommend the establishment of any general system of night signals, to report whether it is, in their opinion, desirable (in addition to the present distress signals) to establish some special warning signals to indicate danger to passing vessels, *e. g.* :

"I am in need of immediate assistance,"

" You are standing into danger,"

" I have encountered ice,"

" I have passed a derelict dangerous to navigation,"

or any other warning signals in the interest of safety; and, if so, what those signals should, in their opinion, be, and by what means they should be made.

The Board of Trade are also pleased to appoint Walter J. Howell, esq., to be secretary to the committee.

STANLEY OF PRESTON.

INTERIM REPORT TO THE SECRETARY OF THE BOARD OF TRADE.

7, WHITEHALL GARDENS, S. W.,
January 15, 1889.

SIR : In compliance with the request of the late president of the Board of Trade, Lord Stanley of Preston, we have carefully considered the matters referred to us by his Lordship's Minute of Reference of the 20th December last (of which a copy is prefixed), and we have now the honor to submit our interim report upon the two salient points covered by the same, viz:

1. THE REVISION OF THE SIGNAL BOOK.

In order to take effective steps to bring the International Signal Book up to date, three of our number, viz, Sir Digby Murray, Sir George Nares, and Admiral Bowden-Smith were deputed to be a subcommittee to undertake this duty, with the assistance of Captain Key, R. N., of the Board of Trade London staff. A revised copy of the book* showing in detail the alterations proposed is submitted herewith (marked A), together with a short explanatory memorandum (marked B) prepared by Admiral Bowden-Smith, in order to indicate clearly the nature of the changes suggested for the improvement of the arrangement of the book, and for bringing it up to date.

We have set out the signals of distress by themselves in an inclosure (marked C); and also nine important urgent signals in an inclosure (marked D).

We have re-arranged important two-flag signals as shown in an inclosure (marked E).

These will all be printed in a permanent place at the beginning of the signal book in the order in which we have given them.

---

* The revised book is at present at the Board of Trade.

We are unanimously of opinion that the alterations and additions we propose will, if adopted, materially increase the usefulness of the Signal Book. It will, however, be necessary to invite and consider the opinions of foreign and colonial governments on the subject, and with that object in view, we think that the book should be set up in type in its revised form, and we suggest that a copy should be sent to the government of each maritime State for its concurrence before any further steps are taken in the matter. When replies have been received from the several foreign and colonial governments, we propose to again meet in order to consider any representations that may be made, and to prepare and submit our final report for your consideration.

2. THE QUESTION OF NIGHT SIGNALING.

We have taken steps to ascertain whether there is a general demand on the part of the mercantile marine for the establishment of some system whereby the signals in the International Code Book may be made by night as well as by day. A copy of a letter of inquiry issued by our directions (together with a summary of the replies received to the same) is appended (marked F).

So far as we have been able to ascertain at present there appears to be no *general* demand on the part of the mercantile marine for the establishment of a general system of night signaling. At the same time we think it advisable to adopt some plan by which a few urgent and important signals may be made by night as well as by day. The signals we have selected for this purpose are shown in the accompanying paper (marked D.)

These signals may be made at night or during fog, either by flashes of white light or by a combination of long and short sounds on the steam-whistle, fog-horn, siren, bugle, etc. In the day-time they will be made by flags. The methods of making these signals are shown in detail in inclosure (D.)

Since the date of Lord Stanley of Preston's minute of reference the board of trade have requested us also to consider and report upon the following points:

" *Whether, in the interests of safety, it is desirable to establish a system of sound-signals to be used by steam-vessels during foggy weather to denote the direction in which they are proceeding.*"

" *Whether, on the same grounds and for the same purpose, it is necessary to establish a system of sound-signals to be used by sailing vessels under like circumstances.*"

" *Whether such system should be limited to crowded waters and narrow seas near coasts; or whether it should be extended to the open seas also.*"

" *If any system is deemed by the committee to be practical, what that system is.*"

These matters will accordingly receive our careful consideration, and will be referred to in our final report.

We have the honor to be, sir, your most obedient servants,

> THOMAS GRAY, *Chairman.*
> HENRY M. HOZIER.
> F. L. McCLINTOCK.
> D. MURRAY.
> G. S. NARES.
> N. BOWDEN-SMITH.
> CHARLES P. WILSON.
> WALTER J. HOWELL,
> > *Secretary.*

To the SECRETARY BOARD OF TRADE.

[Inclosure A.]

The Revised Signal Book (at present at the Board of Trade).

[Inclosure B.]

Memorandum by Admiral N. Bowden-Smith, showing the changes proposed for the improvement of the arrangement of the Signal Book and for bringing it up to date.

1. It is proposed that the British national colors should be omitted from the place they now occupy opposite the title-page, and that certain signal flags shown in the book should be printed in that position.

2. That the "Contents" and "Introduction" should be corrected in accordance with the changes made, and that a few notes shown in an inclosure (marked E) should be inserted against the report of the committee of July, 1855.

3. That, as the national colors printed after page 16 are incomplete, a new and corrected set of colors should be prepared, and that where the colors worn by merchant ships differ from those worn by men-of-war both flags should be shown.

4. That the selection of sentences for the use of vessels, etc., should be omitted from the page preceding the general signals; that the distress signals should be printed in conspicuous type at the top of that page, and that the signals for a pilot should be printed under them on the same page.

5. It is also proposed that the two-flag signals should be regrouped and considerably extended; that they should be headed "Urgent and Important Signals," and that N C should be placed in the first group, as well as in its proper position. Also that where a signal is repeated (such as V L under " boats ") it should be printed in italics. It is further suggested that a few signals should be introduced which could be made at night or during fog, so that if at any future time it should be

considered desirable to introduce a system of night signaling, this may be done without necessitating a further revision of the code signals.

6. That the three-flag signals should be revised and several new ones added relating to cargo, convoy, diver, interpreter, telegraph cable, torpedoes, etc. The obsolete nationalities at page 12 and following pages should be omitted, and the names of other powers substituted as indicated.

Section VII, page 38, relating to boilers and machinery, should be considerably altered as shown, and it is proposed that the table of current coins, etc., now printed at page 69, should in future follow page 72, and that in view of the difficulty of keeping the equivalent values correct, they should in future be omitted from the table.

7. That one geographical list (arranged alphabetically) as reprinted should be inserted at the end of Part I of the Signal Book, and that the second list at page 173 (Part II) should be abolished.

8. That the four-flag signals, under " vocabulary " in Part II, should be amended throughout, and that several important words hitherto omitted should be inserted, as indicated throughout the list.

9. That new significations should be adopted for distant signals, as indicated at page 206, Part III.

10. That the book should be paged consecutively from beginning to end, instead of commencing again at Part II, and that if advertisements are inserted at all in future, they should all be printed at the end of the volume instead of at both ends, as at present.

11. That the names of the men-of-war of the leading maritime states to which symbols have been assigned should be printed in future in the code list bound up at the end of the Signal Book.

[Inclosure C.]

DISTRESS SIGNALS.

The following signals are alone deemed to be signals of distress:

In the day-time.—The following signals, numbered 1, 2, and 3, when used or displayed together or separately, shall be deemed to be signals of distress in the day-time:

    1. A gun fired at intervals of about a minute;
    2. The International Code signal of distress indicated by N C;
    3. The distant signal, consisting of a square flag having either above or below it a ball, or anything resembling a ball.

At night.—The following signals, numbered 1, 2, and 3, when used or displayed together or separately, shall be deemed to be signals of distress at night:

    1. A gun fired at intervals of about a minute;
    2. Flames on the ship (as from a burning tar barrel, oil barrel, etc.);

3. Rockets or shells, of any color or description, fired one at a time, at short intervals.

NOTE.—*It will be seen that we have also provided that the signal N C may be made during day or night by a rocket or shell which bursts in the air with a loud report.*

PILOT SIGNAS.

[To be made by ships wanting a pilot.]

In the day-time.—The following signals, numbered 1 and 2, when used or displayed together or separately, shall be deemed to be signals for a pilot in the day-time, viz:

1. To be hoisted at the fore, the Jack or national color usually worn by merchant ships, having round it a white border, one-fifth of the breadth of the flag; or
2. The International Code pilotage signal indicated by P T.

At night.—The following signals, numbered 1 and 2, when used or displayed together or separately, shall be deemed to be signals for a pilot at night, viz:

1. The pyrotechnic light commonly known as a blue light every fifteen minutes; or
2. A bright white light, flashed or shown at short or frequent intervals just above the bulwarks, for about a minute at a time.

[Inclosure D.]

URGENT OR IMPORTANT SIGNALS

Which may be made at night or during fog, either by flashes of white light or by a combination of long and short sounds on the steam-whistle, fog-horn, siren, bugle, etc. In the day-time they will be made by flags.

Instructions for the use of flashing or sound signals.

1.

With flashing signals the lamp must always be turned towards the person addressed.

2.

To attract attention, a series of rapid short flashes or sounds should be made and continued until the person addressed gives the sign of attention by doing the same.

If, however, it is supposed that the person addressed can not reply, the signal may be made after a moderate pause, or, under certain circumstances, the communication may be made direct without preparatory signs.

3.

After making a few rapid short flashes or sounds as an acknowledgment, the receiver must watch, or listen attentively until the communication is completed, when he must make the sign indicated below, showing that the message is understood.

4.

If the receiver does not understand the message, he must wait until the signal is repeated.

5.

Duration of short flashes or sounds...............1 second.
Duration of long flashes or sounds................3 seconds.
Interval between each flash or sound..............1 second.

Answer, or "I understand"......— – — – — – — – etc.

SIGNALS.

NP I want assistance. Please remain by me....... _ __
JK You are standing into danger................... _ _ __
PG Beware of derelict, dangerous to navigation.... _ _ _ __
QO Have encountered ice......................... _ __ __
PD The way is off my ship, you may feel your way
        past me............... ....,...... _ __ _
JB Stop, or heave to; I have something important
        to communicate .... _ __ _ _
PR Am disabled. Communicate with me........... _ _ __ _

When a vessel is in "tow," the following flashes or sounds may be made from her to the tug or towing vessel:

KR Steer more to port .... _ _
KS Steer more to starboard .... _

[Inclosure E.]

URGENT OR IMPORTANT SIGNALS.

[To be made by two flags.]

NOTE.—NC should only be hoisted when vessel is in extreme danger. (*See* Merchant Shipping Act, 1873, section 18.)

	ASSISTANCE.		DISTRESS.
NC	**In distress. Want immediate assistance.**	NC	**In distress. Want immediate assistance.**
	(*This signal may also be made by day and by night with a rocket or shell which bursts in the air with a loud report.*)		(*This signal may also be made by day and by night with a rocket or shell which bursts in the air with a loud report.*)
HB	Vessel indicated wants immediate assistance.	ND	Can not save the ship. Take people off.
HC	No assistance can be rendered	NF	I must abandon the vessel.
HD	We are coming to your assistance.	NG	Rudder disabled. Will you assist me into port indicated.
HF	Am on shore. Likely to break up Require immediate assistance.	NH	Ship disabled. Will you tow me into port indicated?
HG	Do you require further assistance.	NJ	I am unmanageable.
HJ	Do not require further assistance (*See* WANTS.)	NK	I am in danger, or shoal water; direct me how to steer.
		NL	I am driving; no more anchors to let go.
	BOATS.	NM	I am attacked; want assistance.
HK	Send a boat.	NP	I want assistance. Please remain by me.
HL	No boat or boats available.	NQ	I will remain by you.
HM	Boat in distress, adrift or capsized.	NR	I have sprung a leak.
HN	Do not attempt to land in your own boats.	NS	Leak is gaining rapidly.
HP	I am sinking, or on fire, send all available boats to save passengers and crew.	NT	I am sinking.
HQ	Send lifeboat to save crew.		
HR	Boat is going to you.		**COLLISION, SHIPWRECKED CREW, ETC.**
VL	*Want or wants boat or boats immediately.*	NV	Have been in collision.
		NW	Vessel seriously damaged; wish to transfer passengers.
	COMMUNICATE.	PB	Have you been in collision?
HS	Close.	PC	Has the vessel with which you have been in collision proceeded on her voyage?
HT	Allow no person on board. Allow no communication.	PD	The way is off my ship, you may feel your way past me.
HV	Be very careful in your intercourse with strangers.	PF	Have shipwrecked crew on board; will you let me transfer them to you? *Number to follow, page 73.*)
HW	Open, or "Proceed on your voyage."	NT	*I am sinking.*
JB	Stop or heave to; I have something important to communicate.		
			DERELICT SHIP.
	DAMAGE OR ACCIDENT.	PG	Beware of derelict, dangerous to navigation.
JC	Damaged or sprung mast; can not carry sail.	PH	Have you seen derelict?
JD	Damaged rudder, can not steer.	PJ	Saw derelict in lat ——— long ———. *For lat. and long. see pages 21-24. Date to follow if necessary, page 28.*
JF	Have lost all boats. Can you take crew off.		
JG	Accident; want a surgeon.		**DISABLED STEAMER REPORTING DAMAGE.**
JH	Man overboard. (*See* DISABLED STEAMER.)	PK	Engines completely disabled.
		PL	Engine disabled; can repair do. in — hours. *Number to follow, page 73.*
	DANGER OR CAUTION.	PM	Have broken main shaft.
JK	You are standing into danger.	PN	Have lost screw, or screw disabled.
JL	You are in a dangerous or unsafe position	PQ	One screw disabled; can work the other.
JM	You are within reach of the guns, or of batteries.	PR	Am disabled. Communicate with me.
JN	The attempt is dangerous.		
JP	Appearances are threatening; be on your guard.		**DRAUGHT OF WATER AND PILOT.**
JQ	Stranger (*or vessel indicated*) is suspicious.	PS	What is your draught of water?
JR	Bar is impassable.	PT	Want (or wants) a pilot; can one be obtained?
JS	Have obtained soundings.		(Answer "yes" or "no.")
JT	Am aground.		
MT	Boats should endeavor to land where flag is waived or light shown.		
MV	Look-out will be kept on the beach all night.		
MW	Lights or fires will be kept at the best place for coming on shore.		
NB	Keep a light burning.		

URGENT OR IMPORTANT SIGNALS—continued.

DIRECTIONS TO A VESSEL UNDER WAY.

·JV	Stand off; get an offing.
JW	Tack instantly.
KB	Increase speed. Make more sail.
KC	Stop engines. Heave to.
KD	Go astern. Heave all aback.
KF	Reduce speed. Shorten sail.
KG	Stand on.
KH	Bear up instantly.
KJ	Wear instantly.
KL	Not room to wear.
KM	Heave to, head off shore.
KN	Haul your wind on starboard tack.
KP	Haul your wind on port tack.
KQ	Keep to windward.
KR	Steer more to port. (*To be kept flying until course is sufficiently altered*)
KS	Steer more to starboard. (*Ditto.*)
KT	Steady the helm.
KV	Steer after me.
KW	Steer course indicated.
LB	Channel dangerous without a pilot.
LC	Buoys or marks are not in their proper position.
LD	Leave the buoy or beacon to port.
LF	Leave the buoy or beacon to starboard.
LG	Keep on the port shore or side of channel.
LH	Keep on the starboard shore or side of channel.
LJ	Keep in the center of channel.
LK	Do not anchor on any account.
LM	Do not come into less than —— feet.
LN	Run on the beach. Beach the vessel where flag is waved or light shown.
LP	Anchor instantly.
LQ	Anchor as convenient.

DIRECTIONS TO A VESSEL AT ANCHOR.

LR	Hoist the Blue Peter.
LS	Get steam up (report when ready).
LT	Keep steam ready.
LV	Steam is ready.
LW	Weigh and proceed as ordered.
MB	Weigh, out, or slip; get an offing.
MC	Veer more cable.
MD	Let go another anchor.
MF	Shift your berth; your berth is unsafe.
MG	Cut away your masts.
MH	Hold on until high water.
MJ	You will be aground at low water.
MK	Lose no time in shoring up.

DIRECTIONS FOR SAVING CREW.

ML	Remain by the ship.
MN	Quit the vessel as fast as possible.
MP	Do not quit the ship until the tide has ebbed.
MQ	Landing is impossible.
MR	Look out for rocket line.
MS	Endeavor to send a line.

FIRE.

PV	I am on fire.
PW	With immediate assistance fire can be extinguished.
QB	Fire is extinguished. (*See* BOATS; DISTRESS.)

ICE SIGNALS.

QC	Have encountered ice.
QD	Have passed ice in latitude and longitude indicated. (*See pages* .)
QF	Ice between 30° and 35° of long.
QG	Ice between 35° and 40° of long.
QH	Ice between 40° and 45° of long.
QJ	Ice between 45° and 50° of long.
QK	Ice between 50° and 55° of long.
QL	Ice between 55° and 60° of long.
QM	Ice between 60° and 65° of long.

LETTERS AND MAILS.

QN	Will you take letters?
QP	Have you letters, mails, or dispatches for me, or vessel indicated?
QR	Have letters, mails, or dispatches for you (*or vessel indicated*)

LIGHTERS.

QS	Require lighter, or lighters. (*Number to follow, V more than one, page 73.*)
QT	Lighter, or lighters, are going to you.
QV	There are no lighters available.
QW	Lighter is adrift.

MAST-HEAD AND SIDE LIGHTS.

RB	Your mast-head light is out, or wants trimming.
RC	Your port side light is out, or wants trimming.
RD	Your starboard side light is out, or wants trimming.

ORDERS, REPORTING SHIP.

RF	Where are you from?
RG	Where are you bound?
RH	Indicate name of signal station.
RJ	Your original orders are cancelled. I am directed to inform you to proceed to ——. (*Geographical Table, see page 81.*)
RK	Your orders are as ——.
RL	Proceed to port indicated. (*Geographical Table, page .*)
RM	Shall I telegraph your owners?
RN	I will telegraph for your orders if you will wait reply.
RP	I have telegraphed for your orders.
RQ	Can you await reply?
RS	Will await reply.
RT	I have orders to telegraph your passing.
RV	Have you any message or telegraphic communication for me?
RW	Report me to owners.
SB	Report me to Lloyd's.
SC	Send my message by signal letters instead of writing it at length.
SD	Forward reply by telegraph to signal station indicated. (*Geographical Table, page .*)

PILOT.

PT	*Want (or wants) a pilot; can one be obtained?* (*Answer* "Yes" *or* "No.")

POSITION OF SHIP, LAT. AND LONG.

SF	What is my position by bearings?
SG	What is the name of light-house, or light-ship, in sight, or on bearing indicated?
SH	What is your latitude at present time? (*For Latitude Table, see page* 21.)
SJ	What is your longitude at present time? (*For Longitude Table, see page* 23.)

SIGNAL FLAGS, SEMAPHORE CIPHER.

SK	Repeat ship's name; your flags were not made out.
SL	Repeat your signal, or place it in a more conspicuous position. It is not understood.
SM	Can not make out your flags, come nearer, or make distant signal.*
SN	Repeat signal from word indicated.
SP	I am going to repeat signal from word indicated.
SQ	You may work the semaphore.
SR	Following signal (or communication) is in cipher.†
ST	Give me the key to cipher.‡
SV	Cipher is ended.

* *See* Distant Signal Code, page 206, Part III.
‡ This may be pre-arranged, etc.

† Cipher will continue until the person signaling hoists SV.

URGENT OR IMPORTANT SIGNALS—continued.

	STEAM WHISTLE OR SIREN.
SW	Blow steam whistle or siren at intervals.
TB	Shall signal with steam whistle, or siren, during fog or darkness.

TORPEDO, TORPEDO BOATS.

TC	Is there danger of mines or torpedoes ?
TD	Beware of torpedoes. The channel is mined.
TF	Beware of torpedo boats.
TG	Have you seen torpedo boat or boats. ?
TH	Saw torpedo boat, or boats, at or near ——. (*Geographical Table, see page* 81.)

TOW TUGS.

TJ	I wish to be taken in tow.
TK	Shall I take you (*or ship indicated*) in tow ?
TL	Will take you (*or ship indicated*) in tow.
TM	Can not take you (*or ship indicated*) in tow.
TN	Tug is going to you.
TP	There are no tugs available.
NH	*Ship disabled, will you tow me into port indicated?*
VT	*Want or wants steam-tug or tugs.*

TOWING, OR BEING TOWED.

See also under "Hawser" and "Tow," Alphabetical Table.

TQ	Are towing cables, or is cable fast ?
TR	Towing cable, or cables, is, or are, fast.
TS	Reduce speed, you are towing me too fast.
TV	You can proceed at any speed.
TW	Veer more of the towing cable, or cables.
VB	Shorten-in towing cable, or cables.
VC	Cast off towing cable, or cables.
VD	Towing cable, or cables, is, or are, cast off.
VF	Towing cable, or cables, is, or are, damaged or stranded.
VG	Stop engines to adjust towing cables.
JH	*Man overboard.*
KR	*Steer more to port. (To be kept flying until course is sufficiently altered.)*
KS	*Steer more to starboard. (Ditto.)*

	WANTS.
VH	Want water immediately.
VJ	Want (or wants) assistance; mutiny.
VK	Want (or wants) immediate medical assistance.
VL	Want (or wants) boat or boats immediately.
VM	Want (or wants) provisions immediately.
VN	Want (or wants) coal immediately.
VP	Want (or wants) an anchor.
VQ	Want (or wants) an anchor and cable.
VR	Want (or wants) a cable.
VS	Want (or wants) police.
VT	Want (or wants) steam-tug or tugs. *If more than one, number to follow, page 73.*
VW	Want (or wants) immediate instructions.
WB	Want (or wants) hands.
WC	Want chart or plan of channel, harbor, etc.
WD	

	WAR NEWS.
WF	Is war declared, or has war commenced ?
WG	War is declared, or has commenced.
WH	War between —— and ——.
WJ	Armistice has been arranged.
WK	Is peace proclaimed ?
WL	Peace is proclaimed.

	WEATHER.
WM	What is weather forecast ?
WN	No weather report.
WP	North cone hoisted.
WQ	South cone hoisted.
WR	Bad weather is expected. (*See compass signals*)
WS	Storm center (in direction indicated); probable course towards (direction indicated).
WT	
WV	

[Inclosure F.]

Abstract of replies received to the following letter, dated January 20, 1888.

SIGNALS.

BOARD OF TRADE (MARINE DEPARTMENT),
London, S. W., January 20, 1888.

I have the pleasure to forward, for your information, the inclosed copy of the order of reference to the committee which has been appointed by Lord Stanley, of Preston, to consider and report upon questions affecting the International Code of Signals.

The committee are very desirous of obtaining the opinions of ship-owners, and of the mercantile marine generally, upon the points referred to in paragraphs 2, 3, 4, 5, and 6 of the order of reference, and I am to request that you will be good enough to favor me (for the information of the committee), and at as early a moment as may be convenient to you, with any observations in the matter which your experience, or that of the officers in your employment, may enable you to offer.

I am, your obedient servant,

THOMAS GRAY,
Chairman of the Committee.

Upon the following points, viz:

(1) To bring the International Signal Book up to date.

(2) To report whether the time has arrived when it may be deemed
    desirable to establish a system whereby the signals in the
    International Code Book may be made by night as well as
    by day.

(3) To report whether there is a general demand on the part of the
    mercantile marine for such a system ; and, if so, what system
    should be adopted.

(4) To report (if a system whereby the signals in the International
    Code Book could be made at night were established) whether
    any danger is likely to arise therefrom owing to the induce-
    ment it might afford to ships to approach one another closely
    at night for the purpose of signaling.

(5) To report whether there ought to be any, and, if so, what re-
    striction on the use of night signals, especially in crowded
    waters, as, for instance, the English and Irish Channels.

(6) If the committee do not recommend the establishment of any
    general system of night signals, to report whether it is, in
    their opinion, desirable (in addition to the present distress
    signals) to establish some special warning signals to indicate
    danger to passing vessels, e. g.,
    "I am in need of immediate assistance,"
    "You are standing into danger,"
    "I have encountered ice,"
    "I have passed a derelict dangerous to navigation,"
    or any other warning signals in the interest of safety ; and,
    if so, what those signals should, in their opinion, be, and by
    what means they should be made.

Persons, firms, societies, etc., applied to for observations.	Date of reply.	2. Whether the time has arrived for establishing a system whereby the signals in the International Code Book may be made by night as well as by day?	3. If there is a general demand for such a system, what system should be adopted?	4. If such a system were established, whether any danger is likely to arise therefrom owing to the inducement it might afford to ships to approach one another too closely at night for the purpose of signaling?	5. To report whether there ought to be any, and, if so, what restrictions on the use of night signals, especially in crowded waters?	6. Is it desirable to establish some special warning signals to indicate danger to passing vessels. If so, what should they be and by what means should they be made?
Devitt and Moore. MacIvor, C.	Jan. 23, 1888 Jan. 25, 1888	Thinks it would be a Yes; thinks such a system should be arranged.	good thing to have night Very little occasion for it in time of peace. Recommends system of Captain Wall and Lieutenant Sellners.	signals placed on a proper footing. Does not anticipate additional danger.	As the advisability of communicating by night occurs so seldom, is undesirous of placing special restrictions on masters	Yes, by lamps, for distress signals, only rockets or portfires should be used.
Shaw, Savill and Albion Company, Limited, per J. McKirby, marine superintendent.	Jan. 28, 1888 Feb. 3, 1888 Feb. 6, 1888	No. (thinks vocabulary needs altering, so that sentences bearing on the same subject should be grouped together).	Is not aware of any demand. Recommends the Morse system, if any is adopted.	Yes, decidedly; by diverting attention of the officer of the watch.	Such restrictions would render any system valueless.	Thinks the Roman candle should be used solely for urgent international (and not for private) signaling. For certain signals, suggests combinations of red, white, and green stars, which could be discharged from a revolver.
Inglemere, (Evans E.J., chief officer)		Thinks such a system would be little used, as he has never seen even the present distance signals used.	A system worked by lights would be more confusing than useful.	Would not increase safety, and would probably lead indirectly to accidents.	Signals should not extend beyond the present private signals, and an extension of danger or distress signals.	Rockets as private signals should be abolished. Suggests a code of 18 danger and distress signals commencing with a rocket. (In prepared to draw up a more detailed code.) Recommend a rocket of a distinct character as a "caution," and "distress" signal, and strongly urge that the use of rockets for any other purpose should be forbidden.
General Ship-owners Society.	Jan. 30, 1888	No.	No general demand.	Think there is great danger in the multiplication of lights.		
Orient Steam Navigation Company, Limited.	Jan. 31, 1888	Not desirable.	No demand.	Would in all probability cause confusion.	Any use of night signals in crowded waters would probably result in disaster.	Present distress signals ample.

Persons, firms, societies, etc. applied to for observations.	Date of reply.	2. Whether the time has arrived for establishing a system whereby the signals in the International Code Book may be made by night as well as by day?	3. If there is a general demand for such a system, what system should be adopted?	4. If such a system were established, whether any danger is likely to arise therefrom owing to the inducement it might afford to ships to approach one another too closely at night for the purpose of signaling?	5. To report whether there ought to be any, and, if so, what restrictions on the use of night signals, especially in crowded waters.	6. Is it desirable to establish some special warning signals to indicate danger to passing vessels. If so, what should they be, and by what means should they be made?
Union Steam Ship Company, Limited.	Jan. 31, 1888 / Apr. 9, 1888	Submit the opinions of their senior commanders.				
Inclosure No. 1 (Larner G., master mariner).		No	No general demand.	Yes	Does not approve of a general system of night signaling, but if adopted thinks it should be restricted in crowded waters.	Thinks warning signals of extraordinary importance desirable, but is not prepared to suggest their character.
Inclosure No. 2 (Bainbridge, W., master mariner).		Yes	A general demand only among the higher grades in the service. Recommends the "Morse" system, applied by means of flags by day, lamps by night, and steam whistle in fog.	No	Yes, at first; until the system is well established.	Strongly recommends the four signals mentioned.
Inclosure No. 3 (Griffin, E., master mariner).		Yes	Think there is a growing demand.	No	Should be restricted to urgent signals only, which should be clearly laid down.	Yes; a few urgent ones should be clearly laid down.
Inclosure No. 4 (Hoste, H. S., master mariner).		If the time has not arrived, thinks it soon will.	Has never found need for night signals, but if adopted, should recommend the "Morse."	No	Vessels do not find it necessary to signal in crowded waters, except on very special occasions.	Yes; by means of a rocket or a rocket signal, followed by combinations of three or four lights.
Inclosure No. 5 (Leigh, R. A., master mariner).		Yes	Is not aware of a general demand. If a system were adopted, suggests the flash system.	No need for close approach with the flash system.	Must be considered when the system is decided upon.	Recommends four signals to be made by means of cannon and rockets, avoiding lanterns.
Inclosure No. 6 (Owen, H., master mariner).		Yes	Yes; by means of the flashing system, with a good lantern.	No; as the ship in danger could signal "You are approaching me too closely."	No; but to avoid crowding of signal stations pyrotechnic signals should be used, as at present.	Yes; by means of blue, white, and red pyrotechnic fires.

Respondent	Date						
Inclosure No. 7 (Travers, H. D., master mariner).	......	Yes......	......	No......	......	No........	Recommends three additional distress night-signals, made by means of red globe lamps and red and green fires. By day a black ball to be hoisted in addition to flag signals. At present, many private signals too closely resemble the statutory distress signals.
Inclosure No. 8 (McLean, W. A., master mariner).	......	No......	Yes. Recommends "Morse" flashing system.				Yes; by means of combinations of white lights.
Peninsular and Oriental Steam Navigation Company.	Feb. 1, 1888	Think it doubtful, as the subject does not form a part of Board of Trade examination of masters and mates for certificates. Recommend system of flashing lights for night signaling, as in royal navy, but think about three years' notice would be necessary, so that applicants for, and holders of, certificates could be examined in the interval.	No......	Are not aware of any general demand. Rather the contrary.	There is some element of danger, but not to any great extent.	Yes; if night signals are used generally.	If adopted, should be restricted to urgent cases only.	A few, not exceeding six, additional signals would be of advantage—to be used only in extreme circumstances, and made by means of bright and colored lamps, vertical, horizontal, and diagonal, with a detonating signal to attract attention.
New Zealand Shipping Company, limited, per Hallett, E. V., marine superintendent.	Feb. 3, 1888	Thinks a few simple ones, to be used in cases of great emergency would be of advantage.		Thinks there is no general demand.	There would be some, but not to any extent.		Such signals should be used only in cases of great emergency.	Yes, by means of bright and colored lights, vertical, oblique, and diagonal, with a detonating signal to attract attention. Recommends Colomb's flashing lights, and thinks a knowledge of this system should be encouraged, it being little understood at present.
MacGregor, Jas. (MacGregor, Gow & Co.).	Feb. 8, 1888	No general desire to extend the system of signals in the International Code Book to the night.			Great danger might arise.		Such restrictions would be difficult.	Recommends special signals to distinguish danger might be apprehended.
Ismay, Imrie & Co.	Feb. 8, 1888	No........		Not aware of any......	Yes......		Only signaling of the most necessary kind should be allowed in crowded waters.	It may be desirable. If so, think that signals of distress, warning, or urgent need might be made at night by means of white and red lamps.

Persons, firms, societies, etc., applied to for observations.	Date of reply.	2. Whether the time has arrived for establishing a system whereby the signals in the International Code Book may be made by night as well as by day?	3. If there is a general demand for such a system, what system should be adopted?	4. If such a system were wished, whether any danger is likely to arise therefrom owing to the inducement it might afford to ships to approach one another too closely at night for the purpose of signaling.	5. To report whether there ought to be any, and, if so, what restrictions on the use of night signals, especially in crowded waters.	6. Is it desirable to establish some special warning signals to indicate danger to passing vessels. If so, what should they be and by what means should they be made?
London and North-western Railway Company.	Feb. 9, 1888	Yes	If a demand is found to exist, recommend a portable flashing lamp on the "Morse" system.	Do not anticipate any ..	Think that when officers know where they are and tugs are pitiful the guns would not be much used.	Yes.
Cunard Steam-ship Company, Limited.	Feb. 11, 1888	Not desirable				No.
Henderson Brothers (Anchor line).	Feb. 13, 1888	Yes. They also submit reports of three of their experienced commanders who have not communicated with each other on the subject.	Yes. The dot and dash telegraphic code exemplified by means of colored flashing lights.	Yes, to some extent. In order to obviate danger and prevent delay recommend that a ship desiring to signal should make the wish known by firing guns.	No; provided that the firing of the signal gun precedes signaling.	Recommends six warning signals on dot and dash system.
Inclosure No. 1 (Brown, W., master mariner).		Recommends the dot and dash system for signals. In fog at anchor, by bell. (blasts.)		in which the code is deficient. These could be repeated by the other ship to insure accuracy.	At night, by flashes.	In fog when under way, by ...
Inclosure No. 2 (Campbell, A., master mariner).		Yes	Yes; and suggests the "dot and dash" system.	Yes; and therefore the utmost caution would be necessary in their use.	Utmost care would be necessary in the use of light and sound signals in the vicinity of light-houses in the English and Irish Channels.	Present distress signals sufficient, but suggests certain ... a red rocket with red ... being used for the purpose.
Inclosure No. 3 (Hedderwick, J., master mariner).		Yes	Think there is a desire. Suggests the use of red and white flashes.	Yes; and therefore increased caution would be needed.	Any system requiring restriction should be adopted.	Recommends a ... to be called important communications, distinguished by day by flag, the ensign at the fore, and at night by hoisting a red light at the fore and signaling with red and whi...
Royal Mail Steam Packet Company.	Feb. 15, 1888	Occasionally night signals might prove useful.	No. If adopted, caution would have to be used to prevent confusion.	Yes		

Respondent	Date					
Telegraphic Construction and Maintenance Company, limited.	Feb. 16, 1888	Yes	Think there is no general demand, but recommend the "Morse" system, with colored lights and the steam whistle or fog-horn for sound signals.	Not with ordinary care.	Think that night signaling with colored lamps at pilot stations should not be used except in cases of extreme urgency.	Think that P, danger signals should be emphasized by the firing of guns or by detonating signals in such manner as to be taken for other signals. No one distinctive signal to cover certain sentences, other by specially good red lamps, guns, fits, or detonating signals, and that hrs should be examined in the "also" code.
Chamber of Shipping of the United Kingdom.	Mar. 6, 1888	No	No	Think there is great danger in the multiplication of lights.		Think Colonel "Hill's" proposals that the direction a ship is steering should be indicated by steam-whistle signals is worth consideration.
Allan, J. and A. (Allan Line).	Mar. 21, 1888	Suggest that sailing vessels should have better lights, so that steamers would be able to perceive them at a greater distance, and recommend that steamers should have two white mast-head lights and a colored light added when they are towing. They also submit reports from twenty-one of their commanders.				
Inclosure No. 1 (Allan, J. A., master mariner).		No	No	No	No	Thinks a few special warning signals necessary to be made by combinations of the "Coston" Pyrotechnic light if confusion with private signals can be avoided. For a general system recommends the flash system of the navy.
Inclosure No. 2 (Ambury, J., master mariner).		It is very desirable	Not aware of any general signal, but if used should be made by powerful lights. Pyrotechnic lights being so variously used as private signals, would same idea.	No; if caution is observed.	It would be difficult to make restrictions.	Present distress signals are sufficient. The signal "I am in need of immediate assistance" should be followed by a gun in very urgent cases. There should also be signals for warning other vessels of danger.
Inclosure No. 3 (Barrett, A., master mariner).		Yes	Is not aware of any general signal, but recommends "Eastways" system of lights.	No; but caution would be necessary.	Should be restricted to cases of great necessity only.	Additional signals should be very simple. Urgent signals should be preceded by a distress signal.
Inclosure No. 4 (Bentley, J., master mariner).		No	No	Yes; especially in crowded channels.	(See No. 4)	Yes; by means of red, green, and white lights.

Persons, firms, societies, etc., applied to for observations.	Date of reply.	2. Whether the time has arrived for establishing a system whereby the signals in the International Code Book may be made by night as well as by day?	3. If there is a general demand for such a system, what system should be adopted?	4. If such a system were tried, will there any danger is likely to arise therefrom owing to the inducement it might afford to ships to approach closely at night for the purpose of signaling?	5. To report whether there ought to be any, and, if so, what restrictions on the use of night signals, especially in crowded waters.	6. Is it desirable to establish some special warning signals to indicate danger to passing vessels. If so, what should they be, and by what means should they be made?
Allan, J. and A. (Allen Line). Inclosure No. 5 (Brown, J., master mariner).		Yes	Is unable to say. Thinks that red and green lights should be used exclusively for side lights. Recommends the of range-colored lights for night signals.	No; for vessels could signal at a distance instead of approaching to hail as they now sometimes do.	No; as they would be of most use in narrow channels.	Yes. Recommends five additional urgent signals. Thinks that pyrotechnic lights, rockets, etc., should not be used, as causing confusion with present private signals.
Inclosure No. 6 (Carruthers, R., master mariner).		Yes; but it should only be used for "warnings."	Has not heard it expressed. Suggests the Mot lights in place of ball, pennant, and square flags, with general code signal to attract attention	Not if a distinct code signal can be adopted.	Should be restricted to warning or relief signals.	(As in No. 3.)
Inclosure No. 7 (Dalziel, W., master mariner).		There ought to be some system, but not a complete code made by too many different colored lights.	Yes; to be made by red and White lights only.	Yes	Should be restricted in crowded waters to urgent signals only.	Yes; by means of red and white lights shown in different positions.
Inclosure No. 8 (Dunlop, W., master mariner).			Is not aware of any general demand.	Yes	Should be restricted to urgent signals only in narrow waters.	Yes. Red, green, and White lights in place of ball, pennant, and flag, but the number and variety of private signals now in use would render any
Inclosure No. 9 (France, J., master mariner).		No, unless a very simple system can be adopted.	No	Yes	No	red, green, and White lights to be used for urgency and and signals. Present distress signals sufficient. Ends "Wymke's" system.
Inclosure No. 10 (Hughes, R. H., master mariner).		Yes	Yes. Recommend the navy system of flashing lights.	No occasion for vessels to approach danger ously near.		

Inclosure					Remarks
Inclosure No. 11 (James, D. J., master mariner).	Thinks the time has arrived.	Not aware of any general demand.	No: If precautions are taken.	No	Present distress signals should not be changed. Recommends blue, white, and red lights for urgent signals. Recommends eight additional urgency signals. Thinks there should be a new distinct fog-signal for indicating a vessel's course.
Inclosure No. 12 (McDougall, A., master mariner).	Yes	Yes. Recommends a system of red, white, and green flashes, but does not approve of a system increasing the number of lights to be encountered.	Yes: unless the flashes are powerful enough.	Yes. Vessels signaling should not approach each other nearer than 1 mile, and night signals should not be used except in urgent cases either in channels or at sea.	
Inclosure No. 13 (Macnicol, A., master mariner).		No	Yes	Yes	Recommends a few additional simple warning and urgency signals.
Inclosure No. 14 (Moore, R. P., master mariner).	Not necessary to adopt the whole code for night signals.	Knows of no general demand.	Yes	Night signals should only be used in open waters.	Recommends the four additional signals given in the order of reference made by means of red and white globe lamps.
Inclosure No. 15 (Park, J., master mariner).	Yes	Not aware of any general demand. Recommends bright blue and red lights placed vertically as warning signals.	No: If precautions are taken.	Certainly not. Action in urgent cases may be hampered by restriction; some risk must be run in order to save life.	Present distress rocket-signal sufficient. (See reply to No. 3 for warning signals.)
Inclosure No. 16 (Richardson, W., master mariner).	Thinks that any system introduced would have to have warning of danger ahead.	better not to have them. Recommends rockets or a strong light, often repeated, for distress signals.	be made by means of lights, and as the glare of light would be blinding it would be	It is at all times desirable to	would be blinding it would be It is at all times desirable to
Inclosure No. 17 (Ritchie, J., master mariner).	No	No	Yes	Night signals should be used only in urgent cases.	Any special night signals should be used only by ships in distress and for saving life.
Inclosure No. 18 (Smith, W. H., master mariner).	No	Has not heard any general demand expressed. Thinks some flashing system, such as the "Morse," would be the best system if any is adopted.	Not if caution is used	Not if proper precautions are adopted.	Yes, an explosive rocket to warn vessels approaching danger, also as a means of attracting attention previous to important signaling.
Inclosure No. 19 (Stephen, J. G., master mariner).	Yes	Recommends a system of colored lights.	Yes; therefore should only be used in urgent cases.	Should not be used except in the interest of safety.	Thinks warning signals might be made by means of colored lights placed vertically, the signal to be preceded by a bomb rocket to attract attention.
Inclosure No. 20 (Watts, R. S., marine superintendent).	Yes	Thinks not. On the contrary, practical men dread a system that would increase the number of lights.	Yes. But the danger would be partly obviated by forbidding complimentary signaling.	Recommends a deck flare for attracting attention, to be used exclusively in urgent cases.	Refers to inclosure by Mr. Eastaway the second officer of the Cressawan, containing colored plan of night signals, which would meet all cases.

Persons, firms, societies, etc., applied to for observations.	Date of reply.	2. Whether the time has arrived for establishing a system whereby the signals in the International Code Book may be made by night as well as by day?	3. If there is a general demand for such a system, what system should be adopted?	4. If such a system were established, whether any danger is likely to arise owing to the means it must afford to ships to approach at night for the purpose of	5. To report whether there ought to be any, and, if so, what restrictions on the use of night signals, especially in crowded waters?	6. Is it desirable to establish some special warning signals to indicate danger to passing vessels. If so, what should they be, and by what means should they be made?
Allen, J. and A. (Allen Line). Inclosure No. 22 (Wylie, H., master mariner).		No.	No.	No.	Rockets should not be allowed in crowded waters except as signals of distress.	When field ice is encountered, recommends a warning signal to be made by means of burning six blue lights consecutively.
Smith, G., & Sons.	Mar. 22, 1888	Thinks it would be a mistake. Now that steamers are employed the necessity of speaking one another is done away with.	No.	There is danger when large steamers approach each other.	Signaling should be forbidden in crowded waters, except in urgent cases or in need of pilot.	If distress and warning signals are adopted they should be of a distinct character.
Holt, A., Liverpool.	Apr. 24, 1888	After ... subject with Mrs ... qualified to form an opinion, has somewhat hesitatingly come to the conclusion that the proposal ought not be carried out at present.				
Aberdeen Local Marine Board.	Jan. 27, 1888		No demand			Yes. The distress signal should be a thoroughly distinctive one. Suggest a competition for best code of signals.
London Local Marine Board.	Jan. 28, 1888	Yes; to a limited extent.	Not aware of any	Danger might arise by withdrawing the attention of the watch, and a general system would become a dead letter, as the night watch consists usually of only one officer and the "look-out."	Night signals should be available in all waters and under any circumstances.	Recommends two additional distress signals: (1) red and white flare asking for immediate assistance, and (2) red and blue flare for warning other vessels of danger.

Board	Date					
Dundee Local Marine Board.	Feb. 1, 1888	No.	No demand.	Yes.	Think that private signals of such a nature for distress signals, should not be permitted.	Present distress or danger signals ought to be simplified in a simple manner, to show nature of circumstances in which vessel is placed.
North Shields Local Marine Board.	Feb. 3, 1888	Present distress signals sufficient. Further night signals undesirable.				Suggest a system of signaling for steamers by means of high and low notes on whistles, to be used in fog or danger.
Greenock Local Marine Board.	Feb. 9, 1888	Not required unless for cases of danger, or when in fog.	Not aware of any.			
South Shields Local Marine Board	Feb. 13, 1888	No.	No.	Yes.	Rockets should be forbidden for private and other signals, and used exclusively for distress signals.	Present distress signals are sufficient.
Leith Local Marine Board.	Feb. 14, 1888.	Submit a report, in which they concur, from the Scottish Ship-masters' Association.		Yes.		Suggest three additional warning signals for crowded waters by long and short blasts on the steam whistle or horn.
Inclosure (Scottish Ship-masters' Association).		Yes.	There is only a limited dmd. The majority of the Association are in favor of the "Morse" flashing system. Mrs approve of the fog-whistle, fog-horn, or fog-bell being used on the "Morse" system.	In any case night signaling should be restricted to urgent cases only.		
Cork Local Marine Board.	Feb. 15, 1888.	Yes.	There is no general demand, because it would increase cost of outfit and give . . . Recommend . . . fire alls, Roman candles, . . . as not . . . signals, but think . . . should not be made compulsory.	No.	No.	Recommend five signals in addition to those named in the order of reference, and suggest the use of fire-balls.
Newcastle Local Marine Board.	Feb. 15, 1888.	May be desirable, but they are opposed to any extended or elaborate system of night signals.	No.	Yes.		
Dublin Local Marine Board.	Mar. 21, 1888.	Yes, if it can be done safely.	It should not offer an inducement to run into danger.			Recommend a simple system of urgent danger and distress signals, to be made by means of red, white, and green globe lamps. Such signals are desirable.

Persons, firms, societies, etc., applied to for observations.	Date of reply.	2. Whether the time has arrived for establishing a system whereby the signals in the International Code Book may be made by night as well as by day?	3. If there is a general demand for such a system, what system should be adopted?	4. If such a system were desired, whether any danger is likely to arise therefrom owing to the means it might afford only to ships at night for the purpose of signaling?	5. To report whether there ought to be any, and, if so, what restrictions on the use of night signals, especially in crowded waters?	6. Is it desirable to establish some special warning signals to indicate danger to passing vessels. If so, what should they be, and by what means should they be made?
Liverpool Local Marine Board. Inclosure No. 1 (Liverpool Steamship Owners' Association).	Mar. 23, 1888.	Inclosed copies of replies from three associations.				
		No	No	Yes	Night signals should be restricted to urgent cases only, especially in crowded waters.	Yes; by means of red and white lamps.
Inclosure No. 2 (Mercantile Marine Service Association).		Yes	Yes. A simple system on the "Morse" principle.			Desirous of a signal to indicate the course being steered by another vessel.
		(They suggest that all the points should be referred to the International Conference proposed by the United States.) They suggested to the United States consul that the Conference should be held in England.)		Yes		
Inclosure No. 3 (Ship ... Association, Liverpool).		No. It would be very undesirable, because it would increase the number of lights.	No	Yes		and a night signal to date which way a vessel is steering.
Plymouth Local Marine Board.	Mar. 29, 1888.	No	No	Yes		Some special warning night signals seem desirable.
Belfast Local Marine Board.	Apr. 10, 1888.					
Inclosure (Porter, W., J.P.)	Apr. 11, 1888.	Suggests for revision of signal code that a voyage exceeding one hundred days and degree and should be 1 and to one hoist. Geographical and spelling vocabularies require enlargement. limits of longitude				
Glasgow Local Marine Board.	Apr. 13, 1888.	Suggest that further ation of this ject should be deferred until Mr. al Signals Conference proposed by the States is held.				
Hull Local Marine Board.	May 8, 1888.	Submit opinions of ship-owners and masters as follows.				
Inclosure No. 1 (Bailey and Leetham).	May 8, 1888.	If adopted, should not be compulsory.	No	Yes; dangers of collision and strandings increased.	Yes; rockets should be used only as distress signals.	Yes, in certain cases. Say one distinctive signal denoting ice or other danger ahead.

Inclosure	Date					
Inclosure No. 2 (Briggs, Hy., Sons & Co.), No. 3 ..., and No. ...	May 8, 1888	No.				
Inclosure No. 4 (Good, Allman, and Duncan).	May 8, 1888	Think from inquiries made that additional signals would cause more confusion.				
Inclosure No. 5 (Jackson, Beaumont, & Co.).	May 8, 1888	Yes.	Not sufficiently experienced to give detailed opinion.			
Inclosure No. 6 (Lofthouse, C. M. & Co.).	May 8, 1888	Think it important that steamers should be able to communicate by night as well as by day.	No.	No.	Yes; increase of lights very dangerous in crowded waters.	Yes. Submit sketch of iron frame for four special warning signals.
Inclosure No. 7 (Moran, Wm. & Co.).	May 8, 1888	Not aware of any improvements they could suggest.			Yes.	
Inclosure No. 8 (Ringrose, W. C. L.).	May 8, 1888	Think it desirable.	That signals for this purpose should be hoisted well clear of regulation lights.	Not if confined to urgent, etc., matters.	Yes; night signaling should be confined to the more urgent and important matters.	
Inclosure No. 9 (Woodhead, T. D. & G.).	May 8, 1888	Thinks a system of night signals to firms who have a large fleet of steamers would be of much service.				
Inclosure No. 10 (Coyne, master mariner).	May 8, 1888	Doubtful.	Thinks not.	Yes.	Yes; only to be used by ship in distress.	Yes; the simplest possible.
Inclosure No. 11 (Halbey, D. T., master mariner).	May 8, 1888	No.	No demand.	Very dangerous in crowded waters.	The greatest restrictions.	Thinks that no additions to present distress signals are desirable.
Inclosure No. 12 (Kelsey, Thos., master mariner).	May 8, 1888	Yes.	Yes; signals to be made with colored lamps.	No.	Signals should not be kept out longer than necessary.	Thinks a red flare would answer all purpose.
Inclosure No. 13 (Lee, Rd., master mariner).	May 8, 1888	Yes.	Yes. Suggests red, green, and white lights shown vertically and otherwise.	Should be limited, or would prove dangerous in narrow waters.	Thinks it should be restricted to reporting ships' danger and urgent signals.	Yes; six special signals by means of colored lights.
Inclosure No. 14 (Peters, A. R., master mariner).	May 8, 1888	Yes.	Yes. Suggests colored lights shown horizontally, vertically, and otherwise.	No.	Yes. Should be confined to reporting ships, and to danger and urgent signals.	Thinks some alteration ought to be made in the signal for a vessel not under command.

Persons, firms, societies, etc., applied to for observations.	Date of reply.	2. Whether the ... tie has arrived for ... ling a ... gem whereby the ... ins in the Intal ... Book may be ... mie by ... light as well as by day?	3. If there is a general demand for such a system, what system should be adopted?	4. If such a system were established, whether any danger is likely to arise therefrom owing to the inducement it might afford to ships to approach one another too closely at night for the purpose of signaling?	5. To report whether there ought to be any, and, if so, what restrictions on the use of night signals, especially in crowded waters.	6. Is it desirable to establish some special warning signals to indicate danger to passing vessels. If so, what should they be, and by what means should they be made?
Belfast Local Marine Board—Continued. Inclosure No. 15 (Tether, Rd. E., master mariner).	May 8, 1888	Not desirable	No	Great danger, especially in crowded waters.	The most stringent restrictions to signals affecting the near navigation or the immediate safety of the ships in communication.	Present signals are all that are required.
Inclosure No. 16 (Walskitt, J., master mariner).	May 8, 1888	Present signals answer all requirements.				
Inclosure No. 17 (Winship, C., master mariner).	May 8, 1888	Not advisable to adopt such a system, the present system being all that is required.				

[Inclosure G.]

Note showing proposed alteration at pages xv and xvi of the signal book.

[Extract from the report of a committee of 1855.]

"First, its comprehensiveness and distinctness, the *combination of the signs expressing the nature* of the signal made—[two * flags or symbols in a hoist always meaning either *danger* or *urgency*]—and the signals throughout being arranged in a consecutive series, so that any individual signal, whether a word or a sentence, may readily be found; secondly, that the flags and pennants are so arranged as by their position to characterize the signals made; thus,

    *[" In signals with two signs—

      "The burgee *uppermost* represents .... "*Attention* signals."
      "A pennant *uppermost* .... "*Compass* signals."
      "And a square flag *uppermost* represents .... "*Danger* signals."]

    " In signals composed of four signs—

      " The burgee *uppermost* represents.................. "*Geographical.*"
      "A pennant *uppermost* .... "*Vocabulary.*"
      "And a square flag *uppermost* represents .... "*Ships' names.*"

"and thirdly, that the arrangement of the code is such *as to hold out to foreigners the same advantages* that it affords to our own marine."

This committee [of 1888] have slightly departed from the recommendations contained in the last part of the above report as follows, viz:

Instead of the words† in brackets, as above, this committee have adopted the following words:

†[Two flags in one hoist mean attention and demand, compass, and urgent or important signals, which are now classed into three groups, according to the sign which is uppermost, as follows, viz:

    A two-sign signal with—

      The burgee uppermost represents .... Attention or demand.
      A pennant uppermost represents .... Compass signals.
      A square flag uppermost represents .... Urgency or importance.]

SUPPLEMENTARY INCLOSURE TO INTERIM REPORT.

Since the publication of Parliamentary Paper, No. C. 5695, the following additional replies to the letter dated January 20, 1888 (Inclosure F), have been received.

Persons, firms, societies, etc., applied to for observations.	Date of reply.	2. Whether the time has arrived for establishing a system whereby the signals in the International Code book may be made by night as well as by day?	3. If there is a general demand for such a system, what system should be adopted?	4. If such a system were adopted, whether any danger is likely to arise therefrom owing to the inducement it might afford to ships to approach one another too closely at night for the purpose of signaling?	5. To report whether there ought to be any, and if so what, restrictions on the use of night signals, especially in crowded waters?	6. Is it desirable to establish some special warning signals to indicate danger to passing vessels. If so, what should they be, and by what means should they be made?
British India Steam Navigation Company. Inclosure No. 1 (W. H. Aitkinson, marine superintendent, Calcutta).	Jan. 10, 1889	Such signals are desirable, but without special training would be of little use.	Submit the opinions of their marine superintendents and commanders. Knows of no special desire for such a system. The only safe system would be the Morse.	No serious danger, as they would not be much used.	If the system adopted was Morse flashing signals there need not be any restriction.	Very difficult to make special night danger signals. Experts alone would understand the Morse system, and colored lights are generally objectionable through risk of confusion with side lights, but a small number of danger signals might be made with red and white lights.
Inclosure No. 2 (G. Stevenson, master mariner).		Time has arrived for the system to be established.	No knowledge of general demand for such a system, but if one is adopted, the flashing light, with Morse alphabet, is most suitable.	Apprehends no danger on this score.	Pronounced signals, as red, blue and red lights, now used as private signals, should be set apart for pilot and danger signals, and arrangements of red lights. Should be prohibited in English and Irish waters.	
Inclosure No. 3 (John J. Lewis, Lieut., R. N. R.).		Time not yet arrived for establishment of such a system.	Has heard of no demand for such a system.	Great danger may arise through inducement to ships to close with each other.	neis maniin pilot generally.	Night signals should be adopted. Morse telegraph might be used. Steam whistles by steamers and flashing lanterns by sailing ships with guns.
Inclosure No. 4 (C. R. Kendall, master mariner).		Night signals should be adopted.	Flash signals best as colored lights are easily mistaken.	It is possible that vessels might close with one another through several reasons.	Can give no answer.	Does not know what system should be adopted. It is desirable that special warning signals be instituted.

Inclosure					
Inclosure No. 5 (A. P. Turner, master mariner).	Time has arrived for the adoption of such a system.	No general demand for systems. Morse flashing signals most convenient.	Dangers would arise from vessels closing.	Restrictions should be made in crowded waters, and their use allowed only in urgent cases.	It is desirable to establish warning signals. Rockets and blue lights best.
Inclosure No. 6 (J. R. Gaven, master mariner).			Without great prudence there would be danger of vessels closing.	Colored-light signals unnecessary in narrow waters, or where much traffic prevails.	Gun and rocket signals best. Every steamer might carry white, red, and green globe lamps, with which a number of permutations might be made.
Inclosure No. 7 (H. B. Smith, master mariner).	Time has arrived for night signals to be established.	Great need of system. A simple flashing system, such as used in royal navy, best.	No danger would arise from properly established system.	No restriction should be placed on use of night lights, provided no confusion were possible with lights in common use.	It is absolutely necessary to establish warning signals; if possible, whole International Code of night lights.
Inclosure No. 8 (J. P. Livingstone, master mariner).	Number of night-signals insufficient.	Suggests use of "symbols," which would only necessitate the lamps showing colors at present used (see flashing light system). Morse to error and would take too long.		Is not in favor of general night signaling in crowded waters.	Warning signals should be introduced.
Inclosure No. 9 (E. C. Russell, master mariner).	It is desirable to establish a system of night signaling, but doubts the safety of such signals.	There is a signal demand, and for such a system, especially in urgent cases; i.e. the Colomb's flashing signals.	Danger might arise from signals being misread; no necessity for vessels approaching closely.	Should be restricted to urgent signals in narrow waters.	If any warning signals be used they must be simple. Colomb's night signals or the Morse code.
Incl use No. 10 (T. Johnston, master mariner).	Has no suggestion to offer; thinks present system sufficient.			Great danger might arise in crowded waters by use of signals.	A few simple warning signals might be used.
Inclosure No. 11 (R. D. Dougherty, master mariner).	Thinks it is not desirable to establish night signaling.		Night signaling would add to danger.	Every restriction should be put on bright light signaling.	Special warning signal might be established by colored lights on Morse system of flashing signals.
Inclo No. 12 (John Beeamy, master mariner).		No general demand for any system.			Warning signals would be beneficial.
Incl No. 13 (J. W. ..., master mariner).	Answer in the negative.	Answer in the negative.	Sees no danger from this point of view.	Restrictions would be required in narrow waters.	
Inclosure No. 14 (T. A. ..., master mariner).	Considers night signaling impracticable and unnecessary.	Thinks demand is not great.		Might prove dangerous in narrow waters.	One or two warning signals beneficial; rockets and blue lights best.

SUPPLEMENTARY INCLOSURE TO INTERIM REPORT—Continued.

Persons, firms, societies, etc., applied to for observations.	Date of reply.	2. Whether the time has arrived for establishing a system whereby the signals in the International Code book may be made by night as well as by day?	3. If there is a general demand for such a system, what system should be adopted?	4. If such a gun were used, whether any danger is likely to arise therefrom owing to the light it would afford to ships to approach too closely at night for the [?] of [?]?	5. To report ought to be by [?], and if so, [?] on the use of night [?], only in crowded waters?	6. Is it desirable to establish some special warning signals to indicate danger to passing vessels. If so, what should they be, and by what means should they be made?
British India Steam Navigation Company—Continued. Inclosure No. 15 (A. Hansen, master mariner).		Sees no necessity for night signaling, except in war times.	No demand.		Would be dangerous in crowded waters.	A few simple urgent signals desirable by means of rockets and steam whistling on Morse system. Use of rockets as private signals should be disallowed.
Inclosure No. 16 (A. W. Mann, master mariner).		No.	No special demand.	Would be dangerous.	Very dangerous in crowded waters, such as English and Irish channels, Straits of Gibraltar, etc.	Desirable to adopt the signal, "You are standing into danger," two guns, followed by two red places, one at the bow, other at stern; distant signals to be hoisted at fore and main.
Inclosure No. 17 (J. Stone, master mariner).		Time has not yet come.	No.	Yes.		A few warning signals might be useful.
Inclosure No. 18 (J. Henderson, master mariner).		This system could not be used on board ships, only from the shore or light vessels.			The fewer lights used in crowded waters the better, such as channels off Ushant, Finisterre, Lisbon, etc.	In time of peace no signals are needed; during a war they might be necessary. Suggests flashing lights, using Morse alphabet for letters of International Code.
Inclosure No. 19 (A. A. Fyfe, master mariner).		No general system is advisable.	Short system, by means of red, green, and white lights, would be of use in cases of emergency.	Night signaling a fruitful source of collision.	Should be restricted to actual cases of necessity.	Is advisable to have something more definite than present distress signals.

Inclosure No. 20 (A. E. Withers, master mariner).	Such a system has long been wanted.	Unable to state; Morse code by night, and sound.	Good white light with Morse code boat.	With a flashing light restrictions unnecessary in localities named, communications most desirable.	Some urgent signals advisable; proposes two red pyrotechnic lights, verified, followed by white flashing light in Morse code.
Inclosure No. 21 (James Smith, master mariner).	Time not yet come.	No particular demand; Morse alphabet best.	There would be no occasion for ships to close.	No restrictions necessary.	Distress signal at present in use would indicate, "Need of immediate assistance," "You are standing into danger," and "I have encountered ice," might be adopted by use of rockets and blue lights together, or guns and blue lights together. Signal "I have passed a derelict dangerous to navigation" unnecessary.
Inclosure No. 22 (R. N. Sayers, master mariner).	Time not yet come.	No general demand.	Very great danger from collision.	Dangerous in crowded waters, and ought to be restricted to ships signaling to signal stations only.	Other sentences to indicate danger, distress, or urgency should be used instead of the ones mentioned. Gives Trinity House system, consisting of numbers shown before a box light, as an illustration of what might be done.
Inclosure No. 23 (W. H. Hutchinson, marine superintendent, London).	No special benefit to be derived from establishing night signals for the International Code.	No demand as far as he is aware.	No particular danger to be apprehended from vessels closing, as no vessels would go out of their way to signal.	In crowded waters night signaling would be a danger in itself.	Present signals quite sufficient, and are thoroughly understood.

ADDITIONAL REPORT OF THE COMMITTEE ON SOUND-SIGNALS.

Resolved, That the former Committee on Sound-Signals consider and report the specific cases in which new fog-signals should be adopted and to report specific signals for such cases.

WASHINGTON, *November* 21, 1889.

To Rear-Admiral S. R. FRANKLIN, U. S. Navy,
  President of the International Marine Conference, etc.:

SIR: Agreeably with the reference of the Conference on November 8, for the Committee on Sound-Signals to consider and report the specific cases in which new fog-signals should be adopted and to report specific signals for such cases, we beg to submit that in the opinion of the committee it is desirable to adopt the sound-signals mentioned in the following report for compulsory or permissive use as advised.

The sound-signals at present authorized or adopted by the Conference, to be used during fog, mist, falling snow, or heavy rain, are—

Whistle or siren:

  One long blast of about four seconds' duration, "a steam-vessel under way."
  Two such long blasts, "a steam-vessel not at anchor, but stopped and having no way upon her."

Fog-horn:

  One blast, "a sailing vessel on the starboard tack."
  Two blasts, "a sailing vessel on the port tack."
  Three blasts, "a sailing vessel with the wind abaft the beam."

Bell:

  Rung continuously for about five seconds, "a vessel at anchor."
  One blast on fog-horn and bell rung alternately. To indicate a fishing vessel off the coast of Europe, north of Cape of Finisterre, dredging, employed in line-fishing, with her lines out, or using drift-nets and being attached to them.

156

The sound-signals at present authorized and those adopted by the Conference to be made by steam-vessels when in sight of one another are—

One short blast, "I am directing my course to starboard."

Two short blasts, "I am directing my course to port."

Three short blasts, "I am going full speed astern."

In choosing characters for additional signals the committee have acted on the principle that—

1. Although efficient mechanical fog-horns, capable of producing sounds of varying duration, are increasing in numbers on board both sailing and fishing vessels, many fog-horns are at present incapable of producing long as well as short sounds.

2. A signal consisting of long sounds is not sufficiently distinctive from one made up of "short" sounds to enable characters consisting of similar sounds but of different durations being readily read without liability of mistake. It is only when sounds of different durations are combined in one signal that they are sufficiently distinguishable apart.

3. The sirens of many light-houses and light-vessels sound characteristic high and low notes of different pitch, and this custom is increasing; the committee, therefore, consider it desirable that such characters should be solely used to distinguish fixed sea or coast dangers, and that all signals made by a moving or stationary sea-going vessel should be characters in one tone or key.

The most unmistakable and easily remembered sound-signals—like those now authorized—consist of a single sound or a combination of sounds of equal lengths; and the committee advise the adoption of such characters for any new signals made by one vessel wishing to warn another of her presence, whether she is under way, not under command, or at anchor in a fair-way at sea.

One, two, or three sound blasts on a fog-horn are already in use by sailing vessels under way.

It is not laid down what the length of these blasts should be, but, by the construction of the fog-horns used in the past, they are necessarily blasts of equal duration; we submit that they should be so regulated and termed short blasts.

The one, two, or three short blasts on the whistle or siren of a steam vessel communicating with another vessel, which is in sight of her, might be mistaken for a similar number of sounds on the fog-horn of a sailing vessel unless the instruments are unmistakably different in tone. And the one "long" blast of a steam vessel under way in a fog, etc., may, in certain cases, be mistaken for the one "short" blast helm signal by a steam vessel; but inasmuch as all these signals have been in use for many years without fault being found with them by mariners the committee are not prepared to advise any change in their characters.

The two "long" blasts on a whistle or siren, recently adopted by the Conference, to indicate a steam vessel not at anchor but stopped and having no way upon her might, in some cases, be mistaken for a steam vessel's two "short" blasts helm signal to another vessel in sight. To make these signals as distinct as possible the committee recommend that the words "*two such long blasts*" should be altered to "*two prolonged blasts.*"

The Conference having provided in Article 13 that a steam-vessel hearing apparently before the beam the fog-signal of a vessel, the position of which is not ascertained, shall, so far as the circumstances admit, "stop her engines." We recommend that similar wording should be adopted in Article 12, sec. (*b*).

The committee are of the opinion that it is undesirable to adopt as a character any combination of more than four sounds, either of equal or of varying duration, except they are so numerous and continuous as to be unmistakable.

Acting on this principle they have chosen the following characters for compulsory use during fog, etc., when another vessel is not in sight:

Three blasts on a whistle or siren to denote a steam-vessel when her engines are going full speed astern. The committee recommend the adoption of the above wording in lieu of the present wording in Article 19, "I am going full speed astern."

Two short blasts repeated once, with a short interval between the pair of blasts, on a whistle, siren, or fog-horn, to denote respectively a vessel under steam or sail towing another vessel; and the same character for permissive use to denote also, if necessary, a vessel being towed.

The continuous sounding of any fog-signal, or, while the fog-horns in use are capable only of making single blasts, any number of short blasts greater in number than four, following each other in quick succession on a fog-horn, to denote a vessel in distress.

Considering that it is immaterial to an approaching vessel what the impediment is that she necessarily has to get out of the way of, and that a similar character signal of one blast on the fog-horn alternating with a ring of the bell has long been the authorized and established signal for fishing-boats fishing on the coasts of Europe north of Cape Finisterre, the committee have chosen two prolonged blasts on a whistle or fog-horn, alternating with the ringing of a bell, to denote a vessel at anchor in a fair-way at sea, and have adopted the same character to denote a vessel not under command.

The committee are informed that in the London river four short blasts on a steam-vessel's whistle denotes that the steam-vessel is unable to comply with the regulations and alter course to get out of the way of a neighboring vessel which is in sight in consequence of being dangerously near the side of a narrow channel-way, and the steam-vessel thereby demands that the other vessel should get out of her way. Such being the case, they have considered it unadvisable to adopt the same character as a signal for another purpose at sea.

The characters referred to above practically exhaust the combination of easily-remembered sounds of equal duration, and it follows that for further signals characters combining long and short sounds must be chosen.

The committee consider it desirable to distinguish the few special "communication" signals asked for by mariners from the warning or danger-signals by adopting combination characters commencing with a short sound, and on this principle they have chosen the characters mentioned below.

Short, long, short; ▪ ▬▬▬ ▪ to denote "my engines are stopped; you may feel your way past me."

Short, short, long; ▪ ▪ ▬▬▬ to denote "a pilot-vessel;" or, "I want a pilot."

We are of opinion that Article 12, prescribing what sound-signals apparatus should be carried by vessels, should be limited to vessels above 20 tons gross tonnage, smaller sailing vessels and boats being allowed to make any efficient sound-signal.

We have received evidence that improved mechanical fog-horns are now obtainable at a reasonable expense, and that such horns are largely used; especially is this the case on board of the vessels fishing on the banks of Newfoundland, where, in addition to the safety of the vessel, the interests of those engaged in fishing are increased in accordance with an increase in the efficiency of their fog-horns, which are used for signaling to their out-lying boats when fishing at a distance from the parent vessel.

With a view to insuring as much as possible the efficiency of all fog-horns, we recommend that the words "*a bellows or other,*" in Article 12, be eliminated in order to prevent as much as possible the use of inferior instruments.

In agreement with the decision already come to by the Conference, we recommend the use of a gong in lieu of a bell in Chinese and other waters where such instruments are in common use on board vessels; but inasmuch as a large number of light vessels in other waters use such instruments to sound a special signal indicating their position as a warning mark defining a neighboring sea danger, the committee invite the consideration of the Conference to the desirability of not allowing a gong to be used in such waters.

In accordance with our recommendations as above, we suggest for the consideration of the Conference the following readings of the articles in the regulations :

Addition to Article 9. A pilot-vessel wishing to attract attention may sound on her fog-horn, whistle, or siren, three blasts, viz, short, short, long, with intervals of about one second between them.

ARTICLE—(*k*). In fog, mist, falling snow, or heavy rain-storms, a drift-net vessel attached to her nets, and a vessel when trawling, dredging, or fishing with any kind of drag-net, and a vessel employed in line-fishing with their lines out, shall at intervals of not more than one minute make a blast with her fog-horn, *followed by ringing her* bell.

SOUND-SIGNALS FOR FOG, ETC.

ART. 12. A steam-ship shall be provided with a whistle or siren, sounded by steam or other efficient substitute for steam, so placed that the sound may not be intercepted by any obstructions, and with an efficient fog-horn to be sounded by mechanical means, and also with an efficient bell.* A sailing vessel of 20 *tons gross tonnage* and upwards shall be provided with a similar fog horn and bell.

Sailing vessels and boats of less than 20 tons gross tonnage shall not be obliged to be provided with a mechanical fog-horn, but if not so provided they shall make with any other instrument an efficient sound-signal at intervals of not more than one minute.

ARTICLE 12. (b) A steam-vessel not at anchor, but *stopped* and having no way upon her, shall sound, at intervals of not more than two minutes, two such *prolonged* blasts with an interval of about one second between them.

(e) *A steam-vessel, when her engines are going full speed astern, shall sound on her whistle three short blasts.*

(f) *A vessel, if a steam-vessel, at anchor in a fair-way at sea, shall, at intervals of not more than two minutes, sound two prolonged blasts with her whistle or siren, followed by ringing her bell ; or, if a sailing-vessel, two blasts with her fog-horn, followed by ringing her bell.*

(g) *A steam-vessel and a sailing vessel when towing shall, at intervals of not more than two minutes, instead of the signal provided for under sections (a) and (c) of this article, sound on the whistle, siren, or fog horn, three blasts in succession, viz, one prolonged blast followed by two short blasts. A vessel towed may also give this signal on her fog-horn but not on her whistle or siren.*

(h) *A steam-vessel wishing to indicate to another " The way is off my ship ; you may feel your way past me," may sound on her whistle or siren three blasts, viz, short, long, short, with intervals of about one second between them.*

PILOT SIGNALS.

SEC. 3. *A vessel wanting a pilot may sound on her fog-horn, whistle, or siren three blasts in succession, viz, short, short, long, with intervals of about one second between them.*

SOUND-SIGNALS FOR VESSELS IN SIGHT OF ONE ANOTHER.

ART. 19. In taking any course authorized or required by these regulations a steam-vessel under way shall indicate that course to any other ship which she has in sight by the following signals on her whistle or other steam-sound signal, viz:

One short blast to mean " I am directing my course to starboard."

Two short blasts to mean " I am directing my course to port."

Three short blasts to mean " *My engines are* going full speed astern."

---

* In all cases where the regulations require a bell to be used, a drum may be substituted on board Turkish vessels, *and a gong where such articles are used on board small sea-going vessels.*

LIGHTS AND SIGNALS TO ATTRACT ATTENTION.

ART. —. Every ship may, if necessary, *in order to attract attention*, in addition to the lights which she is by these regulations required to carry, show a flare-up light, or use *any* detonating signal *that can not be mistaken for a distress signal.*

DISTRESS SIGNALS.

ART. 27. When a ship is in distress and requires assistance from other ships or from the shore, the following shall be the signals to be used or displayed by her, either together or separately; that is to say:
In the day-time—

1. A gun fired at intervals of about a minute.
2. The international code signal of distress indicated by N C.
3. The distant signal, consisting of a square flag, having either above or below it a ball or anything resembling a ball.
4. Rockets or shells *bursting in the air with a loud report*, and throwing stars of any color or description, fired one at a time, at short intervals.
5. *A continuous sounding with any fog-signal apparatus.*

At night—

1. A gun fired at intervals of about a minute.
2. Flames on the ship (as from a burning tar-barrel, oil-barrel, etc.)
3. *Rockets or shells, as described under day-signals.*
4. *A continuous sounding with any fog-signal apparatus.*

SPAUN,
Delegate for the Austro-Hungarian Government.
AUG. SCHNEIDER,
Delegate for Denmark.
G. S. NARES, *Chairman of Committee,*
Delegate for Great Britain.
R. SETTEMBRINI,
Delegate for Italy.
T. SALVESEN,
Delegate for Norway.
VAN STEYN,
Delegate for The Netherlands.
J. W. SHACKFORD,
Delegate for the United States.

S. Ex. 53, pt. 3——11

REPORT OF COMMITTEE ON SYSTEMS AND DEVICES.

Resolved, That a committee, to be known as the Committee on Systems and Devices, shall be appointed by the President, and that it shall be the duty of the committee to examine and report upon any system or device connected with the business of the Conference, of which a written description, illustrated by plans whenever necessary, is furnished, and that only such as are favorably reported by the committee shall appear before the Conference.

COMMITTEE.

Belgium . . . . Mr. THO. VERBRUGGHE.
France . . . . Mr. H. VETILLART.
Great Britain . . . . . Admiral N. BOWDEN-SMITH.
Mexico . . . . Commodore A. O. MONASTERIO.
United States . . . . . Mr. S. I. KIMBALL.

WASHINGTON, *October* 31, 1889.

Rear-Admiral S. R. FRANKLIN, U. S. N.,
   President International Marine Conference:

SIR: In compliance with a resolution made by the International Marine Conference, we have considered all systems and devices which have been laid before us up to the 30th instant, on which day, in accordance with the ruling of the said Conference, we closed our examination, and do now report as follows:

We have considered thirty-seven different proposals on night signaling, etc., at sea, but whilst glad to notice that this important subject is receiving so much attention, and thanking the authors of the various systems for their trouble, we have not seen any plan equal to the Morse, which is already in use in many navies, including those of the United States, France, and Great Britain.

This system necessitates the employment of a trained signal-man, but is otherwise inexpensive, as it only requires one flashing lamp for night-work, and the steam-whistle or other sound-signal for fog. It can also be used with or without a code book.

Ten papers on preventing collisions at sea have come before us, but we do not consider it necessary to lay them before the Conference.

We have examined twenty-five papers on various subjects, and consider that those numbered 2, 5, 9, 17, 20, and 25, under "miscellaneous," are interesting. The sheets showing the maneuvering powers of ships under various speeds, and numbered 20, are well worth the attention of every one interested in this subject.

The committee are of opinion that, considering the importance of general division 5, "Saving Life and Property at Sea," and the number of devices which have been presented, it would appear desirable to appoint a special committee to consider that subject, composed, as far as possible, of delegates who have made a study of the matter, and therefore the propositions dealing with "Life-Saving Apparatus" have not been considered.

Furthermore, it might be necessary, in some cases, to carry out some practical experiments.

We inclose herewith forms showing the subjects dealt with, the names of the author or inventor, and our remarks thereon.

N. BOWDEN-SMITH, *Chairman,*
Delegate from Great Britain.
THO. VERBRUGGHE,
Delegate from Belgium.
H. VETILLART,
Delegate from France.
A. O. MONASTERIO,
Delegate from Mexico.
S. I. KIMBALL,
Delegate from United States.

SIGNALS.

No.	Name and address of writer.	Subject.	Remarks of committee.
1	Maritime Electric Manufacturing Company.	Search light	Will be considered in life-saving section.
2	E. M. Brown, 1285 Broadway, New York.	Electric-light illuminating	Not within scope of the Conference.
3	John M. Hayward, Newfoundland.	Night signaling, A B C system.	Examined.
4	Aug. Watson, 218 Twelfth street, northwest, Washington, D. C.	Storm and flood signaling	Do.
5	Chas. Oatman, 131 Cambridge Place, Brooklyn, N. Y.	Signal lantern	This appears a good lamp and is well reported on by United States naval officers.
6	A. F. Ward, Philadelphia, Pa.	Semaphoric color signals	Examined.
7	W. H. Ward, Monongahela City, Pa.	Nautical signals, ocean telegraph.	Do.
8	John Milne, 53 Cedar street, New York.	Method and devices for signaling.	Do.
9	J. M. Batchelder, 1210 Massachusetts avenue, Washington, D. C.	Submarine signals	Do.
10	A. S. Harrison, Burgoyne Cottage, Carona road, Burnt Ashe Park S. E., London, England.	Stellar code of signals	Do.
11	Wm. G. Spiegel, New York	Marine signals	Do.
12	Chas. E. Bridge, captain and acting signal officer, Eleventh Brigade, National Guard, State of New York.	Conversation between vessels at sea.	Do.
13	J. L. Fleischer, inspector coast lights, Denmark.	Relation between light and attached fog-signals.	Does not come within the scope of the Conference.
14	Jos. Wall, commanding steamship Montreal, Dominion Line, Liverpool, Eng.	Distress and intercommunication signals.	Examined.
15	T. R. Elton, 7 Diamond Harbor road, Calcutta.	Maritime-code of signals	Proposing the changing of the color of flags, which the committee does not think advisable.
16	G. W. Robertson, Mt. Vernon, Ind.	New system of signals	Does not come within the scope of the Conference.
17	Wm. M. Crowley, Salt Lake City, Utah.	Signaling	Examined.
18	John H. Mowe, 1503 Pennsylvania avenue, Washington, D. C.	System of signals	Do.
19	H. Lathamer, commanding German steam-ship Hungaria.	System of night signals	Do.
20	Baker & Roberts, Providence, R. I.	Night code of marine signals.	Do.
21	S. F. Aminoff	Signal flags	The proposed system has several advantages, but it is not advisable to change color of the flags which have been known for so many years.
22	Mr. Coston, 136 Pearl street, New York.	Night-signaling chart	Examined.
23	F. C. Johnson	Night-signal system	Do.
24	Curtis Tilton, 419 Walnut street, Philadelphia.	Flash-light system	Do.
25	Crosby Automatic Signal Company, Providence, R. I.	Automatic signal apparatus.	Not to be considered by Conference unless course-indicating signals are introduced.
26	Gartner-Harris, Savannah, Ga.	Marine signals	Same as No. 25.
27	O. C. Hansen, care Gabriel Fedde, 71 Stone street, New York.	Light-house fog-horn	Not within the scope of the Conference as regards light-houses, but is worth a trial on board ship.
28	Ferdinand Forster, care Thos. Drew Stetson, 23 Murray street, New York.	Sound-signals	Examined.
29	Lieut. Fletcher, U. S. Navy	...do	Do.
30	A. Van Vliet, Paterson, N. J.	System of throwing out colored bullets in a fog.	Do.
31	D. Ruggles, Fredericksburg, Va.	Signaling with guns, rockets, etc.	Do.
32	Mr. James, Imperial Japanese Navy.	Helm signal-lights	Do.
33	Rear-Admiral Luce, U. S. Navy.	Proposing additional lights, etc., to light-houses.	Not within the scope of the Conference.
34	John Maurice, 1245 California avenue, Chicago, Ill.	Proposing system of lights for determining distance of ships.	Examined.

SIGNALS—Continued.

No.	Name and address of writer.	Subject.	Remarks of committee.
35	W. H. Hawkes, Putney, London.	System of signaling with rockets.	Examiner.
36	Jacob & Walker, London	High and low tone whistle for fog.	Do.
37	H. H. Dotty, 11 Queen Victoria street, London.	Claims to be a lamp of great intensity without using a wick. Model submitted.	Committee can not pronounce an opinion without comparing this lamp with others at sea.

COLLISIONS.

1	F. Della Torre, Baltimore	Eophone	Examined.
2	....	A system of India rubber rollers.	Do.
3	John F. Schults	Captive balloons to be used in a fog.	Do.
4	Arturo de Marcoartu	International institution to diminish the casualties at sea.	Contains neither systems nor devices.
5	Fairman Rogers	Suggests that all wheels should be made to work the same way, and the adoption of one apparatus by which pushing the handle and the index ahead means go ahead, and pushing it astern means go astern.	Examined.
6	J. McAdams & Sons, New York	Marine brake	Do.
7	John Ria, Brooklyn, N. Y	Collision pad	
8	W. T. L. Wharton	Diagram relating to collisions.	These diagrams are well worth consideration of Conference. (See Miscellaneous, No. 20.)
9	Steamer *Florence*, New York....	Marine brake	The invitation to view the *Florence* should be read to the Conference.
10	William Pilcher, London, W	Models for teaching the rules of the road.	Not within scope of Conference.

MISCELLANEOUS SUBJECTS.

1	Bainbridge-Hoff, commander, U. S. Navy, Washington.	Letter proposing list of subjects to be considered by Conference.	Already disposed of. No action necessary.
2	Littlehales, Division of Chart Construction, Washington.	Referring to Divisions 1, 2, 10, and 11 of Conference.	Might be read to the Conference when those subjects are considered.
	Letters on similar subjects from C. M. McCartney and S. W. Witzel, lieutenants U. S. Navy; also from Gustave Herrie.	Referring to Divisions 1,2,10, 11, and 12.	Might be read when those subjects are considered, except paper on Division 1, which is not necessary.
3	Consul Catlin, of Zurich	Proposing a Swiss maritime flag.	Not within scope of the Conference.
4	John C. Morgan, Philadelphia..	Various matters	Examined.
5	Northern Maritime Conference, Copenhagen.	Memorandum with pamphlet on the the general subjects of programme.	Pamphlet should be distributed to the members of the Conference.
6	F. Della Torre, Baltimore	Letter and plan relating to Division 10.	Examined.
7	A. L. Woodworth, Virginia Iron-Works, Norfolk, Va.	Automatic alarm-buoy	Do.
8	Maj. A. Stewart Harrison, London.	Sound stella signals; night, day, and fog.	Do.
9	Lieut. M. L. Wood, U. S. Navy..	International buoyage	Appears to be a well considered and simple system.
10	S. A. Philipsen, Copenhagen....	......do	An account of systems now in existence and suggestions.
11	I. Leveielle, Montreal	Additional improved safety-rudder.	Does not come within scope of Conference.
12	R. W. Allen	A jury-rudder	Not within the scope of Conference.
13	Report of U. S. Naval Engineers.	Kunstader's combined rudder and swiveling screw.	Not within the scope of Conference.
14	N. H. Borgfeldt, Brooklyn.......	Nautical distance-indicator for use in fog.	Examined.

MISCELLANEOUS SUBJECTS—Continued.

No.	Name and address of writer.	Subject.	Remarks of committee.
15	S. N. Carvalho, New York......	Plan for dissipating fog by flames of carbonized oxy-hydrogen gas.	Not within scope of Conference. no experiments having been reported.
16	M. E. Chamberlain	Suggests firing colored rockets to avoid collision.	Examined.
17	James Lawson, London.........	Lamp for the masthead, fitted with red and green shades, capable of being worked from the deck to indicate which side it is intended to approach a vessel.	Might be laid before Conference if any system of helm-signals is adopted.
18	Various writers. No covering letter.	Various matters	Examined.
19	Capt. P. Talbot Peterson, New York.	A running commentary on the rules and other topics in connection with the Conference.	Do.
20	Capt. W. J. L. Wharton, R. N., London.	Charts with tables showing the maneuvering powers of ships.	Worth the consideration of every one interested in this subject.
21	Hydrographic Office, U. S. Navy Department.	Bundle of papers bearing on every subject before the Conference.	These papers were presented to us the last day of our sitting, having been previously considered by the Committees on Lights and Fog-Signals, and as some of them appear to contain matters of interest, we would recommend their being placed at the disposal of the members of the Conference.
22	American Ship-Windlass Company, Providence, R. I.	Referring to steam capstan windlasses, etc.	Not within scope of the Conference.
23	H. B. Cox, New Haven, Conn...	Proposing a new system of lamps and electric buoy.	Committee can not pronounce an opinion without seeing them at sea.
24	John Spiers, by Watson & Hagen, New York.	Proposition for stopping leaks in vessels built of iron or steel.	Not within scope of the Conference.
25	Curtis Tilton, Philadelphia	White flash stern-light with model.	Worth the consideration of Conference if occulting stern light is introduced but we would prefer that the occultation was made by a shade.

REPORT OF COMMITTEE ON LIGHTS FOR SMALL CRAFT.

RESOLUTION.

Resolved, That a committee of nine be appointed to consider and report on the lights to be carried or shown on small vessels, pilot-vessels, and fishing vessels.

COMMITTEE.

Belgium	Mr. VERBRUGGHE.
China	Capt. A. M. BISBEE.
Denmark	Mr. SCHNEIDER.
France	Captain LANNELUC.
Germany	Capt. CHRISTIAN DONNER.
Great Britain	Mr. GRAY.
Japan	Lieutenant BABA.
Netherlands	Captain HUBERT.
United States	Captain NORCROSS.

WASHINGTON, *November* 8, 1889.

To Rear-Admiral S. R. FRANKLIN, U. S. Navy,
President of the International Marine Conference, etc. :

SIR: The Committee on Lights for Small Craft, pursuant to the resolution adopted by the Marine Conference instructing the said committee to consider and report as to rules for the lights to be carried or shown on small vessels, pilot-vessels, and fishing vessels, have agreed upon a report, which, having adopted unanimously, or by a majority of votes, they respectfully submit, in the form of proposed amendments to the present international regulations.

The committee are unanimously of opinion that the part of the present Article 10, which precedes subsection (*a*), applying to fishing vessels and boats when in the sea off the coast of Europe, lying north of Cape Finisterre, should be omitted. The amendments submitted are therefore proposed as applicable to all waters without distinction.

THOMAS GRAY, *Chairman.*
Delegate for Great Britain.
THO. VERBRUGGHE,
Delegate for Belgium.
A. M. BISBEE,
Delegate for China.
AUG. SCHNEIDER,
Delegate for Denmark.
HENRI LANNELUC,
Delegate for France.
CHR. DONNER,
Delegate for Germany.
R. BABA,
Delegate for Japan.
D. HUBERT,
Delegate for The Netherlands.
JAS. W. NORCROSS,
Delegate for the United States.

ART. 7. Whenever, as in the case of small vessels *under way* during bad weather, the green and red side lights can not be fixed, these lights shall be kept *at hand*, ready for use; and shall, on the approach of or to other vessels, be exhibited on their respective sides in sufficient time to prevent collision, in such manner as to make them most visible, and so that the green light shall not be seen on the port side nor the red light on the starboard side, *nor if practicable more than two points abaft the beam on their respective sides.*

To make the use of these portable lights more certain and easy, the lanterns containing them shall each be painted outside with the color of the light they respectively contain, and shall be provided with proper screens.

ART. 8. No alteration.

ART. 9. (a) A pilot-vessel, *whether under sail or steam,* when engaged on her station on pilotage duty, shall not show the lights required for other vessels, but shall carry a white light at the masthead, visible all round the horizon, and shall also exhibit a flare-up light or flare-up lights at short intervals, which shall never exceed fifteen minutes.

When approaching a vessel to put a pilot on board, or where there is risk of collision with another vessel, such pilot-vessel shall have at hand two lights, which may be the side lights, one red and one green, so constructed that they can be flashed instantaneously, which shall be kept either in their places, screened, or at hand, always ready for use, and shall flash one of them (in order to show the direction in which she is heading) in sufficient time to prevent collision, so that the red light shall only be shown on the port side and the green light only on the starboard side.

(*b*) *A pilot-vessel of such a class as to be obliged to go alongside of a vessel to put a pilot on board may show a white light instead of carrying a white light at the masthead.*

Such vessels shall also not be obliged to carry the side lights proposed for larger pilot-vessels, but in this case they shall have ready at hand a lantern with a green glass on the one side and a red glass on the other side, and on approaching a vessel to put a pilot on board, or on approaching to or being approached by a vessel, such lantern shall be exhibited in sufficient time to prevent collision, so that the green light shall not be seen on the port side nor the red light on the starboard side.

(*c*) A pilot-vessel, *whether under sail or steam,* when not engaged on her station on pilotage duty, shall carry lights similiar to those of other vessels.

Article 10. *Paragraph* (*a*) *of this article applies only to boats and vessels propelled by sails or oars of less than 20 tons gross tonnage, and only to such boats and vessels when they are under way. It therefore applies also to fishing-vessels of less than 20 tons gross tonnage when they are not actually engaged in fishing, but are under way.*

(*a*) Boats and vessels of less than 20 tons *gross* tonnage shall not be obliged to carry the colored side lights; but every such boat and vessel shall, *if she do not carry such colored side lights,* have ready at hand a lantern with a green glass on the one side and a red glass on the other side, and on approaching to or being approached by another vessel such lantern shall be exhibited in sufficient time to prevent collision, so that the green light shall not be seen on the port side nor the red light on the starboard side.

NOTE.—*Paragraph* (*b*) *of this article applies only to vessels under steam of less than 40 tons gross tonnage, and only to such vessels when they are under way. It therefore applies also to fishing vessels under steam of less than 40 tons gross tonnage when they are not actually engaged in fishing, but are under way.*

(*b*) *A vessel of less than 40 tons gross tonnage when under steam shall not be obliged to carry the lights prescribed for other vessels under steam, but if she does not carry such lights she shall carry on or in front of her foremast or on or in front of her funnel or somewhere in the fore part of the vessel where it can best be seen, and at a height above the gunwale of not less than 9 feet, a bright white light visible for at least 2 miles, so constructed as to show over an arc of the horizon of twenty points of the compass, so fixed as to throw the light ten points on each side of the vessel, namely, from right ahead to two points abaft the beam on either side; and such vessel shall further carry either (1) side lights visible for at least 1 mile or (2) a lantern with a green glass on the one side and a red glass on the other, so constructed that it will show an unbroken green light over an arc of the horizon of ten points of the compass from right ahead to two points abaft the beam on the starboard side, and an unbroken red light over an arc of the horizon of ten points of the compass from right ahead to two points abaft the beam on the port side. This lantern shall be carried at not less than 3 feet below the white light before mentioned.*

ARTICLE —. (*a*) All fishing vessels and fishing boats of 20 tons *gross* tonnage, or upwards, when under way and when not required by the following regulations in this article to carry and show the lights therein named, shall carry and show the same lights as other vessels under way.

(*b*) All vessels *and boats* when engaged in fishing with drift-nets shall exhibit two white lights from any part of the vessel where they can be best seen. Such lights shall be placed so that the vertical distance between them shall be not less than 6 feet and not more than 10 feet; and so that the horizontal distance between them measured in a line with the keel of the vessel shall be not less than 5 feet and not more than 10 feet. The lower of these two lights shall be the more forward, and both of them shall be of such a character and contained in lanterns of such construction as to show all round the horizon, on a dark night with a clear atmosphere, for a distance of not less than 3 miles.

NOTE.—*The following subsections* (*c*) *and* (*d*) *and* (*e*) *of this article only apply to vessels engaged in trawl-fishing, by which is meant the dragging of an apparatus along the bottom of the sea attached to any vessel in motion.*

(*c*) *All vessels under steam when engaged in trawling, having their trawls in the water and not being stationary, in consequence of their gear getting fast to a rock or other obstruction, shall carry on or in front of the foremast, and in the same position as the white light which other steam-ships are required to carry, a lantern showing a white light ahead, a green light on the starboard side, and a red light on the port side, such lantern to be so constructed, fitted, and arranged as to show an unbroken white light over an arc of the horizon of four points of the compass, an unbroken green light over an arc of the horizon of ten points of the compass, and an unbroken red light over an arc of the horizon of ten points of the compass, and it shall be so fixed as to show the white light from right ahead to two points on the bow on each side of the vessel, the green light from two points on the starboard bow to four points abaft the beam on the starboard side, and the red light from two points on the port bow to four points abaft the beam on the port side. Such vessels shall also carry a white light in a lantern, so constructed as to show a clear and unbroken light all round the horizon, the lantern containing such white light to be carried lower than the lantern showing the green, white, and red lights, as aforesaid, so, however, that the actual distance between them shall not be less than 6 feet nor more than 12 feet.*

(*d*) *All sailing vessels of 7 tons gross tonnage and upwards, engaged in trawling, having their trawl in the water and not being stationary in consequence of their gear getting fast to a rock or other obstruction, shall carry a white light in a lantern so constructed as to show a clear and unbroken light all round the horizon, and also provide a sufficient supply of red pyrotechnic lights, which shall each burn for at least thirty seconds, and shall, when so burning, be visible for the same distance under the same conditions as the white light. The white light shall be shown from sunset to sunrise. One of the pyrotechnic lights shall be shown on approaching to or being approached by another vessel, in sufficient time to prevent collision.*

All lights mentioned above shall be visible at a distance of 2 miles.

(e) *Sailing-vessels of less than 7 tons gross tonnage engaged in trawling, having their trawl in the water, and not being stationary in consequence of their gear getting fast to a rock or other obstruction, shall not be obliged to carry the white light mentioned in section (d) of this article, but if they do not carry such light, they shall have at hand a lantern showing a bright white light, and shall, on approaching to or being approached by another vessel, exhibit it where it can best be seen in sufficient time to prevent collision; and instead of showing a red pyrotechnic light they may show a flare-up light.*

(*f*) *All* vessels *and boats* when employed in line fishing with *their* lines *out and attached to their lines, and when not at anchor or stationary,* shall carry the same lights as vessels when engaged in fishing with drift-nets.

(*g*) If a vessel *or boat* when fishing becomes stationary in consequence of her gear getting fast to a rock or other obstruction, she shall show the light and make the fog-signal for a vessel at anchor.

(*h*) Fishing vessels and boats may at any time use a flare-up in addition to the lights which they are by this article required to carry and show. All flare-up lights exhibited by a vessel when trawling or fishing with any kind of drag-net shall be shown at the after part of the vessel, excepting that, if the vessel is hanging by the stern to her *fishing gear, the flare-up lights* shall be exhibited from the bow.

(*i*) Every fishing vessel and every boat when at anchor between sunset and sunrise shall exhit a white light visible all round the horizon at a distance of at least 1 mile.

(*k*) Fog-signals not discussed.

REPORT OF THE COMMITTEE UPON GENERAL DIVISIONS 2, 4, AND 6 OF THE PROGRAMME.

Resolved, That the President appoint committees on the several general divisions of the programme, except general divisions 3 and 5.

MOTION.

Mr. GOODRICH (United States). That the several committees be increased each by two, and that the Committee on Collocation also be increased by two members.

The following are the committees appointed in accordance with the above resolution and motion:

Committee No. 1.

To examine and report upon the subjects contained in general divisions 2, 4, and 6 of the programme proposed by the United States Delegates.

Brazil	Capt. SALDANHA DA GAMA.
China	Com. CHEN NGEN TAO.
Costa Rica	Don MANUEL ARAGON.
France	Captain LANNELUC.
Germany	Captain DONNER.
Great Britain	Mr. GRAY.
Italy	Captain SETTEMBRINI.
Norway	Captain SALVESEN,
United States	Captain SAMPSON.

GENERAL DIVISION 2.

REGULATIONS TO DETERMINE THE SEAWORTHINESS OF VESSELS.

(*a*) Construction of vessels.
(*b*) Equipment of vessels.
(*c*) Discipline of crew.

172

(*d*) Sufficiency of crew.
(*e*) Inspection of vessels.
(*f*) Uniform certificates of inspection.

GENERAL DIVISON 4.

UNIFORM REGULATIONS REGARDING THE DESIGNATING AND MARK-
ING OF VESSELS.

(*a*) Position of name on vessels.
(*b*) Position of name of port of registry on vessels.
(*c*) Size of lettering.
(*d*) Uniform system of draft marks.

GENERAL DIVISION 6.

NECESSARY QUALIFICATIONS FOR OFFICERS AND SEAMEN, INCLUD-
ING TESTS FOR SIGHT AND COLOR BLINDNESS.

(*a*) A uniform system of examination for the different grades.
(*b*) Uniform tests for visual power and color blindness.
(*c*) General knowledge of methods employed at life-saving stations.
(*d*) Uniform certificates of qualification.

WASHINGTON, *December* 5, 1889.

To Rear-Admiral SAMUEL R. FRANKLIN, U. S. Navy,
President International Marine Conference, Washington, D. C.:

SIR: The committee appointed to examine and report upon the subjects contained in general divisions 2, 4, and 6 of the programme proposed by the United States Delegates, beg to submt the following report.

GENERAL DIVISION 2.

REGULATIONS TO DETERMINE THE SEAWORTHINESS OF VESSELS.

(*a*) Construction of vessels.
(*b*) Equipment of vessels.
(*c*) Discipline of crew.
(*d*) Sufficiency of crew.
(*e*) Inspection of vessels.
(*f*) Uniform certificates of inspection.

1. It is the opinion of the committee that, upon the subjects contained
in the sections of this division, no international rule could be made
which would secure beneficial results. It is thought that the Conference would be limited in each case to a recommendation fixing a minimum for the objects which it is desired to secure under each of these
sections. If such a minimum were made the legal requirement it would

have an injurious effect upon the present standard of efficiency in many countries.

2. In other countries, where such efficiency does not exist, it is thought that it will be best secured by the same means which have secured it elsewhere, leaving each nation to modify such means in ways which will best adapt them to the particular methods of the respective governments.

3. Again, it is found that the present rules existing in different countries upon several of these questions are different in many respects, though probably equally efficient. It would, therefore, become necessary in forming an international rule in such cases to recommend changes in the existing rules of several countries which to some of them might be impracticable. This is thought to be undesirable. However, the committee earnestly recommend that—

4. All vessels, whether propelled by steam or sail, should possess a margin of strength over and above that which is required to enable them to perform the work for which they were designed and built. A chain, a bridge, or any other structure, the failure of which would entail the loss of human life, invariably has a considerable reserve of strength provided; in other words, the admitted working load is always much less than the computed strength, or the strength ascertained by actual test; certainly it is no less important that the hull of a vessel should contain a similar reserve.

5. To attempt to formulate rules for the construction of vessels of all sizes and for all trades would far exceed the province of this committee, and besides, any arbitrary rules would probably much hamper the advance in design and the method of construction.

6. Therefore, to obtain as much as seems to be practicable in this direction, it is desirable to rely upon efficient and oft-repeated inspection, when upon the least indication of distress or of rupture showing, very substantial additions should be made before the vessel is allowed to again proceed to sea.

7. Ocean-going steam-vessels which carry passengers should be additionally protected by having efficient bulk-heads so spaced that when any two compartments be filled with water the vessel will still remain in a seaworthy condition, and two at least of the amidships bulk-heads should be tested by water pressure to the height of the deck next above the water-line.

GENERAL DIVISION 4.

UNIFORM REGULATIONS REGARDING THE DESIGNATING AND MARKING OF VESSELS.

(a) Position of name on vessels.
(b) Position of name of port of registry on vessels.
(c) Size of lettering.
(d) Uniform system of draft marks.

1. *The name of every registered merchant vessel shall be marked upon each bow and upon the stern, and the port of registry of every such vessel shall be marked upon the stern.*

These names shall be marked in Roman letters in a light color on a dark ground, or in a dark color on a light ground, and to be distinctly visible.

The smallest letters used shall not be less than four (4) inches high.

2. *The draft of every registered vessel shall be marked upon the stem and stern post in English feet or decimeters, in either Arabic or Roman numerals. The bottom of each numeral shall indicate the draft to that line.*

GENERAL DIVISION 6.

NECESSARY QUALIFICATIONS FOR OFFICERS AND SEAMEN, INCLUDING TESTS FOR SIGHT AND COLOR-BLINDNESS.

(a) A uniform system of examination for the different grades.
(b) Uniform tests for visual power and color-blindness.
(c) General knowledge of methods employed at life-saving stations.
(d) Uniform certificates of qualification.

1. *Every man or boy going to sea as a seaman, or with the intention of becoming a seaman, should be examined for visual power and color-blindness; and no man or boy should be permitted to serve on board any vessel in the capacity of seaman, or where he will have to stand lookout, whose visual power is below one-half normal or who is red and green color-blind.*

2. *Every man who shall qualify as an officer or as a pilot of a registered vessel after the adoption of these rules, except engineer officers, shall be required to have a certificate that he has the necessary visual power and that he is not red and green blind. He shall also have a certificate that he is familiar with the regulations for preventing collisions at sea, and with the duties required of him in co-operating with a life-saving station in case his vessel is stranded.*

3. *It is recommended that each country provide means which will enable any boy or man intending to go to sea to have his eyes examined for visual power and color-blindness, and to obtain a certificate of the result; also to enable the master of any vessel to have the eyes of any of his crew tested for the same purpose.*

It is the opinion of the committee that defective visual power and color-blindness are sources of danger at sea, the first both by day and night, because of the inability of the short-sighted to see objects at a sufficient distance. Color-blindness is a source of danger, more especially at night, because of the inability of a color-blind person to distinguish between the red and green side lights. The inability on the part of an officer or look-out to distinguish the color of buoys may be a cause of accident in broad daylight.

It is the opinion of the committee, however, that tests for these defects need not be enforced in the cases of masters and mates who already occupy such positions.

The committee purposely avoid making any recommendation as to the methods to be used in making such tests for visual power and color-blindness, or in conducting the necessary examinations for officers. It is thought that the desired objects will be best secured by leaving each country to employ the methods which may seem most suitable.

CHEN NGEN TAO.
MAN'L ARAGON.
CHR. DONNER.
JAMES WIMSHURST.
H. SETTEMBRINI.
W. T. SAMPSON, *Chairman.*
CAPT. H. LANNELUC.
CAPT. L. SALDANHA DA GAMA.
T. SALVESEN.

REPORT OF THE COMMITTEE UPON THE SUBJECT OF A UNIFORM LOAD-MARK.

GENERAL DIVISION 3 OF THE PROGRAMME.

RESOLUTION.

Resolved, That the Chair appoint a committee of seven upon the subject of a uniform load-mark, general division 3 of the programme.

MOTION.

Mr. GOODRICH (United States). That the several committees be increased, each bv two, and that the Committee on Collocation also be increased by two members.

COMMITTEE.

Brazil	Capt. J. CORDOVIL MAURITY.
Chili	Lieutenant BEAUGENCY.
China	Lieutenant CHIA NI HSI.
Great Britain	Mr. GRAY.
France	Captain RICHARD.
Germany	Dr. SIEVEKING.
Italy	Captain SETTEMBRINI.
The Netherlands	Captain HUBERT.
United States	Mr. GRISCOM.

GENERAL DIVISION 3.

DRAFT TO WHICH VESSELS SHOULD BE RESTRICTED WHEN LOADED.
Uniform maximum load-mark.

WASHINGTON, *November* 26, 1889.

To Rear-Admiral S. R. FRANKLIN,
President of the International Marine Conference, etc.:

SIR: Your committee, having been appointed to report on the subject of a uniform load-mark, have first of all endeavored to obtain as much information as could be collected on this very important question.

The British law, as laid down in the Merchant Shipping Act, 1876 (39 and 40 Vict., c. 80), gives certain powers to the Board of Trade to detain British and foreign vessels which, by reason of overloading or improper loading, are unfit to proceed to sea without serious danger to human life. These powers may be put into force against foreign ships when they have taken on board all or any part of their cargo at a port in the United Kingdom, and are, whilst at that port, unsafe by reason of overloading or improper loading.

With the intention of carrying out this law in a way consistent with the interests of the mercantile community on the one side and with the regard due to protection of life and property on the other side, certain general rules, after careful investigations instituted by a load-line committee appointed by the president of the Board of Trade, as well as by the Board of Trade, have been framed with the purpose of ascertaining whether a ship be overloaded or not. These rules assign to ships a freeboard, which, according to the experience collected on the subject, is considered sufficient to prevent dangerous overloading without unduly interfering with trade, and they contain tables assigning such freeboard as is suitable for vessels of the highest class in Lloyd's Register or of strength equivalent thereto, and which is to be increased for ships of inferior strength.

The above-mentioned rules have proved to be a good standard upon which to determine the proper loading of British vessels which are classed in Lloyd's Register, or for other vessels the particulars of whose strength and fitness to carry any particular cargo can easily be ascertained by the surveyors of the Board of Trade.

As regards foreign ships, however, which are loading in the United Kingdom, and which are either not classed in Lloyd's Register, or the particulars of which can not be ascertained without a minute examination, the difficulty exists that the law which intends to guard against the dangers arising from overloading can not be enforced without serious disadvantages to the owners of ships and cargoes consequent upon the difficulty of ascertaining whether the ships are fit to carry the cargo in question.

For these reasons it appears to be obvious that it would be very desirable if means could be found to ascertain, in a simple and easy way and without loss of time, the fitness of any vessel loading in a port of the United Kingdom to load a particular cargo.

These remarks naturally apply also to vessels loading elsewhere, because it is a very high and important interest, common to all nations, to take every possible measure for the protection of life and property against the dangers arising from overloading.

For these reasons it appears to deserve very serious attention whether, by providing for a certain load-line to be marked on sea-going ships, a trustworthy and simple method could be arrived at for deciding whether a loading vessel should be detained for overloading or ought to be allowed to go to sea.

The British Government has recently invited the attention of other governments to this question. But inasmuch as up to the present no progress has been made in this matter, the question arises whether something could be done to expedite an understanding by any action on the part of the Conference now here assembled.

Now, as far as your committee have been able to ascertain, the laws of many maritime nations contain provisos for dealing with the question of overloading, and enabling the local authorities to detain over-laden ships. But nowhere, except in Great Britain, as far as is known, have statutory rules been introduced for the purpose of ascertaining whether a ship be fit to carry a certain cargo by a load-mark or load-line.

In order to arrive at such laws and to enforce them, it would appear to be necessary to induce the governments of the maritime nations not only to institute investigations similar to those made in Great Britain above referred to, but also to establish a sufficient staff of competent officials to insure the universal compliance with the laws to be given, and to establish courts of appeal authorized to decide on complaints against unjust detention, and to award damages to the ship-owners and shippers of cargo in case of an unjustifiable detention.

It appears to your committee that this would be surrounded with very serious difficulties, as it depends upon the varying cònditions of each country whether the Governments would think it advisable to take steps in this direction or not. It must be kept in mind that a great dis-play of scientific labor, and morever a heavy expenditure of money, would be necessary to introduce a system similar to that which is used in Great Britain. Besides, it could be questioned whether it be necessary to make a law on load-lines or load-marks in order to guard against the danger of overloading, because it might be said that suffi-cient safeguards are given by the responsibility of the ship-owners towards the shippers of the cargo, and to their insurers, and by the control exer-cised by the undewriters and the various institutions for classing ships. There may also be circumstances peculiar to certain countries, as for example, the fact that the goods which they export generally are light goods only, which do not endanger the stability of a ship, which may operate in favor of non-interference on behalf of the respective Govern-ments.

Your committee are led to believe that on these grounds, notwith-standing the advantages which would be connected with the introduc-tion of a uniform system of load-marks, this matter is not ripe for consideration by this Conference, and that it ought to be left to the ne-gotiations to be carried on between the Governments of the maritime nations.

We beg to remark in concluding, that this report has been sanctioned by the undersigned members of your committee, unanimously, and that Mr. Thomas Gray, who has been prevented from reading and signing it by the necessity of his departure, has nevertheless expressed his concurrence with its general views.

SIEVEKING,
Chairman of Committee.

J. MAURITY.

R. BEAUGENCY.

CHIA NI HSI.

E. RICHARD.

R. SETTEMBRINI.

D. HUBERT.

CLEMENT A. GRISCOM.

REPORT OF THE COMMITTEE ON LIFE-SAVING SYSTEMS AND DEVICES.

RESOLUTION.

Resolved, That a committee of seven, to be known as the Committee on Life-Saving Systems and Devices, shall be appointed by the President; that it shall be the duty of the committee to examine any system or device connected with the saving of life and property from shipwreck presented on or before the 12th instant of which a written description, illustrated by plans when necessary, shall be furnished, and that only such matters as are favorably reported by the committee shall be brought before the conference; that the committee shall submit a report when General Division 5 of the programme shall be reached for consideration.

MOTION.

Mr. Goodrich (United States). That the several committees be increased, each by two, and that the committee on collocation also be increased by two members.

COMMITTEE.

Belgium	Mr. VERBRUGGHE.
China	Captain BISBEE.
Chili	Rear-Admiral VIEL.
France	Captain RICHARD.
Germany	Consul-General FEIGEL.
Great Britain	Captain WYATT.
Spain	Lieutenant SEOANE.
The Netherlands	Captain VAN STEYN.
United States	Mr. KIMBALL.

WASHINGTON, *December* 5, 1889.

Rear-Admiral S. R. FRANKLIN, U. S. Navy,
President of the International Marine Conference, etc.:

SIR: The Committee on Life-Saving Systems and Devices, appointed under a resolution of the Marine Conference, were at first in doubt whether the terms of the resolution gave them authority to consider and report upon all the topics embraced in General Division 5 of the programme, but the subsequent action of the Conference in appointing committees to report upon all the subjects of the other divisions, yet making no further provision for those of General Division 5, seemed clearly to imply that it was intended that this committee should deal with them. They have accordingly done so, and herewith submit their report. The various subjects will be taken up in their order upon the programme.

1. SAVING OF LIFE AND PROPERTY FROM SHIPWRECK AT SEA.

"(a) DUTIES OF VESSELS AFTER COLLISION."

What these duties are is obvious enough. Common humanity requires that colliding vessels should remain by each other and render all needed assistance so long as they can do so consistently with their own safety. Experience shows, however, that masters of vessels frequently take advantage of the circumstances attending such disasters to escape from the scene without identification, in order to avoid responsibility. Several of the maritime nations have, therefore, imposed upon them the legal obligation of performing these natural duties. The extent to which they are evaded where such legal requirement does not exist is probably not generally appreciated. The committee have had before them statistics of one such country, which show that in 8 per cent. of the collisions reported the master of one of the vessels left the other to take care of herself and her people, and got away without being known. In these instances there was loss of life upon some of the vessels so abandoned, some went down, and all suffered damage. . It would seem, then, that any effective measure which might prevent such a practice, or make it less frequent, would not only be in the interest of humanity, but also aid in securing justice in regard to the rights of property. The committee, therefore, are of the opinion that in case of collision between two vessels, the master or person in charge of each vessel should be required, so far as he can without danger to his own vessel, crew, or passengers, to stay by the other vessel until he has ascertained that she has no need of further assistance, and to render to the other vessel, her master, crew, and passengers, such assistance as may be practicable and necessary in order to save them from any danger caused by the collision; and also to give to the master or person in charge of the other vessel the name of his own vessel, and of her port of registry, or of the port or place to which she belongs, and the names of the ports and places from which and to which she is bound.

So far as the committee can learn, the laws of those countries which have taken action upon the subject are to the above effect, substantially agreeing in defining the duties of masters, although the infraction of the law is differently dealt with in the different countries.

In expressing the foregoing opinion the committee are unanimous, but a minority think the Conference should indicate what, in their opinion, the penalty of failure to comply with the duties prescribed should be. The majority, however, do not deem this necessary, believing that the consequence of disobedience to their laws can and will be properly taken care of by the several governments, without suggestion from the Conference.

For the information of the Conference, the enactments of Great Britain upon the subject, which prescribed severer penalties for disregard of the duties imposed than those of any other nation, are appended to this report. (See Appendix A.)

"(b) APPARATUS FOR LIFE-SAVING TO BE CARRIED ON BOARD SHIP. (LIFE-BOATS, LIFE-PRESERVERS, LIFE-RAFTS, PUMPS, AND FIRE-EXTINGUISHING APPARATUS.)"

The Government of Chili has made the most liberal provision that the committee have knowledge of for the safety of life on shipboard, requiring her vessels to be furnished with boats sufficient in number and capacity to afford the greatest security possible to everybody on board in case of disaster. (See Appendix B.) The committee, however, do not regard the universal application of this provision as practicable under existing conditions; they believe that the basis upon which an agreement between the several nations is most likely to be established is to be found in the "Rules of the Board of Trade" of Great Britain, under the "Merchant Shipping (Life-saving Appliances) act of 1888," which are to go into effect on March 31, 1890. These rules provide for almost all cases that may arise under the vicissitudes of navigation, while they are sufficiently elastic to admit of adjustment to the various conditions existing in the countries interested without violating their spirit. (See Appendix C.)

The committee also recommend the extension of the principle of these rules to all smaller craft as far as practicable, and that each vessel of this class should carry at least one life-buoy of approved pattern and material, and for every person on board an efficient life-belt or jacket.

The means of extinguishing fire on vessels has become to a considerable extent a matter relating to their construction, and the observation of members of the committee is that in most vessels recently built great care is taken to make due provision in this respect, it being for the interest of the owners to do so. Most of the maritime nations have also enacted laws which provide for a suitable equipment of pumps and other devices. Perhaps, therefore, there is now no great necessity for action upon the subject by the Conference. However this may be, it would be impracticable for the committee to prescribe any definite system, as it would involve a careful classification of vessels and a thorough study of a variety of apparatus, the necessary information and data for which it would be impossible to procure, properly consider, and report upon in season to be of avail to the Conference.

"(c) THE USE OF OIL AND THE NECESSARY APPARATUS FOR ITS USE."

There has been placed before the committee much matter relating to this subject, consisting chiefly of reports from vessels that have used oil for calming dangerous seas, accounts of trials and experiments made under various conditions, deductions drawn from such reports and experiments, and directions for the application of oil under various conditions and circumstances.

An examination of this material and the information the committee already possessed have led to the conclusion that there need be no longer any doubt that the proper application of oil is efficacious on the open sea, but that there are conditions under which the action of breaking waves is not thereby much, if at all, modified. Its effect on the surf over bars at the mouths of rivers and those lying off beaches is especially doubtful. A circular letter relative to the "use of oil at sea," issued by the Board of Trade of Great Britain, says: "In a surf, or waves breaking on a bar, where a mass of liquid is in actual motion in shallow water the effect of the oil is uncertain, as nothing can prevent the larger waves from breaking under such circumstances, but even here it is of some service." Other official documents declare that in an exhaustive series of experiments no effect whatever was produced upon the surf breaking over the outlying bars of beaches.

The committee are of the opinion that all sea-going vessels should be supplied with a proper quantity of animal or vegetable oil (which seems to be more effective than mineral), and with suitable appliances for its distribution. For ordinary voyages the quantity need not be large. The best means of distributing it that have been brought to the attention of the committee appear to be those specified by Vice-Admiral Cloué, published in a circular issued by the French Government. (See Appendix D.)

"(d) UNIFORM INSPECTIONS AS TO b AND c."

If the maritime nations should agree upon uniform requirements in respect to life-saving apparatus to be carried on board ship, and to the use of oil and the necessary apparatus for its use, uniform inspections might perhaps be advantageous, but it would be impossible to formulate an adequate system for this purpose without knowing definitely what these requirements might be, and even then it would be doubtful, considering the great diversity of administrative methods and machinery in different countries, whether any practicable system could be devised that would be acceptable to all.

2. SAVING OF LIFE AND PROPERTY FROM SHIPWRECK BY OPERATIONS FROM SHORE.

The committee have had before them a number of valuable papers describing the organization and methods of institutions for the saving of life from shipwreck, and indicating the extent and results of their work. These will be found in Appendices E and F. An examination of them clearly shows that these institutions are all managed by men whose hearts are in their work, and who may be trusted to use every means known to them for perfecting the apparatus and methods employed for the rescue of unfortunates cast upon their shores. The organization of the service in each country must necessarily vary according to the condition and temper of the people and the character and habits of the coast population from which the men constituting the effective life-saving force must be drawn. It is therefore deemed impracticable to formulate any definite rules which would be applicable to all alike.

It appears desirable, however, that the officers of every organization should study the features of the others in order that they may adopt such improvements as seem suitable for their own. Some of the establishments appear to have been brought to a high degree of excellence.

It seems desirable that careful attention should be given to the frequent drilling and exercising of life-saving crews. It is also deemed important that a watch or patrol should, whenever practicable, be established upon dangerous coasts at night, and during thick weather by day, not only for the early discovery of wrecks, but in order to warn off vessels that may be incautiously standing into danger. Coast guards are established in various countries for the prevention of smuggling, and where this is the case they can be utilized to give timely notice and assistance to life-saving crews, or even to constitute such crews, as is already done in some countries.

With regard to special varieties of life-boats and other appliances, the committee believe that the matter can be safely trusted to the judgment and discretion of the officers in charge of the life-saving institutions of the several countries. The requirements vary so greatly upon different coasts that boats and appliances effective in one place are often ill adapted or useless in another. Besides, the preferences of the men employed have to be considered, they usually having greater confidence in particular models because they are accustomed to them. Confidence in the appliances a crew is required to use is, in general, an admitted essential to success. No one can judge of these matters so well as the officers whose duty it is to study the local conditions, and who are thoroughly acquainted with the prejudices and habitudes of the men.

It is desirable that officers of life-saving institutions should generally communicate freely with each other with reference to any improvements that may occur to them, either in apparatus, methods, or organization, with a view both to the diffusion of information concerning such matters, and to establishing an international comity with regard to a beneficent work.

With reference to subsection d, ("uniform means of transmitting information between stranded vessels and the shore,") the committee would say that co-operation between mariners upon a wrecked vessel and those who wish to assist them upon shore is of the highest importance. The most earnest attempts at aid may be rendered nugatory if the shipwrecked are not aware of what is required of them. In order to secure this co-operation various means have been devised in maritime countries, such as attaching tally-boards to the lines of the beach apparatus; the publication of instructions in the official log-books distributed to vessels; the issuing of pamphlets or cards of such instructions, or the very excellent method of posting in the forecastle, or some convenient place in a vessel, a durable placard showing by illustrations the manner in which life-saving lines are to be secured on board, and giving necessary instructions relative thereto.

All these measures are good, but the instructions have not been as generally distributed among vessels of all nationalities as they should be, and with a view to the universal diffusion of this information, it is recommended that a uniform system of issuing and distributing such instructions be adopted by the several maritime nations.

The committee are also of the opinion that the instructions generally issued do not adequately provide for co-operation between the ship and the shore, and that they should be supplemented by a few simple signals for the purpose of direct communication. The international code can often be used in the day-time, but a still more simple system should be provided for the few signals required. It is believed that the signals absolutely necessary can be reduced to very few, and that the adoption and publication of such a system would be of great benefit in the emergencies of shipwreck.

If it be determined to establish an international code of night signals, such as is referred to in general division 8 of the programme ("night signals for communicating information at sea"), the signals needed for communicating at night between wrecked vessels and the shore ought to be incorporated therein. If it should prove impracticable to adopt a system of night signals for the international code, it may yet be worth considering whether the few signals needed for use at wrecks ought not to be adopted. Such a system is recommended by the committee, and will be found described in detail in the fourth resolution at the close of this report. Every signal there mentioned has been found necessary in emergencies that have actually arisen in service.

3. OFFICIAL INQUIRIES INTO CAUSES AND CIRCUMSTANCES OF SHIP-WRECKS AND OTHER CASUALTIES.

For countries which have not already provided by legislative enactments for official inquiries into the causes and circumstances of ship-wrecks or other accidents to vessels that are of serious importance, the adoption of such laws is recommended, as it is believed that they are the most effective means by which masters and officers of vessels can be impressed with a proper sense of the serious responsibility that rests upon them, and that they therefore constitute one of the most important safeguards for life and property afloat that it is possible to devise. They would also add to the efficiency of laws designed to prevent the sending out of unseaworthy and overloaded vessels where such laws exist, and where they do not, would, to a certain extent, operate in their stead. They would, moreover, give information which might be of great value in showing the general causes and distribution of wrecks, and indirectly indicate the methods by which casualties might be averted or lessened.

The committee have formulated the foregoing recommendations into the following propositions, which are submitted for the consideration of the Conference:

1. *In every case of collision between two vessels, it shall be the duty of the master or person in charge of each vessel, if, and so far as he can do so without danger to his own vessel, crew, and passengers (if any), to stay by the other vessel until he has ascertained that she has no need of further assistance, and to render to the other vessel, her master, crew, and passengers (if any), such assistance as may be practicable, and as may be necessary in order to save them from any danger caused by the collision; and also to give to the master or person in charge of the other vessel, the name of his own vessel, and of her port of registry, or of the port or place to which she belongs, and also the names of the ports and places from which and to which she is bound.

2. *Resolved*, That the Conference approve of the principle of the "Rules made by the Board of Trade of Great Britain under the Merchant Shipping (Life-Saving Appliances) Act, 1888," relating to boats and appliances to be carried on board ship for saving life; and recommend that the several Governments adopt measures to secure compliance with this principle in regard to such boats and appliances for vessels of 150 tons and upwards, gross tonnage.

It is also recommended that the principle of these Rules be extended to all smaller craft, as far as practicable; and that each vessel of this

---

* NOTE.—This proposition is stated in the form and language of the "New Section" proposed November 26, 1889, to be added to the "Rules of the Road;" the consideration of which the Conference voted to postpone, pending the presentation of this report.

class should carry at least one life-buoy of approved pattern and material, and for every person on board an efficient life-belt or jacket.

3. *Resolved,* That the Conference recommend that the several Governments require all their sea-going vessels to carry a sufficient quantity of animal or vegetable oil, for the purpose of calming the sea in rough weather, together with suitable means for applying it.

4. *Resolved,* That the Conference recommend that all institutions for saving life from wrecked vessels prepare uniform instructions to mariners with reference to their co-operation with those attempting their rescue from the shore, and that said instructions include the following signals:

Upon the discovery of a wreck by night the life-saving force will burn a red pyrotechnic light or a red rocket to signify: " You are seen; assistance will be given as soon as possible."

A red flag waved on shore by day, or a red light, or rocket, or red Roman candle displayed by night, will signify, " Haul away."

A white flag waved on shore by day, or a white light slowly swung back and forth, or a white rocket or white Roman candle fired by night will signify, " Slack away."

Two flags, a white and a red, waved at the same time on shore by day, or two lights, a white and a red, slowly swung at the same time, or a blue pyrotechnic light burned by night, will signify, " Do not attempt to land in your own boats. It is impossible."

A man on shore beckoning, by day, or two torches burning near together by night, will signify, " This is the best place to land."

Any of these signals may be answered from the vessel as follows : In the day time—by waving a flag, a handkerchief, a hat, or even the hand ; at night—by firing a rocket, a blue light or a gun, or by showing a light over the ship's gunwale for a short time and then concealing it.

And it is recommended that the several Governments take measures to keep all their sea-going vessels supplied with copies of such instructions.

5. *Resolved,* That the Conference recommend that the several nations provide by legislative enactments for official inquiry into the causes and circumstances of all shipwrecks and other serious casualties happening to their vessels.

The committee have examined a large number of devices and projects relating to the saving of life from shipwreck, a list of which will be found below. Many of them indicate considerable ingenuity, and their number and variety show the great amount of interest and attention that this subject is receiving. The committee have consulted them freely in reaching conclusions relative to the topics placed before them, but have not deemed it advisable to make specific recommendations regarding any particular device or plan, believing that such action is not expected of them by the Conference. Furthermore, to reach conclusions with regard to many of them would involve experiments or trials beyond the power of the committee. To recommend those whose merits are already known to the committee or which require no such tests might be unfair to the others.

> S. I. KIMBALL, *Chairman.*
> *Delegate for the United States.*
> THO. VERBRUGGHE,
>> *Delegate for Belgium.*
> O. VIEL,
>> *Delegate for Chili.*
> A. M. BISBEE,
>> *Delegate for China.*
> E. RICHARD,
>> *Delegate for France.*
> A. FEIGEL,
>> *Delegate for Germany.*
> HENRY WYATT,
>> *Delegate for Great Britain.*
> VAN STEYN,
>> *Delegate for the Netherlands.*
> B. VEGA DE SEOANE,
>> *Delegate for Spain.*

Devices and projects submitted to the committee.

No.	Name and address of writer.	Subject.	Remarks of committee.
1	James W. Crabbe, New York·..	Life-boats and passage-ways on steamers.	Examined. Referred to Committee No. 1.
2	Tucker-Kayess and Harrison...	Life-saving direction rocket ..	Examined.
3	Mr. Bing, Christiana, Norway. Forwarded by Mr. Flood.	Apparatus for discharging oil..	Do.
4	G. N. McKibben, 46 W. Fifty-first street, New York.	Oil-distributing cartridge.......	Do.
5	Aloha Vivarttaa, 75 South street, New York.	Regarding life-saving service ...	Do.
6	T. L. Reed, Laporte City, Iowa ..	Device for detaching and controlling life-buoys.	Do.
7	Henry Hentz, 8 South William street, New York.	Recommends that vessels carry line-throwing projectiles.	No description or device.
8	R. F. Hunter, 225 East Capitol street, Washington, D. C.	Cunningham life-saving rocket.	Examined.
9	A. G. Sorensen, Stockholm, Sweden.	Recommends that relief ships be stationed at suitable points on the Atlantic Ocean.	Do.
10	John Wainwright, Wilmington, Del.	Recommends the use of oil to calm the sea.	Proposes no system or device.
11	John Ericson, Sabine Pass, Louisiana.	Automatic oil-distributor for ships.	Examined.
12	Albert H. Walker, 274 Main street, Hartford, Conn.	Sea-oiling rocket and sea-oiling projectile.	Do.
13	Daniel Ammen, rear-admiral, U. S. Navy.	Balsa life-raft	Do.
14	Hunt and Bartleman, 22 Congress street, Boston, Mass.	Hunt's life-line projectile and gun. Hunt's sea-flames or life-buoy flares.	Do.
15	Miller and McCorvie, Arrowtown, Otago, New Zealand.	Device for conveying a line ashore by means of a kite.	Do.
16	D. R. Dawson, 57 Meadowside, Dundee, Scotland.	Gun for throwing life-lines and signals.	No description or model submitted.
17	A. Van Vliet, 50 North First street, Patterson, N. J.	Suggests that lights should be projected through fog.	Not within the scope of committee.
18	A. G. Belden & Co., 145 Maiden Lane, New York.	Wave-quelling oil..............	Examined.
19	Stewart Newell, 121 West Fifteenth street, New York.	Proposes that vessels patrol the principal routes of European travel to afford relief to distressed vessels.	Do.

Devices and projects submitted to the committee—Continued.

No.	Name and address of writer.	Subject.	Remarks of committee.
20	Jno. R. Winton, North Carolina..	Patent signals to prevent collisions at sea.	Examined.
21	Alfred St. Leger, Hobart, Tasmania.	Proposes use of bows and arrows for effecting line communication between wrecked vessels and the shore, and between vessels at sea.	Do.
22	Cavendish S. Lapalio, Smollet street, Abury, N. S. Wales.	Anti-colliding safety check for vessels.	Not within the scope of committee.
23	Capt. D. R. Post, Deep River, Conn.	Suggests use of extra light when off Cape Horn.	Do.
24	A. B. Wyckoff, lieutenant, U. S. Navy.	Advocating the use of oil at sea..	Examined.
25	— Wyckoff, 263 Ninth street, N. E., Philadelphia, Pa.	Imperishable floating safe	Not within the scope of committee.
26	J. T. Walker, captain U. S. Army, New York.	Refers to establishment of a system of international deepsea light-houses.	Examined.
27	Robert McDonald, New York...	Venetian shutter for stopping leaks and repairing damaged hulls.	Examined. Referred to Committee No. 1.
28	T. B. Viele	Patent for stopping leaks in vessels.	Do.
29	N. C. Jessup, Suffolk Co., N. J...	Patent life-boat.................	No description or device.
30	Thomas Raftery, New York ...	Ship's fenders..................	Examined. Referred to Committee No. 1.
31	Armistead Rust, Ensign, U. S. Navy.	Device for improved life-buoy..	Examined.
32	A. D. Newell, New Brunswick, N. J.	Floating life-line carrier........	Do.
33	American Patent-Right Corporation. Philadelphia, Pa.	Leak-stopper after collision.....	Examined. Referred to Committee No. 1.
34	David Kahnweiler, 146 Worth street, New York.	Improved patent life-preserver and metallic life-raft.	Examined.
35	Alfred Marshall, Woodbury, N. J.	Directions for putting on life-preserver.	Do.
36	Philip Hichborn, naval constructor, U. S. Navy.	Franklin life-buoy	Do.
37	J. R. Selfridge, Lieutenant, U. S. Navy.	Supply box to be carried in life or quarter boats.	Do.
38	New York Branch Hydrographic Office. Mersey Docks and Harbor Board. National Board of Marine Underwriters, New York. Philadelphia Maritime Exchange. Liverpool Humane Society.	Views on programme of subjects.	Do.
39	Steamer *Old Point Comfort*. Bay Line steamer *Georgia*. Nova Scotia ship *Sapphire*.	......do	Do.
40	Sergeant Paul Daniels, U. S. Signal Service. Mr. R. B. Forbes. Mr. D. A. Nash, Pilot Commissioner, New York. Oelrichs & Co., agents North German Lloyd Steam-ship Company.	......do	Do.
41	Branch Hydrographic Offices— New York, Norfolk, Boston, San Francisco, and Baltimore	General information gained in interviews with masters of vessels.	Do.
42	Branch Hydrographic Office, Philadelphia.	Views on programme of subjects.	Do.
43	Branch Hydrographic Office, Portland, Oregon.	......do.....................	Do.
44	Geo. P. Blow, Ensign, U. S. Navy	Report on subjects to be considered by the Conference.	Do.
45	George Learman, 33 South street, New York.	Standard self-detaching davit fall hook.	Do.
46	Wm. C. Foulks, 153 North Fifteenth street, Philadelphia, Pa.	Bow propellers to aid in steering.	Not within the scope of committee.
47	David W. Low, Gloucester, Mass.	Life-saving apparatus for boats.	Examined.
48	F. Olaf Larsen, Copenhagen ...	Oil-distributing bag	Do.
49	Branch Hydrographic Office, New York.	Views on various points in programme of subjects.	Do.
50	Northern Maritime Conference, Copenhagen.	Memorandum on general subjects of programme.	Do.
51	W. Guthrie, Chicago, Ill........	Suggests use of carbonic acid gas in extinguishing fire.	Received too late for consideration by committee.
52	H. F. Coombs, St. John, New Brunswick.	A narrative of dangers of the sea	Examined.

APPENDIX A.

DUTIES OF MASTERS IN CASE OF COLLISION.

[Extract from " merchant shipping act, 1873."]

SEC. 16. In every case of collision between two vessels it shall be the duty of the master or person in charge of each vessel, if and so far as he can do so without danger to his own vessel, crew, and passengers (if any), to stay by the other vessel until he has ascertained that she has no need of further assistance, and to render to the other vessel, her master, crew, and passengers (if any), such assistance as may be practicable and as may be necessary in order to save them from any danger caused by the collision; and also to give to the master or person in charge of the other vessel the name of his own vessel, and of her port of registry or of the port or place to which she belongs, and also the names of the ports and places from which and to which she is bound.

If he fails so to do, and no reasonable cause for such failure is shown, the collision shall, in the absence of proof to the contrary, be deemed to have been caused by his wrongful act, neglect, or default.

Every master or person in charge of a British vessel who fails, without reasonable cause, to render such assistance or give such information as aforesaid, shall be deemed guilty of a misdemeanor, and if he is a certificated officer an inquiry into his conduct may be held, and his certificate may be canceled or suspended.

APPENDIX B.

EXTRACT FROM THE LAWS OF CHILI.

[Translation.]

CHAPTER III.—Small boats.

ARTICLE 13.

The vessels to which Article 1 refers shall keep empty, in good state for service, and ready to be launched at sea at any moment, the number of small boats in proportion to the crew, specified below:

Crew of 2 to 5 men, including the captain, 1 boat, with capacity for 10 men.

Crew of from 6 to 10 men, including the captain, 2 boats, with capacity for 20 men.

Crew of from 11 to 20 men, including the captain, 3 boats, with capacity for 40 men.

Crew of from 21 to 30 men, including the captain, 4 boats, with capacity for 50 men.

Crew of from 31 to 50 men, including the captain, 4 boats, with capacity for 70 men.

Crew of from 51 to 70 men, including the captain, 5 boats, with capacity for 100 men.

Crew of from 71 to 100 men, including the captain, 6 boats, with capacity for 150 men.

For each gang of 30 men exceeding one hundred, a larger boat shall be required with a capacity for 50 men.

In order to determine the capacity of a boat, its tonnage shall be considered; the capacity for one individual being reckoned equal to each fraction of .15 of a ton contained, if it is a double-benched boat, and .25 if it is single.

ARTICLE 14.

The dimensions of each one of the boats may vary according to the discretion of the ship-owner, providing always that none of the boats equipped shall be of less than $1\frac{1}{2}$ tons' burden, and that the total shall reach the tonnage required by regulation according to the number of individuals of its equipment.

Nevertheless, those vessels that carry a crew of more than 40 men shall replace at least one of its boats by a life-saving boat which can conveniently accommodate 30 men.

ARTICLE 15.

All the boats of the equipment shall be fitted out completely and in good condition, the captains seeing that the oars, masts, and yards are found fastened to the thwarts, and the sails and tools properly arranged in sacks and cases, in order that in an emergency they may be adjusted without difficulty in the several boats to which they belong.

Equal care shall be taken that they are kept clean, painted, and covered, and that they are washed sufficiently to prevent their becoming dry.

The loss, damage, or destruction of the small boats must be repaired at the first available station.

APPENDIX C.

REPORT MADE TO THE BOARD OF TRADE BY THE COMMITTEE APPOINTED BY THAT BOARD IN PURSUANCE OF "THE MERCHANT SHIPPING (LIFE-SAVING APPLIANCES) ACT, 1888" (51 AND 52 VICT., C. 24).

[Presented to both houses of Parliament by command of Her Majesty.]

LIFE-SAVING APPLIANCES COMMITTEE,
7 Whitehall Gardens, London, S. W., April 11, 1889.

To the Right Hon. Sir MICHAEL E. HICKS BEACH, Bart., M. P.,
President of the Board of Trade.

SIR: In compliance with the request contained in your minute of the 12th of November, 1888, we have the honor to report that we have carefully considered the matters referred to in the second schedule of the "Merchant Shipping (Life-saving Appliances) Act, 1888," viz:

"(1) The arranging of British ships into classes, having regard to the services in which they are employed, to the nature and direction of the voyage, and to the number of persons carried.

"(2) The number and description of the boats, life-boats, life-rafts, life-jackets, and life-buoys to be carried by British ships, according to the class in which they are arranged and the mode of their construction; also the equipments to be carried by the boats and rafts and the methods to be provided to get the boats and other life-saving appliances into the water; such methods may include oil for use in stormy weather.

"(3) The quantity, quality, and description of buoyant apparatus to be carried on board ships carrying passengers, either in addition to or in substitution for boats, life-boats, life-rafts, life-jackets, and life-buoys."

We now submit herewith rules which we have prepared, and which we advise should be made under the act. These rules if adopted will, we think, insure that ships of different classes shall be provided with such appliances for saving life at sea as (having regard to the nature of the services in which they are employed and the avoidance of undue incumbrance of the ship's decks) are best adapted for securing the safety of their crews and passengers.

As we are, fortunately, unanimous in our recommendation of the rules submitted, we do not think it necessary to trouble you with any account of the reasons that have led to our conclusions further than to state that we have throughout proceeded on the assumption that we had simply to arrange British ships into classes, having regard among other matters to the larger or smaller number of persons they are likely to carry, and to advise what life-saving appliances can properly be provided for the ships of each class.

We have, etc.,

THOS. H. ISMAY, *Chairman.*
J. G. S. ANDERSON, *Vice-Chairman.*
DONALD KENNEDY.
G. A. LAWS.
NATHL. DUNLOP.
G. ELDRIDGE.
WM. JOHN.
GEO. ARMSTRONG.
JOHN LEES.
HY. JNO. WARD.
MATTHEW CALLAGHAN.
TOM SUMNER LEMON.
S. I. DaCOSTA.
C. R. TATHAM.
JAS. B. BUTCHER.

WALTER J. HOWELL,
Secretary.

P. S.—We have shown some appreciation of the importance of efficient subdivision of ships in class 1, division A, par. *g*, of these rules, but we consider it our duty to further express our sense of the

S. Ex. 53, pt. 3——13

importance of the question, and to recommend that it should be investigated by a committee of duly-qualified persons, the subject as a whole having been held to be outside the scope of the reference to this committee.

THOS. H. ISMAY, *Chairman.*
J. G. S. ANDERSON, *Vice-Chairman.*
DONALD KENNEDY.
G. A. LAWS.
G. ELDRIDGE.
WM. JOHN.
GEO. ARMSTRONG.
JOHN LEES.
HY. JNO. WARD.
MATTHEW CALLAGHAN.
*
S. I. DaCOSTA.
C. R. TATHAM.
JAS. B. BUTCHER.

WALTER J. HOWELL,
Secretary.

RULES MADE BY THE BOARD OF TRADE UNDER "THE MERCHANT SHIPPING (LIFE-SAVING APPLIANCES) ACT, 1888" (51 & 52 VICT. C. 24), TO COME INTO FORCE ON THE 31ST MARCH, 1890.

[At the Council Chamber, Whitehall, this 28th day of June, 1889.]

Present: The right honorable Sir Michael E. Hicks Beach, Bart., M. P.

In pursuance of the provisions of the merchant shipping (life-saving appliances) act, 1888, the Board of Trade do hereby make the annexed rules relating to life-saving appliances. These rules shall come into effect on the 31st March, 1890.

M. E. HICKS BEACH.

"MERCHANT SHIPPING (LIFE-SAVING APPLIANCES) ACT, 1888."

For the purposes of these rules, British ships shall be arranged into the following classes:

---

* NOTE.—Mr. T. S. Lemon is now absent abroad.

CLASS 1.—DIVISION A.

RULES AND TABLE FOR STEAM-SHIPS CARRYING EMIGRANT PASSENGERS SUBJECT TO ALL THE PROVISIONS OF THE "PASSENGERS ACTS."

(*a*) Ships of this division shall carry boats *placed under davits*, having proper appliances for getting them into the water, in number and capacity not less than are given in the following table; the boats to be equipped and of the description defined in the general rules appended hereto.

(*b*) Provided that no ship of this division shall be required to carry more boats so placed than will furnish sufficient accommodation for all persons on board,

(c) Masters or owners of ships of this division claiming to carry fewer boats than are given in the following table must declare before the collector or other officer of customs, at the time of clearance, that the boats actually placed under davits are sufficient to accommodate all persons on board, allowing 10 cubic feet of boat capacity per Rule 2, page 9, for each adult person, or " statute adult."

(d) Table for Class 1 (Division A).

Gross tonnage.	Minimum number of boats to be placed under davits.	Total minimum cubic contents of boats to be placed under davits. L.×B.×D.×.6.	Gross tonnage.	Minimum number of boats to be placed under davits.	Total minimum cubic contents of boats to be placed under davits. L.×B.×D.×.6.
1.	2.	3.	1.	2.	3.
9,000 and upwards.	14	5,250	4,000 and under 4,250	8	2,800
8,500 and under 9,000	14	5,100	3,750 and under 4,000	8	2,700
8,000 and under 8,500	14	5,000	3,500 and under 3,750	8	2,600
7,750 and under 8,000	12	4,700	3,250 and under 3,500	8	2,500
7,500 and under 7,750	12	4,600	3,000 and under 3,250	8	2,400
7,250 and under 7,500	12	4,500	2,750 and under 3,000	6	2,100
7,000 and under 7,250	12	4,400	2,500 and under 2,750	6	2,050
6,750 and under 7,000	12	4,300	2,250 and under 2,500	6	2,000
6,500 and under 6,750	12	4,200	2,000 and under 2,250	6	1,900
6,250 and under 6,500	12	4,100	1,750 and under 2,000	6	1,800
6,000 and under 6,250	12	4,000	1,500 and under 1,750	6	1,700
5,750 and under 6,000	10	3,700	1,250 and under 1,500	6	1,500
5,500 and under 5,750	10	3,600	1,000 and under 1,250	4	1,200
5,250 and under 5,500	10	3,500	750 and under 1,000	4	1,000
5,000 and under 5,250	10	3,400	500 and under 750	4	800
4,750 and under 5,000	10	3,300	250 and under 500	2	400
4,500 and under 4,750	8	2,900	150 and under 250	2	300
4,250 and under 4,500	8	2,900			

NOTE.—Where in vessels already fitted the required *cubic contents* of boats placed under davits is provided, although by a smaller *number* of boats than the *minimum* required by this table, such boats shall be regarded as complying with these rules.

(e) Not less than half the number of boats placed under davits shall be boats of section A, page 9, or section B, page 9. The remaining boats may also be of such description, or may, in the option of the ship-owner, conform to section C, page 9, or section D, page 9, provided that not more than two boats shall be of section D.

(f) If the boats placed under davits in accordance with the foregoing table (d) do not furnish sufficient accommodation for all persons on board, then additional wood, metal, collapsible or other boats of approved description (whether placed under davits or otherwise) or approved life-rafts shall be carried.

Subject to the provision contained in paragraph b of these Rules, such additional boats or rafts shall be of at least such carrying capacity that they and the boats required to be placed under davits by table d provide together in the aggregate double the *minimum* cubic contents required by column 3 of that table.

All such additional boats or rafts shall be placed as conveniently for being available as the ship's arrangements admit of, having regard to the avoidance of undue incumbrance of the ship's deck, and to the safety of the ship for her voyage.

(*g*) When ships are divided into efficient water-tight compartments, so that, with any two of them in free communication with the sea, the ship will remain afloat in moderate weather, they shall only be required to carry additional boats or life-rafts of one-half of the capacity required by paragraph *f* of these rules.

(*h*) In addition to the life-saving appliances before mentioned ships of this division shall carry not less than one approved life-buoy (Rules 11*a*, or 11*b*, pages 10, 11) for every boat placed under davits. They shall also carry approved life-belts (Rule 10, page 10) or other similar approved articles of equal buoyancy suitable for being worn on the person, so that there may be at least one for each person on board the ship.

CLASS 1.—DIVISION B.

RULES FOR SAILING SHIPS CARRYING EMIGRANT PASSENGERS SUBJECT TO ALL THE PROVISIONS OF THE "PASSENGERS ACTS."

(*a*) Ships of this division shall carry boats in accordance with the table *d* provided for Division A of this class, and such boats shall be, as far as practicable, placed under davits, with proper appliances for getting them into the water, to the satisfaction of the Board of Trade officer; such of these boats as are not placed under davits being so carried that they can also be readily got into the water to the satisfaction of the Board of Trade officer.

(*b*) If the boats so carried do not furnish sufficient accommodation for all persons on board, then additional life-saving appliances shall be supplied as for ships in Division A of this class.

(*c*) Provided that no ship in this division shall be required to carry more boats than will furnish accommodation for all persons on board.

(*d*) Approved life-belts (Rule 10, page 10) or other similar approved articles shall be carried as required for ships of Class 1, Division A, and also one life-buoy (Rule 11*a* or 11*b*, pages 10, 11) for each boat of wood or metal.

CLASS 2.—DIVISION A.

RULES FOR FOREIGN-GOING STEAM-SHIPS HAVING PASSENGER CERTIFICATES UNDER THE "MERCHANT SHIPPING ACTS."

Ships of this division shall be subject to the same requirements as those in Class 1, Division A.

CLASS 2.—DIVISION B.

RULES FOR FOREIGN-GOING SAILING SHIPS CARRYING PASSENGERS, BUT NOT SUBJECT TO ALL THE PROVISIONS OF THE "PASSENGERS ACTS."

Ships of this division shall be subject to the same requirements as those in Class 1, Division B.

CLASS 3.—DIVISION A.

RULES FOR FOREIGN-GOING STEAM-SHIPS NOT CERTIFIED TO CARRY PASSENGERS.

(a) Ships of this division shall carry, on each side, at least so many and such boats of wood or metal placed under davits (of which one on each side shall be a boat of Section A, page 9, or of Section B, page 9), that the boats on each side of the ship shall be sufficient to accommodate all persons on board. They shall have proper appliances for getting the boats into the water.

(b) They shall carry approved life-belts, as required for ships of Class 1, Division A.

(c) They shall carry not less than six approved life-buoys (Rule 11a or 11b, pages 10, 11).

CLASS 3.—DIVISION B.

RULES FOR FOREIGN-GOING SAILING SHIPS NOT CARRYING PASSENGERS.

(a) Ships of this division shall carry boats in accordance with the table provided for Class 1, Division B, and in addition thereto one good serviceable boat of Section D, page 9. Such boats shall be, as far as practicable, placed under davits, with proper appliances for getting them into the water to the satisfaction of the Board of Trade officer; such boats as are not placed under davits being so carried that they also can readily be got into the water to the satisfaction of the Board of Trade officer.

(b) They shall carry approved life-belts, as required for ships in Class 1, division B, and also one life-buoy (Rule 11a or 11b, pages 10, 11), for each boat of wood or metal.

CLASS 4.—DIVISION A.

RULES FOR STEAM-SHIPS HAVING PASSENGER CERTIFICATES UNDER THE "MERCHANT SHIPPING ACTS" AUTHORIZING THEM TO CARRY PASSENGERS ANYWHERE WITHIN THE HOME TRADE LIMITS; THAT IS TO SAY, BETWEEN PLACES IN THE UNITED KINGDOM OR BETWEEN THE UNITED KINGDOM AND PORTS IN EUROPE BETWEEN THE RIVER ELBE AND BREST.

(a) Ships of this division shall carry boats placed under davits in accordance with the rules and table provided for ships in Class 1, Division A.

(b) If the boats placed under davits in accordance with this requirement do not furnish sufficient accommodation for all persons on board, then additional approved boats or approved life-rafts shall be supplied as for ships of Class 1, Division A.

(*c*) Provided that if (having regard to the avoidance of undue incumbrance of the ship's deck, and to the safety of the ship for her voyage) it is not practicable for a ship of this division to carry additional approved boats or approved life-rafts as are required for ships of Class 1, Division A, *f*, the deficiency so caused may be made up by the supply of an equivalent number of approved buoyant deck seats or other approved buoyant deck fittings to the satisfaction of the Board of Trade officer.

(*d*) Ships of this division shall carry not less than six approved life-buoys (Rule 11 *a* or 11 *b*, pages 10, 11).

(*e*) They shall also carry, in addition to the boats and appliances required above, approved life-belts (Rule 10, page 10) or other similar approved articles of equal buoyancy suitable for being worn on the person, so that there may be at least one for each person on board the ship.

CLASS 4.—DIVISION B.

RULES FOR STEAM-SHIPS IN THE SAME TRADES NOT CERTIFIED TO CARRY PASSENGERS.

(*a*) Ships of this division shall carry, on each side, at least so many and such boats of wood or metal placed under davits (of which one on each side shall be a boat of Section A, page 9, or of Section B, page 9), that the boats on each side of the ship shall be sufficient to accommodate all persons on board. They shall have proper appliances for getting the boats into the water.

(*b*) They shall carry approved life-belts as for ships of Class 1, Division A.

(*c*) They shall carry not less than four approved life-buoys (Rule 11 *a*, or 11 *b*, pages 10, 11).

CLASS 4.—DIVISION C.

RULES FOR SAILING SHIPS IN THE SAME TRADES NOT CARRYING PASSENGERS.

(*a*) Ships of this division shall carry a boat or boats of wood or metal, at least sufficient for all persons on board, and in such a position as to be readily got into the water, to the satisfaction of the Board of Trade officer. Each boat shall be provided with one gallon of vegetable or animal oil in a vessel of an approved pattern for distributing it in the water in rough weather.

(*b*) They shall carry an approved life-belt (Rule 10, page 10) for each person on board.

(*c*) They shall carry at least two approved life-buoys (Rule 11*a* or 11*b*, pages 10, 11.)

CLASS 5.

RULES FOR STEAM SHIPS HAVING PASSENGER CERTIFICATES AUTHOR-
IZING THEM TO CARRY PASSENGERS WITHIN CERTAIN SPECIFIED
LIMITS OF THE HOME TRADE; THAT IS TO SAY, ON SHORT SPECIFIED
PASSAGES ALONG THE COASTS OF THE UNITED KINGDOM, OR BE-
TWEEN GREAT BRITAIN AND IRELAND, OR BETWEEN GREAT BRITAIN
OR IRELAND AND THE ISLE OF MAN.

(a) Ships of this division shall, according to their tonnage, carry
boats placed under davits, as required by the table for ships in Class
1, Division A.

(b) If the boats placed under davits in accordance with the above
requirements do not furnish sufficient accommodation for all persons
on board, then additional boats or approved life-rafts shall be supplied
as for ships of Class 1, Division A.

(c) Provided that if (having regard to the avoidance of undue incumbrance of the ship's deck, and to the safety of the ship for her voyage)
it is not practicable for a ship of this division to carry additional approved boats or approved life-rafts as required for ships of Class 1,
Division A, the deficiency so caused may be made up by the supply of
an equivalent number of approved buoyant deck-seats or other approved buoyant deck-fittings to the satisfaction of the Board of Trade
officer.

(d) Ships of this division shall also carry approved life-belts (Rule
10, page 11) or other similar approved articles of equal buoyancy suitable for being worn on the person, so that there may be at least one for
each person on board the ship.

(e) At least one approved life-buoy (Rule 11a or 11b, pages 10, 11)
shall also be provided for each boat of wood or metal carried by the
ship, but in no case shall less than six approved life-buoys be provided.

CLASS 6.

RULES FOR STEAM-SHIPS CARRYING PASSENGERS ON SHORT EXCUR-
SIONS OR PLEASURE TRIPS TO SEA, OR IN ESTUARIES OR MOUTHS
OF RIVERS DURING DAYLIGHT, OR ACROSS THE STRAITS OF DOVER.

(a) Ships of this class shall carry at least two boats of Section A,
page 9, or Section B, page 9, placed under davits, and with proper appliances for getting them into the water.

(b) They shall also carry other boats, approved buoyant apparatus
(Rule 9, page 10) [and] [or] approved life-belts (Rule 10, page 10), sufficient (with the boats) to keep afloat all the persons on board the ship.

(c) At least four approved life-buoys (Rule 11 a or 11 b, pages 10, 11)
shall be carried.

CLASS 7.

RULES FOR STEAM-SHIPS CARRYING PASSENGERS ON RIVERS [AND] [OR] LAKES, BUT NOT GOING TO SEA OR INTO ROUGH WATERS.

(*a*) Ships of this class shall carry one boat in such a position that she can readily be got into the water. They shall also carry approved buoyant apparatus (Rule 9, page 10) or approved life-belts (Rule 10, page 10) and approved life-buoys (Rule 11, page 10) at least sufficient, together with the boat, to keep afloat all persons carried on board.

(*b*) At least four approved life-buoys shall be carried.

NOTE.—*A discretion to be exercised by the Board of Trade officer to relieve ferry-boats in narrow waters from the operation of Rule A of this class.*

GENERAL RULES.

NOTE.—*All boats shall be properly equipped as provided by these rules.*

(1) *Boats:*

Section A.—A boat of this section shall be a life-boat properly constructed of wood or metal, having for every 10 cubic feet of her capacity computed as in 2 at least 1½ cubic feet of strong and serviceable inclosed air-tight compartments, such that water can not find its way into them.

Section B.—A boat of this section shall be a life-boat properly constructed of wood or metal, having inside and outside buoyancy apparatus together equal in efficiency to the buoyancy apparatus provided for a boat of Section A. At least one-half of the buoyancy apparatus must be attached to the outside of the boat.

Section C.—A boat of this section shall be a life-boat properly constructed of wood or metal, having some buoyancy apparatus attached to the inside [and] [or] outside of the boat equal in efficiency to one-half of the buoyancy apparatus provided for a boat of Section A or Section B. At least one-half of the buoyancy apparatus must be attached to the outside of the boat.

Section D.—A boat of this section shall be a properly constructed boat of wood or metal.

Section E.—A boat of this section shall be a boat of approved form and material, which may be collapsible.

(2) *Cubic capacity.*—The cubic capacity of a boat shall be deemed to be her cubic capacity, ascertained (as in measuring ships for tonnage capacity) by Stirling's rule; but as the application of that rule entails much labor the following simple plan, which is approximately accurate,

may be adopted for general purposes, and when no question requiring absolutely correct adjustment is raised :

Measure the length and breadth outside and the depth inside. Multiply them together and by .6; the product is the capacity of the boat in cubic feet. Thus, a boat 28 feet long, 8 feet 6 inches broad, and 3 feet 6 inches deep will be regarded as having a capacity of $28 \times 8.5 \times 3.5 \times .6 = 499.8$, or 500 cubic feet. If the oars are pulled in row-locks the bottom of the row-lock is to be considered the gunwale of the boat for ascertaining her depth.

(3) *Number of persons for boats of Section A.*—The number of persons a boat of Section A shall be deemed fit to carry shall be the number of cubic feet ascertained as in 2 divided by 10. Thus, a boat whose cubic contents are 500 cubic feet is deemed to be sufficient for 50 adult persons. The space in the boat shall be sufficient for the seating of the persons carried in it and for the proper use of the oars.

(4) *Number of persons for other boats.*—The number of persons a boat of Section B, C, D, or E shall be deemed fit to carry shall be the number of cubic feet ascertained as in 2 divided by 8.

(5) *Appliances for lowering boats.*—Appliances for getting a boat into the water must fulfill the following conditions: Means are to be provided for speedily detaching the boats from the lower blocks of the davit tackles; the boats placed under davits are to be attached to the davit tackles and kept ready for service at any moment; the davits are to be strong enough and so spaced that the boats can be swung out with facility; the points of attachment of the boats to the davits are to be sufficient away from the ends of the boats to insure their being easily swung clear of the davits; the boats' chocks are to be such as can be expeditiously removed; the davits, falls, blocks, eye-bolts, rings, and the whole of the tackling are to be of sufficient strength; the boats' falls are to be long enough to lower the boat into the water with safety when the vessel is light; the life-lines fitted to the davits are to be long enough to reach the water when the vessel is light; and hooks are not to be attached to the lower tackle blocks.

(6) *Equipments for the collapsible or other boats and for life-rafts.*—In order to be properly equipped each boat shall be provided as follows:

(*a*) With the full (single-banked) complement of oars, and two spare oars.

(*b*) With two plugs for each plug-hole, attached with lanyards or chains, and one set and a half of thole-pins or crutches attached to the boats by sound lanyards.

(*c*) With a sea anchor, a baler, a rudder and a tiller, or yoke and yoke lines, a painter of sufficient length, and a boat-hook. The rudder and bailer to be attached to the boat by a sufficiently long lanyard and kept ready for use.

(*d*) A vessel to be kept filled with fresh water shall be provided for each boat.

(*e*) Life-rafts shall be fully provided with a suitable equipment.

(7) *Additional equipment for boats of Section A and Section B.*—In order to be properly equipped, each boat of Sections A and B, in addition to being provided with all the requisites laid down in 6, shall be equipped as follows (but not more than four boats in any one ship require to have this outfit):

(*a*) With two hatchets or tomahawks, one to be kept in each end of the boat, and to be attached to the boat by a lanyard.

(*b*) With a mast or masts, and with at least one good sail, and proper gear for each.

(*c*) With a life-line, in loops run around the outside of the boat and securely made fast.

(*d*) With an efficient compass.

(*e*) With one gallon of vegetable or animal oil, in a vessel of an approved pattern, for distributing it in the water in rough weather.

(*f*) With a lantern trimmed, with oil in its receiver sufficient to burn eight hours.

(8) *Number of persons for life-rafts.*—The number of persons that any approved life-raft for use at sea shall be deemed to be capable of carrying shall be determined with reference to each separate pattern approved by the Board of Trade; provided always, that for every person so carried there shall be at least three cubic feet of strong and serviceable inclosed air-tight compartments, such that water can not find its way into them. Any approved life-raft of other construction may be used, provided that it has equivalent buoyancy to that hereinbefore described. Every such approved life-raft shall be marked in such a way as to plainly indicate the number of adult persons it can carry.

(9) *Buoyant apparatus.*—Approved buoyant apparatus shall be deemed sufficient for a number of persons to be ascertained by dividing the number of pounds of iron which it is capable of supporting in fresh water by 32. Such buoyant apparatus shall not require to be inflated before use, shall be of approved construction, and marked in such a way as plainly to indicate the number of persons for whom it is sufficient.

(10) *Life-belts.*—An improved life-belt shall mean a belt which does not require to be inflated before use, and which is capable at least of floating in the water for twenty-four hours with 10 pounds of iron suspended from it.

(11) *Life-buoys.*—An approved life-buoy shall mean either—

(*a*) A life-buoy built of solid cork, and fitted with life-lines and loops, securely seized to the life-buoy, and capable of floating in the water for at least twenty-four hours with 32 pounds of iron suspended from it; or

(*b*) A strong life-buoy of any other approved pattern and material, provided that it is capable of floating in the water for at least twenty-four hours with 32 pounds of iron suspended from it,

and provided also that it is not stuffed with rushes, cork shavings,
or other shavings, or loose granulated cork, or other loose material,
and does not require inflation before use.

(12) *Position of life-belts and life-buoys.*—All life-buoys and life-belts shall be so placed as to be readily accessible to the persons on board, and so that their position may be known to those for whom they are intended.

APPENDIX D.

AU SUJET DU FILAGE DE L'HUILE.

[Ministère de la Marine et des Colonies. Cabinet du Ministre. 2e bureau: Mouvements de la flotte et opérations militaires.

PARIS, *le 6 août* 1887.

Le Ministre de la Marine et des Colonies, à MM. les Vice-Amiraux commandant en chef, Préfets maritimes ; Officiers généraux, supérieurs et autres, commandant à la mer.

MESSIEURS, l'attention du Département a été appelé à diverses reprises, sur la question de l'emploi de l'huile pour diminuer les effets d'une mer agitée.

Le vice-amiral Cloué a notamment résumé ses recherches et ses observations dans un intéressant mémoire, inséré dans les *Annales hydrographiques* et dans la *Revue maritime et coloniale*, en 1887, et auquel je vous prie de vous reporter.

La diffusion de l'huile sur une grosse mer paraît exercer parfois des effets surprenants, et je suis frappé, comme le vice-amiral Cloué, des résultats qui auraient été obtenus dans certaines circonstances. Je désire, en conséquence, faire procéder à l'étude de ce phénomène, et, afin de m'appuyer sur des données précises et revêtues d'un caractère officiel, je vous prie de faire exécuter, à bord des bâtiments sous vos ordres, des essais sur le filage de l'huile dans les diverses circonstances de la navigation.

Vous voudrez bien m'adresser ultérieurement un compte rendu détaillé de ces expériences, en me faisant part de vos appréciations sur l'application qui pourrait être faite dans la pratique du principe dont il s'agit pour la préservation des navires ou des embarcations.

Je ne crois devoir vous donner aucune instruction de détail ; vous trouverez, dans le mémoire du vice-amiral Cloué, les indications nécessaires pour vous guider.

Recevez, etc.

BARBEY.

PARIS, *le 13 octobre 1888.*

Le Ministre de la Marine et des Colonies, à MM. les Vice-Amiraux com-mandant en chef, Préfets maritimes; Officiers généraux, supérieurs et autres, commandant à la mer.

MESSIEURS, comme suite à la circulaire du 6 août 1887, j'ai l'honneur de vous adresser ci-jointe une note sur le filage de l'huile, rédigée d'après les indications du vice-amiral Cloué, et qui paraît un complé-ment utile de l'ouvrage sur la matière déjà délivré à tous les bâtiments de l'État, aux termes de la circulaire du 14 juin 1888 (B. O.).

Plusieurs des opérations qui y sont décrites n'ont pas encore reçu, tout au moins dans une mesure suffisante, la sanction de l'expérience et sont simplement signalées, sur la proposition de cet officier général, à l'attention des navigateurs.

Il importe, en vue de l'étude complète de cette intéressante question, de continuer activement les essais et de rechercher tous les perfection-nements réalisables.

Je désire, en conséquence, que les commandants continuent à employer ce procédé, lorsque les circonstances de leur navigation s'y prêteront, en tenant compte des recommandations de la note ci-jointe.

Ils devront noter avec soin toutes les applications qu'ils auront pu faire, en indiquant les moyens mis en usage, la durée de l'immersion des sacs, l'espèce et la quantité d'huile employée, la route du navire, la direction et la force du vent, et celles de la mer, etc.

Tous ces renseignements, ainsi que les résultats obtenus, devront être résumés dans un rapport qui me sera transmis sous le présent timbre, à la date du 1er janvier et du 1er juillet de chaque année, ou au désarme-ment du bâtiment.

Recevez, etc. KRANTZ.

NOTE SUR LE FILAGE DE L'HUILE.

Une étude attentive des résultats obenus dans les nombreuses expé-riences qui ont eu lieu sur le filage do l'huile pour calmer les brisants a permis d'établir les meilleures conditions dans lesquelles ce mode de protection peut être utilement employé.

La Note ci-après, qui indique l'état actuel de la question, est divisée en trois parties, savoir:

I.—Mode d'emploi de l'huile.

II.—Huiles à employer.

III.—Circonstances dans lesquelles l'usage de l'huile est recom-mandé.

I.—*Mode d'emploi de l'huile.*

On a reconnu qu'une très petite quantité d'huile permet de couvrir une grande étendue d'eau d'une pellicule grasse suffisante pour empêcher les brisants de se former. Il a même été constaté que l'huile employée ainsi par petites quantités produit l'effet le meilleur et le plus prompt, les gouttes d'huile s'étendant sur l'eau avec une rapidité prodigieuse. Il est donc nécessaire d'égoutter l'huile, et le moyen qui a été reconnu jusqu'ici comme le plus simple et devant être préféré est l'emploi de sacs de forme allongée faits avec de la toile à voile. On prend, par exemple, un de ces sacs que l'on remplit d'étoupe saturée d'huile, on complète en versant de l'huile par-dessus l'étoupe, on ferme avec soin le sac, qui doit être solidement ralingué, et on le met à la traîne à l'aide d'un cartahu frappé sur une cosse tenant, du côté de l'ouverture à la ralingué du sac. Le fond et la partie postérieure du sac sont percés de trous faits à l'aide d'une grosse aiguille à voile.

Pour que les sacs puissent rester trois ou quatre heures à la mer avant qu'il soit nécessaire de les remplacer, il faut que leur capacité soit d'une dizaine de litres, en tenant compte du volume occupé par l'étoupe. Il n'y a donc pas dans chaque sac beaucoup plus de 5 à 6 litres d'huile.

A l'ancre ou à la cape, la forme des sacs importe peu; des navires et des embarcations ont employé un simple bas avec un plein succès. Mais il n'en saurait être de même lorsque le bâtiment a de la vitesse; la forme allongée est alors la meilleure, comme par exemple celle d'une gargousse de canon ou même celle d'un très gros saucisson.

Les cuvettes des poulaines ont été utilisées avec profit, concurremment avec les secs à huile et même sans eux. On les remplit, comme les sacs, d'étoupe saturée d'huile sur laquelle on verse en suite quelques litres d'huile. On a obtenu un très bon résultat en laissant pendre sous les poulaines des lanières d'étoupe, sortes de morceaux de faubert, à travers lesquelles l'huile suintait jusqu'à la mer.

II.—*Huiles à employer.*

Il y a lieu de signaler la supériorité reconnue des huiles de poisson et en premier lieu de celles de baleine. Les huiles d'olive, de colza, de lin, de sésame ne viennent qu'en seconde ligne.

Les huiles de coco, se figeant très vite, ne peuvent pas être employées avec succès dans les hautes latitudes.

Les huiles minérales sont inférieures aux autres comme trop légères; elles on cependant donné quelquefois de bons résultats.

En général les huiles un peu épaisses et visqueuses, telles que celles provenant des résidues de machines à vapeur et de machines-outils dans les usines, produisent de très bons effets; les essences de térébenthine et même le vernis ont été employés aussi avec un certain succès. Cependant il ne faut pas que les matières grasses cessent d'être parfaitement liquides; il serait mauvais de prendre celles qui se présenteraient sous la forme de cambouis; de nombreuses expériences ont prouvé que le suintement se fait alors difficilement et que les gouttes d'huile trop épaisse sont bien plus longues que les autres à s'étendre sur l'eau; l'effet produit est alors inutile, car le navire s'est déjà éloigné quand la zone de protection est établie,

III.—*Circonstances dans lesquelles l'usage de l'huile est recommandé.*

Les diverses circonstances de mer dans lesquelles l'usage de l'huile peut être utile sont les suivantes :

1° A l'ancre.... { Navire ou bateau mouillé.
——————————— amarré bord à quai.

2° A la mer.... { Navire vent arrière.
—————— vent de la hanche.
—————— vent largue ou du travers.
—————— vent de bout.
—————— à la cape ou en dérive sans voiles.

3° .... { Embarcation ou bateau de sauvetage à la mer en marche.
Embarcation ou bateau capeyant sur une ancre flottante.

4° .... Mettre à la mer une embarcation pour sauvetage et la rehisser à bord par gros temps.

5° .... Franchir une barre.

6° .... Remorquage.

1° NAVIRES À L'ANCRE.

Lorsqu'un navire se trouvera au mouillage dans un endroit non abrité, il pourra, dès que la mer commencera à se lever, fouetter une poulie double sur la chaîne, en dehors de l'écubier, passer dans chaque clan de la poulie un cartahu, puis filer 15 ou 20 mètres de chaine et amarrer à l'un des cartahus une bouée portant un sac à huile.

Un hâle-à-bord frappé sur la bouée donnera le moyen de renouveler le sac lorsqu'on le jugera nécessaire, et le second cartahu permettra de faire rapidement cette opération.   Si le navire est pourvu d'un beaupré et à plus forte raison d'un bout dehors de foc assez long, il sera probablement suffisant de suspendre le sac à son extrémité jusqu'à toucher l'eau.

Lorsqu'une embarcation affalée à la côte sera forcée de mouiller pour faire tête à la mer, elle pourra prendre la précaution de frapper sur son câblot, près du grappin, une poulie munie d'un va-et-vient, sur lequel sera fixé un sac à huile.

Si le navire (ou l'embarcation) était amarré à un quai exposé à être battu par la mer, on pourrait élonger dans le vent un grappin ou une ancre légère, portant la poulie avec le va-et-vient.   On obtiendra le meilleur résultat en halant près de l'ancre ou du grappin une bouée portant un sac à huile.   En effect, si le sac était fixé près de l'ancre, par une profondeur de quelques mètres, l'huile devrait, avant de s'étendre, employer un certain temps pour remonter à la surface, et ce temps serait perdu pour l'effet qu'on désire produire.

Afin d'être sûr d'avoir toujours en place un sac à huile fonctionnant bien, il est entendu que la poulie tenant à l'ancre doit être double et munie par conséquent de deux cartahus, de manière qu'on puisse envoyer un sac à huile auprès de la poulie au moment où l'autre est hâlé à bord.

2° NAVIRES À LA MER.

Navires vent arrière.—Lorsqu'un navire fuyant devant le temps risque de recevoir par l'arrière un dangereux coup de mer, il pourra pendre à l'avant, à chaque bossoir, un sac à huile touchant l'eau. L'avant du navire, en fendant la mer, la repousse de chaque côté, et l'huile étendue à la surface forme le long du bord une bande unie large de plusieurs mètres et une sorte de chemin huileux derrière le navire.

Si ces deux sacs étaient insuffisants, ce qui est peu probable, on devrait pendre deux autres sacs vers les grands porte-haubans, un de chaque bord.

Sur les bâtiments à hélice, on ne doit jamais pendre les sacs à la poupe, de peur qu'ils ne s'engagent dans le propulseur.

Navires vent de la hanche, vent largue, vent de travers.—Il faut, dans ce cas, établir un brise-lames huileux à quelques mètres, parallèlement au navire. Dans ce but, on établit au bossoir un espars ou arc-boutant faisant saillie de 6 ou 8 mètres en dehors; on a eu soin de fouetter sur son extrémité une poulie double dans laquelle passent deux légers cartahus, remorquant chacun un sac à huile, ce qui permet d'en avoir toujours un dehors.

Si, avec une grosse mer du travers, l'espars ne suffisait pas pour écarter suffisamment la bande d'huile, on emploierait un flotteur divergent portant un sac à huile. Il y a lieu de supposer que ce moyen suffirait même avec une grosse mer venant un peu de l'avant du travers.

Avec certaines mers fortes, lorsque le navire a une très grande vitesse, la mise en place de l'arc-boutant peut être très difficile et, si l'on s'y prend un peu tard, elle peut même être dangereuse. Il y aurait sans doute avantage, dans ce cas, à utiliser la vergue de misaine brassée convenablement.

Autant que possible, il faut que les sacs soient disposés de manière à traîner sur l'eau sans sauter; il faut aussi éviter qu'ils ne plongent trop, car l'huile ne s'étend et ne produit son effect qu'à la surface, et le temps qu'elle emploierait à y remonter serait du temps perdu.

Navires vent debout ou presque vent debout.—Plusieurs navires filant 10 ou 11 nœuds contre un gros temps ont réussi à se préserver des coups de mer en suspendant simplement des sacs à huile à l'avant ou en faisant égoutter de l'huile par les poulaines. Ce procédé, qui a réussi à un très petit nombre de capitaines, ne serait certainement pas suffisant pour tous les navires; il pourrait être remplacé par le suivant: Établir à l'avant une pompe puissante capable de lancer contre un coup de vent, à une quinzaine de mètres de distance, un jet d'eau *dense* contenant quelques gouttes d'huile. Au besoin, on s'aiderait d'un fort espars s'avançant en dehors et contre lequel s'appuierait le tuyau de la pompe. S'expression *dense* veut dire que le jet reste cylindrique depuis sa sortie du tuyau jusqu'à l'eau ; autrement le vent renverrait l'eau à bord.

La pompe lancerait, par exemple, 1,000 litres d'eau à la minute, et un petit mécanisme introduirait, avant que le jet ne sorte du tuyau, 3 ou 4 centilitres d'huile à la minute, ce qui ferait une consommation de 1 lit. 80 à 2 lit. 40 d'huile à l'heure. L'huile, en arrivant à la surface de la mer, prendra sans doute sa place immédiatement.

Navires à la cape ou en dérive sans voiles.—Bien des navires ont obtenu un excellent résultat à la cape en suspendant un sac à huile au bossoir du vent. Cependant il serait peut être utile, sur un grand navire, de suspendre à l'eau le long du bord plusieurs sacs à une quinzaine de mètres l'un de l'autre.

Lorsqu'un bâtiment à vapeur fait une avarie grave de machine, il tombe en travers et reste dans cette position, surtout s'il est très long; c'est alors une épave exposée à tous les coups de mer.

Pour le préserver des paquets de mer qui pourraient embarquer, on peut pendre du côté du vent des sacs à huile distants entre eux d'environ 15 mètres en ayant soin de les renouveler de deux en deux toutes les trois ou quatre heures. Si le vent renvoyait les sacs à bord, même lestés il suffirait de les pendre sous le vent; la dérive ne tarderait pas à faire passer le champ d'huile au vent.

3° EMBARCATION OU BATEAU DE SAUVETAGE À LA MER EN MARCHE.

Une embarcation, un bateau de sauvetage, par exemple, peut marcher contre certaines mauvaises mers avec succès en plaçant droit devant un espars portant un sac à huile. Mais cette manœuvre ne peut pas toujours réussir, et comme il n'est pas probable qu'on puisse installer sur un aussi petit bâtiment la pompe dont on a parlé plus haut, les embarcations légères devront renoncer à affronter de fortes mers debout.

Une embarcation, un bateau non ponté, fuyant vent arrière devant la lame, pourra suspendre son sac à huile à l'avant, à l'extrémité d'un espars et traînant légèrement à l'eau, ou bien près de l'arrière de manière à ne pas l'engager dans le gouvernail.

Une embarcation, un bateau de sauvetage peut marcher avec grosse mer du travers en employant un espars orienté à 45° de la direction de l'avant et traînant un sac à huile dont la remorque passe dans une poulie fixée à l'extrémité de cet espars.

EMBARCATION CAPEYANT SUR UNE ANCRE FLOTTANTE.

Lorsqu'une embarcation isolée est surprise par un fort vent qui ne lui permet plus de porter de la voile et est menacée par une grosse mer sur une eau trop profonde pour mouiller, elle peut avoir recours à une ancre flottante sur laquelle elle s'amarre et à l'abri de laquelle elle peut dériver. Cette ancre flottante est ordinairement faite avec une drôme composée des mâts, vergues et même des avirons. Il est souvent utile de laisser pendre à l'eau, sous cette drôme une des voiles de l'embarcation et d'en retenir la partie inférieure à l'aide d'une écoute venant à bord. Un sac à huile peut être installé sur l'ancre flottante à l'aide d'une poulie dans laquelle passe un va-et-vient, de manière à pouvoir facilement changer le sac lorsque l'huile s'épuise.

4° METTRE UNE EMBARCATION À LA MER ET LA REMBARQUER PAR GROS TEMPS.

Voici à ce sujet la manœuvre recommandée. Cette opération ne devra se faire que protégée par un champ d'huile qui écarte tout brisant. L'embarcation devra, en outre, être munie de tout le gréement nécessaire au filage de l'huile.

Sur un bâtiment à vapeur.—Le navire étant stoppé ne tardera pas à venir en travers au vent ; il sera probablement plus avantageux d'amener l'embarcation du côté du vent, à cause de la dérive du navire qui laissera au vent le champ d'huile.

Sur un bâtiment à voiles.—Le navire en panne donne nécessairement une forte bande. On devra probablement amener le canot sous le vent. Il faudrait alors mettre les sacs à huile à l'eau de ce côté. Les mouvements du navire feront sans doute assez élargir le champ d'huile pour que l'embarcation soit mise à l'eau sur une mer sans brisants. On pourrait du reste, avec un espars muni d'un sac, élargir la bande d'huile sous le vent de manière à avoir un espace uni suffisant pour l'embarcation.

*5° FRANCHIR UNE BARRE.

La meilleure méthode à employer est d'avoir un sac à huile pendu à l'extrémité de l'espars poussé droit devant et un autre sac à la remorque à l'arrière, de manière qu'il ne puisse se pendre dans le gouvernail ou dans l'hélice, s'il s'agit d'une embarcation à vapeur.

6° REMORQUAGE.

Le filage de l'huile sera alors un puissant auxiliaire, car si le remorqueur ne parvient pas à se garantir complètement des coups de mer par l'avant, il sera en très bonne position pour filer l'huile de manière à en garantir entièrement le remorqué, ce qui allégera beaucoup le travail des remorques en leur évitant les secousses qui les compromettent et qui fatiguent, en outre, l'arrière du remorqueur et l'avant du remorqué.

APPENDIX E.

ORGANIZATION AND METHODS OF THE UNITED STATES LIFE-SAVING
SERVICE.

[Read to the Committee on Life-Saving Systems and Devices, International Marine
Conference, November 22, 1889, by S. I. Kimball, General Superintendent of the
Service.]

The sea and lake coasts of the United States, exclusive of the coast of
Alaska, have an extent of more than 10,000 miles. There are to-day
upon these coasts two hundred and twenty-six life-saving stations, one
hundred and sixty-five of which are on the shores of the Atlantic, eight
on the shores of the Gulf of Mexico, eight on the shores of the Pacific, and
forty-five on the shores of the great lakes. There is, besides, a station
at the falls of the Ohio River at Louisville, Ky. These stations are
located at selected points of danger to shipping, and vary somewhat in
character, according to their environment and the nature of the service
demanded of them. On some portions of the coast they are placed only at
long intervals, while upon others they form chains of contiguous posts
within communicating distance of each other.

From the eastern extremity of the coast of Maine to Race Point on Cape
Cod, a distance of 415 miles, there are but sixteen stations, ten of these
being located at the most dangerous points on the coast of Maine and
New Hampshire, which, although abounding with rugged headlands,
islets, rocks, reefs, and intricate channels that would naturally appear
to be replete with dangers, are provided with numerous harbors and
places of shelter in which, upon short notice, vessels can take refuge.
The portion of the Massachusetts coast included, although less favored
with safe resorts, enjoys the excellent guardianship of the Massachusetts Humane Society—a venerable institution, operating under the volunteer system. On account of this protection, the general Government
has deemed it proper to place its stations within this territory only at
points where wrecks are unusually frequent; at least, until other dangerous parts of the coast shall have been provided for.

Cape Cod, a narrow strip of sand, stretches directly out into the ocean
some 40 miles, then abruptly turns to the north for an equal distance,
and, like a threatening arm, fiercely menaces the commerce of the principal port of New England. Its eastern borders of shifting sand-bars
fringe an unbroken line of sandy beaches which have become the burial-
ground of unnumbered craft. Here ten stations are located nearly equi-
distant, and designed to co-operate with each other.

From Monomoy—the elbow of the Cape—to Montauk Point, a distance of 110 miles, the coast is again somewhat similar to that of Maine,
and is provided with but nine stations.

The ocean shores of Long Island and New Jersey, one about 120 and
the other 130 miles in length, form nearly a right angle, one side of

which faces southeasterly and the other easterly, the vertex being at the entrance to the harbor of the great commercial metropolis of the nation. The southern portion of the New Jersey coast also borders the entrance to Delaware Bay, which is traversed by the shipping of Philadelphia and Wilmington. The coast-line throughout nearly its whole extent consists of a narrow strip of sand beach, varying in width from a quarter of a mile to 5 miles, and separated from the mainland by narrow thoroughfares that sometimes expand into considerable bays. This strip is unbroken except by shallow inlets connecting the ocean with the inland waters, and by the entrance to New York Harbor, as before stated. At a distance of from one to four hundred yards from the shore it is bordered by outlying sand-bars, over which, in violent storms, immense walls of surf continually form and break. Its shores, exposed to all easterly storms, are constantly skirted by vessels bound into and out of the ports of New York, Philadelphia, and Wilmington, and by craft of the coasting trade. Their sands have always levied a fearful tribute upon the passing commerce, and are literally strewn with the half-buried and decaying skeletons of wrecked vessels, while the graveyards of the coast villages and settlements abound with unmarked mounds that tell a sorrowful tale of the destruction of human life. Here, therefore, the number of stations is increased, thirty-nine being placed upon the coast of Long Island and forty upon the New Jersey coast.

A similar formation marks the coast from Cape Henlopen to Cape Charles, and from Cape Henry to Cape Fear. On the first of these sections, a distance of 116 miles, sixteen stations are located, while from Cape Henry to Cape Hatteras, a stretch of 121 miles, there are twenty-three stations. These guard a portion of the ocean commerce of Philadelphia, all that of Baltimore and Norfolk, and the coastwise shipping.

Between Cape Hatteras and Cape Fear, 175 miles, six stations are placed, for the protection of the commerce of Beaufort and Wilmington, N. C., and for the benefit of coasting vessels liable to disaster upon these stormy capes.

From Cape Fear as far south as the peninsula of Florida there are no stations, with the exception of one on Morris Island, at the entrance to Charleston Harbor, their protection not being needed, for the reason that the westerly trend of the coast from Cape Hatteras to Florida takes it distant from the track of vessels not bound to or from the local ports. The climate is also much milder than in the higher latitudes, being almost perennial summer; consequently, shipwrecks are less frequent.

On the coast of Florida, when vessels strand, they usually come well up to the shore, so that sailors find little difficulty in reaching the land. Until of late, however, these shores were almost uninhabited, and mariners cast upon them were exposed to the terrors of starvation and thirst. On this account there are provided for their relief ten stations of an exceptional type, denominated houses of refuge. There is, how-ever, a completely equipped station at Jupiter Inlet, a somewhat dangerous point.

Along most of that portion of the coast of the Gulf of Mexico lying within the United States, the water is shoal for a great distance from shore, the soundings regular, and the coast-line generally low, marshy, or sandy. The dangerous gales are the "northers," so well known to seamen who frequent the Gulf, and these force vessels off and not on shore, except where a portion of the coast of Texas runs nearly north and south. This portion is exposed to the effects of these storms, especially if the wind is a little quartering from the east, and here are appropriately established four stations. There is also a station at the entrance to Galveston Harbor, where many vessels have been wrecked upon the bar, and at unusually exposed points two others.

The Pacific coast is not a dangerous one. From the southern bound-ary of the United States, as far north as San Francisco, the climate is remarkably bland, and shipwrecks are of rare occurrence. The re-mainder of the coast-line, extending northward to the Straits of Fuca, is very regular, bold, and unbroken, and contains but few harbors. The prevailing winds are mostly from a common quarter, blowing not towards the shore, but southward, along its line, with almost the reg-ularity of monsoons. The weather, therefore, is easily forecast, and navigation can not in general be regarded as hazardous. There are, however, a few extremely dangerous points, mostly situated at the en-trances to the important ports. These are guarded by eight stations.

The cluster of inland seas known as the Great Lakes contains an area of about 80.000 square miles, and has a coast line within the limits of the United States of nearly 2,500 miles. These seas are open to navi-gation about eight months in the year; at other times being closed by ice, although one or two steamers cut their way across Lake Michigan at intervals throughout the winter. There are few natural harbors, but a large number of artificial ones. These are formed at the mouths of rivers by extending piers from their banks out into the lake for a considerable distance and dredging the bottom between. The lakes are generally tranquil, but at certain seasons are visited by violent gales which throw their fresh waters into furious convulsion with a sud-denness unknown upon the ocean. Vessels unable to hold their own against the severity of these storms, being land-locked and with scant sea room, are likely to be left with only the choice between stranding wherever they may be driven and seeking refuge in the harbor that seems most accessible. The latter course is naturally the one taken. To effect an entrance within the narrow space between the piers at such times with sailing vessels, and even with steamers, is frequently a task of extreme difficulty, and the luckless craft are liable to strand upon the bar on one or the other side of the piers and meet their destruction. At some of these harbors many disasters occur in a single day.

The numerous severe gales attending the opening and closing of navigation in the early spring and late fall cause great numbers of wrecks from the enormous shipping of the lakes. As the strandings usually occur near the harbors, however, the number of stations required is not so large as it would be if they were distributed more generally along the shore. The number at present is, as I have stated, forty-five.

At Louisville, Ky., dangerous falls occur in the Ohio River, across which a dam has been constructed with two wide openings or chutes to facilitate the descent of vessels, the ascent being accomplished through a canal provided with locks. This dam is a source of danger to boats attempting to cross the river to the city of Jeffersonville, as they are liable to be sucked down by the chutes or swept over its verge. Larger vessels are also exposed to danger if they become disabled or unmanageable. For this reason it has been found advisable to moor here a floating station of a unique character.

The remaining few stations are located at various points which have seemed to need their protection. There are eight stations now in course of construction, and twenty others authorized to be hereafter built at various isolated points of danger. When these are completed, this form of protection will have about reached the practical limit of the present necessities of our commerce.

The stations upon the ocean beaches are generally situated among the low sand-hills common to such localities sufficiently back of high-water mark to be safe from the reach of storm-tides. They are plain structures, designed to serve as barracks for the crews and to afford convenient storage for the boats and apparatus. Most of those upon the Long Island and New Jersey coasts have been enlarged from the boat-houses put up to shelter the boats and equipments provided for the use of volunteers before regular crews were employed. Those built later are more comely in appearance, while a few, located conspicuously at popular sea-side resorts, make some pretensions to architectural taste. They are all designated by names indicating their localities.

In the majority of stations the first floor is divided into four rooms; a boat-room, a mess-room (also serving for a sitting-room for the men), a keeper's room, and a store-room. Wide, double-leafed doors and a sloping platform extending from the sills to the ground permit the running out of the heavier equipments from the building. The second story contains two rooms; one is the sleeping-room of the men, the other has spare cots for rescued people and is also used for storage. The more commodious stations have two additional rooms—a spare room and a kitchen. In localities where good water can not be otherwise obtained cisterns are provided for water caught from the roof. There surmounts every station a lookout or observatory, in which a day watch is kept. The roofs upon the stations on those portions of the coast exposed to view from the sea are usually painted dark red, which makes them distinguishable a long distance off shore. They are also marked by a flag-staff 60 feet high, used in signaling passing vessels by the International Code.

The stations (other than the house of refuge) are generally equipped with two surf-boats (supplied with oars, life-boat compass, and other outfits), a boat-carriage, two sets of breeches-buoy apparatus (including a Lyle gun and accessories), a cart for the transportation of the apparatus, a life-car, twenty cork jackets, two heaving sticks, a dozen Coston signals, a dozen signal rockets, a set of the signal flags of the International Code, a medicine-chest with contents, a barometer, a thermometer, patrol lanterns, patrol checks or patrol clocks, the requisite furniture for rude housekeeping by the crew and for the succor of rescued people, fuel and oil, tools for the repair of the boats and apparatus and for minor repairs to the buildings, and the necessary books and stationery. At some of the stations the Hunt gun and projectiles are supplied, and at a few the Cunningham rocket apparatus. To facilitate the transportation of boats and apparatus to scenes of shipwreck a pair of horses is also provided at stations where they can not be hired, and to those stations where the supplies, mails, etc., have to be brought by water a supply boat is furnished.

All the stations on the ocean coast of Long Island, twenty-nine stations on the coast of New Jersey, nine stations on the coast between Cape Henlopen and Cape Charles, and all the stations between Cape Henry and Hatteras Inlet are connected by telephone lines.

The few lake stations located upon the sand beaches are similar in all respects to those upon the sea-coast, but those situated at the harbors differ from them in that room is provided for a heavy life-boat and for a small boat for quick work in the immediate vicinity of the station. The buildings are usually located not far from the water's edge, behind one of the piers of crib-work forming the sides of the harbor entrance. An inclined platform, upon which are laid two tramways for the launching of the boats, extends from the boat-room down to the water through an opening cut in the pier. Cradles or cars are provided, on which the boats are kept mounted and by which they can be put afloat with the men at their oars in half a minute. Exit for the surf-boat wagon and apparatus cart is also provided in the rear of the building, in case it should be necessary to transport them along the shore. These stations usually have telephone connection with the systems of the adjacent towns.

The houses of refuge on the Florida coast are simple dwellings, not unlike those common at the south, with capacity sufficient for the residence of a family, and for the temporary shelter of as many as are likely to need it. The distance between them averages 26 miles, and at each mile along the coast are placed guide posts indicating the distance and direction to the nearest station. The houses are supplied with cots and provisions sufficient to succor twenty-five persons for ten days. No boats or apparatus are provided, except a small galvanized iron boat for the use of the keeper.

The floating station at Louisville is a scow-shaped hull, on which is a house of two stories surmounted by a lookout. Besides the housekeeping furniture there are but few equipments; two boats called lifeskiffs, and two reels, each with capacity to hold a coil of 5-inch manilla rope, and so placed in the boat room that a line can be speedily run out from either, or, if desired, that they can be rolled out of the boat-room, with the lines upon them, for use elsewhere. The station is usually moored above the dam at a place which will afford the readiest access to boats meeting with accident, but it can be towed from place to place when necessity requires, as was the case in the great floods of 1883-'84, when it was of incalculable service in rescuing people from the upper stories and roofs of their inundated dwellings, and in distributing food to the famishing. On these two calamitous occasions the crew of this station rescued and took to places of safety over 800 imperiled persons, men, women, and children—among them many sick and infirm—and supplied food and other necessaries to more than 10,000.

The station buildings upon the coast are all constructed with a view to withstand the severest tempests. Those located—as many necessarily are—where they are liable to be undermined or swept from their positions by the ravages of storms and tidal waves, are so strongly put together that they may be overthrown and sustain but trifling injury. There are instances on record where they have been carried a long distance inland—in one case a half a mile—without sustaining material damage. This substantial construction also enables them to be easily and cheaply moved when threatened by the gradual encroachment of the sea, which, upon many sections of the coast, effects in the course of years great changes in the configuration of the coast line.

Since the establishment is closely related to commerce and the collection of the revenue, it is attached to the Treasury Department, which discharges all executive functions of that character. It has, indeed, from its earliest inception, been formed and fostered by that Department. The present system was established in 1871, upon the New Jersey and Long Island coasts, by a code of regulations under the authority of somewhat scattered and fragmentary legislation. Acts of Congress passed since that time have extended it to embrace the entire ocean and lake coasts, which are divided into twelve districts, limited in general by prominent natural or political boundaries.

The chief officer of the Service is the General Superintendent, whose appointment is made by the President and confirmed by the Senate. No one is eligible to the position who is not familiar with the means employed in the service for the saving of life and property from shipwreck. The law places no limit upon the tenure of this officer, which is therefore subject to the pleasure of the President. He has general charge of the Service, and of all administrative matters connected with it. His compensation is $4,000 per annum. An assistant general superintendent, appointed by the Secretary of the Treasury, assists him, and in his absence performs his duties. His compensation is $2,500 per annum.

The office of the General Superintendent is in Washington, where, to assist in the transaction of business, are employed a corps of clerks, a civil engineer, a topographer and hydrographer, and a draughtsman. To assist the General Superintendent in investigating devices and inventions for the improvement of life-saving apparatus there has been formed a Board on Life-Saving Appliances, composed of experts selected from the Life-Saving Service and others. It is their duty to examine and report upon such devices as may be submitted to them.

The next official in rank to the General Superintendent is the Inspector, an officer detailed from the Revenue-Cutter Service upon the request and recommendation of the General Superintendent. His headquarters are in New York City. Besides making periodical inspections of the stations, he performs such other duties in connection with the conduct of the service as the General Superintendent may direct. Nearly all the self-bailing and self-righting life-boats are built in New York, and most of the apparatus is manufactured there. He is, therefore, required to inspect and superintend the work upon these. Under the system pursued by the Government for making purchases of goods for its use, a large proportion of the outfits and supplies for the stations are obtained in that city, and these he is also required to inspect. An assistant inspector is detailed to the office of the Inspector, and in his absence acts for him. Such other assistance as is found necessary is also allowed.

An assistant inspector is also detailed from the Revenue-Cutter Service for each district. He is authorized to perform within his district any of the duties of the Inspector under the latter's direction. He visits each station monthly during the " active season," and upon each visit, in addition to the ordinary routine of inspection, he examines and practices the crews in their duties. On his first tour after the opening of the stations in each year, he examines the keepers and men as to the required qualifications, reporting for dismissal any found wanting. Upon each succeeding visit he makes a similar examination of all persons who have entered the service since his previous visit. He makes special visits to any of the stations when necessary. Whenever a shipwreck attended with loss of life occurs within the domain of the service, an assistant inspector is detailed to carefully investigate all the circumstances connected with the disaster, with a view of ascertaining its cause, and whether the officers or employés of the service have been guilty of neglect or misconduct. The results of these investigations are published in the annual reports. The Inspector and assistant inspectors receive no other compensation than that pertaining to their rank in their own corps.

Each district is under the immediate charge of a superintendent, and for the coast of Rhode Island—a portion of the third district, widely separated by water from the other portion and from the adjacent district, but not large enough to form a district by itself—there is an assistant superintendent. These officers must be men of good character and correct habits, not less than twenty-five nor more than fifty-five years of age when appointed; able to read and write English readily, and have sufficient knowledge of accounts to properly transact the district business. They must be residents of the respective districts for which they are chosen, familiar with the line of coast embraced within them, and conversant with the management of life-boats and other life-saving appliances. They are rigidly examined as to these qualifications by the General Superintendent and the Inspector. They are disbursing officers and paymasters for their respective districts, and are required to enter into bonds varying in amount from $10,000 to $50,000, according to the fiscal responsibility placed upon them. They are also *ex officio* inspectors of customs. They conduct the general business of their districts, look after the needs of the stations, make requisition on the General Superintendent for station supplies, repairs, etc., and upon receipt of authority see that these are furnished. They visit the stations at least once a quarter to acquaint themselves with their condition. On these occasions they pay off the crews and make such other disbursements as are authorized. As inspectors of customs they look after the interests of the Government in reference to dutiable property wrecked within their jurisdiction, and see that the keepers of stations perform their duties in respect thereto. Their compensation ranges from $1,000 to $1,800 per annum, and is designed to be proportionate to the extent of their duties and to the degree of fiscal responsibility incumbent upon them severally.

Each station has a keeper who has direct control of all its affairs. The position held by this officer will be recognized at once as one of the most important in the Service. He is, therefore, selected with the greatest care. The indispensable qualifications for appointment are that he shall be of good character and habits, not less than twenty-one nor more than forty-five years of age; have sufficient education to be able to transact the station business; be able-bodied, physically sound, and a master of boat-craft and surfing. He is usually nominated by the district superintendent, the initial step being left to that officer because of the extensive acquaintance he is supposed to have with the class of men from which the choice must be made, by reason of long residence among them and because of the degree of responsibility resting upon him for the condition and conduct of his district. So much depends, however, upon the selection, that an effort is made to eliminate, as far as possible, the chance that any political, social, or personal interests shall intentionally or unintentionally enter into it. In the vicinity of nearly all the stations there are numbers of fishermen and wreckers who have followed their callings from boyhood and become expert in the handling of boats in broken water, and among these there is usually some one who, by common consent, is recognized as a leader *par excellence.* He is the man it is desirable to obtain for keeper, unless there be some fault of character which should exclude him. The nomination is accompanied by a statement of the reasons which guided the district superintendent in his choice, and a certificate of the candidate's physical soundness, made by a surgeon of the Marine Hospital Service, after careful examination. Before granting his approval the General Superintendent submits the nomination to the district inspector for his views, and if after thorough inquiry he concurs, the General Superintendent approves and the appointment is made. If he does not concur, and his stated reasons seem to justify his conclusion, the General Superintendent takes such action as he deems best, either calling upon the district superintendent to submit another nomination, or visiting the locality himself and seeking out the proper person. It is gratifying to be able to state, and it is an evidence of the singleness of purpose and strict appreciation of duty which actuate both the district officers, that difference of opinion in reference to a nomination has rarely arisen between them.

It is not found difficult to fill vacancies that occur among the keepers at old stations, or along that portion of the coast where the stations are contiguous. Either from the crew where the vacancy exists, or from a neighboring one, there is selected the most competent surfman, the merits of all having been ascertained by inspection and drill and recorded in the central office. Rarely, it is considered for the best advantage and welfare of the service to take some person from without; in which case the district officers are required to set forth specifically all the facts upon which this conclusion is based. The original selection of keepers for new stations remote from others is less easily determined.

The keepers are required to reside constantly at their stations; are intrusted with the care and custody of the station property, for which they are accountable; and govern the station premises. They are captains of their crews; exercise absolute control over them (subject only to the restriction of the regulations of the Service and the orders of superior officers); lead them and share their perils on all occasions of rescue, taking always the steering oar when the boats are used, and directing all operations with the apparatus. They are also *ex officio* inspectors of customs, and as such take care of the Government interests in relation to dutiable goods on wrecked vessels, until the arrival of other customs officers. By law they are also made guardians of all wrecked property until relieved by the owners or their agents, or until instructed by superior authority as to its disposition.

No crews are employed at houses of refuge, but the keepers and their families travel after storms as far as practicable along the shore in both directions from the stations, searching for persons possibly cast ashore.

A daily journal or log is required to be kept at every station, weekly transcripts of which the keeper sends through the district superintendent to the General Superintendent, who is thus kept advised of all that transpires. Immediately after the occurrence of a wreck the keeper furnishes a complete report of every detail of interest concerning the disaster, and from time to time various other reports are required of him. Any false statement made in the books or reports subjects him to instant dismissal.

The Secretary of the Treasury is authorized to grant the keepers a compensation not to exceed $800 per annum. The maximum amount is paid only to one or two, whose stations are so isolated that they are obliged to secure an associate to reside with them when the crews are off duty, and to such keepers as have remarkably distinguished themselves by bravery and effective service. The usual salary paid is $700 per annum; to keepers of houses of refuge, only $400.

The law provides that the stations on the Atlantic and Gulf coasts shall be opened and manned for active service from the 1st day of September in each year until the 1st day of the succeeding May, and those on the lake coasts from the opening to the close of navigation, usually from about the 15th of April to about the 15th of December. On the Pacific coast the period is left discretionary with the General Superintendent. The time during which the stations are manned is designated the " active season." Four of the stations on the Pacific coast are kept open the year round, experience having shown that disasters in their neighborhood occur more frequently from local causes than from stress of weather, and are about as liable to happen at one season as at another. For similar reasons a crew is kept continuously at the Louisville station.

The number of men composing the crew of a station is determined by the number of oars required to pull the largest boat belonging to it. There are some five-oared boats in the Atlantic stations, but at all of them there is at least one of six oars. Six men, therefore, make up the regular crews of these stations, but a seventh man is added on the 1st of December, so that during the most rigorous portion of the season a man may be left ashore to assist in the launching and beaching of the boat and to see that the station is properly prepared for the comfortable reception of his comrades and the rescued people they bring with them on their return from a wreck; also to aid in doing the extra work that severe weather necessitates. Where the self-righting and self-bailing boat which pulls eight oars is used, mostly at the lake stations, a corresponding number of men is employed.

The crews are selected by the keepers from able-bodied and experienced surfmen residing in the vicinity of the respective stations. This privilege is granted the keepers in view of the obvious necessity for mutual confidence between a leader and his followers in hazardous enterprises involving their own lives and the lives of others, and in view

of the strict responsibility to which each keeper is held for the good re-
pute of his station and the conduct of its affairs.

In the absence of strong counteracting inducements these considerations would naturally lead to the choice of the very best men to be had.
It was early found, however, that political, social, and family influences
were often strong enough to so control the selection as to materially
affect the efficiency of a crew. To oppose them certain regulations were
established, the most important of which provided that the selection of
keepers and crews should be made solely with reference to their fitness
and without regard to their party affiliations. This, after being enforced for several years, received in 1882 the sanction of Congress,
being at the same time extended to the appointment of district superin-
tendents and inspectors. This enactment greatly aids successful resistance to the most insidious and potent evil that has ever threatened the
welfare of the service. Another important regulation forbids a keeper
to take into his crew his brother, father, or son, except where adherence
to the rule would be detrimental to the service. This was found necessary to countervail the quite natural inclination of keepers to provide
situations for their near kinsmen, even to the serious detriment of the
strength and *morale* of the station force.

Protected by these and a few less noteworthy safeguards, the method
adopted for manning the stations has filled them with the very pick
and flower of the hardy race of beachmen who inhabit our shores. No
better evidence of the virtue of the plan can be desired than the fact
that during the eighteen years it has governed the selection of the men
not one has shown the white feather, while the pages of the annual
reports of the service are crowded with the records of gallant deeds
that have made them famous throughout the land.

Upon original entry into the Service a surfman must be not over
forty-five years of age, and sound in body, being subjected to a rigid
physical examination by a surgeon of the Marine Hospital Service.
He is afterwards examined as to expertness in the management of boats
and matters of that character by the inspector of the district. The
regulations setting forth his duties being read to him, he is enlisted by
signing articles by which he agrees to reside at the station continuously
during the "active season," to perform such duties as may be required
of him by the regulations and by his superior officers, and also to hold
himself in readiness for service during the inactive season, if called
upon. Desertion entails a forfeiture of his wages, to be exacted in the
discretion of the General Superintendent. His compensation is $50
per month during the "active season," and $3 for each occasion of serv-
ice at other times. Beyond the wages mentioned the surfmen receive
no allowances or emoluments of any kind, except the quarters and fuel
provided at the stations. Their food and clothing they themselves
supply.

No person belonging to the Service is permitted to hold an interest in any wrecking apparatus, or to be connected with any wrecking company; nor is he entitled to salvage upon any property he may save or assist to save.

A surfman can not be discharged from the Service without good and sufficient reason. For well-proven neglect of patrol duty, or for disobedience or insubordination at a wreck, the keeper may instantly dismiss him; in all other cases special authority must be first obtained from the General Superintendent.

In case a keeper or surfman becomes disabled by injury received or disease contracted in the line of duty, he is entitled to receive his full pay during the continuance of the disability, if it does not exceed one year, and upon the recommendation of the General Superintendent the Secretary of the Treasury may extend the time for a second year, or a part thereof, but no longer in any case. If any keeper or surfman loses his life by reason of injury or disease incurred in the line of his duty, his widow or children under sixteen years of age may receive for two years the pay that the deceased would have if alive and in the Service. If the widow remarries or a child arrives at the age of sixteen, the amount that would have been paid to the one or the other goes to the remaining beneficiaries, if any. It will be seen at once that this beneficence affords certain advantages to the widow which the ordinary pension does not furnish, inasmuch as the death of her husband does not add to her grief the misfortune of financial embarrassment by cutting off or diminishing the family income at a time when the funeral expenses make an unusual demand upon it.

At the opening of the "active season" the men assemble at their respective stations and establish themselves for a residence of eight months. They arrange for their housekeeping, usually by forming a mess, taking turns by weeks in catering and cooking, although at some of the stations they engage board of the keeper at a rate approved by the General Superintendent. These preliminaries being settled the keeper organizes his crew by arranging and numbering them in their supposed order of merit, the most competent and trustworthy being designated as No. 1, the next No. 2, and so on. These numbers are changed by promotion as vacancies occur, or by such re-arrangement from time to time as proficiency in drill and performance of duty may dictate. Whenever the keeper is absent, No. 1 assumes command and exercises his functions.

The rank of his men being fixed, the keeper assigns to each his quarters and prepares station bills for the day watch, night patrol, boat and apparatus drill, care of the premises, etc. For the purpose of watch and patrol, the district officers establish patrol limits as far as practicable along the coast in both directions from the stations, marking them by distinct monuments, and a description of the beats thus laid out is sent to the office of the General Superintendent. The day watch is kept from sunrise to sunset by a surfman daily assigned to this duty, who is usually stationed in the lookout, and who, if the patrol limits can not be seen from there, goes at least three times a day far enough along the shore to bring them into view. During thick and stormy weather a complete patrol like that at night is maintained. At the harbor stations on the lakes, at the river station at Louisville, and at other places where accidents are frequent, there is connected with the lookout a gong, by means of which the crew is alarmed when occasion requires. The day watch keeps a record of all passing vessels.

For the night patrol the night is divided into four watches—one from sunset to 8 o'clock, one from 8 to 12, one from 12 to 4, and one from 4 to sunrise. Two surfmen are designated for each watch. When the hour for their patrol arrives they set out in opposite directions along the coast, keeping as near as practicable to the shore, as far as the ends of their respective beats. If within communicating distance from an adjacent station, each patrolman proceeds until he meets another from the next station and gives him a metallic check marked with his station and crew number, receiving in exchange a similar one. The checks thus collected are examined by the keeper, recorded in the journal, and returned to their proper stations the next night. If a patrolman fails to meet his fellow from the adjacent station, after waiting a reasonable time at the usual place of meeting, he continues his journey until he either meets him or reaches that station and ascertains the cause of the failure, which, on his return, he reports to his keeper, who makes a record of it in his journal.

At isolated stations each patrolman is required to carry a clock within which is fixed a dial that can be marked only by means of a key which also registers the time of marking. This key is secured to a post at the end of his beat, and he is required to reach it and bring back the dial properly marked.

Each patrolman is equipped with a beach-lantern and several red Coston hand-lights. Upon the discovery of a wreck, a vessel in distress, or one running dangerously near the shore, he ignites by percussion his hand-light, which emits a brilliant red flame. This serves the double purpose of warning the people on the vessel of their danger and of assuring them of succor if they are already in distress.

For every week-day a regular routine of duties is appointed. For Monday, it is drill and practice with the beach-apparatus and overhauling and examining the boats and all apparatus and gear; for Tuesday, practice with the boats; for Wednesday, practice with the international code of signals; for Thursday, practice with the beach apparatus; for Friday, practice in the method adopted for restoring the apparently drowned; and for Saturday, cleaning house. Whenever anything prevents the regular performance of any of these duties, the fact must be entered upon the station journal, with a full explanation, and the omitted exercise performed at the first opportunity.

For practice with the beach apparatus there is provided near each station a suitable drill ground, prepared by erecting a spar, called a wreck-pole, to represent the mast of a stranded vessel 75 yards distant (over the water if possible) from the place where the men operate, which represents the shore. At drill the crew is mustered in the boat-room, and each man, upon his number being called, salutes the commanding officer and recites in proper sequence every act he is to perform in the exercise as prescribed in the Service manual. At the proper words of command they all fall into their allotted places at the drag-ropes of the apparatus-cart and draw it to the drill ground, where they perform the remainder of the exercise, which consists in effecting a mimic rescue by rigging the gear and taking a man ashore from the wreck-pole in the breeches-buoy. The officer conducting the drill carefully notes the time which elapses from the moment he gives the initial command "action" until the rescued man sets foot upon the shore.

If in one month after the opening of the "active season" a crew can not accomplish the rescue within five minutes it is considered that they have been remiss in drilling, or that there are some stupid men among them. They are cautioned that if upon the next visit of the inspector a marked improvement is not shown some decisive action will be taken to secure it. This usually produces the desired effect. In many of the districts a spirited rivalry exists between the stations for excellence in this drill. It has been executed without error by several crews in two minutes and thirty seconds. I confess I was incredulous of the posibility of such a feat until I witnessed it myself; but even this is perhaps less surprising than the time attained at some of the night drills, when, without lights other than the moon and stars, the shot has been fired, the apparatus set up, and a man brought ashore from the wreck-pole in three minutes. Of course, nothing like such celerity can be expected in effecting rescues at actual shipwrecks, when storms, currents, surf, the motion of the vessel, the lack of skillful co-operation on the wreck, and many other unfavorable elements conspire to obstruct progress, and the practice of timing the drill was instituted, not so much with the expectation of materially hastening the work of rescue, as with the design of giving the men the utmost familiarity with the stowage of the apparatus in the cart, with its uses, and with the method of handling it.

How well this purpose is fulfilled has been repeatedly illustrated on occasions of rescue, but never better than in the memorable storm of February 3, 1880, which wrought general ruin and devastation upon the coast of New Jersey and strewed her shores with wrecks. In the very height of that terrible tempest, at the dead of night, the crews of three separate stations rescued without mishap the people on four different vessels by means of the apparatus, set up and worked in almost utter darkness, the lanterns of the surfmen being so thickly coated with sleet that they emitted only glimmers of light so feeble that the lines and implements could not be seen. These and the other rescues achieved in that storm excited such public admiration that the State legislature unanimously passed resolutions commending the skill and bravery of the station crews.

Boat practice consists in launching and landing through the surf, and at least a half hour's exercise in handling the oars under the keeper's directions.

Drill in signalling is conducted by interrogating each surfman as to the meaning of the various flags, the definitions of two, three, and four flag-hoists, the distinguishing flag or pennant of each hoist, the use of the code book, and by actual conversation carried on by means of two sets of miniature signals provided for each station. Frequent practice is also had between the stations and revenue vessels.

The method adopted for restoring the apparently drowned is formulated into four rules which each member of the crew commits to memory. In drill he is required to repeat these and afterwards illustrate them by manipulations upon one of his comrades. The medicine-chest is also opened and he is examined as to the use of its contents.

The proficiency of every keeper and surfman in the several branches of qualification in which he is thus trained, as ascertained in the drills conducted by the district inspectors on their monthly visits, is marked by those officers in their drill-books upon a scale of ten; and transcripts of this rating are transmitted to the General Superintendant, who is thus kept constantly informed of the effectiveness of the corps.

The ultimate means employed by life-saving institutions to rescue people from stranded vessels are everywhere essentially the same. The tumultuous waters between the wreck and the shore are either crossed by a life-boat sent out to the imperilled people or are spanned by strong lines by which a breeches-buoy or other vehicle is passed back and forth. There are many kinds of life-boats, however, and various devices for effecting line-communication. The type of boat in most general use in our Service, although properly entitled to be called a life-boat, is distinctively known as the surf-boat, and this term will be applied to it in the remarks which follow upon this topic. There are several varieties of this type, all developments of the boat found in use among the shore fishermen or surfmen of the Long Island and New Jersey coasts for crossing the surf on the outlying sand-bars in their daily blue-fishing when the first boat-houses or stations were placed there. Three varieties, respectively designated the Beebe, the Higgins & Gifford, and the Beebe-McLellan surf-boat, from the names of the persons who devised the modifications which characterize them, are the only ones furnished to the stations in recent years. They are all constructed of white cedar with white-oak frames, and their dimensions are from 25 to 27 feet in length, $6\frac{1}{2}$ to 7 feet beam, 2 feet 3 inches to 2 feet 6 inches depth amidships, and 1 foot 7 inches to 2 feet 1 inch sheer of gunwale. Their bottoms are flat, with little or no keel, and have a camber of $1\frac{1}{2}$ or 2 inches in 8 feet each side of the midship section.

S. Ex. 53, pt. 3——15

They draw 6 or 7 inches of water, light, and weigh from 700 to 1,100 pounds. They are propelled with six oars, without sails, and are expected to carry, besides their crews, from ten to twelve persons, although as many as fifteen have been landed at a time in a bad sea. Their cost ranges from $210 to $275. There is no great difference between the Beebe and the Higgins & Gifford boat, except that the former has more sheer and is clinker-built, while the latter is of carvel construction. The Beebe-McLellan boat is the Beebe boat with the self-bailing quality incorporated. This feature has been added within the past two years, and but few of them have yet been put in service. All of these boats are so light as to be readily transported along the shore; they can be launched in very shallow water, and in the dexterous hands of our surfmen are maneuvered in the breakers with marvelous ease and celerity. This facility of handling is of great advantage when working in proximity to wrecks, enabling the boat to evade collision with floating wreckage, and to quickly slip up alongside a stranded vessel at a favorable moment and receive its freight, while it is easily fended off from contact with the lurching hull.

These boats, of one variety or other, are supplied to nearly all the stations in the Service, and on the Atlantic sea-board they are relied upon almost exclusively. Indeed, the shores of soft, yielding sand without roads, and the flat beaches covered with but little depth of water for a considerable distance seaward, which almost uniformly mark the coast from Cape Cod to Cape Fear, preclude the use of boats of greater weight and draught. Even at those stations where the most approved self-righting and self-bailing boats are furnished, the surf-boats are generally preferred by the life-saving crews for short distances and when the number of imperilled people is not large. In executing the work required at minor casualties, such as aiding to float stranded craft by carrying out anchors, running lines to tugs, etc., they are especially handy and by their use a vast amount of property has been saved.

As respects safety they will compare favorably with any other boats. During the eighteen years they have been in the hands of our crews they have been launched 6,730 times in actual service, and have landed 6,735 persons from wrecked vessels. In all this service they have capsized but 14 times. Six of these instances were attended with loss of life, the number of persons perishing being 41, of whom 27 belonged to the service and 14 were shipwrecked people.

Among other life-boats, the self-righting and self-bailing boats of the Royal National Life-Boat Institution of Great Britain, the honored mother and mentor of all existing life-saving organizations, are unquestionably pre-eminent. They are the product of a century's devoted study and experiment with unstinted means, dating from the time the London coach-maker first conceived the idea of a life-boat. Their wonderful achievements have formed the theme of song and story, shed merited luster upon the institution which fostered their development, and stimulated the formation of kindred organizations equipped with their models throughout christendom. I learn from the annual reports of the institution that during the same period of eighteen years her boats have capsized 21 times attended by loss of life, the number perishing aggregating 75, of whom 68 were life-boatmen and 7 shipwrecked people. The number of capsizes unattended with loss of life I could not ascertain, except by an exhaustive search through the detailed accounts of all the occasions of service, but I find by the official report of the inquiry into the circumstances of the accidents to the Southport and St. Anne's life-boats in December, 1886, made to the Board of Trade by Sir Digby Murray, Bart., and captain, the Hon. H. W. Chetwynd, of the Royal navy, chief inspector of life-boats for the institution, that during the previous thirty-two years, the self-righting boats of the institution had been launched in actual service 5,000 times, whereby 12,000 lives were saved, and that on these occasions 41 of the boats had capsized, 23 of the accidents being unattended with loss of life, while 18 were accompanied with fatal results. The number of persons lost was 88, 76 being life-boatmen and 12 shipwrecked people. The report further states that "the 76 life-boatmen lost represented about 1 in 850 of the men afloat in the life-boats on service, and the capsizes 1 out of each 120 launches on service." In the case of our capsized surf-boats the 27 men lost represented 1 in 1,744 of the men afloat in the surf-boats on service, and the capsizes 1 out of each 480 launches on service. But as the saving of property is an incidental duty imposed upon our crews, the surf-boats, although they are not used in saving cargoes, are doubtless often launched under conditions more favorable than generally fall to the lot of the boats of the institution, and therefore the number of launches does not afford a satisfactory basis for comparison. Let us therefore take another basis. The number of lives saved by the life-boats is stated, as we have seen, at 12,000—in round numbers, probably. Calling the number saved by the surf-boats 6,500 in round numbers, we find, then, 1 capsize of the surf-boat to every 464 persons saved, a difference in its favor of 172. The self-righting boat lost 1 life to every 136 saved, the surf-boat 1 to every 158 saved, a difference of 22 in its favor. Of the life-boatmen afloat, 1 to 850 were lost by the self-righting boat, 1 to 1,109 by the surf-boat, a difference of 259 in favor of the latter. In the life-boat 1 man of the crew is lost for every 157 lives saved, in the surf-boat 1 for every 240 saved, a difference in favor of the surf-boat of 83.

Since 1876 there have been put into the United States Service 37 self-righting and self-bailing life-boats of the model of a boat received from the Royal National Life-boat Institution. They are all nearly reproductions of the boat sent to us. They are 29 feet 3 inches in length, 7 feet 7 inches beam, 3 feet 1$\frac{1}{4}$ inches deep amidships, 1 foot 10 inches sheer of gunwale, straight-bottomed, pull 8 oars, and weigh about 4,000 pounds each. This great weight is made necessary by the device of a heavy iron keel to aid in securing the self-righting quality. They have made on service 471 trips and saved 584 persons; they have capsized on service 4 times, once with fatal results, 5 lives, all ship-wrecked people, being lost. These figures produce results similar to those already reached in reference to the life-boats used in Great Britain. The boats have capsized once in each 118 trips, and once in rescuing every 146 persons, and one life has been lost from the boats to every 117 saved.

There are two other varieties of self-righting and self-bailing boats in the service—the Richardson and the Dobbins. They are modifications of the life-boat just described, though considerably lighter. They have not been used often enough to furnish any practical basis of comparison, but have given good results so far.

Notwithstanding these figures it would be unwise to hastily conclude that the surf-boat of either variety mentioned is the best life-boat for all conditions of service. Among the boats at present employed in life-saving institutions I know of none that can justly be denominated the best life-boat. The type that is best for one locality may be ill-adapted or entirely unfitted for another, and a boat that would be serviceable at one time might be worse than useless at another in the same locality.

On the larger portion of the Atlantic sea-board boat service at wrecks is not very distant from the shore, and the chief danger lurks in the line of surf which must be crossed and in the breakers on outlying shoals. For this service the surf-boat is easily transported on its carriage through the loose and trackless sands of the strand to a point as near the wreck as possible, is quickly unloaded, and at a favorable time is launched in a minute. The keeper steers with a long steering oar, and with the aid of his trained surfmen, intent upon his every look and command, maneuvers his buoyant craft through the surf with masterly skill. He is usually able to avoid a direct encounter with the heaviest breakers, but if he is obliged to receive their onset meets them directly "head on." His practiced hand immediately perceives any excess of weight thrown against either bow and instantly counteracts its force with his oar as instinctively and unerringly as the skilled musician presses the proper key of his instrument. He thus keeps his boat from broaching-to and avoids a threatened capsize. The self-righting boat is more unwieldy and not so quickly responsive to the coxswain's tactics, and is therefore not so well adapted to our general work.

The usual conditions of service in the United Kingdom are probably different. The excursions the life-boats make on service are said to be more extended, and exposure to violent gales for long periods upon the open sea more frequent. Our surf-boats, it is true, venture upon outlying shoals covered with breakers, such as the Nantucket Shoals, off Massachusetts, and the Diamond Shoals, off Cape Hatteras, but it is likely that there is no such locality within the scope of our Service so fatal as the terrible Goodwin Sands, which are often visited by the boats of the Royal National Life-Boat Institution, and where they have accomplished so much noble work. There are doubtless other important differences in the requirements of service with which I am not acquainted. Probably, therefore, the conditions are so diverse that no just conclusion as to the superiority of the two boats can be drawn from the results of their experience, and I have given these results in comparison, not with a desire to establish such a conclusion, but to show that the United States Service has provided quite as effective means for dealing with the conditions presented to it as the most eminent organization of other countries has for its conditions, and because I thought they might be of service in the deliberations of the committee in considering some of the topics of the division of the programme referred to it, and, further, because I thought they might aid in the efforts always being made by life-saving institutions and by individuals to improve the safety of life-saving boats. Where long excursions are to be undertaken and the service is exceptionally hazardous, the men undoubtedly feel safer in a self-righting boat, and, having this in view, it has been introduced into many of our stations, where it may be found side by side with the surf-boat, the choice being left to the keepers to' take either, as the occasion seems in their experienced judgment to demand.

Self-righting and self-bailing are properties unquestionably desirable in any boat designed to be used in saving life, provided they can be obtained without too greatly impairing other necessary qualities. May it not be a question worthy of consideration whether these properties and the means of propulsion by sails can not be advantageously incorporated into the surf-boat without materially increasing its weight and draught, and whether such a boat would not be found to be better adapted to perform the general services of life-boats than those which sit deeply in the water, and which, on that account and because of their great weight, are less agile in action and more difficult to transport and launch? Already, as I have said, the self-bailing property has been successfully applied by Lieutenant McLellan, and is hailed with delight by our crews; the addition of sails has also been accomplished by the use of a center-board, and I am able to add that I believe the self-righting quality is on the verge of successful application. One boat of this kind is already built, and with slight changes, which seem entirely practicable, I believe will satisfactorily solve the problem, at least so far as to answer all the purposes of our Service. When this result is attained, why may not self-bailing and self righting boats supplant the inferior boats now carried upon passenger vessels for life-boats? And why, since it has been found that the self-bailing principle can be applied to a model thoroughly convenient to be carried on shipboard, may not these vessels even now be supplied with self-bailing boats, in which the liability to capsize is greatly diminished by reason of their ability to immediately free themselves of any water they may ship?

For effecting line communication with stranded vessels our Service chiefly employs the Lyle gun, named after Capt. D. A. Lyle, of the Ordnance Department of the United States Army, who devised it. It is to be found in every station except the houses of refuge. But the Hunt gun, devised by Mr. Edmund S. Hunt, of Massachusetts, and the Cunningham rocket, invented by Mr. Patrick Cunningham, of the same State, have been recently furnished to a few stations where the outlying bars are so far off shore that vessels may possibly strand beyond the range of the Lyle gun. This has been done, not in the belief that the beach-apparatus can be effectually used at any distance beyond this range, but with the hope that a line, if thrown from the shore to a wreck, might be used to effect the passage of a boat or a life-car, or that some other means for rescue might be improvised. The Lyle gun is of bronze, with a smooth 2½-inch bore, weighs, with its carriage 185 pounds, and carries a shot weighing 17 pounds. This projectile is a solid elongated cylinder 14¼ inches in length, into the base of which is screwed an eye-bolt for receiving the shot-line, the bolt projecting sufficiently beyond the muzzle of the gun to protect the line from being burned off in firing. When the gun is fired the weight and inertia of the line cause the projectile to reverse. The shot-lines used are of three sizes, designated by the numbers 4, 7, and 9, being respectively $\frac{4}{32}$, $\frac{7}{32}$, and $\frac{9}{32}$ of an inch in diameter. Any charge of powder can be used up to the maximum of 6 ounces. A range of 695 yards has been obtained with the No. 4 line under favorable circumstances. The range of the larger line is, of course, proportionately diminished. The No. 4 is only used where the vessel is thought to lie beyond the range of the larger lines, for the reason that it is not strong enough to sustain the hauling of the whip line on board—and an intermediate line has to be supplied, requiring the expenditure of time and strength—and because it is not so easily hauled upon by the shipwrecked sailors as the larger one. The Hunt gun is also of bronze, of about the same size and weight as the Lyle, and not very different from it, except that it has a bore an inch larger and is attached to its carriage-bed at the cascabel instead of resting on trunnions. Indeed, the peculiarity of the Hunt system is not in the gun, but in the projectile, which could be fired just as well from the Lyle gun if the latter were of sufficient caliber. This projectile consists of a cylindrical tube of tin, into one end of which is soldered a solid hemispherical piece of lead, which, when the projectile is placed in the gun, rests upon the cartridge, and upon discharge reverses its position like the Lyle shot and goes foremost. The shot-line, being fastened into a staple in the center of the inside surface of this piece of lead, is coiled in the tube until the cavity is nearly filled, being kept in place by a coating of paraffine, which is sufficiently adhesive for the purpose, but does not materially retard its paying out as the projectile flies. The tube has a capacity for 320 yards of No. 4 line. In the outer end is placed a diaphragm of pasteboard with a circular hole in its center three-quarters of an inch in diameter through which a portion of the other end of the line hangs out. When the missile is placed in the gun 4 or 5 inches protrude beyond the muzzle. Upon this portion four trapeziform wings are soldered at regular intervals to control the flight. Before firing the protruding end of the incased line is tied to another line coiled in a can, or otherwise so arranged as to permit it to be taken out without entanglement. When the discharge takes place the line in the can by its inertia and weight causes the line in the projectile to pay out, and when the latter is exhausted furnishes the supply for the remainder of the flight. The range obtained is about 40 yards greater than can be had with the Lyle projectile. The Massachusetts Humane Society uses this system altogether. The United States Service prefers the Lyle system, because where extreme range is not required it conveys a larger and stronger line to the shipwrecked; because it does not require the use of an intermediate line for hauling on board the whip line (Mr. Hunt claims that the line he uses is strong enough, but I should not dare to trust it), and because the projectile can be used any number of times, while the Hunt projectile after once being fired, either in drill or service, has to be returned to the manufacturer to be refilled, or a new one must be obtained, involving expense and trouble.

The Cunningham rocket system may be said to be an application of the Hunt projectile to a rocket. It consists of a powerful rocket, at the rear end of which is a female screw that receives the pointed end of a sheet-iron tube 5 feet 9½ inches in length and of equal diameter with the rocket. This tube is packed with 800 yards of No. 4 shot-line, which is connected with a shore-line in the same manner as in the Hunt system, and is paid out in flight as from the Hunt projectile. The tube also takes the place of the stick in other rockets. The shore-line can be of any size. The range of the rocket with a No. 4 shore line is from 700 to 1,000 yards, which is diminished with other lines according to their sizes. With any line it exceeds that of any other rocket I have seen.

Several considerations have determined the choice of the gun for general use in the Life-Saving Service in preference to the rocket, among which are the following:

(1) Within its range it performs the desired service equally as well as any rocket at much less expense. The cost of the Lyle gun and all its appurtenances, exclusive of projectiles, is $87.83. The lowest cost of any efficient rocket with appurtenances that I know of is not much less. The only expense attending the use of the gun is the cost of the cartridge, say half a dime, except when occasionally a shot is lost, which can be replaced for $2. When a rocket is fired several dollars are expended. These facts are of consequence when considered in connection with the utility of frequent drilling.

(2) The gun is very easily handled and readily prepared for firing. Everything can be done almost as well in the dark as in the light, and,

if the weather be cold, without taking off the mittens. The manipulation of the rockets I have seen and experimented with is not so simple.

(3) A rocket must be given considerable elevation in firing, whereby the line is carried high in the air—usually far above the stranded vessel—where it is exposed to the force of the wind, making it liable, in falling, to float wide of the mark and fail to drop across the vessel. The gun, on the other hand, can be given any elevation—even be depressed below a horizontal position if fired from a cliff—and the charge of powder can be graduated according to the distance the vessel lies from the shore, thereby greatly reducing the chance of failure.

A recent incident admirably illustrates the adaptability of the gun to exceptional situations. In the great storm of September last the keeper of the Hunniwell's Beach Station, on the coast of Maine, was notified that a wrecking crew of fifteen persons who were at work upon a vessel which had some time before struck upon Glover's Rock, some 5 miles distant from the station and out of sight, had hoisted a signal of distress. He put a heaving-stick, the Lyle gun, a shot-line, a whip-line, a breeches-buoy, and a spare line into the surf-boat, and with his crew set out for the rock. Arriving, he found the wreckers in danger of being engulfed by the growing sea, and that the boat could not approach near enough to enable him to reach the rock with the heaving-stick. He therefore anchored his boat, set the shot-line box on the stern, lashed the gun upon the after thwart, loaded it with a 1-ounce cartridge of powder, and fired, casting the line almost into the hands of the imperiled men. It was found impossible, however, to take them off with the breeches-buoy without great risk of their being dashed upon the projecting points of the rock. Fortunately there was a small dory upon the rock, by means of which, with the use of the line, the whole number was drawn in six trips safely to the surf-boat, which took them ashore through a sea which the keeper describes as as heavy as he ever saw. In the same storm the crew of the Lewes Station, Delaware, fired the gun from the upper window of a fish-house and landed the crew of a vessel into the loft with the breeches-buoy.

For a vehicle in which to transport people from a wreck to shore after line communication has been established, the breeches-buoy is generally used as in other countries. The life-car (which I believe to be the invention of Mr. Joseph Francis, of New Jersey, although this is disputed by Capt. Douglas Ottinger, of the Revenue Marine Service, who claims to have devised it) is sometimes taken, however, especially where many persons are to be landed, and where the distance is too great to use the breeches-buoy. The car is a covered boat, made of corrugated galvanized iron, furnished with rings at each end, into which hauling-lines are bent, whereby the car is hauled back and forth on the water between the wreck and the shore without the use of any apparatus. It is supplied, however, with bails, one near each end, by which it can be suspended from a hawser and passed along upon it like the breeches-buoy, if found necessary, as is sometimes the case where the shore is abrupt. The cover of the boat is convex, is provided with a hatch, which fastens either inside or outside, through which entrance and exit are effected. Near each end it is perforated with a group of small holes, like the holes in a grater, punched outward, to supply air for breathing, without admitting much if any water. It is capable of containing six or seven persons, and is very useful in landing sick people and valuables, as they are protected from getting wet. On the first occasion of its use it saved two hundred and one persons.

In all other respects than those noted the beach-apparatus is the same as is used elsewhere.

A difficulty that has not infrequently seriously obstructed the operations of rescue, and which, I suppose, is familiar to all institutions which use the apparatus, is the inability of the ship's company to intelligently and promptly co-operate with the rescuing force. Improvidence has been imputed to sailors as a characteristic to an extent that is probably unjust. However that may be, it is certain that as a rule they do not in advance make the preparation for the emergencies of shipwreck that instinctive regard for their own safety would be expected to prompt. One would naturally suppose that every intelligent sailor, at least every officer of a vessel, aware that there existed upon the coasts of nearly every country stations supplied with means of aiding their rescue if they should unhappily be cast ashore, would carefully acquaint himself with the methods employed. This is so far from being the case that tedious delays in the work of deliverance are frequently occasioned by their ignorance, which in some instances in the history of our service have nearly proved fatal. The inscriptions printed in English and French upon the tally-boards or tablets which are sent out with the whip-line and hawser are explicit enough as to what is to be done after they are received, but they can not always be read, sometimes on account of darkness, sometimes because no one on board is familiar with either the French or the English language. Again, I have known instances in which sailors did not even know what to do with the shot-line sent them, and have with difficulty been made to understand that they were to haul it aboard. In dealing with this trouble we have followed the example of the rocket service of the Board of Trade in England and published a pocket manual containing complete instructions for co-operating with the station crews and showing by plain cuts the manner of setting up the parts of the apparatus sent on board. To this is added a list of the stations, with their locations, and other useful information relating to the service. Each book is provided with a receptacle for cards, papers, etc., which makes the officers of vessels glad to get them and carry them in their pockets on account of the convenience they afford for the care of their small papers. Their value has been illustrated on several occasions of rescue, when the captains have stood, book in hand, and given directions from it as the operations progressed.

This device, however, has only partially remedied the evil. The distribution is not sufficiently general; in several nations not being made at all. I understand that in England and some other countries a knowledge of these matters is required as a qualification in officers of vessels. If the other maritime nations would also require this, the difficulties experienced would largely disappear. Emergencies arise, however, where, although the sailors well understand the part they have to take, progress would be greatly facilitated if there were some means of communicating between them and their co-operators on the shore, particularly at night. Such means would be advantageous not only on such occasions, but at other times, as when the shipwrecked, lured by the comparatively smooth appearance of the surf as viewed from seaward, attempt to land in their own boats, while it can be plainly seen from the shore that the venture must be fatal. I think I can safely say that more lives are now lost within the scope of station operations through these attempts than from any other cause.

The telephone lines which now extend along nearly all those portions of the coast on which contiguous stations are located make it easy to quickly concentrate the crews of two or more stations at any point where additional force is required, as in the case when several wrecks occur at the same time in the same neighborhood; and the double equipment at each station expedites this concentration by permitting the re-enforcing crew to come unencumbered. A notable illustration of the benefit of such a combination of crews was the work achieved near Cape Henlopen in the great storm of September 10, 11, and 12 last, one of the most destructive that has ever visited our coast, when the crews of three stations, under the leadership of Captain Clampitt, of the Lewes Station, rescued the crews of 22 stranded vessels—194 persons—by the use of every form of rescuing appliance; 23 being landed with the surf-boats, 16 with the self-righting life-boat, 135 with the breeches-buoy, and 20 with the life-car—not a life being lost.

The telegraph and railroad systems of the country are also used to secure the services of the crews at scenes of rescue far remote from their stations. On two occasions the Cleveland crew has been called to Cincinnati, Ohio, and Newport, Ky., a distance of 240 miles, to render aid to the sufferers from inundations in the Ohio Valley. On the first occasion 1,200 persons were succored, on the second over 800. The crew of the Sturgeon Bay Ship-Canal Station, Lake Superior, was once called at night to Chocolay Beach, near Marquette, Mich., a distance of 110 miles. Proceeding by special train running at the highest attainable speed, and taking with them their beach apparatus and boat, they reached the beach at midnight, and through a blinding snow-storm and in spite of bitter cold, were able to board two stranded vessels and rescue 24 persons after every effort of the citizens had failed. Shorter journeys of from 15 to 30 miles by rail are frequently undertaken, especially where the railway skirts the shore, as it does on many parts of the coast.

At isolated stations, where aid from another station is not available, the keepers have authority to accept the assistance of volunteers, who are paid $3 each per day upon the certificate of the keeper, approved by the district superintendent.

After rescue the shipwrecked people are taken to the station and provided with every comfort it affords. They find hot coffee and dry clothing awaiting them, with cots for those who need rest and sleep. If any are sick or maimed, as is frequently the case, they are nursed and cared for until sufficiently recovered to safely leave; in the meantime medical aid is called in if practicable. For wounds and ailments requiring only simple and well-known remedies, recourse is had to the medicine-chest, which is stocked with restoratives and medicines that can be safely used and provided with a hand-book of directions. The sojourner also finds at hand a very fair library of books to relieve the tedium of his enforced detention.

The dry clothing is taken from a supply constantly kept on hand by the Woman's National Relief Association, an organization established to afford relief to sufferers from disasters of every kind, and the libraries are the donations of the Seamen's Friend Society and of sundry benevolent individuals. Several newspaper publishers send their papers regularly to many of the stations. The food is prepared by the keepers or the station messes, who are re-imbursed by the recipients if they have the means; if not, by the Government.

Occasionally unfortunate victims of shipwreck reach the shore to all appearances dead. In such cases the life-saving crews attempt their restoration according to the method for restoring the apparently drowned, in which they have been drilled as already described. When the Service was first organized we adopted the system then, and I believe, still employed by nearly all life-saving organizations. It is known as the Hall-Silvester method, containing features of each of the systems formulated by Dr. Marshall Hall and Dr. H. R. Silvester. A discussion of the subject in the Life-Boat Journal (February number, 1873), in which the "direct method," as it is called, recommended by Dr. Benjamin Howard, of New York, was brought to my attention, led to the adoption of the latter system with some slight modifications suggested by Dr. John M. Woodworth, late Surgeon-General of the United States Marine Hospital Service. Dr. Frank Baker, professor of anatomy in the medical department of Georgetown University, who is also connected with the Life-Saving Service, has at my request made a very thorough examination of the various systems, and has submitted an exhaustive report upon them. He states his general conclusion as follows:

"The different methods all have in view the expulsion of the vitiated air in the lungs and the introduction of fresh. To effect this, respiratory movements are stimulated. Hall does this by turning the patient on his face and compressing the thorax by pressure on the back, then turning him on the side and allowing the thorax to expand. The expulsion of air is but slight, but it is an excellent method of expelling fluids from the stomach and lungs. In Silvester's method the arms are first stretched at full length upward beside the head, then carried downward, pressing the elbows against the thorax. These motions are thought to alternately expand and contract the chest. It is difficult to understand how the first movement can produce an effective expansion, as the scapulæ are not fixed, and the muscles passing directly from the arms to the chest are inserted so high up on the thorax as to have but little, if any, effect. The second movement produces an expulsion of air, but not as effectively as in the method of Howard, by which the lower thorax and the abdomen are compressed, the diaphragm consequently pushed up, and the lungs emptied. This method is believed to be more efficient than any other that has been employed. No active inspiratory movement is made, the expansive resiliency of the chest-wall springing back after compression being sufficient."

During the twelve years in which the "direct method" has been practiced in the Service one hundred and eighteen cases have come under the treatment of our crews. In this number of attempts at resuscitation sixty were successful and fifty-eight unsuccessful. In some of the successful instances several hours elapsed after the patient was taken from the water before natural respiration was induced. Success has followed even after the patient had been pronounced dead beyond hope by reputable physicians. As to the results obtained by other methods I have been unable to secure any information.

Next to the success of the Service in saving life that of its efforts in the saving of property is conspicuous. This is accomplished in getting vessels afloat when stranded, a work in which the surfmen are experts; in extricating them from dangerous situations; in pumping them out when leaking; in running lines between wrecked vessels and tugs when it can not be done with ordinary boats; in rendering assistance in various ways, and in warning off vessels standing into danger. In the majority of casualties the surfmen succeed in saving the vessels and cargoes without any other aid than that of the ships' crews. When this is impossible they act in conjunction with the revenue-cutters—which are equipped for rendering assistance in such cases—if these vessels are available, or assist, if necessary, any other relief sent.

The tabular statistics published in the annual reports of the Service show, in reference to imperiled property, only the amount imperiled, the amount saved, and the amount lost within the field of station operations; but, in order to convey here a better idea of the value of the labors of the life-saving crews, I have had prepared a statement of their salvage work during the years 1888 and 1889. This statement shows that in 1888 the station crews saved, without any outside assistance, 194 vessels, valued, with their cargoes, at $1,495,550. The number of persons on board was 898. The number of vessels which they assisted other effort in saving was 88, the value involved being $2,170,500, and the number of persons on board 654. The aggregate number of vessels, therefore, which they saved and assisted to save was 282, the amount of property involved $3,666,050, and the number of persons ön board 1,552. They also rendered assistance of less importance to 210 other vessels. In 1889 the crews saved, without outside assistance, 172 vessels, valued, with their cargoes, at $1,127,295. The number of persons on board was 823. The number of vessels which they assisted other effort in saving was 85, the value involved being $2,114,535, and the number of persons on board 623. The aggregate number of vessels, therefore, which they saved and assisted to save in this year was 257, the amount of property involved $3,241,830, and the number of persons on board 1,446. Assistance of minor importance was rendered to 253 other vessels. For all this it must be remembered they received no salvage.

But their usefulness as salvors of property does not end here. By the aid of the telephone lines, all of which are connected with telegraph stations, they give to the maritime exchanges and underwriters early notice of disasters, with information as to the condition of the vessels, the extent of additional aid required, if any, etc., or send directly to the nearest available place for tugs or other needed help, thus securing prompt assistance where delay would involve serious and perhaps fatal consequences. More valuable than this, perhaps, is the service rendered both to humanity and commerce in the prevention of disasters by the warning signals of the night and day patrol. Of course no estimate of the lives and property saved in this manner can be made. We only know the number of such warnings given. Last year they were 217. They have reached as high as 240 in a year, and during any of the last six years have not been less than 200.

It is pertinent to inquire what it costs to maintain this system, and whether the results produced are proportionate to the outlay. The expenditures vary considerably from year to year, as do also the aggregate results produced, the difference depending upon the number of new stations added to the establishment and upon numerous contingencies. A summary of the expenditures and operations of any one year would therefore but imperfectly answer the inquiry. Such a statement, however, will be found interesting in other respects, and I give it in regard to the last fiscal year, as extracted from the annual report, not yet printed: The total expenditures were $965,907.18, all but $163,454.03 of which was expended in the payment of the compensation of the officers and men and that of the clerical force—$712,567.95 being paid to the keepers and surfmen alone. There were 378 disasters to documented vessels within the scope of the Service. There were on board these vessels 3,106 persons, of whom 38 were lost. The estimated value of property involved was $6,343,880. Of this amount $4,995,130 was saved and $1,348,750 lost. The number of vessels totally lost was 63. In addition to the foregoing there were 150 casualties to smaller craft—sailboats, row-boats, etc.—on which were 320 persons, of whom only 4 were lost. The property involved in these instances is estimated at $72,895, of which $59,310 was saved and $13,585 lost.

The results of all the disasters within the scope of the Service aggregate, therefore, as follows:'

Number of disasters	528
Value of property involved	$6,416,775
Value of property saved	$5,024,440
Value of property lost	$1,362,335
Number of persons involved	2,426
Number of persons lost	42
Number of vessels totally lost	63

To this statement should be added 787 shipwrecked persons succored at the stations, the number of days' succor afforded being 1,732.

There were landed by the surf-boats 435 persons, by the self-righting life-boats 74, by the river life-skiffs (at Louisville) 56, by other station boats 179, by the breeches-buoy 193, by the life-car 10, by other means 40. There were besides 24 persons rescued who had fallen from wharves, piers, etc. The details relative to the saving of property, etc., having already been stated.

It may be mentioned that the loss of life from documented vessels last year was unusually large. The year before it was only 12. The average loss per annum since the introduction of the present system is 26.

The following is a general summary of the statistics of disasters that have occurred within the scope of the Service from the introduction of the present system in 1871 to the close of the last year:

Number of disasters	4,924
Value of vessels	$55,473,190.00
Value of cargoes	$26,246,584.00
Value of property involved	$81,719,774.00
Value of property saved	$60,352,092.00
Value of property lost	$21,367,682.00
Number of persons involved	42,864
Number of lives lost	*505
Number of persons succored	7,903
Number of days' succor afforded	20,837
Cost of maintaining the Service	$9,172,208.86

We would probably obtain a better idea of the relation between the cost of maintenance and the results by taking the aggregate during the seven years since the adoption of the present rate of wages, commencing July 1, 1883, and afterwards giving the average per station. In 1883 there were 194 stations; 1884, 201; 1885, 203; 1886, 211; 1887, 218; 1888, 222; 1889, 225; making a total of 1,474 stations. The general cost and results may be summed up as follows:

Cost during seven years	$5,791,184.05
Number of disasters	3,232
Value of property involved (vessels and cargoes)	$52,441,120.00
Value of property saved	$42,286,800.00
Value of property lost	$10,154,320.00

*This includes 30 lost from undocumented vessels (small craft).

Number of persons on board	27,766
Number of persons lost	196
Number of shipwrecked persons succored at the stations	4,831
Number of days' succor afforded	12,402
Number of disasters resulting in total loss of vessels	482

The average number of stations was 210, and the average annual cost of maintenance per station was therefore $3,928.89. Other average results per station per annum are as follows:

Number of disasters	2.19
Value of property involved	$35,577.42
Value of property saved	$28,688.47
Value of property lost	$6,888.95
Number of persons involved	18.97
Number of persons saved	18.84
Number of persons lost (being one person to every seven stations)	.13
Number of persons succored	3.27
Number of days' succor afforded	8.41
Number of disasters resulting in total loss of vessels (being one to every three stations)	.33

It is to be regretted that no data exist from which a definite comparison of the results of disasters to vessels upon the coasts, before and after the establishment of stations thereon, can be drawn. Unfortunately no provision of law was made for the collection of statistics pertaining to disasters beyond the scope of the service until 1874, when authority was given to gather them. From the time, however, that the present life-saving system began its work upon the coasts of Long Island and New Jersey, in 1871, all-important data relating to casualties within its province have been secured. In 1849 and 1850, as I have before stated, the Government had erected upon these coasts boat-houses containing surf-boats and other life-saving appliances, each in charge of a keeper, for such effort as might be volunteered on occasions of shipwreck (a system somewhat similar to other existing volunteer systems), and although no definite record of the results of this experiment was kept, it is known that many lives were saved through the facilities it afforded. The number lost can not be ascertained. I have positively learned, however, of the loss of 512 persons during the twenty years from 1850 to 1870, and have authentic information that these figures indicate but a fragment of the reality. Yet they afford the basis for some comparison. They give, for instance, an average annual loss of at least 25 lives. During the eighteen years of the existence of the present system the number lost upon this section of the coast has been 119, an annual average of only 7—a reduction of about 80 per cent.—which would doubtless be largely augmented if the facts could be ascertained, and this, notwithstanding the number of disasters has greatly increased as a consequence of the growth of the commerce of the country, particularly that of New York and Philadelphia.

It will be observed, too, that the ascertained loss of 512 lives during the twenty years of the volunteer system, although confined to a very small section of the coast, is greater than that upon all the dangerous coasts which have come under the protection of the present system during the last eighteen years. Yet this latter number (505) includes 30 lives lost from undocumented vessels (small craft), while the former does not embrace such. It also contains the lives of 28 wreckers lost from the steam-ship *Circassian* in 1876, on the Long Island coast, for whose rescue the breeches-buoy apparatus had been set up, but was deliberately and against the keeper's protest cast overboard by the wrecker in charge, for fear that his men would become frightened and avail themselves of it as the storm increased, while he hoped to float the vessel at high tide. If these be deducted the number will be reduced to 447, and yield an average annual loss for the entire service less than that upon the New Jersey and Long Island coasts alone under the volunteer system. I may here remark that in making up the annual record of the loss of life under the present system, care has always been taken to include every instance that could with any degree of fairness be said to have occurred within the field of the operations of the service; the doubtful cases have been counted in, and among them are others than those specified above that could be deducted with equally good reason.

I have thus endeavored to present a sketch of the organization and methods of the Life-Saving Service of this country and to convey an accurate idea of its effectiveness. Doubtless the system appears to be an expensive and elaborate one, but it must be remembered that, putting aside entirely the consideration of the value of human life, which is beyond computation, it saves many times its cost in property alone, and that it fulfills the functions usually allotted to several different agencies. It rescues the shipwrecked by both the principal methods which human ingenuity has devised for that purpose, and which in some countries are practiced separately by two distinct organizations; it furnishes them the subsequent succor which elsewhere would be afforded by shipwrecked mariners' societies; it guards the lives of persons in peril of drowning by falling into the water from piers and wharves in the harbors of populous cities, an office usually performed by humane societies; it nightly patrols the dangerous coasts for the early discovery of wrecks and the hastening of relief, thus increasing the chances of rescue and shortening by hours intense physical suffering and the terrible agony of suspense; it places over peculiarly dangerous points upon the rivers and lakes a sentry prepared to send instant relief to those who incautiously or recklessly incur the hazard of capsizing in boats; it conducts to places of safety those imperiled in their homes by the torrents of flood, and conveys food to those imprisoned in their houses by inundation and threatened with famine; it annually saves, unaided, hundreds of stranded vessels with their cargoes from total or partial destruction, and assists in saving scores of others; it protects wrecked property, after landing, from the ravage of the elements and the rapine of plunderers; it extricates vessels unwarily caught in perilous positions; it averts numerous disasters by its flashing signals of warning to vessels standing into danger; it assists the customs service in collecting the revenues of the Government; it pickets the coast with a guard, which prevents smuggling, and, in time of war, surprise by hostile forces. I might considerably extend the catalogue of its beneficent offices. I could tell of the valuable aid it has rendered to scientific research; of its contributions of rare specimens to the department of marine zoology in our National Museum; of the hotels, dwellings, mills, and other structures it has saved from destruction by fire; of its timely detection and prevention of burglaries and robberies, and of many other services inuring to the public benefit which it has incidentally rendered. But I must not detain the committee longer. I have made a heavy draft upon its time and patience, which nothing but the importance of the subject would justify. The Conference sits in council charged with the responsibility of devising means to secure, if possible, a greater measure of safety to those who go down to the sea in ships. It is a responsibility of the gravest nature, in which we have an important share. We are to study the different methods of dealing with the contingencies of shipwreck; to compare the results of our individual experience and observations, and deduce for the consideration of the Conference such rules of action as seem to us practicable and best for common adoption. Of course, it is not apprehended that it is possible, or perhaps even desirable, that the diverse systems and methods pertaining to the various life-saving institutions of the world should be made uniform, but if the Conference could have the benefit of a full exposition of all of them, perhaps some of the best features of each system might be selected and recommended for general extension. Under these considerations and with this view I have felt that I ought not to omit, even at the risk of being tiresome, the mention of anything essential to afford a just conception of the general character and scope of our service, which is so unlike all other organizations established for similar purposes.

APPENDIX F.

MEMORANDA RELATING TO LIFE-SAVING INSTITUTIONS ON THE COASTS OF EUROPE.

The following information and statistics have been collected with reference to institutions for the saving of life from shipwrecks in various European countries:

AUSTRIA.

[Translation.]

*   *   *   *   *   *   *

There are in this empire neither public nor private life-saving institutions, such as exist in the United States of America, because conditions on the east coast of the Adriatic do not render such institutions necessary.

In cases of wrecks or other disasters, the health officers of the port are bound to adopt the required measures to offer the first assistance to the endangered persons, and to secure, if possible, ship and cargo, to which end they use the boats, anchors, and ropes which are at their disposal.

Of these officers or harbor police, those stationed at Trieste, Lussin-piccolo, Zara, and Spalato are provided with steamers, and the one at Rovigno has a sail-boat, to offer effective assistance in the saving of life.

The harbor police at the remaining ports are empowered to hire private boats and help in case their means of rendering assistance are insufficient.

Aside from these there are life-saving boats, especially constructed for the purpose, stationed in four ports on the coast of Istria where traffic is greatest, which serve at the same time as guard-ships to the revenue officers; namely, at Umago and Cittanova, on the west coast of Istria, the life-boats III and V, built respectively in 1876 and 1878, at Rabaz; on the east coast of Istria, life-boat No. I, built in 1876; and at Fare-sina, on the island of Cherso, life-boat No. II, built in 1883.

These boats are always kept in a state ready for use at a moment's notice, are perfectly sea-worthy, and are adapted, when properly manned, to saving life at sea.

The above-named officers and men of the harbor police report by telegraph each disaster taking place in their respective districts to the chief of the marine department, who, according to circumstances, adopts further measures for saving the vessel in distress.

There are no special publications issued or any reports made by the above-named officers. The chief of the marine department simply collects the data as furnished by each station relative to name and tonnage of vessels, location and cause of accident, damage and loss of life sustained, and publishes these annually in the Annuario Marittimo.

Nor is the life-saving service at sea on the coasts of the Hungarian monarchy entrusted to a special institution, but is performed by the harbor police, supplied for this purpose with the necessary crews, boats, and material.

The publications treating of life-saving appear in the annual reports of the royal Hungarian marine department at Fiume, in the official weekly newspaper, and in the monthly series of the "Reports of the Royal Hungarian Ministry of Commerce."

* * * *

Vienna, November 13, 1888.

For the minister of foreign affairs.

M. PASETTI.

BELGIUM.

The life-saving service, established since 1838, is a state institution.

The Government alone bears all the expenses for material, crews, and staff necessitated by the organization and maintenance of the service.

The life-saving stations are scattered along the whole coast for a distance of 65 kilometers.

There are stations at Adinkerke, Nieuport, Ostende, Blankenberghe, and at Knocke. A new one is in course of erection at Coq, between Blankenberghe and Ostende.

At Nieuport and Blankenberghe there is a station on both sides of the harbor, as well as at Ostende, where there is a large life-boat, which is towed by one of the Government tugs in case a vessel should be in distress in the offing.

Each boat's crew consists of a cockswain, one or two assistants, and from seven to twelve rowers.

There is a life-boat at each of the stations provided with all the necessary apparatus and appliances for assisting crews and vessels in distress, always ready to be launched.

A wreck gun and projectiles are placed at the disposition of the chief of the station for the purpose of establishing line communication with the shore when the state of the sea prevents even insubmersible boats from approaching the wreck.

The boats and apparatus are stored in sheds, situated in places easiest of access to the beach. Each station has a supply of medicine and surgical appliances. The care of shipwrecked crews is superintended by the physician attached to the station.

DENMARK.

Direction of the life-saving Service of North Jutland.

LEMVIG, *September* 20, 1889.

In herewith returning the inquiry of the Treasury Department at Washington in relation to various points connected with the life-saving service on the Danish coasts, which inquiry was received together with the communication of the ministry of the 17th instant, I would state as follows:

The institutions in this country for the rescue of the shipwrecked are that of North Jutland, that of Bornholm, and that of Möen.

As regards the Life-Saving Service of North Jutland, I would refer to the list of stations and persons employed thereat, which appears in the report of the last fiscal year.

The expense of the Life-Saving Service is defrayed by the State exclusively.

The number of life-saving stations will be found in the inclosed Notice to Navigators.

As regards the operations for the year up to March 31, 1889, within the scope of the life-saving stations of Jutland, I would state:

The number of cases of stranding was 73.

The value of the property saved and lost on these occasions is unknown to me, and no information can be given on this subject.

The number of persons shipwrecked on the occasions of the aforesaid 73 strandings was 742.

The number of persons rescued, 737.

Four shipwrecked persons perished on the coast when the vessel went to pieces, which it did before assistance could be rendered, and during a collision with one of the light-ships on the coast a seaman belonging to the crew of the colliding vessel was killed by a falling spar; thus 5 men in all perished.

As shipwrecked persons are not cared for at Danish life-saving stations, for the reason that sufficient accommodations are afforded by the neighboring inhabitants, the inquiries on this subject are not applicable to the state of things in this country.

The number of vessels totally lost during the aforesaid fiscal year was 40.

As regards the result obtained from the time of the establishment of our Life-Saving Service, computed from April 15, 1851, to March 31, 1887, I will refer, as far as Jutland is concerned, to the following extract from the Director's List of Strandings, and will answer the inquiries as follows:

The whole number of vessels stranded during the above-named period was.. 2,208
The number stranded in 1887-'88 was.. 62
The number stranded in 1888-'89 was.. 73

Total... 2,343

The value of those vessels, as already stated, is unknown.
According to the extract the number of shipwrecked persons was 17,356
For 1887-'88 add 411
For 1888-'89 add 742

Total 18,509

According to this, up to March 31, 1887, the number of shipwrecked persons
who were rescued was 16,381
In 1887-'88 the number of persons rescued was............................... 398
In 1888-'89 the number of persons rescued was.............................. 737

Total... 17,516

Up to March 31, 1887, the number of those lost was 975
In 1887-'88 the number of those lost was 13
In 1888-'89 the number of those lost was 5

Total... 993

From April, 1857, up to March 31, 1887, the number of vessels totally lost
was 1,550
In 1887–'88 the number of vessels totally lost was 43
In 1888–'89 the number of vessels totally lost was 40

    Total 1,633

In addition to the... 18,509
    shipwrecked persons previously mentioned, the crews on board of 180
    "dead" vessels which were driven in up to March 31, 1889, were........ 1,046

    Total 19,555

From the "dead" vessels driven upon the coast the number of persons who
    perished in the open sea was 259
Before the stranding of not "dead" vessels took place the number of those
    who perished at sea was 35

    Total 294

Although the 294 persons last mentioned did not come under the information desired by the Treasury Department, I have nevertheless thought proper to furnish information concerning that portion of the "dead" vessels driven in and concerning other persons who lost their lives at sea.

* * * * * * *

A number of the foregoing data have been taken from the annual reports of the operations of the life-saving service, while others have been taken from other sources.

The concise information desired by the Department at Washington, a portion of which is herewith communicated, is not found in the aforesaid reports or in any other documents that are known to me.

    Very respectfully,

                              A. ANDERSEN.

THE MINISTRY OF THE INTERIOR.

EXTRACT FROM THE LIST OF STRANDINGS AT THE LIFE-SAVING STATIONS OF JUTLAND.

[Prepared by Vice-Consul A. Andersen, Director of the Life-Saving Service of Jutland.]

INTRODUCTORY REMARKS.

Before the Life-Saving Service was organized in Jutland, in the year 1852, means were adopted at certain points on the coast for the rescue of shipwrecked persons. Consequently, the list prepared includes shipwrecks on the west coast of Jutland for the period commencing April 20, 1851. The enumeration is continued up to March 31, 1887, and includes portions of the Cattegat coast.

The first printed report concerning the operations of the Life-Saving Service in this country appeared in the year 1858. As it was considered desirable, and even important on several accounts, that the list should embrace, as far as possible, all the losses that had occurred within the scope of the life-saving stations, even before the issue of the first report, efforts were made to collect the necessary data on this subject.

This had special reference to the so-called "dead" vessels, i. e., vessels driven ashore without any living persons on board, concerning the fate of whose crews the yearly reports could, as a rule, contain no information from the nature of the case.

Concerning the crews of 126 out of 173 "dead" vessels embraced in the list, of which the number of men saved in the open sea was 735, and that of those who perished in the open sea was *293, total 1,028, some information was obtained only by way of exception.

The fact that it was found possible to obtain some of these data after the lapse of a comparatively long period of time, is due in a great measure to the obliging disposition which the inquiries in question met with, almost without exception, among the local authorities on the coast, as well as among the Danish Consuls-General, Consuls, and Vice-Consuls in foreign countries, at the Record Office of Shipping, at the Bureau Veritas, at the editorial office of the "Berlingske Tidende," etc.

The aforesaid crews belonging to "dead" vessels, which, as already remarked, consisted of 1,028 men, are not taken into consideration in these observations, because the life-saving stations were unable to exert any influence over their fate.

The number of cases of stranding given in the list from folio 1 to 111, is 2,214. Of these no information could be obtained concerning 43, and in 6 cases the operation was repeated at the place of stranding, and is mentioned a like number of times in the list. The number of stranded vessels concerning which information was obtained was thus 2,165, to wit:

Flag.	Folio.	Rescued.	Lost.	Per cent. lost.	Vessels stranded.
Danish in the list	116–132	2,014	113	5.31	413
Norwegian	133–149	2,157	100	4.43	336
Swedish	150–159	1,640	111	6.34	191
German	161–181	3,887	211	5.15	490
English	182–196	3,334	272	7.54	358
Dutch	197–207	1,251	44	3.40	215
Russian	208–211	1,384	36	2.53	80
French	215–218	520	42	7.47	64
American		105	0		8
Belgian		11	0		3
Portuguese	220	19	0	3.24	2
Spanish		12	6		2
Italian		18	0		2
Austrian		14	0		1
From vessels nationality not ascertained		15	40		
		16,381	975		2,165
The coast life-boats rescued from Danish fishing vessels		123			
Total		16,504	975		2,165

* Thirty-one men of this number, although they perished in the open sea, did not belong to "dead" vessels.

If the last-named fishermen, rescued by life-boats, are not counted, the average percentage of persons who perished on the coast will be 5.62 of the number of persons shipwrecked.

The fact that the percentage of those lost is so different for the different flags, is to be attributed to various circumstances. The heavy loss of the English is principally due to their well-known disposition to attempt to land with their own boats. The low percentage of the Dutch is to be attributed to their flat-bottomed vessels, which were able to come nearer to land than others of the same size but with sharper bottoms, and the case was the same in respect to the Russians when the frigate *Alexander Newsky* was stranded with a numerous crew on board.

The number of vessels stranded, which were known, was...................... 2,165
The number of those concerning which no information could be obtained was. 43

2,208

The number of those got afloat (including 9 dead vessels) was 658
While those totally lost were.. 1,550

Total 2,208

In addition to these strandings a number of vessels ran aground in the course of the year, but succeeded in getting afloat again by their own efforts, without having any connection with the land.

According to folio 111 the number of persons rescued by life-boats was 2,136
And by fishermen 123

2,259

By the rocket apparatus 2,145
And with rocket apparatus previously to 1851.......................... 12

2,157

With both combined 68

Total 4,484

They are thus divided:

Established.	Life-boats.	Rocket apparatus.	Both combined.	Total.	Established.	Life-boats.	Rocket apparatus.	Both combined.	Total.
1850-'51	......	12	......	12	1870-'71	57	35	39	131
1851-'52	......	18	......	18	1871-'72	62	30	10	102
1852-'53	4	35	......	39	1872-'73	69	39	......	108
1853-'54	38	12	......	50	1873-'74	92	101	......	193
1854-'55	49	10	......	59	1874-'75	89	50	......	139
1855-'56	7	101	......	108	1875-'76	14	45	......	59
1856-'57	21	23	......	44	1876-'77	57	32	......	89
1857-'58	13	8	11	32	1877-'78	88	97	......	185
1858-'59	25	133	......	158	1878-'79	96	15	......	111
1859-'60	40	19	......	59	1879-'80	142	30	......	172
1860-'61	90	120	......	210	1880-'81	77	106	3	186
1861-'62	9	47	......	56	1881-'82	175	64	......	239
1862-'63	86	75	......	161	1882-'83	74	55	......	129
1863-'64	83	95	......	178	1883-'84	100	54	......	154
1864-'65	49	48	......	97	1884-'85	88	207	......	295
1865-'66	54	56	......	110	1885-'86	101	45	......	146
1866-'67	31	110	......	141	1886-'87	86	35	......	121
1867-'68	70	110	......	180					
1868-'69	34	35	......	69	Total......	2,259	2,157	68	4,484
1869-'70	89	50	5	144					

The number of life saving stations in Jutland on the 1st day of April. 1888, was 44, 3 of which were substations, under the management of men residing in the neighborhood.

The aforesaid operations took place at the following life-saving stations :

Name.	Estab-lished.	Life-boats.	Rocket appara-tus.	Both com-bined.	Total.
Aalbeck......................	1860	66	....	....	66
Skagen.......................	1852	162	15	....	177
Gl. Skagen	1869	272	11	....	283
Kandesterderne...............	1852	150	5	....	155
Tverated	1866	70	....	....	70
Nörre Tornby.................	1852	149	17	....	166
Lönstrup.....................	1852	82	9	....	91
Lökken	1852	177	·1	....	178
Blokhus ....'...........	1852	87	3	....	90
Slettestrand	1852	7	8	....	15
Thorupstrand................	1857	51	23	....	74
Lildstrand	1852	30	26	....	56
Hanstedholm.................	1852	37	54	....	91
Klitmöller...................	1852	56	201	....	257
Nörre Vorupöre...............	1852	75	175	....	250
Lyngby	1882	....	19	....	19
Hedegaardene................	1852	....	47	....	47
Vesteragger..................	1852	46	440	5	491
Aggerkanal (finished 1874).....	1852	117	....	....	117
Thyborön	1852	47	243	....	290
Flyvholm	1852	104	252	....	356
Ferring	1860	....	92	....	92
Tuskjär	1852	74	131	11	216
Thorsminde	1882	....	3	....,.....	3
Fjand	1858	....	109	....	109
Vedersö......................	1852	46	60	5	111
Söndervig	1857	....	38	....	38
Söuderlyngvig...............	1852	....	38	....	38
Haurvig.....................	1860	....	33	....	33
Bjerregaard	1852	....	59	....	59
Nymindegab..................	1857	18	16	39	73
Hennegaard..................	1852	....	5	....	5
Blaavand....................	1852	125	....	....	125
Svenske Knolde..............	1877	5	....	....	5
Rindby......................	1862	22	....	....	22
Fornaes	1870	....	7	....	7
Osterby	1871	88	5	5	98
Vestero	1875	73	....	....	73
Anholt	1878	....	23	....	23
And in 1850–1851		....	12	....	12
Total....................	....	2, 259	2, 157	68	4, 484

In operations of this kind, extending over a period of thirty-six years, there were, of course, some cases of disaster. Of these we will mention the capsizing of four life-boats while attempting to rescue ship-wrecked persons, on which occasion 11 boatmen and 12 of the persons who had been taken into the boats perished; also four capsizings, which caused the death of 8 men, who were in boats, going through the life-saving drill.

The work done by the persons employed at the life-saving stations of Jutland (who, on the 31st of March, 1887, were 39 overseers and 391 boatmen and assistants) may be divided as follows:

Four overseers and 41 boatmen and assistants took part in the rescue of from 4 to 6 shipwrecked persons.

Four overseers and 48 boatmen and assistants took part in the rescue of from 11 to 20 shipwrecked persons.

Six overseers and 53 boatmen and assistants took part in the rescue of from 21 to 30 shipwrecked persons.

Seven overseers and 51 boatmen and assistants took part in the rescue of from 31 to 50 shipwrecked persons.

Three overseers and 59 boatmen and assistants took part in the rescue of from 51 to 70 shipwrecked persons.

Four overseers and 32 boatmen and assistants took part in the rescue of from 71 to 100 shipwrecked persons.

Four overseers and 26 boatmen and assistants took part in the rescue of from 101 to 200 shipwrecked persons.

Four overseers took part in the rescue of from 201 to 417 shipwrecked persons.

Twenty-two boatmen and assistants took part in the rescue of from 201 to 491 shipwrecked persons.

In connection with the foregoing concise statement of the nationality of the stranded vessels, the following details are given:

Stranded vessels under the Danish flag.

The number of vessels, with crews, that were totally lost was......	240	
Without crews (dead vessels)...	16	
		256
The number got afloat was...		157
Total		413
Rescued by boats belonging to life-saving stations ....men..	245	
Rescued by the rocket apparatus of life-saving stations ......do...	165	
Rescued by both apparatus combined............... ....do...	8	
		418
Rescued by private boats from land...........................do...	310	
Rescued by other private assistance from land.................do...	250	
Rescued by getting vessels afloat and by their own efforts (including bringing to land) ....men..	994	
Rescued by both methods combined ....do...	42	
		1,596
Lost when vessel went to pieces.............................do...	75	
Lost in attempting to land by their own efforts...............do...	10	
Killed or washed overboard during stranding.................do...	28	
		113
Total...		2,127
Percentage of persons lost on the coast = 5.31.		
To the crews belonged, moreover, the men rescued in the open sea..	25	
And those lost in the same	58	
		83
Total		2,210

Vessels stranded under the Norwegian flag.

Totally lost, with crew..	212
Without crew (dead vessels)	44
	256
Got afloat..	80
Total	336

Rescued by boats belonging to life-saving stations .... men..   398
Rescued by rocket apparatus belonging to life-saving stations.do...   431
Rescued by both apparatus combined .... do...   5   834

Rescued by private boats from the land....................... ....do...   252
Rescued by other private help from land .... do...   141
Rescued by the vessels being got afloat and by their own efforts (in-
     cluding bringing to land) .... men..   864
Rescued by both methods combined .... do...   66   1,323

                                                              2,157

The number of those who perished when the vessel went to pieces
     was   53
The number of those who perished in attempting to land   23
The number of those killed or washed overboard during the strand-
     ing, was   24   100

     Total   2,257
Percentage of those who perished on the coast = 4.43
To the crews belonged, moreover, those rescued in the open
     sea .... men..   331
And those lost in same .... do...   128   359

     Total   2,616

Vessels stranded under the Swedish flag.

Totally lost with crew......................................   133
Without crew (dead vessels)   8   141

Got afloat   50

Total .... ..:..   191

Rescued with boats belonging to life-saving stations........men..   292
Rescued with rocket-apparatus belonging to life-saving stations.do...   213   505

Rescued by private boats from land ....do...   218
Rescued by other private help from land....................... do...   82
Rescued by vessels being got afloat and by their own efforts (including
     bringing to land) .... men..   790
Rescued by both methods combined .... do...   45   1,135

     Total   1,640
Lost when vessel went to pieces............................men..   44
Lost in attempting to land by their own efforts ....do...   18
Killed or washed overboard during stranding ....do...   49   111

     Total   1,751
   Percentage of those lost on the coast = 6.34.
To the crews belonged also those rescued in the open sea......do...   51
And those lost in same.. do...   17   68

     Total...do...........   1,819

Vessels stranded under the German flag.

Totally lost, with crew	328	
Without crew (dead vessels)	23	
		351
Got afloat with a crew	136	
Without crew (dead vessels)	3	
		139
Total		490
Rescued by boats belonging to life-saving stations ....men..	493	
Rescued by rocket-apparatus belonging to said stations ....do..	543	
		1,036
Rescued by private boats from land ....do...	511	
Rescued by other private help from land ....do...	225	
Rescued by vessels being got afloat and by their own efforts (including bringing to land) ....men..	2,002	
Rescued by both methods combined ....do...	113	
		2,851
Total		3,887
Lost when vessel went to pieces ....men..	132	
Lost in attempting to land by their own efforts ....do...	32	
Killed or washed overboard during stranding..............do...	47	
		211
Total		4,098
Percentage of those lost on the coast = 5.15.		
To the crews belonged also those rescued in the open sea.....men..	100	
And those lost in same ....do...	43	
		143
Total		4,241

Vessels stranded under the English flag.

Totally lost, with crew ....vessels..	193	
Without crew (dead vessels) ....do...	26	
		219
Got afloat, with crew ....do...	134	
Without crew (dead vessels) ....do...	5	
		139
Total		358
Rescued by boats belonging to life-saving stations ....men..	456	
Rescued by rocket-apparatus belonging to same ....do...	397	
Rescued by both apparatus combined.......................do...	50	
		903
Rescued by private boats from land ....do...	351	
Rescued by other private help from land ....do...	142	
Rescued by vessels being got afloat and by their own efforts (including bringing to land).........................men..	1,739	
Rescued by both methods combined ....do...	199	
		2,431
		3,334

Lost when vessels went to pieces ....men..   120
Lost while attempting to land by their own efforts............do...   114
Killed or washed overboard during stranding ....do...   38
                                                                              272

    Total   3,606
  Percentage of those lost on the coast = 7.54.
To the crews belonged also those rescued in the open sea .....men..   189
And those lot in same ....do...   39
                                                                              228

    Total...   3,834

Vessels Stranded under the Dutch flag.

Totally lost, with crew..   164
Without crew (dead vessels)   4
                                                                              168
Got afloat   47

    Total   215

Rescued by boats belonging to life-saving stations ....men..   113
Rescued by rocket-apparatus belonging to same ....do...   164
Rescued by both apparatus combined.......................do...   5
                                                                              282
Rescued by private boats from land ....do...   182
Rescued by other private help from land ....do...   86
Rescued by vessels being got afloat and by their own efforts (includ-
    ing bringing to land)..men..   622
Rescued by both methods ....do...   79
                                                                              969
                                                                              1,251
Lost when vessel went to pieces...............................do...   14
Lost in attempting to land by their own efforts ....do...   6
Killed or washed overboard during stranding ....do...   24
                                                                              44

    Total   1,295
  Percentage of those lost on coast = 3.40.
To the crews belonged also those rescued in the open sea .....men..   22
And those lost in same   2   24

    Total   1,319

Vessels stranded under the Russian flag.

Totally destroyed, with crew..   58
Without crew (dead vessels)   4
                                                                              62
Got afloat...   18
                                                                              80

Rescued by boats belonging to life-saving stations ....men..   .91
Rescued by rocket-apparatus belonging to same...............do...   155
                                                                              246
Rescued by private boats from land ....do...   568
Rescued by other private help from land.... ....do...   267

Rescued by vessels being got afloat and by their own efforts (including bringing to land)..men.. 289
Rescued by both methods combined ....do... 14
————
1,138
————
1,384
Lost when vessel went to pieces...........................do... 24
Lost in attempting to land by their own efforts..............do... 5
Killed or washed overboard during stranding.............do... 7
————
36
Total.. 1,420
Percentage of those lost on the coast=2.53.
To the crews belonged also those rescued in open sea ....men.. 28
And those lost in same.................................do... 6
————
34
Together 1,454

Vessels stranded under the French flag.

Totally lost, with crew....................................... 44
Without crew (dead vessel) 1
————
45
Got afloat.. 19
————
64
Rescued by boats belonging to life-saving stations............men.. 18
Rescued by rocket-apparatus belonging to same..............do... 66
————
81
Rescued by private boats from land ....do... 24
Rescued by other private help from land ....do... 68
Rescued by vessels being got afloat and by their own efforts (including bringing to land) ....men.. 315
Rescued by both methods combined.........................do... 29
————
436
————
520
Lost when vessel went to pieces............................do... 25
Lost in attempting to land by their own efforts............do... 13
Killed or washed overboard during stranding.............do... 4
————
42
Total... 562
Percentage of those lost on the coast=7.47.
To the crews belonged also those rescued in the open sea................... 6
Together 568

Stranded vessels of other nationalities.

Totally lost, with crew....................................... 10
Without crew (dead vessel) 1
————
11
Got afloat with crew... 6
Without crew (dead vessel) 1
————
7
————
18
Rescued by boats belonging to life-saving stations............men.. 30
Rescued by rocket-apparatus belonging to life-saving stations..do... 11
————
41

Rescued by private boats from land......................men..   13
Rescued by other private help from land ....do...   2
Rescued by vessels being got afloat, and by their own efforts (in-
  cluding bringing to land)...............................men..   123
                                                                            138
                                                                            179
Lost in attempting to land by their own efforts......................do...   6
    Total   185
    Percentage of those lost on the cost = 3.24.
To the crews belonged also those rescued in the open sea ....men..   83
    Together   268

FRANCE.

The services appear, for the most part, to be performed by the *Société Centrale de Sauvetage de Naufragés*, founded in 1865. From the journal of that society (*Annales du Sauvetage Maritime, tome xxiv,* 1889) it is seen that the society is supported mainly by voluntary contributions, having, however, a subsidy from the Government. The society has 422 stations on the coasts of France and Algeria, employing 2,000 persons, most of whom are also employed in the customs service. Seventy-seven of the stations are provided with life-boats. From its foundation to October 1, 1889, the society has saved by means of its boats and apparatus 4,561 persons and 286 vessels. It has besides assisted 175 vessels and given rewards for saving the lives of 823 persons.

GERMANY.

German Society for the saving of the shipwrecked.

MARTINI STRASSE, No. 41,
BUREAU OF MANAGEMENT, *September* 17, 1889

*   *   *   *   *   *   *

The entire life-saving service on the German coasts is under the management of the German Society for the Rescue of the Shipwrecked. This society is located at Bremen, and was founded May 29, 1865.

The following statements will furnish information concerning the organization of the society. It is under the patronage of His Majesty William II.

The presiding officers of the society are:

(*a*) Consul W. H. Meyer, president.

(*b*) Dr. Marcus, a senator, who acts as president in the absence of Mr. Meyer.

(*c*) Capt. H. Steengraft, a member of the society; all of whom are residents of Bremen.

The officers of the society are:

(*a*) Capt. G. Pfeifer, inspector.

(*b*) Mr. Otto Kroll, accountant; and the undersigned.

The society is a private one, and is entirely supported by voluntary contributions.

The society has 111 life-saving stations. Of these 66 are on the Baltic and 45 on the North Sea. Forty-three stations are double stations, provided with a boat and rocket apparatus; 51 are only boat stations, and 18 are only rocket stations.

* * * * * * *

(a) The whole number of disasters to vessels on the German coast in 1888-'89, from April 1 to March 31, was 43.

(b) The whole number of persons that were on board of these 43 vessels was 281.

(c) Of whom 254 were rescued.

Of these 95 were saved by their own efforts; 67 were saved by other vessels; 46 were saved by private assistance from shore, and 46 were saved by the life-saving apparatus; 26 having been rescued by life-boats, and 20 by the rocket apparatus.

(d) 27 persons perished.

From the foundation of the society, May 29, 1865, up to April 1, 1889, 1,743 were rescued by life-saving stations. Of these, 1,452 were rescued by life-boats, and 291 were rescued by rocket apparatus.

The whole number of the vessels wrecked on the German coasts during this time was 1,892, with 10,208 persons on board. Of these, 9,404 were rescued, so that 804 persons perished.

We would here remark that the data given, *sub numeris*, (5) and (6), have been taken solely from the statistics collected by our society for its own use.

Fuller statistics of disasters to vessels on the German coasts are prepared and published by the Imperial German Statistical Bureau. (Statistics of the German Empire, published by the Imperial Statistical Bureau, new series, vol. 42, part 1, for the year 1888; vol. 35, part 1, for the year 1887, and comparative tables, published at the same place, of "Disasters to vessels on the German coast in the years 1883-1887," October number of the Monthly Statistical Reports of the German Empire, year 1888, also separately printed.)

* * * *

Very respectfully,

Dr. BOISSELIER,
Secretary General.

GREAT BRITAIN.

The life-boat service is mainly under the charge of the Royal National Life-boat Institution, founded in 1824. Their stations, now numbering 293, are managed by volunteer crews. An annual salary is paid to a coxswain and an assistant for each boat. The other boatmen are paid a fixed sum for each occasion of service and drill. The coxswain and assistant are also paid a like sum in addition to the regular salary.

During 1888, 26 vessels and 626 lives were saved by them, and 174 rewards were given for saving lives by fishing and other boats. The total number of lives saved since the foundation amounts to 35,043, including lives saved each year by boats not belonging to the institution, but which were rewarded by it for their services.

The rocket service is in the hands of the Board of Trade, and was organized under its present system in 1855. On the 30th of June, 1888, there were 302 rocket stations, as well as 374 stations where belts and lines are provided for the rescue of those accidently falling into the water. From July, 1856, to June, 1887, there were saved by the rocket apparatus 11,080 persons. The operations on wrecks are conducted by the coast guard, who also patrol the coast.

Other stations also exist under charge of various local corporations and private parties.

HOLLAND.

AMSTERDAM, *September* 30, 1889.

Bijlagen.

1. All documents published.
2. Nominal list of all those who constitute the local direction.
2. List of the stations with boats and rocket apparatus.

Het Bestuur der Noord- en Zuid-Hollandsche Redding-Maatschappij aan Treasury Department, Office of General Superintendent, U. S. Life-Saving Service, Washington, D. C.

Agreeable to your writing of the 21st July last, we have the honor of furnishing the following information, and to inclose a copy of all printed documents published by us, with lists for more complete details.

1. Names and locations of all institutions having for their object the saving of life from shipwreck.

1. *Noord- en Zuid-Hollandsche Redding-Maatschappij,* at *Amsterdam.*

2. *Zuid-Hollandsche Maatschappij tot Redding van Schipbreukelingen,* at *Rotterdam.*

As to last-mentioned company, we can not give you any information. You should direct your request to that company at Rotterdam.

2. The organization of each including the names and functions of their officers.

The organization will appear from the inclosed documents, whereas the names and functions of our officers are noted on an inclosed list (first list).

3. How supported, whether by the Government wholly, or in part, or by the contributions of private citizens entirely.

The company is erected and maintained only by contributions of private persons, without any assistance from Government.

4. Number and location of each life-saving station with the apparatus used at each; as life-boat, rocket, or other line-throwing apparatus.

See annexed list (second list).

To afford any specification about property can not be done. Our company, according to statutes, has in view exclusively the saving of persons.

We may answer your inquires about last year as follows:

1. Total number of disasters, 16.

6. Total number of persons saved, 46 with salvage means; 37 in other ways.

7. Total number of persons lost, 25.

8. Total number of shipwrecked persons succored at stations, two men at Scheveningen.

9. Total number of days' succor afforded, 16.

10. Number of vessels totally lost, 7 ships, amongst which one with the whole crew.

Since the whole period of the erection of the company we can only state that since 1824 (year of the establishment) till last December, 1888, 3,193 persons were saved.

Hoping to have complied with your wishes as far as possible, we have the honor of remaining, most respectfully,

THE DIRECTION OF THE NORTH AND SOUTH HOLLAND LIFE-SAVING COMPANY.

A. J. VAN VOLLENHOVEN,
Secretary.

SECOND LIST.

No.	Stations.	Boat.	Apparatus.
1	Loosduinen	Life boat	Rocket apparatus.
2	Scheveningen	...do	Do.
3	Fatwijk a-zee	...do	Do.
4	Noordwijk a-zee	...do	Do.
5	Zandvoort	...do	Do.
6a	Yumiden (north)	...do	Do.
6b	Yumiden (south)	...do	Do.
7	Wijk a-zee	...do	Do.
8	Egmond a-zee	...do	Do.
9	Petten	...do	Do.
10	Callanssoog	...do	Do.
11	Huisduinen		Do.
12	Helderschen Zeedijk	Life-boat	
13	Nieuwediep	...do	
14	Tekel—Koog	...do	Rocket apparatus.
15	Tekel—Hooksdorp	...do	
16	Tekel—Hoorn	...do	
17	Terschelling—Oostereind	...do	Rocket apparatus.
18	Terschelling—Midaland	...do	
19	Terschelling—west	...do	
20	Ameland (Nes)	...do	
21	Ameland—Hollum	...do	
22	Schiermonnikoog	...do	
23	Modderyat	...do	
24	{Flieland—Posthuis / Flieland—Dorp	} 3 life-boats	Rocket apparatus.

ITALY.

The principal life-saving institution is the *Società Italiana per prov-vedere al Soccorso dei Naufraghi*, which has its headquarters at Rome. The society has under its control 10 stations, 8 of which are life-boat stations, 2 rocket stations.

There are besides a number of local societies for giving aid to ship-wrecked people or for resuscitating the apparently drowned. Such are the *Società Ligure de Salvamento*, which has 16 huts of refuge; the *Società Livornese di Soccorso degli Asfittici*, at Leghorn, and the *Società Veneziana di Soccorso degli Asfittici*, at Venice.

RUSSIA.

[Translation.]

Society established under the Supreme Patronage of Her Majesty the Em-press for Saving Life on Waters.

No. 783.]   St. Petersburg, Ministry of Ways Building,
OFFICE OF THE SECRETARY,
September 9, 1889.

Sir: In a communication, addressed, on the 3d of August last, to the secretary of this society, Mr. N. O. Mikhnievich, you request certain information concerning the organization and functions of the society.

In the absence of Mr. Mikhnievich, I have the honor to submit the following:

1. The object of the society is to give assistance to all persons in dis-tress on the seas, lakes, and rivers within the boundaries of Russia.

2. The society is composed of honorary members (by election); actual members, who contributed not less than 100 rubles in a single payment, or who contribute annually not less than 5 rubles, and co-operating members, who contribute not less than $1 each year. The business of the society is managed by a principal board, located at St. Petersburg; 46 district boards, located in the principal cities of Russia, and a num-ber of local boards established in various towns and villages. The or-ganization and duties of these institutions are specified in sections 14-25 of the constitution of the society, a copy of which is inclosed herewith.

3. The society is supported mainly by private contributions, but it also receives from the state treasury an annual subsidy of 25,000 rubles, in addition to various supplies not infrequently furnished to the life-saving stations, without charge, from Government stores.

4. The society has 2 cruiser stations, 10 rocket stations, 49 boat sta-tions on seas, 41 boat stations on lakes and rivers, 73 winter stations, 72 substations, 6 light-houses, 60 refuges, and 657 posts.

The location of each of these establishments and a detailed statement of the boats and appliances possessed by each will be found in the list, hereto annexed, of all the life-saving establishments of the society up to January 1, 1889.

I am able to furnish statistical data only as to some of the particulars indicated in your letter, touching the operations of our life-saving establishments for the last year, viz: The number of persons rescued during the year by the summer stations on seas, was 159; by river and lake stations—summer, 48; winter, 76; by substations, 20; by posts and refuges, 45; in all, 348 persons. The number of days of assistance afforded by sea-stations proper was 25,038.

As regards the total number of disasters, persons imperiled, and lives and vessels lost, I have to state that the information received by the principal board is incomplete and fragmentary. As to the value of property involved, saved and lost, no information reaches the board, inasmuch as the saving of property is not only outside of the proper duties of the life-saving establishments of the society, but is expressly prohibited.

The total number of persons saved by the establishments of the society during the period of its existence up to the present year was 6,378.

.* * * * * * *

Accept, dear sir, the assurance of my perfect consideration,

V. ROOTKOVSKI,

Assistant Secretary.

The SUPERINTENDENT OF THE U. S. LIFE-SAVING SERVICE.

[Translation.]

The organization of the crews of life-saving stations within the jurisdiction of the society, and the system of compensation for the performance of the duties assigned to such crews, are subject to some variation, according to local circumstances and the degree of interest in the work of life-saving which may be awakened among the inhabitants of the various localities along the coasts and shores.

At all stations the keeper (*ataman*) has full charge of the property, and full command over the crew, invariably recruited by himself. The keepers direct the use of the boats on all occasions and take the helm or steering oar. As a general rule the keepers, whether of boat stations or of rocket stations, call out the crews and direct all their movements at drills, inspections, firing of rockets, and life-saving operations.

Under the existing rules the compensation of life-saving crews is determined by the district boards. At present the keepers at most stations receive a salary at rates varying from 36 to 60 rubles per annum. Higher salaries are allowed to keepers of such stations only where the whole crews are salaried. In the Estland district, however, no fixed compensation is allowed either the keepers or the oarsmen, who do the work assigned them from an exalted sense of Christian duty. With very few exceptions the stations in that district are well kept and work quite satisfactorily; still even in that district two or three crews are found that perform their duties with indifference, if without protest—a fact which shows the impossibility of relying in all cases solely upon appeals based upon the exalted nature of the work of saving the life of fellow-men, and seems to prove the necessity of securing a definite pecuniary compensation both to the keepers for their continuous labor and care and to the oarsmen when on duty.

The most effective system of compensation is that adopted in the Lief-land district. There the keepers are allowed from 36 rubles (winter stations) to 60 rubles (sea-board stations) per annum. For every drill or inspection the oarsmen, the keeper, and the assistant keeper receive 2 rubles each, and for every rescuing expedition 5 rubles each, and in addition thereto a premium of 10 rubles to be equally divided among them all for every person saved. Since the first organization of this society the stations of the Liefland district have always worked quite successfully and have been kept in examplary order.

In the Courland district a similar scheme of compensation has been adopted for boat stations, while at the rocket stations, the crews of which are fixed at four oarsmen and one keeper, a premium of 10 rubles, to be divided between them, is allowed for each working of the apparatus, whether on drill, inspection, or rescuing service. In cases of especially successful life-saving performances, the amount of the premium may be increased by the district board, or a recommendation be made to the central board for special reward. In this district the stations are kept in good order, improving from year to year, and operate quite satisfactorily.

In most of the districts along the coasts of the White, Black, and Azov Seas, and also along the shores of the great lakes, the rates of compensation of the crews are not definitely settled, and even in those localities where compensation has been fixed the amounts allowed are wholly insufficient. Thus, for drills each man is allowed from 30 to 50 copecks, and in no case more than 80 copecks, and for life-saving expeditions not more than 2 rubles, without any premium for lives saved. While the men at these stations not unfrequently display heroic zeal, they sometimes fall short of the mark.

At the Ansheron station, on the Caspian Sea (originally established by the local board of Baku, under the supervision of the Caucasus district board, but at present wholly within the jurisdiction of the Baku district board), a station situated in a locality destitute of population, where it was found necessary to build a house for the crew and to keep a horse for the hauling of fresh water, fire-wood, and provisions, the keeper and his six oarsmen receive a salary all the year round; the keeper about 25 rubles and the men about 15 rubles per month each. The keeping of this station costs the society about 2,500 rubles a year. Its life-saving exploits often deserve high commendation.

The Poti station, which also belonged until last year to the jurisdiction of the Caucasus district board, was managed upon nearly the same plan as the Ansheron station. The keeper and the oarsmen received fixed monthly salaries all the year round. The cost was about 2,000 rubles a year. No satisfactory account can be given of the workings of this station. In regard to its present organization under the management of the Kutais district board no reports have as yet been received by the central board.

From the above data, and an examination of the reports of district and local boards, as well as from information furnished by the corps of inspectors, the following general conclusions may safely be drawn: That the character of the men employed at the life-saving stations must be recognized as the principal factor in the problem of bringing such establishments into a state of due efficiency, and that fixed compensation in amounts corresponding with the labor and risk involved must be acknowledged as the best means of securing the right kind of men. It may be noticed, in this connection, that the risk incurred by the life-saving crews is in a certain degree lightened by the provisions of the existing regulations for mutual insurance. Unfortunately, some of the district boards fail to forward to the central board the requisite assessments or insurance premiums, and, as a consequence, the chief officers of the service find it possible in only very few cases to call to the attention of the crews the existence of a right to insurance. This uncertainty can not fail to detract in some measure from the efficiency of the service.

N. SOUSLOV,
Central B. Inspector.

———

SPAIN.

Spanish society for the saving of the shipwrecked.

MADRID, *October* 3, 1889.

S. I. KIMBALL, Esq.,
General Superintendent Life-Saving Service, Washington:

SIR: I have received your letter dated 2d of August, and I have the honor to send you the information that this society can give in reference to maritime rescue in Spain. As the purpose of the institution is only to save life, it does not collect statistics of the value of the cargoes of the vessels either lost or saved, and, though we have tried to obtain such data, we have been prevented by the fact that no statistics exist in the ministry of the navy, to whom the captains of vessels transmit the information of the disasters.

*   *   *   *   *   *   *

I am, with the highest consideration and respect, your devoted servant,

FRANCO DE PAULA PAVÍA,
The President, Vice Admiral.

[Translation.]

"The Spanish Society for Saving the Shipwrecked," founded in 1880.

1st. In Spain the life-saving service is composed of *"The Spanish Society for Saving the Shipwrecked,"* whose superior council and central board reside in Madrid, and the *"Guipuzcoa Maritime Life-Saving Society,"* which has its chief bureau in San Sebastian. The latter society was merged into the Spanish Society in December, 1880.

2d. The organization of the society is described in detail in chapter second of the statutes approved in general session July 12, 1885. The superior council is constituted as follows: *Honorary Presidents,* Hon. Ministers of the Navy, of Public Works, War, and the Treasury, and the Hon. Admiral of the Navy. The *Active President,* His Excellency Sor Don Francisco de P. Pavia, Vice-Admiral and Senator. *Honorary Vice-Presidents,* Matritense, President of the Economical Society, and His Excellency, Señor Don Juan Romero y Moreno, Rear-Admiral. *Active Vice-Presidents,* His Excellency, Señor Don Eduardo Saavedra, Engineer and Academician; His Excellency, Señor Don Hilario de Nava, Inspector-General of Naval Engineering and Deputy to the Cortes; His Excellency, Señor Don Francisco Coello, Colonel of Engineers and Academician; His Excellency, the Duke of Victoria, Senator and Director of Railroads in the South.

* * * * * * *

The duties recommended to the central and to the local boards are defined in the respective regulations.

3d. The society is founded on national charity, and being declared by law, on the 12th day of January, 1887, to be of public utility, the Government granted it a subsidy of $8,000 for the maintenance and preservation of the material which by the said law was given into its charge. In October, 1888, on account of economy in all public expenses, the subsidy was reduced to $7,200 per annum.

4th. The society has the following stations:

Supplied with life-boats and apparatus for throwing ropes: *Guipúzcoa,* two boats and four apparatus for throwing rope; *Portugalete,* one boat and one apparatus for throwing ropes; *Barcelona,* Idem, Idem; *Cádiz,* Id., Id.; *Vinaroz,* life-boat, —, and apparatus for throwing ropes; *Torrevieja,* boat and apparatus for throwing ropes; *Algeciras,* Id., Id.; *Laredo,* life-boat and apparatus for throwing ropes; *Sanlúcar de Barranceda,* boat and apparatus for throwing ropes; *Arecibo,* Id., Id.; *San Juan de Puerto Rico,* Id., Id.; *Palamós,* Id., Id.; *Tarragona,* boat, life-boat, and apparatus for throwing ropes; *Denia,* boat and apparatus for throwing ropes; *Gijón,* Id., Id.; that is to say, a total of fifteen stations with boats and rope-throwing apparatus.

Supplied with one boat: Station at *Cape Palos,* station at *Correpedo, Rosas, Villannera* and *Settin, Puerto de la Selva, Cadaqués Ybiro-Ria del Barquero, Candás,* one life-boat. *Serilla,* Id. Pending an application, two boats. Total, twelve.

Supplied only with apparatus for throwing ropes: *Santander*, two apparatus; *Rivadeo*, one; *Blanes*, one; *Tarifa*, one; *Cartagena*, one; *Rivadesella*, one; *Palma de Mallorca*, two: *Alardia*, one; *Felanitz*, one; *Soller*, one; *Torredembarra*, one; *Cambrils*, one; *Ceuta*, one; *San Felix de Guixols*, one; *Coruña*, two; *Corcubión*, one; *Garrucha*, one; *Llanes*, one; *La Escala*, one. Total, twenty-two.

There are, besides, an unlimited number of guns, large Torres life-buoys, ropes, cables, Legrand hooks, and life-preservers at the stations of *Ferrol, Huelva, Puerto de Santa Maria, Santurce, Toledo, Vigo*, and at the light-houses of *Estaca de Vares*, Islands of *Lisaigas, Finisterre, Alboran, Columbretes*, and *Buda Island*.

STATEMENT OF SERVICES RENDERED BY THE STATIONS DURING THE YEAR 1888.

The subject of questions 1 and 5 of this part of the interrogatory do not relate to the society, whose only object is to save lives, and the data comprehended by them do not exist at the ministry of the navy which keeps no record of them.

Number of persons saved by the society directly 187
Saved by the apparatus of the society 173
Number of persons who perished of those rescued by the society 0
Number who perished of those not rescued by the society 28
Number of shipwrecked rescued at the stations 187
Number of days they were succored 11
Number of vessels totally lost not known but about usually .... 70 per cent.

SERVICES RENDERED BY THE STATIONS SINCE THE CREATION OF THE SOCIETY.

Number of persons directly saved by the society 571
Saved without the apparatus of the society 841
Number of persons who perished of those aided by the society 0
Number who perished not rescued by the society 148
Number of wrecked persons aided at the stations 571
Number of days in which aid was given.. 57
Number of nights in which shipwrecks took place 25
Madrid, *October* 5, 1889.

FRANCISCO DE P. PAVÍA,
President, Rear-Admiral.

UNITED STATES.

Besides the service maintained by the Government, an account of which will be found in Appendix E, there is the Massachusetts Humane Society, supported by voluntary contributions. This society was founded in 1786, and has seventy-eight stations on the coast and rivers of Massachusetts, besides some twenty stations at which minor apparatus, such as life-buoys, ladders, and lines, are kept. During the last year they saved 123 lives and assisted 5 vessels, besides giving 111 rewards and 26 certificates for brave service.

REPORT OF COMMITTEE UPON GENERAL DIVISIONS 7 AND 8 OF THE PROGRAMME.

Committee No. 2.

To consider and report upon General Divisions 7 and 8.

Denmark	Mr. GARDE.
France	Captain LANNELUC.
Germany	Captain DONNER.
Great Britain	Admiral BOWDEN–SMITH.
Hawaii	Mr. H. A. P. CARTER.
Portugal	Mr. SOUZA ROZA.
Sweden	Captain MALMBERG.
The Netherlands . . .	Captain HUBERT.
United States	Captain SHACKFORD.

GENERAL DIVISION 7.

LANES FOR STEAMERS ON FREQUENTED ROUTES.

(*a*) With regard to the avoidance of steamer collisions.
(*b*) With regard to the safety of fishermen.

GENERAL DIVISION 8.

NIGHT SIGNALS FOR COMMUNICATING INFORMATION AT SEA.

(*a*) A code to be used in connection with the International Code Signal book.
(*b*) Or a supplementary code of limited scope to convey information of special importance to passing vessels.
(*c*) Distress signals.

264

LANES FOR STEAMERS ON FREQUENTED ROUTES.

WASHINGTON, *December* 6, 1889.

Rear-Admiral S. R. FRANKLIN, U. S. Navy,
    President of the International Marine Conference, etc.

SIR: Committee No. 2 beg leave to report on General Division No. 7, entitled, "Lanes for Steamers on Frequented Routes," that after consideration of various routes they concluded to report only upon the North Atlantic route, between ports of North America and ports of Northern Europe, as the route upon which there was apparently the greater demand for such lanes, if such could be advantageously laid down on any ocean or sea.

It appears that the adherence of fast steam passenger vessels to certain southerly routes would tend to the avoidance of fog and ice, and the committee adopted a resolution to the effect that it was desirable, during the spring and summer months, that such vessels should follow a southern route which would clear the banks of Newfoundland, and be likely to be clear of fog and ice, but when it came to proposing any plan to make such ocean lanes compulsory, the committee found the subject one of such difficulty that they do not recommend a proposition of that nature.

The difficulty of enforcing the present rule providing for moderate speed in thick weather, suggests what greater difficulties would be met with in enforcing lane routes if made compulsory, and it was not thought desirable to lay down routes by international agreement unless they were to be made compulsory for swift steamers.

Routes that might be proposed would be in danger of invasion by ice during the spring and summer months, and at all times would be crossed by sailing vessels and steamers going north and south. If laid down on parallels of latitude which seemed to favor one seaport at the expense of another, or the ports of one country at the expense of the ports of another country, they would arouse opposition that would probably prevent their adoption.

It is possible that, even in the near future, vessels may be employed of such power and speed that all such considerations may have to give way to the paramount consideration of safety; but, so far as shown to the committee, present conditions do not seem to justify an international agreement to that effect. It was not shown to the committee that collisions in mid-ocean between fast ocean steamers had taken place, or that the danger was great enough to justify enforced adherence to certain lanes. Collisions between fast steamships, so far, have occurred nearer the coasts, where all tracks must converge.

The committee believe, however, that the voluntary establishment of, and adherence to, particular routes by the different steamship companies for different seasons of the year is very desirable. In fact, the committee are of opinion that such action by the steamship companies, with the experience to be gained thereby, would be quite essential before any concerted action by the maritime powers could be profitably taken.

The committee therefore strongly recommend that the companies interested should, by mutual agreement, after consultation together, establish routes for the different lines, and make them public, in order that the hydrographic offices of the various governments may publish them for the information of navigators.

The committee have considered the opinions of several persons in the printed matter that has been laid before them. With the exception of one or two definite propositions, the literature before the Conference does not show how such lane routes could be laid down. Even those containing such propositions arrive at the conclusion that such routes could not be made compulsory. In Appendix A will be found extracts or copies of the papers laid before them.

SUBSECTION *b*: With regard to the safety of fishermen upon the North Atlantic Ocean, the committee are of opinion that their safety would be best promoted by unceasing vigilance on the part of the fishermen, and by careful compliance by all with the present rules for the prevention of collisions, especially as to the. efficiency of lights and sound-signals. If lanes were established which carried the fast steamers clear of the banks frequented by the fishermen it might promote such a sense of security on their part as would tend to carelessness with reference to the rules as at present laid down,' and lead to danger from the slower vessels which would still frequent the banks.

During the months when the fishing-vessels most frequent the Banks the fear of encountering fog and ice leads many of the steamers to go south of them.

Quick passages are what the steam-vessels aim at in response to the public demand for swift passenger and mail service, and if they were compelled to obey existing rules regarding moderate speed in fogs at all times and in all places they would avoid the banks still more in order to go clear of fogs; and thus it seems that the solution of the problem before the committee, namely, of how to induce steam-ships of great speed to take safer routes to avoid fogs, ice, and danger of collision with fishermen and other vessels, is in compelling obedience to the present rules regarding moderate speed in thick weather. The enforcement of · these rules would make it for the interest of such vessels to take routes comparatively clear of fogs and ice and thus attain the end which compulsory legislation might fail to do.

In Appendix B will be found some correspondence regarding the dangers of fishermen upon the banks, from which it will be observed that vigilance regarding lights and sound-signals have been found efficient safeguards in most instances.

AUG. GARDE,
Delegate for Denmark.

HENRI LANNELUC,
Delegate for France.

CHRISTIAN DONNER,
Delegate for Germany.

N. BOWDEN-SMITH,
Delegate for Great Britain.

H. A. P. CARTER,
Chairman of Committee,
Delegate for Hawaii.

T. DE SOUZA ROZA,
Delegate for Portugal.

FREDERICK MALMBERG,
Delegate for Sweden.

D. HUBERT,
Delegate for The Netherlands.

JOHN W. SHACKFORD,
Delegate for the United States.

APPENDIX A.

LANES FOR STEAMERS ON FREQUENTED ROUTES.

[Extract from letter written by C. A. Griscom, président of International Navigation Company, November 21, 1889.]

There can be no doubt that the risk of collision is the principal danger to be apprehended in the navigation of modern steam-ships, and no one thing will contribute more to lessen this risk than the establishment of lane routes in the now already crowded North Atlantic.

My own view is that the lanes we have adopted are the most prudent, viz, to keep south of 42 when crossing the meridian of 50, from the 15th February to the 15th of August, and a safe distance south of the Virgins the rest of the year, separating east-bound and west-bound tracks at the meridian of 50° about one degree.

While we pursue this practice with the steamers under our management—some twenty-six—the good effect thereof is, of course, almost negative, so far as the lane feature is concerned, because the practice is not general.

[Extract from letter written by W. Bussius, N. G. Lloyd, S. S. *Werra*, April 13, 1889].

I would say that in the vicinity of Long Island, Nantucket, and St. George's shoal grounds, I think it absolutely necessary to establish lanes for steam-ships apart. This can be done very easily, even if astronomic observations are not at hand and the position of a ship doubtful.

A westward-bound ship to keep north; that means in 40 to 35 or 30 fathoms of water by soundings, when thick weather prevails. Here the ship will find pilots as their position is in this line.

An eastward-bound ship ought to steer from Sandy Hook east by south one-quarter south to the 90-fathom soundings, then east on deep soundings. This will cause steamers to go safely almost 50° west, if the eastward-bound steamers keep warm water during summer, or, say, in latitude 41°. I have proved it dozens of times that in summer a distance of 80 to 90 miles is gained eastward by the Gulf Stream between Sandy Hook and Scilly, if I kept well to the southward. I shall not fail to run these Southern routes this summer.

[Extract from letter written by Arthur W. Lewis, master S. S. *City of New York*, 1889.]

With regard to perfect safety, lane routes, especially on the Atlantic, are greatly to be desired.

During the ice season on the Atlantic ships bound east ought to make the lane routes in the great circle that crosses lat. 40° N., long. 50° W.; those coming west lat. 41° and 50° W.

Northern routes about 40 miles south of Virgins, bound west, to latitude 43° and long. 50° bound east.

Fisherman on the Grand Banks, as well as in other portions of the globe, ought to have defined grounds to operate in and out of them, and to be there at their own risk.

[Extract from letter written by Captain Horatio McKay, of the Cunard steam-ship *Aurania*, March, 1889.]

In regard to my opinions about ocean tracks, lengthened experience only serves to emphasize present views, * * * namely: Definite easterly and westerly tracks, more or less south of the Banks. I am still strongly impressed with these conclusions, notwithstanding the steady adherence to the northerly route by the great majority of steam-ship lines.

PROPOSAL AS TO LANES FOR STEAMERS.

It can hardly be doubted that lanes or tracks for coming and going steam-ships would in a great measure tend to increase the safety of navigation, and that such tracks might be laid down, not only on the large oceans, but also on many of the local waters, in this case considering the North Sea, the Baltic, the English Channel, etc., as local waters. The advantage derived from such tracks would not only consist in the fact that steamers would avoid to a certain extent the danger of meeting other steamers end on, but also that the chart would give warning to the navigator whenever another track was crossing his, as well as that it might be expected that sailing vessels would do their best to keep out of these tracks, especially in the night-time. Nevertheless, whenever a discussion upon the subject has taken place it has always been argued that, taking in consideration the difference in tonnage, speed, load-line, etc., of screw-steamers, in fact, the difference as to the sea-going qualities between different ships, it would hardly be fair to force all steamships, under all circumstances, to follow a prescribed track from which they were not permitted to deviate.

Admitting, however, that it would be unfair to lay down compulsory tracks for steam-ships, would it not tend to the safety of navigation if tracks were laid down on all charts? If such tracks, marked, *Non-compulsory tracks for screw-steamers*, their position being, of course, decided by the various maritime powers, were laid down on all charts it can hardly be doubted that the steam-ships, if possible, would follow them voluntarily, and that the sailing vessels would do their best to keep out of them. The black line in the chart would of itself be a warning to the mariner every time he looked at it.

My proposal would therefore be that such non-compulsory tracks for screw-steamers should be laid down on all charts whenever it was found possible to do so, while, as a matter of course, I shall not offer any opinion about the way in which the work should be divided between the different seafaring nations.

Copenhagen, September 9, 1889.

JACOB HOLM,
Master Mariner.

OCEAN LANE ROUTES.

10 WATER STREET, LIVERPOOL,
November 12, 1889.

SIR: We beg to hand you annexed copy of a letter addressed by our senior, under date 1st January, 1876, to the secretary of the North Atlantic Steam Traffic Conference here, relative to the adoption of the lane routes advocated by Lieutenant Maury, U. S. Navy, *vide* inclosed tract chart.

At the time this letter was written a way could not be found to secure unanimity among the various lines interested, and there has continued up to the present time considerable divergence of practice in regard to the tracks followed by the steamers employed in this much-frequented ocean highway, which neutralizes in a great measure the advantages, in point of safety, that may be derived from the adoption of well-defined routes by certain lines.

We have been disappointed not to see any reference to this subject in the cable reports of the proceedings of the Conference, and should be sorry if the sittings were to close without so important a question being included in the deliberations, especially as Lieutenant Maury's proposals offer so simple and efficacious a remedy.

We sincerely trust that the Conference may have seen their way to deal with this long-standing difficulty, and that regulations may be adopted which may tend still further to promote the safe navigation of the North Atlantic.

We remain, sir, your obedient servants,

ISMAY, IMRIE & CO.

LANE ROUTES.

WHITE STAR LINE,
Liverpool, January 1, 1876.

GRAY HILL, Esq.,
Secretary North Atlantic Steam Traffic Conference:

DEAR SIR: Referring to the failure to agree upon an international rule obliging all steamers passing between Europe and North America to follow fixed lane routes (which, personally, I much regretted at the time), and having since given a good deal of consideration to the matter during four transatlantic passages, made within the past eighteen months, I have determined, as far as practicable, with the company's steamers, to follow Maury's steam lanes, and would suggest that a conference be called, to consist of a nautical and lay representative from such of the European lines as may respond to an invitation to be issued by the North Atlantic Steam Traffic Conference, and that a committee thereof make a joint report, to be unanimously adopted, the responsibility of non-agreement to rest with those who do not accept the committee's recommendation.

These lanes, if generally adopted, would, I think, materially lessen the risks of collision and ice.

Pending the discussion of this subject on the part of the Conference, the commanders of the White Star steamers are instructed to follow the routes named.

I am, dear sir, yours, faithfully,

THOMAS H. ISMAY.

[Report of Ensign George P. Blow, in charge of Branch Hydrographic Office, New York City, on General Division No. 7.]

There can be no doubt as to the great desirability of establishing a system of ocean lanes for vessels navigating much-frequented routes. While such lanes can obviously be followed only by steamers, their importance is probably much greater to vessels depending upon sail alone. By adopting such a system of well-defined routes the steam tonnage of all nations will concentrate at certain points, leaving the rest of the ocean free to sailing vessels, thus greatly diminishing the risk of collision. The captain of a vessel disabled or in need of provisions or water would then know at once where to go to get assistance and would shape his course accordingly. Fishermen would carry on their hazardous occupation without the constant fear of being run down by one of the great ocean racers, and pilot-boats could cruise across the track of incoming steamers with an absolute certainty of meeting them. It would be a comparatively easy matter to keep these lanes free from wrecks, derelicts, or other obstructions; and, as all passengers are carried by steamers, the safety of life at sea would be much better protected than at present.

Speaking in general terms, therefore, the proposed ocean lanes should be as nearly as possible great circle courses, making a liberal allowance for all rocks, shoals, islands, and other natural obstructions. Care should also be taken to lay down these routes so as to avoid the ice and fog limits, and not to pass through the great fishing-grounds. The outward and homeward bound tracks should be about one degree or 60 miles apart, so as to avoid all possibility of vessels getting on the wrong lane. Where practicable the lanes should be arranged so that all vessels follow the old rule of keeping to the right, and in passing keep each other on the port hand. This rule should apply also to inland waters and along the coasts from headland to headland. Thus a vessel passing through Long Island Sound would keep to the southward when going east, and to the northward when coming west. Coasting vessels leaving the land on the starboard side would keep as near inshore as the safety of navigation would allow; while those having the land on the port or left side would take a parallel course at least 5 miles further off shore, or as far out as the limit of visibility of the different lights would allow. Where these routes cross fishing-grounds frequented by a very large number of vessels a detour should be made, if possible. These lanes should be mapped out by the nations whose shipping is most directly interested.

It is believed that the use of these ocean lanes can not be made obligatory, and can only be recommended to navigators, as it would be impossible to enforce any law requiring vessels to use them.

With regard to the ocean lanes in the North Atlantic Ocean, the following is respectfully submitted.

The great dangers to be avoided are:

(1) Foggy weather and the consequent danger of shipwreck and col-lision.

(2) Collision with icebergs.

(3) Collision with derelicts.

(4) Collision with fishermen.

In laying out the ocean lanes,· therefore, it is necessary to carefully avoid passing through the portions of the ocean where these dangers are the greatest, and at the same time to utilize the force of the Gulf Stream, where possible.

By plotting the southern limit of fogs and ice for each month of the year it has been found that great circle-courses from Boston, New York, Delaware Bay, and the Chesapeake Bay to latitude 40° north, longi-tude 50° west, all pass clear of the fog limits for nearly the whole year and through the southern limits for the rest of the time. These courses also pass entirely clear of the fishing-grounds and ice limits, and may be considered as safe. Similarly great circle-courses from latitude 40° north, longitude 50° west, to the Straits of Gibraltar, English Channel, etc., also pass clear of the fog limits. These courses are further to the southward than the dotted course laid down on the chart, and which is the very shortest practicable route, but they have the great advantage of being in the full strength of the Gulf Stream, which more than makes up for the loss going east. The homeward-bound trip to the westward is more to the northward, so as to keep to the right and also to avoid the Gulf Stream. In this case, latitude 41° north, longitude 50° west, is taken as the point of concentration, as shown on the chart. In certain seasons of the year vessels can go further north than this with safety, and will undoubtedly do so in spite of whatever ocean lanes may be selected. It is recommended, therefore, that the steamers bound east be required to go to the southward of the courses laid down, and that steamers bound to the westward shall be required to keep to the northward of the course shown on the chart. It is thought that this will have the desired effect. The difference between the shortest course (dotted lines) and the course laid down is only about 180 miles. If steamers are required to go at the rate of half speed in fog, and this law is really ʼenforced, as it should be, there will be no trouble in ar-ranging the ocean-lane system, for it will be both to the interest and comfort of the captain, the interest of the owners, and the comfort and safety of the passengers, to take the route laid down. This is the only way in which the ocean-lane system can be enforced, by enforcing the law limiting the speed of vessels in a fog.

The captains of all large steamers are both willing and anxious to keep clear of the fishermen, fog, and ice, but are required by the owners to make quick trips. To do so they must go to the northward on their trip west, and are compelled to take the risk of running at from 15 to 20 knots an hour through thick fog in order to save time.

[Captain Kennedy, formerly in command of the S. S. *Germanic.*]

Captain Kennedy strongly advocates the use of the ocean lanes, and suggests for vessels bound east that they should cross the meridian of 50° west, between 41° and 42°, while vessels bound to the westward should cross between 42° and 43°. This would not only tend to lessen the danger of collisions with other steamers, but it would enable the fishermen on the banks to keep clear of the ocean routes in good weather, and all vessels, in case of being disabled, to know where to go for assistance. The case of the *Danmark* is a very good illustration of this point.

[Sergeant Paul Daniels, U. S. Signal Service.]

To avoid collisions, it is suggested that steamers on frequented routes should be compelled to observe the following rules:

Steamers going east should make their course on a parallel of latitude which would carry them a little more north or south of the course which the west-bound steamers would be likely to take; also the trans-atlantic steamers should be required to keep at least 60 miles to the southward of the George's banks, thereby keeping clear of fishermen.

[D. A. Nash, Pilot Commissioner of New York.]

Fixed routes or lanes for fast steamers, especially between Atlantic ports, are very desirable.

[Report of D. T. Terrell, Ensign U. S. Navy (in charge of Branch Hydrographic Office, Portland, Oregon), concerning opinion of seafaring men whom he has interviewed.]

All recognize the advisability of lanes of traffic in much frequented seas, and especially recommend lanes across the Newfoundland Banks, and the prohibition of vessels crossing in any other track at night or during thick weather.

[New York Branch Hydrographic Office.]

Lanes for steamers on frequent routes, as England-New York.

(*a*) Permanent lanes can not be prescribed for the regular lines, as the conditions of ice are not alike every year. A general agreement, however, would be desirable, resulting in rules requiring every steamer to follow a *northerly* course to *New York* and a *southerly* course from *New York, i. e.,* of the 50 degree longitude (Newfoundland Banks), coming *from* Europe *northerly* and going *to* Europe *southerly.*

The total avoidance of the fishermen on the Banks is impossible.

[Philadelphia Maritime Exchange.]

Adopt lanes for steamers on frequented routes, which shall be 50 miles apart in mid-ocean, and which shall avoid known fishing-grounds, especially the Banks of Newfoundland.

S. Ex. 53, pt. 3——18

[William. C. Whittle, captain Bay Line steamer *Georgia.*]

I believe that the establishment of "*lanes" for steamers on frequented routes*, going in opposite directions, would greatly promote safety of life and property. I question the feasibility of absolutely maintaining such "lanes," but in proportion as the number of steamers meeting is decreased the chances of collision would be lessened.

The navigators, however, should be warned not to presume upon the effort to establish these "lanes," or lulled into any feeling of security, or any lack of vigilance, upon the hypothesis that a lane system is maintained. They should be cautioned that although a man may be in his "lane," if he meets a steamer he must not arrogate to himself any rights or privileges not given him by the "Rules of the Road."

[General information gained in interviews with masters of vessels at the branch hydrographic office, Boston.]

In the matter of "lanes for steamers on frequented routes" there will undoubtedly be great opposition to any move in this direction. Most steamer captains are thoroughly convinced that the ocean belongs especially to them, and that they have a perfect right to go on it where they please. Notwithstanding the fact that a few hours at the most will cover the difference between the route passing clear of the Banks of Newfoundland to the southward and a more northerly route—crossing, say, about the middle of the Bank—with the additional advantage in favor of the former that there is very much less likelihood of encountering fog, many masters of steamers persist in following the route across the Banks, regardless of the lives of the fishermen who depend on these same Banks to furnish a living for themselves and families. I can see no reason why steamers should not be obliged to follow certain routes, differing for the different seasons of the year. It would frequently cause a slight lengthening of their voyages, but would very greatly increase the safety of ocean travel. In the summer, or ice season, the prescribed route should pass clear of the tail of the Banks to the southward. In the winter, or safe season, it should pass near Cape Race. If it is decided that steamers must cross the Banks, then a specified route across them should be prescribed, and fishermen should be required to keep clear of this track. In deciding this question, in reference to the Banks of Newfoundland and other similar localities, preference should undoubtedly be given to the rights of the fishermen. The only practical solution of the question of lane routes with regard to the avoidance of collisions between steamers is by the separation of the eastern and western routes by a degree at least, but it is claimed by many masters of vessels that it would not work in practice. In thick or foggy weather, with no observations to verify the position, no vessel could be sure that she was in the right path. During heavy weather vessels are very likely to be driven out of their way. In various ways vessels are likely to find themselves not only out of their own track, but directly in the track of steamers going in the opposite direction. On the other hand, in the case of steamers proceeding in the same direction the difference in speed is often so great as to render a collision between them almost as serious as if they had met bows on. There is, of course, a possibility that any one or all these things may occur, but, to my mind, they detract nothing from the wisdom of the proposed separation of the routes; there could be no more danger than under the present condition of things, under which steamers apparently follow a go-as-you-please policy, and there is every reason to believe that the proposed system would operate to the greatest possible advantage. Ordinarily there would be no excuse for a master of a vessel to fail to keep his ship in the proper track, and under no circumstances would there be any more danger than at present exists at all times at sea.

[Discussion before the U. S. Naval Institute, Annapolis, Md., on collisions at sea.]

Lieutenant McCARTENEY. * * * The recommendation of the employment of different routes for eastward and westward bound vessels is not the least important of the suggestions made, but the difficulty has been to have these recommendations followed, each captain being naturally desirous of shortening his voyage as much as possible.

There can be no doubt how greatly the adoption of a route to go and another to return will conduce to safety. With these routes, varying with the season, and sufficiently separated to avoid the possible danger of a vessel which is following one from drifting into the other, from not having had observations for two or three days, the chances of collision will be much lessened. The U. S. Hydrographic Office, in its monthly publication of the Pilot Chart, has for a long time earnestly advocated this subject, and each month calls special attention to the best transatlantic steam-ship routes.

In his annual report to the Bureau of Navigation the Hydrographer says: "Every effort has been made to collect the latest and most reliable data concerning ice in the vicinity of the Grand Banks, but very few reports have been made of this great danger south of the parallel of 45° north. The transatlantic routes as laid down on the Pilot Chart seem to have been adopted by the Boston steam-ship lines more generally this year than ever before, which accounts in part for the scarcity of ice reports. Many captains have been inclined to regard the recommendations as unnecessarily cautious, but such illustrations as the collision of the *Geiser* and *Thingvalla* affords have convinced the most skeptical of their value. The routes of the various transatlantic steam lines are slowly but surely drawing together, and while in all probability they will not reach the extreme limit for ice-season travel recommended by the Chart, they will approximate to it, and the adoption of one path each way for all will be a great improvement." An objection raised to the Pilot Chart routes by Captain Banaré, of the French hydrographic office, is that they are not widely enough separated, thus giving opportunity for the possible error previously mentioned, due from lack of observations, wild steering, etc.; but this is a very minor point, and could be easily remedied when certain fixed limits have been adopted and vessels rigidly required to observe them.

In the second part of "Les Collisions en Mer," recently published in the *Annales Hydrographiques*, Captain Banaré says that "in giving to navigators a regulation that offers a guaranty of security the tendency would be to diminish the watchfulness on board ship by raising a feeling of false confidence on the part of the captain, from the certainty which he would have that all vessels moving in the contrary direction would follow the official route; also that the lengthening of one of the routes, which would be the natural consequence of the adoption of the double track, could be another element of danger, inasmuch as all vessels would then maintain an exaggerated speed, not only in foggy weather, but at all times, so that the number of collisions, instead of diminishing, would be considerably increased." It is hardly probable that, should such routes be adopted, a captain would take upon himself the responsibility of leaving his proper track, knowing that in case of collision he or his company would be held responsible for the loss of life and property incurred. Still less would this be apt to occur in thick weather.

Ensign HAYDEN. "If it were possible to determine for each voyage a route to go and another to return, the chances of collision would be greatly diminished. But a similar project, applicable only to steamers, and which does not prohibit the crossing of the routes, has raised so many objections that it appears to be abandoned. Notwithstanding, there are localities like those of the Banks of Newfoundland, for instance, where we find a great number of vessels assembled unable to maneuver and for whom it is desirable to enforce some special conservative (protective) measures."

This question of the best regulation of steam traffic across the Grand Banks seems to be one of the most important as well as difficult problems that can come before the Marine Conference, and I am inclined to doubt whether this or any other Conference will be able to agree upon and enforce any set of regulations that will improve, to any appreciable extent, the present status of affairs. Nevertheless, it should be thoroughly considered from every point of view, and an international tribunal is the only one that can properly do so. Moreover, the results of the deliberations of the Conference in other directions—its decisions as to lights, fog-signals, and rules of the road—have such an important bearing upon this question that its consideration may best be taken up after other points have been definitely decided.

From my connection with the publication of the Pilot Chart, I have of necessity considered this subject very carefully, and perhaps, on that account, more fully appreciate the difficulties in the way of the adoption and enforcement of any hard-and-fast regulations or restrictions regarding transatlantic steam navigation. So many things enter as factors in the problem, and with such constantly varying force, that I must deprecate the hasty adoption of any of the specious and plausible schemes that look so well on paper and yet would never work in practice.

"The longer any one studies a vast subject," says Professor Bryce in The American Commonwealth, "the more cautious in inference does he become." The world-renowned Maury even proposed a plan of "lane-routes," and, although it has still a prominent existence on paper, yet it has not now, and really never did have, any particular force in practice.

With the Pilot Chart for December, 1887, there was published a brief discussion of this subject, and certain routes were recommended. The plan thus initiated has been adhered to since that date, so far as recommendations go, and a brief *résumé* may therefore be of interest.

Eastward Bound.—Follow this track, or nothing to the northward of it. Leaving New York, steer for latitude 40° 26′ N., longitude 73° 46′ W., thence ESE. ¼ E. to the 100-fathom line, then deep soundings, and off-soundings, crossing 60° W. in 42° N. and 50° W. in 45° N.; thence follow the great circle, crossing 40° W. in 48° 01′ N., 30° W. in 49° 56′ N., 20° W. in 50° 55′ N., and 10° W. in 50° N.

Westward Bound.—Follow this track, or nothing to the southward of it. Cross 10° W. in 51° 10′ N.; thence following the great circle, crossing 20° W. in 51° 16′ N., 30° W. in 50° 28′ N., 40 W. in 48° 46′ N., and 50 W. in 46° N. Cross 60° W. in 43° N., 69° W. in 40° 38′ N.; then keep inside 30 fathoms, steering to cross 74° W. in 40° 30′ N.

With the addition of a route from the English Channel (course about west by north), joining the west-bound route in about long. 20° W., and the shifting of both routes to the southward during the ice season, this plan has been consistently and persistently recommended on the Pilot Chart, and many letters of approval have been received from practical navigators and others. The main feature of this plan is, it will be noticed, to *keep to the right* of a narrow central belt, whose limits are accurately defined, both graphically and by means of a detailed printed description. Westward-bound vessels are thus enabled to take advantage of the Labrador current, shaving Cape Race, if they choose, and eastward-bound vessels can go as far south as they please, to take advantage of the Gulf Stream and the easterly drift-current in mid-ocean. At the same time, in the central belt the danger to the fishing fleet and other vessels is at a minimum; to the north of this belt danger is to be looked for principally from the *east,* and to the south of it from the *west.*

Neglecting the fact that different ports of departure and arrival must always interfere with this or any other plan, I may refer to certain other difficulties that may or may not prove insuperable. In the first place, there is the self-evident truth that this great highway of steam navigation, the connecting link between the old world and the new, is of vast and steadily increasing importance. Even now, although it is traversed yearly at almost railway speed by vessels intrusted with more than a million human lives, and property of an aggregate value of fully a billion dollars, the inventive genius of the age is devoting its best energies toward meeting the demand for better, larger, faster and safer vessels. The steam-ship that breaks the record, and carries the pennant for the best passage, becomes famous, and her success is heralded to the four corners of the earth. Now, this fact indicates "a condition, not a theory;" it means that there is a *demand* that must be considered and complied with, and regulations that lose sight of or attempt to discountenance it are as absurd as would be an attempt to regulate, by statute, the speed of railroad trains.

Again, general averages regarding the limits of ice off the Grand Banks are often of no earthly use so far as any particular season is concerned. The present season, for instance, has been a marked exception, almost no ice at all having been reported. The usual or normal limit of drifting ice can not, therefore, be considered, and we must base our routes upon the conditions that actually exist, as reported by incoming vessels or by telegraph from St. John's. Another important element is the fact that the mails are given to the fastest vessels. One steamer may take a safer route, traverse a slightly longer distance, and lose the mails. This very thing happened only last year, when the *Werra* was beaten a few hours by the *Servia*, and Captain Bussius complained that he had followed the route recommended, and lost the mail in consequence. This question should therefore be carefully considered, and postal regulations framed accordingly.

Last, but by no means least, all possible reasonable precautions should be taken to avoid unnecessary danger to the brave fishermen who follow their hazardous occupation on the Grand Banks and adjacent fishing grounds, constantly exposed, in their little sailing vessels, to all the dangers of this stormy coast, and surrounded half the time by dense fog that gives them scant notice of the approach of one of the rushing ocean grey-hounds, whose sharp bow would cut them through like a knife. In this connection let me quote from Capt. J. W. Collins, of the U. S. Commission of Fish and Fisheries, whose long experience and intimate acquaintance with all the circumstances of the case render his opinion of great value. Captain Collins says, in a letter dated Washington, April 12, 1889: "So far as any plan is concerned to secure the safety of fishermen upon the Banks by the recommendation of definite lanes of travel for ocean steamers, I give as my opinion that it would add much to the safety of fishermen if lanes could be established during the greater part of the year which would take the steamers south of the Grand Banks. From March to November there is a large fleet fishing upon the Grand Bank, aggregating somewhere from 500 to 700 vessels, belonging to the United States, British North American Provinces, France, and Portugal. A comparatively small number of vessels, principally from the United States, fish upon the Grand Bank throughout the year. The fishing-grounds extend from about 42° 57′ north latitude, which is practically the southern limit for halibut, to the northern margin of the Bank, and some times even beyond it. I appreciate the obstacles which might be met with in an attempt to prohibit steam-ships from crossing the Grand Bank, since I realize the force of your statement that the Banks can not be 'fenced in.' I think, however, that, considering the danger incident to the crossing of the Banks in the spring, summer, and autumn, when fogs are prevalent, it would be vastly to the advantage of the fishermen, and an act of humanity, if the steam-ship lanes could be arranged to pass south of the Grand Bank from March to November. In winter, the vessels fishing upon the Grand Bank are generally collected about its southern extremity, where they go to fish for halibut. I would say that at that season the danger to fishing vessels would not be so great, if steamers are to cross the Grand Bank any how, if the crossing were made north of the forty-fourth parallel of north latitude, or about where it is limited on the chart you have sent me. A very slight deflection, to avoid the southern point of Banquereau, would take the ships clear of all fishing-grounds resorted to west of the Grand Bank, and would carry them far enough north so that they would not come in contact with the majority of the fleet, at that time fishing on the latter Bank. I have drawn in, roughly, lines which I would suggest for spring, summer, and autumn travel, from March to November, so arranged that the northernmost would just clear the southern prong of the Grand Bank. I most earnestly hope that the steam-ship companies may be disposed to adopt some system which will relieve the fishermen from the perils now encountered by them in consequence of transatlantic steamers crossing the Banks. It seems that this might be done without material disadvantage, for the presence of ice enforces the deflection I have suggested for a part of the year, and there would only remain a comparatively short time when the transatlantic trade would have to diverge from the courses heretofore followed in late summer and autumn."

These considerations seem to me to be the principal ones that have an important bearing on the question, and serve to illustrate its complexity and the difficulty of a practical solution that will be advantageous all around. Evidently, conflicting interests must be considered, and a compromise effected, or else the whole thing left *in statu quo*. When we consider, however, the enormous importance of transatlantic steam navigation; the demand for great speed and quick passage; the fact that the shortest route is close to Cape Race; that storms, fog, and ocean currents enter as a factor less and less every year; that a single great ocean steam-ship, carrying the transatlantic mail, and straining every nerve to lessen the gap that separates the old world from the new, represents almost, if not quite, as great a value, in number of lives and amount of property, as the entire fishing-fleet of every nationality—considering all these things, I must say it seems to me that all other interests are necessarily subordinate, and any regulations likely to be effective must be framed accordingly.

WASHINGTON, D. C.

APPENDIX B.

BOSTON, *October* 17, 1889.

The honorable SECRETARY OF STATE,
        Washington, D. C.:

SIR: Learning of the proposed conference of nations on the subject of maritime regulations, George V. Steele, esq., president of the Gloucester Mutual Fishing Insurance Company, in the interest of American fishing vessels, addressed a circular to many masters of fishermen asking information as to the dangers of the fishing banks caused by steamers. A few specific answers were received, many remain unanswered. I transmit at his request the accompanying circular and answers for your consideration.

I am, very respectfully,

CHAS. L. WOODBURY.

[Circular.]

JUNE 26, 1889.

Have any vessels disappeared under circumstances which induce the opinion that they have been run down by any steamer or steam-ship and are a total loss?

Do you know of any that have had narrow escapes?

Give the names of such vessels, the date and situation when last seen, and also state the circumstances so far as you have learned them.

[Replies.]

"I have several times narrowly escaped being struck by steamers in thick weather, both while lying at anchor and under sail, on and in the neighborhood of fishing grounds. In some instances the steamer has been almost upon me before her way could be stopped or course changed. I have no particular instance in mind.

"SAMUEL HILTZ."

"On northeast part of Georges had very narrow escape from being run down by steamer at night, it being thick fog at the time. She came within 75 feet, and would have run over the vessel if it had not been for our torches and horns. This was last February, in schooner *Carl Schurz.*

"JOHN CONSTANCE, *M.*"

"Schooner *Golden Hind*, in 1885, on southern edge of Georges, at night, had a narrow escape from collision with steamer. We were lying-to, and steamer came so near that we hauled up the boat to leave the vessel, but after showing our torch and making a noise, she kept off.

"RUBEN CAMERON."

"Schooner *James A. Garfield*, in 1886, in longitude 60°, latitude 43° 30′, had narrow escape from being run down by steamer at 10 o'clock p. m. She came within 25 feet of the vessel, and changed her course when we showed our torch.

"THOMAS BOHLIN, *M*."

"I don't know of any vessel being run down by a steamer, but have had several narrow escapes from steamers going at full speed across the Banks.

"CHAS. PETERSON, *P*."

"Have been master to the *Grand Banks* ten years. The passage of steamers across the Banks is, in my opinion, very dangerous, and I have no doubt that vessels have been run down by steamers in foggy weather. Have seen steamers daily when fishing on the Banks, and have heard their whistle in foggy weather.

"JOHN GAUEVILLE."

NIGHT-SIGNALS FOR COMMUNICATING INFORMATION AT SEA.

WASHINGTON, *December* 6, 1889.

Rear-Admiral S. R. FRANKLIN, U. S. Navy,
President of the International Marine Conference, etc.:

SIR: With regard to subsections (*a*) and (*b*) of General Division 8, the committee have considered systems of night-signals with ordinary colored lights, but the objection exists that they cannot be seen so far as a white light. It is the opinion of the committee that night-signaling at sea can better be carried on by a system of long and short flashes from a white light than by any system in which colored lights are used.

The committee have concluded that the systems of signaling by pyrotechnic lights which have been brought to their notice are too expensive for general use.

The committee have had before them "A supplementary code of limited scope to convey information of special importance to passing vessels," which has been prepared by a committee of the British Board of Trade and has been presented by the British Government to the various powers for their consideration.

Your committee, after careful consideration, suggest that the Conference recommend the adoption, for optional use, of that suplementary code, with the following change, which will become necessary if the Conference adopt the signal suggested by the joint committee on "Pilot-Signals, viz: To strike out signal P G, "Beware of derelict dangerous to navigation," and substitute in its place N P, "I want assistance. Remain by me." Appendix A contains this supplementary code as amended.

To illustrate the importance attached to the subject of night-signals the committee refer to the great number of proposals on that subject mentioned by the report of the committee on Systems and Devices.

That part of the proposed amendment to Article 27, entitled extra amendment No. 6, which reads as follows—

" Vessels in want of a pilot have to display their national flag with a white border or make the signal indicated by P T at the fore.

"At night, together or separately.

"The pyrotechnic light, commonly known as a blue light, every fifteen minutes, or a bright white light, flashed or shown at short intervals just above the bulwarks for about a minute at a time,"—

which was referred to this committee, the committee find is already included in the International Code Signal Book under the head of "Pilot Signals." The committee therefore recommend no further action on the amendment.

With reference to the twenty-third amendment to Article 4, viz, "A tug wishing to offer her service to a vessel shall exhibit to such vessel, in addition to the ordinary lights, a white and red flare-up alternately," which was referred to this committee, the committee beg leave to report that they do not think it expedient to allot any special signal to vessels of this class.

Subsection (c) referring to distress signals was not considered, as it has been disposed of by the Conference.

In compliance with the resolution of the Conference referring to this committee, assisted by the Committee on Sound-Signals, the subject of fog-signals to be allotted to pilots and to vessels seeking pilots, the joint committee met and decided upon the following signals:

For vessels requiring pilots—a prolonged blast followed by a short blast, ▬▬▬▬ ▬.

For pilots wishing to offer their services—short blast followed by a long blast, ▬ ▬▬▬▬.

And the committee recommend that they be inserted in the International Code Book under the "Pilot-Signals."

While considering the subject of signals to convey information of special importance to passing vessels, the decision of the conference in adding to the signals now in use, consisting of short and long blasts, the favor in which such signals seem to be held, and the convenience which an extended use of such signals would be to mariners, have led the committee to consider the benefits which might accrue from the more general use of the Morse system now in use by the navies of various powers.

Up to the present time no better system seems to have been devised for signaling purposes; it is one which can be used under all circumstances, it is readily acquired by young persons of ordinary ability, and is already taught on some training ships. If its use were encouraged it might lead to the study of the code by more young men qualifying as officers of the Merchant Marine, or as signal men, and thus come into more general use.

Such studies are beneficial in developing the intellectual activity of seamen, and every accomplishment of the kind acquired and made necessary by the requirements of the service helps to develop the *morale* of the sailor.

To thus encourage the use of the system the committee suggest to the Conference that the complete alphabet of the Morse Code be inserted in the International Code Book for optional use.

AUG. GARDE,
Delegate for Denmark.

HENRI LANNELUC,
Delegate for France.

CHRISTIAN DONNER,
Delegate for Germany.

N. BOWDEN-SMITH,
Delegate for Great Britain.

H. A. P. CARTER,
Chairman of Committee, Delegate for Hawaii.

T. DE SOUZA ROZA,
Delegate for Portugal.

FREDERICK MALMBERG,
Delegate for Sweden.

D. HUBERT,
Delegate for the Netherlands.

JOHN W. SHACKFORD,
Delegate for the United States.

The undersigned desire to record that in signing the above report they do so without prejudice to the opinions they hold as to the desirability of giving special signals to use with fog-horns on board pilot-vessels.

CHRISTIAN DONNER,
Delegate for Germany.

N. BOWDEN-SMITH,
Delegate for Great Britain.

T. DE SOUZA ROZA,
Delegate for Portugal.

FREDERICK MALMBERG,
Delegate for Sweden.

D. HUBERT,
Delegate for the Netherlands.

APPENDIX A.

A SUPPLEMENTARY CODE OF THE BRITISH BOARD OF TRADE.

[As amended and recommended.]

Important signals which may be made at night or during fog, either by flashes of white light or by a combination of long and short sounds on the steam-whistle, fog-horn, siren, bugle, etc.

[In the day-time they will be made by flags.]

INSTRUCTIONS FOR THE USE OF FLASHING OR SOUND SIGNALS.

1.

With flashing signals the lamp must always be turned towards the person addressed.

2.

To attract attention, a series of rapid short flashes or sounds should be made and continued until the person addressed gives the sign of attention by doing the same.

If, however, it is supposed that the person addressed can not reply, the signal may be made after a moderate pause, or under certain circumstances, the communication may be made direct without preparatory signs.

3.

After making a few rapid short flashes or sounds as an acknowledgment, the receiver must watch, or listen attentively until the communication is completed, when he must make the sign indicated below, showing that the message is understood.

4.

If the receiver does not understand the message, he must wait until the signal is repeated.

5.

Duration of short flashes or sounds	1 second.
Duration of long flashes or sounds	3 seconds.
Duration of prolonged sound	4 to 6 seconds.
Interval between each flash or sound	1 second.
Answer, or "I understand"	━━ ━ ━━ ━ ━━ ━ ━━ ━ etc

SIGNALS.

JK	You are standing into danger	━ ━ ━━
NP	I want assistance. Please remain by me	━ ━ ━ ━━
QC	Have encountered ice	━ ━━ ━
PD	The way is off my ship, you may feel your way past me	━ ━━ ━
JB	Stop, or heave to; I have something important to communicate	━ ━━ ━ ━
PR	Am disabled. Communicate with me	━ ━ ━━ ━

When a vessel is in "tow," the following flashes or sounds may be made from her to the tug or towing vessel:

KR Steer more to port .... ▬ ▬
KS Steer more to starboard.. ▬

PILOT SIGNALS DURING FOG.

For vessels requiring pilots .... ▬▬▬ ▬
For pilots wishing to offer their services......................... ▬ ▬▬

REPORT OF THE COMMITTEE UPON GENERAL DIVISIONS 9, 10, 11, AND 12 OF THE PROGRAMME.

COMMITTEE No. 3.

To consider and report upon General Divisions 9, 10, 11, and 12:

Austria-Hungary	Lieut. SANCHEZ DE LA CERDA.
China	Captain BISBEE.
France	Mr. RIBIÈRE.
Germany	Captain MENSING.
Great Britain	Admiral NARES.
Norway	Mr. FLOOD.
Siam	Mr. VERNEY.
Uruguay	Dr. ALBERTO NIN.
United States	Captain SAMPSON.

GENERAL DIVISION 9.

WARNINGS OF APPROACHING STORMS.

(*a*) The transmission of warnings.
(*b*) The uniformity of signals employed.

GENERAL DIVISION 10.

REPORTING, MARKING, AND REMOVING DANGEROUS WRECKS OR OBSTRUCTIONS TO NAVIGATION.

(*a*) A uniform method of reporting and marking dangerous wrecks and derelicts.

(*b*) The division of labor, cost, and responsibility among the several maritime nations, either by geographical apportionment or otherwise—
Of the removal of dangerous derelicts.
And of searching for doubtful dangers with a view of removing them from the charts.

GENERAL DIVISION 11.

NOTICE OF DANGERS TO NAVIGATION.

Notice of changes in lights, buoys, and other day and night marks.

GENERAL DIVISION 12.

A UNIFORM SYSTEM OF BUOYS AND BEACONS.

(a) Uniformity in color of buoys.
(b) Uniformity in numbering of buoys.

WASHINGTON, D. C., *December* 28, 1889.

Rear-Admiral S. R. FRANKLIN, U. S. Navy,
 President International Marine Conference, etc.:

SIR: In submitting their report the committee have thought it the most convenient plan to deal separately with each of the General Divisions which have been discussed and considered by them.

GENERAL DIVISION 9.

WARNINGS OF APPROACHING STORMS.

(a) The transmission of warnings.
(b) The uniformity of signals employed.

(a) THE TRANSMISSION OF WARNINGS.

The committee understand that the various meteorological offices in Europe are in frequent and intimate communication, and interchange telegraphic information for the purpose of weather forecasting on that side of the Atlantic Ocean, while the meteorological offices of the United States and the Dominion of Canada act in concert on the Western side, and also, that a similar custom prevails in many Eastern countries.

The preparation of the weather forecasts and the transmission of warnings regarding expected storms must, by the very nature of the subject, be dealt with locally; and it is, in the opinion of the committee, very questionable whether any useful purpose would be gained by the adoption of uniformity of methods except so far as the general progress of scientific knowledge indicates the direction of possible improvement, and this, it is hardly necessary to say, is more likely to be secured by work carried on independently rather than under any uniform system.

(b) THE UNIFORMITY OF SIGNALS EMPLOYED.

Storm-warning signals were first introduced in the interests of the shipping or fishing-vessels lying at anchor in harbor or proposing to put to sea. Lately the same warning-signals have been freely extended to coast stations with a view to give information regarding the weather to passing vessels. Inasmuch as these may be local or foreign traders, the committee are of opinion that such signals should, as far as possible, be in international agreement.

The established signals originally in use in Europe are evidently founded on the seaman's knowledge of the "law of storms," and, while warning him of an approaching cyclone, indicate whether the northern or southern portion is expected to pass over the district. Experience proves that this was practically sufficient information for the masters of vessels in the neighboring harbor who would know whether the cyclone was approaching or had passed, but it is scarcely sufficient for coasting vessels, especially those proceeding on a course at right angles to the direction in which the cyclone is moving.

In the opinion of the committee it is therefore desirable that storm-signals displayed at coast stations should give to passing vessels some further information as to whether storms are approaching or have passed the station, and, in reference to this, the committee desire to call attention to the fact that this want has been supplied by the system now in use in the United States. The German system indicates four directions from which a storm is expected, and whether its probable course is to the right or the left. (See Appendix C.)

In dealing with this matter the committee have had the advantage of hearing the views of General A. W. Greely, the Chief Signal Officer in charge of the United States Weather Bureau, and he has summarized them in a memorandum contained under cover of a letter dated December 23, 1889, both of which are appended to this report and to which the committee desire to draw special attention. (See Appendix A.)

It will be seen that, in this memorandum, General Greely has indicated the practical reasons for adopting, in lieu of cone-shaped signals, the use of colored flags for notifying storm warnings on the coasts of the United States, which, it is claimed, can be seen (except in very calm weather) at a greater distance and by means of which additional information can be given.

The committee consider that this subject is of such a technical nature that they are not prepared to express a decided opinion upon it. They recommend, however, the Conference to invite the various maritime countries to consider the best practical mode of signaling by day, whether by shapes, colored or black, by flags, or by the two combined, and by night by means of lights, colored or white, arranged to represent distinctive forms.

Together with the memorandum alluded to General Greely inclosed a copy of General Orders, No. 29, dated from the Signal Office, War Department, November 11, 1889, from which a paragraph is quoted, and also a paper of diagrams showing the storm, cautionary, and wind-direction signals in use in the United States. These signals are reproduced in Appendix B to this report.

S. Ex. 53, pt. 3——19

In recapitulation the committee recommend the Conference to invite the maritime countries interested to take into consideration the establishment of a uniform system of indicating storm warnings by day and by night, and that such a system should, as far as possible, include signals indicating whether the storm is approaching or has passed the station.

APPENDIX A.

WARNINGS OF APPROACHING STORMS.

SIGNAL OFFICE, WAR DEPARTMENT,
Washington City, December 23, 1889.

CHAIRMAN OF COMMITTEE No. 3,
International Marine Conference, Washington, D. C.:

SIR: In compliance with the verbal request of your committee, I have the honor and pleasure to herewith transmit a brief statement setting forth the methods in vogue giving storm warnings, which is a concise reduction to writing of the statements made by me before your honorable committee.

I also transmit a brief statement showing the system of storm-warning signals used in other countries. This statement depends on the official publications in this office, and in the case of some countries, as you will notice, is twelve years old. If more time had been available, possibly later information might have been obtained from some of these countries. As will be observed, Great Britain has modified its system by abandoning the drum. Portugal, also, which officially adopted the English system, though it is doubtful if it ever went into practical use, has replaced it by a system composed entirely of flags. The suggestions from Portugal are pertinent and forcible—that a common system should be used.

Regretting that I have not been able to give more definite and exact information to the International Congress which you represent, and regretting also that the urgency of action has given so brief a time for this summary, I am, with the greatest respect,

Yours, sincerely,

A. W. GREELY,
Brigadier-General and Chief Signal Officer.

EXPLANATION OF THE SYSTEM OF STORM WARNINGS USED IN THE UNITED STATES.

The system recognizes the fact that the sailor has the right to expect information regarding coming gales, first, whether they are expected to be of moderate severity or of considerable violence; second, whether the storm has passed him or is approaching him; and, thirdly, whether he is in the northerly or southerly quadrant of the more dangerous winds attending an approaching storm, or in the northern or southern quadrant of the high winds following in the rear of a storm.

With this in view, the first object has been obtained by recognizing the fact that danger is largely represented by the red color, so that the more violent storms are represented by a square red flag, which has in the center a small square of white.*

A yellow flag with a white center indicates light storms.

In order to indicate whether the storm center is approaching or has not passed the station a red pennant is used, which thus indicates winds in the front quadrants of the storm, which generally are from south to northeast and are considered the most dangerous on the American coast. In like manner a white pennant indicates that the storm has passed the station, and that high, clearing winds are expected from the north to the southwest.

In order to convey most simply to the sailor whether the expected winds will be in the northerly quadrant or in the southerly quadrant, the plan has been followed of having the pennant (whether red or white) above the square flag when winds are expected from the northerly quadrant, as naturally the sailor judges that anything which is *above* should indicate the north. Similarly winds from the southerly quadrant are shown by placing the pennant (whether white or red) under the square flag.

An additional signal, known as the "information signal," is displayed for the benefit of the mariner about to sail. It is a yellow pennant, and indicates that the Signal Office is in possession of information which may or may not be valuable. For instance, it very frequently occurs that vessels can sail, not only with perfect safety but with great benefit, in certain directions from the port, while on other courses dangers and delays would follow.

It may be stated that experiments have indicated to this office the decided superiority of flags with color over forms, such as spheres and cylinders. Unless the cylinders, cones, and balls are very large they can not be distinguished under average conditions more than 2 to 2½ miles, and observation has confirmed the theoretical knowledge that during the warm part of the day, or under any conditions where vertical air currents obtain, the distortion of the forms is so great as to render them indistinguishable and uncertain even at moderate distances. Experiments have also shown that the reds, blues, greens, and dirty whites tend to show up as black, and that the only light color which holds its visibility as a color at any considerable distance is yellow. It would thus appear that the red, being a pronounced danger

---

* This small center of white is not a desirable or necessary part of the flag, and it was only adopted for reasons of economy, in order to utilize a large number of flags of this pattern which are on hand for use in army signaling.

color, and the yellow are the most suitable colors for storm-warning signals.

The white pennant now in use by the United States could, with advantage, be replaced by the yellow pennant, but it was not adopted owing to the prejudice which obtains in Southern ports against the yellow flag, and the fear that the display of the solid yellow, such as is used in the pennant, might be mistaken for a "yellow-fever flag." The large yellow flag *having a white center* is not so liable to misinterpretation.

The various systems of cautionary or storm signals in use by the several meteorological services are about as follows, as far as we are able to judge from the information contained in this office:

The system used by the London meteorological office for the British Isles, as described by Mr. Scott in 1887, was as follows: The day cautionary signal consisted of a cone, 3 feet high and 3 feet wide at the base. Hoisted with the point downward, it indicated that a gale was probable from the south, and hoisted with the point upward to indicate that the gale would probably be from the north. Cautionary night signals of this system consisted of three lanterns, arranged in the form of a triangle representing the outline of a cone. The signals are cautionary, and the fact that such notice has been received at any station is made known by hoisting the cone, the meaning of which is a warning to sailors and others interested to "look out; it is probable that bad weather of such and such a character is approaching you." In every case some of the principal reasons which have led to the hoisting of signals are briefly explained in the telegram, which should always be kept posted up for public inspection while the signal is flying. The central meteorological office issues to ports and fishing stations, approved by the Board of Trade, notices of approaching storms near the coast of the British Islands.

The system now in use in the British Islands is based upon the system adopted by Admiral Fitz Roy in 1862, only it is less complicated. The Fitz Roy system consisted of the north and south cones and combinations of these for day signals, and lanterns arranged in the form of a triangle or parallelogram to represent the cone and drum. The cone and drum were hoisted together—the cone above the drum, with the vertex up—when the gale was expected to be first to the north and afterward shifting to some other quarter. The position of these symbols was reversed when the storm was expected to set in first from the south.

The Canadian system consists of a cone or cone and drum for the day signals, while the night signals consist of two lamps.

The meteorological department of the government of India uses the following system of cautionary signals: Day signal No. 1, to indicate bad weather, or a warning signal, a ball. No. 2, a storm or danger signal, a drum. For a night signal No. 1, or bad weather signal, three white lights arranged in a vertical line. No. 2, storm or danger signal, two white lights arranged in a vertical line.

In a report on weather telegraphy, by Robert H. Scott, secretary of the permanent committee, the following replies relative to the systems of signals employed in the various countries for the announcement of storm warnings were received in 1877, and later information has not been received relative to some of these systems of signals:

Russia.—Drum and cone, with lamps for night signals.

Sweden.—Storm warnings not in use.

Norway.—In some places balls or flags. No official or uniform system. No night signals.

Denmark.—No storm warnings.

Holland.—The Æroklinoscope, for the direction and force of the expected wind. Sheets on which are noted the winds actually blowing, barometer heights, temperature, etc.

Belgium.—No storm warnings.

France.—Drum and cone. No night signals.

Austria.—No storm warnings.

Turkey.—By signals. The reports are exhibited in the harbor offices.

Mauritius.—Flags and ball, with lamp for night signals.

New South Wales.—Admiral Fitz Roy's. No night signals.

Victoria.—None at present. The English system is to be adopted.

WARNING STORM-SIGNALS IN USE ON THE COAST OF PORTUGAL SINCE AUGUST 1. 1888.

At all the semaphore stations the state of weather is communicated to passing vessels by the signals of the commercial code, which, being known to all mariners, is used in view of the fact that there is no international code of storm-signals. This system indicates the force of the wind, on a scale of one to six and also its direction to eight points.

It is suggested from Portugal, that the system of signals should be common for all coasts and also very simple; that one flag should indicate the section of the coast predicted for, a second the direction of the wind, and a third flag or a triangle the force of the wind.

GENERAL ORDERS, }   SIGNAL OFFICE, WAR DEPARTMENT,
No. 29.   }   *Washington, November 11, 1889.*

*   *   ?   *   *   *

III.—INFORMATION SIGNAL.

In obedience to the wishes of a large number of vessel owners, ship captains, and others interested in navigation, the Chief Signal Officer has adopted a signal known as the "Information Signal," and forming one of the system of "storm, cautionary, and wind-direction signals."

The "information signal" consists of a yellow pennant, of the same dimensions as the red and the white pennants (wind direction signals), and when displayed indicates that the local observer has received information from the central office of a storm covering a limited area, dangerous only for vessels about to sail to certain points. The signal will serve as a notification to ship-masters that the necessary information will be given them upon application to the local observer. The use of this signal will begin December 1, 1889.

It is believed that the display of the "information signal" will, in many instances, obviate the necessity for the display of the "cautionary signal" (yellow flag with white center).

APPENDIX B.

UNITED STATES SIGNAL SERVICE WIND SIGNALS.

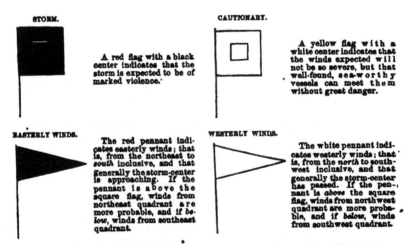

STORM.

A red flag with a black center indicates that the storm is expected to be of marked violence.

CAUTIONARY.

A yellow flag with a white center indicates that the winds expected will not be so severe, but that well-found, sea-worthy vessels can meet them without great danger.

EASTERLY WINDS.

The red pennant indicates easterly winds; that is, from the northeast to *south* inclusive, and that generally the storm-center is approaching. If the pennant is above the square flag, winds from northeast quadrant are more probable, and if below, winds from southeast quadrant.

WESTERLY WINDS.

The white pennant indicates westerly winds; that is, from the *north* to southwest inclusive, and that generally the storm-center has passed. If the pennant is *above* the square flag, winds from northwest quadrant are more probable, and if *below*, winds from southwest quadrant.

By night a red light will indicate easterly winds and a white light above a red light will indicate westerly winds.

A. W. GREELY,
Chief Signal Officer.

NOTE.—Hoisting signals for each quadrant is an opinion only, offered to aid the public, as the predictions upon which they are based are only made for easterly or westerly winds.

APPENDIX C.

SYSTEM OF STORM WARNINGS USED IN THE GERMAN EMPIRE.

The system of cautionary signals adopted in the German Empire is as follows:

1. A ball means caution!
2. A cone hoisted point down—storm from the SW.!
3. A cone hoisted point up—storm from NW.!
4. Two cones hoisted points down—storm from SE.!
5. Two cones hoisted points up—storm from NE.!

One square flag hoisted, together with these shapes, means that the wind will probably turn to the right—(N. E. S. W.); two flags, pointed in the same way, mean that it will probably turn to the left—(N. W. S. E.).

Night signals are not in general use.

APPENDIX D.

*OPINIONS OF OFFICERS AND OTHERS, SUBMITTED FOR THE CONSID-
ERATION OF THE MARITIME CONFERENCE.*

[Report of Ensign George P. Blow, U. S. Navy, in charge of branch hydrographic
office, New York City, on General Division 9.]

"(a) THE TRANSMISSION OF WARNINGS."

Warning of approaching storms should be immediately telegraphed to the seat of government of each country or island over which the gale is expected to pass, or the shipping of which will be exposed to danger. As soon as this report is received, it should be turned over to the meteorologist for elaboration and correction. With a knowledge of the local action of such gales in the past, together with a careful consideration of the meteorological conditions then existing, a very accurate forecast of the weather may be made. This forecast or warning should then be telegraphed to all the sea-board cities, life-saving stations, light-houses, and, where possible, to the light-ships. (In the near future it is believed that all light-ships will be connected with the shore by submarine cables, which will make it possible to display these storm signals.) Printed bulletins in English, French, German, Spanish, and Italian, giving a brief description of the approaching storm, should also be posted in all the exchanges, custom-houses, and other places where ship-masters are known to congregate.

Warning signals should be hoisted at each signal station, light-house, life-saving station, and light-ship within the threatened district.

"(b) THE UNIFORMITY OF SIGNALS EMPLOYED."

It is of great importance that the signals employed for this purpose be the same all over the world. The captain or mate of a foreign vessel may not be able to read the bulletins giving warning of an approaching storm, or may not be in a position to see it, but if an international system be adopted he will have ample warning from the signal station before leaving port. There are many systems of signals used in different countries for the purpose of giving timely warning of danger to the captain about to leave port, or coasting along the shore from light-house to light-house. Some of these depend upon the number and color of flags, others upon the position of different shapes suspended from masts and yards, and others again upon the semaphore system. Flags are not suitable for the purpose, as they are only extended in a breeze and are of no use in a calm. It is found to be impossible to distinguish colors in misty or foggy weather or where the bunting is old and discolored, even when the flags are extended to the full limit in a stiff breeze. Flags can not be read even under favorable circumstances when the wind is blowing either towards or away from the observer. It is believed that the best results can be obtained from a modification of the semaphore system, and the following rough plan is respectfully suggested :

The arm of the semaphore will be used to denote the *direction* from which the gale or storm may be expected, while the *shapes* suspended from the end of the arm will denote the relative force of the wind. These semaphores should be established at all signal stations, lighthouses, and, where practicable, on every light-ship, and they should be as large as the surrounding conditions will admit. They should be painted such colors as can best be distinguished. At night the direction of the arm of the semaphore will be shown by *three colored lights*, according to the amount of danger to be apprehended from the approaching storm.

INFORMATION SIGNAL.

It sometimes happens that a severe storm is raging on some other part of the coast, but is not expected to pass over certain sections. It is very important that all vessels about to sail from ports in this section, however, should be warned of these gales. · Thus, a cyclone in the Gulf of Mexico may not reach the northern ports of the United States, and storm signals would not be displayed in Boston, but only along the Gulf coast. It is essential that all vessels about to go south be warned of what is approaching. The information signal is displayed for this purpose at all signal stations where there are vessels likely to sail for the dangerous district. The "information signal" simply calls attention of ship-masters about to leave port that a severe gale is raging at some other place, and advises him to call at the station and obtain further information, read the weather bulletins and telegrams, and consult the weather bureau before sailing. To signal this information would necessitate such a complicated code as to make the whole system unintelligible. The information signal should be made with the semaphore arm unshipped or concealed, as it is not intended to give the direction of the wind, but simply to state that information can be obtained by calling at the branch hydrographic office, or signal office. It is suggested that this signal be given by unshipping the semaphore arm and placing it across the semaphore frame by day, and by three *white* lights forming an equilateral triangle by night.

STORM SIGNALS.

For moderate gale a cone is suspended from the semaphore's arm instead of the ball by day, and the two green lights mark the direction of the semaphore's arm instead of the two red lights by night.

[*William C. Whittle, captain Bay-Line steamer Georgia.*]

(*a*) I think that much good would result from an *interchange* of opinions between passing vessels and when one vessel meets another. I think it would be well to communicate *warnings* of bad weather or *assurances* of good.

(*b*) *As no system of communicating* could be intelligible without uniformity, all classes of information should be communicated under an *international code* for such purpose.

The arrangement of such a code should be made by a conference of authorities on maritime matters, and international legislation obtained for its enforcement.

[Report of D. T. Terrill, ensign, U. S. Navy (in charge of Branch Hydrographic Office, Portland, Oregon), concerning opinions of sea-faring men whom he has interviewed.]

The Signal Service of the United States leaves but little to be desired in the way of improvement. Its flags convey accurately the information desired.

Stations showing warning flags should be established where all vessels could receive the latest information before putting to sea.

[Extract from letter written by Edw. Gittins, secretary of the Mersey docks and harbor board, August 26, 1889.]

Storm warnings are received by telegrams from the meteorological office at London, and signals, consisting of a cone, are exhibited in a prominent position for the information of parties concerned in shipping. Copies of the telegrams are also posted in various public places.

[Extract from "North Sea Pilot," Part IV, fourth edition, 1887.]

WEATHER SIGNALS.—The following local signals have been adopted at the principal ports and shipping places on the coast of France, in addition to the established storm warnings:

1. A flag, of any color, indicates: Weather doubtful, barometer inclined to fall.

2. A short pendant (cornet) indicates: Appearance of bad weather, heavy sea, barometer falling.

3. A pendant indicates: Appearance of better weather, barometer rising.

4. A ball above cornet indicates: The entrance of the port has become dangerous, be careful.

5. A ball below cornet indicates: The life-boat is coming out.

WEATHER SIGNALS.—Signals, in connection with the telegraph station on the Skaw, are made at the mast-head by means of a black cone and cylinder, and remain hoisted for thirty-six hours after the receipt of the dispatch from the meteorological institution at Christiania; they signalize great atmospheric disturbances that may threaten the neighboring coasts in the North Sea and in the Baltic.

A cylinder over a cone with the point down: A gale threatened from the south.

A cylinder under a cone with the point up: A gale threatened from the north.

A cylinder alone: A gale, without indicating the direction.

[Extract from Baltic Pilot, second edition, 1888.]

STORM WARNINGS are regularly transmitted to the stations at Libau, Windaw, Riga, Pernau, Baltic Port, Revel, Hangö, Helsingfors, and Kronstadt, from the chief observatory at St. Petersburg. The signals are made with a cone and a drum. When the cone is hoisted point downwards it indicates that strong winds may be expected from SE. to NW. by the south; point upwards, that strong winds may be expected from NW. to SE. by the north. At night the storm warnings are signaled by three lanterns in the form of a triangle, with the point either up or down, corresponding with the day signals.

APPENDIX E.

STORM-WARNING SIGNALS EMPLOYED BY SOME OF THE NATIONS REPRESENTED AT THE INTERNATIONAL MARINE CONFERENCE.

Where not particularly mentioned, night signals are not made.

1. AUSTRIA-HUNGARY:
   Storm-warning signals have been discontinued.

2. CHILI:
   White pendant, with red ball in center above black ball, indicates fair weather.
   Black ball indicates rain.
   Two black balls, one below the other, indicate expected gale.
   Black ball above white pendant, with red ball in center, indicates changeable weather.

3. CHINA:

Storm warnings are only displayed at Shanghai by the private observatory at Zi-ka-wei, near Shanghai. For this purpose 10 flags and 2 pendants, differing from those used in the International Signal-Book, are used, the flags always in combinations of two. The code comprises 90 sentences, from 10 to 99, all relating to the weather.

4. DENMARK:

No storm-warnings are given.

5. FRANCE:

Cone, point down: Strong winds from the south may be expected.

Cone, point up: Strong winds from the north may be expected.

Drum over cone, point down: Very strong winds from the south may be expected.

Cone, point up over drum: Very strong winds from the north may be expected.

Besides these, the state of weather in the open sea is indicated by displaying a flag, a broad pendant, or a pendant of any color, meaning, respectively: Doubtful weather; barometer tends to falling, bad weather; weather appears to be moderating.

6. GERMANY:

A ball indicates caution.

A cone hoisted point down indicates storm from the SW.

A cone hoisted point up indicates storm from the NW.

Two cones hoisted points down indicate storm from the SE.

Two cones hoisted points up indicate storm from the NE.

One square flag hoisted together with these shapes, indicates that the wind will probably turn to the right, N.E.S.W.; two flags, shown in the same way, indicate that it will probably turn to the left, N.W.S.E.

Signals denoting state of weather in the open sea at different points are displayed by an instrument specially constructed for this purpose at Cuxhaven, mouth of the Elbe.

Night signals are in use at some stations, red lanterns being employed.

7. GREAT BRITAIN:

(a) *United Kingdom:*

Cone, point down: Strong winds from the south may be expected.

Cone, point up: Strong winds from the north may be expected.

Night signals—Three lanterns of any color shown in the form of a triangle, point down: Strong winds from the south may be expected.

7. GREAT BRITAIN—Continued.

(*a*) *United Kingdom*—Continued.

Three similar lanterns shown in the form of a triangle, point up: Strong winds from the north may be expected.

(*b*) *British Colonies :*

1. Chittagong: A ball in daytime, or three lights placed vertically at night, indicate a dangerous hurricane with center near Akyab, and which will probably advance towards Chittagong.

A drum in daytime, or two lights placed vertically, indicate a hurricane with a corresponding sea advancing rapidly towards Chittagong.

2. India: See Appendix A, page 9.

3. Hong-Kong: A black drum [if shown by the police hulk, accompanied by a gun], indicates bad weather expected.

4. New South Wales: The same signals as in the United Kingdom are used here.

5. Queensland ; The signal shown at the top of the signal-mast indicates direction of wind, according to International Signal-Book.

The signal shown at south end of yard denotes force of wind.

The signal hoisted at north end of yard denotes state of sea.

6. South Australia: A blue flag denotes, barometer indicates bad weather.

7. Mauritius: White flag with horizontal blue stripes below a ball: Prepare for bad weather.

A red flag below a ball, take lower yards and top-masts down.

8. ITALY:

Day signals the same as in France. Night signals the same as in Great Britain.

9. JAPAN:

One red ball in daytime, or one red lantern at night: Strong winds from direction yet undecided may be expected.

One red cone, point down, in daytime, or three red lanterns shown in the form of a triangle, point down, at night: Strong winds from the south may be expected.

One red cone, point up, in daytime, or three red lanterns shown in the form of a triangle, point up, at night: Strong winds from the north may be expected.

10. MEXICO:

A red flag : A norther may be expected.

11. NORWAY:

Day and night signals the same as in Great Britain.

12. PORTUGAL:

Day and night signals the same as in Great Britain. At several points of the coast signals are made informing passing vessels of the state of the weather in the Bay of Biscay, or in the south by the international code.

13. RUSSIA:

Day and night signals the same as in Great Britain.

14. SPAIN:

On the coast of the mother country different systems of storm warnings are in use.

Philippine Islands :

1. A black drum: A disturbance exists at some distance.
2. A black cone, point up: Fresh winds between south and west may be expected.
3. A black cone, point down: Fresh winds between east and south may be expected.
4. A black cone, point up, above a black drum: Violent winds, probably from between south and north through west.
5. A black cone, point up, below a black drum: Violent winds, probably from between north and south through east.
6. A black ball: Violent storm; entrance of ships into port forbidden.

15. SWEDEN:

No storm-warning signals made.

16. THE NETHERLANDS:

Instead of bodies or shapes The Netherlands make use of an instrument called the Aëroklinoscop to indicate the weather. It consists of a pillar supporting a beam painted half red and half white, having a ball painted in a similar way, suspended at the white arm. The beam can be turned by a handle around a *central axis* in a horizontal direction and inclined, by an iron rod, to a certain angle. With this instrument the difference in barometric pressure between any of four stations in The Netherlands is shown in the following way: The red part of the beam is pointed to the northern station, and the white part to the southern station. The arm is inclined *pro rata* of the difference in the barometer readings at the two points selected as having the largest amount of difference. The maximum of inclination is reached at about 49°, corresponding to a barometic difference of 7 mm. (1 mm. difference in pressure being equal to an inclination equal to 7°). If the white arm is up, then the barometer is higher in the south, and *vice versa.*

16. THE NETHERLANDS—Continued.

At night a lantern is hoisted, the light of which illuminates the apparatus; remembering the rule that the wind will probably blow from a direction nearly perpendicular to the line connecting the point of highest with the point of lowest pressure, and from the left of an observer, looking to the latter, and remembering, moreover, that the force of the wind depends on the amount of difference between the barometric readings in these places, the sailor is enabled to judge for himself what kind of weather may be expected.

17. UNITED STATES:

See Appendix A, page 290.

GENERAL DIVISION 10.

REPORTING, MARKING, AND REMOVING DANGEROUS WRECKS OR OBSTRUCTIONS TO NAVIGATION.

(a) A uniform method of reporting and marking dangerous wrecks and derelicts.

(b) The division of the labor, cost, and responsibility among the several maritime nations, either by geographical apportionment or otherwise:

Of the removal of dangerous derelicts;

And of searching for doubtful dangers with a view of removing them from the charts.

The heading of this division leaves it doubtful whether the Conference expect the committee to consider measures dealing with dangerous wrecks and obstructions in territorial waters as well as on the high seas.

The committee are of opinion that it is not necessary or desirable to propose international action regarding territorial waters, except the marking of wrecks, which subject is treated under General Division 12.

(a) A UNIFORM METHOD OF REPORTING AND MARKING DANGEROUS WRECKS AND DERELICTS.

Wherever the word "wreck" is used in this report it is meant to designate "*an abandoned vessel aground*," and wherever the word "*derelict*" is used it is meant to designate "*a vessel afloat permanently abandoned*."

Wrecks are not always to be considered a source of danger to navigation. When lying outside of fair-ways, as, for instance, on dangerous sands, or on coral reefs, they may even contribute to the safety of navigation by becoming conspicuous day marks; but when they are lying in fair-ways, in water of not sufficient depth to allow vessels to pass without striking the hull or spars of the wreck, they become a serious danger to navigation.

Derelicts are always a danger to navigation, as other vessels may run into them without any warning, particularly at night or during thick weather. Since January 1, 1889, five collisions with derelicts are known to have taken place in the North Atlantic Ocean alone, by one of which lives were imperiled. (See Appendix A, page 315.)

Undoubtedly the number of lives and the value of property lost through collision with derelicts at sea has been very considerable, and such losses might be greatly reduced if proper steps were taken to clear the seas of such dangers.

Other dangerous obstructions (icebergs, newly discovered shoals, reefs, etc.), would seem to be included under the heading of "General Division 10," and although not alluded to in paragraph (*a*) should, in the opinion of the committee, be discussed here, as they may constitute the most serious of all the dangers dealt with in this division.

Reporting dangerous wrecks and derelicts.

The danger caused by wrecks and derelicts might be considerably lessened, if their exact position were known to the mariner. For obvious reasons it is often most difficult to attain this end completely. Much, however, would be gained if as accurate a report as possible were secured and brought to the notice of mariners without loss of time.

Regarding the manner in which such reports should be brought to the central office in charge of the distribution of "Notices to Mariners," the committee propose the following resolutions:

1. That it is advisable to make it the duty of any of the officers, or of the crew of a wreck or derelict, to report, as soon as possible after landing, to the nearest harbor authority, if necessary through their consul, as follows:

(*a*) Name of the vessel abandoned.

(*b*) Her distinguishing number.

(*c*) Name of her home port, port from which she sailed, and place of destination.

(*d*) General description of vessel and her rig.

(*e*) Place where abandoned (latitude and longitude as near as possible).

(*f*) Weather and current experienced before leaving the vessel, and in case she was a derelict, the direction in which she would most likely drift.

(*g*) Whether or not it is intended to take any steps towards her recovery.

2. That a similar report should be made to the same authorities by the master of any vessel sighting a wreck or derelict, and a suitable entry made in the ship's log.

3. Such reports should be published in "Notices to Mariners," the daily press, and, if necessary, by giving telegraphic information to the ports which it most concerns.

Reporting other obstructions to navigation, as icebergs, newly discovered shoals, reefs, etc.

Regarding the manner in which such reports should be transmitted to the proper authorities, the committee propose the following resolution:

4. That it is advisable to make it the duty of every commander or master of a vessel to report the fact that an iceberg or dangerous field ice has been sighted, or a shoal, reef, or other obstruction has been discovered, to the harbor authorities or the hydrographic office of that country to which the port next reached belongs, giving a full description of the obstruction, and all facts that may lead to the determination of its position; for instance, the time elapsed since the last reliable astronomical observation, and the rate of the chronometer. If the obstruction be a shoal or reef, the depth of water actually obtained by sounding on it should be given. Also when land is in sight the position of any off-lying shoal or reef should be determined by compass bearings of fixed objects in view; the error of the compass being stated, with information as to how and when that error was observed. Angles should also be taken between such objects, and a drawing of the coast and the position of the observer be added.

Regarding the reporting of ice met with in the vicinity of the New-foundland Banks by signal from a vessel to other vessels, the committee are aware that an "ice code" has been published by a private individual which, according to his own statement, is rather extensively used amongst the steamers employed in the regular trade between the port of New York and the ports of northern Europe.

This code seems to offer some advantages, but as there was no evidence before the committee, showing whether its use had been found to be beneficial or otherwise, they were unable to decide whether the introduction of this code or a similiar one could be recommended.

Marking Wrecks and Derelicts.

As it appears impracticable in most cases for the master and crew of a sunken vessel to mark the wreck in any effective manner, no such obligation should be imposed on them; and it would also be a great burden, aside from the peril of the undertaking, to compel a passing vessel to mark a derelict. Neither does it seem feasible that any national government should assume such a duty; but so far as possible, means should be employed by which derelicts may be recognized at first sight, and with this end in view, the committee recommend the adoption of the following resolution:

5. That whenever practicable it shall be the duty of the crew before

abandoning a vessel (a) to hoist some distinctive signal, as: B O F, "abandoned by the crew," or O R T G, "Derelict," or a ball, shape, or other similar mark, where it can best be seen, and where it should not be mistaken for any other authorized signal; (b) to let go the sheets and halliards of such sails as are not furled.

Marking other Obstructions.

At present it seems impracticable to mark shoals, reefs, etc., whether they be well known or only newly discovered, with the exception of those lying near the coasts of countries having a maritime commerce, and we consider it unnecessary to press for their being marked in other localities where they can be readily avoided by the exercise of ordinary skill and the usual precautions known to navigators; for this reason the committee have no proposition to submit to the Conference beyond the introduction, so far as possible, of a uniform system of buoyage.

(b) THE DIVISION OF THE LABOR, COST, AND RESPONSIBILITY AMONG THE SEVERAL MARITIME NATIONS, EITHER BY GEOGRAPHICAL APPORTIONMENT OR OTHERWISE, OF THE REMOVAL OF DANGEROUS DERELICTS; AND OF SEARCHING FOR DOUBTFUL DANGERS WITH A VIEW OF REMOVING THEM FROM THE CHARTS.

1. Derelicts, etc., on the High Seas.

A geographical apportionment of the waters of the globe amongst the different maritime nations, in order to divide the labor and cost of removing wrecks and derelicts, or searching for doubtful dangers, can not be recommended for adoption.

In the open sea, with the exception of a part of the North Atlantic, derelicts and dangerous wrecks are exceedingly rare, and as these parts of the ocean are, comparatively speaking, not much frequented by vessels, the danger accruing from such obstructions is not one to warrant the expenditure of such sums of money as would be necessary to institute a regular service, sufficient to insure their removal from regions of such enormous extent. The news of having sighted a derelict is often a week or more old before it is received by the authorities; a rescuing steamer can often not be on the spot for another week; the position given is in many cases not accurate; and in most parts of the sea the drift of the derelict is exceedingly uncertain. It is, therefore, a most difficult task for a vessel sent out to search for a derelict to find it; and the expense incurred by such expiditions may often be out of all proportion to the small chance of finding and removing one.

The geographical apportionment of the waters of the oceans might, besides this, easily lead to the supposition that the limits so defined would circumscribe, moreover, the sphere of political interest of the respective governments.

S. Ex. 53, pt. 3—— 20

2. *Derelicts in the North Atlantic.*

In the North Atlantic, particularly in that part of it bordering the North American coast, westward of a line drawn from the Bermuda Islands to Cape Race, Newfoundland, derelicts are so frequently met with that they must be considered a serious danger to navigation.

As in these waters the vessels whose safety is imperiled by their existence are exceedingly numerous, the number of persons on board of them very large, and the value of these ships and their cargoes very great, and as, moreover, the chances for locating derelicts, and for determining the direction of their drift, are particularly favorable, the committee propose that the various maritime powers should come to some agreement respecting their removal.

In case this proposition should be entertained, it is submitted that the respective powers should also come to some understanding regarding the proprietary rights which may still exist, whether in the ship or in her cargo.

Besides this, it seems desirable to point out that, amongst other matters that will necessarily have to be considered, it would be well to take steps to prevent the destruction of derelicts that might readily have been saved, and to make sure that, in case destruction has been decided upon, no evidence of crime should be destroyed also.

3. *Wrecks and derelicts in coast waters.*

Regarding wrecks and derelicts in coast waters outside the territorial limits, the committee submit that the duty of marking, and if necessary of removing, wrecks, or such portions of them as obstruct navigation, has already been generally acknowledged by the governments whom it concerns, and therefore no further propositions have to be made in this regard.

It has, however, been brought to the notice of the committee that governments who by treaty have acknowledged the exterritoriality of subjects of other powers and of their property are sometimes very much hampered by the consideration of private interests in their action regarding the removal of wrecks, even when the value of the wreck and cargo is very small and there is scarcely a possibility that salvage operations can be successfully undertaken. The committee are therefore of opinion that a resolution should be adopted to the following effect: That in such cases the consul or consuls shall not have the right of withholding his or their consent to the destruction of a wreck, or parts thereof, if it is shown that the wreck constitutes a danger to passing vessels, and if there is no apparent possibility that it will be removed within a reasonable time by the owners or by the insurance companies interested.

As to derelicts in coast waters, there seems to be little doubt but that private enterprise, in order to secure salvage, will prove sufficient to remove any of them; for this reason it would seem to be unnecessary that any proposition should be made which would interfere with the established custom.

There was in the opinion of the committee some doubt regarding the meaning of the word "responsibility" used in the heading. They consider, however, that no government would acknowledge any responsibility for the waters under discussion which had not been made the subject of some formal agreement entered into after negotiations by the usual diplomatic methods.

4. *Searching for doubtful dangers with a view of removing them from the chart.*

The greater part of these dangers have been entered on the charts from the reports of single ships, and under the assumption that it is often better to do so rather than have the mariner entirely unwarned, though such reports may have appeared from the very first of doubtful accuracy. In order to make sure that these dangers do not exist, it has been conclusively shown by experience that it is not sufficient to sail across the alleged position, but that it is necessary, at the same time, to take extensive soundings, to prove beyond a doubt that nowhere in the vicinity of the alleged danger anything but deep water is found, and that it is therefore justifiable to remove the danger from the chart. This has become the acknowledged custom of the different hydrographic offices.

In order, therefore, to make such searches effectual, ships employed for this purpose should be fitted out with deep-sea sounding apparatus. Ordinary war vessels are not usually supplied with such means, but only surveying vessels or vessels fitted out for scientific exploration. Such vessels will, as a matter of course, receive from their respective governments instructions to search for dangers of this kind whenever they find them located in a position near which their special mission will take them. What is, however, most wanted at present are accurate surveys on coasts newly opened to trade and commercial enterprise, in order to detect dangers whose existence is entirely unsuspected. The number of these that are yearly discovered (ninety last year), many by the expensive process of losing a ship on them, proves incontestably how imperfect the surveys of the world are.

To divert ships engaged in such surveying work to scour the ocean in order to verify doubtful reports under international engagements would be to practically stop the production of improved surveys. Under these circumstances the committee cannot recommend any action in the matter.

If masters of vessels, when seeing indications of shallow water, would act in accordance with the resolution we have placed before the Conference on page 304 instead of passing on their course without any examination or even taking a cast of the lead, the number of these dangers reported as doubtful would be greatly lessened.

RESOLUTIONS REGARDING GENERAL DIVISION 10, SUBMITTED FOR THE CONSIDERATION OF THE CONFERENCE.

1. That it is advisable to make it the duty of any of the officers, or of the crew of a wreck or derelict, to report, as soon as possible after landing, to the nearest harbor authority, if necessary through their consul, as follows:

(a) Name of the vessel abandoned.

(b) Her distinguishing number.

(c) Name of her home port, port from which she sailed, and place of destination.

(d) General description of vessel and her rig.

(e) Place where abandoned (latitude and longitude as near as possible.)

(f) Weather and current experienced before leaving the vessel, and in case she was a derelict, the direction in which she would most likely drift.

(g) Whether or not it is intended to take any steps toward her recovery.

2. That a similar report should be made to the same authorities, by the master of any vessel sighting a wreck or derelict, and a suitable entry made in the ship's log.

3. That such reports should be published in "Notices to Mariners," the daily press, and, if necessary, by giving telegraphic information to the ports which it most concerns.

4. That it is advisable to make it the duty of every commander or master of a vessel to report the fact that an iceberg or dangerous field ice has been sighted, or a shoal, reef, or other obstruction has been discovered, to the harbor authorities or the hydrographic office of that country to which the port next reached belongs, giving a full description of the obstruction, and all facts that may lead to the determination of its position; for instance, the time elapsed since the last reliable astronomical observation, and the rate of the chronometer. If the obstruction be a shoal or reef the depth of water actually obtained by sounding on it should be given. Also when land is in sight the position of any off-lying shoal or reef should be determined by compass bearings of fixed objects in view; the error of the compass being stated, with information as to how and when that error was observed. Angles should also be taken between such objects, and a drawing of the coast and position of the observer be added.

5. That whenever practicable it shall be the duty of the crew before abandoning a vessel (a) to hoist some distinctive signal, as: B C F, "Abandoned by the crew," or C R T G, "Derelict," or a ball, shape, or other similar mark, where it can best be seen, and where it should not be mistaken for any other authorized signal; (b) to let go the sheets and halliards of such sails as are not furled.

6. That the different maritime powers interested in the navigation of that portion of the North Atlantic Ocean bordering the American coast, and situated westward of a line drawn from the Bermuda Islands to Cape Race, Newfoundland, be invited to come to an agreement respecting the removal of derelicts in these waters under due official supervision.

7. That in countries which, by treaty, have acknowledged the exterritoriality of subjects of other powers and their property, the consul or consuls concerned shall be instructed not to withhold his or their consent to the destruction of a wreck or parts thereof, if it is shown that the wreck constitutes a danger to passing vessels, and if there is no apparent possibility that it will be removed within a reasonable time by the owners or the insurance companies interested.

APPENDIX A.

REPORTING, MARKING, AND REMOVING DANGEROUS WRECKS OR OBSTRUCTIONS TO NAVIGATION.

[Report of Ensign George P. Blow, U. S. Navy, in charge of branch hydrographic office, New York City, on General Division 10.]

"(a) A uniform method of reporting and marking dangerous wrecks and derelicts."

An international telegraphic exchange should be established for this purpose. The position of every dangerous wreck or derelict should be reported by telegraph to the government of each of the maritime nations as soon as received. Every government should immediately telegraph this information to each of its sea-port cities, together with such additional information as may be necessary. In the case of "wrecks" it should be the duty of the government within whose jurisdiction the wreck is located to properly mark it and to immediately notify the other governments by telegraph that such has been done. The marks employed for this purpose should be wreck-buoys or "watch-vessels." These marks should be kept in position until the wreck has been removed or destroyed, or has ceased to be a danger to navigation. When this is the case telegraphic notice of the removal of the mark should be given. If possible, due notice of the removal of any "wreck-buoy," or "watch-vessel," shall be given in advance. Wreck-buoys should be painted green and should carry a cage of the same color made in the shape of a cube. The name of the wreck should be plainly marked on the buoy or "watch-vessel." The buoy should be a lighted one, if possible, and should show *two green lights*. The "watch-vessel" should be painted green, with the name of the wreck plainly marked on each side in white. By day-time two green cubes should be hoisted, one above the other, and by night two green lights should be shown in the same position.

It would be impossible to mark derelicts unless they should be on soundings and could be anchored. The only thing that can be done is to warn mariners of their probable position, and offer inducements to passing vessels to destroy them or bring them into port.

"(b) The division of labor, costs, and responsibility among the several maritime nations, either by geographical apportionment or otherwise."

"(b 1) Of the removal of dangerous derelicts."

It is the manifest duty of each nation to police its own waters and to keep them free from derelicts, wrecks, or other obstructions. The policing of the high seas becomes much more complicated and difficult. An attempt to apportion certain sea areas to each nation would meet with great opposition and innumerable complications, except in waters like the North Atlantic. In the latter case, where the great bulk of the commerce of the world is concentrated, the immediate coasts are occupied by a few powerful civilized maritime powers, both capable and willing to assist in clearing the ocean of dangers. Along the African coasts, or among the islands of the Pacific, however, it would be impossible to carry out such an apportionment.

According to almost universal custom and law, if a vehicle breaks down in a street or road it is the duty of its owner to remove it at once, so as not to obstruct the highway. A derelict vessel occupies the same position as an abandoned carriage in a road; often valueless to its owner, but a source of constant danger to others. It should be the duty of the government whose flag the vessel flies to send out, and either bring her into port, or destroy her. As above stated, the North Atlantic can, with great ease, be divided into certain areas, and each section can be policed by one of the Great Powers. This action is earnestly advocated. But for the other oceans this idea is not deemed practicable. Some inducement should be given to vessels to bring derelicts into port or destroy them. Time is valuable to seamen as well as to those on shore, and a liberal allowance should be paid for the destruction of one of these floating wrecks. In case of a vessel floating bottom up, only a short time is required to pierce her bottom and sink her, but a timber-ladened vessel would require torpedoes or dynamite to break her up.

It is suggested that a liberal sum be paid the captain and crew of any vessel who destroys a derelict. Proof of the actual destruction of the wreck would, of course, be required before payment. This sum should be paid by the government under whose flag the derelict originally sailed. It is believed that if such an inducement should be offered many vessels would destroy derelicts, and thus greatly reduce the danger of navigation.

A still further inducement should also be offered by decreeing that the salvage on an abandoned vessel (after a certain limit of time) be the total value of the vessel and cargo. This would pay a steamer for towing a derelict into port.

"(b 2) Or of searching for doubtful dangers with a view of removing them from the charts."

With the exception of the North Atlantic Ocean any geographical apportionment would be impossible, as above stated; and the number of *doubtful* dangers in the Atlantic is so small that there is really little need for such an apportionment. Probably the best and simplest way of accomplishing the desired object would be for an international agreement to be made between all the maritime powers for the continuous prosecution of this work. Each government should pledge itself to employ one or more properly equipped vessels in this work and to give the other powers full reports of the results obtained from time to time. The number of vessels employed should depend upon the amount of commerce, and be in direct proportion to the foreign trade of the nation. No attempt should be made to coerce any power into investigating certain sections, as it is believed that the country most interested should make the investigations, and each should be free to choose its own field of operations. These vessels would, of course, be required to search for and destroy wrecks or derelicts in the vicinity of their working grounds ; or, when so ordered, to cruise specially for these dangers and remove them.

It is believed that such an agreement will be much more readily made and kept than one depending upon geographical apportionment, and that better results will follow its adoption.

[Report submitted by the U. S. Hydrographic Office on General Division 10.]

(*a*) As regards aids to navigation, a uniform method of reporting and marking dangers is absolutely necessary; much trouble has been experienced in this division because no system prevailed; time, labor, and confusion would be saved if a uniform method would be adopted and adhered to.

The bearings should be given from seaward, or towards the object, as the mariner sees it. Whether true or magnetic, the variation used should be stated.

(*b*) A uniform method of spelling geographical names, based upon the spelling adopted by the nation to which the place belongs, leaving the pronunciation out of consideration, except in those languages where it becomes necessary by reason of the characters used to represent sounds (Chinese and Japanese) should be adopted.

The maritime community would be benefited greatly by the use of a universal geographical dictionary, in which the spelling of names would be universal, the pronunciation to be in parentheses, according to the usage of the principal nations interested.

A uniform system of reporting the characteristics of lights should be adopted, and the visibility should be upon a basis common to all nations. As to the former, the words intermittent and occulting are cases in point. There is no proper distinction between the two; the word occulting is doubtful to some, and intermittent is preferable. In our light lists it includes the term occulting.

As to the visibility, the elevation of the focal plane of the light above high-water level is given, and the distance of the sea horizon due to that elevation, or the distance it may be seen from the deck of an ordinary vessel. With us 15 feet is used; the English, 14 feet; the Italians, 18 feet; the French, $4\frac{1}{2}$ meters (about 15 feet), and so on.

Every nation should have attached to its hydrographic service small vessels especially fitted for and adapted to blowing up or otherwise destroying dangerous derelicts. Reports of the existence of these dangers to navigation should be regularly made, as they are to the division of marine meteorology of this office, and their location and general drift shown upon some such publication as our own pilot-chart, whence they could be easily followed and destroyed.

Searching for doubtful dangers.—These "doubtful dangers" have always been a bug-bear to navigators, especially in the Pacific Ocean, owing to contradictory reports as to position and conflicting evidence as to their existence.

In the original reports, the chief trouble lay with the disagreement of the Dutch charts with those of other nations, but latterly they have adopted the same longitude as the British Admiralty.

Duplication and discrepancies doubtless arose in the position of these dangers, depending upon the authority used. Since the telegraphic determinations of longitude, in 1881–'82, in the East Indies, China, and Japan, discrepancies in the positions of actually existing dangers should not occur.

If a plan could be agreed upon whereby the Pacific could be divided into districts and apportioned among the various naval powers represented at the Conference, and a thorough survey of such allotted positions be made by each, this question could be definitely settled, a source of doubt removed, and a feeling of security obtained in the navigation of these waters. The division of labor, cost, and responsibility could be easily arranged. In spite of the fact that the Atlantic Ocean is so well surveyed many doubtful dangers exist there as well, and this service should be so extended as to include *all* the waters of the globe.

Very respectfully,

CHAS. M. McCARTENEY,
Lieutenant, U. S. Navy.

I propose that each nation shall keep clear of wrecks and other obstructions to navigation her own shores and the shores of her dependencies out to the 100-fathom line; and that the work of investigating reported dangers and removing wrecks and derelicts on the high seas of the world, outside of this line, be assigned to contractors by oceans, and be paid for by all the nations carrying on trade upon such ocean in combined proportion to the tonnage afloat and to the commerce carried on in importation and exportation.

A proposed geographical apportionment is also submitted. In this the principle is supposed to hold good that each maritime nation is bound to remove all wrecks and derelicts which are dangerous to navigation, and also to verify or disprove the existence of any doubtful dangers reported in the past or future whenever such wrecks, dangers, or derelicts are situated within —— miles of its main coasts, or a like distance from any of its off-lying islands. Outside of this —— mile limit, the ocean, according to this scheme, is to be regarded as international region, and on the map the districts have been allotted by taking into account the resources of the respective governments and their facilities for reaching the allotted region from the home or the colonial stations.

The inner or —— mile limit has not been indicated generally on the map, as it is supposed to apply equally to all coasts and islands, except in cases where the nation or government controlling a coast is known to be without a navy, and without sufficient resources to do the required work efficiently. In such a case the government to which the district contiguous to the —— mile limit is assigned is to do the work on such conditions as may be satisfactorily arranged between the two governments involved.

It is not claimed that the details of such a plan are here presented; the object has been to present the apportionment in general form, so that it may be available as a basis for the discussion of such a plan.

Very respectfully,

G. W. LITTLEHALES.

[Opinion of Wm. C. Whittle, captain Bay-Line Steamer *Georgia.*]

(*a*) A UNIFORM METHOD OF REPORTING WRECKS AND DERELICTS.

As all maritime legislation should have for its object the removal of dangers, everything tending to secure that end should be done.

All vessels on arriving in port should report the position of any source of danger, and, as far as possible, its condition.

In case of a derelict, any vessel removing or destroying (if not worth saving) such a source of danger should be remunerated for it.

In the urgency for expedition in trade, it would be unreasonable to expect, unfair to require, and impossible to enforce upon any trader the delay and expense, solely *pro bono publico,* the work that action in this matter would necessitate.

It should be required of the merchant vessel to report obstructions of any character, and the duty of taking further action should devolve on the Government in such a way, and under such a system, as their concerted wisdom should determine.

(b) It is not an easy matter to determine an equitable system among maritime nations as to *expense, responsibility,* and *labor* of searching for, locating, or removing derelicts or dangerous obstructions, but it would seem but just that all such expense, etc., no matter by whom incurred, should fall on the nation in the service of whose citizens the derelict was employed. A fund to meet such obligations should be provided by law, and expended under direction of a legally established authority.

A coast-guard of Government vessels for searching out such derelicts, and taking action upon their being reported, should, in my judgment, be established, and a system of telegraphing such reports, with positions, etc., to the nearest port to the locality of the obstruction should be arranged for.

[Extract from letter written by Edw. Gittins, secretary of the Mersey docks and harbor board.]

Information as to wrecks within the port of Liverpool is at once given to the pilotage office in this city, and by telegrams to the outlying pilot stations.

A wreck is denoted by a watch-vessel and a wreck-buoy, both painted green, with the word "wreck" marked thereon in white letters. Owing to the narrow tidal waters of the river and the approaches thereto, these are stationed in the tidal line of a wreck.

Provision is made in the rules hereinbefore referred to with regard to the signals to be displayed by vessels marking the position of .wrecks.

Obstructions to the navigation of the port of Liverpool are dealt with by the Mersey board under the powers conferred upon them by section 11 of "the Mersey Docks act, 1874."

Under an act which has just been obtained by the Mersey board, the marine surveyor is required to certify that, in his judgment, a wreck is an obstruction to the safe and convenient navigation and use of the port, before the wreck can be dealt with by the board.

[Report of D. T. Terrill, Ensign, U. S. Navy (in charge of Branch Hydrographic Office, Portland, Oregon), concerning opinion of sea-faring men whom he has interviewed.]

The reporting system of the U. S. Hydrographic Office gives universal satisfaction. Every master should be required to report position of all wrecks sighted by him to the consul of his Government in foreign ports, and to the nearest hydrographic office in home ports.

Each naval squadron should have a vessel specially fitted to destroy obstructions to navigation.

(b) No suggestions made.

List of collisions of vessels with derelicts in the North Atlantic since January, 1889.

1. April 20, 1889. Latitude 38, 10 N., longitude 66, 30 W., British S. S. *Cuban* ran into a water-logged vessel. Had one plate bent by the blow; cut into the derelict about 13 feet.

2. June 28. American schooner *John S. Davis*, in latitude 34, 42 N., longitude 64, 18 W., collided with a large three-masted vessel. The *Davis* rebounded after collision and passed within 5 feet of her. In the morning found a small piece of spruce pine stuck in the bows.

3. Schooner *W. B. Herrick*, of Boston, with cargo oak staves, from Portland, for Cardenas, Cuba, struck a derelict at 4 a. m., on the 29th of January, 365 miles WNW. of Bermuda, apparently the wreck of a three-masted schooner, with mainmast and mizzenmast gone and foremast standing. It was blowing hard from NNW. at the time, and the schooner was running under a two-reefed mainsail only in a high sea when she struck the derelict bow on, shaking the vessel from stem to stern; after pushing the obstruction away, 2 feet of water in the hold were discovered with the water rapidly increasing against the continued pumping of captain and crew, the vessel soon water-logged and filled the cabin, galley, and forecastle, and the heavy seas continually washing over the decks, so that only the after-house was left dry, on which the captain's wife, a few stores, and the boat's gear were placed. On 1st of February, at about 4 a. m, made signal to a passing steamer, supposed to be the S. S. *Orinoco* for New York, which lay by the schooner for some time in the dark, but later on became separated. No other vessel sighted. The island was made on the evening of the 2d instant, and the schooner towed into anchorage on the 3d, all on board completely exhausted, having lived on such canned goods available, and on some brackish water. The provisions and water had been lost, the deck-load and everything about the deck having been sacrificed in the first endeavors to keep the ship afloat.—Bermuda Royal Gazette, February 5, 1889.

4. October 15. British schooner *Forest Fairy*, in latitude 40, 59 N, longitude 33, 40 W, struck and passed over a submerged wreck, doing considerable damage.

5. December 16. Schooner *Cornelius Hargraves* collided with a capsized vessel near Cape Henry. Put into Norfolk and discharged some of her cargo of coal. Not much damage done.

[Extract from " Memorandum prepared by the Committee of the Second Northern Maritime Conference," Copenhagen.]

INTERNATIONAL AGREEMENTS FOR PREVENTING THE DANGERS OF FLOATING WRECKS.

The discussion, mentioned in the introduction, page 2, on the question : " What can be done to diminish the danger which threatens the

navigation by floating wrecks?" led to the result that the following resolution was passed:

"That the committee of the Conference should recommend to the
Governments of the Northern States the issuing of instructions to their
men-of-war similar to an order issued by the British "Board of Admiralty," which runs thus:

"Should any of Her Majesty's ships fall in with any water-logged
vessel abandoned at sea, and constituting danger to navigation, the
same should be examined, and unless it appears that the cargo is
composed of such large balks of timber as to be of themselves a danger
if released to float, or unless the position of the wreck is such as to make
it probable that she may be presently towed into port, every effort
should be made to sink or otherwise destroy her; and that this resolution should be brought to the knowledge of the Maritime Congress,
which is to be held at Washington in April, 1889."

In doing this the committee think it advisable to add the following
main points of the said discussion:

The desirability of the introduction of an international agreement,
whereby the above-named *British* arrangement could be universally
adopted, was shown by statistical dates extracted from the excellent
and most useful "Pilot Charts of the North Atlantic Ocean," published
monthly at the United States "Hydrographic Office," and which are
sent, free of charge, to mariners, on application to the Hydrographer at
Washington.

The yearly increasing number of *reported* floating wrecks seems to be
quite astonishing, viz, in 1884 the number was 162; in 1885, 176; in
1886, 215; but in 1887 the number amounted to 305. It is evident that
such numbers of derelicts constitute a most dangerous obstruction to
the navigation, the more so as the longevity of some derelicts has been
proved to be almost incredible; for instance, a schooner, *Twenty-one
Friends*, which was abandoned in March, 1885, has been reported twenty-
two times, the last time in December same year; the drift of this derelict in eight months ten days has exceeded a distance of 3,500 miles.
Another derelict, the Italian bark *Vicenzo Pirota*, which was abandoned
in September, 1887, has been reported eleven times, the last time at the
end of April, 1888, having thus drifted upwards of seven months, and
was then apparently in a good condition, and being directly in the track
of commerce, it is probable that she will continue to be reported for a
long time. To the dangers derived from derelicts must now be added
the drifting logs of the great Canadian timber raft, dense masses of
which are still to be met with in the Gulf Stream. This timber raft,
which was lost in December, 1887, on a voyage from Nova Scotia to
New York, consisted of about 27,000 logs from 30 to 100 feet in length,
chained together in the form of a cigar. This sea-monster had a length
of 560 feet, breadth 65 feet, depth 38 feet, draught of water 19 feet,
weight about 1,100 tons. According to the latest reports, parts of it

have drifted in five months a distance of about 1,560 miles. From an international standpoint it is rather startling to see that nothing can be done to prevent a single individual from sending to sea, for the sake of gain, such an unseaworthy monster, which for a long time will make the navigation of the whole North Atlantic Ocean unsafe to the ships of all nations.

In connection with these remarks there was, naturally enough, given some statistical dates extracted from the monthly lists of shipwrecks, etc., published by the "Bureau Veritas." It was hereby shown that from 1884 till the end of 1887, that is, in four years, 176 sailing-ships and 23 steamers had totally disappeared in the North Atlantic Ocean. There must certainly be a great probability for the supposition that many of these ships, whose fate ever will be unknown, have been lost by collision with floating wrecks, as it appears from the remarks in the "Pilot Charts" that not a few cases of collision have occurred from contacts with abandoned water-logged timber-ships, after which, for instance, four of the ships were abandoned in a sinking state, though the crews were saved.

At the Conference in 1887, held in *London*, by the "Association for the Reform and Codification of the Law of Nations," a question intimately connected with this matter was treated in a very interesting manner by Rear-Admiral Colomb, viz, "Under what circumstances is it justifiable to destroy shipping property at sea," and where the following resolution in this respect was adopted:

"That in the opinion of the Conference, derelict private property at sea ought only to be destroyed where there is an evident danger to navigation, and the vessel is unlikely to be salved."

From the examples cited it seems that the best manner to destroy a derelict is by blowing her up, as the burning of such wrecks, particularly when they are water-logged timber-ships often has failed.

In the said "Pilot Charts" are also for every month laid down special "Transatlantic Steam-ship Routes" for *Eastward* and *Westward* bound steamers. The hope expressed on page 11, that the plan as to "Ocean Lane Routes," originally proposed by the world-renowned American scientific navigator, Lieutenant Maury, will have the support of the honorable Congress, seems, therefore, to have got the very best basis.

Finally, the "Committee of the Second Northern Maritime Conference" avail themselves of this opportunity to conclude this memorandum with an expression of their sincere thanks to the *Government of the United States* for the benefit bestowed to the navigation of the North Atlantic Ocean by the publishing in the said liberal manner of the above-named invaluable "Pilot Charts."

COPENHAGEN, *September*, 1888.

GENERAL DIVISION 11.

NOTICE OF DANGERS TO NAVIGATION.

Notice of changes in lights, buoys, and other day and night marks.

(*a*) A uniform method of taking bearings, of designating them (whether true or magnetic), and of reporting them.

(*b*) A uniform method of reporting, indicating, and exchanging information by the several maritime nations—to include the form of notices to mariners.

(*c*) A uniform method of distributing this information.

All notices of changes in lights, beacons, buoys, and other day and night marks require not only to be brought to the notice of the public of that country in whose waters these changes have taken place, but also to all other maritime nations, so that the authorities may be enabled to impart information for the benefit of their own sea-faring population.

This is usually done by publications to which the generic title of "notices to mariners" has been applied. They are either issued whenever occasion demands it, or at regular intervals, with an extra edition when necessary.

They may further be divided into (*a*), those published by the department of naval affairs of the different countries, or under its direction, by the hydrographer; (*b*) those published by the authorities, central, provincial, colonial, or local, in charge of the light-houses, beacons, and buoys.

The publications mentioned under (*a*) are intended for the use of the mariner only, and the committee do not consider it advisable to insist on any change regarding form or arrangement of "notices to mariners."

What has been said regarding the publications mentioned under (*a*) is true as well regarding those mentioned under (*b*). These "notices to mariners" are mainly intended for internal and local use in each country, and supply information not to mariners only but to local officials, such as light-house keepers, inspectors of buoys, and others; and, considering that they are published for very different objects, and to be used by men of very different classes and occupations, the committee do not consider it feasible to insist upon uniformity in matters of detail.

(*a*) A UNIFORM METHOD OF TAKING BEARINGS, OF DESIGNATING THEM (WHETHER TRUE OR MAGNETIC), AND OF REPORTING THEM.

Taking bearings.—In all countries, as far as we know, except Italy and Norway, the custom prevails that all bearings in "notices to mariners," and in "light lists," in order to locate a danger or to determine the limits of a light-sector, are given from seaward, that is, from the danger indicated towards the fixed objects by which its position is determined, or from the outer limit of visibility of a light towards the light-house.

This mode of taking bearings has the advantage that it is in agreement with the mode in which they are used by the mariner, and the committee recommend that the resolution in this behalf appended to their report be adopted by the Conference with a view to this custom being made universal.

Designating bearings, whether true or magnetic.—The adoption of a uniform method of designating bearings, whether true or magnetic, offers the advantage that bearings given in the publications of any country can be transferred verbatim to similar publications issued in any other country without the necessity for any alteration or calculation. This is of importance in preparing publications the value of which depends in no small degree on the possibility of issuing them immediately after any changes have been made which require to be notified to mariners.

All the evidence, however, which has been laid before your committee, tends unmistakably to the conclusion that it would be inexpedient for any country suddenly to adopt a new system of designating bearings in the place of one which has been sanctioned by the custom of many years, and has become an essential part of the system of navigation generally adopted and taught in the nautical schools of the various countries.

It has also to be borne in mind that such a change concerns not only experts and scientific men, who can easily understand and adapt a new system to their requirements, but, in the vast majority of cases, it would affect seamen whose knowledge of matters regarding navigation is inseparably connected with the methods with which they have been familiar all their lives, and to whom any change of the kind indicated would be confusing and dangerous.

For these reasons the committee do not propose the adoption of a uniform method of designating bearings by giving them either true or magnetic.

Uniformity might have been attained in another way, *i. e.*, by giving bearings both true and magnetic. It was shown, however, that the advantages of such a plan would be more than counterbalanced by a large increase in the bulk of the text, and by the possibility of errors amongst sea-faring men unaccustomed to any but a single system, and who might mistake one set of bearings for another when read in a hurry.

Having regard to these difficulties the committee do not propose to advise any action in this matter in the direction of uniformity beyond recommending that in all "notices to mariners" and "light lists" intended for exchange with other nations, whenever true or magnetic bearings are given, the variation shall be inserted.

Bearings to be given in degrees or in points and fractions thereof.—It seems that in the majority of maritime nations the custom prevails that all bearings are given in degrees. This has the advantage that if the variation, which is always expressed in degrees, has to be applied in order that the bearings be entered on a chart, or when the variation has to be corrected for time elapsed since the date when it was determined, the result is more accurate than if the bearings were expressed in points.

On the other hand, it has to be borne in mind that the "Notices to Mariners" and "Light Lists" which are most universally used, retain the custom of giving bearings in points and fractions thereof.

After a full discussion of this large and intricate question, the committee decided to adopt the following resolution:

That the bearings for cuts of different colored sectors of lights, or of bearings of lights defining a narrow channel, should be expressed in degrees where practicable.

Counting the degrees.—The custom adopted universally in geodesy is that of counting the degrees from the north to the right (or with the sun), beginning with 0 to 360°. In one country the steering compasses are also so marked; and directions with reference to the course of the vessel are so expressed. This method offers certain advantages, but it is contrary to the custom of the large majority of mariners, and on this account the committee propose that the number of degrees used in designating bearings should be counted from north and south to east and west, beginning with 0 and ending with 90°.

North and south are universally designated by the letters N and S. But east is in some countries designated by the letter O, and west in others also by the same letter—O. In order to make these designations uniform the committee propose that all countries adopt, for use in the publications under consideration, the letter E to designate east and the letter W to designate west, in uniformity with the rules adopted already for publications of meteorological offices.

Designating distances.—The committee advise that: Distances should be expressed in nautical miles and fractions thereof. The word "cable" should mean the tenth part of a nautical mile.

(b) A UNIFORM METHOD OF REPORTING, INDICATING, AND EXCHANGING INFORMATION BY THE SEVERAL MARITIME NATIONS, TO INCLUDE THE FORM OF NOTICES TO MARINERS.

1. *Reporting dangers to navigation, change of lights, etc.*—Reports of dangers discovered should be made as promptly and accurately as possible, and should be addressed to the proper authorities. This has been pointed out already in the committee report upon General Division 10, page 304.

2. *Indicating dangers, changes of lights, etc.*—(a) Several countries refer the longitude given in the publications under consideration to a prime meridian, whose difference from the meridians of Greenwich or Paris, on which most charts in use by mariners are constructed, may be unknown to a sailor. In such a case, though he may have become

acquainted with the fact of the discovery of a danger, the establishment of a light-house, etc., he may be unable to enter such information, with sufficient correctness, on his chart.

The committee, therefore, propose that in all notices which refer to any other prime meridian but that of Greenwich or of Paris, the difference in longitude between such meridians should be inserted.

(b) The visibility of a light is given in different ways. In some countries the number of miles given refer to the visibility of light in clear weather or in ordinary weather; in others, the visibility refers to a mean state of the atmosphere, *i. e.,* one which may be expected at that particular locality in fifty cases out of one hundred. The committee had not sufficient evidence before them to decide as to the advantages of the two plans for general adoption ; they, however, consider it desirable to bring the subject before the conference in order that the attention of the different maritime powers should be called to it.

(c) In some "Light Lists" the geographical range of a light is given, *i. e.,* the distance resulting from the height of a light above high water, in connection with the curvature of the earth, together with or without the additional distance calculated for an observer supposed to be elevated above the sea at a certain height; in other "Light Lists" the actual visibility of a light is given without any regard to the height of the light or the elevation of the observer; in some publications the lesser of the two distances is given, and in other cases both together.

Each of these methods offers some advantage, and it seems inexpedient, as at the present moment, to propose uniformity in this respect.

It appears advisable, however, to adopt a standard height for the observer wherever the geographical range of a light is given in "Light Lists" or in "Notices."

The committee therefore propose that the height of 5 meters be generally adopted in all countries where the metric system is in use, and that in other countries, where this is not the case, the height should be 15 feet of the measure of the country. This height seems to the committee the best suited to the present requirements of navigation. The difference between these measures is of no practical importance.

(d) The lights of light-houses are classified at present in "Orders," according to the size of the lantern, or, if dioptric, according to the diameter of the apparatus, though, in this respect, there exists considerable difference.

Since the introduction of the electric lights this classification has become inaccurate, and from a seaman's point of view, misleading, for under its rules a third-order electric light generally is much more powerful than a first-order oil or gas light. Uniformity in this respect is desirable, and the committee therefore propose that the several maritime powers interested should be requested to consider the question in order to establish, if possible, a uniform classification of lights on the basis of the power of the light as seen by the mariner. At the same time it would be desirable to bring about a uniform classification as regards their character.

3. *Exchanging information by the several maritime nations.*—It has become the custom for the hydrographic offices of the different maritime countries, with few exceptions, to ask for any information regarding their publications ("Notices to Mariners," "Light Lists," "Charts," "Sailing Directions,") by direct application to the hydrographic offices of other countries, and to give such information in the same way.

It is not easy to see how this information could be so speedily and conveniently given in any other way. But the committee are not aware that this usage has ever been sanctioned by the proper authorities. They have on this account thought it well to call the attention of the Conference to this fact, and they submit that permission to exchange information regarding these publications direct, without the intervention of the foreign offices, should be granted to all central hydrographic offices in the home countries as well as those in the provinces, colonies, and dominions, and also to those central offices which administer the light-houses, beacons, and buoys of a country, and which publish such information. A list of the offices referred to in this paragraph, which are known to the committee, will be found in Appendix B.

Some maritime powers are without any special hydrographic department. In such cases it would be well to designate some other office, for instance that of harbor-master of their principal ports, who could be addressed if occasion occurs.

In some countries the "Notices to Mariners" are published only in newspapers. It would be well if such notices were sent to the different hydrographic offices of the world.

Contemplated changes in lights and buoys should be brought to public notice, if convenient, before the date on which such change is proposed to be made.

(c) A UNIFORM METHOD OF DISTRIBUTING THIS INFORMATION.

The information contained in "Notices to Mariners" is now brought to the knowledge of the seafaring population by sending copies of the same to the different shipping offices and consulates, and to captains of the navy, and to masters of the merchant fleet. The committee have no evidence before them which points to the fact that the measures taken by each country do not fully satisfy the requirements of those interested.

RESOLUTIONS PROPOSED TO THE MARITIME CONFERENCE REGARDING GENERAL DIVISION 11.

In recapitulation, the committee recommend the Conference to invite the several maritime powers to consider the following resolutions with a view to establishing uniformity in the subjects treated in "Notices to Mariners" and "Light Lists:"

1. That all bearings should be given from seaward.

2. That the bearings of cuts of different colored sectors of lights or bearings of lights defining a narrow channel should be expressed in degrees where practicable.

3. That all bearings expressed in degrees should count from north and south, from 0° to 90°, towards east and west.

4. That in designating bearings, the letter E shall designate east, and the letter W shall designate west.

5. That whenever bearings are given, the variation of the compass at the place should be stated.

6. That distances should be expressed in nautical miles and fractions thereof. The word " cable " should mean the tenth part of a nautical mile.

7. That whenever the longitude of a position is given, it should be stated which prime meridian is adopted, and if other than that of Greenwich or Paris, the difference of longitude should also be stated.

8. That in defining the visibility of a light, it should be stated whether the distance is for " clear," or " mean " state of the weather.

9. That where the geographical range of a light is given, it should be calculated as seen at high water from an observer 15 feet or 5 meters above the sea.

10. That a uniform classification of lights, based on luminous intensity and on the character as seen by the mariner, should be adopted.

11. That the central offices that issue "Notices to Mariners" or " Light Lists" should be permitted to correspond direct on such subjects.

12. That from countries where " Notices to Mariners" are published only in newspapers, copies of such papers should be sent to the various hydrographic offices.

APPENDIX A.

NOTICE OF DANGERS TO NAVIGATION.

[Report of Ensign George P. Blow, U. S. Navy, in charge of Branch Hydrographic Office, New York City, on General Division 11.]

"(a) A uniform method of taking bearings, of designating them (whether true or magnetic), and of reporting them."

All bearings should be taken with an aledade placed directly over the compass, if possible. If not possible, however, the bearing should be carefully taken with respect to the ship's head, noting carefully the compass course at the same time, and, after being verified, should be referred to the compass.

All bearings should be magnetic and should be given in degrees and minutes of arc from north or south around to east or west. Thus NNW. would be N. 22° 30′ W. and SW. by W., S. 56° 15′ W.

"(b) A uniform method of reporting, indicating, and exchanging information by the maritime nations, to include the form of notices to mariners."

As previously stated, a telegraphic exchange should be established for the purpose of forwarding valuable information. Less important information could be sent by regular mail, as is now the case. The information thus received should be distributed according to its value and importance. Thus storm-warnings should be telegraphed to all the coast cities in the country, while notice of anticipated changes in lights would be given to the press and also issued in the regular way, as "Notices to Mariners."

The present form of notices to mariners issued by the United States Hydrographic Office fills all the requirements and has given general satisfaction. It is to be regretted, however, that there are two kinds—one issued by the Coast Survey and another by the Hydrographic Office—even in this country. For the sake of simplicity, economy, and uniformity, only one set should be published. If the notices to mariners of each country could be published in English, French, and German their value would be greatly increased, as they could be read and understood by nearly all ship-masters.

"(c) A uniform method of distributing this information."

Information received by the different governments will be utilized in the way in which seems most desirable by the officials charged with that work. It is believed to be impossible to secure uniformity in this respect, although it is greatly to be desired.

[Reports submitted by the U. S. Hydrographic Office on General Division 11.]

(a) A uniform method of taking and reporting bearings should be used, as above stated. With us, and the French as well, the true bearing is used; it is the most economical, and, could dependence *always* be placed upon the accuracy of the observer reporting, it would be preferable.

But while to the educated navigator there should be no chance of wrong application of the variation, the generality of the merchant marine have a deep-rooted aversion to the use of true bearings.

The variation changes so slowly that the smallest change in the text of a report or book of sailing directions as to courses and bearings would vary so little (less than one-eighth point or about 1°) that the best instruments used in modern navigation would hardly detect it in less than eight years in Great Britain and Northwest Europe; fifteen years in the North Atlantic Ocean and the United States; twenty years in the South Atlantic Ocean; forty years in the Indian Ocean, and of fifty years in the Pacific Ocean (data obtained from Mr. Littlehales). Of course there are many arguments for and against the use of both, but I think that possible errors would be avoided by the use of the magnetic bearings.

(*b, c*) The consular service would be of great value in reporting, indicating, and exchanging information. If regular reports were made and forwarded to the various hydrographic offices by the consuls in the sea-port cities, much would be done towards the universal dissemination of nautical information. Ship-masters could obtain the printed reports in the form of notices to mariners from the maritime exchanges, boards of trade, and such like institutions, as is done in our country through the medium of the branch hydrographic offices, which have done so much to spread this knowledge. It should be part of the consular duty—not left to his volition, but compulsory—to send weekly reports, which would be transferred to the hydrographic offices, and thence issued in the form of notices and extracts, of which, I think, our own system is an excellent illustration.

As to General Division 12 *a* and *b*, a uniform system in color and numbering of buoys and beacons will be adopted, and it is practically almost generally agreed to and in use over the world, especially as to the main features common to all in marking channels, etc.

Very respectfully,

CHAS. M. McCARTENEY,
Lieutenant, U. S. Navy.

———

The mariner is principally concerned in making the land and in taking his departure from it, and in entering and leaving port. All lights, beacons, bouys, and land and sea-marks are established as means to these ends.

In general, the directions for making use of these signals and guiding marks are arranged for approaching the land and entering port, and the reversing of them serves for departing. In conformity, then, with the methods of giving directions in general, it seems expedient that all bearings having reference to marks for navigation should be given from seaward. And as a further amplification of this uniform method, all bearings taken upon fixed objects for the purpose of locating wrecks, shoals, and the like should also be given from seaward, thus:

Rock awash, Morro Castle, Havana, S. ⅜ W. 6¼ miles.

Sunken wreck, Isle of Wight Light-house, England, NE. 10 miles.

The virtue of the use of the true bearing in nautical books and charts appears only when the subject is viewed from the standpoint of economy. But it is questionable whether economy can be successfully urged as an argument in its favor. As the direction of the magnetic meridian at a given place changes with the lapse of time, angular values of fixed directions referred to it must also change, and make corrections necessary in books and on charts where these directions are set down.

The expense and labor of making corrections on charts from this cause is inconsiderable, and, if the argument has any force, it must be with reference to books. It would be laborious and expensive to correct

the bearings and courses in sailing directories by hand; and it is believed that the changing of these bearings would entail quite as much
expense, if new editions of books were issued, through these changes in
the text alone. If, however, the change which occurs in the direction
of the magnetic meridian, and consequently in the value of a magnetic
bearing or course, during the lifetime of an ordinary book of sailing directions is not sufficient to alter appreciably the reading of the text,
then, as far as concerns nautical works, which are overhauled and re-
issued from period to period, the true and magnetic bearings stand upon
the same footing with regard to the necessity for change. Let us suppose that, in a given book, the bearings all read to the nearest one-
eighth point. The smallest change of which the text of this book could
take account may be assumed to be somewhat less than one-eighth of
a point, say one degree. This book could then be said to need change,
as to the bearings and courses given in it, by an amount which the best
instruments used in modern navigation could detect, at the end of eight
years in Great Britain and Northwestern Europe; of twelve years in the
South Atlantic Ocean; of fifteen years in the North Atlantic Ocean; of
twenty years in the West Indies; of forty years in the East Indies; and
of fifty years in the Pacific Ocean.

The most rapid changes in magnetic bearings happen, at this secular
period of the earth's magnetic state, to have their seat where there is
the greatest activity in those changes of which nautical directories take
cognizance; and it is probable that a volume of sailing directions em-
bracing the British Isles would need extensive revision, amounting almost to a rewriting of the work, at the end of eight years, from the accumulation of necessary corrections not brought on by changes in the
magnetic bearings.

All manuals on the deviation of the compass and all graphical and
mechanical methods of applying the deviation of the compass, at least
in English literature upon this subject, proceed upon the assumption
that the magnetic bearing or magnetic course is to be found, and not the
true or astronomical, and, therefore, that it is the magnetic which is given
in sailing directions.

Probably the most useful and most universally known graphical
method of changing the distorted readings of a compass under the local
influence of a ship's magnetism, to a standard condition in which it is
comparable with all other bearings is Napier's diagram, which is arranged solely for the conversion of compass into magnetic courses, and
the reverse. Such graphical processes as this are arranged for safe and
efficient usage amongst men possessed of a minimum of theoretical
knowledge, to which class the great majority of seafaring men belong.
While it may be an easy matter for such men as we find performing the
duties of navigators in the navies of the world so far to generalize the
method employed in Napier's diagram, or any other device, as to pass
from compass to true course, and the reverse, by using the total error

instead of the deviation alone, yet it is manifest that this is not to be expected of mariners in general.

Sailing directions and charts should conform to the ideas and methods advanced in standard nautical educational works.

Very respectfully,

G. W. LITTLEHALES.

[Opinion of William C. Whittle, Captain Bay-Line Steamer *Georgia.*]

Notice of changes in lights, buoys, and other day and night marks.

Whenever it shall be deemed expedient to change any of such marks, whose existence is known as a guide to navigators in coming into any port or on any coast from sea, a notice of such change should be given to an "International Maritime Commission" ninety days before such change is made, so that all foreign boards of trade can be notified and all vessels warned. A similar notice should be given to the Board of Trade in the country in which the contemplated change is made.

In the inland waters of any country, where any such change is contemplated, a notice of at least —— days before such change is consummated should be given.

All foreign vessels should be required to take a *pilot*, and by that means avoid the dangers resulting from inland changes.

(*a*) A uniform method of taking bearings, designating and reporting them.

It is to be accepted that every navigator knows the error of the compass by which he navigates, and it would greatly simplify the proper promulgation of the information if he would reduce all bearings taken to the true bearing, freed from magnetic deviation or error of his compass, so that any navigator or master receiving the report, and, in turn, knowing the error of his own compass, can reduce the reported bearings to his compass bearings and be guided thereby.

(*b*) *Under the International Code of Signals* all vessels should be empowered and required to give any and all assistance to others in giving notice of dangers, changes, etc.

(*c*) *A uniform method of distributing information* would be for all Boards of Trade, Light-House Departments, Coast Surveys, and Boards of Marine Inspectors to communicate with the "*International Maritime Commission,*" upon whom the duty of cognizance and action should fall in any changes and causes of danger.

[Opinions and suggestions of various experienced mariners obtained by Sergeant Paul Daniels, U. S. Signal Service.]

An international and uniform method of taking bearings, of designating and reporting dangers to navigation, changes in lights, buoys, and other day and night marks, also an international and uniform method of reporting, indicating, and exchanging information by the several maritime nations to include the form of notices to mariners, as well as an international and uniform method of distributing this information, should be adopted.   All bearings and their designations should be *true* and *not magnetic*.

[Report of D. T. Terrill, Ensign, U. S. N., (in charge of Branch Hydrographic Office, Portland, Oregon), concerning opinion of seafaring men whom he has interviewed.]

(*a*) Bearings should be given by vessels in points and eighths, magnetic, and by Government offices in degrees and minutes, true.   Whenever points are used let magnetic bearings be understood, and where degrees are used let true bearings be referred to.

(*b*) The U. S. Hydrographic Office form of notices to mariners are all that could be desired, and give universal satisfaction.

(*c*) Through branch hydrographic offices is the only practicable method.

APPENDIX B.

LIST OF THE HYDROGRAPHIC OFFICES OF THE COUNTRIES REPRESENTED IN THE MARITIME CONFERENCE, AND OF SUCH OTHER OFFICES WHICH PUBLISH "NOTICES TO MARINERS" AND "LIGHT LISTS."

[Where both classes of the offices mentioned exist, the Hydrographic Office is marked (*a*).]

1. AUSTRIA-HUNGARY:
   (*a*) Hydrographisches Amt der kaiserlichen und königlichen Kriegs Marine, Pola.*
   (*b*) Kaiserlich königliche Seebehörde, Trieste.
2. BELGIUM:
   L'administration de la Marine, 38 Boulevard Bischofsheim, Brussels, Belgium.
3. BRAZIL:
   (*a*) Repartiçao Hydrographica do Brazil, Rio de Janeiro.
   (*b*) Repartiçao Geral dos Pharóes do Brazil, Rio de Janerio.
4. CHILI:
   (*a*) Oficina Hydrográfica de Chile, Santiago.
   (*b*) Inspeccion general de Faro i Valisas, Valparaiso, Chile.
5. CHINA:
   (*a*) No Hydrographic Office.
   (*b*) Coast Inspector's Office, Custom-House, Shanghai.
6. COSTA RICA:
   No particular office.   The hydrographic work is intrusted generally to the Oficina Principal de la Direccion de Obras Publicas, San José, Costa Rica.

7. DENMARK:

Det Kongelige Sokartarkiv, Copenhagen, Denmark, regarding shoals and sailing directions; and regarding other information, Marine ministerets Admiralitets Departement, Copenhagen, Denmark.

8. FRANCE:

(a) Service hydrographique de la Marine, 13 rue de l'université, Paris.

(b) Direction des Phares et Balises, 43 Avenue du Trocadéro, Paris.

9. GERMANY:

Hydrographisches Amt des Reichs Marine Amtes, Berlin, 9 Matthäirkirchstrasse.

10. GREAT BRITAIN AND COLONIES:

A. *United Kingdom :*

(a) Hydrographic Office, Admiralty, London.

(b) Trinity House, London (for England). Northern Light-House Commissioners, Edinburgh (for Scotland). Irish Light-House Commissioners, Dublin (for Ireland).

B. *Colonies:*

(1) *India*—Bombay: Marine Department, Bombay Castle, Bombay. Calcutta: Port-office, Calcutta. Madras: Presidency, Port-office, Madras.
Ceylon: Colonial Secretary's Office, Colombo.
Mauritius. } Notices published in Government
Strait Settlements. } Gazette.
Australian Colonies.—South Australia: Marine Board Offices, Port Adelaide. Victoria: Department of Ports and Harbours, Melbourne. New South Wales: Marine Board Office, Sydney. Queensland: Department of Ports and Harbours, Brisbane. Tasmania: Marine Board Office, Hobart. New Zealand: Marine Department, Wellington, and Harbor Board Office, Auckland.

(3) *Hong Kong:* Notices are published in the Hong Kong Government Gazette.

(4) *Canada and Vancouver :* Department of Marine, Ottawa, Canada.

(5) *Newfoundland :* Board of Works, St. John, Newfoundland.

(6) *West India Islands :* Colonial Secretary's Office, Nassau, N. P., West Indies.

(7) *Cape of Good Hope:* Harbor Master's Office.

(8) *Natal :* Harbor Master's Office.

11. GREECE:

Chef de la division des Phares, Athens, Greece.

12. HAWAII:

No particular office. Information should be addressed to His Excellency the Minister of the Interior, Honolulu, Hawaiian Islands.

13. HONDURAS:

There is no special central hydrographic office in this country. Information may be procured by applying to the military commandants of the Atlantic ports of Cortez, Trujillo, Roatan, and the Pacific port of Amapala.

14. ITALY:

(a) Ufficio Idrografico della Regia Marina, Genoa.

(b) Ufficio del Genio Civile (at the different ports in question.)

15. JAPAN:

(a) Suyero Kioku [Hydrographic office of the Imperial Japanese Navy Department] Tokio, Japan.

(b) Light-House Office, Department of Communications, Tokio, Japan.

16. MEXICO:

No particular office. Information should be addressed, Departamento de Marina—Secretaria de Guerra y Marina, Palacio Nacionál, Mexico City.

17. NORWAY:

(a) Den geografiske Opmaaling, Christiania, Norway.

(b) Fyrdirektionen, Christiania, Norway.

18. PORTUGAL:

No particular office. For information address: Mr. Francisco da Costa e Silva, General Secretary of the Department of Marine, Lisbon.

19. RUSSIA:

For all information: Hydrographic Office of the Marine Ministry, St. Petersburg.

For information regarding the Black Sea: Hydrographic Office of the Black Sea, Nicolaieff, South Russia.

For information regarding Eastern Siberia: Hydrographic Office of Wladivostock, Wladivostock, East Siberia.

20. SIAM:

Captain Richelieu, R. Siamese Navy, Bangkok.

21. SPAIN:

In the mother country: Direccion de Hidrografia, Allaca 56, Madrid.

In the dependencies: Comandante general de Marina, Hábana (for the 5 provinces of Cuba and Puerto Rico), and Comandante general de Marina, Manila, for the Philippine Islands.

22. SWEDEN:

(a) Kungl. Sjökarteverket, Stockholm.

(b) Kungl. Lotsstyrelsen, Stockholm.

23. THE NETHERLANDS:

Home office, Marine Department, Hydrographic Office, S' Gravenhage.

Netherlands India: Marine Department, Hydrographic Office, Batavia, Java.

24. TURKEY:

Administration générale des Phares de l'Empire Ottomane, Constantinople.

25. UNITED STATES OF AMERICA:

(a) Hydrographic Office of the United States Navy, Washington, D. C. (both for information regarding home ports and abroad); United States Coast and Geodetic Survey, Washington, D. C. (for information regarding home ports).

(b) Light-House Board of the United States, Treasury Department, Washington, D. C.

26. URUGUAY:

Hydrographic Office of Uruguay, care of Comandante de Marina y Capitan-General de Puerto, Montevideo, República des Uruguay.

27. VENEZUELA:

No particular office. For information address the "Capitanias de Puertos" at La Guaira, Puerto Cabello, Coro, Maracaibo, Barcelona, Cumaná, Margarita (Isla), y Ciudad Bolivar ó Angostura.

GENERAL DIVISION 12.

A UNIFORM SYSTEM OF BUOYS AND BEACONS.

(a) Uniformity in color of buoys.

(b) Uniformity in numbering of buoys.

Owing to the absence of a uniformity in buoyage, mariners, up to very recent times, seldom attempted to navigate a district by means of the buoyage unless they were specially well acquainted with the local system. But now that a certain degree of uniformity on a fundamental basis prevails, mariners in general are more induced to navigate their vessel, trusting to it and the chart of the district; it therefore becomes of greater importance that such uniformity should be extended as far as possible.

Two principal characters are used for distinguishing buoys and beacons, color and shape.

The first object to be attained, from an international point of view, is uniformity. For that purpose color is the best means, as applying to all systems of whatever kind, while the shape admits numerous exceptions. The color is also applicable in all countries and with little expense, whereas the immediate adoption of shape would involve changes of several existing systems. Moreover, experience has proved that very many, if not the majority of channels, are now buoyed with sufficient distinctness without resorting to difference of form.

For these reasons, and while the opinion prevails that, at night and in thick weather, difference in form is a better means of distinction than difference of color, your committee advise that uniformity in color should be adopted as a general rule, and that the use of shape should remain optional.

While, in the opinion of some members, the single colors of black and red are not so distinctive in contrast as a single color used in connection with a parti-color, experience gained in many buoyage districts, and particularly where used in conjunction with form, has proved that these dark colors are sufficiently distinctive for the safe navigation of districts where a more complicated system is not necessary. Single-colored buoys are also more readily and cheaply repainted than party-colored buoys. We therefore recommend that the largely used red and black colors should be adopted generally for marking respectively the starboard and port sides of single channels.

Many districts, however, require a more complicated system of buoyage, to identify the several neighboring channels one from the other, such as the entrances of rivers with numerous channels like the Thames, the outlying shoals off the coast of the North Sea, the numerous shoals separated from each other by complicated channels such as in the Baltic Sea, etc.

In some of such districts a party-colored buoy is used with much advantage as a port-hand buoy. In a few, a single black color is used as a starboard-hand buoy. Inasmuch as a single black color is in general use as a port-hand buoy in neighboring districts visited by the same shipping, we suggest that the authorities of such countries should be invited to consider the great general advantages to shipping that would result from the adoption of uniformity in color by discontinuing this dangerous custom of using a black color to denote a starboard-hand as well as a port-hand buoy.

In some countries white is used as a distinctive color, and with advantage when contrasted with a dark background. As this practice can not lead vessels into danger, we hesitate to advise that it should be compulsorily interfered with.

We are of opinion that where form is adopted the two shapes "conical" and "can" are appropriate for marking the starboard and port sides of a channel, a spar-buoy taking the place of the can in certain cases.

These forms are practically used in the United States, Germany, Canada, India, and Great Britain. But the various countries are not all in agreement as to which side of the channel is to be marked by a conical buoy and which by a can or spar-buoy.

It follows that one or more of the countries would necessarily have to re-arrange their system, but if the work were done gradually, the committee believe that this could be performed at a minimum of expense in no way comparable with the great advantage that would result to navigation.

In connection with such a change of system we are informed that an extensive re-arrangement in buoyage was recently carried out by Great Britain, the different shapes being changed from one side of the channels to the other side, the change being brought about without any casualty to navigation.

As regards top-marks, we recommend that those countries whose buoyage is based on color alone should, whenever top-marks are used to denote sides of a channel, use conical or can-shaped marks on the existing buoys or beacons.

We are of opinion that the mode of distinguishing buoys from each other by names, numbers, or letters should be left to the decision of the various countries, but that all numbers and letters should be in consecutive order, commencing at the seaward end of the district.

The committee are of opinion that districts where the buoyage is so complicated as to have led the authorities to adopt a compass system of marking, such as in the Baltic Sea, can not, with a view to general uniformity, be coupled with the simpler systems found sufficient elsewhere; they therefore hesitate to recommend a fundamental change in such districts. But, after studying the "Sailing Directions" and the publication of Mr. S. A. Philipsen, Copenhagen, on "Beaconage and Buoyage of Different Nations," which presents graphically the plans adopted by several nations, particularly those interested in the navigation of the Baltic Sea, the committee find that the systems now in use, so far as color and top-marks are concerned, are so similar that they recommend the conference to suggest to the countries interested the desirability of the adoption of one uniform system, at least as regards color.

The committee understand that the following are the colors and top marks at present in use in the various districts using the compass system to define the bearing of the mark or buoy from the danger it indicates:

Marks on the *North* side of a shoal:

Norway ....
Sweden .... } .. Black.

Russia .....
Finland .... } .. White.
Denmark ..

Marks on the *South* side of a shoal:

Norway .... White.

Sweden ....
Russia .....
Finland .... } .. Red.
Denmark ..

Marks on the *East* side of a shoal:

Norway........Black.
Sweden ....Black, with a white horizontal band.
Russia...........Red, with white horizontal bands.
Finland........Half red and half white horizontal.
Denmark ......Red.

Marks on the *West* side of a shoal:

Norway.... }
Denmark .. } ..White.

Russia.........White and black horizontal bands.
Finland ....Half white and half red horizontal.
Sweden........Red.

Marks on a *Middle ground*, with fair-way channels on either side:

Norway........Black and white horizontal bands.

Finland.... }
Denmark .. } ..Red and white horizontal bands.

Russia.........Black.

Top-marks:

On buoys or marks on the *North* side of a shoal:

Norway........Brooms turned downwards.
Russia.........Broom or brooms not systematically arranged.
Finland........A pole without a top-mark.
Sweden ....A ball.

On buoys or marks on the *South* side of a shoal:

Russia.....
Finland....
Norway.... } ..Broom turned upwards.
Sweden....

On buoys or marks on the *East* side of a shoal:

Norway........Broom turned downwards.
Finland........A pole without a top-mark.
Sweden ....A ball.
Russia.........Two brooms { Upper one turned upwards.
Lower one turned downwards.

On buoys or marks on the *West* side of a shoal:

Norway........Broom turned upwards.

Sweden.... }
Finland.... } ..Broom turned downwards.

Russia.........Two brooms { Upper one turned downwards.
Lower one turned upwards.

On marks on a *Middle ground* with fair-way channels on either side:

Norway.... }
Russia..... } ..A ball.

Finland........A cross.

Owing to the difficulty in choosing a fourth single color, green being universally used to denote a wreck, it practically becomes necessary, in arranging for a general system, if four distinct modes of coloring are adopted to mark the four cardinal bearings of or from a shoal, to resort to one or more party-colors to be used in conjunction with red, black, and white.

On the principle of using four colors to mark the four sides of a shoal, the committee put forward the following scheme, based on the least change that would be necessary in altering the present systems to a uniform plan; and they recommend the Conference to bring it to the notice of the countries interested, as an example showing that uniformity is attainable if they will agree to consider the subject:

All shoals, marked on the compass system, to be marked—
On the *North* side by a single black or white color.
South side by red.
East side by half red and half white combined.
West side by half white and half black combined.

On rocks in fair-way, with channels on either hand, to be marked black or red, with horizontal bands.

If such colors were adopted, then the following changes of color would be necessary:

The marks on the *North* side of a shoal would remain colored black or white as they now are in all countries using the compass system.

The marks on the *South* side of a shoal would in—
Norway, have to be changed from white to red.

The marks on the east side of a shoal would in—
Norway, have to be changed from black to half red and half white.
Sweden, have to be changed from black and white to half red and half white.
Denmark, have to be changed from red to half red and half white.

The marks on the west side of the shoal would in—
Norway } have to be changed from white to half white and half
Denmark } black.
Sweden, have to be changed from red to half white and half black.
Finland, have to be changed from white and red to half white and half black.

The marks on a rock in fair-way, with channel on either side, if a white horizontal band is generally adopted, would in Russia have to be changed from black to black or red with white horizontal bands, in agreement with the other countries.

The committee advise the Conference to invite the various powers interested to consider the following general principles, which they put forward as a basis on which to build up a uniform international buoyage system for districts other than those where the compass system is in use.

The term starboard-hand shall denote that side of a navigable channel which is on the right hand of the mariner entering from seaward;

the term port-hand shall denote that side which is on the left hand under the same circumstances.

Color.—Buoys defining the starboard-hand shall be painted a single red color. Buoys defining the port-hand shall be painted a single black color, or a party-color. Buoys defining middle grounds shall be painted with horizontal bands.

Form.—Wherever form is used as a distinctive character. Buoys defining the starboard-hand shall be conical, and those defining the port-hand shall be can or spar.

Top marks.—Countries where form is not used as a distinctive character for buoys, may adopt as another distinctive feature for the buoys on either side of a channel, top-marks resembling a cone to be used on the starboard side, or a cylinder on the port side of a channel.

Numbers and letters.—Numbers, letters, and names may be painted on the buoys, but they must never be so large as to interfere with their distinctive coloring. Wherever numbers and letters are used they shall be in consecutive order, commencing from seaward.

Buoying and marking of wrecks.—(*a*) All buoys and the top sides of vessels used for the marking of wrecks, shall be painted green with a suitable white inscription. (*b*) Where it is practicable, by day one ball shall be exhibited on the side of the vessel nearest the wreck, and two placed vertically on the other side; three fixed white lights similarly arranged, but not the ordinary riding light, shall be shown from sunset to sunrise.

> SANCHEZ DE LA CERDA,
> A. M. BISBEE,
> RIBIÈRE.
> MENSING, *Chairman.*
> G. S. NARES,
> S. W. FLOOD,
> FREDERICK W. VERNEY,
> ALBERTO NIN,
> W. T. SAMPSON.

APPENDIX A.

PROPOSED PLAN FOR INTERNATIONAL BUOYAGE BY LIEUT. M. L. WOOD, U. S. N., U. S. COAST AND GEODETIC SURVEY.

U. S. COAST AND GEODETIC SURVEY OFFICE,
Washington, D. C., October 15, 1889.

Rear-Admiral S. R. FRANKLIN, U. S. N.,

President United States Delegation, International Marine Conference:

SIR: I have the honor to propose the following system of international buoyage for discussion before the International Marine Conference, convening in this city October 16, 1889.

The plan proposed, while of course differing in some respects from that of any nation, will, it is believed, come as near as any toward giving a simple, unmistakable method of indicating to a stranger the direction in which to move a vessel in order to maintain the best water and avoid dangers.

Owing to the difficulty at times experienced in locating a buoy by means of its color, from peculiar conditions of light and background, any plan which will be independent of color, while sacrificing no good characteristics, would seem to be preferable to any other which is mainly dependent upon color as the chief feature in distinguishing buoys in entering harbors.

On the other hand, as there are times when shapes are uncertain during fogs and thick weather, when buoys are close aboard but the outlines are indistinct, a plan which relies altogether on shape alone would seem to be inferior to a plan which admitted a distinguishment by color while losing the benefits of no other good quality.

For these reasons, in the plan proposed, it is considered an essential that the double identification by both shape and color should be used when it is possible, and, in fact, this is fully provided for.

Owing to various positions of ports and channels with reference to the cardinal points of the compass, even in the same country, and possibly in the same harbor, any plan which necessitates both a reference to the compass and to a chart before its warning can be translated into the practical result of changing a vessel's course, and owing to the fact that if a buoy is placed with reference to the east and west or north and south side of the same channel, its meaning may be reversed, it would seem decidedly better to place buoys so that at all times their meanings are the same, by their indication of the *right* and *left* side of a channel, irrespective of any reference to the compass.

If buoys can be so placed that when a mariner distinguishes one ahead he will know precisely what is to be done to take his vessel in the best water, without any mental process involving even a small expenditure of time, it would seem for the best in every way to adopt such a system.

To carry out these views the following plan is proposed for discussion:

Fair-way or channel-buoys to be of *elongated* or *spar* shape, except in shoal water, where nun-shaped buoys can be used, painted in perpendicular *white and black* stripes, to be of either wood or iron, depending upon the importance of the channel and the size required. In all cases, these buoys to indicate the channel-line, or line of deepest water, and they should be passed close to on either hand.

Obstruction buoys or those marking characteristics in the channel which should be avoided, such as sunken ledges, wrecks, or points separating channels, to be *nun* or *can* shaped, with a perch or broom projecting from the top, painted in *red and black* in horizontal stripes.

S. Ex. 53, pt. 3——22

These buoys to be given a good berth and passed on either side. The lower end of an obstruction with a good channel on both sides to be marked by a *can*-buoy with broom, and the upper end by a *nun*-buoy with broom. When one channel is the better, both buoys to be of the shape to indicate the side of the best channel on which they are placed.

Starboard-hand buoys in entering to be *pointed-top* shape, or *nun*-shaped, and painted RED, with even numbers in white paint in main channels and black paint in secondary.

Port-hand buoys in entering, to be square topped, can-shaped, painted black with odd numbers in white paint in main channels, and in red paint in secondary channels.

Main channels to be marked by the largest sized buoys used in the harbor, secondary channels by smaller sized buoys of the same shapes, and minor channels by spar-buoys.

Sea-buoys off the entrances to harbors to indicate initial points for entering, to be of either can or nun, red or black, or white and black in perpendicular stripes, with the name of the port in white letters, and to be either automatic, bell, or whistling buoys, depending upon locality. When a skeleton bell-buoy is used to mark the entrance to a harbor, a *watch-buoy*, painted either red or black, will be placed just inside the bell-buoy, with the name of the port painted in white letters.

It is quite important to reduce the shapes and colors of buoys to the minimum in order to prevent confusion, and at the same time leave no ambiguity in the directions a buoy gives to a stranger.

It will be noticed that, in the plan proposed, in channels the buoys are distinguished both by shape and color, and that either one will locate the buoy with respect to the channel; also that when the color or shape of the buoy is made out ahead, all there is to be done is to change the vessel's course so as to pass the proper side of the buoy, when a further identification can be made by its number when passed as close to as necessary.

There is no change of meaning in any position of the buoy, and hence no uncertainty in the way in which the helm should be shifted.

The only thing that is required to be known is whether the vessel is entering or leaving port, to decide which side to leave the buoy in passing; and, in fact, if all ports were buoyed in this manner, and the buoys were in sight, it would not even be necessary to know the name of the port—all that would be necessary would be to follow the buoys as seen with the certainty that if they were properly placed the best water would be followed.

It will also be noticed that the only buoys having projections in the shape of perches or brooms are those placed to mark dangers or obstructions—the horizontal-striped buoys—the reason for this being that there will be less necessity for vessels passing close to them, and hence less danger of the perch or broom being carried away and the distinctive characteristic of the buoy's outline being lost, though of course the color of the buoy would still remain.

When a buoy is placed to mark a point at the opening of a *secondary channel* branching off from the main channel, it is painted black and red in horizontal stripes with a perch or broom on the top, but it can be a *nun* shape to mark a point between the main channel and a secondary channel on the starboard side, and a *can-buoy* to mark the point between the main channel and a secondary channel on the port side of the main channel, in entering from the sea.

This system includes three shapes of buoys—*can*, *nun*, and *spar* or elongated.

The only colors are *red, black*, and *red and black* in horizontal stripes, and *white and black* in perpendicular stripes.

With these shapes and colors, if the color of the buoys be indicated on the charts, the shapes can be indicated by a single letter ("*C.*," "*N.*," or *S.*"), an advantage which is quite important.

Trusting that this system may meet with the approval of the Conference as an idea for discussion, if not for adoption,

Very respectfully,

M. L. WOOD,
Lieutenant, U. S. Navy,
Assistant, U. S. Coast and Geodetic Survey.

[Report of Ensign George P. Blow, U. S. Navy, in charge of Branch Hydrographic Office, on General Division 12.]

"(*a*) Uniformity of color of buoys."

"(*b*) Uniformity in numbering of buoys."

The subject of a uniform system of buoys and beacons is one of the most important questions which will be discussed by the Marine Conference. The need of a simple and uniform system of buoys has long been felt by sea-faring men, and many suggestions have been made and many systems worked out to accomplish this object. Some of these systems have been too elaborate and costly to adopt. The system selected should be that which secures absolute uniformity with the fewest changes to the greatest number of Governments.

Buoys and beacons should be distinguished from each other in as many ways as possible, paying due regard to economy and utility. Thus, it is not sufficient to depend upon "color" alone, for at night or in misty weather color can not be distinguished. Buoys and beacons should be distinguished by color, shape, number (letter or name), and, lastly, by carrying some distinctive form or shape of cage-work on the end of a short staff. This "shape" or signal will be really the most direct and the simplest way of distinguishing the different classes of buoys. In many rivers and harbors where buoys are subjected to rough handling or exposed to ice the paint gets rubbed off, and color can not be distinguished, even by day-time and under the most favorable conditions. At night and in thick weather color can not be distinguished at all, and it becomes absolutely necessary to provide some simple and inexpensive way of making a buoy so that it can be recognized from its shape. It is proposed, therefore, to place a shape or "signal" on the top of each buoy or beacon for the purpose of assisting still further in its identification. These "signals" must be of such a size and shape as to prevent any possibility of error, and must also be so formed as to allow the ice or other obstructions to pass over them without injuring them. For buoys the signals should be made of cage-work, so that they will be very light and will not afford any material resistance to the wind or sea. Light angle-iron will be the best, strongest, and cheapest material to use for this purpose. The size of the signal should depend upon the class and size of the buoy upon which it is to be placed, but in general terms it should be as large as the existing conditions will allow.

For beacons the same shapes or signals should be used, but as there is no reason for limiting the weight or surface exposed to the wind they should be made larger, and the frame should be covered in with sheet-iron instead of being merely cage-work.

Speaking roughly, there are only three classes of buoys, although there are several sizes and varieties to each class. All buoys may be classed as "can-buoys," "nun-buoys," or "spar-buoys." The signals must be so designed that they can be fitted to any class of buoy.

In coloring buoys the great majority should be of some solid color. If a buoy is to be repainted with one color it will not be necessary to take it up to do the work, but a small boat can be sent out and any one can do the painting. Elaborately striped or checkered buoys would require to be taken up every time it was necessary to repaint them, and would thus greatly increase the expense and difficulty of keeping them in order.

As before stated, in selecting any system to be adopted universally, great care should be taken to select that one which will necessitate the fewest changes. The United States and Canada are buoyed on the same system, and have, together, probably more buoys than any three or four other nations. Besides this, the system closely resembles that in use in France, Scotland, and other countries. It is believed, therefore, that a modification of the United States system will be the best to adopt for an international system. The modifications consist of the addition of signal cages on each buoy, so as to add an additional means of identifying them. It is also thought better not to insist on that portion of the United States system which requires nun-buoys to be used on the starboard side and can-buoys on the port side of the channel, as these buoys are frequently used for other purposes, and such a distinction is likely to cause confusion and disaster.

In providing for an international system only the regular buoys should be provided for. Special buoys should be allowed for special purposes, but should be given some distinctive mark which, under no consideration, should in any way resemble the regular "signals," coloring, etc.

The buoys provided for are the following:

1. Starboard-channel buoys (to be left on starboard side on entering port).

2. Port-channel buoys (to be left on port side on entering port).

3. Mid-channel buoys (to be passed close to).

4. Obstruction buoys (channel on either side).

5. Wreck buoys (to mark wrecks, etc.).

6. Mooring buoys (for mooring or anchorage purposes).

7. Quarantine buoys (quarantine station).

The following is the system proposed:

1. STARBOARD-CHANNEL BUOYS.
[To be left on starboard hand on entering port.]

Color.—Red (now used in United States, Canada, France, and Scotland, etc.), with a white horizontal band, 1 foot wide, at the top (now used in France).

Lettering, etc.—To be numbered with *even* numbers, beginning from seaward and numbering in regular order up the river or harbor (now used in United States, Canada, and France).

Signal.—An inverted triangular pyramid, painted white, and made in the form of a cage. To be constructed of light angle-iron and to be in altitude about twice the length of one side of the base.

2. PORT-CHANNEL BUOYS.
[To be left on port hand on entering port.]

Color.—Black (now used in the United States, Canada, France, Scotland, Holland, and Belgium).

Lettering, etc.—To be numbered with *odd* numbers from seaward up the river or harbor in regular order (now used in United States, Canada, and France).

Signal.—A double cone painted black, to be made of angle-iron in the form of a cage, and to be in length about three times its greatest diameter.

3. MID-CHANNEL BUOYS.
[To be passed close to on either side.]

Color.—To be painted in white and black vertical stripes (now used in United States and Canada).

Lettering, etc.—To be lettered with large Roman capital letters, A, B, and C, etc., beginning from seaward and continuing in regular order up the river or harbor.

Signal.—To carry a plain white staff *without* any signal.

4. OBSTRUCTION BUOYS.
[To mark a shoal, middle ground, rocks, etc., may be passed on either side.]

Color.—Red and black horizontal stripes (now used in United States, Canada, France, Scotland, etc.).

Lettering, etc.—To be plainly marked in large white letters with the name of the obstruction which it marks (now used in Scotland and France).

Signal.—A large cage-work sphere or ball (with ice guards) constructed of light angle-iron, the upper hemisphere to be painted red and the lower black.

5. WRECK BUOYS.

[To mark a wreck or temporary obstruction.]

Color.—Solid green (used in England, Scotland, etc.).

Lettering, etc.—To be plainly marked in large white letters with the name of the wreck or obstruction which it marks.

Signal.—A large cage-work cube, secured by one of its corners. The cube to be constructed of light angle-iron and to be painted green.

6. MOORING AND ANCHORAGE BUOYS.

[For mooring purposes or to mark anchorages.]

Color.—Solid white (used in France, New York City, etc.).

Lettering, etc.—To be marked in plain black letters with its name or the purpose for which it is placed in position.

Signal.—None.

7. QUARANTINE BUOY.

[For marking the quarantine limits and sometimes for mooring purposes.]

Color.—Solid yellow (used in the United States and Canada).

Lettering, etc.—To be marked with black letters with name and object for which placed.

Signal.—None.

Beacons should be painted, lettered, and numbered on the same system and should carry signals of the same shape. The signals should be made of light sheet-iron, however, and not of cage-work.

In the above cases it is understood that the numbers shall be "Arabic" and the letters "Roman," so as to secure uniformity.

[William C. Whittle, Captain Bay Line steamer *Georgia.*]

A uniformity in system of buoys and beacons is very conducive to safety in navigation, and while all foreign vessels should be required to take a pilot, such uniformity in buoys, beacons, etc., should be international.

(*a*) *The ordinary rule* of red buoys being on the left-hand side of the channel and black buoys on the right-hand side as you descend a river or approach the ocean or bay into which it flows, is a good one, and should be international.

(*b*) *In the numbering of buoys,* likewise, it is necessary to maintain uniformity with odd numbers on the right and even numbers on the left side of all channels or rivers as you descend towards the mouth or

ocean. This numbering should, in my opinion, commence at the mouth
of the river or bay and increase as you ascend, with the smallest number at the mouth and the largest at the highest marked point up the
river.

[Opinions and suggestions of various experienced mariners, obtained by Sergeant
Paul Daniels, U. S. Signal Service.]

The present system of buoys and beacons, the manner of numbering
them, and the color of these buoys is satisfactory to most mariners;
black and white perpendicular stripes is the best method for coloring
buoys, because it is much easier to distinguish them at sea than any
other colors.

Uniformity in buoyage is very desirable. Experience in this harbor also shows that it will be an improvement to have all star-
board-buoys of a fixed *shape* as well as color, and all port-buoys of a
different fixed *shape* and color, so that a red buoy may be known as
such even if it is *not* red, the color having been scraped off by ice or
sea-wear.

[Extract from report of D. T. Terrill, Ensign U. S. Navy (in charge of Branch
Hydrographic Office, Portland, Oregon), concerning opinions of seafaring men
whom he has interviewed.]

The United States system of buoyage gives general satisfaction.
Nun-buoys should always be found on one side of the channel, can-
buoys on the other; spar-buoys on the same side as nun-buoys should
have their upper ends pointed, while those on the opposite side
should be squared off. All turn-buoys should have cages.

[Extracts from "Beaconage and Buoyage of Different Nations," by S. A. Philipsen.]

In continuation with the explanation of the "International System
of Beaconage and Buoyage" presented by me, I beg to propose the
paragraphs in the system placed in the following order:

1. The mariner when approaching the coast must determine his
position on the chart, and must note the direction of the main stream
flood-tide.

2. The term "Starboard Hand" shall denote that side which would
be on the right hand of the mariner, either going with the main
stream of flood, or entering a harbor, river, or estuary from seaward.

The term "Port Hand" shall denote the left hand of the mariner
under the same circumstances.

3. Buoys, showing the pointed top of a cone above water shall be
called "Conical," and shall always mark the north side of the channel.

4. Buoys, showing a flat top above water shall be called "Can,"
and shall always mark the south side of the channel.

5. Buoys, showing a domed top above water shall be called "Spherical," and shall always mark the east side of the channel.

6. Buoys, showing only a mast above water shall be called "Spar-buoys," and shall always mark the west side of the channel.

7. Buoys, having a tall central structure on a broad base, shall be called "Pillar-buoys," and shall mark the outer and inner ends of middle grounds.

8. Buoys having a round "conical" structure on a domed "spherical" base shall, like other special buoys, such as bell-buoys, gas-buoys, automatic sounding buoys, be placed to mark special positions either on the coast, or in the approaches to harbors, river inlets, etc.

9. Conical buoys, marking the north side of the channel (south side of the shoal) shall always be of white color.

10. Can buoys, marking the south side of the channel (north side of the shoal) shall always be of black color.

11. Spherical buoys, marking the east side of the channel (west side of the shoal) shall always be of green color.

12. Spar buoys, marking the west side of the channel (east side of the shoal) shall always be of red color.

13. Pillar buoys, marking inner and outer ends of middle grounds, shall be distinguished by horizontal stripes of black and red color.

14. Buoys, placed to mark special positions, shall be painted in black and white perpendicular stripes.

15. Surmounting beacons such as staff and globe, etc., shall always be painted of one black color, they may be applied on either side of the channel seamarks at the discretion of the authority having jurisdiction, "exempli gratia," as in § 12 "Uniform System of Buoyage for the United Kingdom."

16. Buoys on the same side of a channel, estuary, or tide-way may be distinguished from each other by names, letters, or numbers, even numbers, 2—4—6, etc., on the starboard or right hand side, and odd numbers 1—3—5, etc., on the port or left hand side from seaward.

17. Buoys, intended for moorings, etc., may not be of shape and color like the seamarks above described.

18. Buoys, for marking submarine telegraph cables shall be of yellow color with the word "telegraph" painted thereon in black letters.

BUOYING AND MARKING OF WRECKS.

19. Wreck buoys in the open sea or in the approaches to a harbor or estuary, shall be colored yellow, with the word "Wreck" painted in black letters on them.

20. When a wreck-marking vessel is used it shall, if possible, have its top sides colored yellow, with the word "Wreck" in black letters thereon, and shall exhibit, by day: Three balls on a yard 20 feet above the sea, two placed vertically at one end, and one at the other, the single ball being on the side nearest to the wreck. By night:

Three white Fixed Lights, similarly placed, but not the ordinary riding light.

21. In narrow waters or in rivers, harbors, etc., under the jurisdiction of local authorities, the same rules may be adopted, or at discretion, varied as follows:

When a wreck-marking vessel is used she shall carry a crossyard on a mast with two balls by day placed horizontally not less than 6 nor more than 12 feet apart, and two lights by night similarly placed. When a barge or open boat only is used, a flag or ball may be shown in the day time.

22. The position in which the marking-vessel is placed with reference to the wreck, shall be at the discretion of the local authority having jurisdiction.

NOTE.—In Russia no buoys are used as seamarks in the open sea; to comply with the system proposed, it is only necessary to alter the color of the seamarks actually in use accordingly.

REPORT OF THE COMMITTEE UPON GENERAL DIVISION 13 OF THE PROGRAMME.

RESOLUTION.

Committee No. 4.

To consider and report upon General Division 13:

Belgium	Mr. VERBRUGGHE.
Chili	Admiral VIEL.
Denmark	Mr. SCHNEIDER.
France	Captain RICHARD.
Germany	Dr. SIEVEKING.
Great Britain	Mr. HALL.
Guatemala	Mr. FERNANDO CRUZ.
Sweden	Captain MALMBERG.
United States	Mr. GRISCOM.

GENERAL DIVISION 13.

THE ESTABLISHMENT OF A PERMANENT MARITIME COMMISSION.

(a) The composition of the Commission.

(b) Its powers and authority.

THE ESTABLISHMENT OF A PERMANENT INTERNATIONAL MARINE COMMISSION.

WASHINGTON, *November* 26, 1889.

Admiral S. R. FRANKLIN,

President of the International Marine Conference, etc. :

SIR: Your committee have considered the above matter, and beg to report as follows:

At the commencement of our proceedings we invited our colleagues and the secretaries to the Conference to furnish us with the proposals, if any, prepared by Governments of the several powers taking part in the Conference, or of any private societies or persons, bearing upon the subject in question. We have not succeeded in ascertaining that there are any such proposals in existence save the documents set out in the appendices hereto, A, B, C, D, and E.

We have considered whether such a commission could be instituted with a practical result, and in such a manner as to lead to its adoption by the maritime powers.

However desirable such a result would be, a majority of your committee do not believe it to be possible to carry it into effect, and are of

346

opinion that it can not be regarded as one of practical feasibility at the present time.

We have also decided, by a majority of votes, that it is not possible to create an International Tribunal to try questions of collisions between subjects of different nationalities.

In coming to this conclusion, we have been guided, amongst others, by the following considerations:

An International Commission could not be invested with any legislative power. It would be a consulting body only, constituted with the view of preparing universal legislation on maritime matters of international importance. Apart altogether from the difficulties connected with the formation of such a body, the questions as to its domicile, as to who are to be its members, and how and by whom the members are to be compensated for their labors—difficulties which by themselves seem to be entirely unsurmountable for the present—it seems to your committee that such a consulting body of experts would not serve the purpose for which it is intended to be created, viz, that of facilitating the introduction of reforms in maritime legislation, because the advice given by such a commission would not in any way enable the Governments of the maritime nations to dispense with the necessity of considering the subjects laid before them and laying the proposals made to them, if adopted, before the legislative bodies of the different States.

The consequence of instituting a body like that in question on the contrary would, it appears, be this: That merely another investigation of any scheme proposed with a view to reforming international maritime laws would have to be gone through before the opinions of the Governments could be taken, and thus the course of procedure as it is now—by correspondence between the different Governments—would be made more complicated instead of being simplified. For these reasons your committee beg to propose to resolve:

That for the present the establishment of a permanent International Maritime Commission is not considered expedient.

We have the honor to be, sir, your obedient servants,

TH. VERBRUGGHE,
Delegate for Belgium.
OSCAR VIEL,
Delegate for Chili.
E. RICHARD,
Delegate for France.
F. SIEVEKING,
Delegate for Germany.
CHARLES HALL, *Chairman,*
Delegate for Great Britain.
F. MALMBERG,
Delegate for Sweden.
CLEMENT A. GRISCOM,
Delegate for United States.

I regret that I am unable to sign this report, as its general tenor varies too much from the views entertained by the maritime associations in my country on the important question mentioned in General Division 13 of the programme.

I have endeavored to explain the views in this respect of the said associations, as well as my own opinion, in a letter to the present committee, which is laid before the Conference as Appendix C to the committee's report.

AUG. SCHNEIDER,
Delegate for Denmark.

APPENDIX A.

MEMORANDUM CONCERNING A PROPOSED PERMANENT INTERNATIONAL MERCHANT SHIPPING COMMISSION.

[Prepared by the Committee of the Second Northern Maritime Conference, September, 1888.]

INTRODUCTION.

At the second Conference (the first was held in Gothenburg in the year 1883) of northern (Swedish, Norwegian, Finnish, and Danish) delegates from various ship-owners'),* master mariners', underwriters', etc., associations and societies held in *Copenhagen* in the first days of July, 1888—under the leadership of C. F. Tietgen, esq., chairman of the Copenhagen Chamber of Commerce, and in the presence of several ministers of state, foreign ministers and consuls, government maritime officials, etc.—the proceedings commenced with the discussion of the following question:

"*On the establishment of a Permanent International Merchant Shipping Commission.*"

After a full discussion the following resolution was adopted unanimously:

"The development of the shipping trade which has taken place during the last years, having given rise to a great number of questions of which the satisfactory solution is of the utmost importance to the trade,

"The Conference resolves:

"*That this object best can be attained by the establishment of a Permanent International Commission—and requests the committee of the Conference to present a memorandum to this effect to the Maritime Congress which is to be held at Washington in the last days of April next year and to apply to the*

---

* Representing a merchant fleet of above 2,000,000 register tons, the Scandinavian vessels thus to be placed as No. 3 on the list, No. 1 being the English, No. 2 the United States, No. 4 the German, and No. 5 the French merchant fleet.

governments of the northern states to submit the said resolution with their recommendation to the great European powers and the United States of America."

In compliance with the first part of this resolution the committee has appointed the undersigned to inquire into and report on the question, and in fulfillment of this request we now have the honor to present this memorandum to the said Congress, and in doing so we propose to divide the memorandum in four parts, viz:

Part I, containing the main points of the discussion; Part II, containing a detailed statement of the development of international maritime agreements, with notes referring to Part III, consisting of an Appendix, containing the necessary information as to the respective merchant shipping laws and regulations, the opinions or proposals of influential societies or experts, and references to the nautical works made use of. For the sake of convenience we have also divided Part II in four divisions:

(*a*) Under division 1 we have collected and propose to treat the international agreements *which have been adopted by the governments of almost all maritime states,* as " The rule of the road at sea," " The international code of signals," " Signals of distress and for pilots," " International tonnage measurement," etc

(*b*) Under division 2 we propose to discuss some other merchant shipping laws or regulations, in the adoption of which by the other maritime states Great Britain has taken an interest, which, as yet, has nearly been without result; for instance, the laws on " Official inquiries into shipwrecks, strandings," etc.; " Preventive regulations as to the sending to sea of ' unseaworthy ships'"; " The British system of marking and lettering of the names of ships and their home ports, register-tonnage and draught scale of feet," etc.

(*c*) Under division 3 we propose to give an outline of some other mercantile shipping affairs of a more private judicial nature, which in our opinion seem well adapted to be considered as being of an international character, and, therefore, ought to be treated with due regard to such character.

(*d*) In division 4 we have wound up our views as to the usefulness of the proposed Permanent International Merchant Shipping Commission, its eventual composition, mode of action, expenses, etc.

Lastly, in Part IV, we propose to state the reasons for another resolution, which we are charged by the Conference to bring to the knowledge of the Congress, namely, about the question, " What can be done to diminish the danger which threatens the navigation by floating wrecks ?" which, also, was discussed during the Conference.

PART I.

GENERAL REMARKS AS TO THE DEVELOPMENT OF INTERNATIONAL MARITIME AGREEMENTS, STATED IN ORDER TO SHOW THE DESIRABILITY OF A PERMANENT INTERNATIONAL MERCHANT SHIPPING COMMISSION.

It is a well-known fact, that it is only lately that the merchant shipping has thoroughly felt the inconvenience of the discrepancies in the rules by which its relations in the different countries have been regulated. In former times the navigation of the seas was moving in narrower tracks, more regularly laid down, in such a manner that it was in its whole character in a less degree international, and it is, properly speaking, first, when the enormous development of the steam navigation took place that efforts were awakened for reforms which could liberate the navigation from its many checks.

Gradually, as the commercial intercourse has increased, the navigation is getting more and more cosmopolite, and the ship owners and merchants of all nations are associated in such a manner that to the commercial world it is an indifferent matter whether the goods are transported in the ships of one nation or another. A well-equipped and well-manned ship, with an able and active master, will make her way in the freight market, whether it is in the coasting or the foreign trade, without any other regard than to the master's capability to fulfill a contract cheaply and punctually.

The natural consequence hereof seems to be that it is in a high degree to be wished for, and in certain respects necessary, that all laws and regulations concerning shipping and navigation are drawn up as uniform as it in any way can be accomplished; in short, that in the navigation of the ocean, the highway at sea of all nations, a universal law system should be obeyed. By such an arrangement a multitude of common interest will, by and by, be created, and thereby the world will have found the right although a slow and difficult way by which, at least, the probability of long-lasting wars will be somewhat diminished.

It has hitherto been extremely difficult to get reliable information as to the register tonnage of the merchant fleets in former times. Fortunately this want has lately been for a great deal removed by a memorandum entitled, "Statistique Internationale. Navigation Maritime," issued in 1887, by the chief of the Norwegian Statistical Bureau, Mr. A. N. Kiaer. From this interesting exposé permit us to give a few extracts, viz:

In 1850 the entire register tonnage of the North American and the European merchant fleets (of vessels above 20 tons register) was a little above 7,000,000 tons, of which only about 200,000 tons were steam-ship tons; in 1860 the tonnage of these fleets had increased to about

11,500,000 tons register, of which about 750,000 were steam-ship tons, and in 1886 it may be estimated at about 18,000,000 tons, of which about 7,500,000 were steam-ship tons. Thus, for the last twenty-five years the total tonnage has increased about 57 per cent., but in steam-ship tons about 900 per cent. Forty years ago the total tonnage did not reach the present steam-ship tonnage, and when it is remembered that every steam ton performs the work of at least 3 sailing tons, the increase must be said to have been quite gigantic. The three cardinal points which characterize the last forty, and especially the last twenty-five years, are thus: an enormously increased register tonnage, an increased use of big ships instead of small ones, and the creation of a gigantic steam-ship fleet.

A natural consequence of the above-named mighty changes in all shipping affairs has been an intensely felt desire of additions to and improvements in the laws and regulations under which the navigation formerly could live and thrive, but which can not give satisfaction any more, and though reforms were rather tardily introduced in the different countries as a consequence of the slow working of the State machinery, it must be admitted that their governments on the whole have showed zealousness and activity in meeting the wishes of the mercantile community, and most of the newest maritime laws bear the testimony thereof, though it is not an easy task to reconcile the necessities of the State with the claims which commerce and navigation means to be entitled to put in. But even this does not suffice, for, the more lively the intercourse between the nations has been, the more international character the navigation gains, the more the above-named want has been felt, and a necessity has arisen for better uniformity of the different laws. When a ship makes a freight contract to the fulfillment of which the assistance for a foreign court of justice must be sought or caused by a collision or a casualty, it comes under foreign jurisdiction; the owner or the master will probably see their intentions and acts weighed and judged according to rules they do not know, and which do not agree with the basis for their dispositions. This has caused and will continue to cause inconveniences of different kinds; therefore, year by year, the want grows to obtain regulations having validity everywhere in the world, which can complete the laws of the individual country and arrange the international side of the shipping affairs.

While the governments in other matters of international character have displayed great energy for the creation of agreements—for instance: The international *Meter convention*, concluded in Paris May 20, 1875; the international *Telegraph convention*, concluded in St. Petersburgh July $\frac{12}{30}$, 1875 (revised in Berlin September 17, 1885); the international *Post convention*, concluded in Paris June 1, 1878; the international *convention for the protection of Submarine Telegraph Cables*, concluded in Paris March 14, 1884; The Sugar Bounties convention, concluded in

London August 30, 1888—they seem to take up a much more reserved position as to the creation of international merchant shipping regulations.

The *Belgian* Government forms an exception herefrom in the latest time, for example, it will be remembered that it in the spring of 1885 invited all maritime powers to send delegates to a "Congrès international de droit commercial," to be held in Antwerp the 27th of September the same year. Many maritime questions of great consequence were here discussed, with intimate knowledge of the matters and with great ability, but in this respect we must confine us to refer to the excellent report named "Actes du congrès international de droit commercial" (D'anvers, 1885). Even this invitation seems to have been treated with a certain reluctance, which may be proved by the fact that several maritime countries were not represented at all, and that it can not be seen that any of the delegates present have, in an official manner, expressed any opinion as to the questions under discussion. In private circles steady efforts have, however, been made for the solution of the said questions, particularly by the "Association for the Reform and Codification of the Law of Nations," with headquarters in *London*. As a private institution this association must confine its labors to the formation of propositions or recommendations to the authorities, and besides work for the propagation of its transactions and papers, and, therefore, the highest point to which it has reached is giving the impulse to reforms in some directions.

As it must be admitted that *Great Britain* is in possession of the most accomplished maritime laws, drawn up with the greatest practical knowledge of the subject, the first general question which is steadily put forward is, how this great maritime country has ruled in this or that nautical question. In these respects it can not be denied that England, especially in the latter years, has experimented in the interest of all other countries with great sacrifices of painstaking labor and capital. Of course the natural explanation of these sacrifices is partly her mighty merchant fleets, with a tonnage at least as large as the tonnage of the fleets of all other countries together, and partly that the relations of this fleet are embraced with an interest and love, of which the like can not be found in any other country. It is therefore both natural and prudent that the more or less insignificant maritime countries on the whole, and where it can be done without giving up their independence or peculiarities, subordinate themselves to the British systems. In these circumstances the principal cause must be sought in the fact that the other maritime countries hitherto tacitly have conceded to *Great Britain* the leadership through its "Board of Trade" of almost all maritime transactions and agreements of an international character, and this has particularly been the case since the "B. o. T." by the "Merchant Shipping Act, Amendment Act of 1862, Articles 58, 59, 60, and 61" had, according to issued "Orders in Council," acquired power to treat vessels belonging to States having adopted certain British maritime laws or regulations in the same manner as English vessels are treated. In accordance herewith the "Board of Trade" has gradually with great energy and on the whole with success got the *British rule of the road at sea*, the *English-French code of signals*, and although with doubtful modifications, the "*Moorsom's*" *system of tonnage measurement* adopted in almost all maritime countries, which thereby have acquired advantages of consequence, for which the whole maritime world must be to *Great Britain* thankful, and it ought not here to be passed in silence that the thanks in this respect particularly must be directed to the well-known secretary to the Marine Department of the "Board of Trade," Thomas Gray, C. B., who for more than a generation has worked unflinchingly for the promotion of international maritime matters, not only in his official situation, but also through numerous treatises in newspapers and periodical nautical magazines.

Though the above-named agreements may be considered as being of very great international value, still they are incomplete and there is an everywhere felt and constantly growing want for different other international agreements; nevertheless, the years pass by without sufficient regard being paid to such wants, and it may therefore be asked: What can be the cause why all these efforts both from official as well as private sources have given so comparatively poor results? Our answer to this question is: The cause must simply be sought in the want of a central institution, whose duty it is to follow and lead the development of the maritime affairs and which at the same time can be the joining link between navigation, as far as it is international, and the marine government departments of the different countries.

Though England, as before said, hitherto has been the natural leader, it has even for this mighty maritime power been an unsolvable task to lead sufficiently, quickly, and steadily, and this is not difficult to explain. Firstly, the British "Board of Trade" must be won for this or that reform, which may often be hard work enough. Next, if it succeeds, the "Board" begins to act by writing to the British foreign office, which again writes to the foreign offices of the other countries and these again to a number of departments in the respective countries, which also have to procure the opinions of existing institutions or of commissions especially appointed for the purpose, and the answers have to go the same long way back again to the "Board of Trade" and for every little change proposed by any of the countries, the question must often repass the same way. How can it be otherwise than such a machinery works too heavily to be satisfactory for the wants of the navigation at the present times, and how can it be wondered at that the above-named government department hesitates a long time before it moves, and, generally first does so, when the public opinion has gained such strength that it can not longer be ignored?

And last not least, there are the parliamentary difficulties to overcome, but of this delicate side of the question later more under Part II.

The natural and, in our opinion, the only way to conquer all such difficulties will be that the maritime powers agree to establish the herein proposed: "*Permanent International Merchant Shipping Commission.*"

Such a commission, consisting of experienced Delegates from all maritime nations, would form a sort of united representation for the common shipping interests of all such nations; it would have to watch over these interests and to test the propositions which might be presented for its consideration from different quarters, and to their furtherance formulate such proposition as joint resolves to the Governments represented. The commission, as consisting of experts on every nautical subject, would be in possession of so much knowledge from all countries of the matters, that every question taken up by it would be sure of getting an universal and serious treatment; the difference of opinion which now is the cause of never-ending correspondence, would, through a quiet personal discussion at the meetings of the commission in most cases be smoothed down without difficulty, and it would thus be far easier than now to come to harmony about anything sound and good. And in like manner, as every one interested in shipping affairs would feel satisfied, knowing that an institution exists whose duty it is to watch the development, and to whom they could address their wishes, sure of their being taken into consideration, and not shelved in the archives of one department or another, the Government would acquire a mighty support in carrying through a certain maritime reform. A proposition—unanimously agreed to by the commission, which accordingly should appear as the unanimous expression of the opinion of the experts in the whole civilized world—a Government would always easier carry through than its own perhaps one-sided views, even if these are supported by private resolutions. And finally, when a proposition appears as the outcome of the labors of the whole commission, in which all nations have an equal part, there would be no room for mutual jealousy between the States to appear and embroil what, on its merits, deserves to be furthered.

For the better proof of our statements, as well as of the necessity of the said Commission, we propose in the following Part II separately to treat the existing or proposed international maritime agreements as described in the introduction.

PART II—DIVISION I.

EXISTING INTERNATIONAL MARITIME AGREEMENTS.

A.

"INTERNATIONAL REGULATIONS FOR PREVENTING COLLISIONS AT SEA."

Half a century ago, as it is well known, there did not exist any written law or regulation for the prevention of collisions between ships at sea. There was then only a general "custom of the sea," which prescribed that sailing ships going with a free wind should give way to close-hauled ships, and that of two close-hauled ships the close-hauled *port-tack* should give way to the close-hauled *starboard-tack*. But of course such primitive state could not last when steam-ships commenced to plow the seas, and when the navigation on the whole was becoming livelier. At first it was mostly in narrower fair-ways that the want of more comprehensive and distinct rules was felt, and the single States therefore issued regulations, which certainly were of more or less mutual likeness, but yet were not the result of mutual negotiations. Only *England* and *France* concluded agreements as to common rules, what is easily explained by their joint interests in the navigation of the Channel.

It is not our intention here thoroughly to represent the development of the rule of the road, as such may easily be found in several excellent treatises on this subject, of which we particularly refer to the most complete and instructive ones we know, named in the Appendix, under note 1. For our purpose it will be sufficient to go back to 1863, when *England* succeeded in gaining the adhesion of the other seafaring nations to the English-French rules of the same year (Order in Council, January 9, 1863). Since then twenty-five years have passed, but a jubilee these rules could not hold, and those who believed that their development under the leadership of *England* should advance in a safe and satisfactory track must have felt somewhat disappointed. The rules of 1863, with the supplemental or explanatory provisions of 1868 to article 13 of the rules (Order in Council, July 30, 1868), remained in force sixteen years; but these English-French—now international—rules were constantly the object of criticism and attacks from different sides, and a revision was at last found unavoidable, which took place in 1879 (Order in Council, August 14, 1879). Nevertheless, shortly after a supplemental order, dated March 24, 1880, was passed, putting off Article 10, relating to the lights of fishing vessels, and in lieu thereof Article 9 of the regulations, authorized by Order in Council, 1863, was substituted. By the revised rules of 1879 no fundamental changes took place. The rules continued unaltered in substance, but some points which required elucidation were improved, and some other points, where experience had shown that additions were necessary, were also provided for. (See Appendix, note 2.) Nevertheless, these revised rules had some weak points. One of these was Article 5, " Day and night signals for steamships not under command," by which the same signals should be given by a steam-ship, which, in consequence of accident to her machinery or steering gear, or for any other reason, is not under command, as by a steam-ship laying or picking up a telegraph cable. Against this confounding intimacy, which might lead to dangerous misunderstandings, the telegraph companies naturally enough protested and proposed different and distinct signals in both cases. That Article 10 had been put off, as before mentioned, was also very unsatisfactory, and the consequence was that instead of the rules of 1879, the rules of 1884 (Order in

Council, August 11, 1884), were issued. By these rules Article 5 was changed as proposed, but the new Article 10, "Lights and signals for fishing vessels," had the same unfortunate fate as the former rule. The owners of fishing vessels protested with much energy against the system of lights ordered by this article, and as the British Board of Trade did not see its way to enforce these provisions against the wishes of several influential members of Parliament, it gave its sanction through a "Supplemental Order in Council," dated December 30, 1884, to a new and complicated system, the so-called "Grimsby Duplex-System." The same unfortunate story was repeated, the fishing representatives, backed up by the same members of Parliament, would not adopt this system, but insisted on the undisturbed carriage of the sole *bright white light* when fishing, as prescribed by the rules of 1863, and in addition, in case of "trawlers," of a red flare-up. The Board of Trade did not find it prudent to resist this renewed parliamentary pressure, and therefore gave the matter up, as will be seen by the "Supplemental Order in Council," dated June 24, 1885, by which the last-named system was allowed for sailing trawlers. The consequence of these wavering orders is, that *English,* and probably also other *trawlers,* may be met with in the North Sea carrying *when fishing* either:

(1) The common colored side lights (eventually also a white top-light);

(2) Two top-lights, the upper red and green on the sides and the lower bright white (the Grimsby Duplex-System); and finally,

(3) A bright white top-light and occasionally a red flare-up.

It appears, however, that German, Dutch, Belgian, and Danish "trawlers" only use the last named light-signal.

It can not be denied that the leadership of *England* in this respect has been rather misleading, as it repeatedly obliged the other maritime governments to rescind their regulations expressly adopted on the recommendation of the Board of Trade, but the worst feature is that the confusion which at present reigns may easily lead to loss of life by collisions between fishing vessels and other vessels.

Nevertheless, almost all maritime powers have step by step adopted the British rules of 1884 (with the exception of the said Article 10)—for instance *Norway* by a royal ordinance, dated January 28, 1885, *Sweden* by a royal ordinance, dated February 20, 1885, the *United States of America* by an Act of Congress, dated March 3, 1885, *Holland* by a royal edict, dated June 26, 1885, *Denmark* by a royal decree, dated February 18, 1887.

Unfortunately, the question of lights for fishing vessels has not been the only weak point in the leadership of *England.* The criticisms on the one side, and the deplorable experience as to the number and character of the increased collisions on the other side, has driven *England* from revision to revision, and yet the matter is still in such a plight that almost all other countries agree that the rules are in need of improvements and additions. Both the system of lights (see Appendix, note 3) and the system of fog-signaling (see Appendix, note 4) are insufficient, and though the rules commonly, and in our opinion rightly, are considered as based on "sound, practical, and seamanlike" principles, not a few of their articles still want elucidation and additions (see Appendix, note 5).

The cause of this unfortunate situation of these rules is mainly, as far as we are able to judge, that *England*, in spite of suggestions made by *France* and *Russia* (see Appendix, note 1, under "Parliamentary papers"), has refused to treat the matter in an International Conference, stating that such proceeding would be "undesirable." All transactions in this respect have, therefore, been conducted by correspondence through the troublesome ways formerly described; the propositions or proposals made from different countries have, therefore, not undergone the intimate inquiry they had deserved, and the rules have undoubtedly suffered thereby. For a comparison, what would be the fate of a law when the mode to frame it was not by exchanging opinions through a debate in Parliament, but in such a manner that every member should write to the speaker, and he alone had to formulate the law according to all these writings! And yet, in fact, such proceeding is now the ordinary way, and therefore the situation is as it is, and no advance will be made before this method is totally changed.

An instance illustrating that the above-named proceedings in the present steam age may be called "slow coach driving," we may name the time spent before the adoption as an international agreement of the article 16 of Merchant Shipping Act, 1873, "Duties of masters in case of collision" was accomplished.

Here *Great Britain* has not failed in her calling, but has strenuously and repeatedly recommended its adoption. Though the desirability of such a provision seems self-evident, as it is dictated by simple regard to the sake of humanity, it took fifteen years before it was universally adopted. We believe *Norway* was the first, by merchant shipping law, dated June 3, 1874; then *Germany*, by a royal decree, dated August 15, 1876, and, lastly, we are sorry to say, *Denmark*, by a law of March 23, 1888.

Another side of this question, being intimately connected with the inquiries as to collisions, we have found in a British "Merchant Shipping Bill" of March, 1884, which we regret was not passed. This is the matter treated in Article 79, which we think would have been very well suited for adoption as an international prescription. We, therefore, think it advisable to reproduce this article with only a slight modification of the first lines, viz:

"As soon as possible, and at the latest twenty-four hours after a collision with any other ship has occurred, every master of a ship shall make or cause to be made an entry in the official log-book, containing a full report, stating the circumstances under which the collision oc-

curred. and which ought to be certified by sign-manual by the officer of
the watch, the helmsman, and the look-out."

" Such entry shall, in particular, give information as to—

(a) " The course and speed of the ship when the other ship was first
seen, and the direction and force of the wind."

(b) " The estimated bearing and distance of the other ship when first
seen. "

(c) " The light or lights, or, if the collision occurred during daylight,
the apparent course of the other ship when first seen."

(d) " Any alteration in the lights or course of the other ship before
the collision, and the distance at which such alteration occurred."

(e) " The steps taken on board the master's own ship to avoid a collision, and the estimated distance at which such steps were respectively
taken."

(f) " The parts of each ship which first came into contact."

(g) " The master's opinion as to the cause of the collision."

We are firmly convinced that such an international arrangement
would be of very great consequence for the inquiries and judgments by
the proper tribunals in collision cases, particularly between ships belonging to different countries. The want of such an arrangement con-
tributes probably much to the present ingenious formulation of marine
declarations by the so-called " sea lawyers," which, as a rule, are more
misleading than leading. In our opinion, the agreement mentioned
here would often be a sure preventive against such erroneous practice.

Under the revised rules of 1884 the " *signals of distress*" are taken up
under a new Article 27. Substantially the same signals were introduced
by Merchant Shipping Act, 1873, section 18, and, on the recommendation of *Great Britain*, gradually adopted by the other maritime countries, for instance, by *Germany*, according to a royal decree of February
26, 1876, and these signals must, therefore, now be considered as internationally adopted; the only change introduced by the said article is,
that while the act prescribed as a night signal of distress "rockets
or shells of any color or description," * * * the article prescribes "rockets or shells *throwing stars* of any color or description." * * * This addition is certainly an improvement, as two or more rockets, without stars,
fired simultaneously, are used as distinguishing signals for the mail-
packets and other passenger liners in pursuance of section 21 of the
"Merchant Shipping Act Amendment Act, 1873," and might, therefore,
formerly have been mistaken for signals of distress. Nevertheless,
we find in the "Instructions for surveyors of ships," edition 1887,
issued by the " Board of Trade," under article 48, " statutory distress
signals," the signals specified in the act of 1873, reprinted without any
mention of the above-named change, but this is certainly rather misleading, at least for a foreign inquirer.

The " Signals for a Pilot," by Article 19 of the "Merchant Shipping
Act, 1873," the "Board of Trade" has also by degrees got internationally adopted, and these signals have since remained unchanged.

"THE DIFFERENCE IN THE COMMAND TO THE HELM."

Identical nautical terms for these commands are of the utmost consequence for the practical and safe use of the "Rule of the Road." Until 1874, terms having the same meaning were everywhere in use. But since that time an unfortunate change has taken place, as in all French ships, German, Austro-Hungarian, and Italian Government ships, and partly in Swedish ships. "Port," or "Helm to port," means that the helm shall be put in such a way that the ship turns to port or to the left, while this command in the other maritime countries, according to the old tradition, means that the helm shall be put in such a way that the ship turns to starboard or to the right. The above-named change has created a confusion which already has led and probably will continue to lead to deplorable collisions, with loss of life, particularly as it has been proved by law court suits in collision cases that there are still pilots to be found who are not aware of what command is to be used in the ships of the various nations. It is, therefore, in the highest degree to be wished for that harmony should be procured in such a manner that the command derived from the time when steering was effected by a tiller, should be abolished—so much more, as this practice is directly at variance with the commonly used signs to the helmsman, viz, beckoning with the hand to the right for altering the course to starboard, and *vice versa*—but as *England* hitherto has been unwilling to hear of any change in this respect, it would in our opinion be far better meanwhile to adhere to the ancient British custom. To leave no room for mistakes in the future the wording of the only article in the whole of the Regulations which used to contain the injunction to "port the helm" (Article 15), has been altered to "that each shall alter her course to starboard."

That the "Northern Conference" does not stand alone in its wishes for improvements in the "Rule of the Road" we could prove by many examples, but for the present we will confine us to cite a part of a resolution we have found in the report of the eleventh conference (in 1883) of the "Association for the Reform and Codification of the Law of Nations," viz:

" *That it is desirable that the Powers should agree in establishing an International Court of Appeal whose decisions might be sought by the Powers themselves in case of conflict in the interpretation or application of the international laws and regulations to collisions at sea.*"

"*That, to obviate all risks of mistranslation, it is desirable that the Maritime Powers should appoint an International Commission, composed of carefully selected experts, to prepare and publish, with the sanction of such Powers, an authentic polyglot text of the regulations and code of law above referred to.* "

In the report of the thirteenth conference (London, 1887) of the said association the following resolution was also carried:

" That a committee of five, with power to add one member from each maritime nation, be appointed by the chairman to inquire into the best mode of preventing collisions at sea, and to report thereon to this association at the next Conference."

While, in principle, agreeing with these resolutions, proposed and carried by eminent *English* experts, we are decidedly of opinion that their aim would be far better attained if these matters were taken in hand by the herein proposed *"Permanent International Commission."*

Finally we permit us to express the hope that the honorable Congress will not lose sight of the plan for diminishing the chances of collisions laid down as early as in 1856 by the world-renowned American scientific navigator, Lieutenant Maury. As it is well known, he laid down on the charts of the Atlantic Ocean two lane routes for the regular steam traffic between New York and Europe; the northward, for from Europe coming, and the southward, for from North America going steamers, divided by a belt 50 miles broad under Cape Clear, and gradually increasing to 200 miles on 50° western longitude.

By following the advice of Mr. Maury, all steamers coming from or going to the Channel would be sure to avoid each other: nay, even those from or to Brest and Nantes going steamers would, by making a small detour and seeking these routes, obtain the like security under the passage. But not only that such a benefit would be obtained, this ingenious author says, all sailing ships would be, by keeping outside of this belt, considerably secured, and if circumstances carried them there they would have a yet stronger occasion to be still more attentive. He winds up with about these words: "It is self-evident that such a plan does not in the least permit the neglect of the sailor's best support: his *log*, his *lead*, and the *look-out.*"

Some steam-lines, as the Cunard and the White Star, advertise, as it is well known, that their steamers take the lane routes, recommended by Lieutenant Maury, on both the outward and homeward passages, but such cautious navigation is rather an exception than a rule.

This question has been much under discussion in the Scandinavian nautical circles, and some experienced navigators recommend that not only between North America and Europe, but also in the Channel and in the Sound, such rules ought to be internationally adopted. For instance, it has been suggested that in the Channel all through-going steamers coming from the west should keep in the outline of the offing of the English lights, and from the east they should keep closer to the English coast; and that in the Sound such steamers coming from the south should go through the "Flintrännan," and to the east of the isle of "Hven," while all such steamers coming from the north should go along the coast of "Zealand," and through the "Drogden."

When it is remembered that it has been proved by a report, dated April 16, 1884, drawn up by a committee of experts appointed by the "Society of Arts" in London, that the English-American mail-packets under the passage in the open ocean, even in *foggy weather*, steam along with full speed, and that this is now between 15 and 20 knots, and that the increase of such steamers has been enormous, and that there is no probability of such racing being put a stop to, we are strongly of opinion that something more definite must be done in the direction recommended by Lieutenant Maury. If his advices *thirty* years ago, as we believe, were sound and good, they must certainly be the highest wisdom nowadays, having regard to the facts mentioned under Part I, page 3. We therefore hope that it will be taken into consideration whether the principle laid down in article 21 of the present rules "that in narrow channels every steam-ship shall, when it is safe and practicable, keep to that side of the fairway or mid-channel which lies on the starboard side of such ship" could not in some way or other, under a coming revision of the rules, be modified so as to serve as a guide for the navigation in other fair-ways, at least for steamers in regular passages.

B.

"INTERNATIONAL CODE BOOK OF SIGNALS."

The "Board of Trade," having always taken a great interest in sea-signaling, appointed in 1855 a committee "to inquire into and report upon the subject of a code of signals to be used at sea," and in the following year a signal book was submitted, based on the principle of the present code; but it was first in the year 1864, after it had undergone a revision by an Anglo-French commission, that it gained international acknowledgment, and it is now adopted both by men-of-war and merchant vessels of all nations. This code book has now been issued in ten or eleven different languages, and almost all sorts of communications can now be exchanged between ships and with signal-stations without regard to the language spoken by the crew. So far all was well, but the development of the commercial and shipping affairs has been so vast these twenty years that a code which was then sufficient is not so any more. There are constantly created new maritime inventions and nautical terms, as well as ports and maritime places, whose names ought to be added, but experience has amply shown that it is very difficult for other countries than *England* to get such improvements or additions introduced. Perhaps this is partly owing to the manner—rather difficult to understand for a continental observer—in which this book is issued in England. It seems to be prepared under the authority of the "Board of Trade," but its editor is "The Registrar-General of Shipping and Seamen," and it is, as well as the "Code List," printed and owned by the "Shipping and Mercantile Gazette." While this undertaking is half governmental and half private, the establishment and management of signal stations on the English coast seem to be quite private, as almost the whole of them are at present owned by "Lloyd's" or "Shipping Gazette." Pressed from various sides the "Board of Trade" in 1884 asked the maritime countries to send in proposals for a revision of the Code Book, but only as regards changes in coins, weights, and measures, and changes or additions to the geographical signals; but it does not appear that the proposals have been adopted but in an almost imperceptible degree. A great lacuna in the code is also that it does not contain any system of "night-signals," though several well-considered plans have been submitted to the "Board of Trade." (See "Appendix," Note 6.) "Rocket-signals" from light-houses to distressed ships, as introduced by the *Dutch* government from July, 1888, we think ought also to be adopted as international signals.

The " Board of Trade " has in the beginning of this year appointed a committee of delegates and experts from that department, the Trinity House, Lloyd's, etc., with Mr. Thomas Gray, C. B., as chairman, to report on this matter, particularly to bring the International Signal Book up to date, and to advise " whether the time has arrived when it may be deemed desirable to establish a system whereby the signals in the International Code Book may be made by night as well as by day."

No doubt this matter has now been put in the very best hands, but, as we have stated under Part I, the changes proposed will have to go the described long and weary international way several times before anything can be settled, while, if the herein proposed *permanent commission* existed, everything would be finished much quicker, and certainly at least as well.

" *Also, this matter would, therefore, in our opinion, be well served by being put under the wings of the said Commission.*"

C.

"INTERNATIONAL TONNAGE MEASUREMENTS."

The following remarks are, on the whole, a reproduction of a memorandum published in the English language by *the Danish " Board of Customs* " in the autumn, 1878, and as it was considered necessary—on account of the agreements concluded between the various maritime powers, having adopted the British measurement system, as to the mutual recognition of the national tonnage measurement—or at least suitable to the purpose, that any reform which may bring along with it an alteration in the registered tonnage that existed at the time when the agreement was concluded should be made a matter of mutual communication between the countries concerned; this memorandum was presented to the governments of the principal maritime States as an explanation of the reasons which led *Denmark* to give up the so-called "British Rule" (the 32 percentage deduction of the gross tonnage of screw steamers) and only to use the so-called " Danube Rule," proposed by the International Tonnage Commission of Constantinople, 1873, and adopted by the European Commission of the Danube from January 1, 1877, as well as by the Suez Canal Company from July 1, 1878.

The present British measurement system, commonly called "Moor-som" system, after its inventor, the first surveyor-general for tonnage in *England*, was introduced in that country by the "Merchant Shipping Act," 1854, Article XX–XXX, from the 1st May, 1855.

This system consists, as is well known, in all its simplicity therein that the cubic contents of all inward spaces, as well under the decks as of the permanent and covered-in erections on the uppermost deck, are measured with as great mathematical exactness as the circumstances on board ships may permit. The sum of the cubic contents thus ascertained, converted into tons register à 100 cubic feet, makes the gross register-tonnage. From this tonnage, again, is deducted the sum of the tonnage of certain partitioned-off spaces in the ships, as crew and engine-room spaces. The rest, then, shows the net register-tonnage of the ship, which, as it is well known, in most cases constitutes the norm, after which dues are levied on the shipping.

Directly after the emanation of the Merchant Shipping Act Amendment Act (1862), mentioned in the introduction, the British "Board of Trade," enabled by article 60 of this act, issued a memorandum accompanied by an invaluable treatise on the subject by Mr. Moorsom, called "Review of the laws of Tonnage," London, 1853, in which the prominent qualities of the British system were explained, and the international advantages obtained by its adoption were shown.

As the net register-tonnage forms the norm according to which the different dues on shipping are calculated, and as the great differences which then existed between the tonnage measurement of various countries led to great loss of time, expenses, and troubles of different kinds by the continuous remeasurements every time a ship discharged or loaded abroad, it was manifestly a great benefit *England* bestowed on the whole maritime world by the aforesaid step.

Nevertheless, the negotiations to bring about so desirable a result have lasted for many years, and only after long and patient discussion they have resulted in the present approximation to uniformity of practice.

In the *United States of America* the "*Moorsom*" system was introduced from the 1st January, 1865, but at first only with regard to the gross tonnage. By a new act of August 5, 1882, the net register-tonnage was also there established as the norm, as by this act deductions for crew-spaces and engine-room according to the "Danube Rule" were allowed.

By degrees the system was adopted by the European maritime powers; thus by—

Denmark	Oct. 1, 1867.
Austria-Hungary	Sept. 1, 1871.
Germany	Jan. 1, 1873.
France	June 1, 1873.
Italy	July 1, 1873.

Sweden ....Apr. 1, 1875.
Holland and Spain........................Jan. 1, 1876.
Norway ....Apr. 1, 1876.
Finland ....June 1, 1877.
Greece ....July 1, 1878.
Russia....................................Jan. 13, 1880.
Belgium ....Jan. 1, 1884.
Outside *Europe* the system has been adopted by:
Chili ... .Jan. 1, 1875.
Argentine Republic.......................Jan. 1, 1877.
Japan ....July 1, 1884.

DEDUCTION FOR SPACES OCCUPIED BY OR NECESSARY FOR THE PROPELLING POWER IN STEAMERS.

According to Merchant Shipping Act, Art. XXIII, this deduction is computed after the result of the measurement of all spaces that are occupied by or necessary for the proper working of the engines and the boilers (the coal bunkers *not* included), and when—

(*a*) The tonnage of these spaces so ascertained in *screw*-steamers is above 13 but under 20 per cent., and in paddle-*wheel* steamers above 20 but under 30 per cent. of the gross tonnage of the ship a deduction of respectively 32 and 37 per cent. of the gross tonnage is allowed.

(*b*) In all other cases, but now seldom met with, the deduction is computed by adding to the tonnage of the above-mentioned spaces 75 per cent. for screw-steamers and 50 per cent. for paddle-wheel steamers.

It may here be well to note that the rule (*b*) is identical with the so-called "Danube Rule," but that, nevertheless, the rule (*a*) only bears the name of the "British Rule."

More than thirty years these curious and complicated percentage rules ha e been in force; thus there has been a superabundant opportunity to prove how unsatisfactory and irrational the results found out in this way may be.

This has, for instance, been proved by many examples shown in the explanatory tables of the Danish measurement memorandum, but it will here be too prolix to repeat such examples. Of course, the faults of the "British Rule" are well-known in *England*, and as a proof hereof we may mention that Mr. Thomas Gray, in his evidence before the select committee on the Tonnage Bill of 1874, in this respect made use of the following noteworthy expressions:

"*It is indeed an anomaly that a great maritime country like England can not get rid of a few bad features in an otherwise excellent measurement law, which, instead of being a pattern to the other nations of the world, thereby is made a thing they should most avoid.*"

Among a number of essays on "Merchant Shipping Legislation," published in the "Nautical Magazine" for 1871, Mr. Gray has given further elucidation of this question, which, in his usual way, is as sound in its reasonings as it is clearly put. Herein the "British Rule" is denounced as irrational and absurd. In the same "Magazine" for 1887, in an article on "Saving Life at Sea," a striking example as to the impossibility of using the net registered tonnage according to the "British Rule" for any practical purpose whatever is mentioned thus: "* * * the steamer *Bournemouth*, which went ashore in a passage from Torquay to Bournemouth and was certified to carry at sea 372 passengers, was 232 tons gross *but* under 7 tons register * * * and was free from inspection simply because her builders and owners possessed contrivances and ingenuity enough to avail themselves to the fullest extent of the vagaries in the laws governing register-tonnage, and brought that in her case down to below seven."

In "the Shipping and Mercantile Gazette" we have also found a very pertinent letter, dated October 1, 1887, on this subject from one on the question of register tonnage "completely puzzled" writer, who winds up his remarks as follows:

"* * * A glance at the "Mercantile Navy List" will soon convince the most skeptical that this is no overdrawn statement. For example: There is one whose gross tonnage is 135 tons, net tonnage *nil*; another, gross tonnage 116 tons, net tonnage *nil*; another, gross tonnage 160, net 17 tons; and another 244 tons gross and 33 tons net; and some of these are paddle-wheelers, taking up the room of at least two ordinary vessels. How these figures are arrived at it is impossible for any one not being an expert or a conjuror to say; but it is possible, with a little more practice in this direction, that some steamers may be reduced *to so many tons less than nothing*, and then the question may arise if harbor authorities will have to pay them for the privilege of entry, and at the same time be liable in case of damage, should any occur, through defective moorings or a stray order from a harbor-master."

Finally, we find in the report of the last (1881) British "Royal Commission on Tonnage" the following statement:

"* * * *In the case of the steam-tug Clyde, of Greenock, her tonnage is registered as minus 4.64, her gross tonnage being 87.72 tons and her deductions 92.36. We have it in evidence that this vessel occupies space in harbors and docks without the authorities being able to levy any dues whatever upon her for the accommodation she enjoys.*"

Of course the builders of steam-ships have made themselves thoroughly acquainted with such vagaries, and it is now almost always the case that, in countries which make use of the "British Rule," the actual engine-room is given such a size as to be just above 13 per cent. of the gross tonnage, thereby acquiring the right of the 32 per cent. reduction, but also not seldom thereby doing damage to the proper construction of the engine-room, and, of course, causing considerable loss as to the light, harbor, and dock dues, and last, not least, it is prejudicial in the highest degree to the sailing-ships. The professional experts are, therefore, everywhere extremely anxious of getting rid of such a rule, which owes its too long existence only to the circumstance of being inserted in a maritime law of *Great Britain* and to the particular difficulties in changing that law.

It can not, therefore, be said that the following assertion, used in the Danish memorandum in the winding up of the comparisons between the different rules, is unfounded, viz:

"That the ' British Rule' is most deficient as to accurateness and equity."

. The British " Board of Trade," being fully aware of the inconvenience in this respect, has made most strenuous efforts for introducing a reform, but has hitherto totally failed in every such attempt.

Thus, already in the year 1860, the obnoxious rules for the deduction for propelling power were abolished in an administrative way. Several steam-ship companies, which thought their interests threatened, brought the question before the English courts of justice, whereby the improved mode of proceeding was reversed. In the year 1867 a memorandum, entitled " Observations on the Admeasurement of Tonnage," drawn up by the aforesaid marine secretary, Mr. Thomas Gray, C. B., was issued by the " Board of Trade," and presented for the consideration of other maritime countries, showing among other things, the fallacies of the " British Rule," and recommending the adoption of a rule by which the cubic contents of the herein-mentioned spaces (bunkers included) could be ascertained.

In consequence hereof, in 1871, a "Tonnage Bill" was laid before the Parliament, by which it was moved to introduce the later so-called " German Rule" (*i. e.*, the deduction for the propelling power in steamers fixed by cubical measurement of all spaces occupied by or necessary for the engine, boilers, and shaft-trunk, as well as of *the permanent coal-bunkers*), but this bill was not passed.

It was also *England* which caused the appointment of the International Tonnage Commission of Constantinople, 1873. The proposals of this Commission were looked forward to with great expectation as likely to be conducing to an agreement about the establishment of a universal tonnage measurement, but these expectations have only been partly fulfilled. The debates and the proposals of this Commission are inserted in a voluminous memorandum (Procès verbaux) issued by the Turkish ministry of foreign affairs in December, 1873, but how interesting the work may be in a scientific point of view, nevertheless, the proposals founded thereon have, as it seems, a good deal to be wished for, as to their usefulness in a practical point of view.

However, as a result hereof, and in accordance with the proposals of the above-named committee of 1874, in the same year a new "Tonnage Bill" was presented where it was moved to introduce the rule recommended by the said Commission, namely, the "Danube Rule" (*i. e.*, the deduction fixed by cubic measurement of all spaces occupied by or necessary for the engine, boilers, and shaft-trunk, with an addition of 75 per cent. thereof as amends for the coal-bunkers *not* being measured). Nor was this motion carried either, because the parliamentary commission, which had to examine the same, had given it such form as the Government could not approve.

Again in 1880 a "Royal Commission on Tonnage" was appointed, whose painstaking labors are laid down in an exceedingly clear and concise report (with a voluminous "minutes of evidence"), dated August 25, 1881 (Parliamentary Paper, C., No. 3074, 1881).

On the deduction for propelling power in steamers this Commission says:

"As regards the operation of the law in respect of the deduction of space in steamers for propelling power, we find a general concurrence of opinion that the existing allowances are neither equal in their operation, nor based on any sound principle discernible under the present conditions of steam navigation." This opinion was backed up by some very lucid tables. The proposal in this respect was that the owners of steamers should have the option to claim as deduction for propelling power either the application of the "Danube Rule" or the "German Rule," but with the provision that this deduction in screw-steamers should not exceed 33 per cent. and in paddle-steamers 50 per cent. of the gross tonnage. On the base of this report a "Tonnage Bill" was in the beginning of 1884 presented, but was soon withdrawn by the Government, and has not as yet again been laid before the Parliament.

Nevertheless, the requirements of the Danube Commission and the difficulties with the Suez Canal Company made it impossible for *England* to leave this matter alone, and by a convention, dated February 5, 1878, the proposals of the Constantinople Commission became obligatory for the company.

In accordance with this arrangement there are also issued special certificates of tonnage for the Suez Canal, in which the deduction is ascertained by the "Danube Rule;" the formula hereto being adopted by all maritime countries. Herein it may be hoped that the germ to an international tonnage certificate is to be found.

We think it must be admitted that it can not with justice be said that the "Board of Trade" has failed its calling in this matter, but that the fault is to be found in the British parliamentary system.

When it is considered how the English experts, as shown above, have treated their own measurement rules for the deduction for propelling power, it is not to be wondered at that these rules have not fared better in other countries. Nevertheless, some of these—for practical reasons, and, namely, to be in full accordance with the mightiest maritime power—have adopted the "British Rule;" several chose to follow the "German Rule," introduced by *Germany* by its "Schiffsvermessungs-Ordnung vom 5 Juli, 1872 sections 16 and 17" (see "Appendix," Note 7); and the rest adopted the "Danube Rule."

At present the situation is as follows:

(1) The "British Rule" is the legal rule in English, French, Finnish, Italian, and Austro-Hungarian ports;

(2) The "German Rule" is the legal rule in German, Swedish, Norwegian, Russian, and Belgian ports;

(3) The "Danube Rule" is the legal rule in North American (United States), Danish, Dutch, Egyptian, Greek, and Spanish ports, as well as for the passage of the Suez Canal and the river Danube.

The reasons why the last named rule is recommended by the experts are:

(a) That it was already introduced by the "Merchant Shipping Act," 1854, Article XXIII, b, and therefore must be said to be well known, though not often used in practice;

(b) That the deduction according to this rule is so ample that very seldom any steamer will suffer from its application;

(c.) That by its application no opportunity is given for the inquiries which are necessary by the application of the "German Rule" as to what may be considered as *permanent* or *not* permanent bunkers, and which makes the last named rule so obnoxious both to owners, masters, and surveyors (see Appendix, Note 7).

One drawback to the "Danube Rule" must not be left unmentioned here. As well known, great iron houses are as a rule built on the upper deck to give protection to the proper engine-room, and for the admission of light and air. In case of such houses not forming a part of, and not being inclosed in other erections, they are not measured at all, but if not so built, it is the rule that they are considered as belonging to the engine-room under the upper deck, and their tonnage augmented with 75 per cent. in like manner as the tonnage of the proper engine-room. But by such proceeding a disposition is created to increase the size of such deck engine-houses beyond what is necessary or expedient, and a way is thus opened to a fatal misuse of the "Danube Rule." To prevent such abuse, it is evident that only the actual tonnage of the engine-house on deck, *as included in the gross tonnage*, ought, in such cases, to be added to the engine-room deduction, and not, as the "Danube Rule" at present prescribes, also with 75 per cent. of such a separate partitioned-off space on the upper deck or betwixt-decks in addition.

Finally, we are of opinion that the recommendation of the British "Royal Commission," that the deduction for propelling power shall not exceed 33 per cent. of the gross tonnage of any *screw-steamer*, in some cases will be rather too narrow. The bad effects of the present deficiency in the "British Rule" of any limitation at all has been amply represented before, as it may lead to the absurd result that the net tonnage can be reduced to *nil*.

In the United States, Denmark, Germany, Norway, and Russia this limit is therefore fixed at 50 per cent. of the gross tonnage; but with such a deduction, in addition to the deduction for screw-spaces, no injustice can be said to be done to any steamer, while at the same time any misuse is prevented.

As the *net registered tonnage* for steamers above 1,000 tons gross, estimated under the "British Rule," is, on the average, about 10 per cent. less than the same tonnage according to the "Danube Rule" and about 16 per cent. less than after the "German Rule," there exists at present a deplorable inequality as to the international norm for the calculation of the dues on steam-shipping. The advantages of an international register-tonnage are therefore for a great deal lost, as, of course, net register-tonnage, after the "British Rule," is not recognized in countries having adopted either the "Danube" or the "German Rule." Originally, in the agreements, concluded about the recognition of the tonnage measurements, no notice was taken of the varieties in the modes of measurement and in the deduction for the propelling power in steamers.

In the later agreements a change has taken place in that respect, and generally it has been determined that only the gross tonnage for steamers shall be recognized, and that the engine-room deduction in every special case shall be determined according to the rules in force in the respective countries. Partial remeasurements were accordingly re-introduced, carrying with them the former loss of time and other troubles, though, of course, in a diminished degree.

On the other side, where the "British Rule" is the norm, reduction by remeasurement to this rule from the "German" or the "Danube Rule" is allowed. Although it can not be denied that such an arrangement is quite correct, experience, however, has shown that it is not much made use of, on account of either ignorance or fear of detention.

In order to prevent the drawbacks of such partial remeasurements, the tonnage certificates issued in *Denmark* since the 1st of October, 1878, besides the tonnage computed after the "Danube Rule," have under a special head been provided with the officially recorded tonnage details, according to the two other rules.

The same arrangement has also been adopted in *Sweden* and *Norway*, and as such statements, according to special agreements, respectively, are taken for good in most countries, no remeasurement takes place, and consequently the inconveniences of the different methods are not so much felt by steamers belonging to these countries.

But, besides the above-described difference as to the deduction for the *propelling power*, there exist several other discrepancies, which exercise a more or less disturbing influence on the size of the respective registered tonnage. One of these is:

"DEDUCTION FOR SPACES FOR THE ACCOMMODATION AND USE OF THE CREW."

Concerning the deduction for separately partitioned-off spaces for the accommodation and use of the ship's officers and crew, there are at present three systems in operation, viz:

S. Ex. 53, pt. 3——24

(1) The *English* rule, according to "Merchant Shipping Act Amendment Act," 1867, Article 9, by which—under certain conditions as to
arrangements and size in respect to the number of the crew—such deduction is allowed with the full-measured tonnage of said spaces, *without any limitation whatever.*

Besides in *Great Britain,* this rule is followed in *Sweden* and *Norway.*

(2) The *German* rule, according to "Schiffsvermessungs-Ordnung,
July 5, 1872," sections 11 and 15, whereby the total deduction for crew
spaces must not surpass 5 per cent. of the gross tonnage. (See Appendix, note 7.)

Navigation spaces, as well as *cook houses* and *privies,* are considered as
not belonging to the *crew* spaces, and are, in general, left out of consideration altogether.

This rule is adopted in *Russia* and *Austria-Hungary.*

(3) The *International* (Constantinople) *Tonnage Commissions* or the
"Danube Rule," according to which the total deduction for *crew spaces,*
also, must not surpass 5 per cent. of the gross tonnage, but with the
difference, that *navigation spaces* as well as *cook houses* and *privies*
are here considered as belonging to the *crew* spaces, and therefore are
added to these, and limited as above mentioned. No conditions as to
size or arrangement in respect to the number of the crew are made here.

This rule is adopted by the *United States, France, Holland, Belgium,
Spain,* and *Greece,* as well as by the *Danube Commission* and *Suez Canal
Company.*

In *Denmark* this rule is also followed, but only for ships above 1,000
tons gross. In every case the conditions as to size and arrangement,
according to the above-named Merchant Shipping Act 1867, Article 9, are
strictly enforced. For vessels with a gross tonnage below 1,000 tons a
per cent. deduction, *rising in an inverse proportion* to the ship's size is
allowed, as it has been proved by numerous measurements of crew spaces
that a limitation of 5 per cent. for smaller vessels is unjustifiably little,
provided that the sanitary regulations shall be duly attended to. Experience
has also shown that the deduction for *navigation spaces, cook houses,* etc.,
ought to have *special limitations,* and consequently not, as according to
the "Danube Rule," to be included in the deductions for crew spaces.
As well known, the number of crew and, consequently, the size of the
crew space do not increase in the same proportion as the size of the
vessel. For instance, while the crew of a sailing ship of 50 tons, as a
rule, consists, besides the master, of 3 men, the crew of a sailing ship
of 500 tons does not number 30, but, in general, only 15 men. Consequently, for the first-named ship, according to the "Danube Rule," a
deduction of only 0.8 ton for each man will be allowed, while, on the
contrary, for the latter a deduction of 1.7 ton for each man will be
allowed, that is to say, more than the double; this dispositon can not,
however, be said to be proportionate or equitable; the reverse ought
obviously rather to be the case.

In order to prevent the misuse, caused by an unlimited deduction, a certain limitation is unavoidably necessary, and as no plan more practical has been proposed, the only expedient left seems to be, as it is done in the following table, to adopt a deduction increasing in an *inverse* proportion to the size of the ships, and this deduction ought to be so ample, that each ship may, as far as possible, be indemnified for the space, which, in general, is required or appropriated for the accommodation of the crew, answering to the size of the ship; moreover, the deduction ought to be so adjusted that the regulations with respect to the spaciousness of the forecastle should not be counteracted by the tonnage-measurement rules as to the limitation of the deductions.

In *England* as in *Denmark* it is, namely, prescribed, that for each man, who is to be accommodated in the crew spaces, shall be allotted a space, the cubic content of which must be 0.72 ton, at least. The maintenance of this requirement—which is as moderate as well may be, as, for instance, can be seen by the circumstance that in barracks a minimum space about 5 times as large is required for each man—would be rendered highly difficult by too narrow limitations. The circumstance that the ship's owner knows that the whole space allotted for the accommodation and use of the crew is not included in the dutiable net tonnage, will evidently contribute exceedingly much to a satisfactory solution of the question in hand. In a time, when the attention is more and more turned to the unsatisfactory sanitary conditions existing on board many vessels, it seems unadvisable to prescribe too narrow rules with regard to measure and duty-free crew spaces (see Appendix, note 7).

The following table shows how this problem has been solved in *Denmark*, and we hope the Congress will be good enough also to look into this side of the intricate tonnage-measurement question. At the first glance this table probably will look rather complicated, but ten years' experience has shown that it works very well, and that the augmented reckoning caused thereby is next to nothing in relation to all the other tonnage computations :

Gross tonnage.	The deduction for all crew-spaces must not exceed—	The deduction for all navigation-spaces must not be exceeded—
For ships above 1,000 tons...	The total deduction must not exceed 5 per cent. of the gross tonnage.	
1,000 to 500 tons..............	6 per cent. of the gross tonnage. The total deduction must not exceed 50 tons.	1 per cent. of gross tonnage.
500 to 300 tons	7 per cent. of gross tonnage and not over 30 tons.	5 tons.
300 to 200 tons	8 per cent. of gross tonnage and not over 21 tons.	4 tons.
200 to 100 tons	9 per cent. of gross tonnage and not over 16 tons.	3 tons.
100 to 50 tons	10 per cent. of gross tonnage and not over 9 tons.	2 tons.
50 to 30 tons	11 per cent. of gross tonnage and not over 5 tons.	2 tons.
30 to 10 tons	14 per cent. of gross tonnage and not over 3.3 tons.	1 ton.
Under 10 tons	18 per cent. of gross tonnage and not over 1.4 tons.	

As the size of the crew-spaces varies between 3 or 10 per cent. of the ship's gross tonnage, corresponding inequalities are created as to the norm for the dues on shipping. A consequence hereof is again that the countries which have adopted the 5 per cent. limitation are suffering under a corresponding pregravation in comparison with the countries which allow deductions for crew-spaces without any limitation at all. An inequality which is contrary to the agreements concluded, and which could easily be prevented.

As little as the *net registered tonnage*, on account of the above-named deductions for propelling power and crew-spaces, can at present be considered to be in a satisfactory state as to equality, as little the *gross registered tonnage* is identical for vessels under different flags having one or more of the following special constructions:

" *Incomplete covered or closed-in deck shelter spaces.* "

The said British " Royal Commission " recommends in its report (see paragraph 44, d):

"*That gross tonnage should be made to include all permanently covered and closed-in spaces above the uppermost deck, and that erections with openings either on deck, or coverings, or partitions that can readily be closed-in, should also be included in gross tonnage, but that skylights of saloons, booby hatches for the crew, light-and-air spaces for the boiler and engine rooms when situated above the uppermost deck, as well as erections for the purposes of shelter, such as turtle-backs, open at one end, and light decks supported on pillars and uninclosed, should not be measured for the purpose of their contents forming part either of the gross or register tonnage. Cargo carried under such erections should continue to be measured for dues under the act of 1876, the same as if stowed on the open deck.*"

In a theoretical point of view, it is just, and in accordance with the " Moorsom " system, to include, as proposed by the Commission, in the dutiable tonnage all permanent spaces on or above the uppermost deck, regardless of these spaces being but incompletely closed-in, in as far as the actual openings of those spaces can be closed or choked.

In most countries—at all events in countries whose steamers have a lively business in carrying deck passengers and live cattle—it has, however, practically been found impossible to work upon this principle, as, by this means necessary contrivances to shelter passengers and cattle, when on deck, against shipment of seas and inclemency of the weather would be hindered, and at the same time, the proper means to secure life and property at sea be counteracted.

That scarcely any other question relating to tonnage measurement has given rise to so much dispute as this highly difficult question will be seen by the following outline of its history.

In default of *English* rules in this respect, officially advertised, a number of examinations on board English steam-ships have been under-taken in Danish ports, by which it has been found that the English measurement-surveyors up to 1875 practically have adopted the plan that when "any part of the deck below the shelter-deck was not covered in then the shelter-deck spaces were not measured, and, on the contrary, when the shelter-deck was unbroken and continuous, then the shelter-deck spaces were always measured."

How favorable so ever such a distinction really was to the steam-ship owners it did not satisfy them, and the question was, therefore, in 1872, brought before the English courts of justice for decision, whereby, nevertheless, the above-mentioned mode of proceeding seems to have been reversed, but whereby also a deplorable confusion in this question was created, which will be seen by a "Board of Trade" circular, No. 28, July, 1875, communicating the judgment of the House of Lords in the case of the steam-ship *Bear*, and showing its consequences.

It appears therefrom that the attempts to settle the question in *administrative way* have failed, and that it, therefore, will be necessary to judge and treat every case according to its special qualities. However, as it can not with certainty be seen from the said circular what the mode of proceeding ought to be, this vagueness has led to a very unsatisfactory state of things, the lamentable consequences of which, on account of the importance of the question, are more or less felt by all countries that have adopted the "Moorsom" system.

By examination of a great number of English steam-ships, however, it has been found that according to the English praxis, the following two conditions for exemption were *at first* required, viz:

(1) "That the shelter or covering deck should be broken through by complete transversal intersections, and

(2) "That on or above the shelter-deck should not be placed such heavy apparatus as steam-cranes and capstans for the unloading of cargo or weighing of the ship, nor permanent deck-houses for passengers or crew."

To the former condition it is, as it seems with good reason, objected, that by such intersections the strength of the upper part of the ship will be considerably weakened, without it being prevented, that the condition may be rendered illusory if the said openings, immediately after the measurement has taken place, shall be covered or closed in by planks from above and by ports on the sides, which, by means of caulking and screw-bolts, can be made almost completely water-tight.

Of the latter condition complaints have likewise been made on account of several disastrous accidents having been caused thereby, as in case of the unloading or weighing apparatus being placed under the shelter-deck it will be impossible for the man working these apparatus to have the necessary control with what is going on about him.

The consequence of these remonstrations has been that these conditions could not be maintained, and as the "Board of Trade" has not yet succeeded in carrying through any of the bills which it has repeatedly laid before the Parliament in this respect, this question is in an highly unsatisfactory state, and as no rules generally valid and suitable to the purpose exist, the practical treatment is different in the different countries. In consequence of the lively Anglo-Danish maritime intercourse, *Denmark* follows the English practice at any time as near as possible, but in *Sweden*, and particularly in *Norway*, the conditions for exemption of deck-shelter spaces are more severe; in *Germany* they seem, in certain respects, to be treated somewhat easier (see Appendix, Note 7); but dissimilarities as high as from 10 to 30, per cent. of the gross tonnage are hereby created between steamers under different flags; nevertheless, their net registered tonnage is usually taken for good in pursuance of the wording of the agreements.

The "Board of Trade" has, however, as soon as possible, taken care to neutralize the noxious effect that necessarily must be the consequence of the above-mentioned decision pronounced by the English supreme court by inserting in the "Merchant Shipping Act," 1876, section 23, the following preventive regulation:

" If any ship, British or foreign, other than home-trade ship, carries as deck cargo, that is to say, in any uncovered space not included in the cubical content forming the ship's registered tonnage, timber, stores, and other goods, all dues payable on the ship's tonnage shall be payable as if there were added to the ship's registered tonnage the tonnage of the space occupied by such goods at the time at which such dues became payable." * * *

It is easy to see that by this regulation not only the construction of imperfect and less seaworthy shelter-decks, but also the increasing, and in many instances dangerous, carrying of deck cargo is counteracted, as no real profit is to be gained thereby, and the temptation to elude the tonnage-measurement law in this manner is, therefore, as far as concerns Great Britain, almost done away with.

Sure enough, in the end of the year 1876, the *British Government* sent an invitation to the maritime powers which had adopted the "Moorsom" system to introduce the above-mentioned rule as to measurement of deck cargoes, contending that this provision ought to be regarded as an appendix to that system, and in such a manner that the deck cargoes in foreign vessels should be measured in the loading ports, and that the measured tonnage should be proved by the issuing of an official special tonnage certificate in every case, but, as far as it is known, none of the said countries has, as yet, followed this invitation, and it must also be admitted that this proposal is connected with several practical difficulties.

Also, this important tonnage question is therefore waiting for its solution by the herein-proposed "International, Permanent Merchant Shipping Commission."

" *Double-bottom water ballast arrangements.*"

To the other pending tonnage questions is lately added one more, namely, whether the water-ballast space in the double-bottom should or should not be exempted in all cases, howsoever it may be constructed. The reasons for the wishes as to such exemption are known to be:

That it is not freight-earning space, that cargo can not be carried in it, that the double-bottom is a source of strength and safety, that vessels have been saved from foundering through being so built, that in the case of heavy cargoes it is found advantageous by raising the weight, and that vessels so constructed do not require dock or harbor facilities for loading and unloading ballast.

On the other side it is argued, that although double-bottom spaces may not be used for the stowage of cargo, they often practically contribute to freight-earning, inasmuch as the entire hold in such case is available for light cargo, whereas a portion of the hold in a ship not fitted with water-ballast would be unremuneratively occupied by stone or other material for ballast. It is also manifest that a ship fitted with a double bottom on the bracket or cellular system is externally a larger ship, and is capable of carrying more dead-weight cargo, with a given freeboard, than a ship of the same internal dimensions, and of precisely the same tonnage, constructed without a double bottom, or with double-bottom water-ballast on the "McIntyre" system, and lastly, that this wished-for exemption is contrary to the principle governing the "Moorsom" system.

In view of these different opinions no hard and fast rule has, as yet, been laid down in any country; but meanwhile, in *England, Sweden,* and *Denmark,* the practice has grown up that such spaces are not only exempted in cases where the double-bottom is constructed on the "cellular" (the bracket or longitudinal) system, that is, where the floor-plates form the upper bottom, and where this bottom is hermetically closed and continuously running fore and aft, but in *Germany* it seems that water-ballast spaces between the double bottom are exempted without any condition whatever. (See Appendix, note 7.)

We are inclined to think that the last rule is better than the first one, as this may lead to anomalies and complaints from ship builders and others interested. If to the last rule were added, that the deduction should only be given with 50 per cent. of the tonnage of such spaces, we think that the opposite meanings might be somewhat reconciled. Such inequality in the treatment is, of course, unfortunate, as it may lead to differences in the respective gross tonnage of from 5 to 10 per cent. *As the "Board of Trade" does not see its way to take the lead, this question is also waiting for an international solution.*

"Measurement of Hatchways."

It has appeared by experience, besides the many attempts that have been made to elude the "Moorsom" system, that it has been contrived to fit up not to be measured holds in large hatchways. As thereby the seaworthiness of the ship is diminished, partly with regard to the strength of the deck and the whole structure, partly with regard to the stiffness of the ship, the "Board of Trade," to prevent such misuse, in September, 1876, issued a measurement-circular, which prescribes that hatchways of whatever height are to be measured, "in order that the proportion their tonnage bears to the gross tonnage of the ship may be ascertained, and that the excess, if any, above one-half per cent. of such gross tonnage may be added to the register-tonnage of the vessel."

This example was from 1878 followed in *Denmark*, but as this does not appear to be the case in several other countries, the consequence is one more, though comparatively insignificant, difference in the respective gross tonnage.

As shown in the statements above, the net registered tonnage for screw-steamers built according to the same design with quite the same external dimensions, measured in the harbors of the various countries, may vary on account of—

(1) The different rules for the deduction for the *propelling power* with until 16 per cent. of the net registered tonnage;

(2) The different rules for the deduction for *crew-spaces* with until 5 per cent. of that tonnage;

(3) The different treatment of *deck-shelter spaces* with until 25 per cent. of the gross registered tonnage;

(4) The different treatment of *water-ballast spaces* in double bottom with until 5 per cent. of that tonnage.

Accordingly the difference altogether may be for *screw-steamers* until 50 per cent., and this, notwithstanding the "Moorsom" system, forms the common principle for the tonnage measurement in the respective harbors.

As before said, the censure for the unsatisfactory state, seen from an international stand-point, of the "Tonnage Rules" as well as of the "Rule of the Road," can not with justice be brought home to the "Board of Trade," as it has been shown that this overburdened department again and again has presented to the British Parliament "Bills" for the development and improvement of the said rules, but such bills are constantly wrecked there, as the Government, as before mentioned, have not been able to break the obstinate resistance which the influential ship-owner party raises against every proposal which is thought to touch at this party's pecuniary interests, without the least regard being paid to international agreements.

"*In view of this state of things we are decidedly of opinion that this important question will never find its solution without being drawn in under the auspices of an 'International Permanent Merchant Shipping Commission.'*"

D.

"MISCELLANEOUS MARITIME AGREEMENTS."

Under this partition may be noted some practical agreements, which owe their existence to the interest *England* has taken to their international adoption, viz:

I. Reciprocal arrangements as to the disposal of the estates of deceased seamen;

II. Agreements as to the reciprocal surrender of deserted seamen from merchant vessels;

III. Reciprocal arrangements as to the relief of distressed seamen in certain cases;

IV. Reciprocal agreements concluded in pursuance of the "Merchant Seamen (Payment of Wages and Rating) Act," 1880, Art. 5, to prevent "unauthorized boarding of ships." By these agreements the evil influence caused by the presence of "boarding masters" and their "runners" on board arriving ships, in order to induce the crew to desertion, has been counteracted in a very effective way;

V (a). The international convention relative to the police of the fisheries in the North Sea, dated Hague, May 6, 1882;

V (b). The international convention respecting the liquor traffic in the North Sea, dated Hague, November 16, 1887.

The deliverance to the care of an " International Permanent Merchant Shipping Commission " of questions relating to such practical reciprocal agreements would, no doubt, be received with thankfulness from all parties concerned.

DIVISION II.

Under this division are treated the following merchant-shipping laws and regulations, in the adoption of which by other maritime states *Great Britain* has taken an interest, which, as yet, to our regret, has been met with but too slight adherence.

E.

"OFFICIAL WRECK INQUIRIES."

In this important matter *England* has also been the true leader, having got her eminent system for such inquiries introduced as early as in 1854 ("Merchant Shipping Act," 1854, part VIII), which was further improved and completed by a series of "Amendment Acts" of 1855, '62, '73, and '76, as well as by the "Shipping Casualties Investigation Act," 1879.

These inquiries of casualties at sea have been of great service to the whole maritime world, partly as a lesson or a warning to the sailors, and partly as constituting the fundament for the development of the newest side of the merchant shipping legislation, and especially in respect to prevention of the use of unseaworthy ships. At first there was a good deal of opposition against these laws by some maritime circles and shipmaster's societies, but this was little by little silenced when, by the information contained in the reports, the benefits were known which could be re-opened from such inquiries when they are led and published by experts.*

---

*In a work entitled "Wreck Inquiries," by Walter Murton, esq., solicitor to the Board of Trade, published in 1881, is given a most complete information of the whole machinery of these inquiries, and which, in the English maritime press, has got the very best reception, as indispensable for every one who has to do with law-court cases of shipping casualties.

England has therefore several times invited the other maritime countries to adopt her system in order to procure uniform information by specified formulas for the different classes of casualties occurring on the coasts of the various countries; but this well-founded invitation has, on the whole, not been met with the adherence it deserves.

In the *Scandinavian* countries already, in 1876, commissions were appointed to consider and report on the English system, and in *Denmark* "Bills" based on her commission's proposals were presented three times to the "Rigsdag" (the last time in 1883), but none of these bills were passed.

On the contrary, it must be admitted that *Germany*, by its " Reichsgesetz vom 27. Juli 1877 betreffend die Untersuchung von Seeunfällen," has got introduced a most excellent system in this respect, which can be learned by the perusal of the " Entscheidungen des Ober-Seeamts und der Seeämter des deutschen Reichs," published yearly by the "Reichsamt des Innern." *

Acknowledging the usefulness of such inquiries, the first "Scandinavian Maritime Conference" (of 1883) discussed this matter, and the following resolution was unanimously carried :

" *The conference find it advantageous for the sea-trade :*

(1) " *That the circumstances by all accidents at sea, which have led to loss of property of greater consequence, or have caused loss of life, should be the object of an official inquiry by experts;*"

(2) " *That by such inquiries in the three northern Kingdoms, as soon as possible after the casualty, there ought to be drawn up as far as possible uniform statements as to the details of such casualty;*"

(3) "*That these statements should be statistically treated by the proper departments, and the results published.*"

In the report of the Twelfth Conference (in 1881) of the "Association for the Reform and Codification of the Law of Nations," we find that the following resolutions were carried as to "Official investigations of maritime casualties :"

(1) " *That this association deems it advisable that the results arrived at by the competent authorities in the investigation of maritime casualties, if of general interest, be communicated between the respective Governments ;*

(2) " *That this association deems it advisable that the authorities intrusted with the investigation of maritime casualties, if empowered to deprive the masters of their certificates, ought also to be allowed a discretion to suspend only the certificate for a certain limited time.*"

While in principle agreeing with the above resolutions, we are decidedly of opinion that their aim will not in a discernible future be attained *without this important matter being taken in hand by the herein-proposed Commission.*"

_____

* A very clear and concise statement of the "German" system is represented in a work by "Statsanwalt" Julius Cæsar, entitled " Handbuch der deutschen Reichsgesetzgebung betreffend die Seeunfälle, deren Untersuchung und Verhütung " (Bremen, 1882.)

F.

"OFFICIAL SURVEY AS TO THE SEAWORTHINESS OF MERCHANT VESSELS."

The regulations in this respect must, according to their nature, be said to be of an international character in so far as a country which has introduced severe controlling provisions as to seaworthiness of her own vessels for the case of competition must be anxious to know that other maritime countries have introduced similar provisions for their vessels. This seems to be the natural explanation why *England* has shown so great an interest for getting her legislation in this respect, and particularly the provisions in the Merchant Shipping Act, 1876, Article 13, respecting an "official load-line," accepted in other countries.

In consequence of suggestions from *England* in this respect to the *Scandinavian* countries, commissions were appointed there (in 1876) to inquire into and report on the English system of survey of merchant ships by Government officials.

In *Denmark* "Bills" founded on her commission's report were presented to the "Rigsdag" in the years 1880, 1881, and 1883, but were not passed, the principal cause being that in none of the surrounding countries any serious interest for the introduction of the English system was shown.

After the British "Load-line Committee" of 1883, in the beginning of 1885, had submitted its report on this matter to the "Board of Trade," this department, in the spring of 1886, renewed their invitation to the other maritime countries as to an international adoption of the proposals of the committee with regard to the fixing of an official load-line.

In April, 1887, the British Government has further notified to foreign governments that clauses 13 and 24 of the Merchant Shipping Act, 1876, which have heretofore been in abeyance, are now to be applied to foreign vessels. Clause 13 provides that, subject to certain modifications, the Board of Trade shall have power to prevent the *overloading* of foreign vessels, which may load in whole or in part in British ports. Clause 24 prohibits all vessels, whether British or foreign, from carrying into British ports *deck cargoes of heavy timber* during the *winter* months. The effect of this new regulation will be that in respect to vessels loading in British ports, and vessels arriving with deck cargoes of timber at British ports, the same rules will be applied to foreign vessels which have hitherto applied to British vessels only. Of course, this will remove a grievance of which British ship-owners have complained, that they had to compete with foreigners who were left without restrictions as to the quantity of cargo they might carry. From a continental stand-point this provision has, however, its great drawbacks, as it, without adherence from other countries, may be cause of serious protests, international difficulties, and endless correspondence; but, of course, everything will depend on the manner in which this provision is carried through in practice. As far as we know it has as yet been enforced with great moderation.

We believe that it is a general opinion in the small maritime countries that the English system of survey is too complicate and would be too costly, also that it is not so necessary in such countries, where, of course, the shipping affairs are more uniform and quiet, and where the ship-owners may be said to be living in glass houses, and are therefore controlling each other, so that Government interference is not so much needed. Nevertheless, we are inclined to think that some control—on the principles laid down by the Merchant Shipping Act, 1876, and the Merchant Shipping (Carriage of Grain) Act, 1880—ought to be introduced, particularly in respect to the loading of vessels; but as long as *Germany* and *Russia* will not move, there seems to be very little probability that the *Scandinavian* countries will take the lead in this matter.

In our opinion this is also a right stand-point as to the question of surveys for seaworthiness by Government officials, as this preventive matter is a true international question, which only can be solved by an International Commission, as proposed by the Conference.

In this opinion we are glad to see that we are in the very best accordance with the British " Royal Commission on loss of life and property at sea" (see final report, dated 27th August, 1887, "Parliamentary Paper," O, 5227, 1887), which, with regard to the loading and seaworthiness of *foreign* vessels, reports: " * * * We think that the Board of Trade has acted wisely in endeavoring to secure by negotiation that the same measures shall be applied to foreign vessels by their own governments and local authorities rather than by attempting to enforce our regulations upon foreign vessels."

" *We recommend, therefore, that Her Majesty's Government should take immediate steps to invite a conference of maritime states to consider how far it may be possible to agree on identical rules for the loading of merchant vessels, and also what measures can be mutually agreed on for enforcing such regulations.*"

G.

"AGREEMENTS FOR PREVENTING THE TRANSFER OF UNSEAWORTHY VESSELS TO THE FLAGS OF OTHER NATIONS."

An arrangement intimately connected with the foregoing question, which has been very effective in aiding the " Board of Trade " in its endeavors to prevent the use of unseaworthy vessels, has been attained by the above-named agreements, which that department has carried through with success and impartiality.

According to these agreements no British ship can be transferred to another flag before a certificate of survey upon the condition of the vessel in question, showing that no objection exists on the grounds of unseaworthiness to the transfer, has been issued by a "Board of Trade" surveyor and has been presented to the consuls of the respective countries.

At the same time, as fraudulent or colorable transfers are hereby counteracted, such maritime countries as have not got introduced provisions against the use of unseaworthy vessels have escaped the danger of being overrun by such vessels heretofore under the English flag.

Similar agreements might also with advantage as to the security of life and property at sea be concluded between other maratime countries.

H.

"UNIFORM MARKING AND LETTERING OF NAMES OF SHIPS, PORT OF REGISTRY, REGISTER TONNAGE, AND DRAUGHT SCALE OF FEET."

In this respect the "Board of Trade" has recommended the universal adoption of the rules according to Merchant Shipping Act 1873, art. 13, as to the above-named marking, after which the name shall be marked on each of the ship's bow, and her name and the name of her port of registry on the stern. The last prescription is generally enforced in most countries but not the first, which, nevertheless, must be said to be very useful for the better control with a ship's whereabouts. In addition hereto the number denoting her registered tonnage shall be cut in on her mainbeam, and a scale of English feet denoting the ship's draught of water shall be marked on each side of her stem and of her stern-post. As there is no probability that England will give up her feet-measure, while on the other side most countries have adopted the meter-measure, we think it advisable that the ship's draught should be marked by both these unities of measure, and that a record of the draught of water of any séa-going ship, as well as the extent of her clear-side, when leaving port, should always be noted in the log-book.

The marks of nationality on the mainbeam, which a few countries (for instance, the "Scandinavian") still retain, we think had better be left out, as such marking has never been universally adopted and the certificate of registry ought to be considered sufficient to prove the nationality and identity of a vessel.

Also this matter would be better off if taken care of by the said Commission.

J.

"UNIFORM CONDITIONS AS TO THE RIGHT TO CARRY THE NATIONAL FLAG."

It is a well-known fact that the legislation in some maritime countries as to these conditions is so elastical that foreigners very easily can get their ships transferred to the registers of such countries, and as such irregularity under a naval war may lead to complications of a dangerous character for the neutral powers, it seems to us that some uniform fundamental rules in this respect would be very useful. Though the British rules, according to Merchant Shipping Act, 1854, Part II, Art. XVIII, "Description and ownership of British ships," generally have been adopted as the pattern, nevertheless these rules in other countries have been more or less changed, but generally not for the better. It would carry us too far to point out such deviations in detail for every country, and we admit that it is a most difficult task to formulate these rules in such a manner that they can not be eluded either by *pro forma* bills of sale and secret not registered mortgages, or by the starting of share companies with men of straw as managers. However, we think that something ought to be done in this respect, *but also that the only institution that could solve this problem would be the proposed International Commission.* The same remarks are valid for the form and contents of the certificates of registry in the different countries, which will be evident by a look into the valuable collection of such papers, which the British "Board of Admiralty" has published in May, 1886. Some of them are curiously impractical as to the information most needed, and, where no measurement bill is included, give very little enlightenment as to the controlling of the dutiable register tonnage. In our opinion there ought to be an international agreement in this respect, prescribing that the spaces above the uppermost deck that are measured into gross tonnage should be specified with their contents on the certificates of registry or measurement bills, and that the spaces whose contents are deducted from gross tonnage should in like manner be specified on these papers. Though it might be useful, it will not be necessary that the registry machinery should be the same in every country; it would, nevertheless, for the lightening and security of purchase and sale of shipping property, be desirable that the most important deeds of property, as the bill of sale and the builder's certificate, should be made more alike as to form and contents.

In the transactions of the "Antwerp Congress" of 1885 will be found a proposal of Mr. *Smekens*, president of a Belgium tribunal of commerce, as to uniform provisions for registration of mortgage of ships, etc., and partly for the form and content of the registers, which, in our opinion, is very noteworthy. In the *Scandinavian* countries special commissions have lately prepared new registry "Bills," which, to all practical purposes, are quite alike.

It would certainly not be amiss if also these questions were to be taken care of by the said commission.

K.

"UNIFORM CONDITIONS RESPECTING THE QUALIFICATIONS FOR THE ACQUIREMENT OF MASTER'S, MATE'S, AND ENGINEER'S CERTIFICATES OF COMPETENCY."

Although the safe and successful carriage of passengers and property in the oversea or the foreign trade mainly depends on the same qualifications as to skill and knowledge of the officers of whatever nation it may be, we are not aware that any serious step has been made by the British Government or any other government in order to establish certain uniform fundamental provisions in the above-named respect. Nevertheless, most of the continental regulations, as the German "Bekanntmachung" of September 25, 1869, the Swedish decree of November 22, 1878, and the Dutch decree of January 18, 1886, bear witness that the *British* regulations as to the examination of masters, mates, and engineers—according to the Merchant Shipping Acts, 1854, Articles 131-140, and 1862, Articles 5-11, together with Board of Trade's regulations of 1868, and later circulars—have been adopted as a pattern, though not sufficient to be considered as being uniform, but as it would only be waste of time and space here to point out in detail the existing divergences, particularly as to the conditions for the age, and the time served at sea of the applicants, we must confine us to express a hope that at least these conditions should be made similar, as well as the regulations for the admission of foreigners to command and pilot vessels. The *British* regulations in the last-named respect are the most liberal known, as a sailor of whatever nationality, *who fulfills the English requirements*, can command a British ship and pilot such ship or a foreign ship, even in British compulsory waters. These liberal regulations we should be glad to see internationally adopted. Certainly by the Merchant Shipping Bill laid before Parliament in 1887, it was proposed to take away from the masters and mates of foreign ships the privilege of proving their competency to pilot their own ships, and thus obtaining a certificate which exempts them from compulsory pilotage; but as the "Select Committee on Pilotage" in their report, dated August 3, 1888, recommend that the granting of pilotage certificates to aliens should be continued, it is probable that the above-named truly British regulations will not be allowed to be interfered with.

L.

GENERAL UNIFORM SYSTEM OF BUOYAGE."

The report of the committee delegated by the Conference, which, under the presidency of the *Duke of Edinburgh*, in 1882, was held upon a proposal to establish such a system (see "Parliamentary Paper, C. 3622, 1883"), contains in its minutes of evidence a series of opinions from experts in favor of an international system of beaconage and buoyage as a valuable assistance to the navigator, which, therefore, would prove a benefit to the shipping. One member of the commission proposed a system for the marking of shoals based on the compass bearings to be shown by different variations in the coloring of the buoys.

As, however, the colors very often are difficult to discern at a distance, several inventors have tried to solve the problem by a combination of different forms and colors of the sea-marks.

In "Annalen der Hydrographie," 1887, such system will be found, entitled "Einheitliche Betonnungs-System unter besonderer Berücksichtigung des Deutchen Betonnungs-Systems."

In the "Appendix," under Note 8, we propose to give a short outline of an international system proposed by a *Danish* expert, who has lately published an interesting book with numerous designs, entitled "Beaconage and Buoyage of Different Nations," which will be presented to the Congress by the said author.

M.

"UNIFORM QUARANTINE REGULATIONS."

If the motto of the old and renowned "Nautical Magazine" that "the seas but join the nations they divide" is a truth, the artificial barriers against the free intercourse which most continental powers raise by their too severe and often vexatious quarantine regulations for the prevention of the introduction of contagious diseases, must be regarded as a curious contradiction and a serious mistake. Though this, also, generally has been freely admitted, the history of the international quarantine conferences held in Paris, 1851 and 1859, in Constantinople 1866, and in Vienna 1874, as well as the transactions of the "Association for the Reform and Codification of the Law of Nations" (see 7th report, 1879), shows how extremely difficult it is to come to an understanding on this matter, as the very divergent views of various countries in regard to sanitary precautions have hitherto rendered it impossible to secure a general consent to principles which might form the basis of a convention to regulate quarantine. *Great Britain,* however. continues to protest against the continental systems and to recommend her own hitherto successful system, according to the "Order in Council" of July, 1873, and the "Public Health Act," 1875; but we are not aware that any noticeable regard has been taken to this advice.

Therefore we can not come to any other conclusion than the said Commission would also in this question prove to be the best anchor-hold.

DIVISION III.

"UNIFORMITY IN DIFFERENT PRIVATE JUDICIAL MERCANTILE MARINE MATTERS."

Several mercantile marine questions of a more private judicial nature have often in the last fifteen years been discussed at the conferences of the different associations mentioned before, and have thus given occasion for a number of able speeches and interesting reports enough to fill a whole library, but what in practice has been attained by these otherwise invaluable transactions is indeed very little. Though we agree in the opinion that most of these questions are well adapted to be considered as being of an international character, and therefore, with benefit to the commercial world, should be treated with due regard to such character, we do not intend to reproduce such transactions as this would exceed our resources, and besides would not suit the limited plan for this memorandum.

Nevertheless, for the sake of completeness, we beg leave to give the following short outline of the history of a few of the most debated of these matters.

N.

"INTERNATIONAL UNIFORMITY IN THE LAW OF DAMAGES CAUSED BY COLLISIONS AT SEA."[*]

At the first Northern Maritime Conference (1883) this subject was discussed at great length, and the inconveniences of the present confusion, caused by the existing discrepancies, were amply shown, to the remedy of which several well-considered proposals were approved, but as the same matter also has been treated in the very best manner at the "Antwerp Congress" of 1885 (see the report, pages 130–146, and 296–318), we prefer to quote the resolutions there adopted, viz:

"L'abordage dans les ports, fleuves et autres eaux intérieures, est réglé par la loi du lieu où il se produit."

"L'abordage en mer, entre deux navires de même nationalité, est réglé par la loi nationale."

"Si les navires sont de nationalité différente, chacun est obligé dans la limite de la loi de son pavillon et ne peut recevoir plus que cette loi lui attribue."

"Si l'abordage a eu lieu dans les ports, fleuves et autres eaux intérieures, on applique, quand aux fins de non-recevoir et aux prescriptions, la loi du lieu où il s'est produit."

"Si l'abordage a eu lieu en mer, le capitaine conserve ses droits en réclamant dans les formes et délais prescrits par la loi de son pavillon, par celle du navire abordeur, ou par celle du premier port de relâche."

" En cas d'abordage de navires, s'il y a faute commise à bord des deux navires, il est fait masse des dommages, lesquels sont supportés par les deux navires, dans la proportion de la gravité qu'ont eue les fautes respectivement constatées comme cause de l'événement."

" Si l'abordage a été causé par une faute commise à bord d'un seul navire, le dommage est supporté entièrement par lui."

" Si l'abordage est fortuit ou douteux, chaque navire supporte son dommage, sans répétition."

In want of a leader with authority, which the proposed commission expectingly would yield, this important question has, however, as yet, not advanced a whit.

---

[*] The "Nautical Magazine" for 1881 contains a series of articles on this subject by F. W. Raikes, esq., M. A., L. L. M., barrister at law. In these interesting and complete articles is represented the historical development of the laws regulating this matter, with an extract of the laws in force in this respect in the most important maritime countries, and finally, suggestions for a general code of maritime law on this subject.

O.

At the "Antwerp Congress" of 1885 (see the report, pages 146–151, and 304–314), the following resolutions were adopted on this subject:

" L'assistance maritime dans les ports, fleuves et autres eaux intérieures est rémunérée d'après la loi du pays où elle se produit."

" L'assistance en mer est rémunérée d'après la loi de l'assistant."

" L'indemnité d'assistance ou de sauvetage doit être déterminée surtout en prenant pour base les circonstances suivantes : le zèle déployé, le temps employé, les services rendus au navire, aux personnes et aux choses, les dépenses faites, le nombre des personnes qui sont intervenues activement, le danger auquel ces personnes ont été exposées, le danger, qui menaçait le navire, les personnes ou les choses sauvées, enfin, la valeur dernière des objects sauvés déduction faite des frais."

" Les passagers dont la vie a été sauvée ne doivent pas contribuer à la rémunération spéciale d'assistance."

" Tout contrat fait durant le danger est sujet à rescision."

" N'a aucun droit à l'indemnité de sauvetage ou d'assistance celui qui a imposé ses services, qui, notamment, est monté sur le navire sans l'autorisation du capitaine présent."

" Le capitaine, qui rencontre un navire, même étranger ou ennemi, en danger de se perdre, doit, s'il le peut, venir à son aide et lui prêter toute assistance, sous des péualités à comminer par la loi."

One of the English delegates, Sir John Gorst, Q. C. M. P., the present parliamentary under-secretary of state for India, recommended particularly the second resolution for adoption, with the following noteworthy words :

" Je n'hésite pas à me prononcer en faveur de la loi de l'assistant. Il faut encourager l'assistance, réagir contre l'égoïsme, si disposé à ne pas se déranger pour prêter secours à autrui. Il faut au moins que celui qui se dévoue ne soit pas privé, par une législation étrangère parcimonieuse de la juste rémunération de ses peines. Vous encouragerez l'assistance et vous sauverez beaucoup de vies humaines en admettant que, en cas de conflit des lois, c'est celle de l'assistant qui prévaut."

As another English delegate, Sir Travers Twiss, Q. O., heartily seconded this, with acclamation accompanied expression, it is to be hoped that the British Government will take an interest in the furtherance of this truly international question.

P.

After many years of indefatigable labor the before-mentioned "Association," at a meeting at Antwerp in 1877, succeeded in getting adopted the so-called "York and Antwerp" rules to form the basis for a uniform treatment of general average cases, and continual efforts have ardently been made to gain common adhesion to these rules, so that at present in charter-parties and bills of lading of numerous ships a clause is inserted that they are to be applicated, and most assurance companies have submitted to them.   But it is a natural consequence of the manner in which the " York and Antwerp" rules were created, that, though they are both practical and suggestive, they are not complete; they comprise only the most frequently occurring and most debated points, but do not give any information as to numerous general average questions, and even within this limited ground there is room for deviating interpretations, so that they in no wise compensate the want of a uniform law of general average, though their adoption and application in the practical life must be admitted to be a promising step in the right direction.

Of course this important question continues to be discussed at the meetings of the said "association " (see, for instance, its report for 1885), and was also treated at the " Antwerp Congress" of 1885 ; but it will carry us too far from our plan here to repeat these most interesting transactions.*

Q.

INTERNATIONAL UNIFORMITY IN THE LAW OF AFFREIGHTMENT AND BILLS OF LADING.

For a number of years there has also been worked assiduously by many corporations and authors in maritime law to smooth down the existing discrepancies as to the rules of affreightment.   At first the attention was directed particularly to some of the most glaring differences in the maritime laws of the respective countries—as, for instance, to distance-freight—but, in the course of time, it seems that practical men have arrived at the conviction that it is more important to come to an agreement as to the limits the laws ought to fix for the private-contract liberty in this matter.   The charter-party being a contract between the ship-owner and the freighter, there is no reason why they should not have a great liberty to agree on the conditions for the use of the vessel ; nevertheless, there are some reciprocal duties and rights which are deeply rooted in the nature of the relation between them and are a necessary sequel of it, and which it should not be allowed any one of the interested parties one-sidedly to abolish by a clause in the charter-party or bill of lading.

In *England*, where the legislation puts a very great and extensive liability on the owners, these, in the course of time, have, by additions

---

* In a work, entitled " The Law of General Average, English and Foreign " (fourth edition, London, 1888,) by Richard Lowndes, esq., average adjuster, all the subjects in this matter are treated in an exhaustive and interesting way, and, therefore, will be found useful as a trustworthy and able guide on all matters relating to the law of general average and its adjustment.   In the appendices are quoted the laws that have been or still are in operation throughout the maritime world.

and additions to the said ship's papers, tried to put off every sort of liability. To prevent such abuse the aforesaid "Association" took the matter in hand and tried to gather all the interests for a common, reasonable bill of lading, which could form the basis of a further development of the question as to a universal law of affreightment. At the meeting in Liverpool, 1882, a draft was agreed on, but as it was considered as being too moderate as to the liabilities of the ship-owners, and, besides, from a theoretical point of view, was found to be contending against the scientific principles of law, this question was again put under debate in *Hamburg*, 1885, where a new draft was agreed on. Now it was the ship-owners' turn to be dissatisfied; none of them would introduce this normal bill of lading, and for the third time it must be rearranged in *London*, 1887, where the following resolution was carried:

" *That the following principle, adopted by the Conference, of this association held in Liverpool in* 1882, *be now confirmed and adopted as the basis of discussion. That the principle of the common form of bill should be this: that the ship-owner, whether by steam or sailing ship, should be liable for the faults of his servants in all matters relating to the ordinary course of the voyage, such as the stowage and right delivery of the cargo and other matters of this kind ; but, on the other hand, the ship-owner should be exempt from liability for everything which comes under the head of accidents of navigation, even though the loss from these may be indirectly attributable to some fault or neglect of the crew.*"

By this resolution a result has been arrived at which on the whole agrees with that which, in the mean time, had been attained by similar transactions in the *United States of America*, and which, in our opinion, is as good as it is possible to attain by private exertion, as the ship-owners retain liability for everything respecting the equipment and seaworthiness of the ship, the stowing, preservation, and proper delivery of the cargo, but are exempted from all consequences of accidents occurring during the voyage, whether they are a consequence of *vis major* or of the faults or errors of the master or the crew. Much contest might be avoided by a universal adoption of this bill of lading; but there is still much left to be done. There is doubt and disagreement amongst the lawyers as to what may be acceptable or not for stipulation in the bills of lading. In fact, it is not known if this bill, which now tries to work its way for acknowledgment in the business world in the different countries, will be taken for good by this or that court of justice, and, therefore, there still exists an insecurity which ought not to be found in a matter so important for the general intercourse but which first can be done away with *when the international legislation* steps in.

Finally, it may perhaps be expedient here to mention that a *Scandinavian merchant shipping commission*, in 1887, has submitted to the respective governments a scheme to fuse their sea laws, by which the three distinct codes, each very ancient and original, will bring up for future use a fresh code, made up of the best parts of each.

DIVISION IV.

"THE PROPOSED INTERNATIONAL PERMANENT MERCHANT SHIPPING COMMISSION."

In addition to our general remarks in Part I as to the usefulness, etc., of the said commission, we beg leave here to give a few suggestions as to its eventual composition, mode of action, and expenses.

In the like manner, as provided for by the latest international conventions (see the Post Convention, dated Paris, June 1, 1878, article 16, and the Revised Telegraph Convention, dated Berlin, September 17, 1885, article 14), a permanent international merchant shipping "Bureau" should be established in *London*, with a staff consisting of a chief secretary, two assistant secretaries, and the necessary number of clerks, etc. This bureau—which should be the intermediate link between the governments as to the regular and general communications respecting the international sides of merchant shipping questions—would, under the control of the commission, have to collect and arrange all sorts of informations in respect to international maritime laws or regulations, to prepare the proposals received from the contracting governments, maritime institutions, or private persons, to be laid before the delegates of the commission, and, on the whole, to perform the different inquiries or other special tasks intrusted to it by the commission. It should take charge of all the necessary publications, the reports of the conferences held by the commission, and the correspondence (in the English language) with the commission or its subcommittees, as well as with the different maritime institutions and the public in general.

The chief-secretary should attend the conferences of the commission, and take part in the discussion, but without right of voting.

The "Bureau" to prepare a yearly report (in the English language) of its works and to forward it to the administration of the contracting States.

The common yearly expenses of this "Bureau" might probably be estimated at the same sum as proposed for the expenses of the "Bureau" of the "International Customs Tariff Commission" at Brussels. The sum to be participated by the contracting States in proportion to the *gross registered tonnage* of their merchant *steam*-fleets, but otherwise in the manner settled by the other international conventions.

The "Permanent Merchant Shipping Commission," to be composed of two or three delegates from each of the contracting States, of which one should be an expert in practical maritime questions and the other an expert in maritime law. The Commission to hold conferences with intervals of at least two years, alternately in the capitals of the six most important maritime States. The expenses of these conferences to be borne in equal proportions by the contracting States.

For the sake of convenience we shall finally recapitulate the questions mentioned under the foregoing divisions as eventually belonging to the domain of the said Commission:

A. International regulations for preventing collisions at sea.
B. International code book of signals.
C. International tonnage measurement.
D. I. Reciprocal arrangements as to the disposal of the estates of deceased seamen.
   II. Agreements as to reciprocal surrender of deserted seamen from merchant vessels.
   III. Reciprocal arrangements as to the relief of distressed seamen in certain cases.
   IV. Reciprocal agreements as to the prevention of "unauthorized boarding of ships."
   V. (a.) The international convention relative to the police of the fisheries in the North Sea.
      (b.) The international convention respecting the liquor traffic in the North Sea.
E. Official wreck inquiries.
F. Official survey as to the seaworthiness of merchant vessels.
G. Agreements for preventing the transfer of unseaworthy vessels to the flags of other nations.
H. Uniform marking and lettering of names of ships, port of registry, register tonnage, and draught scale of feet.
J. Uniform conditions as to the right to carry the national flag.
K. Uniform conditions respecting the qualifications for the acquirement of master's, mate's, and engineer's certificates of competency.
L. General uniform system of buoyage.
M. Uniform quarantine regulations.
N. International uniformity in the law of damages caused by collisions at sea.
O. Uniform salvage regulations.
P. International uniformity in the law of general average.
Q. International uniformity in the law of affreightment and bill of lading.

FINAL REMARKS.

As this memorandum has only been based on information which every one could have acquired by studying the official or other publications having appeared the last twenty years respecting maritime matters or problems, and as we are not in connection with any Government department in possession of the necessary intimate knowledge to international communications of similar kind, it may be that negotiations have taken place between the different Governments about questions as to other merchant shipping matters of an international character; nevertheless, we hope we have represented the most important of them, and in every case enough to prove to the maritime public that here is still a rich field to be found for the improvement of the existing agreements and for the adoption of new ones.

Having witnessed the establishment of the conventions mentioned in the introduction (page 4), which in our opinion are far less important in respect to the security of life and property, we have no doubt that this plan in times to come will be a reality.

We hope, also, that we have stated enough to show that the *sea traffic* now-a-days has a well-founded claim; that the further development of its many-sided relations ought not any longer to be left to the initiative and labors of private persons, howsoever earnest and energetic they may be, and how great appreciations they deserve; that it will not suffice that the important questions which will never find their final solution, but—even when solved for a time—will claim attention again before long, on account of the never-ending development of the shipping trade, and which, at all times, are of so great consequence for the international intercourse, separately and at long intervals are made the object for diplomatic correspondence between the Governments, but that the traffic requires a *permanent central organ*, which can collect the endeavors and lead them in a rational direction, having the duty and right to speak, and being able to give its expressions the necessary weight, where it is expedient to break the resistance which old customs or abuse may put up against every progress.

Even if this plan should meet with difficulties, it is not the quantity of these which is decisive, where there is a question of reform, but it is the worth and importance of the reform itself. Every reform will have difficulties to overcome, but if it is a good one, at last it will make its way, and this will also be the case here; but every one who has the welfare of the sailor and the behoof of the sea-traffic at heart ought to contribute his part, that too long a time is not lost before it happens. And it ought not to be forgotten that the realization of this plan aims at something more than the satisfaction of the behoof of the material interests; for it is through progress of this kind that the way shall be paved for a better mutual understanding between the nations, for better relations between them, and for a better comprehension of the truth that all the peoples of the earth, in spite of their national peculiarities, have got by Providence a common work to do and a common aim to strive for—*the development of the whole mankind to a life in peace and harmony.*

Therefore we finish by expressing a hope that the honored Congress will yield its valuable assistance to the furtherance of the objects aimed at by this memorandum.

Copenhagen, September, 1888.

C. F. TIETGEN,
Chairman of the Copenhagen Chamber of Commerce.
N. JACOBSEN,
Manager of the Copenhagen Marine Insurance Association.
N. J. JESPERSEN,
Inspector of the Bureau Veritas.
AUG. SCHNEIDER,
Chief Registrar of Shipping.

APPENDIX B.

*RÉFORME DE LA LOI INTERNATIONALE DU 4 NOVEMBRE 1879 SUR LES
COLLISIONS EN MER ET CRÉATION DE TRIBUNAUX MARITIMES IN-
TERNATIONAUX.*

[Pétition au Parlement Français et lettre aux présidents des Chambres de commerce
françaises et étrangères, par Albert Riondel, capitaine de frégate en retraite, officier
de la Légion-d'Honneur.]

PRÉFACE.

Depuis plus de deux ans nous nous occupons exclusivement des questions de collisions en mer et droit maritime.

L'approbation presque unanime que nos propositions ont rencontrée,
auprès de deux Gouvernements étrangers, de quatre grandes Chambres
de Commerce et de deux Congrès internationaux, nous décide à faire un
nouveau pas en avant.

Nous publions dans ce mémoire les divers documents officiels que
nous avons reçus. Nous les faisons précéder d'une pétition à la Chambre des Députés et au Sénat. Nous demandons respectueusement au
Parlement de prendre l'initiative de la réforme; elle consiste en deux
points principaux :

1º La création de tribunaux internationaux pour juger les litiges
maritimes entre navires de nationalités différentes ;

2º La modification urgente de la loi internationale du 4 novembre
1879.

Nous nous adressons ensuite aux présidents des Chambres de commerce des capitales des seize puissances ayant adhéré à la loi citée plus
haut, ainsi qu'aux présidents des autres Chambres de commerce de
France.

Nous leur demandons également de vouloir bien approuver les propositions de la Chambre de commerce de Paris et de voter, en outre, une
clause additionnelle ; celle-ci serait, à notre avis, un remède efficace et
le moyen certain (comme le demande cette Chambre) "de résoudre ces
questions internationales de si haut intérêt et de satisfaire aux besoins
de la grande famille du monde commercial."

L'Avant-Propos, qui précède immédiatement les documents officiels,
expose les diverses phases de la question.

Nous limitons à ce cadre restreint la publication que nous faisons aujourd'hui.

Nous réunirons plus tard, dans un nouveau mémoire, toutes les études
que nous avons insérées dans la presse depuis "la collision du *St.
Germain* et du *Woodburn*."

ALBERT RIONDEL.

PÉTITION À LA CHAMBRE DES DÉPUTÉS ET AU SÉNAT.

J'ai l'honneur de placer sous les yeux de la Chambre des Députés et
du Sénat les documents suivants ; ils touchent à la création de tribu-

naux internationaux maritimes et à la réforme de la loi internationale des abordages du 4 novembre 1879.

Je demande respectueusement au Parlement Français :

De vouloir bien approuver les propositions de la chambre de commerce de Paris, dans sa séance du 13 juillet 1885 ; cette Chambre a transmis, ce jour-là, au ministre du commerce "un avis tendant à ce que le Gouvernement Français *s'entende* avec les gouvernements étrangers *pour résoudre ces questions internationales de si haut intérêt.*

Le président de la dite Chambre m'écrivait le 9 novembre 1885 : " La Chambre ayant statué dans un sens *conforme* à vos propositions ne peut que vous donner connaissance de ses résolutions."

Ces dernières sont au nombre de trois :

1° La première est relative à la manœuvre qui est imposée (en cas de collision) au navire isolé rencontrant à la mer un groupe de bâtiments réunis ensemble par des remorques. Le navire isolé est libre de ses mouvements ; il devra désormais *se déranger* de sa route et céder le pas au groupe qui *continuera* la sienne.

2° Les deux autres résolutions sont résumées dans le passage suivant : " La Chambre de commerce estime en conséquence que *non-seulement* la création de tribunaux internationaux s'impose pour les besoins de la grande famille du monde commercial, mais qu'il conviendrait surtout que toutes les nations eussent un même code maritime."

Les documents du deuxième dossier annexe montreront aux représentants de la nation que les résolutions de la Chambre de commerce de Paris (saisie de mes propositions le 1er mai 1885) avaient été également approuvées, presque sans réserve, par le gouvernemment d'Athènes ; les trois grandes Chambres de commerce de France : Marseille, Bordeaux et le Havre, et le gouvernement des Etats-Unis.

Il s'agit de la protection de la vie sur mer ; il faut diminuer, dans une large mesure et dans le plus bref délai, le nombre toujours croissant des désastres maritimes qui déciment et jettent dans le deuil et la misère tant de familles de toutes les nations.

Je demande respectueusement au Parlement et au Gouvernement Français de prendre la cause en mains et de se mettre à la tête de la réforme.

Cherbourg, le 15 décembre 1885.

Commandant ALBERT RIONDEL.

———

[Lettre adressée par M. le commandant Albert Riondel, aux présidents des Chambres de commerce étrangères et françaises.]

MONSIEUR LE PRÉSIDENT :

J'ai l'honneur de vous adresser respectueusement les documents suivants ; je vous prie de vouloir bien les soumettre à l'appréciation de la Chambre de commerce. J'espère, en raison de l'intérêt même de la question, que la Chambre voudra bien examiner avec bienveillance les propositions que je prends la liberté de soumettre à sa haute attention.

Les deux gouvernements des États-Unis et de Grèce * m'ont donné leur approbation complète. Les quatre Chambres de commerce françaises de Paris, Bordeaux, le Havre et Marseille ont été également du même avis.

Les lettres qui m'ont été écrites par le secrétaire général du congrès d'Hambourg et par M. le baron de Lambermout, ministre d'État de sa Majesté le roi des Belges et président du Congrès d'Anvers† témoignent aussi de l'intérêt des deux Conférences internationales au sujet de mes propositions.

La Chambre de commerce de Paris demande à tous les gouvernements de s'entendre " pour résoudre ces questions internationales de si haut intérêt." Elle trouve "que non-seulement la création des tribunaux internationaux s'impose pour les besoins de la grande famille du monde commercial, mais qu'il conviendrait surtout que toutes les nations *eussent un même code maritime."*

Ce langage trouvera son écho dans toutes les chambres de commerce ; il se répercutera partout et accomplira la réforme. C'est un devoir d'arrêter le flot de ces hécatombes maritimes incessantes, qui frappent si cruellement les familles des différentes nations. "A un titre quelconque, soit par profession, soit pour leurs affaires ou leurs plaisirs," elles ont plusieurs de leurs membres qui voyagent sur le terrible élément, sous les diverses latitudes ; on leur doit des garanties et la sécurité.

Dans ma 3e note au Congrès d'Anvers, j'ai demandé, à *titre permanent*, la réunion d'une commission internationale composée de seize membres, appartenant aux seize puissances ayant adhéré à la loi internationale du 4 novembre 1879.

Cette commission aurait *pleins pouvoirs*, nommerait elle-même son *président*, se réunirait au point qu'il indiquerait et quand il le jugerait utile. N'étant pas trop nombreuse, composée d'hommes compétents, elle ferait de bonne besogne et l'harmonie règnerait dans son sein.

Cette commission ferait le projet de la loi internationale uniforme, si justement réclamé par la Chambre de commerce de Paris. Elle s'occuperait enfin de toutes les questions relatives aux moyens de prévenir les collisions en mer.

Cette commission internationale, une fois nommée, ne serait *jamais* dissoute.

Le 17 mars 1884, dans ma brochure du *Saint-Germain* et du *Woodburn*, j'exprimais cette idée dans les termes suivants: " La loi internationale du 4 novembre 1879 a été faite pour prévenir les abordages à la mer. Elle doit toujours rester ouverte au progrès. Chaque évènement malheureux devrait être étudié avec soin et servir d'enseignement pour

---

* Le Gouvernement Russe (d'après une correspondance de Saint-Pétersbourg du 28 novembre publiée par le journal *Le Soleil*) vient également d'approuver mes propositions (*voir au second dossier*).

† Les comptes-rendus ne sont pas encore publiés.

l'avenir. Il est nécessaire que l'expérience si chèrement acquise ne soit pas perdue."

Si vous partagez cette manière de voir, je solliciterai de votre haute bienveillance la faveur de proposer à la chambre de commerce l'adoption de la clause suivante :

"La Chambre de commerce de ——— adopte complètement les propositions de la Chambre de commerce de Paris ; elle demande la nomination *immédiate* d'une commission internationale composée de 16 membres, appartenant aux 16 puissances adhérentes à la loi du 4 novembre 1879.

"Cette commission devra être permanente ; elle nommera son président qui aura pleins pouvoirs de la convoquer et de la réunir là où il le jugera utile ; elle préparera (comme le dit la Chambre de Paris) "la solution de toutes ces questions internationales d'un si haut intérêt;" elle étudiera avec soin les collisions nouvelles où elle trouvera "un enseignement salutaire pour les prévenir à l'avenir."

Recevez, je vous prie, monsieur le président, l'assurance de mon très profond respect.

ALBERT RIONDEL,
18 *quai Caligny, à Cherbourg,*

———

AVANT-PROPOS.

Dans la nuit du 25 au 26 août 1883, vers 2 heures ¼ du matin, le paquebot français *Saint-Germain* rencontra un groupe de deux navires anglais, à 30 milles dans le sud de Plymouth, le vapeur *Recovery* remorquant le *Woodburn.*

La collision eut lieu : le *Woodburn* sombra et 18 hommes de son équipage disparurent après l'abordage.

Des circonstances particulières nous ont fait étudier cette affaire ; d'abord, dans la presse locale de Cherbourg ; plus tard, dans une brochure publiée à Paris, 19, quai St.-Michel, chez Léon Vanier, éditeur ; elle porte le titre de : Collision du *Saint-Germain* et du *Woodburn* et ses conséquences, par Albert du Hailly.

La brochure a été inscrite, depuis, sous notre véritable nom, par ordre du ministre de la marine, sur les exemplaires qui ont été déposés dans les bibliothèques de ce département.

La Compagnie transatlantique eut connaissance des articles du *Phare de la Manche,* qui avaient été reproduits par les journaux du Havre ; elle nous fit remercier par son capitaine du *Saint-Germain.*

La brochure avait paru au mois d'avril 1884. Au mois de décembre, nous l'adressâmes par l'intermédiaire des ambassadeurs à Paris, aux seize puissances maritimes adhérentes à la loi internationale du 4 novembre 1879 ; douze de ces ministres voulurent bien nous répondre et envoyer notre livre à leurs gouvernements.

Quelques mois après, les ambassadeurs d'Italie et d'Espagne, ainsi que les ministres des États-Unis et des Pays-Bas, nous firent parvenir les remerciements de leurs gouvernements.

Ces différentes pièces constituent le premier dossier.

Jusqu'au 13 avril 1885, nous n'avions encore reçu que des témoignages d'estime; ils n'avançaient pas cependant la question de la réforme internationale.

La date du 13 avril 1885 a été le point de départ d'un progrès sérieux; ce jour-là, M. Morton, ministre des États-Unis, à Paris, a posé les bases de la réforme; elle ne peut plus se faire attendre longtemps désormais.

M. Morton disait dans le second paragraphe de sa lettre: "Vous me demandiez de soumettre votre travail à l'appréciation de mon gouvernement; je l'ai fait et M. le secrétaire d'État m'adresse aujourd'hui une copie de la correspondence échangée à ce sujet avec le secrétaire du trésor et le commissaire de la navigation. Vous verrez par cette correspondance, que je m'empresse de vous adresser, que votre proposition a été étudiée sérieusement et dans un esprit tout à fait sympathique."

Le secrétaire d'État, de son côté, en transmettant le rapport du commissaire de la navigation, se servait de ces termes: "Le département donne *pleinement* son assentiment à ces idées."

Le rapport du commissaire de la navigation est véritablement remarquable; il démontre d'une manière irréfutable la nécessité urgente de constituer, à bref délai, des tribunaux internationaux pour juger les litiges maritimes entre nations différentes.

Le Gouvernement de Grèce faisait aussi étudier nos propositions; il approuvait également la création des tribunaux internationaux maritimes et se déclarait "tout disposé à prendre part aux travaux de la Conférence, quand les puissances décideraient d'en convoquer une."

Étant en possession de ces documents, la pensée nous vint de les communiquer aux trois Chambres de commerce maritimes du Havre, Marseille et Bordeaux. Nous adressâmes un peu plus tard le même dossier à la Chambre de commerce de la Capitale.

Nous avons trouvé, dans ces quatre grandes assemblées commerciales, l'accueil le plus empressé et le plus courtois; elles ont approuvé sans réserve toutes nos propositions.

La Chambre de commerce de Paris s'est exprimée avec une grande énergie, dans sa délibération du 13 juillet 1885; on peut s'en faire une idée par le passage suivant de la lettre qui nous a été écrite le 9 novembre 1885 par son président: "La Chambre de commerce estime, en conséquence, que non-seulement la *création des tribunaux internationaux s'impose* pour les besoins de la grande famille du monde commercial, mais qu'il conviendrait surtout que toutes les nations eussent un *même code maritime.*"

La netteté et la précision de ce passage sont complétées par le dernier paragraphe de la lettre: "Par ces motifs, la Chambre de commerce de Paris, à la date du 13 juillet 1885, a transmis à M. le ministre du commerce un avis tendant à ce que le Gouvernement Français s'entende avec les gouvernements étrangers pour résoudre ces questions internationales de si haut intérêt.

"La Chambre ayant statué déjà dans un *sens conforme* à vos propositions ne peut que vous donner connaissance de ses résolutions."

Ce qui caractérise surtout cette décision, c'est la demande directe et officielle adressée au Gouvernement Français par la Chambre de commerce de la Capitale.

Le gouvernement est prié de résoudre immédiatement " ces questions internationales de si haut intérêt."

Il s'agit de protéger la vie sur mer; le vœu du commerce de Paris sera exaucé, car il est partagé par l'opinion unanime des autorités citées plus haut.

En même temps que nous nous adressions aux chambres de commerce, nous consultions également les deux grandes compagnies maritimes des messageries et transatlantique ; elles emploient un nombreux personnel de marins, et leurs bâtiments ont eu plusieurs fois des collisions ; la dernière, avec son *Saint-Germain*, venait d'avoir, dans le jugement de Londres du 7 décembre 1883, des ennuis sérieux. Nous espérions donc qu'elles s'intéresseraient à la question.

La Compagnie des messageries, dans sa lettre du 5 mai 1885, nous a répondu: "Nous n'avons dû que prendre connaissance avec intérêt du dossier que vous nous avez transmis ; mais les questions qui s'y trouvent traitées dépassent évidemment la sphère de notre action ; c'est seulement en s'adressant au Département de la Marine que M. Riondel peut, suivant nous, espérer arriver à une solution en ce qui touche les sujets spéciaux qui font l'objet de son travail."

La Compagnie transatlantique n'a exprimé aucune opinion.

Toutes ces différentes pièces composent le second dossier.

Le président de la Chambre de commerce du Havre nous avait donné le conseil, dans sa lettre du 18 juin 1885, de nous mettre en relations avec deux congrès internationaux qui devaient se réunir : le premier, le 18 août, à Hambourg, et le second, à Anvers, le 27 septembre 1885. Nous avons suivi ce conseil ; par l'intermédiaire des deux consuls de France dans ces deux villes, nous nous sommes mis en relations avec les présidents des deux conférences ; nous avons trouvé chez eux l'accueil le plus encourageant.

Le président du Congrès d'Hambourg, M. le docteur Sieveking, président du Tribunal civil supérieur des villes hanséatiques, a mis une grande insistance, pour nous engager à aller traiter, en personne, la question devant la Conférence ; c'est ce qui nous a déterminé à faire le voyage de Paris, et à adresser, au président du Conseil et aux deux ministres des affaires étrangères et de la marine, une demande qui n'a pas été accueillie.

Nous avons résumé en quatre notes séparées qui ont été envoyées au président du Congrès d'Anvers, les diverses propositions qui résultaient, non seulement de l'étude de la collision du *Saint-Germain* et du *Wood-burn*, mais encore des divers travaux que nous avons faits plus tard, jusqu'à la fin de septembre. Nous n'avions présenté qu'une seule note à la première conférence de Hambourg.

Nous n'avions pas dû communiquer aux deux congrès les résolutions de la Chambre de commerce de Paris ; ces deux assemblées auraient sans doute pris des conclusions du même genre.

Comme nous l'avons dit plus haut, la Chambre de Paris avait statué le 13 juillet ; mais ce n'est que par la lettre de son président (datée du 9 novembre), que nous avons eu connaissance de ses résolutions.

Les comptes-rendus des deux Congrès ne sont pas encore publiés ; on ne connait pas leurs résolutions ; toutefois, les deux lettres qui nous ont été écrites, par le secrétaire-général de la Conférence d'Hambourg, l'honorable M. Alexander, et par le baron de Lambermont, ministre d'État de Sa Majesté le roi des Belges, sont un témoignage manifeste de l'intérêt que les deux grandes assemblées internationales ont bien voulu porter à la question ; elles vont insérer les documents que nous avons soumis respectueusement à leur haute et bienveillante attention.

Ces pièces constituent le troisième dossier.

Une correspondance de Saint-Pétersbourg du 28 novembre (journal *Le Soleil*) annonce que la première de nos propositions vient d'être adoptée par l'assemblée générale des commandants d'escadre, des amiraux et capitaines de navires, qui s'est réunie dans ce but à Cronstadt.

APPENDIX C.

GENERAL DIVISION 13.—*"THE ESTABLISHMENT OF A PERMANENT MARITIME COMMISSION."*

(*a*) The composition of the Commission.

(*b*) Its power and authority.

As a member of the Committee appointed to consider and report on the above-named Division, I beg to submit for the consideration of this Committee the following remarks:

SECTION *b*. The problem to determine the power and authority of any International Commission has always been considered to be most difficult to solve, and this seems particularly to be the case when a Commission shall have to do with maritime matters.

The Second Northern Marine Conference held at Copenhagen, July, last year—which consisted of about 200 delegates from the greater part of all existing maritime institutions in Norway, Sweden, Denmark, and Finland, and which represented a merchant fleet of a registered tonnage between 2,000,000 and 3,000,000 tons, ranging in order of all merchant fleets as the second or third—unanimously passed a resolution by which the establishment of a " Permanent International Marine Commission " with a Bureau, was recommended, and also that a memorandum to this effect should be presented to the present " International Marine Conference" at Washington.

This memorandum, which also has been distributed to the distinguished members of this Committee, will clearly show that it was not the intention of the Northern Conference that the proposed "International Marine Commission," with permanent Bureau, should have any power or authority at all, and therefore in no way would interfere with the sovereignty of the different contracting powers. On the contrary it should only form the connecting link between the different maritime Governments and countries in all maritime matters of an international character. It should also be composed as much as possible in conformity with the Commisssions or Conferences and their permanent bureaus, established under the Conventions about an international "Meter" Measure, about the international "Postage," and the international "Telegraphy," which have acted with so much benefit to international intercourse.

As before said, the " Northern Conference" of 1888 proposed both a permanent international marine commission, *consisting of delegates* from all maritime nations, and a permanent " Marine Bureau."

Though in accordance with the principle of these proposals, I think it expedient, at present, by the experience gained during the sittings of the present Conference, only to offer some suggestions as to the establishment of a permanent international marine department or bureau. The views entertained on the composition and mode of action of a "Permanent International Maritime Commission" seem at present to vary too much. For instance, in a report presented to the present Conference by several French marine societies, dated Havre, August 6, 1889, it is recommended (page 104–126) to establish a " Tribunal Suprême International établi en pays neutre, et composé de magistrat internationaux pour juger *souverainement,* en fait et en droit, les jugements nationaux en dernier ressort, qui lui seraient déférés. * * *"

As far as I know the general opinion is, that the time for such an institution has not come, and will not come for many years.

In the report presented by the branch hydrographic office, New York City, it is only said about the permanent commission mentioned in Division b:

"The establishment of such a commission is to be generally desired, and much good can be done by providing for an annual meeting for the purpose of regulating maritime affairs."

"The composition of the commission and its powers and authority should be settled by the Conference, and can become a part of the international agreement."

Maybe the present International Conference will not be actually dissolved, but only adjourned, in order to assist in the further steps necessary for carrying into effect its proposals and recommendations, and so for some time at least could perform the part of an international maritime commission.

In consideration of these circumstances the following remarks only apply to the establishment of an international department or bureau, which of course would have no other power or authority than that which would result from the knowledge that all international maritime matters taken up by such an institution would be treated with impartiality and by the best practical and scientific experts which can be procured in the whole world.

Section (a). As to the formation of the said institution I particularly wish to draw the attention of the committee to the rules for the inter national bureaus established according to the " Réglements annexés á la convention postale internationale, Paris, June 1, 1878, Art. 16, et á la convention télégraphique internationale de St. Petersburg. Revision de Berlin le 17 Septembre, 1885," et à l'Union internationale pour la publication des tarifs douaniers. Bruxelles, 1888.

In accordance with the principles laid down in these regulations the international department in question should be established in a great maritime city—presumably in London—and should, if no international marine commission is established, be under the supervision of the foreign office in the country where it is domiciled. This department would then be the intermediate link between the Governments as to the regular and general communications respecting the international sides of merchant shipping questions. Its principal duty should be to collect and arrange all sorts of information in respect to international maritime laws or regulations, to prepare the proposals received from the contracting Governments, maritime institutions, or private persons, for the consideration of future international marine conferences, and on the whole to perform the different inquiries or other special tasks in-trusted to it by the contracting powers. It should take charge of all the necessary publications and the correspondence with the different Governments, as well as with the different maritime institutions and the public in general.

The department should also prepare a yearly report of its labors and forward it to the maritime departments in the contracting States.

It should have a staff consisting of a chief secretary, three or four assistant secretaries, and the necessary number of clerks, etc.

The chief secretary should attend the future maritime conferences and take part in the discussion, but without the right of voting.

The common yearly expenses of this institution might probably be estimated at about 300,000 francs yearly, which is 200,000 francs higher than the yearly expenses for the international postage bureau at Berne, and 175,000 francs higher than the expenses for the bureau of the intended "International Custom Tariff Commission" at Brussels; but having regard to the importance of the maritime department, its more costly residence, and the practical trials with light and fog apparatus, etc., which must be expected, it is not safe to estimate the yearly ex- penses at a lower sum. This sum might, perhaps, be defrayed by the contracting powers in proportion to the number of their merchant ships above 100 tons gross tonnage, or in the manner settled by other inter- national conventions.

If it is asked who should appoint the officers belonging to such an institution, I should think that the simplest way would be to advertise over the whole world that an international maritime department is to be established with secretaries and clerks, and then, if no international maritime commission is in existence, leave it to delegates from the con- tracting powers, nominated expressly for that purpose, to make the selection among the applicants. The voting might perhaps be given according to the above-named proportion, and the said delegates would no doubt be careful to select the officers from different countries in or- der to secure the greatest possible knowledge of the different languages.

As will be seen, there is nothing new or original in this plan, as it is only continuing in well-known and tried paths laid down by earlier in- ternational conventions.

That such an institution would be a great benefit for all the countries which do not own such an excellent department as the "British Board of Trade," is self-evident. Almost every maritime reform which is asked for in the different countries must be considered also from an interna- tional point of view, but at present it is often rather difficult to get the necessary information in this respect; while, if such a department existed, in a short time and in a most reliable manner, the necessary information would easily be obtained. This would no doubt assist the various Governments considerably in carrying through the proposed new maritime laws, as certainly the advice and recommendations from such an international institution would be listened to with respect, and, if otherwise acceptable, followed by the legislative assemblies. I should also think that if such a department had existed before the present Conference took place, much labor and time would have been spared. Many important questions raised, which are now dropped, in want of any institution to get them inquired into and tried, would also then get a proper treatment. For instance, in looking into the valuable report of the "Committee on Systems and Devices," I find the following re- marks on several proposals on night-signaling, etc.:

No. 5. "This signal-lantern appears a good lamp, and is well reported on by U. S. Naval officers."

No. 27. "Light house fog-horn." "Not within the scope of the Con- ference as regards light-houses, but is worth a trial on board ship."

No. 37. "Lamp without a wick." "Committee can not pronounce an opinion without comparing this lamp with others at sea."

S. Ex. 53, pt. 3——26

No. 23. "New system of lamps and electric buoy." "Committee can not pronounce an opinion without seeing them at sea."

No. 25. "White flash stern-light with model." "Worth the consideration of Conference if occulting stern-lights are introduced."

Here the question must strike every one, Who is to take care of these recommendations and who is to make the necessary trials?

As a member of the "Committee on Sound-Signals," I have also had the opportunity of looking into a great part of the seventy or eighty inventions or proposals as to fog-signals. Though some of these must be considered as valuable, and when the time is ripe perhaps will be introduced in practice, I am afraid that no official notice will be taken of them, and that they therefore will be lost to the maritime world. On the contrary, if such an international institution existed, all such proposals and plans would be forwarded to it, registered there, compared with other proposals in the same direction, and, if possible, tried in practice. If the department should be unable to do so with its own means, there would certainly be many maritime countries which willingly would, on an application to them from the department, take the matter in hand and get the wished-for trials executed.

The reports from the other committees have not yet been laid before the Conference, and it is therefore not easy to know if the matters treated by them have been found to be of such a character that they ought to be arranged by international agreements, or should be left only to be made by local rules. If the questions are to be arranged according to international agreements, I do not see how it at present can be done, whereas, if the said international department existed, the valuable recommendations could be instantly acted on and carried into effect in a comparatively short time.

If it is asked what maritime matters, other than those contained in the programme, would by and by come under the care of said department, I should wish to draw the attention of the committee to the fact that, in the opinion of the oft-mentioned Northern Conference, there are several other matters which are of such a character that they ought to be arranged according to international agreements.

Of such matters there are named and shortly treated in the memorandum presented to the present International Conference the following:

1. International tonnage measurement.

2. Agreements for preventing the transfer of unseaworthy vessels to the flags of other nations.

3. Uniform quarantine regulations.

4. International uniformity in the law of damages caused by collision at sea.

5. Uniform salvage regulations.

6. International uniformity in the law of general average.

7. International uniformity in the law of affreightment and bills of lading.

I only mention these questions in order to show that there are a number of international maritime questions which should be prepared by a department of the said kind to be laid before future International Maritime Conferences.

The maritime institutions in the north of Europe take the greatest interest in this question, and the standing committees of the Northern Maritime Conferences have expressly wished that I should do my best to gain the good will of the present International Conference for the plan herein mentioned. I therefore sincerely hope that this important committee will see its way to meet the wishes of the Northern Conference by recommending the establishment of an international institution of the described kind.

Finally, I may add that the Scandinavian ship-owners have so keenly felt the want of a headquarters that they, in this year, have established a common central maritime bureau at Copenhagen, wholly at their own expense.

Washington, November 25, 1889.

AUG. SCHNEIDER,
Delegate for Denmark.

The COMMITTEE APPOINTED TO CONSIDER AND REPORT ON GENERAL DIVISION 13.

APPENDIX D.

RAPPORT SUR LE PROGRAMME DE L'AMIRAL FRANKLIN, PRÉSIDENT DE LA CONFÉRENCE MARITIME INTERNATIONALE DE WASHINGTON.

UNION SYNDICALE MUTUALISTE DES INSCRITS MARITIMES DU HAVRE ET SYNDICATS DE NAVIGATEURS FRANÇAIS ADHÉRENTS.

[Par M. T. Augé, capitaine au long cours, président de l'Union Syndicale Mutualiste des Inscrits Maritimes du Havre, membre de plusieurs sociétés savantes.]

CHAPITRE XIII.—COMMISSION INTERPERMANENTE, SA COMPOSITION, SES POUVOIRS ET LES TRIBUNAUX INTERNATIONAUX.

La mer libre n'est la propriété de personne, elle est d'un usage commun à tous les peuples navigateurs. Le développement de la navigation avec les engins modernes, les richesses immenses que l'on confie à la mer, les bienfaits économiques, qui en résultent pour tous les peuples de la terre, ont nécessairement de tous les temps appelé l'attention des gouvernements civilisés sur l'usage que les navigateurs font et doivent faire de cette mer libre, qui n'est et ne saurait être, ni le patrimoine commun des peuples maritimes, ni le patrimoine particulier d'aucune nation.

Chaque nation, chaque peuple maritime, a le droit de faire dans la mer libre tout ce qui lui convient, à la condition cependant de ne pas nuire à la liberté d'autrui.

Et c'est de ce principe vrai, que découle le droit incontestable pour les gouvernements maritimes de régler impersonnellement et dans un intérêt commun, l'usage de cette mer libre, usage, nous l'avons dit, qui ne doit avoir pour bornes que la liberté des autres ; de là, la condition essentielle que tous les peuples qui naviguent soient soumis à cette loi commune qui règle l'excercice que l'on doit faire de cette propriété neutre, qui ne saurait avoir un maître et dont l'usage est imprescriptible.

La Conférence doit donc être composée des représentants de tous les peuples maritimes, et ses pouvoirs peuvent alors s'exercer légitimement, sur tous les actes de la navigation, qui ont un caractère d'intérêt général commun à tous les navigateurs, pour l'usage qu'ils font de cette mer libre ; en un mot, pour protéger la liberté d'autrui, dans l'exexcice de sa propre liberté.

Et, c'est pour cela qu'il est nécessaire aujourd'hui en présence des dangers que font courir les bateaux rapides aux autres navigateurs, que les nations civilisées se réunissent, pour poser les bases d'un code international commun à tous les peuples maritimes ; et établissent des règles fixes pour les conflits internationaux qui peuvent surgir dans cette mer libre et pour éviter les catastrophes fréquentes qui font gémir l'humanité.

La Conférence de Washington d'après le programme na pas d'autre but.

Pour arriver à des résultats pratiques, nous pensons qu'après la vérification des pouvoirs des délégués la Conférence devrait se diviser en cinq commissions, et siéger en permanence jusqu'à ce qu'une solution définitive sorte de ses travaux :

1° Une commission révisant le règlement international de 1884 composée de marin-manœuvriers ayant exercé de longs commandements à la mer à la voile et à la vapeur ;

2° Une commission pour examiner les signaux visuels de jour et de nuit, phoniques etc. Composée de marins-timoniers, car il faut pour cela être spécialiste, avoir des connaissances particulières sur cette partie du programme ;

3° Une commission de marins-ingénieurs, étudiant la navigabilité des navires, le tirant d'eau, les bouées et balises, enfin tout ce qui concerne le génie maritime ;

4° Une commission de marins-hydrographes, étudiant le tracé des routes d'aller et de retour sur les cartes à l'usage des rapides, pour les points les plus fréquentés par ces sortes de navires ;

5° Une commission de marins-légistes, pour établir les règles qui doivent prévenir les conflits, et régler tout ce qui concerne la procédure, entre navires de nations différentes.

Les cinq spécialités ci-dessus indiquées se rencontreront certainement dans les délégués des seize nations adhérentes, et à cette condition, l'œuvre de la Conférence sera féconde et pratique, nous ne saurions en douter ; la nomination des délégués des États-Unis et la spécialité connue des membres qui la composent, nous est un sûr garant du succés, si les autres nations, comme il n'y a pas lieu d'en douter, s'inspirent des mêmes idées, et des mêmes sentiments.

Nous allons, dans ce dernier rapport, traiter les réformes et les créations qui nous semblent nécessaires, sans toucher au droit des gens, pour arriver à la solution pratique du problème qu'à notre avis devra résoudre la cinquième commission de la Conférence.

Cette grave question de juridiction internationale est une des plus délicates qu'ait à traiter le Congrès, et cependant elle est des plus nécessaires et des plus urgentes á résoudre ; nous croyons que, sans froissement aucun, elle peut être résolue d'une manière équitable et pratique, sans empiéter sur les droits souverains de chacune des puissances contractantes.

Prétendre créer des tribunaux internationaux à un ou deux degrés, dans les grandes métropoles maritimes, ne nous paraît pas pratique.

Il suffirait, selon nous, d'un tribunal suprême international établi en pays neutre, et composé de magistrats internationaux pour juger *souverainement*, en fait et en droit, les jugements nationaux en dernier ressort, qui lui seraient déférés. La procédure serait simple et peu coûteuse ; elle aurait lieu sur requête, sans ingérence d'avocats ni d'avoués.

Les documents de la cause, les dits, les contre-dits fournis par les parties, le tribunal prononcerait souverainement dans un délai déterminé.

Ce tribunal aurait dans sa compétence, au point de vue des réparations civiles, toutes les contestations résultant de délits et de quasi délits, par suite de violation du règlement international relatif aux collisions.

Pour les tribunaux nationaux, devant connaître de ces réparations civiles jusqu'en dernier ressort, une simple règle de procédure, qui se pratique même souvent dans les pays hors d'Europe par nécessité, devenue générale, suffirait, à notre avis, comme réforme des tribunaux nationaux, pour juger les questions d'abordages.

On a parlé de célérité dans les affaires de ce genre, en matière de procédure maritime devant les tribunaux de commerce français, et même ailleurs, comme devant l'amirauté anglaise, la procédure est ce qu'il y a de plus sommaire et de plus rapide.

En France, un procès maritime n'est point long ; il a d'abord la priorité pour le rôle ; il ne faut que le temps moral et nécessaire pour l'instruction ; ce sont parfois le ou les experts qui ne sont pas prêts pour leur rapport, ou même le plus souvent les avocats des parties qui font remettre l'affaire.

N'importe quels tribunaux que l'on créerait sous n'importe quelle dénomination, ces tribunaux ne pourraient moralement être plus expéditifs que nos tribunaux de commerce, successeurs de nos anciennes amirautés.

Ces tribunaux ont-ils toujours, en *fait*, toute la compétence nécessaire pour prononcer sur des faits purement techniques ?

Parfois, selon la composition du tribunal, et toujours, par des experts techniques ayant beaucoup navigué.

Par là, on comprend le rôle considérable que jouent les experts dans les questions maritimes internationales soumises à l'appréciation des tribunaux, questions spéciales s'il en fut, car, quiconque n'a pas navigué ne peut se rendre un compte bien exact des *faits* purement techniques qu'il peut être appelé à juger. Nous sommes sur ce point en désaccord avec les arrêts de la Cour de cassation du 2 juillet 1828 et 13 décembre 1842.[*]

Dans la vie ordinaire, bien que l'on n'exerce pas une profession, l'ensemble des connaissances générales que l'on peut posséder, permettent d'avoir un aperçu de cette profession. La vue, les relations, les entretiens avec des hommes compétents, la vérification d'un fait, toujours facile et possible par soi-même, peuvent permettre à tout homme éclairé, d'avoir une idée de la chose qui est soumise à son appréciation, ou à son jugement.

Ce serait une grande erreur de croire qu'il peut en être ainsi des faits techniques passés à la mer entre ciel et eau. L'équipage lui-même, rompu au métier, souvent ne peut se rendre compte, sur le coup, de la situation et des causes qui ont pu motiver une manœuvre de préférence à une qui semblait naturellement indiquée, et les magistrats consulaires ou autres qui ne son pas de la partie, malgré leur plus grande science juridique, il faut bien le dire, sont certainement ignorants des causes qui ont déterminés les *faits* qu'ils sont appelés à juger, ne les connaissant que par le rapport des experts.

La pierre angulaire de toute procédure pour des faits maritimes se rattachant aux collisions, réside dans l'intégrité des experts et dans la fidélité litérale de la traduction des documents servant de base légale au procès. Le rapport des experts en ces matières est généralement homologué, c'est donc ces derniers qui en *fait* sont les véritables juges, les magistrats prenant leurs décisions sur leurs dires et n'étant et un mot que l'écho de leurs conclusions.

En vain, nous dirait-on, que le droit peut parfois être appliqué différemment à des faits déterminés ; ceci est possible, mais pas en matière d'abordage ; si le contraire a eu lieu, c'est que les documents relatant les faits n'étaient pas les mêmes, et s'ils étaient les mêmes, ils n'étaient pas traduits par la même personne.

Voici, à notre avis, ce qu'il serait important de faire pour que le tri-

---

[*] Ces arrêts disent : " Les juges sont aussi souverains appréciateurs de l'abordage—ils peuvent se dispenser d'avoir recours à une expertise s'ils trouvent dans la cause des éléments suffisants de décision "—nous sommes contraire à cette doctrine, estimant que la justice ne saurait jamais être trop éclairée.

bunal ayant à se prononcer sur un fait international d'abordage donnât une entière garantie d'impartialité aux parties, sans toucher à l'organisation judiciaire.

Il faudrait que dans toutes les affaires de ce genre le rapport de l'affaire fut fait par trois experts et jamais par un seul, avec mission d'arbitre ; procédure *néfaste* que donne à un homme, sans responsabilité, le droit que la loi dénie à un seul magistrat.

Si les parties veulent régler amiablement leur litige, rien de mieux, mais alors quelles nomment leurs arbitres en dehors du tribunal. Les trois experts seraient nommés, un par le tribunal et les autres par chacune des parties

Le défendeur ou l'ajourné assisterait ainsi par *représentation*, à l'instruction de l'affaire, il serait certain de l'exactitude des documents traduits versés aux procès, ainsi que du sens technique des dépositions de l'équipage de l'un ou de l'autre navire.

Les experts pourraient être de n'importe quelle nationalité, à l'exception de celui nommé par le tribunal, bien entendu, que les autres devraient parler la langue dans la quelle le rapport serait fait, c'est là *l'innovation*.

En vain objecterait-on que cela ne modifierait pas le Code, différent, suivant le pays où le litige serait jugé.

Nous répondrons que cette différence de Code, en matière d'abordage, n'a au fond qu'une faible importance, si toutefois elle en a ; que s'il est différent quant aux règles de procédure, il ne l'est radicalement jamais au fond ; que toutes les nations policées ont dans leurs lois ce principe d'équité et de justice : que quiconque par sa faute porte préjudice à autrui est tenu de le réparer. Or, le principal est l'appréciation de la faute, c'est-à-dire de connaître laquelle des deux parties·a violé le règlement international ; le Code particulier de chaque pays, si différent qu'il soit, n'a rien à voir à cette constatation du *fait*, qui est universelle.

Il en est de même pour l'évaluation des dommages. Un cas seulement peut offrir certaines divergences pour l'application de la *pénalité ;* c'est quand il y a faute commune ; le mot douteux étant impropre dans ce cas, la répartition des dommages entre les parties n'est pas la même dans les différents Codes. Nous estimons, nous, qu'il est facile d'y remédier ; la faute commune ne pouvant être assimilée aux cas fortuits, il y aurait à prendre un terme moyen ; faire masse des dommages et diviser par moitié, comme l'indique l'art. 407 du Code francais, en changeant cependant, pour plus de clarté, les mots *s'il y a doute dans les causes*, par ceux-ci : *s'il y a faute commune, quand il y aurait doute dans les causes, il y aurait cas fortuit.*

Il est en France une institution vermoulue qui est en contradiction formelle avec les principes qui régissent son gouvernement, qui, lors de l'existence des droits *prohibitifs* de douane, pouvait, selon le dire de bien des gens, avoir sa raison d'être, bien que nous n'en pensions rien. Elle était, disent-ils, l'auxiliaire du fisc pour la surveillance; comme depuis longtemps notre régime douanier a été reformé, que des Docks-Entrepôts ont été créés dans tous les ports, où les matières soumises encore à de fortes taxes entrent ; par la création de ces Docks-Entrepôts, on peut dire que la douane a les navires et les marchandises dans sa main, et par suite, un contrôle facile et constant des déclarations faites à l'entrée par le capitaine.

Cette institution caduque n'a aucune raison d'être ; ses services, vis-à-vis de l'État sont nuls et vis-à-vis du commerce maritime, pour ses rapports avec la douane, inutiles et très onéreux.

La preuve de son inutilité, c'est que nos plus grands armateurs se privent de ses services ; il ne sont donc pas indispensables, un simple commis fait sa besogne.

Et la preuve qu'ils sont très onéreux, c'est que bien des navires étrangers ne veulent plus venir dans certains ports pour ne pas être taxés et rançonnés pour des services que leurs capitaines ou le consignataire du navire peuvent faire !

Cette institution pèse d'un poids considérable sur les relations maritimes de certains ports avec l'étranger et surtout dans les affaires litigieuses, bien que la compétence, en fait, des courtiers maritimes soit toujours contestable, cette ingérence a une influence pernicieuse sur la procédure, les courtiers étant les traducteurs des documents ; les navires sont, en outre, frappés d'une taxe obligatoire par la force des choses, allant en moyenne à un franc par tonneau de jauge, non pas au profit de la navigation, ni des œuvres du port, mais de huit ou neuf personnes, jouissant d'un monopole exclusif, alors que les pouvoirs publics se privent trop souvent de certaines améliorations d'intérêt général, pour ne pas frapper les navires de taxes nouvelles dont ils sont déjà surchargés.

Ce monopole est aujourd'hui le plus grand obstacle au développement du commerce maritime avec l'étranger.

La France et le commerce maritime ont tout à gagner à la disparition de ce scandaleux monopole.

Il y a longtemps que pour l'intérêt économique du pays il ne devrait plus exister.

La France est la seule nation maritime qui ait conservé cette institution surannée. Singulière chose, l'on s'acharne à soutenir qu'elle est nécessaire pour l'intérêt des navires étrangers, quand ces mêmes navires déclarent et proclament qu'elle leur est inutile et agissent même auprès de leurs gouvernements pour qu'ils négocient avec le Gouvernement Français l'abolition de ces charges onéreuses, de courtiers maritimes. Les revendications fréquentes des courtiers devant les tribunaux pour faire respecter leur monopole sont la preuve la plus éclatante de leur inutilité et de leur impopularité.

Ces officiers ministériels, à l'abri de leur monopole, ont seuls le droit de traduire les documents de procédure ou autres, devant les tribunaux de commerce, et c'est pour cette dernière fonction incompatible, moralement avec la première, que la question des courtiers maritimes nous intéresse et que nous nous sommes occupés d'eux dans ce rapport.

C'est comme truchement avec la douane et comme interprètes jurés que nous demandons une réforme radicale ; cette double fonction pèse sur leurs traductions, ces dernières, pour ce qui est des faits, peuvent paraître parfois nébuleuses et équivoques ; et pourraient ainsi changer par leurs indécisions même, la face d'un procès, si les experts chargés de l'examen des *faits* ne connaissaient pas la langue dans laquelle le rapport des capitaines est écrit. Mieux vaudrait une traduction littérale, que la loi et la morale exigent, qu'une traduction qui, quelque fois pourrait avoir la prétention d'expliquer le fond d'une cause qui, par sa nature, ne peut être sérieusement connue du traducteur.

Et, par une anomalie incompréhensible, c'est toujours le courtier truchement du navire, qui traduit les documents du capitaine demandeur ou défendeur dont il est le mandataire, et c'est cette traduction des documents du litige fait par ce mandataire qui sert, et servira de *base* à toute la procédure ; le courtier est souvent à l'insu des magistrats et des experts, juge en sa propre cause. Qu'on examine de près cette question, qui n'a rien de comparable dans aucune législation, et l'on verra le bien fondé de nos observations ; c'est une énormité scandaleuse, qu'on est étonné de voir subsister encore, car les fonctions d'interprètes jurés, cumulées avec celles de *negotiorum gestor* sont immorales.

Nous estimons, dans un intérêt de justice, que les interprètes jurés près les tribunaux compétents pour juger les contestations internationales maritimes dans tous les pays, doivent être des officiers relevant du tribunal, et ces fonctions incompatibles avec celles de mandataire officiel ou officieux du capitaine ou de l'armateur qui est en cause.

C'est en général de la traduction du rapport et de l'interrogatoire de l'équipage, que l'on connait les circonstances de la cause, expliquant les événements ; c'est de la traduction littérale du rapport du Capitaine, narration fidèle des faits que les experts déduiront leurs conclusions.

Comment admettre que ce soit l'homme du demandeur ou du défendeur qui traduise ces *faits* énoncés à un moment où le capitaine ne pouvait prévoir la procédure, témoignage précieux de l'exactitude des faits, et auquel la loi attache une importance capitale.

Malgré toute la délicatesse de son caractère et des fonctions qu'il remplit, un doute doit nécessairement planer sur la traduction d'un courtier maritime qui, dans l'intérêt de son client, dirige la procédure ; difficilement un avocat montrerait au tribunal une pièce, un document qui pourrait être préjudiciable à son client, il ne montrerait que ceux qui pourraient être utiles à sa thèse ; il n'est pas malhonnête pour cela, il défend l'intérêt de son client qui le paye ; le courtier maritime fait de même.

Nous pensons donc qu'il est de la plus grande urgence que le monopole des courtiers maritimes en France soit aboli, et que dans tous les pays maritimes les interprètes près les tribunaux qui jugent les matières maritimes internationales soient des fonctionnaires, attachés au tribunal, n'ayant intérêt, ni moral, ni matériel dans les litiges, n'ayant aucun rapport avec la profession d'agent maritime.

De cette manière, à notre avis, les documents remis aux experts seraient la représentation exacte, littérale des faits arrivés, traduction faite par des hommes complètement désintéressés à la solution positive ou négative du litige, traduction faite sans aucun artifice.   Combien d'abus se sont produits à l'insu de bien des gens, des traducteurs mêmes, dominés qu'ils étaient par les fonctions de mandataire d'une des parties ; ce dédoublement de la même personne dans les fonctions aussi délicates et aussi opposées ne peut être décemment maintenue, il est immoral, la Conférence a le droit d'en demander la suppression.

Voilà, selon nous, dans l'organisation de la procédure des tribunaux nationaux jugeant des questions internationales en matière d'abordage, les réformes à faire pour avoir une justice prompte, peu coûteuse, équitable, sincère et juste, donnant satisfaction aux droits des parties à quelque nation qu'elles appartiennent.

1º Nomination de trois experts, un par le tribunal qui doit connaître le litige, un par chacune des parties, sans obligation de nationalité ; si les parties n'avaient pas désigné leurs experts dans un certain délai, le Tribunal y suppléerait d'office.

2º Traduction des rapports et de l'interrogatoire de l'équipage par des traducteurs jurés autres que les courtiers maritimes ;

3º Compétence de juridiction et de procédure, telle qu'elle existe dans chaque pays pour juger les faits maritimes jusqu'en dernier ressort, en France jusqu'à l'arrêt d'appel, et dans les autres pays par analogie.

Une fois l'arrêt rendu, la partie qui se croirait, malgré les précautions prises que nous avons indiquées, soit pour la traduction, soit pour l'examen des faits être mal jugée, se pourvoirait devant le tribunal supérieur international, qui jugerait, tant en *fait* qu'en *droit*, le litige, et transmettrait par la voie diplomatique au ministre compétent du pays de la partie condamnée, une expédition traduite de la sentence finale. Cette dernière serait exécutée à la requête de la partie conformément aux lois du pays et dans les mêmes formes que l'exécution des arrêts souverains émanant de la juridiction nationale.

Le pourvoi devant le tribunal supérieur international ne serait pas suspensif, l'arrêt serait exécutoire par provision si, provision n'avait déjà été faite, signification du pourvoi serait faite dans les vingt-quatre heures au domicile de l'intimé, domicile indiqué dans l'arrêt, le délai de pourvoi serait d'un mois à partir de la signification de l'arrêt, d'avoué à avoué ou au domicile indiqué du lieu où l'arrêt a été rendu.

Les parties feraient élection de domicile, si elles étaient étrangères, au consulat du lieu de juridiction ou du lieu le plus rapproché qui aurait un consulat.

La transmission de la sentence souveraine, par le président du tribunal supérieur, équivaudrait à une demande d'*exequatur* qui, en vertu du règlement ou du pacte international, ne pourrait jamais être refusé.

Pour les collisions entre navires de guerre ou entre un navire de guerre ou assimilés, et un navire de commerce, l'examen de l'affaire ressortirait directement du tribunal supérieur international, sans passer, bien entendu, par les tribunaux nationaux.

Les procès verbaux et tous les documents conservatoires pour pouvoir ouvrir plus tard l'instance de devant le tribunal supérieur ou autre, seraient faits à la chancellerie du consulat ou du vice-consulat du pavillon; cependant, s'ils étaient faits contradictoirement, on procéderait devant le tribunal compétent du lieu, qui nommerait un expert et les parties, chacun un; ces derniers feraient les constatations, évalueraient les dommages; le navire procéderait à ses réparations, etc.

Le tribunal du lieu n'aurait qu'à donner la sanction légale aux actes, requêtes et ordonnances qui lui seraient remises ou demandées, en un mot comme l'on procède en matière d'avaries dans le port de relâche.

Les avaries n'étant réglées que plus tard, au lieu de reste du navire, dans l'espèce ce serait devant le tribunal supérieur; on agirait de même si ce tribunal du lieu n'était pas compétent pour juger le fond entre navires de commerce.

Il nous semble que de cette façon, aucune nation n'aurait abdiqué le droit de rendre la justice chez elle, conformément à ses lois et à ses mœurs. Le pourvoi devant le tribunal supérieur n'aurait certainement pas lieu dans tous les procès, les parties comme les tribunaux nationaux étant mieux et plus équitablement éclairés par la commission d'experts vraiment internationaux.

On regarderait à deux fois, auparavant de prendre une décision sachant que le tribunal souverain peut casser la sentence ou l'arrêt et le modifier.

Cette juridiction suprême ne serait, en un mot, selon nous, qu'un *arbitre* éclairé, indépendant, d'un conflit d'intérêts internationaux.

Ainsi dans l'affaire du *City of Mecca* avec le bâtiment portugais *Insulano*, il paraît que l'arrêt rendu à Lisbonne fut loin de donner satisfaction à l'Angleterre; comment trancher sans froissement cette difficulté, cette défiance? Par notre système d'experts internationaux, la sentence aurait d'abord pu être différente et en suite, en admettant qu'elle eût été la même, l'Angleterre mieux éclairée, n'aurait peut-être pas fait de récrimination; et, si malgré la Commission d'experts elle avait eu quand même un doute sur l'impartialité de l'arrêt, après avoir épuisé à Lisbonne le dernier ressort, elle se serait adressée au tribunal supérieur international qui, sur le vu des documents de la cause, traduits à nouveaux par des traducteurs jurés, les faits nouvellement examinés par des experts jurés nommés par lui; rapport d'experts qui aurait été communiqué aux parties ou, dans un temps fixé, elles auraient eu la faculté de fournir des contre-dits. La sentence de Lisbonne aurait été maintenue ou réformée en tout ou en partie, et cette nouvelle sentence définitive aurait terminé l'affaire; tous devant s'incliner au prononcé de ce verdict désintéressé.

Si nous ne nous trompons, le ministre anglais, à Lisbonne, demandait à soumettre le jugement à une Cour d'appel internationale, notre manière de voir est au fond, sinon dans la forme, pareille à la sienne.

Reste l'examen de la compétence du lieu où le litige doit être jugé.

Le droit de rendre la justice est un droit souverain que les Nations n'abdiquent pas avec raison facilement.

Or, un navire qui a commis des dommages ou fait des déprédations à un autre navire est nécessairement justiciable de la juridiction compétente du lieu où les dommages et les déprédations ont été commises, sauf à lui, s'il se trouve mal jugé en dernier ressort, d'en appeler au Tribunal supérieur international que nous demandons d'établir, nous entendons par lieu, la zône territoriale comme les ports, rades, fleuves, etc., à la condition qu'un des deux navires, le défendeur, sinon tous les deux, s'arrêtant dans un des ports du souverain de la zône, où les dommages ou les déprédations ont été commis, et puisse y recevoir l'assignation ou même la protestation, peu importe son déplacement ultérieur.

Les dommages faits et les déprédations commis à un navire dans la *mer libre* doivent être justiciables des tribunaux compétents du domicile du défendeur.

Celui qui a commis un crime ou un délit ou quasi-délit, dans la mer libre, est nécessairement justiciable des tribunaux respectifs de son pays, le navire dans la mer libre étant la continuation de la patrie, continuation qui cesse et qui doit cesser dès qu'on est chez un autre souverain, excepté pour les contestations civiles et administratives, entre le capitaine et l'équipage et même les passagers embarqués dans un port du pavillon du navire, le contrat que lie toutes ces personnes entre elles, n'étant pas un contrat *universel* mais un contrat spécial, tenant souvent aux lois intérieures d'un état, comme en France, par exemple, où par *l'inscription maritime*, le capitaine ne peut être autorisé à laisser à l'étranger un homme inscrit; on comprend que si la juridiction du lieu est compétente pour connaître de tous les actes civils que traite un capitaine au point de vue du commerce, en général, et comme conducteur du navire et mandataire de l'armateur. Il n'en est plus de même des contrats qui se forment naturellement par les lois du pays du pavillon, par le seul fait de l'inscription sur le rôle d'équipage. Les hommes ainsi engagés ont accepté la loi spéciale du pays et les tribunaux étrangers au pavillon ne sauraient l'interpréter étant censés l'ignorer, sauf les traités sur les capitulations.

En matière civile et commerciale pour le sujet qui nous occupe, il y a deux domiciles distincts pour le défendeur.

Le domicile du propriétaire du navire, et le domicile conventionnel du capitaine à son bord, et dans le lieu où se trouve le navire au moment des poursuites, peu importe le déplacement antérieur.

On pourrait nous objecter, que souvent il est difficile de savoir lequel est le défendeur; nous répondrons qu'à moins que les assignations soient simultanées, il y en a toujours un qui commence, le second n'est donc demandeur que reconventionnellement et cette dernière qualité ne lui enlève pas celle de défendeur.

Mais, nous ferons encore observer que, dans les affaires qu'on pourrait nous citer comme les deux parties étant demanderesses, elles ne l'étaient précisément que pour échapper aux tribunaux étrangers et être jugées par les tribunaux de leur pays. La chose n'est plus la même, il n'y a que les tribunaux du domicile du *défendeur* de compétents ou ceux du lieu de relâche pour les quasi-délits commis dans la mer libre, et celui du lieu des dommages pour les quasi-délits commis sur le territoire d'un souverain.

Le domicile ainsi établi, il ne peut y avoir aucune contestation fondée sur le pays qui doit connaître du litige, parce qu'il est conforme aux droits des gens en ce que le défendeur n'est privé de ses juges naturels que par son déplacement émanant de sa volonté et de sa liberté.

Ce domicile n'empiète sur aucun droit souverain, bien que le demandeur ait le droit pour un quasi-délit *commis dans la mer libre,* entre le domicile du défendeur et le lieu où relâche le navire poursuivi, ce choix se justifie même par le peu de garantie que pourrait offrir dans certains endroits la juridiction territoriale; mais ce choix n'aggrave pas la situation du défendeur, puisque c'est devant les tribunaux de son pays qu'il sera poursuivi s'il ne l'est au lieu de relâche.

Et quant au conflit qui pourrait exister sur la qualité des parties, il ne serait pas à redouter; ou les arrêts seraient les mêmes, ou ils seraient divergents, celui qui se croirait lésé se pourvoirait devant le Tribunal supérieur international; mais, nous le répétons, nous ne croyons pas au conflit de juridiction, par la seule raison que ce qui les motive actuellement, disparaît par notre système.

Lorsque les dommages auraient été commis en un lieu appartenant à un souverain, à moins d'un accord des deux parties désignant un autre lieu de juridiction de *droit,* la juridiction du lieu serait compétente.

Cette manière d'établir la compétence du lieu nous paraît raisonnable et logique, et nous semble donner la satisfaction nécessaire que réclament des intérêts considérables, tout en respectant les droits souverains; elle offre de rendre une bonne et prompte justice, dont, du reste, si l'on était mal jugé, nous le répétons, le dernier mot appartiendrait au Tribunal international.

Dans certains pays, il n'y a pour les collisions qu'un seul degré de juridiction; en France il y en a deux, cette différence tient uniquement à l'organisation de la procédure dans les différents pays et aussi à la composition du corps judiciaire.

Le mal n'est pas dans un, ni dans deux degrés de juridiction, il est dans des traductions parfois inexactes, si elles ne sont pas littérales, et dans la commission d'experts où l'étranger n'a pas toujours toute la garantie désirable.

On doit désirer aussi la rapidité de la procédure; pour cela, il faut autant que possible la moins compliquer; elle ne l'est pas en France; mais malgré tout, ce qu'il faut, c'est une bonne et impartiale justice; c'est sans doute quelque chose d'aller vite; nous estimons qu'en ces matières, il vaut mieux encore aller bien.

Ces principes nettement établis, ne gêneraient en rien un navire, qui aurait des dommages, pour relâcher, puisque en quelque lieu qu'il se trouverait, il pourrait être légalement arrêté, sans que son gouvernement puisse élever un conflit; il n'aurait aucun intérêt à fuir; le droit d'arrêter un navire existerait sur la présentation de la protestation régulière et, sur requête, tant que l'action ne serait pas prescrite pour la saisie, le président du tribunal pourrait en outre exiger caution du saisissant.

Mais nous estimons aussi que le navire qui relâcherait pour plusieurs raisons et dans l'intérêt même du demandeur, pourrait continuer son voyage, quitte à donner caution égale aux dommages évalués et jusqu'à concurrence de la valeur estimée par la police d'assurance du défendeur; qu'il pourrait donner comme caution, le néantissement de cette même police d'assurance, en tout ou en partie, et empêcherait la saisie, ou enfin une hypothèque, soit du chiffre des dommages estimés, soit de tout le navire, espèce d'hypothèque légale ayant un rang privilégié sur toutes celles existantes, n'ayant avant elle que le privilège de l'équipage et celui des frais qui concouraient depuis le dommage à la conservation de la chose, excepté l'emprunt à la grosse, à moins qu'il ne fut pour ce dernier emprunt décidé autrement entre les parties.

La transcription de cette hypothèque légale, toute provisoire jusqu'à la fin du litige, serait faite sur l'acte de nationalité par le consul du défendeur; s'ils étaient tous les deux demandeurs, ils se garantiraient mutuellement jusqu'à la fin du litige, de cette façon la cession du navire serait impossible pendant la durée du procès.

Un navire qui serait nanti de l'un des moyens que nous avons décrits, n'aurait aucun intérêt à retenir l'autre dans le port, puisque pour une raison d'intérêt public, l'armateur n'est tenu de réparer, civilement, les actes licites ou illicites de son capitaine, que jusqu'à concurrence de la valeur du navire et du fret, sur lequel il faut déduire les privilèges qui l'absorbent presque toujours. Dans l'intérêt général, cette garantie nous parait suffisante. En Angleterre, elle est fixée suivant le tonnage, et il est prévu une augmentation s'il y a mort d'homme.

Il va sans dire que si le navire, ainsi hypothéqué, n'était pas assuré, le bénéficiaire de l'hypothèque aurait le droit de le faire assurer à son profit comme s'il en était le propriétaire, et que dans le cas de nantissement par la police et dans celui de perte du navire, dont la police serait donnée en nantissement, la somme due par l'assurance serait déposée avec un privilège spécial, sauf celui de l'équipage et des frais de justice, jusqu'à ce que le litige fût terminé.

En conséquence de tout ce qui précède, la commission de l'Union syndicale mutualiste des incrits maritimes du Havre formule les vœux suivants :

1° Qu'en matière d'abordage, les protestations soient faites conformément et dans les délais prescrits par la loi du pavillon de celui qui proteste, peu importe de quelle juridiction relèvera l'affaire ultérieurement, nul n'étant censé ignorer la loi de son pays ;

2° Que tous les tribunaux qui ont dans leurs attributions la connaissance des quasi-délits maritimes, contre navires de même nation ou de nations différentes aient auprès d'eux des interprètes jurés ne pouvant exercer les fonctions de courtiers de navires, ni de mandataires des parties ;

3° Qu'aucune procédure relative à une collision ne puisse venir en délibéré devant le tribunal compétent, sans être au préalable précédée d'un rapport fait par une Commission d'experts, composée de trois capitaines nommés : un par le tribunal, et un par chaque partie ; s'il y avait plus de deux parties, pour que le nombre fût toujours impair, le tribunal le rendrait impair en nommant deux experts.

Les experts nommés par les deux ou plusieurs parties pourraient être de n'importe quelle nationalité, à la condition toutefois d'être capitaines et de parler la langue du tribunal. Les ingénieurs, constructeurs, etc., servant à évaluer les dommages, n'auraient pas voix délibérative au rapport, ils seraient adjoints aux experts pour *fixer* les sommes seulement, et sous la responsabilité de ces derniers.

La minorité d'experts opposante aurait toujours la faculté de motiver son opposition dans le rapport ;

4° Que la compétence du lieu de juridiction en matière d'abordage, soit : 1° Le tribunal attributif du lieu où le quasi-délit a été commis ; 2° Le tribunal attributif du domicile de l'armateur ; 3° Le tribunal attributif du lieu de relâche du navire, au moment des poursuites, peu importe, tout déplacement antérieur ou ultérieur, le choix est au demandeur pour les deux derniers cas ; faculté aux parties pour le premier cas, de désigner, par un acte, le lieu qui doit trancher le litige, s'ils ne doivent pas se faire juger par le tribunal du lieu où le dommage a été commis ;

5° Que la procédure dans les domiciles sus-indiqués et dans le lieu où les dommages ont été commis, soit suivie sous les réserves des vœux 1, 2 et 3, conformément aux lois, règles et usages du pays, qui rend la justice jusqu'en dernier ressort ;

6° Que tout navire qui est actionné en réparations de dommages causés par lui, soit dans le lieu où il est actionné, soit dans la mer libre,

puisse continuer son voyage et sa navigation en donnant une caution
égale à la valeur entière du navire évaluée par sa police d'assurance,
ou par trois experts nommés, un par le consul du demandeur et les
autres par chacune des parties, et que la caution soit agréée du demandeur.

Que, de droit, le défendeur puisse offrir comme caution sa police
d'assurance par un *transfert motivé*, ou bien en donnant une hypothèque
légale, un privilège sur le navire n'étant primé que par les frais conservatoires, faits depuis le dommage au jour du règlement définitif.

Cette hypothèque comme le transfert de la police se ferait devant le
consul du défendeur, qui délivrerait au demandeur un duplicata du certificat d'inscription sur l'acte de nationalité indiquant le jour et l'heure,
et enverrait ce certificat au port d'attache, afin qu'aucune cession ne
puisse être faite légalement;

7° Qu'un Tribunal supérieur international jugeant souverainement en
fait et *droit* soit établi en pays neutre, siégeant toujours au nombre de
sept membres, magistrats internationaux, et composée d'une section
d'experts et d'une section de secrétaires (interprètes formant ainsi le
tribunal supérieur international);

8° Que le tribunal suprême, juge sur requête, sans ingérence d'avocats
ni d'avoués, sur la présentation des documents, jugements, arrêts, etc.,
etc.;—toute demande incidente pourrait être jointe au fond. Un nouveau rapport serait fait sur l'affaire par les experts du tribunal supérieur sur le vu des rapports des capitaines et de l'interrogatoire de
l'équipage nouvellement traduits par les secrétaires du tribunal. Le dit
rapport serait signifié aux parties qui auraient un mois pour le contre-
dire et, après ce délai, le tribunal prononcerait souverainement sur le
tout.

9° Que dans toute appréciation de dommages en matière d'abordage,
il y ait un *boni* de 10 pour cent au profit des hommes d'équipage du navire
qui auraient souffert les dommages par pertes d'effets, chômage, rupture
de contrat, excès de travaux, etc., et que dans le cas de blessures graves
ou mort d'hommes, un tarif établisse la pénalité et la réparation civile
pour chacun de ces accidents; les blessés et les ayants droit des décédés,
auraient un privilège sur l'indemnité accordée au demandeur. Les ama-
teurs auraient à faire couvrir ces nouveaux risques s'ils n'aimaient mieux
en supporter eux-mêmes la responsabilité.

10° Que si contrairement à notre manière de voir, par suite de traités
internationaux ou pour d'autres considérations de haute politique,
qu'il ne nous appartient pas d'apprécier les navires postaux étaient assimilés pour *la saisie* et autres faits de juridiction, aux navires de guerre
et relevaient par suite du Tribunal supérieur international dans l'intérêt
de l'indemnisé, après la sentence prononcée, la *subvention postale* serait
saisissable et par privilège jusqu'à concurrence de l'indemnité, intérêts
et dépens accordés au demandeur.

Tels sont les vœux que formule la commission de l'Union syndicale mutualiste des inscrits maritimes du Havre.

Havre, le 1ᵉʳ Juillet 1889.

AUGÉ.

Vu et approuvé les quartorze raports ci-dessus:

Par la Commission d'Études de l'Union Syndicale du Havre:

AUGÉ,

Capitaine au long cours, Membre de plusieurs Sociétés savantes françaises et étrangères, Président et Rapporteur.

E. VOIZARD,

Chevalier de la Légion-d'Honneur, Vice-Président.

V. DUREL,

Capitaine au long cours.

G. LEBOURHIS,

Capitaine au long cours.

CORBIÈRE,

Capitaine au long cours.

Pour le Syndicat des Capitaines au long cours de Marseille:

Le Président, BÉNIGNI,

Capitaine au long cours, Chevalier de la Légion-d'Honneur.

Pour le Syndicat des Capitaines-marins de la Méditerranée:

Le Président, J. BOUSQUET, C. M.

Pour l'Union des Corporations Maritimes du Midi:

Le Président, J. PÉTRIER,

C. A. L.-C. Officier d'Académie.

APPENDIX E.

COLLISIONS EN MER.

[Législation maritime internationale.—Note sur les tribunaux maritimes internationaux; étude de M. Favier avocat; opinion du Gouvernement des États-Unis, Congrès de Milan et d'Hambourg; responsabilité des compagnies. C. Albert Riondel, officier de la Légion d'Honneur.]

A M. FAVIER, *Avocat du Barreau de Cherbourg:*

Je vous dédie cet opuscule en témoignage de mon amitié. Vous avez bien voulu mettre votre expérience et votre science du droit au service de la question internationale des tribunaux maritimes. Je vous en remercie très affectueusement.

Sentiments les plus dévoués,

ALBERT RIONDEL.

PRÉFACE.

Au mois d'août 1883, nous avons étudié la collision du paquebot français *St-Germain* avec le bâtiment anglais *Woodburn* remorqué par le *Recovery*. Nous avons fait de cette étude une brochure. Nous l'avons

adressée à divers gouvernements et aux grandes Chambres de com·
merce françaises de Paris, Bordeaux, Marseille, le Havre et Nantes.
Nous faisions ressortir dans notre travail le vice de la législation actuellle.
Nous demandions la création de tribunaux maritimes internationaux
pour juger les litiges résultant des collisions en mer entre bâtiments de
nationalités différentes.

Le Gouvernement des États-Unis et le Gouvernement de Grèce ap-
prouvèrent le principe et l'utilité de cette création.   Les cinq Chambres
de commerce citées plus haut exprimèrent la même opinion.   Plus tard,
à la suite de 17 conférences faites dans les ports, en 1886, 1887 et 1888,
depuis Bayonne jusqu'à Dunkerque, les autres Chambres de commerce,
les Sociétés de géographie commerciale et les Conseils municipaux
émirent des vœux identiques.

Ces corporations dressèrent des résolutions écrites.   Elles les trans-
mirent directement au Gouvernement Français.   Le Conseil d'Amirauté
fut saisi de la question par l'amiral Aube, ministre de la marine.   Ce
Conseil émit à l'unanimité un avis conforme à celui des Chambres de
commerce au sujet de ces tribunaux.   L'Académie des Sciences, la Commission des pétitions de la Chambre des députés, les Congrès de Nantes,
de Hambourg et de Milan, plusieurs Chambres de commerce Étrangères
se montrèrent également favorables.   Tous ces documents sont publiés
dans deux brochures : la première a été imprimée à Cherbourg en 1886,
sous le titre : *Réforme internationale et tribunaux maritimes internationaux.*
La seconde s'imprime actuellement à Cherbourg chez Biard, 14, rue du
Château ; elle a pour titre : *Les Routes internationales de navigation,* et
elle formera la seconde partie de cet ouvrage.

Un avocat de Cherbourg, jurisconsulte réputé dans la Manche et le
Calvados, très expert dans les questions maritimes—M. Favier—s'est
intéressé à la question qui nous préoccupe.   Il avait assisté à la Conférence que nous fîmes à Cherbourg au mois de juin 1886.   Le travail de
M. Favier constitue la partie principale de cette brochure.   Nous le
faisons précéder d'une note sur les tribunaux maritimes internationaux,
que nous avons lue au VIIIe Congrès des 42 Sociétés de géographie ré-
unies à Nantes, au mois d'août 1886.   Le Congrès émit à l'unanimité un
vœu favorable à l'institution de ces tribunaux.

A la suite du travail de M. Favier, nous insérons le document du
Gouvernement des États-Unis, qui a été la base et le point de départ
de l'agitation française dont nous venons de parler.   Nous publions
après ce document une note relative aux deux congrès de Hambourg et
de Milan qui ont examiné et approuvé les propositions qui leur étaient
soumises.

La création des tribunaux maritimes internationaux a été attaquée
dans un livre récemment paru sur les collisions en mer.   Cet ouvrage
est de M. le commandant Banaré, chef du service des instructions nautiques.   Nous lui répondons dans une note spéciale.

Nous insérons aussi une étude sur la responsabilité des compagnies de navigation et la nécessité d'établir un tarif international protecteur de la vie humaine sur mer.

Nos conclusions sont faites avec beaucoup de réserve. Nous nous bornons simplement à quelques considérations. Notre but est avant tout d'appeler l'attention sur la nécessité de créer, en matière de collisions, des tribunaux internationaux à la place des tribunaux des nationalités, pour régler plus équitablement les litiges entre navires de nationalités différentes.

Le besoin d'une législation nouvelle résulte de l'unanimité des vœux nettement formulés par les intéressés. Le rapport du commissaire de la navigation des États-Unis rend la pensée commune en ces termes : " L'établissement d'un pareil tribunal épargnerait les dépenses, préviendrait beaucoup d'ennuis et apporterait plus d'harmonie dans l'interprétation donnée par les différentes nations aux lois sur les collisions. Il est probable que toutes les nations favoriseraient l'insertion (au moins en substance) de la deuxième clause proposée par M. Riondel et j'incline à recommander son adoption."

La solution pratique des tribunaux internationaux présentera certainement des difficultés, mais elles ne paraissent pas insurmontables à un homme de la valeur et de l'expérience de M. Favier.

D'autres jurisconsultes suivront probablement son exemple at essaieront de résoudre la question.

CRÉATION DES TRIBUNAUX MARITIMES INTERNATIONAUX.

Cette note a été lue, en séance publique, au Congrès de Nantes, le 8 août 1886, par M. le commandant Riondel.

Le Congrès, à l'unanimité, a émis un vœu favorable au projet. Le principe et l'utilité des tribunaux maritimes internationaux pour juger les litiges entre navires de nationalités différentes ont été reconnus :

1° Par les États-Unis, le 4 février 1885 ;

2° Par la Grèce ;

3° Par la Chambre de commerce du Havre ;

4° Par la Chambre de commerce de Paris ;

5° Par la Chambre de commerce de Bordeaux ;

6° Par la Chambre de commerce de Marseille ;

7° Par les Congrès d'Anvers et de Milan ;

8° Par le Conseil de l'amirauté française, le 25 avril 1886. *

Nous avons fait deux conférences dans les grands ports de commerce de Nantes et du Havre, le 18 mai et le 3 juillet 1886.

Ces deux assemblées ont approuvé l'idée.

M. le commissaire-général de la marine qui présidait la Conférence que nous avons faite au Havre, nous écrivait, le 9 juillet : " J'estime que, grâce à vos efforts, la question est assez mûre pour passer de la période des idées et des projets, à l'état définitif, c'est-à-dire à un pro-

---

*Un très grand nombre d'autres Chambres de commerce, françaises et étrangères, se sont associées à ce mouvement, depuis cette époque.

jet de convention internationale à discuter par des délégués de puissances."

Le chef du service de la marine qui assistait à la Conférence du Sport
Nautique de Nantes, le 18 mai dernier, nous écrivait, le 29 juin : "Je
relis l'organisation que vous proposez pour vos tribunaux internationaux d'États ; je la considère comme bonne et pratique. Cela me parait
excellent, et je crois que mon avis sera partagé par tous ceux qui exa-
mineront sérieusement la question."

Le 16 juillet, la Chambre de commerce de Saint-Nazaire nous disait :
" L'exécution de votre très intéressant projet est appelée, croyons-nous
à rendre les plus utiles services."

La Chambre de commerce du Havre ajoutait, le 24 juillet, dans son
dernier paragraphe : "Le Congrès d'Anvers, qui a examiné toutes ces
questions, a émis le vœu que les gouvernements se réunissent et s'en-
tendent pour en faire l'étude."

Un mois auparavant, le Congrès de Hambourg avait examiné nos propositions avec intérêt et pris des résolutions sur deux points. Le Congrès de Milan de 1883 avait approuvé le principe d'une cour d'appel internationale révisant les jugements des tribunaux.

L'Académie des Sciences a été saisie ; elle a nommé une commission
pour étudier l'affaire.

De nombreuses pétitions signées au Havre, à Cherbourg, Nantes,
Paris, Saint-Nazaire, Marseille, ont été adressées à la Chambre des
Députés. Le dépôt a été fait à la tribune par un député de la Loire-
Inférieure, M. le marquis de la Ferronnays.

Cette revue rétrospective indique surabondamment l'intérêt qui s'attache à la question que nous allons présenter brièvement à la haute attention du Congrès.

Le projet n'a rien de définitif. C'est une simple esquisse.

On trouvera une sanction pratique, après examen préliminaire fait
par des jurisconsultes, armateurs et membres de campagnies d'assurances. Les discussions de la presse éclaireront encore le sujet. Les
délégués des puissances viendront ensuite ; ils donneront en dernier
ressort la forme internationale voulue, pratique et définitive, utile aux
intérêts généraux de toutes les nations.

· I.

En droit, nul ne peut être juge dans sa propre cause.

Dans un différend maritime international anglo-français, par exemple,
résultant d'une collision en mer, tous les juges seront anglais, si le navire incriminé relâche en Angleterre.

Au contraire, si le navire aborde en France, tous les juges seront
français.

En un mot, la composition du tribunal dépend uniquement du " has-
sard." Elle influe nécessairement sur la sentence.

La collision du *Saint-Germain* et du *Woodburn*, dans la Manche, en 1883, a démontré la nécessité d'un tribunal international mixte. Nous en avons fait l'objet d'une brochure qui a été approuvée par le Gouvernement des États-Unis et les autorités citées plus haut.

Nous empruntons ici les expressions du commissaire de la navigation, M. Jarvis Patten, dans son remarquable rapport du 31 janvier 1885 : " L'établissement de semblables tribunaux épargnerait des frais, préviendrait beaucoup de soucis et apporterait plus d'harmonie dans l'interprétation donnée par les différentes nations aux lois sur les collisions."

L'honorable commissaire de la navigation dit encore : "Ce serait certainement, de la part des différentes nations adhérentes, un moyen rapide de donner toutes les garanties désirables à la législation."

D'un autre côté, la collision du navire anglais *City of Mecca* avec le bâtiment portugais *Insulano* a été l'objet, pendant huit ans, de plaintes et de réclamations diplomatiques de l'Angleterre.

Cette nation trouvait alors que le tribunal portugais, dans le jugement de cette affaire, avait fait un " déni de justice."

Le ministre anglais à Lisbonne proposa alors la création d'une cour d'appel internationale devant réviser les jugements des nationalités.

Le Congrès de Milan de 1883 approuva l'idée et prit une résolution dans ce sens.

Rien ne serait plus désirable que la création de ces deux degrés de juridictions :

1° Des tribunaux internationaux siégeant sur un certain nombre de points déterminés et limités ;

2° Une cour d'appel internationale siégeant en pays neutre, révisant les jugements des tribunaux internationaux de première instance.

Cette création nouvelle présentera certainement des difficultés de plus d'un genre.

Sont-elles insurmontables ? Nous ne le croyons pas. Dans tous les cas, l'importance du résultat, unanimement reconnue en principe, comme nous l'avons vu, n'impose-t-elle pas le devoir de tenter l'entreprise et de ne reculer qu'après avoir fait les plus grands efforts pour réussir ? Il s'agit d'une œuvre de justice à la fois humanitaire et civilisatrise au premier chef.

Pourquoi n'obtiendrait-on pas une entente sur ce point capital, qui doit tenter et attirer toutes les bonnes volontés, quand on est arrivé à la faire aboutir des conventions internationales aussi ardues et minutieuses que des conventions de pêche, postales, télégraphiques et autres ?

Les difficultés s'aplaniraient avec du temps, de la persévérance, du travail et la volonté de réussir.

Pourquoi, en un mot, une barrière infranchissable s'élèverait-elle de ce côté seulement, quand nous ne la voyons nulle part ailleurs ?

IL.

En Angleterre, les litiges contentieux des collisions sont jugés dans la capitale, à Londres, par "l'Admiralty-Court." Il y a un juge et deux assesseurs, capitaines choisis dans la corporation du "Trinity-House."

En France, au contraire, ces affaires appartiennent aux tribunaux de commerce.

Si la marine anglaise, qui dépasse comme nombre la moitié des autres marines du globe, se contente d'une seule cour établie dans sa capitale, on peut l'imiter sans crainte ; cela simplifie la difficulté et permet de fixer le nombre et le siége des tribunaux internationaux.

Ils seraient établis dans chacune des capitales des pays ayant adhéré à la convention internationale.

Dans le cas d'un litige anglo-français, à juger en Angleterre, par exemple, le tribunal serait international au lieu d'être national. Le jugement serait rendu par trois juges, au lieu d'un juge unique : un juge de chacune des parties intéressées et un juge étranger, pris sur un tableau des nations ayant adhéré à la convention.

Le nombre des juges augmenterait avec celui des parties intéressées. Chacune doit être représentée. Dans tous les cas, le nombre des juges devra rester impair.

Dans le cas que nous venons d'examiner, un litige se jugeant en Angleterre, le jugement serait rendu naturellement dans la langue anglaise. Tout le personnel nécessaire à la justice resterait le même. Il n'y aurait de changé qu'un seul élément : la composition des juges. Mais c'est là le point capital qui donnerait aux parties les garanties d'impartialité qui leur font défaut aujourd'hui.

Les difficultés nous paraissent donc plus apparentes que réelles. Les plénipotentiaires délégués sauront bien les surmonter et cimenter les bases de l'organisation nouvelle. Il faut éviter à l'avenir, comme le dit avec tant d'à-propos M. Jarvis Patten : "que des jugements, même quand ils sont justes, soient suivis de soupçons et de récriminations. On permettra alors à un commandant, en pareil cas, de relâcher dans le port le plus voisin (manœuvre dictée par l'humanité quand la vie humaine est en danger), sans craindre de nuire à ses intérêts."

L'honorable commissaire de la navigation des États-Unis s'exprimait ainsi dans la dernière phrase de son rapport : "Il est probable que toutes les nations favoriseraient l'insertion (au moins en substance) de la deuxième clause proposée par M. Riondel, et j'incline à recommander son adoption."

On ne peut pas approuver la création des tribunaux maritimes internationaux d'une manière plus catégorique. Le chef du Département de la Trésorerie et le Secrétaire d'État des États-Unis approuvaient le rapport de leur commissaire de la navigation (le 4 février 1885), dans une phrase laconique, bien expressive, écrite à M. Riondel : "J'ai l'honneur de vous transmettre la copie d'un rapport du commissaire de la navigation, qui exprime ses idées sur ce sujet, idées auxquelles le département donne pleinement son assentiment. "

La nation des États-Unis est essentiellement maritime et possède le sens pratique des choses. Elle a démontré, dans le rapport de son commissaire de la navigation, l'urgence de la réforme. Comment ne pas être convaincu, après cette lecture, que la vérité est là, et que le reste n'est plus qu'une question secondaire qui sera résolue quand on le voudra !

III.

Les ordonnances de 1681 (livre IV, titre 9, art. 18) et du 29 octobre 1833 (art. 62), imposent aux autorités maritimes et consulaires le devoir de chercher les causes des sinistres maritimes. Une instruction du ministre de la marine, en date du 18 mai 1860, a précisé leurs devoirs. Un questionnaire adopté par une autre décision du 24 mai 1879 a donné de l'uniformité à ces investigations: on ne doit pas se borner à lire aux témoins de l'événement le rapport du capitaine. L'enquête doit être approfondie. Il faut arriver à la découverte de la vérité par tous les moyens possibles. Les commissaires de l'inscription maritime et les consuls procèdent à cet effet à l'examen des papiers de bord et du casernet; on interroge et on presse de questions l'équipage et les passagers. On a recours à des experts assermentés. Dans les consulats, on réclame l'assistance d'un officier de vaisseau, si un navire de guerre est dans le port ou sur rade; ou bien encore, du plus âgé des capitaines au long cours présents dans la localité.

En France, le commissaire de l'inscription maritime appele à l'enquête le directeur des mouvements du port ou le capitaine du port.

Lorsque les naufrages ont lieu à l'étranger, l'instruction est transmise au ministre de la marine, par le consul qui fait connaître les ports sur lesquels les hommes repatriés ont été dirigés.

A leur arrivée en France, ces personnes sont soumises à un nouvel interrogatoire, sur tous les points où elles abordent dans la mère-patrie.

Ainsi donc, il existe deux catégories d'enquête très différentes: les unes sont faites dans le consulat le plus rapproché du lieu du sinistre; les autres sont dressées à l'arrivée sur le sol natal.

Il serait rationnel, si la collision est anglo-française, par exemple, que le consul anglais assistât à l'enquête française, et réciproquement. Il y aurait ainsi des garanties indéniables de justice. Le consul *assistant* aurait droit d'interrogatoire et d'inscription au procès-verbal.

Au point de débarquement, le contrôle de l'enquête serait toujours possible, car il y a des consuls dans la localité même du débarquement de l'équipage ou sur un point très rapproché. On avertirait ce consul du jour et de l'heure de l'interrogatoire.

A l'étranger, sur le lieu de la collision, si un des consuls faisait défaut, il pourrait être substitué par un consul d'une autre nationalité ou par un

officier d'un navire de guerre présent sur les lieux, ou par le capitaine
au long cours le plus ancien, ou bien encore par un notable. Ceux-ci
remplaceraient le consul manquant.

Les marins et armateurs trouveraient certainement dans cette double
enquête contrôlée par les intéressés, au moment même de l'événement
et peu de temps après, des garanties précieuses qui n'existent pas
aujourd'hui.

Cet important dossier formerait la première assise. Envoyé au tribunal maritime international, il lui rendrait d'utiles services.

IV.

Nous n'avons pas voulu entrer dans les détails. Un peu plus tard,
quand la question aura été discutée par les intéressés et par la presse,
il nous restera à formuler, article par article, dans un projet spécial, les
diverses idées qui sont exprimées dans ce mémoire.

Sans chercher à nier les difficultés qu'on rencontrera sur sa route
pour résoudre le problème, afin d'arriver à une entente internationale,
nous avons eu pour but de montrer au Congrès que ces obstacles ne
sont pas insurmontables. Le sentiment du bien public et l'amour de la
justice seront le levier puissant qui, un jour donné, nous l'espérons,
soulèvera toute la charge et rendra ce grand service à la civilisation.

Dans sa délibération du 13 juillet 1885, la Chambre de commerce de
Paris, statuant sur les propositions que nous avions soumises à son
examen, émettait un avis " tendant à ce que le gouvernement s'entendit
avec les gouvernements étrangers pour résoudre ces questions internationales de si haut intérêt."

Nous avons vu plus haut que le Congrès d'Anvers de 1885 avait émis
le même vœu.

Nous demandons respectueusement au Congrès de Nantes de vouloir
bien prendre une résolution semblable.

La Chambre de Paris avait fait précéder son vœu des considérants
suivants : " La Chambre de commerce a constaté la difficulté de déterminer le tribunal compétent pour connaître d'une collision en mer entre
navires de nationalités différentes, et les conséquences graves qui en
résultent, les codes maritimes n'étant pas identiques.

" La Chambre de commerce estime, en conséquence, que non-seulement la création de tribunaux internationaux s'impose pour les besoins
de la grande famille du monde commercial, mais qu'il conviendrait surtout que toutes les nations eûssent un même code maritime."

Le Conseil d'amirauté, dans sa séance du 25 avril 1886, avait émis un
vœu analogue : "Qu'il serait du plus sérieux intérêt qu'un accord pût
être réalisé entre les diverses nations maritimes pour la constitution de
tribunaux internationaux chargés de connaître les litiges entre navires
de nationalités différentes, et de les juger d'après une loi commune."

Le Gouvernement Grec a adopté aussi la même proposition et s'est déclaré " tout disposé à prendre part aux travaux de la Conférence, quaud les puissances maritimes auront décidé d'en convoquer une."

Dans notre mémoire, " Sur la réforme de la loi internationale du 4 novembre 1879 et la création de tribunaux maritimes et internationaux," nous avons proposé (page 9) la nomination d'une commission permanente de personnes techniques.

Elle préparerait la solution de ces questions internationales d'un si haut intérêt; elle étudierait avec soin les collisions nouvelles où elle trouverait un enseignement salutaire pour les prévenir à l'avenir."

Ne serait-ce pas un moyen de faciliter plus tard l'œuvre des plénipotentiaires délégués de la Conférence internationale ? Ces derniers auront à mission de créer définitivement une entente sur cette question importante. Comme le dit la Chambre de commerce de Paris: "la création de ces tribunaux s'impose pour les besoins de la grande famille du monde commercial."

CHERBOURG, 31 *juillet* 1886.

A M. le Commandant A. RIONDEL:

CHERBOURG, le 7 *janvier* 1887.

MONSIEUR LE COMMANDANT:

Voici la note que je vous avais promise.

Elle n'a pas la prétention d'être complète, mais c'est un aperçu des moyens qui me semblent le plus pratiques pour mettre vos idées en application, en ce qui touche l'organisation et la juridiction des tribunaux internationaux.

Il importe de démontrer que cette institution n'a rien d'irréalisable, même au point de vue du courant ordinaire des affaires.

C'est ce que j'ai essayé de faire.

Veuillez agréer, Commandant, l'assurance de mon entier dévouement.

H. FAVIER.

ÉTUDE SUR L'ORGANISATION ET LA JURIDICTION DES TRIBUNAUX MARITIMES INTERNATIONAUX.

[Par M. H. Favier, avocat.]

La nécessité d'une juridiction internationale pour les abordages n'est plus à discuter; elle s'impose. Mais, si elle est admise par tous *en principe* et en *théorie* elle n'en soulève pas moins certaines objections au point de *vue pratique*.

Tous les hommes d'affaires, qui se sont occupés spécialement de questions maritimes, savent qu'en pareille matière, un avantage qu'on ne saurait légèrement sacrifier, c'est la *célérité*. C'est surtout dans le commerce maritime qu'on doit tenir compte de l'adage américain: "Time is money." L'importance des intérêts engagés dans les armements est considérable et un retard de quelques jours dans l'accomplissement du voyage pour lequel un navire est affrété, peut porter une grave atteinte

à des intérêts nombreux. Non seulement le capitaine et l'équipage mais
les armateurs, les chargeurs, les assureurs et souvent d'autres encore
peuvent en éprouver de sérieux préjudices.

Aussi il est un écueil qu'il faut éviter en organisant en cette matière
une nouvelle juridiction, c'est de la placer trop loin des justiciables.

Un abordage survient, le navire abordé relâche dans le porte le plus
voisin. Il faut qu'il y trouve immédiatement une autorité ayant qualité
pour constater l'avarie, sa nature, en rechercher les causes, prescrire et
surveiller les réparations, et mettre le navire à même de continuer son
voyage le plus tôt possible, ou constater son innavigabilité irrémédiable,
afin que le chargement puisse être transbordé sur un autre navire. Il
peut ainsi y avoir des mesures urgentes à prendre pour assurer le sauvetage ou la conservation de la cargaison. S'il fallait, pour toutes ces
mesures, recourir à un tribunal éloigné, les dommages résultant de
l'abordage seraient considérablement aggravés par les retards et les
frais qui en seraient la conséquence inévitable.

Or, les tribunaux internationaux seront nécessairement peu nombreux, et par suite siégeront à des distances très considérables. Il n'est
pas possible d'admettre que pour toutes les questions signalées plus
haut on doive recourir à leur intervention.

Aussi, le soussigné estime-t-il qu'il n'y aurait pas lieu de leur attribuer
compétence pour toutes les mesures d'instruction, qui, pour être effi-
caces, doivent s'effectuer sans retard et sur les lieux mêmes de relâche.

Il serait possible de concilier l'intérêt d'une bonne justice, avec
l'intérêt d'une prompte justice, en restreignant le rôle des tribunaux
internationaux au jugement des questions de responsabilité, et en laissant aux tribunaux nationaux existant actuellement, le soin de présider
aux mesures de conservation et d'instruction, sauf à donner aux
étrangers, dans cette première phase de la procédure, quelques garanties que les législations actuelles ne leur donnent pas.

En conséquence, le projet de traité à soumettre aux délibérations des
diverses puissances, pourrait être formulé ainsi qu'il suit :

Titre 1er.

Article 1er. En cas d'abordage, chacun des capitaines devra, dans
le délai de vingt-quatre heures, déposer au greffe du tribunal du lieu où
il se trouvera, ou bien du port où il relâchera, un rapport détaillé relatant toutes les circonstances de l'abordage.

Dans le cas où il y aurait sur les lieux un Consulat de sa nation, le
capitaine pourra, s'il le préfère, déposer son rapport au dit Consulat.

Article 2. Le délai de vingt-quatre heures courra du moment de
l'abordage, si l'abordage a eu lieu dans une rade ou dans un port ; il
courra du moment de l'arrivée du navire dans le premier port où il en-
trera, si l'abordage a eu lieu en mer.

Article 3. Le rapport sera vérifié par les déclarations des hommes
de l'équipage et des passagers qui seront interrogés et déposeront, sous

la foi du serment, devant le Magistrat ou le Consul qui aura reçu le rapport.

ARTICLE 4. Les rapports non vérifiés ne sont point admis à la décharge du capitaine, et ne font point foi en justice, excepté dans le cas où le capitaine s'est sauvé seul dans le lieu où il a fait son rapport. La preuve des faits contraires est réservée aux parties.

ARTICLE 5. Le même magistrat ou consul fera, en outre, d'office, toutes les constatations qu'il jugera utiles à la manifestation de la vérité.

ARTICLE 6. Il sera surtout dressé procès-verbal, dont une expédition sera remise au capitaine avec une expédition de son rapport.

ARTICLE 7. Si les deux navires se trouvent dans le même lieu, le capitaine le plus diligent assignera l'autre devant le tribunal du lieu, compétent d'après la loi locale pour les affaires maritimes, aux fins de faire nommer des experts chargés de visiter les deux navires, de constater les avaries, d'en rechercher les causes et de donner leur avis sur les responsabilités encourues. Les experts auront la faculté de s'entourer de tous renseignements et de demander, s'ils le jugent utile, de nouveaux éclaircissements aux hommes des deux équipages et aux passagers.

ARTICLE 8. Les mêmes experts auront pour mission d'indiquer les mesures à prendre, s'il y a lieu, pour le sauvetage des navires ou des chargements ainsi que pour leur conservation.

Ils indiqueront aussi, s'il y a lieu déclarer l'innavigabilité des navires, ou, dans le cas contraire, les réparations nécessaires pour les remettre en état.

ARTICLE 9. Les experts seront au nombre de trois, chacun des capitaines pourra en désigner un; le troisième sera choisi par le tribunal, qui désignerait aussi les autres, dans le cas où ils n'auraient pas été désignés par les capitaines.

Aucune condition de nationalité n'est exigée des dits experts.

ARTICLE 10. Après le rapport des experts, le tribunal statuera sur l'homologation de leur rapport, mais seulement en ce qui touche les mesures à prendre pour la réparation ou la conservation des navires et de leurs cargaisons.

Il prescrira, en outre, d'office ou sur la demande des parties, toutes les mesures d'instruction qui seraient utiles pour éclairer la question des responsabilités, mais en réservant cette question.

Il statuera enfin sur les demandes d'embargo, et fixera, s'il en est requis, les cautions à fournir par celui des capitaines qui voudra continuer son voyage avant la solution du procès.

ARTICLE 11. Si les deux navires ne se trouvent pas dans le même port, chacun des capitaines poursuivra dans le lieu où il se trouvera, par voie de requête, l'accomplissement des formalités nécessaires pour faire procéder à l'expertise; mais, en ce qui concerne seulement son navire et sa cargaison. Il en poursuivra l'homologation aussi par voie de requête. L'autre capitaine, comme toute partie intéressée, pourra, en tout état de cause, intervenir dans la procédure qui deviendrait alors contradictoire.

ARTICLE 12. Les jugements de l'homologation et ceux qui pourraient être rendus sur les incidents de la procédure, seront en premier ressort, mais ils seront exécutoires par prévision, sans caution.

L'appel pourra en être porté devant les tribunaux internationaux dont il va être parlé.

<h2 style="text-align:center">TITRE 2.</h2>

ARTICLE 13. Il est institué dans les pays adhérents au traité, des tribunaux internationaux composé d'un délégué de chacun des États contractants. La présidence appartiendra au délégué de l'État dans lequel siègera le tribunal. Chaque tribunal élira parmi ses membres un vice-président; il choisira, hors de son sein, un greffier. Il désignera aussi un certain nombre d'avoués, chargés de représenter ou d'assister les parties. Le ministère des avocats sera facultatif.

ARTICLE 14. La présence de cinq membres au moins sera nécessaire pour la validité de leurs jugements. En cas de partage, la voix du président sera prépondérante.

ARTICLE 15. Les tribunaux internationaux sont compétents pour statuer: 1° Sur les appels des jugements rendus en conformité des dispositions du titre premier du présent traité; 2° sur les questions de responsabilité en matière d'abordage.

ARTICLE 16. Les appels seront portés devant le tribunal international dans la circonscription duquel se trouvera le tribunal dont la décision sera attaquée.

ARTICLE 17. Le tribunal international pourra statuer séparément sur les dits appels ou joindre les incidents au fond.

ARTICLE 18. La question de responsabilité en matière d'abordage sera portée devant le tribunal international, dans la circonscription duquel le demandeur aura suivi la procédure préliminaire mentionnée au titre premier.

Dans le cas où les deux capitaines se porteraient respectivement demandeurs devant les deux tribunaux internationaux différents, le tribunal saisi le dernier, renverrait l'affaire devant le tribunal premier saisi.

ARTICLE 19. L'instance sera introduite et suivie dans les formes usitées dans le pays, pour les procédures commerciales devant les cours d'appel.

ARTICLE 20. Lorsque les deux navires appartiendront à des nationalités différentes, si le délégué de la nation de l'un d'eux se trouve empêché de siéger, le délégué de la nation de l'autre ne pourra prendre part au jugement à peine de nullité.

ARTICLE 21. Les jugements seront rendus sur le vu des rapports de mer, des expertises et autres documents, sans préjudice des vérifications nouvelles et de toutes mesures d'instruction que le tribunal jugerait utile d'ordonner.

ARTICLE 22. Les décisions des tribunaux internationaux seront en dernier ressort et ne pourront être attaquée que pour vices de forme, incompétences, ou excès de pouvoir.

ARTICLE 23. Il est établi une Cour internationale de cassation devant laquelle seront portés les pourvois, et qui, le cas échéant, devra procéder aux règlements de juges.

ARTICLE 24. Cette Cour sera composée de deux délégués de chacun des États contractants. Elle élira parmi ses membres un président et un vice-président. Elle choisira, hors de son sein, un greffier. La présence de neuf membres au moins sera nécessaire pour la validité de ses arrêts.

ARTICLE 25. Elle statuera sans débat oral, sur le vu des mémoires, des parties et des pièces de la procédure.

ARTICLE 26. Elle sera saisie par voie d'assignation, et les arrêts seront rendus sur le rapport d'un conseiller qui ne pourra appartenir à la nationalité de l'une des parties en cause.

ARTICLE 27. En cas de cassation, la cause sera renvoyée devant un autre tribunal international.

TITRE 3.

ARTICLE 28. Tous les exploits seront signifiés dans la forme usitée dans le pays où la procédure se poursuivra. Ils devront, si la partie interpellée est étrangère à ce pays et n'y a ni domicile réel, ni domicile élu, lui être notifié soit en parlant à sa personne, soit à son domicile réel à l'etranger, soit à bord du navire où elle est embarquée, soit enfin au consulat de sa nation.

ARTICLE 29. La procédure préliminaire et la procédure devant les tribunaux internationaux, ainsi que tous actes ou procès-verbaux sont également soumis quant à la forme aux règlements établis dans les pays où ils sont passés.

ARTICLE 30. La procédure devant la Cour internationale de cassation fera seule exception à la règle qui précéde et fera l'objet d'un règlement que cette Cour elle-même arrêtera.

ARTICLE 31. Les jugements et arrêts rendus en conformité du présent traité, seront exécutoires dans tous les territoires soumis à l'autorité des États contractants, sans qu'il soit besoin d'exequatur.

ARTICLE 32. Néanmoins les arrêts de la Cour internationale de cassation ne pourront être mis à exécution dans chaque État qu'après qu'une expédition en due forme, accompagnée, s'il y a lieu, d'une traduction, aura été soumise, dans le pays où devra se faire l'exécution, au visa de l'autorité qui sera désignée à cet effet par chacun des États contractants.

Il en sera de même des jugements rendus par les tribunaux ordinaires ou par les tribunaux internationaux, mais seulement dans le cas où ils devront être exécutoires dans le territoire d'un État autre que celui dans lequel ils auront été rendus.

ARTICLE 33. Le présent traité ne sera pas applicable en matière d'abordage entre deux navires de la même nation, si ce n'est lorsque les deux navires se trouveront ou relâcheront l'un et l'autre dans un port étranger.

Dans le cas où un seul des navires relâcherait à l'étranger, la procédure préliminaire seule se fera, conformément aux dispositions ci-dessus dans le lieu de relâche et la question du fond sera portée devant la juridiction nationale des dits navires.

OPINION DU GOUVERNEMENT DES ÉTATS-UNIS.

Le document américain a été publié dans notre seconde brochure. Nous le reproduisons, à cause de son importance, dans ce volume où sa présence est nécessaire. Ce rapport a été la cause et le point de départ de l'agitation française dans la question des abordages.

"LÉGATION DES ÉTATS UNIS,
Paris, le 13 avril 1885.

"A Monsieur RIONDEL,
Capitaine de frégate en retraite :

"Par une lettre en date du 15 décembre 1884, vous avez bien voulu m'adresser un travail sur les collisions en mer, dont l'objet était de suggérer diverses modifications à la loi du 4 novembre 1879.

"Vous me demandiez de soumettre ce travail à l'appréciation de mon gouvernement; je l'ai fait et Monsieur le Secrétaire d'État m'adresse aujourd'hui une copie de la correspondance échangée à ce sujet avec le Secrétaire du Trésor et le Commissaire de la navigation.

"Vous verrez par cette correspondance que je m'empresse de vous adresser que votre proposition a été étudiée sérieusement et dans un esprit tout à fait sympathique.

"MORTON,
"Ministre des États-Unis."

[1ᵉ lettre.]

"DÉPARTEMENT DE LA TRÉSORERIE,
"4 FÉVRIER 1885.

"A l'Honorable SECRÉTAIRE D'ÉTAT :

"MONSIEUR : Répondant de nouveau à votre lettre du 19 janvier dernier qui soumettait une communication de M. Riondel, de la marine française, dans laquelle il proposait une réforme des règlements internationaux pour prévenir les collisions en mer, j'ai l'honneur maintenant de vous transmettre la copie d'un rapport du Commissaire de la navigation qui exprime ses idées sur ce sujet, idées auxquelles le *Département donne pleinement son assentiment.*

"McCOLLOUGH."

"RAPPORT DU COMMISSAIRE DE LA NAVIGATION,

. " *Washington*, 31 *janvier* 1885.

" A l'Honorable SECRÉTAIRE DE LA TRÉSORERIE :

"MONSIEUR : J'ai l'honneur de vous accuser réception de la lettre du sous-secrétaire Coon, qui me transmettait, à la date du 24 janvier 1885, une communication du secrétaire d'État, accompagnée d'une lettre de la légation des État-Unis à Paris, et une brochure de M. Riondel, officier en retaite de la marine française. Dans cette brochure, cet officier décrit les circonstances qui ont accompagné la collision entre le paquebot français *Saint-Germain* et le vapeur anglais désemparé *Woodburn* pendant que celui-ci était à la remorque du *Recovery ;* il donne aussi le jugement rendu par les tribunaux.

" Pour répondre à la demande que vous me faites d'un rapport et de mes vues particulières sur la matière, j'expose : qu'après avoir examiné les documents qui m'ont été soumis, et lu avec beaucoup d'intérêt le rapport de M. Riondel, j'estime que la conclusion de ses recherches est de proposer l'addition de deux clauses distinctes à la loi sur les collisions : la première, relative à la sécurité ultérieure des navires remorqués ; la seconde, proposant la création de tribunaux internationaux appelés à connaître des cas de collision en pleine mer entre bâtiments de différentes nations.

" La première clause, demandée comme une garantie nouvelle, pour les navires remorqués, pour éviter les chances de collisions, est la suivante :

"Tout navire, à voiles ou à vapeur, qui rencontre un groupe composé d'un navire remorqueur ayant quelque chose à la remorque, doit changer sa route toutes les fois que les directions du bâtiment isolé et du groupe se croisent de manière à entraîner des risques d'abordage."

"Les règles établies ci-dessus pour des bâtiments à vapeur isolés, sont applicables à des groupes qui se trouveraient dans la position des premiers par rapport aux seconds."

" Le jugement du *Saint-Germain* et du *Woodburn* semble prouver que l'application des mêmes règles, d'une part, à des bâtiments entièrement libres de faire la meilleure route pour éviter un abordage et, d'autre part, à des bâtiments en ayant d'autres à la remorque et n'étant pas complètement maîtres de leurs mouvements, est arbitraire et pourrait être modifiée.

" Il est raisonnable de stipuler que le navire isolé, parfaitement libre de ses mouvements, doit s'éloigner du groupe qui, forcément, n'est maître qu'en partie de ses mouvements.

" Je pense donc que la proposition de M. Riondel d'ajouter cette clause au Code international est *digne d'être prise en considération.*

" Quant à la proposition de M. Riondel d'établir des tribunaux internationaux qui connaitraient des collisions en pleine mer entre des bâ-

timents de nationalités différentes, on peut dire que la question de juridiction est encore incertaine, pour beaucoup de cas, chez les nations
maritimes. Elle engendre parfois beaucoup de mécontentement chez
les deux parties en cause ; elle occasione du désordre et des frais.

" En Angleterre, la cour de l'Amirauté possède la juridiction des procès entre bâtiments étrangers qui s'abordent dans les eaux territoriales.

" Mais quand le fait se produit à plus de trois milles des côtes du
royaume, il n'existe pas d'autre procédé que d'arrêter, partout où on peut
le trouver, le navire qui a causé le plus grand dommage, et de lui in-
tenter une action.

" Cette manière de faire donne naissance à des discussions pour savoir
quel est le tribunal convenable, ce qui soulève un grand nombre de
plaintes, de dénis de justice dans la procédure.

" Il y a peu de temps, un navire américain fut arrêté dans un port
français pour une collision avec un navire autrichien, collision qui s'était
produite quelques mois auparavant dans l'Océan Pacifique. Le navire
américain se rendait au Havre ; l'autrichien à Lisbonne, où son chargement était assuré.

" Les assureurs de la cargaison, qui firent le plus de bruit, voulaient
que le cas fût jugé à Lisbonne, tandis que les propriétaires du navire
maltraité préféraient les tribunaux autrichiens.

" Il y avait par suite, engagés dans cette affaire, les sujets des quatre
nations : États-Unis, Portugal, Autriche et France (pays où le bâtiment
américain fut saisi).

" Après des négociations considérables et de grandes dépenses, il fut
agréé que le cas serait soumis à un tribunal français qui devait être, sans
aucun doute, moins influencé par des préférences nationales ; aucun
citoyen français n'ayant d'intérêts pécuniaires dans cette affaire.

" Mais si le bâtiment américain avait relâché à Lisbonne et qu'il eût
été chargé pour un port d'Autriche, il aurait été arrêté et jugé avec un
Code différent, comme cela pouvait être, par l'un ou l'autre tribunal.

" Les propriétaires, placés dans un port d'Amérique, auraient pu
craindre que justice ne fût pas faite.

" Le cas du *Saint-Germain* et du *Woodburn* est cité par M. Riondel
comme étant un de ceux où le jugement a causé un préjudice, par un
verdict favorable à une des parties dont la nationalité était celle du pays
qui jugeait le litige. Sa proposition d'un tribunal mixte est faite en vue
d'éviter, à l'avenir, que des jugements, même quand ils sont justes, soient
suivis de soupçons et de récriminations.

" La proposition de M. Riondel d'avoir un tribunal maritime international pour exercer son autorité sur les collisions qui se produisent entre
navires de différentes nations, *éviterait*, je le pense, ce malheur et per-
mettrait à un commandant, en pareil cas, de relâcher dans le port le
plus voisin (manœuvre dictée par l'humanité quand la vie humaine est
en danger) sans craindre de nuire à ses intérêts.

" On peut cependant faire l'objection qu'un règlement ou une loi pour l'institution d'un tribunal devant juger les cas des collisions, ne doit pas être inséré dans le Code international qui a seulement pour but de les prévenir.

"Ce serait certainement, de la part des différentes nations adhérentes, un moyen rapide de donner toutes les garanties désirables à la législation.

"L'établissement d'un pareil tribunal épargnerait les dépenses, préviendrait beaucoup de soucis et apporterait plus d'harmonie dans l'interprétation donnée par les différentes nations aux lois sur les collisions.

"Il est probable que toutes les nations favoriseraient l'insertion (au moins en substance) de la deuxième clause proposée par M. Riondel dans les règlements internationaux et *j'incline à recommander son adoption*.

"JARVIS PATTEN."

CONGRÈS DE HAMBOURG, DE MILAN ET DE LONDRES.

Les deux congrès de Hambourg et d'Anvers ont eu lieu en août et septembre 1885.

Le président du premier congrès, M. le docteur Sieveking, président du Tribunal supérieur des villes hanséatiques, dans la première séance, s'exprimait ainsi (Compte-rendu officiel, page 170): "Les propositions faites au Congrès de Milan, en 1883, sont en très grande harmonie avec le projet de M. Riondel, qui mérite la chaleureuse sympathie de tous les membres présents."

Le discours du Président fut suivi de la lecture d'une lettre du Consul-Général de France et d'une note présentée au Congrès par M. Riondel. Nous les reproduisons:

HAMBOURG, *le* 19 *Août* 1885.

MONSIEUR LE PRÉSIDENT:

Monsieur Albert Riondel, capitaine de frégate en retraite de la Marine française, a désiré soumettre au Congrès que vous présidez, divers projets de réforme dont il est l'auteur et qui ont pour but de prévenir les abordages en mer et d'assurer le jugement équitable des litiges qui peuvent résulter des collisions entre navires de nationalités différentes; cet honorable officier ne pouvant, à son grand regret, prendre part, en personne, aux travaux du Congrès. J'ai l'honneur de vous adresser, ci-joint et d'ailleurs à titre purement officieux, le dossier contenant ses propositions, et je ne puis que vous prier de vouloir bien le communiquer à la Commission compétente.

Ces propositions sont les suivantes:

1° Utilité de créer un tribunal international appelé à connaître des cas de collision, en pleine mer, entre bâtiments de différentes nations. Ce tribunal serait composé d'un juge appartenant à chacune des nations en cause, et de deux ou trois juges, désignés par le sort, parmi les autres nations ayant adhéré à la loi internationale;

2° Obligations imposées à tout navire isolé qui rencontre, à la mer,

S. Ex. 53, pt. 3——28

un groupe composé d'un remorqueur et d'un ou plusieurs remorqués de s'écarter de la route suivie par ce groupe;

3° Obligation d'éclairer la queue des groupes de navires remorqués;

4° Responsabilité partielle, en cas de collision, du remorqueur qui remorque un ou plusieurs navires sans feu;

5° Responsabilité entière et *ipso facto*, en cas de collision, du navire qui n'ayant pas allumé ses feux a ainsi privé l'autre bâtiment du feu légal que le règlement international lui accorde pour diriger ses mouvements;

6° Responsabilité correctionnelle des hommes chargés de l'allumage et du bon état des feux;

7° Obligation pour les bâtiments de guerre d'arrêter les navires sans feux et d'en dresser procès-verbal;

Enfin, 8° Attribution par le tribunal juge de la responsabilité de l'abordage, de dommages et intérêts à accorder non seulement aux propriétaires des bâtiments et de la marchandise, mais encore aux victimes de la collision ou à leurs ayants-droit.

Veuillez agréer, Monsieur le président, les assurances de ma haute considération.

Cte. BALUS D'AVRICOURT,
Le Consul-Général de France.

NOTE PRÉSENTÉE AU CONGRÈS INTERNATIONAL DE HAMBOURG EN 1885.

Dans une brochure publiée en 1884 (sous le pseudonyme de Albert du Hailly), chez Léon Vannier éditeur à Paris, 19 Quai St. Michel, et intitulée: Collision du *St. Germain* et du *Woodburn*, j'ai fait les deux propositions suivantes:

1° Utilité de créer un tribunal international pour juger les litiges maritimes.

2° Obligation imposée à tout navire isolé qui rencontre à la mer un groupe (composé d'un remorqueur et d'un ou plusieurs remorqués) de se déranger de sa route afin d'éviter une collision.

1er Point. La juridiction dépend aujourd'hui uniquement du hasard. Dans le cas d'une collision entre français et anglais la juridiction sera anglaise ou française selon que le bâtiment, auteur de la collision, aura relaché en pays anglais ou sur le sol français.

La sentence est toujours attaquée par la partie condamnée avec une certaine apparence de raison.

Il est de principe en droit: qu'on ne peut pas être à la fois juge et partie; un tribunal international ne serait-il pas une chose désirable et un progrès réel?

2me Point. Un groupe est dans l'impossibilité de manœuvrer et d'éviter un danger; chaque navire qui en fait partie, est tenu par l'avant et l'arrière et n'a pas (sauf le remorqueur) la possibilité:

1° De stopper;

2° D'augmenter ou de réduire la vitesse;

3° De marcher en arrière ;

4° De faire une abbattée pratique, prompte et accentuée, pour éviter un danger.

En dehors de ces deux propositions nettement formulées, j'avais également émis (dans plusieurs passages de la brochure) les idées suivantes :

1° Nécessité d'éclairer la queue d'un groupe. La raison est simple. Les trains de chemins de fer son éclairés en tête et en queue; cependant ils ne sont jamais, comme sur mer, susceptibles d'être abordés à droite ou à gauche. Cela s'impose bien plus fortement aux groupes qui sont de vrais trains maritimes.

2° Si les feux ne sont pas allumés, la responsabilité *entière*, en cas de collision, devrait incomber *ipso facto* à ce navire. Quelle que soit la manœuvre de l'autre bâtiment, celui-ci ne peut pas en être déclaré responsable, puisqu'il a *été privé du feu légal* que le législateur lui accorde pour diriger ses mouvements.

3° Le législateur international devrait imposer aux bâtiments de guerre le *devoir* d'arrêter les navires sans feux et d'en dresser procès-verbal.

4° Le remorqueur (qui *remorque* un navire ou des navires sans feux) commet une négligence qui doit le rendre en partie responsable de la collision.

5° Les hommes chargés de l'allumage et du bon état des feux, et qui manquent à ce devoir sacré, doivent être punis, le cas échéant, de la même manière que le garde-barrière, l'aiguilleur, le chef de gare, ou un employé quelconque, quand il arrive une rencontre sur les voies ferrées. Si la responsabilité du capitaine est engagée, il doit être puni aussi. Ces trois dernières clauses s'imposent au nom de la sécurité générale.

La loi internationale du 4 novembre 1879 a été faite pour prévenir les abordages à la mer. Elle doit toujours rester ouverte au progrès. Chaque événement malheureux devrait être étudié avec soin et servir d'enseignement pour l'avenir. Il est nécessaire que l'expérience, si chèrement acquise, ne soit pas perdue.

A. RIONDEL.

Le congrès de Milan mit en relief un point intéressant. Une collision eut lieu en 1885 entre le navire anglais *City of Mecca* et le bâtiment portugais *Insulano*. Le jugement rendu à Lisbonne par le tribunal portugais n'eut pas l'approbation de l'Angleterre. Pendant 8 ans (de 1875 à 1883), une correspondance diplomatique fut échangée à propos de cette affaire entre les deux gouvernements. Les relations se tendirent au point que Lord Granville prononça le mot de "déni de justice." Sir Robert Morier, ministre plénipotentiaire anglais à Lisbonne, fit à ce moment la proposition d'une cour d'appel chargée de réviser les jugements des tribunaux des nationalités.

Le congrès de Milan, saisi en 1883, de cette demande, vota à l'unanimité la résolution suivante: "à toutes les puissances maritimes incombe le devoir d'adopter un code unique de lois, en matière de collisions sur mer, spécialement *en ce qui concerne la juridiction.*"

Le congrès de Londres s'est assemblé au palais de Guildhall, du 25 au 29 juillet 1887. Le secrétaire-général lut dans une des séances, une lettre de M. le Commandant Riondel, en disant que son programme avait déjà été approuvé par le congrès de Hambourg.

Le procès-verbal (page 190) contient ces deux communications que nous reproduisons :

"Monsieur le vice-amiral Jurien de la Gravière a résumé (dans le Compte-rendu de l'Académie des sciences du 20 juin 1887) de la manière suivante, les diverses propositions que je lui avais soumises:

"1° Imposer aux paquebots à vapeur une route d'aller et une route de retour, afin de diviser le courant unique en deux courants parallèles.

"2° Déterminer une vitesse maximum dans les canaux étroits en-temps de brume.

"3° Augmenter la portée de l'éclairage et le mettre en harmonie avec les vitesses d'aujourd'hui.

"4° Etablir des tribunaux maritimes internationaux pour juger les litiges entre navires de nationalités différentes.

"Je soumets respectueusement la question à la Conférence de Londres, dans les termes adoptées par l'illustre et savant amiral Jurien de la Gravière.

"Je ne puis pas me placer sur un meilleur terrain et sous un patronage plus recommandable et plus compétent.

"Je crois même inutile de faire une autre note, plus spéciale et plus développée pour la Conférence de Londres. Je me borne à présenter mes nouveaux travaux.

"Qu'il me soit permis, en outre, de recommander particulièrement à la haute assemblée:

"Ma note sur les tribunaux maritimes internationaux, el celle de la modification des couleurs de l'éclairage.

"Une troisième note sur les signaux de brume et l'utilité d'indiquer la route suivie par un avertissement supplémentaire (le clairon).

* * * * * * *

"Le moyen pratique qui me paraît le plus sûr pour résoudre ces questions est le suivant:

"Nomination immédiate d'une commission technique internationale (un membre par nation adhérente); cette commission préparerait le travail des diplomates chargés un jour de rédiger le projet de loi. On arrêtera ainsi le cours de ces terribles calamités, les collisions en mer, qui croissent et croîtront sans cesse en intensité at en victimes. Il est nécessaire, par un remède énergique et salutaire, d'établir une barrière et de mettre un frein à tant de misères et de douleurs: elles durent depuis trop longtemps.

"La Conférence de Londres accomplira son œuvre en y mettant un terme.

"ALBERT RIONDEL."

L'assemblée vote à l'unanimité la résolution suivante:

"L'attention des autorités compétentes des puissances maritimes doit être appelée sur l'importance de punir toutes les infractions au règlement qui exige un éclairage convenable sur mer."

C'est exactement la 6me proposition que nous avions faite, en 1885, au congrès de Hambourg.

LES TRIBUNAUX MARITIMES INTERNATIONAUX.

JUGÉS PAR LE CHEF DU SERVICE DES INSTRUCTIONS NAUTIQUES.

Les tribunaux maritimes internationaux comptent comme adversaire: M. le chef du service des instructions nautiques de la marine.

Dans son ouvrage sur les collisions en mer récemment publié, il a attaqué cette institution en disant qu'elle était irréalisable.

Nous lui avons répondu en ces termes dans le *Cosmos:*

M. le chef du service des instructions nautiques, au service hydrographique de la marine, a fait paraître récemment le second tome de son ouvrage sur les collisions en mer. Comme le précédent, ce volume sort de l'Imprimerie nationale. Les fonctions de l'auteur et le nom de l'imprimerie donnent à cet ouvrage l'apparence d'une attache officielle. Cependant, cette attache n'existe pas. Le volume qui vient de paraître le déclare en ces termes (page 169):

"Il ne nous paraît pas inutile de dire en terminant que l'initiative des deux parties de ce travail nous est propre et que personne ne nous en a imposé, et ne pouvait d'ailleurs songer à nous en inspirer la rédaction, non plus que les idées ou arguments qui y sont développés."

C'est heureux assurément; cependant il sera difficile au public et surtout aux étrangers de ne pas faire quelques réserves attendu que le ministère a favorisé des expériences, fait construire des instruments spéciaux et mis ses archives et ses renseignements officiels sur la matière à l'entière disposition de l'auteur, chef d'un de ses services.

Ce n'est pas tout. Dans la première partie de l'ouvrage, le chef du service des instructions nautiques déclare : "Qu'il a collationné par la nature de son service *tous* les documents français et étrangers."

Il est fâcheux, dans ces conditions, de faire non seulement des oublis, mais des erreurs de *faits* pouvant tromper et égarer le lecteur. Nous croyons de notre devoir de les mettre en évidence pour tous ceux qui s'occupent de cette cause, et de les signaler en même temps à M. le ministre de la marine. Nous ne parlerons, aujourd'hui, que de ce qui concerne les tribunaux maritimes internationaux; nous nous occuperons une autre fois des routes de navigation, pour montrer qu'elles ont été l'objet des mêmes oublis, d'autant plus fâcheux qu'ils ont été peut-être volontaires.

A la page 106 de son second volume, l'auteur dit que les deux Chambres de commerce de Bordeaux et de Dunkerque sont *opposées* à la création de tribunaux maritimes internationaux. Nous allons édifier le lecteur à ce sujet. Voici la délibération de la Chambre de Bordeaux (22 juillet 1885) :

" La Chambre, partageant l'opinion de son rapporteur, décide que la lettre suivante sera écrite à M. Riondel :

" MONSIEUR :

" La Chambre de commerce de Bordeaux a examiné votre communication avec intérêt ; elle en apprécie le mérite et joint son approbation à celle que le Gouvernement des États-Unis a donnée aux deux proposition que vous formulez relativement aux mesures à prendre pour éviter les collisions, et à la formation de tribunaux maritimes internationaux.

"*Le Président de la Chambre,*
" HUBERT PROM."

La Chambre de commerce de la Rochelle (dans sa délibération du 12 mai 1887), à la suite de considérants, émet le vœu :

* * * Que le Ministère du Commerce et de l'Industrie, après entente avec les autres ministères compétents, prenne l'initiative de conférences internationales avec les représentants des 16 puissances maritimes qui ont adhéré au règlement sur les moyens de prévenir les abordages. Ces conférences devront avoir pour objet :

1° *   *   *   *   *
2° *   *   *   *   *   *   *

3° L'établissement de tribunaux maritimes internationaux chargés de juger les contestations ayant pour cause les collisions en mer entre navires de nationalités différentes ; tribunaux qui seraient composés à la fois de juges de la nationalité de chaque partie et de juges étrangers à l'une et à l'autre, pour départager au besoin les premiers.

Le Président de la Chambre,
MOREL.

A la page 105 du même volume, le chef du bureau des instructions nautiques dit également que la Chambre de commerce de Dunkerque ne veut pas non plus de ces tribunaux maritimes internationaux. C'est une nouvelle erreur. Le 17 juin 1887, la Chambre de commerce, par l'organe de son président, M. Petit, s'exprime ainsi :

" Quant aux tribunaux maritimes internationaux, leur création serait appelée à rendre les plus grands services et mettrait fin aux difficultés résultant du régime adopté jusqu'ici. C'est ainsi qu'en matière d'abordage, les juges appelés à se prononcer sont ceux du pays où relâche le navire abordeur. Or, les codes maritimes des diverses nations n'étant pas identiques, des jugements différents peuvent être rendus pour des faits analogues, suivant la nationalité des juges qui en connaissent. Il y a là évidemment une situation anormale qu'il importe de modifier. La création de tribunaux internationaux, devant lesquels seraient portés les litiges maritimes, en tranchant tout d'abord la question de compétence, donnerait sur ce point aux intéressés toutes les garanties que la justice doit leur fournir ; elle aurait ensuite pour conséquence d'amener tôt ou tard la réforme des codes maritimes dans le sens de l'uniformité, et c'est là un but auquel on doit tendre dans l'intérêt de la marine.

Dans ces conditions, M. le président propose à la Chambre d'appuyer auprès du gouvernement les vœux formulés par M. le commandant Riondel.

La Chambre consultée adopte cette proposition.

Le Président,
A. PETIT.

Voilà qui est catégorique, mais continuons :

A la page 107, l'auteur ajoute que plusieurs autres Chambres de commerce sont du même avis que celles de Bordeaux, de La Rochelle et de Dunkerque ; c'est vrai, mais leur opinion est diamétralement opposée à celle que leur prête le chef de bureau des instructions nautiques ; elles réclament la création de ces tribunaux internationaux.

Chambre de Marseille ; délibération du	30 juin	1885
Paris "	9 novembre	1885
Nantes "	16 octobre	1886
Granville "	27 novembre	1886
Caen	25 janvier	1887
Cherbourg "	29 janvier	1887
Bayonne "	12 juin	1887
Rochefort "		
Calais "	3 juin	1887
Abbeville "	27 juin	1887
Dieppe "	8 juin	1887
Rouen "	9 juin	1887
Cette	25 novembre	1887
Lorient "	17 janvier	1888
Saint-Malo "	5 mars	1888
Le Havre ; lettres du prést.	18 juin	1885
" "	11 novembre	1885
" "	14 avril	1888
Lisbonne "	24 novembre	1886
"	4 décembre	1886
Glasgow . "	10 mai	1886

Dans cette longue liste, nous citerons seulement la délibération de la Chambre de commerce de Nantes ; elle a une importance particulière. Le 16 octobre 1886, le président de cette Chambre, M. Rivron, écrivait :

" J'ai l'honneur de vous faire connaître, Monsieur, que la Chambre de commerce de Nantes n'hésite pas à donner son approbation à l'idée, par vous émise, en faveur de la création de tribunaux maritimes internationaux chargés de prononcer sur les conflits qui se produisent entre navires de nationalités différentes. Nous croyons, comme vous, que l'institution de ces tribunaux rendrait de grands services au commerce ; elle offrirait en un mot, si elle était composée d'après les vues dont vous vous êtes inspiré, toutes garanties d'impartialité et de prompte justice. Elle mettrait fin aux difficultés qui naissent aujourd'hui des questions de compétence dont la solution entraîne souvent des délais excessifs, et elle aurait aussi pour résultat d'assurer l'exécution des jugements.

"La réunion d'une Commission internationale proposée par vous, dans le but d'élaborer une révision de la loi, serait d'une utilité évidente ; elle serait la préface obligée des tribunaux internationaux."

Faisons remarquer que plusieurs sociétés de géographie commerciale et que plusieurs assemblées municipales ont pris des délibérations identiques.   Le Congrès de Nantes (août 1886) où 42 sociétés géographiques se trouvaient représentées, a approuvé à l'unanimité la création de tribunaux maritimes internationaux.

Le Conseil d'amirauté (séance du 24 avril 1886) a émis à l'unanimité le vœu suivant :

"Qu'il serait du plus sérieux intérêt qu'un accord pût être réalisé entre les diverses nations maritimes pour la constitution de tribunaux internationaux chargés de connaître des litiges entre navires de nationalités différentes, et de les juger d'après une loi commune."

Le Gouvernement de Grèce, les Congrès de Hambourg et d'Anvers ont exprimé des avis pareils.

Le Gouvernement des États-Unis disait, 4 février 1885, en parlant du rapport sur cette question de M. Jarvis Patten, commissaire de la navigation : "Le Département de la Trésorerie donne pleinement son assentiment à ces idées."   Or le dit rapport contient ces lignes dans son dernier paragraphe : "Il est probable que toutes les nations favoriseraient l'insertion de la deuxième clause proposée par M. Riondel dans les règlements internationaux, et j'incline à recommander son adoption."

En terminant cet exposé, nous poserons devant le monde maritime, à M. le chef du bureau des instructions nautiques, les questions suivantes :

1° Pourquoi n'a-t-il pas fait connaître tous les documents publiés de cette grande enquête française ?

2° Pourquoi dit-il, en présence de ce dossier qu'il connaissait parfaitement : "C'est compliquer le problème déjà si délicat de la sécurité sur mer, que de vouloir y joindre ces irréalisables propositions de tribunaux inernationaux" (page 108) ?

3° Que croit-il que pensera la marine du passage final (page 169) : "Nous avons cru rendre service aux navigateurs en mettant sous leurs yeux *tous* les éléments de discussion jusqu'ici épars dans les diverses publications françaises et étrangères."

L'auteur des *Collisions en mer* doit à l'opinion publique, il se doit à lui même de répondre à ces questions, Comment fera-t-il ?

L'Imprimerie nationale qui a prêté ses presses aux deux premières parties de son travail pourra aisément publier la troisième.

TARIF PROTECTEUR DES EXISTENCES ET RESPONSABILITÉ DES COM-
PAGNIES.

La Revue de la Marine Marchande, qui partage les idées de M. le chef
du service des instructions nautiques au sujet des routes de navigation,
émet une nouvelle objection contre ces routes :

" Tout en admirant sincèrement les sentiments généreux qui inspirent
les *partisans* des routes de navigation, dit-elle, nous ne pourrons partager leurs convictions que lorsqu 'ils nous auront démontré que les capitaines des paquebots transatlantiques français, anglais et autres sont de
leur opinion."

Ces partisans des routes, on le sait, ce sont : Les Chambres de commerce, les Sociétés de géographie commerciale, les municipalités des
ports et environ 7,000 marins, parmi lesquels les plus éminents. Le
dossier qui le constate embarrasse les ennemis des routes, aussi n'en
parlent-ils jamais ; mais ils ne se bornent pas à cette démonstration
passive.

Au mois de juin 1885, la Commission des pétitions de la Chambre
des Députés, sur la proposition de son rapporteur, M. le Marquis de la
Ferronnays, votait et signait un rapport très favorable aux vœux des
nombreux marins de tous rangs, armateurs, commerçants, Chambres de
commerce, Sociétés de géographie et municipalités des ports ; on y
demandait en premier lieu la double route d'aller et de retour pour les
paquebots. Le rapport en démontrait éloquemment la nécessité.

Immédiatement informées, les grandes Compagnies de navigation se
mirent en campagne ; quelques officiers de marine s'associèrent à ce
mouvement.*

On entreprit de faire revenir sur leur vote les membres de la Commission ; ce but ne fut pas atteint ; le rapport, fort heureusement, avait
été remis à la questure, et il était trop tard pour revenir sur ce qui était
fait.

Les compagnies de navigation sont dans leur rôle, quand elles s'op-
posent de toutes leurs forces à ce qu'on leur impose les nouvelles responsabilités qu'elles encourraient avec des itinéraires obligatoires ; elles
préfèrent garder leur liberté. Des routes internationales garantiraient
sans doute la vie de leurs victimes, mais elles gêneraient leurs mouvements.

N'est-il pas évident, d'autre part, que l'opinion des compagnies com-
mande celles de leurs capitaines ? Ceux-ci ont d'ailleurs cent raisons
pour préférer une situation qui leur permet de suivre l'itinéraire qui
leur convient davantage.

Cependant si, depuis deux ans, le passage du banc de Terre-Neuve
avait été interdit aux paquebots, Granville compterait cinq navires de
plus dans sa flotte ; ses familles de marins ne seraient pas en deuil, on

---

* Lettre de M. de la Ferronnays au président de la Société de géographie de Roche-
fort.

n'aurait pas les veuves et les orphelins des équipages du *Georges-et-Jeanne* du *Saint-Pair* du *Medellin*, etc., etc., coulés par les paquebots sur les lieux de pêche.

Toute règlementation civile ou maritime entrave le libre arbitre; elle crée des responsabilités et une gêne; on ne saurait s'étonner qu'elles ne soient pas goûtées par certains capitaines; mais les doubles voies ne sont pas proposées pour l'agrément des compagnies et de leurs officiers, mais bien pour la protection des personnes et des biens.

Si les compagnies réclament leurs aises et s'élèvent contre toute atteinte à ce libre arbitre, c'est qu'elles veulent décliner toute responsabilité et que ce qui les touche avant tout, c'est de ne pas perdre une heure, de ne pas brûler une tonne de charbon en trop, et que, par suite, le parcours le plus court leur parait le plus favorable; quant aux victimes elles passent après ces considérations; d'ailleurs on compte sur la Providence et sur sa bonne étoile.

Les compagnies sont puissantes, leur influence est considérable; leur opposition constitue donc une barrière difficile à renverser. Mais l'accumulation incessante des sinistres maritimes aura raison de leur résistance et conduira fatalement à l'établissement de routes internationales.

L'auteur de l'article de la *Revue de la marine marchande* parle des *Pilot-charts* (cartes dressées chaque mois par les États-Unis pour les navigateurs de l'Atlantique), et apporte ainsi un argument à notre cause. Jadis on se contentait d'y indiquer la meilleure route pour éviter les glaces flottantes. Depuis plusieurs mois, ces mêmes cartes indiquent une route d'aller et une route de retour pour les navires; de là, à réglementer ces tracés et à les rendre obligatoires, il n'y a qu'un pas; il suffit de vouloir le faire.

L'auteur ajoute:

" La publication de ces cartes est appelée à rendre de grands services aux navigateurs de l'Atlantique nord. Nous savons que ceux-ci tiennent toujours compte de leurs indications; mais ells *empêcheront jamais* les capitaines, soucieux d'arriver vite, de chercher à raccourcir leur route chaque fois que le temps clair leur permettra de ne pas craindre de passer dans des parages où des icebergs ont été signalés par les ' pilot-charts.' "

Cette appréciation n'est pas exacte, nous en sommes convaincus. Les capitaines suivront l'itinéraire devenu obligatoire si on met un prix assez élevé à chaque vie humaine anéantie dans un abordage causé par leur désobéissance à la loi, si on tarife, non seulement la mort, mais les blessures graves et les blessures légères aussi. Une pareille classification, facile à établir, est juste; on doit la faire, fixer un tarif élevé et faire accepter ces mesures dans un accord international. La responsabilité des capitaines n'existe pas aujourd'hui, elle fait défaut à la sécurité des mers; on doit l'établir. Elle sera certainement créée un jour, parce qu'il est équitable, quand on fait des veuves et des orphelins par sa faute, en violant les lois, de prendre la charge de ces infortunés, et de payer au poids de l'or ceux qu'on leur a enlevés.

Les pétitions, qui ont marqué le premier mouvement de l'opinion publique sur cette question, sont couvertes de signatures de capitaines au long cours, de capitaines au cabotage, de pilotes, de marins; des capitaines étrangers ont tenu à apporter aussi leur adhésion. Tous, comme les hautes corporations citées ci-dessus, ont demandé le tracé de routes obligatoires, et c'est ce que constate le rapport de M. de la Ferronnays. En outre, nos illustrations maritimes se sont aussi déclarées en faveur des routes maritimes.

C'est contre cette majorité que luttent les grandes compagnies de navigation, et, jusqu'à present, elles ont été assez puissantes pour la tenir en échec. Leur influence, leur action sur les sphères officielles, leur ont donné cet avantage: mais il ne sera que passager; elles seront vaincues par la force prépondérante de l'opinion publique de mieux en mieux éclairée.

CONCLUSIONS.

LE RAPPORT DU COMMISSAIRE DE LA NAVIGATION AUX ÉTATS-UNIS.

M. Jarvis Patten démontre, dans son rapport du 31 janvier 1885, la *nécessité* de recourir à des tribunaux internationaux.

"L'établissement de ces tribunaux, dit-il, épargnerait des frais, préviendrait beaucoup d'ennuis et conduirait à une plus grande harmonie dans l'interprétation donnée aux lois sur les collisions par les différentes nations.

"Il est probable—ajoute-t-il—que toutes les nations favoriseraient l'incorporation dans le nouveau règlement international, d'une clause semblable à celle que propose le capitaine Riondel pour les tribunaux mixtes."

Dans le cours de ce rapport, le commissaire de la navigation condamne en ces termes les tribunaux des nationalités: "On peut dire que la question de juridiction, dans les cas dont il s'agit, est complètement incertaine chez les nations maritimes. Il en est résulté quelquefois beaucoup de désagréments, de part et d'autre, avec des frais et des ennuis considérables."

Presque toutes les chambres de commerce maritimes de France ont fait entendre le même langage. Leurs résolutions offrent également ce double caractère: elles condamnent ce qui existe. Toutes réclament des tribunaux internationaux. La lecture attentive de ces résolutions est donc très instructive.

En nous appuyant sur les autorités que nous venons de nommer, nous demandons l'établissement de tribunaux maritimes internationaux qui remplaceraient les tribunaux des nationalités.

Nous avons exprimé nos préférences dans la note lue au Congrès de Nantes. Ces vues ont obtenu l'approbation du Gouvernement des États-Unis et des chambres de commerce françaises.

La Chambre de Nantes se prononçait ainsi dans son passage principal : " Si ces tribunaux étaient composés d'après les vues dont vous vous êtes inspiré, ils offriraient toutes garanties d'impartialité et de prompte justice : ils mettraient fin aux difficultés qui naissent aujourd'hui des question de compétence dont la solution entraîne souvent des délais excessifs ; l'institution de ces tribunaux aurait aussi pour résultat d'assurer l'exécution des jugements."

Malgré cela, nous formulons simplement, d'une manière générale dans notre conclusion, la nécessité d'une législation internationale. Nous resterons ainsi dans notre rôle d'officier de marine. Nos travaux peuvent servir, mais les jurisconsultes de droit maritime ont seuls la compétence et les connaissances requises pour résoudre les difficultés pratiques de cette organisation judiciaire. Nous considérons notre tâche comme remplie, après avoir saisi l'opinion publique et réussi à faire partager notre conviction par les plus hautes autorités. Nous avons eu la bonne fortune de voir un homme éminent prendre pied dans la question.

D'autres jurisconsultes marcheront sur ses traces et résoudront un problème dont tout le monde aujourd'hui reconnaît la grande importance. Comment serait-il irréalisable, quand les États-Unis, d'une part, et les commités commerciales et maritimes de notre pays d'autre part, pensent précisément le contraire ?

L'organisation nouvelle rendra surtout des services, si ses rouages sont simples et la justice expéditive. C'est à notre avis un point essentiel, gagner du temps en marine est une qualité à la quelle il faut sacrifier beaucoup. C'est le vrai moyen de garantir les intérêts du commerce. Cette idée a inspiré la note que nous avons présentée au Congrès de Nantes. Elle a certainement entraîné l'adhésion donnée à notre projet par la Chambre de commerce de Nantes et les autres corporations commerciales.

Dans tous les jugements d'abordage, on ne considère généralement que les *pertes matérielles*. Le navire déclaré responsable de la collision est condamné à une juste réparation envers l'armateur lésé dans ses intérêts. Mais ce dommage se compose de *deux* éléments. L'un—le principal—est toujours laissé dans l'oubli. La vie humaine, sacrifiée ou mutilée, a droit cependant à une réparation, au même titre que le propriétaire du navire coulé à fond, ou varié par la faute du capitaine auteur du sinistre. Le tribunal qui ordonne et fixe le *dommage*, après avoir pesé et jugé les circonstances de la cause, a le devoir de faire *deux* parts : celle des intérêts matériels, et aussi, celle des victimes. Tout être humain, en pareil cas, est égal devant la mort. La vie du simple matelot a droit à une indemnité égale à celle de toute autre personne qui périt dans le désatre. Ne devrait-il pas exister un *tarif international* des indemnités accordées aux victimes, pour blessures légères, blessures graves et perte de la vie ?

Le tribunal international *classerait* et appliquerait le dit tarif. L'état récapitulatif de cette équitable et tardive réparation serait déduit du chiffre accordé aujourd'hui *intégralement* aux propriétaires du navire. Les intérêts matériels sont très respectables. L'intérêt du matelot tué ou blessé dans un abordage mérite une protection légale qui, de nos jours, lui fait absolument défaut. * * * Sa *situation* lui interdit absolument le recours à la justice, ce que peut faire l'armateur ou la Compagnie de navigation. Le législateur a par suite le devoir de rétablir l'équilibre du droit et de la justice.

Un litige d'abordage est d'une nature spéciale. Les deux intérêts— matériel et humanitaire—ne doivent pas être *séparés*. Ces considérations sont surtout nécessaires à l'époque actuelle. Dans la lutte insensée des vitesses sur mer et des rivalités commerciales ou postales, le respect de la vie humaine est placé à un rang tout-à-fait inférieur. Les grandes compagnies n'ont *aucune* responsabilité. Au point de vue de la stricte justice, et aussi au point de vue humanitaire, nous demandons instamment, qu'une responsabilité *pécuniaire* leur soit imposée pour chaque vie humaine qu'elles anéantissent avec une insouciance et une imprudence que nous qualifions de coupables. On accomplira ainsi un acte de justice. On diminuera notablement le nombre des collisions en mer.

INTERNATIONAL MARINE CONFERENCE,

WASHINGTON, D. C.,

1890.

REPORT OF THE UNITED STATES DELEGATES.

REPORT OF THE UNITED STATES DELEGATES.

DEPARTMENT OF STATE,
INTERNATIONAL MARINE CONFERENCE,
Washington, February 20, 1890.

Hon. JAMES G. BLAINE,
Secretary of State,
Department of State:

SIR: In pursuance of the directions contained in the Letter of Instructions to the Delegates of the United States, issued by the Secretary of State on February 27, 1889, in regard to "framing a report of the proceedings of the Conference," the United States Delegates have the honor to submit the following report upon the conclusions reached.

The United States Delegates, pursuant to such Letter of Instructions, met in March, 1889, and formulated a programme containing thirteen general divisions, which was approved by the Department of State, and which appear in order below.

The Conference met on October 16, 1889, considered the entire programme and discussed with great care and patience each separate division and clause, in the following order:

GENERAL DIVISION 1.

Marine signals or other means of plainly indicating the direction in which vessels are moving in fog, mist, falling snow, and thick weather, and at night.

RULES FOR THE PREVENTION OF COLLISIONS AND RULES OF THE ROAD.

1. Visibility, number, and position of lights to be carried by vessels.
    (*a*) Steamers under way.
    (*b*) Steamers towing.
    (*c*) Vessels under way, but not under command, including steamers laying cable.
    (*d*) Sailing vessels under way.
    (*e*) Sailing vessels towing.
    (*f*) Vessels at anchor.
    (*g*) Pilot vessels.
    (*h*) Fishing vessels.

S. Ex. 53, pt. 3——29

2. Sound signals; their character, number, range, and position of instruments.

    (a) For use in fog, mist, falling snow, and thick weather, as position signals.

        For steamers under way.

        For steamers towing.

        For sailing vessels under way.

        For sailing vessels towing.

        (These signals to show the approximate course steered if possible.)

        For vessels at anchor.

        For vessels under way, but not under command, including steamers laying cable.

    (b) For use in all weathers as helm signals only.

        For steamers meeting or crossing.

        For steamers overtaking.

        For steamers backing.

    (c) Whether helm signals shall be made compulsory or remain optional.

3. Steering and sailing rules.

    (a) Sailing vessels meeting, crossing, overtaking, or being overtaken by each other.

    (b) Steamers meeting, crossing, overtaking, or being overtaken by each other.

    (c) Sailing vessels meeting, crossing, overtaking, or being overtaken by steamers.

    (d) Steamers meeting, crossing, overtaking, or being overtaken by sailing vessels.

    (e) Special rules for channels and tide-ways, where no local rules exist.

    (f) Conflict of international and local rules.

    (g) Uniform system of commands to the helm.

    (h) Speed of vessels in thick weather.

Under this general division, regarding course-indicating signals for use in fog, mist, falling snow, and thick weather, the Conference, by a call of the roll of countries, unanimously adopted the following resolution:

"*Resolved*, That in the opinion of the Conference it is inexpedient to adopt course-indicating sound-signals in foggy or thick weather; inasmuch as among the other strong reasons presented by the Sound-Signal Committee, if such signals were used in crowded waters, danger would result from the uncertainty and confusion produced by a multiplicity of signals, and from the false security that would be created in the minds of mariners, and if vessels were navigated in dependence on such signals, when neither could see the other, there would be danger that the officer in charge might read the signal incorrectly, or if he read it correctly, would interpret it wrongly."

Regarding rules for the prevention of collisions and rules of the road, the Conference finally approved of the following:

REGULATIONS FOR PREVENTING COLLISIONS AT SEA.

PRELIMINARY.

These Rules shall be followed by all vessels upon the high seas and in all waters connected therewith, navigable by sea-going vessels.

In the following Rules every steam-vessel which is under sail and not under steam is to be considered a sailing-vessel, and every vessel under steam, whether under sail or not, is to be considered a steam-vessel.

The word "*steam-vessel*" shall include any vessel propelled by machinery.

A vessel is "*under way*" within the meaning of these Rules when she is not at anchor, or made fast to the shore, or aground.

RULES CONCERNING LIGHTS, ETC.

The word "*visible*" in these Rules when applied to lights shall mean visible on a dark night with a clear atmosphere.

ARTICLE 1. The rules concerning lights shall be complied with in all-weathers from sunset to sunrise, and during such time no other lights which may be mistaken for the prescribed lights shall be exhibited.

ART. 2. A steam-vessel when under way shall carry—

(a) On or in front of the foremast, or if a vessel without a foremast, then in the fore part of the vessel, at a height above the hull of not less than 20 feet, and if the breadth of the vessel exceeds 20 feet, then at a height above the hull not less than such breadth, so however, that the light need not be carried at a greater height above the hull than 40 feet, a bright white light, so constructed as to show an unbroken light over an arc of the horizon of 20 points of the compass, so fixed as to throw the light 10 points on each side of the vessel, viz, from right ahead to 2 points abaft the beam on either side, and of such a character as to be visible at a distance of at least 5 miles.

(b) On the starboard side a green light so constructed as to show an unbroken light over an arc of the horizon of 10 points of the compass, so fixed as to throw the light from right ahead to 2 points abaft the beam on the starboard side, and of such a character as to be visible at a distance of at least 2 miles.

(c) On the port side a red light so constructed as to show an unbroken light over an arc of the horizon of 10 points of the compass, so fixed as to throw the light from right ahead to 2 points abaft the beam on the port side, and of such a character as to be visible at a distance of at least 2 miles.

(*d*) The said green and red side-lights shall be fitted with inboard screens projecting at least 3 feet forward from the light, so as to prevent these lights from being seen across the bow.

(*e*) A steam-vessel when under way may carry an additional white light similar in construction to the light mentioned in subdivision (*a*) These two lights shall be so placed in line with the keel that one shall be at least 15 feet higher than the other, and in such a position with reference to each other that the lower light shall be forward of the upper one. The vertical distance between these lights shall be less than the horizontal distance.

ART. 3. A steam-vessel when towing another vessel shall, in addition to her side-lights, carry two bright white lights in a vertical line one over the other, not less than 6 feet apart, and when towing more than one vessel shall carry an additional bright white light 6 feet above or below such lights, if the length of the tow measuring from the stern of the towing-vessel to the stern of the last vessel towed exceeds 600 feet. Each of these lights shall be of the same construction and character, and shall be carried in the same position as the white light mentioned in Article 2 (*a*), excepting the additional light, which may be carried at a height of not less than 14 feet above the hull.

Such steam-vessel may carry a small white light abaft the funnel or aftermast for the vessel towed to steer by, but such light shall not be visible forward of the beam.

ART. 4. (*a*) A vessel which from any accident is not under command shall carry at the same height as the white light mentioned in Article 2 (*a*), where they can best be seen, and if a steam-vessel in lieu of that light, two red lights, in a vertical line one over the other, not less than 6 feet apart, and of such a character as to be visible all around the horizon at a distance of at least 2 miles; and shall by day carry in a vertical line one over the other, not less than 6 feet apart, where they can best be seen, two black balls or shapes, each 2 feet in diameter.

(*b*) A vessel employed in laying or in picking up a telegraph cable shall carry in the same position as the white light mentioned in Article 2 (*a*), and if a steam-vessel in lieu of that light, three lights in a vertical line one over the other, not less than 6 feet apart. The highest and lowest of these lights shall be red, and the middle light shall be white, and they shall be of such a character as to be visible all around the horizon, at a distance of at least 2 miles. By day she shall carry in a vertical line one over the other, not less than 6 feet apart, where they can best be seen, three shapes not less than 2 feet in diameter, of which the highest and lowest shall be globular in shape and red in color, and the middle one diamond in shape and white.

(*c*) The vessels referred to in this article, when not making way through the water, shall not carry the side-lights, but when making way shall carry them.

(*d*) The lights and shapes required to be shown by this article are to be taken by other vessels as signals that the vessel showing them is not under command and can not therefore get out of the way.

These signals are not signals of vessels in distress and requiring assistance. Such signals are contained in Article 31.

ART. 5. A sailing vessel under way, and any vessel being towed shall carry the same lights as are prescribed by Article 2 for a steam-vessel under way, with the exception of the white lights mentioned therein, which they shall never carry.

ART. 6. Whenever, as in the case of small vessels under way during bad weather, the green and red side-lights can not be fixed, these lights shall be kept at hand, lighted and ready for use; and shall, on the approach of or to other vessels, be exhibited on their respective sides in sufficient time to prevent collision, in such manner as to make them most visible, and so that the green light shall not be seen on the port side nor the red light on the starboard side, nor if practicable more than 2 points abaft the beam on their respective sides.

To make the use of these portable lights more certain and easy, the lanterns containing them shall each be painted outside with the color of the light they respectively contain, and shall be provided with proper screens.

ART. 7. Steam-vessels of less than 40, and vessels under oars or sails, of less than 20 tons, gross tonnage, respectively, when under way, shall not be obliged to carry the lights mentioned in Article 2 (*a*) (*b*) and (*c*), but if they do not carry them they shall be provided with the following lights:

1. Steam-vessels of less than 40 tons shall carry:
    (*a*) In the fore part of the vessel, or on or in front of the funnel, where it can best be seen, and at a height above the gunwale of not less than 9 feet, a bright white light constructed and fixed as prescribed in Article 2 (*a*), and of such a character as to be visible at a distance of at least 2 miles.
    (*b*) Green and red side-lights constructed and fixed as prescribed in Article 2 (*b*) and (*c*), and of such a character as to be visible at a distance of at least 1 mile, or a combined lantern showing a green light and a red light from right ahead to 2 points abaft the beam on their respective sides. Such lantern shall be carried not less than 3 feet below the white light.
2. Small steam-boats, such as are carried by sea-going vessels, may carry the white light at a less height than 9 feet above the gunwale, but it shall be carried above the combined lantern, mentioned in subdivision 1 (*b*).
3. Vessels under oars or sails, of less than 20 tons, shall have ready at hand a lantern with a green glass on one side and a red glass on the

other, which, on the approach of or to other vessels, shall be exhibited in sufficient time to prevent collision, so that the green light shall not be seen on the port side nor the red light on the starboard side.

The vessels referred to in this article shall not be obliged to carry the lights prescribed by Article 4 (a) and Article 11, last paragraph.

ART. 8. Pilot-vessels, when engaged on their station on pilotage duty, shall not show the lights required for other vessels, but shall carry a white light at the mast-head, visible all around the horizon, and shall also exhibit a flare-up light or flare-up lights at short intervals, which shall never exceed fifteen minutes.

On the near approach of or to other vessels they shall have their side-lights lighted, ready for use, and shall flash or show them at short intervals to indicate the direction in which they are heading, but the green light shall not be shown on the port side nor the red light on the starboard side.

A pilot-vessel of such a class as to be obliged to go alongside of a vessel to put a pilot on board may show the white light instead of carrying it at the mast-head, and may, instead of the colored lights above mentioned, have at hand ready for use a lantern with a green glass on the one side and a red glass on the other, to be used as prescribed above.

Pilot-vessels, when not engaged on their station on pilotage duty, shall carry lights similar to those of other vessels of their tonnage.

ART. 9. Fishing vessels and fishing boats, when under way and when not required by this article to carry or show the lights therein named, shall carry or show the lights prescribed for vessels of their tonnage under way.

(a) Vessels and boats when fishing with drift-nets shall exhibit two white lights from any part of the vessel where they can best be seen. Such lights shall be placed so that the vertical distance between them shall be not less than 6 feet and not more than 10 feet, and so that the horizontal distance between them, measured in a line with the keel, shall be not less than 5 feet and not more than 10 feet. The lower of these two lights shall be the more forward, and both of them shall be of such a character as to show all around the horizon, and to be visible at a distance of not less than 3 miles.

(b) Vessels when engaged in trawling, by which is meant the dragging of an apparatus along the bottom of the sea—

(1) If steam-vessels, shall carry in the same position as the white light mentioned in Article 2 (a), a tricolored lantern so constructed and fixed as to show a white light from right ahead to 2 points on each bow, and a green light and a red light over an arc of the horizon from 2 points on either bow to 2 points abaft the beam on the

starboard and port side respectively; and not less than 6 nor more than 12 feet below the tricolored lantern, a white light in a lantern, so constructed as to show a clear, uniform, and unbroken light all around the horizon.

(2) If sailing vessels of 7 tons gross tonnage and upwards, shall carry a white light in a lantern, so constructed as to show a clear uniform and unbroken light all around the horizon, and shall also be provided with a sufficient supply of red pyrotechnic lights, which shall each burn for at least 30 seconds, and shall be shown on the approach of or to other vessels in sufficient time to prevent collision.

In the Mediterranean Sea, the vessels referred to in subdivision (b) 2, may use a flare-up light in lieu of a pyrotechnic light.

All lights mentioned in subdivision b (1) and (2) shall be visible at a distance of at least 2 miles.

(3) If sailing vessels of less than 7 tons gross tonnage, shall not be obliged to carry the white light mentioned in subdivision b (2) of this article, but if they do not carry such light, they shall have at hand, ready for use, a lantern, showing a bright white light, which shall, on the approach of or to other vessels be exhibited where it can best be seen, in sufficient time to prevent collision; and they shall also show a red pyrotechnic light, as prescribed in subdivision b (2), or in lieu thereof a flare-up light.

(c) Vessels and boats when line-fishing with their lines out and attached to their lines, and when not at anchor or stationary, shall carry the same lights as vessels fishing with drift-nets.

(d) Fishing vessels and fishing boats may at any time use a flare-up light in addition to the lights which they are by this article required to carry and show. All flare-up lights exhibited by a vessel when trawling or fishing with any kind of drag-net shall be shown at the after part of the vessel, excepting that, if the vessel is hanging by the stern to her fishing gear, they shall be exhibited from the bow.

(e) Every fishing vessel and every boat when at anchor shall exhibit a white light visible all around the horizon at a distance of at least 1 mile.

(f) If a vessel or boat when fishing becomes stationary in consequence of her gear getting fast to a rock or other obstruction, she shall show the light and make the fog-signal prescribed for a vessel at anchor, respectively. (*See Article* 15 (*d*), (*e*) *and last paragraph.*)

(g) In fog, mist, falling snow, or heavy rain storms, drift-net vessels attached to their nets, and vessels when trawling, dredging, or fishing with any kind of drag-net, and vessels line-fishing with their lines out, shall, if of 20 tons gross tonnage or upwards, respectively, at intervals of not more than one minute, make a blast; if steam-vessels with the whistle or siren, and if sailing vessels with the fog-horn, each blast to be followed by ringing the bell.

(h) Sailing vessels or boats fishing with nets or lines or trawls, when under way, shall in day-time indicate their occupation to an approaching vessel by displaying a basket, or other efficient signal, where it can best be seen.

The vessels referred to in this article shall not be obliged to carry the lights prescribed by Article 4 (a), and Article 11, last paragraph.

ART. 10. A vessel which is being overtaken by another shall show from her stern to such last-mentioned vessel a white light or a flare-up light.

The white light required to be shown by this article may be fixed and carried in a lantern, but in such case the lantern shall be so constructed, fitted, and screened that it shall throw an unbroken light over an arc of the horizon of 12 points of the compass, viz, for 6 points from right aft on each side of the vessel, so as to be visible at a distance of at least 1 mile. Such light shall be carried as nearly as practicable on the same level as the side-lights.

ART. 11. A vessel under 150 feet in length, when at anchor, shall carry forward, where it can best be seen, but at a height not exceeding 20 feet above the hull, a white light in a lantern so constructed as to show a clear, uniform and unbroken light visible all around the horizon at a distance of at least 1 mile.

A vessel of 150 feet or upwards in length, when at anchor, shall carry in the forward part of the vessel, at a height of not less than 20 and not exceeding 40 feet above the hull, one such light, and at or near the stern of the vessel, and at such a height that it shall be not less than 15 feet lower than the forward light, another such light.

The length of a vessel shall be deemed to be the length appearing in her certificate of registry.

A vessel aground in or near a fair-way shall carry the above light or lights and the two red lights prescribed by Article 4 (a).

ART. 12. Every vessel may, if necessary in order to attract attention, in addition to the lights which she is by these rules required to carry, show a flare-up light or use any detonating signal that can not be mistaken for a distress signal.

ART. 13. Nothing in these rules shall interfere with the operation of any special rules made by the Government of any nation, with respect to additional station and signal lights for two or more ships of war or for vessels sailing under convoy, or with the exhibition of recognition siguals adopted by ship-owners, which have been authorized by their respective Governments and duly registered and published.

ART. 14. A steam-vessel proceeding under sail only, but háving her funnel up, shall carry in day-time, forward, where it can best be seen, one black ball or shape 2 feet in diameter.

<h3>SOUND-SIGNALS FOR FOG, ETC.</h3>

ART. 15. All signals prescribed by this Article for vessels under way shall be given :

1. By "*steam-vessels*" on the whistle or siren.
2. By "*sailing vessels and vessels towed*" on the fog-horn.

The words "*prolonged blast*" used in this Article shall mean a blast of from four to six seconds' duration.

A steam-vessel shall be provided with an efficient whistle or siren, sounded by steam or some substitute for steam, so placed that the sound may not be intercepted by any obstruction, and with an efficient fog-horn, to be sounded by mechanical means, and also with an efficient bell.* A sailing vessel of 20 tons gross tonnage or upwards shall be provided with a similar fog-horn and bell.

In fog, mist, falling snow, or heavy rain-storms, whether by day or night, the signals described in this Article shall be used as follows, viz :

(*a*) A steam-vessel having way upon her shall sound, at intervals of not more than 2 minutes, a prolonged blast.

(*b*) A steam-vessel under way, but stopped and having no way upon her, shall sound, at intervals of not moie than 2 minutes, 2 prolonged blasts, with an interval of about 1 second between them.

(*c*) A sailing vessel under way shall sound, at intervals of not more than 1 minute, when on the starboard tack 1 blast, when on the port tack 2 blasts in succession, and when with the wind abaft the beam 3 blasts in succession.

(*d*) A vessel, when at anchor, shall, at intervals of not more than 1 minute, ring the bell rapidly for about 5 seconds.

(*e*) A vessel, at anchor at sea, when not in ordinary anchorage ground and when in such a position as to be an obstruction to vessels under way, shall sound, if a steam-vessel, at intervals of not more than 2 minutes, 1 prolonged blasts with her whistle or siren, followed by ringing her bell; or, if a sailing-vessel, at intervals of not more than 1 minute, 2 blasts with her fog-horn, followed by ringing her bell.

(*f*) A vessel, when towing, shall, instead of the signals prescribed in subdivisions (*a*) and (*c*) of this article, at intervals of not

---

*NOTE.—In all cases where the Rules require a bell to be used a drum may be substituted on board Turkish vessels, or a gong where such articles are used on board small sea-going vessels.

more than 2 minutes, sound 3 blasts in succession, viz: 1 prolonged blast followed by 2 short blasts. A vessel towed may give this signal and she shall not give any other.

(g) A steam-vessel wishing to indicate to another "The way is off my vessel, you may feel your way past me," may sound 3 blasts in succession, viz, short, long, short, with intervals of about 1 second between them.

(h) A vessel employed in laying or in picking up a telegraph cable shall, on hearing the fog-signal of an approaching vessel, sound in answer 3 prolonged blasts in succession.

(i) A vessel under way, which is unable to get out of the way of an approaching vessel through being not under command, or unable to manœuvre as required by these rules, shall, on hearing the fog-signal of an approaching vessel, sound in answer 4 short blasts in succession.

Sailing vessels and boats of less than 20 tons gross tonnage shall not be obliged to give the above-mentioned signals, but if they do not, they shall make some other efficient sound-signal at intervals of not more than 1 minute.

SPEED OF SHIPS TO BE MODERATE IN FOG, ETC.

ART. 16. Every vessel shall, in a fog, mist, falling snow, or heavy rain storms, go at a moderate speed, having careful regard to the existing circumstances and conditions.

A steam-vessel hearing, apparently forward of her beam, the fog-signal of a vessel, the position of which is not ascertained, shall, so far as the circumstances of the case admit, stop her engines, and then navigate with caution until danger of collision is over.

STEERING AND SAILING RULES.

PRELIMINARY—RISK OF COLLISION.

Risk of collision can, when circumstances permit, be ascertained by carefully watching the compass bearing of an approaching vessel. If the bearing does not appreciably change, such risk should be deemed to exist.

ART. 17. When two sailing vessels are approaching one another, so as to involve risk of collision, one of them shall keep out of the way of the other, as follows, viz:

(a) A vessel which is running free shall keep out of the way of a vessel which is close-hauled.

(b) A vessel which is close-hauled on the port tack shall keep out of the way of a vessel which is close-hauled on the starboard tack.

(*c*) When both are running free, with the wind on different sides, the vessel which has the wind on the port side shall keep out of the way of the other.

(*d*) When both are running free, with the wind on the same side, the vessel which is to windward shall keep out of the way of the vessel which is to leeward.

(*e*) A vessel which has the wind aft shall keep out of the way of the other vessel.

ART. 18. When two steam-vessels are meeting end on, or nearly end on, so as to involve risk of collision, each shall alter her course to starboard, so that each may pass on the port side of the other.

This article only applies to cases where vessels are meeting end on, or nearly end on, in such a manner as to involve risk of collision, and does not apply to two vessels which must, if both keep on their respective courses, pass clear of each other.

The only cases to which it does apply are, when each of the two vessels is end on, or nearly end on, to the other; in other words, to cases in which, by day, each vessel sees the masts of the other in a line, or nearly in a line, with her own; and by night, to cases in which each vessel is in such a position as to see both the side-lights of the other.

It does not apply, by day, to cases in which a vessel sees another ahead crossing her own course; or by night, to cases where the red light of one vessel is opposed to the red light of the other, or where the green light of one vessel is opposed to the green light of the other, or where a red light without a green light, or a green light without a red light, is seen ahead, or where both green and red lights are seen anywhere but ahead.

ART. 19. When two steam-vessels are crossing, so as to involve risk of collision, the vessel which has the other on her own starboard side shall keep out of the way of the other.

ART. 20. When a steam-vessel and a sailing vessel are proceeding in such directions as to involve risk of collision, the steam-vessel shall keep out of the way of the sailing vessel.

ART. 21. Where by any of these Rules one of two vessels is to keep out of the way, the other shall keep her course and speed.

ART. 22. Every vessel which is directed by these Rules to keep out of the way of another vessel, shall, if the circumstances of the case admit, avoid crossing ahead of the other.

ART. 23. Every steam-vessel which is directed by these Rules to keep out of the way of another vessel shall, on approaching her, if necessary, slacken her speed or stop or reverse.

ART. 24. Notwithstanding anything contained in these Rules every vessel, overtaking any other, shall keep out of the way of the over-taken vessel.

Every vessel coming up with another vessel from any direction more than two points abaft her beam, *i. e.*, in such a position, with reference to the vessel which she is overtaking that at night she would be unable to see either of that vessel's side-lights, shall be deemed to be an overtaking vessel; and no subsequent alteration of the bearing between the two vessels shall make the overtaking vessel a crossing vessel within the meaning of these rules, or relieve her of the duty of keeping clear of the overtaken vessel until she is finally past and clear.

As by day the overtaking vessel can not always know with cer-tainty whether she is forward of or abaft this direction from the other vessel she should, if in doubt, assume that she is an overtaking vessel and keep out of the way.

ART. 25. In narrow channels every steam-vessel shall, when it is safe and practicable, keep to that side of the fair-way or mid-channel which lies on the starboard side of such vessel.

ART. 26. Sailing vessels under way shall keep out of the way of sailing vessels or boats fishing with nets or lines or trawls. This Rule shall not give to any vessel or boat engaged in fishing the right of obstruct-ing a fair-way used by vessels other than fishing vessels or boats.

ART. 27. In obeying and construing these Rules due regard shall be had to all dangers of navigation and collision, and to any special cir-cumstances which may render a departure from the above Rules neces-sary in order to avoid immediate danger.

SOUND-SIGNALS FOR VESSELS IN SIGHT OF ONE ANOTHER.

ART. 28. The words *"short blast"* used in this Article shall mean a blast of about one second's duration.

When vessels are in sight of one another, a steam-vessel under way, in taking any course authorized or required by these Rules, shall indi-cate that course by the following signals on her whistle or siren, viz:

One short blast to mean, "I am directing my course to starboard."

Two short blasts to mean, "I am directing my course to port."

Three short blasts to mean, "My engines are going full speed astern."

NO VESSEL, UNDER ANY CIRCUMSTANCES, TO NEGLECT PROPER PRE-CAUTIONS.

ART. 29. Nothing in these Rules shall exonerate any vessel, or the owner or master or crew thereof, from the consequences of any neg-lect to carry lights or signals, or of any neglect to keep a proper look-out, or of the neglect of any precaution which may be required by the ordinary practice of seamen, or by the special circumstances of the case.

RESERVATION OF RULES FOR HARBORS AND INLAND NAVIGATION.

ART. 30. Nothing in these Rules shall interfere with the operation of a special rule, duly made by local authority, relative to the navigation of any harbor, river, or inland waters.

DISTRESS SIGNALS.

ART. 31. When a vessel is in distress and requires assistance from other vessels, or from the shore, the following shall be the signals to be used or displayed by her, either together or separately, viz:

In the day-time—

1. A gun fired at intervals of about a minute.
2. The International Code signal of distress, indicated by N. C.
3. The distant signal, consisting of a square flag, having either above or below it a ball or anything resembling a ball.
4. Rockets or shells as prescribed below for use at night.
5. A continuous sounding with any fog-signal apparatus.

At night—

1. A gun fired at intervals of about a minute.
2. Flames on the vessel (as from a burning tar-barrel, oil-barrel, etc.).
3. Rockets or shells, bursting in the air with a loud report and throwing stars of any color or description, fired one at a time at short intervals.
4. A continuous sounding with any fog-signal apparatus.

The United States delegates recommend the adoption, at as early a date as possible, of these regulations, by act of Congress, for the navigation of all vessels of the United States upon the high seas and in all waters connected therewith, navigable by sea-going vessels, except where local rules are necessary, and it is earnestly recommended that such local rules be made to conform as nearly as possible to the international rules; this act to go into effect upon a date set by the President, such date depending upon acceptance of these regulations by the principal maritime powers represented at the Conference. It is further recommended that these regulations when adopted be printed in the official log-book.

The following resolutions were adopted by the Conference and recommended to the attention of the powers represented thereat in an appendix to the regulations:

"(1) The power of all lights should be expressed by referring them all to one standard, by which the light issuing from the lantern should be measured.

"(2) The minimum power only of each lamp should be definitely fixed, leaving it to the judgment of the parties responsible for fitting out the vessels with proper lanterns to employ lamps of this or greater power.

" (3) The use of incandescent lamps should be permitted; the use of arc lights at present should be excluded for all purposes other than signaling and searching.

" (4) Each lantern should be so constructed that the minimum power of light can be found at every point where the light is to be visible, after the lamp has been fitted with proper screens.

"(5) The lanterns should be so constructed as to insure the light having at least the required minimum power in the ideal line connecting the lantern with the horizon, even though the vessel be heeled one way or the other 10 degrees.

" (6) The color of the glasses by which the coloring of the light is to be produced should be so chosen that, if possible, the red light shall have no admixture of green, nor the green light of red rays, and that both colors can be readily and unmistakably distinguished.

" (7) No detailed description should be internationally adopted for the construction of the lamp or lantern, so that a fair chance may be given to inventors to produce serviceable articles.

" (8) The side lights should be so screened as to prevent the most convergent rays of the lights being seen across the bows more than half a point.

" (9) The side-lights should be placed in steam-vessels not forward of the mast-head light.

" (10) To meet the number of complaints as to the absence of proper lights on sailing vessels, the attention of the powers is called to the better enforcement of the regulations in that behalf.

" (11) All steam-whistles, sirens, fog-horns, and bells should be thoroughly tested as to their efficiency, and should be capable of being heard at a stated minimum distance, and should be so regulated that the tones of whistles and sirens should be as distinct as possible from the sound of fog-horns.

"(12) Steam-vessels should be provided, if possible, with means of blowing off surplus steam when the engines are stopped, in such a manner as to occasion as little noise as possible.

" (13) In clear weather at sea no vessel should attempt to cross the bows of the leaders of any squadron of three or more ships of war in regular formation, nor unnecessarily to pass through the lines of such squadron.

" (14) In every case of collision between two vessels it should be the duty of the master or person in charge of each vessel, if and so far as he can do so without serious danger to his own vessel, crew, and passengers (if any), to stay by the other vessel until he has ascertained that she has no need of further assistance, and to render to the other vessel, her master, crew, and passengers (if any) such assistance as may be practicable and as may be necessary in order to save them from any danger caused by the collision, and also to give to the master or person in charge of the other vessel the name of his own vessel and her port of registry, or the port or place to which she belongs, and also the name of the ports and places from which, and to which, she is bound."

The United States delegates recommend that resolutions 1, 2, 3, 4, 5, 6, 8, 9, and 11 be enacted as laws and embodied at once in the instructions now issued to inspectors of steam-vessels, with the recommendatory clause changed to a mandatory one; and that the subject of the better enforcement of the regulations, as embodied in resolution No. 10, be also provided for by law.

Resolution 13, recommending that single vessels be prevented from crossing the bows of leaders of squadrons of three or more ships of war in regular formation, was first adopted as one of the regulations, having been proposed as such by Great Britain, but, upon reconsideration, on motion of France, it was taken out of the regulations and placed in the appendix thereto, to be brought to the attention of the various powers, owing to its being an entirely new rule and one which would not result in benefit unless adopted and enforced by all maritime governments.

The United States delegates recommend, for the reasons given above, and on account of the possible encroachment of this rule upon the principles of international law, that this section be not placed under the regulations for preventing collisions at sea, at the present time, but that correspondence be carried on with the various powers represented at the Conference in regard thereto; and, that should a unanimous agreement be reached, it be then placed as one of the regulations.

Regarding resolution 14, the standing-by clause, it was adopted by the Conference unanimously under both General Divisions 1 and 5 of the programme, and thereby called to the special attention of the governments.

The United States delegates recommend that it be enacted as a law by Congress, changing the recommendatory clause to a mandatory one, with the addition of the following:

"If he fails so to do, and no reasonable cause for such failure is shown, the collision shall, in the absence of proof to the contrary, be deemed to have been caused by his wrongful act, neglect, or default.

"Every master or person in charge of a United States vessel who fails, without reasonable cause, to render such assistance or give such information as aforesaid, shall be deemed guilty of a misdemeanor, and shall be liable to a penalty of $1,000, or imprisonment for a term not exceeding two years; and, for the above sum, the vessel shall be liable and may be seized and proceeded against by process in any district court of the Untied States by any person; one-half such sum to be payable to the informer and the other half to the United States."

GENERAL DIVISION 2.

Regulations to determine the sea-worthiness of vessels.

(a) Construction of vessels.
(b) Equipment of vessels.
(c) Discipline of crew.
(d) Sufficiency of crew.
(e) Inspection of vessels.
(f) Uniform certificates of inspection.

Under this general division the Conference approved of the following :

" (1) It is the opinion of the Conference that, upon the subjects contained in the sections of this division, no international rule could be made which would secure beneficial results. It is thought that the Conference would be limited in each case to a recommendation fixing a minimum for the objects which it is desired to secure under each of these sections. If such a minimum were made the legal requirement it would have an injurious effect upon the present standard of efficiency in many countries.

" (2) In other countries where such efficiency does not exist, it is thought that it will be best secured by the same means which have secured it elsewhere, leaving each nation to modify such means in ways which will best adapt them to the particular methods of the respective governments.

" (3) Again, it is found that the present rules existing in different countries upon several of these questions, are different in many respects, though probably equally efficient. It would, therefore, become necessary in forming an international rule in such cases, to recommend changes in the existing rules of several countries, which to some of them might be impracticable. This is thought to be undesirable. However, the Conference earnestly recommend that——

" (4) All vessels, whether propelled by steam or sail, should possess a margin of strength over and above that which is required to enable them to perform the work for which they were designed and built. A chain, a bridge, or any other structure, the failure of which would entail the loss of human life, invariably has a considerable reserve of strength provided; in other words, the admitted working load is always much less than the computed strength, or the strength ascertained by actual test; certainly it is no less important that the hull of a vessel should contain a similar reserve.

" (5) To attempt to formulate rules for the construction of vessels of all sizes and for all trades would far exceed the province of this Conference, and, besides, any arbitrary rules would probably much hamper the advance in design, and the method of construction.

" (6) Therefore, to obtain as much as seems to be practicable in this direction, it is desirable to rely upon efficient and oft-repeated inspection, when upon the least indication of distress, or of rupture showing, very substantial additions should be made before the vessel is allowed to again proceed to sea.

" (7) Ocean-going steam-vessels which carry passengers should be additionally protected by having efficient bulk-heads, so spaced that when any two compartments be filled with water the vessel will still remain in a sea-worthy condition, and two at least of the amid-ships bulk-heads should be tested by water pressure to the height of the deck next above the water-line."

The United States delegates recommend, in regard to (a), construction of vessels, that a board of experts be appointed to consider the recommendations made by the Conference, with the view of determining the practicability of establishing suitable rules for the construction of vessels.

As to the sea-worthiness of vessels, it is desirable to rely upon efficient and oft-repeated inspection, when upon the least indication of strain or rupture the vessel should be put in a thoroughly sea-worthy condition before being allowed to proceed to sea.

Regarding the other subdivisions of this general division, laws have been enacted, most of which, however, only refer to steam-vessels.

The United States delegates recommend the revision and the better enforcement of the laws now in existence and the enactment of new ones covering all necessities, especially as to the inspection of sailing vessels, their equipment and appliances; the providing of proper instruments of navigation, compasses, charts, etc.

GENERAL DIVISION 3.

Draught to which vessels should be restricted when loaded.

Uniform maximum load-mark.

Under this general division the Conference adopted the following:

" The Conference first of all endeavored to obtain as much information as could be collected on this very important question.

" The British law, as laid down in the Merchant Shipping Act, 1876 (39 and 40 Vict., c. 80), gives certain powers to the Board of Trade to detain British and foreign vessels which, by reason of overloading or improper loading, are unfit to proceed to sea without serious danger to human life. These powers may be put into force against foreign ships when they have taken on board all or any part of their cargo at a port in the United Kingdom, and are, whilst at that port, unsafe by reason of overloading or improper loading.

" With the intention of carrying out this law in a way consistent with the interests of the mercantile community on the one side and with the regard due to protection of life and property on the other side, certain general rules, after careful investigations instituted by a load-line committee appointed by the president of the Board of Trade, as well as by the Board of Trade, have been framed with the purpose of ascertaining whether a ship be overloaded or not. These rules assign to ships a freeboard, which, according to the experience collected on the subject, is considered sufficient to prevent dangerous overloading without unduly interfering with trade, and they contain tables assigning such freeboard as is suitable for vessels of the highest class in Lloyd's Register or of strength equivalent thereto, and which is to be increased for ships of inferior strength.

" The above-mentioned rules have proved to be a good standard upon which to determine the proper loading of British vessels which are classed in Lloyd's Register, or for other vessels the particulars of whose strength and fitness to carry any particular cargo can easily be ascertained by the surveyors of the Board of Trade.

" As regards foreign ships, however, which are loading in the United Kingdom, and which are either not classed in Lloyd's Register, or the particulars of which can not be ascertained without a minute examination, the difficulty exists that the law which intends to guard against the dangers arising from overloading can not be enforced without serious disadvantages to the owners of ships and cargoes consequent upon the difficulty of ascertaining whether the ships are fit to carry the cargo in question.

" For these reasons it appears to be obvious that it would be very desirable if means could be found to ascertain, in a simple and easy way and without loss of time, the fitness of any vessel loading in a port of the United Kingdom to load a particular cargo.

" These remarks naturally apply also to vessels loading elsewhere, because it is a very high and important interest, common to all nations, to take every possible measure for the protection of life and property against the dangers arising from overloading.

" For these reasons it appears to deserve very serious attention whether, by providing for a certain load-line to be marked on sea-going ships, a trustworthy and simple method could be arrived at for deciding whether a loading vessel should be detained for overloading or ought to be allowed to go to sea.

" The British Government has recently invited the attention of other Governments to this question. But inasmuch as up to the present no progress has been made in this matter, the question arises whether something could be done to expedite an understanding by any action on the part of the Conference now here assembled.

" Now, as far as the Conference have been able to ascertain, the laws of many maritime nations contain provisos for dealing with the question of overloading, and enabling the local authorities to detain overladen ships. But nowhere, except in Great Britain, as far as is known, have statutory rules been introduced for the purpose of ascertaining whether a ship be fit to carry a certain cargo by a load-mark or load-line.

" In order to arrive at such laws and to enforce them it would appear to be necessary to induce the Governments of the maritime nations not only to institute investigations similar to those made in Great Britain above referred to, but also to establish a sufficient staff of competent officials to insure the universal compliance with the laws to be given, and to establish courts of appeal authorized to decide on complaints against unjust detention and to award damages to the ship-owners and shippers of cargo in case of an unjustifiable detention.

" It appears to the Conference that this would be surrounded with very serious difficulties, as it depends upon the varying conditions of each country whether the Governments would think it advisable to take steps in this direction or not. It must be kept in mind that a great display of scientific labor, and moreover a heavy expenditure of money, would be necessary to introduce a system similar to that which is used in Great Britian. Besides, it could be questioned whether it be necessary to make a law on load-lines or load-marks in order to guard against the danger of overloading, because it might be said that sufficient safe-guards are given by the responsibility of the ship-owners towards the shippers of the cargo, and to their insurers, and by the control exercised by the underwriters and the various institutions for classing ships. There may also be circumstances peculiar to certain countries, as, for example, the fact that the goods which they export, generally, are light goods only, which do not endanger the stability of a ship, which may operate in favor of non-interference on behalf of the respective Governments.

"The Conference is led to believe that on these grounds, notwithstanding the advantages which would be connected with the introduction of a uniform system of load-marks, this matter is not ripe for consideration by this Conference and that it ought to be left to the negotiations to be carried on between the Governments of the maritime nations."

The United States Delegates recommend that, for the reasons given above, the subject be left, as the Conference decided, to negotiation between the Governments of the maritime nations.

GENERAL DIVISION 4.

Uniform regulations regarding the designating and marking of vessels.

    (*a*) Position of name on vessels.
    (*b*) Position of name of port of registry on vessels.
    (*c*) Size of lettering.
    (*d*) Uniform system of draft-marks.

Under this general division the Conference agreed to the following rules:

"(1) *The name of every registered merchant vessel shall be marked upon each bow and upon the stern, and the port of registry of every such vessel shall be marked upon the stern.*

"*These names shall be marked in Roman letters in a light color on a dark ground, or in a dark color on a light ground, and to be distinctly visible.*

"*The smallest letters used shall not be less than four (4) inches high.*

"(2) *The draft of every registered vessel shall be marked upon the stem and stern-post in English feet or decimeters, in either Arabic or Roman numerals. The bottom of each numeral shall indicate the draft to that line.*"

The United States Delegates recommend the adoption of these rules and that they be enacted as laws by Congress. This will necessitate but slight changes in the present laws and the enactment of a new law to cover Rule 2.

The United States Delegates recommend that section 4405, Revised Statutes, be made to apply to sailing vessels as well as to steam-vessels.

GENERAL DIVISION 5.

Saving life and property from shipwreck.

1. Saving of life and property from shipwreck at sea.
   (a) Duties of vessels after collision.
   (b) Apparatus for life saving to be carried on board ship. (Life-boats, life-preservers, life-rafts, pumps, and fire-extinguishing apparatus.)
   (c) The use of oil and the necessary apparatus for its use.
   (d) Uniform inspections as to (b) and (c).
2. Saving of life and property from shipwreck by operations from shore.
   (a) Organization of, and methods employed by, life-saving institutions.
   (b) The employment of drilled and disciplined crews at life-saving stations.
   (c) The maintenance of a patrol upon dangerous coasts by night, and during thick weather by day, for warning off vessels standing into danger, and for the early discovery of wrecks.
   (d) Uniform means of transmitting information between stranded vessels and the shore.
   (e) Life-boats, life-saving apparatus and appliances.
3. Official inquiries into causes and circumstances of shipwrecks and other casualties.

Under this general division the Conference passed the following resolutions and recommendations:

"(1) *Resolved,* In every case of collision between two vessels, it shall be the duty of the master or person in charge of each vessel, if, and so far as he can do so without danger to his own vessel, crew, and passengers (if any), to stay by the other vessel until he has ascertained that she has no need of further assistance, and to render to the other vessel, her master, crew, and passengers (if any), such assistance as may be practicable and as may be necessary in order to save them from any danger caused by the collision; and also to give to the master or person in charge of the other vessel the name of his own vessel, and of her port of registry, or of the port or place to which she belongs, and also the names of the ports and places from which and to which she is bound.

"(2) *Resolved,* That the Conference approve of the principle of the 'Rules made by the Board of Trade of Great Britain under the Merchant Shipping (Life-Saving Appliances) Act, 1888,' relating to boats and appliances to be carried on board ship for saving life; and recommend that the several Governments adopt measures to secure compliance with this principle in regard to such boats and appliances for vessels of 150 tons and upwards, gross tonnage.

"It is also recommended that the principle of these Rules be extended to all smaller craft, as far as practicable; and that each vessel of this class should carry at least one life-buoy of approved pattern and material, and for every person on board an efficient life-belt or jacket.

" (3) *Resolved*, That the Conference recommend that the several governments require all their sea-going vessels to carry a sufficient quantity of animal or vegetable oil, for the purpose of calming the sea in rough weather, together with suitable means for applying it.

" (4) *Resolved*, That the Conference recommend that all institutions for saving life from wrecked vessels prepare uniform instructions to mariners with reference to their co-operation with those attempting their rescue from the shore, and that said instructions include the following signals :

" *Upon the discovery of a wreck by night the life-saving force will burn a red pyrotechnic light or a red rocket to signify—'You are seen ; assistance will be given as soon as possible.'*

"*A red flag waved on shore by day, or a red light, red rocket, or red Roman candle displayed by night, will signify—' Haul away.'*

"*A white flag waved on shore by day, or a white light slowly swung back and forth, or a white rocket, or white Roman candle fired by night will signify—' Slack away.'*

"*Two flags, a white and a red, waved at the same time on shore by day, or two lights, a white and a red, slowly swung at the same time, or a blue pyrotechnic light burned by night, will signify—'Do not attempt to land in your own boats. It is impossible.'*

"*A man on shore beckoning by day, or two torches burning near together by night, will signify—' This is the best place to land.'*

"*Any of these signals may be answered from the vessel as follows : In the day-time—by waving a flag, a handkerchief, a hat, or even the hand; at night—by firing a rocket, a blue light or a gun, or by showing a light over the ship's gunwale for a short time and then concealing it.*

"And it is recommended that the several governments take measures to keep all their sea-going vessels supplied with copies of such instructions.

" (5) *Resolved*, That the Conference recommend that the several nations provide by legislative enactments for official inquiry into the causes and circumstances of all shipwrecks and other serious casualties happening to their vessels.

" If the maritime nations should agree upon uniform requirements in respect to life-saving apparatus to be carried on board ship, and as to the use of oil and the necessary apparatus for its use, uniform inspections might perhaps be advantageous, but it would be impossible to formulate an adequate system for this purpose without knowing definitely what those requirements might be; and even then it would be doubtful, considering the great diversity of administrative methods and machinery in different countries, whether any practicable system could be devised that would be acceptable to all.

" The Conference have had before them a number of valuable papers describing the organization and methods of institutions for the saving of life from shipwreck, and indicating the extent and results of their work. An examination of them clearly shows that these institutions are all managed by men whose hearts are in their work, and who may be trusted to use every means known to them for perfecting the apparatus and methods employed for the rescue of unfortunates cast upon their shores. The organization of the service in each country must necessarily vary according to the condition and temper of the people and the character and habits of the coast population from which the men constituting the effective life-saving force must be drawn. It is, therefore, deemed impracticable to formulate any definite rules which would be applicable to all alike. It appears desirable, however, that the officers of every organization should study the features of the others, in order that they may adopt such improvements as seem suitable for their own. Some of the establishments appear to have been brought to a high degree of excellence.

"It seems desirable that careful attention should be given to the frequent drilling and exercising of life-saving crews. It is also deemed important that a watch or patrol should, wherever practicable, be established upon dangerous coasts at night, and during thick weather by day, not only for the early discovery of wrecks, but in order to warn off vessels that may be incautiously standing into danger. Coast-guards are established in various countries for the prevention of smuggling, and where this is the case they can be utilized to give timely notice and assistance to life-saving crews, or even to constitute such crews, as is already done in some countries.

"With regard to special varieties of life-boats and other appliances, the Conference believe that the matter can be safely trusted to the judgment and discretion of the officers in charge of the life-saving institutions of the several countries. The requirements vary so greatly upon different coasts that boats and appliances effective in one place are often ill-adapted or useless in another. Besides, the preferences of the men employed have to be considered; they usually having greater confidence in particular models because they are accustomed to them. Confidence in the appliances a crew is required to use is, in general, an admitted essential to success. No one can judge of these matters so well as the officers, whose duty it is to study the local conditions, and who are thoroughly acquainted with the prejudices and habitudes of the men.

"It is desirable that officers of life-saving institutions should generally communicate freely with each other with reference to any improvements that may occur to them, either in apparatus, methods, or organization, with a view both to the diffusion of information concerning such matters, and to establishing an international comity with regard to a beneficent work.

"With reference to subsection (d), 'Uniform means of transmitting information between stranded vessels and the shore,' the Conference would say that co-operation between mariners upon a wrecked vessel and those who wish to assist them upon shore is of the highest importance. The most earnest attempts at aid may be rendered nugatory if the shipwrecked are not aware of what is required of them. In order to secure this co-operation various means have been devised in maritime countries, such as attaching tally-boards to the lines of the beach-apparatus, the publication of instructions in the official log-books distributed to vessels, the issuing of pamphlets or cards of such instructions, or the very excellent method of posting, in the forecastle, or some convenient place in a vessel, a durable placard showing by illustrations the manner in which life-saving lines are to be secured on board and giving necessary instructions relative thereto.

"All these measures are good, but the instructions have not been generally distributed among vessels of all nationalities as they should be, and with a view to the universal diffusion of this information it is recommended that a uniform system of issuing and distributing such instructions be adopted by the several maritime nations.

"The Conference is also of the opinion that the instructions generally issued do not adequately provide for co-operation between the ship and the shore, and that they should be supplemented by a few simple signals for the purpose of direct communication. The International

Code can often be used in the day-time, but a still simpler system should be provided for the few signals required. It is believed that the signals absolutely necessary can be reduced to very few, and that the adoption and publication of such a system would be of great benefit in the emergencies of a shipwreck.

"If it be determined to establish an international code of night-signals, such as is referred to in General Division 8 of the programme—('Night-Signals for Communicating Information at Sea')—the signals needed for communicating at night between wrecked vessels and the shore ought to be incorporated therein. If it should prove impracticable to adopt a system of night-signals for the International Code it may yet be worth considering whether the few signals needed for use at wrecks ought not to be adopted. Such a system is recommended by the Conference, and will be found described in detail in the fourth resolution above. Every signal there mentioned has been found necessary in emergencies that have actually arisen in service."

Resolution 1 has been already considered under General Division 1.

The United States Delegates recommend that appropriate legislation be had by this Government for carrying into effect the recommendations contained in Resolutions 2 and 3.

As to Resolution 4, it is recommended that the General Superintendent of the Life-Saving Service be instructed to prepare and submit to the various life-saving institutions such instructions as are mentioned in the resolution, to include the signals therein printed in italics, and that if accepted by them they be submitted to the powers represented in the Conference for their consideration, and, if approved, they be printed and copies furnished to all vessels of the United States through the customs officials and the hydrographic offices of the Navy Department at the various ports; also that they be inserted in the new International Code Signal Book, about to be published by the Hydrographic Office, Navy Department, and in the official log-book.

It is recommended that, as to vessels of the United States, the provisions of Resolution 5 be carried out by the enactment of suitable laws.

It is also recommended that the following paragraph be added to section 4290, Revised Statutes:

"In every case of collision, in which it is practicable so to do, the master shall, immediately after the occurrence, cause a statement thereof, and of the circumstances under which the same occurred, to be entered in the official log-book."

GENERAL DIVISION 6.

Necessary qualifications for officers and seamen, including tests for sight and color-blindness.

    (*a*) A uniform system of examination for the different grades.

    (*b*) Uniform tests for visual power and color-blindness.

    (*c*) General knowledge of methods employed at life saving stations.

    (*d*) Uniform certificates of qualification.

Under this general division the Conference approved of the following:

"(1) *Every man or boy going to sea as a seaman, or with the intention of becoming a seaman, should be examined for visual power and color blindness; and no man or boy should be permitted to serve on board any vessel in the capacity of seaman, or where he will have to stand lookout, whose visual power is below one-half normal or who is red and green color-blind.*

"(2) *Every man who shall qualify as an officer of a registered vessel or as a pilot, after the adoption of these rules, except engineer officers, shall be required to have a certificate that he has the necessary visual power, and that he is not red and green blind. He shall also have a certificate that he is familiar with the regulations for preventing collisions at sea, and with the duties required of him in co-operating with a life-saving station in case his vessel is stranded.*

"(3) *It is recommended that each country provide means which will enable any boy or man intending to go to sea, to have his eyes examined for visual power and color-blindness, and to obtain a certificate of the result, also to enable the master of any vessel to have the eyes of any of his crew tested for the same purpose.*

"It is the opinion of the Conference that defective visual power and color-blindness are sources of danger at sea. The first both by day and night, because of the inability of the short-sighted to see objects at a sufficient distance. Color-blindness is a source of danger more especially at night, because of the inability of a color-blind person to distinguish between the red and green side lights. The inability on the part of an officer or lookout to distinguish the color of buoys may be a cause of accident in broad daylight.

"It is the opinion of the Conference, however, that tests for these defects need not be enforced in the cases of masters and mates who already occupy such positions.

"The Conference purposely avoid making any recommendation as to the methods to be used in making such tests for visual power and color-blindness, or in conducting the necessary examinations for officers. It is thought that the desired objects will be best secured by leaving each country to employ the methods which may seem most suitable."

The United States delegates recommend, with reference to Resolution 1, the enactment of the following:

"That every man or boy going to sea with the intention of becoming a seaman shall be examined for visual power and color-blindness, and no such man or boy shall be permitted to serve on board any vessel in the capacity of seaman whose visual power is below one half normal, or who is red and green color-blind, nor shall any person stand look-out on board any vessel who possesses such visual defects."

This variation from the provision of the resolution is recommended in order to avoid working hardship upon old seamen by depriving them of the privilege of pursuing their vocation, notwithstanding defective vision.

With reference to Resolutions 2 and 3 it is recommended that they be enacted into law, and that they be made to apply to enrolled as well as to registered vessels.

It is also recommended that the present system of examination of masters, officers, engineers, and pilots of steam-vessels be revised, and if any defects are found they be remedied; and that examinations as to competency be extended to masters and officers of sailing vessels—the requirements for each grade to be specified and then properly enforced; and that should the examiners find that the capacity, experience, habits of life, and character of the persons examined, are such as to warrant the belief that he can be safely intrusted with the duties and responsibilities of the station for which he makes application, and for which he shall have passed the examination as to qualification, they shall grant him a certificate of competency in the grade for which he shall have qualified; but such certificate shall be suspended or revoked upon satisfactory proof of bad conduct, intemperate habits, unskillfulness or want of knowledge of the duties of the station, or the willful violation of any of the provisions of the navigation laws.

GENERAL DIVISION 7.

Lanes for steamers on frequented routes.

(a) With regard to the avoidance of steamer collisions.

(b) With regard to the safety of fisherman.

Under this general division the Conference approved of the following:

"After consideration of various routes the Conference concluded to report only upon the North Atlantic route between ports of North America and ports of northern Europe as the route upon which there was apparently the greater demand for such lanes, if such could be advantageously laid down on any ocean or sea.

" It appears that the adherence of fast steam passenger vessels to certain southerly routes would tend to the avoidance of fog and ice, and the Conference adopted a resolution to the effect that it was desirable during the spring and summer months that such vessels should follow a southern route which would clear the banks of Newfoundland, and be likely to be clear of fog and ice, but when it came to proposing any plan to make such ocean lanes compulsory, the Conference found the subject one of such difficulty that they do not recommend a proposition of that nature.

" The difficulty of enforcing the present rule providing for moderate speed in thick weather suggests what greater difficulties would be met with in enforcing lane routes if made compulsory, and it was not thought desirable to lay down routes by international agreement unless they were to be made compulsory for swift steamers.

" Routes that might be proposed would be in danger of invasion by ice during the spring and summer months, and at all times would be crossed by sailing vessels and steamers going north and south. If laid down on parallels of latitude which seemed to favor one sea port at the expense of another, or the ports of one country at the expense of the ports of another country, they would arouse opposition that would probably prevent their adoption.

" It is possible that even in the near future vessels may be employed of such power and speed that all such considerations may have to give way to the paramount consideration of safety, but, so far as shown to the Conference, present conditions do not seem to justify an international agreement to that effect. It was not shown to the Conference that collisions in mid-ocean between fast ocean steamers had taken place or that the danger was great enough to justify enforced adherence to certain lanes. Collisions between fast steam-ships, so far, have occurred nearer the coasts where all tracks must converge.

" The Conference believe, however, that the voluntary establishment of, and adherence to, particular routes by the different steam-ship companies, for different seasons of the year is very desirable. In fact, the Conference are of the opinion that such action by the steam-ship companies, with the experience to be gained thereby, would be quite essential before any concerted action by the maritime powers could be profitably taken.

" The Conference, therefore, strongly recommend that the companies interested should, by mutual agreement, after consultation together, establish routes for the different lines, and make them public, in order that the hydrographic offices of the various governments may publish them for the information of navigators.

" The Conference have considered the opinions of several persons in the printed matter that has been laid before them. With the exception of one or two definite propositions, the literature before the Conference does not show how such lane routes could be laid down. Even those containing such propositions arrive at the conclusion that such routes could not be made compulsory.

" With regard to the safety of fishermen upon the North Atlantic Ocean, the Conference are of opinion that their safety would be best promoted by unceasing vigilance on the part of the fishermen, and by careful compliance by all with the present rules for the prevention of collisions, especially as to the efficiency of lights and sound-signals. If lanes were established which carried the fast steamers clear of the banks frequented by the fishermen it might promote such a sense of security on their part as would tend to carelessness with reference to the rules as at present laid down, and lead to danger from the slower vessels which would still frequent the banks.

"During the months when the fishing-vessels most frequent the Banks, the fear of encountering fog and ice leads many of the steamers to go south of them.

"Quick passages are what the steam-vessels aim at in response to the public demand for swift passenger and mail service, and if they were compelled to obey existing rules regarding moderate speed in fogs at all times and in all places they would avoid the Banks still more in order to go clear of fogs; and thus it seems that the solution of the problem before the Conference namely, of how to induce steam-ships of great speed to take safer routes to avoid fogs, ice, and danger of collision with fishermen and other vessels, is in compelling obedience to the present rules regarding moderate speed in thick weather. The enforcement of these rules would make it for the interest of such vessels to take routes comparatively clear of fogs and ice and thus attain the end which compulsory legislation might fail to do.

"From the correspondence placed before the Conference regarding the dangers of fishermen upon the Banks, it will be observed that vigilance regarding lights and sound-signals have been found efficient safeguards in most instances."

The United States delegates give their approval to these conclusions, and recommend that the fishermen on the Grand Banks be required to use more powerful lights, do away with tho old mouth fog-horn, and provide their vessels with the modern mechanical ones, which are more powerful and can be sounded by every man or boy employed on board.

These vessels should be inspected to see that they comply with the above recommended requirements.

GENERAL DIVISION 8.

Night signals for communicating information at sea.

(a) A code to be used in connection with the International Code Signal book.
(b) Or a supplementary code of limited scope to convey information of special importance to passing vessels.
(c) Distress signals.

Under this general division the Conference concluded as follows:

"With regard to subsections (a) and (b) of General Division No. 8, the Conference have considered systems of night-signals with ordinary colored lights, but the objection exists that they can not be seen so far as a white light. It is the opinion of the Conference that night-signaling at sea can better be carried on by a system of long and short flashes from a white light than by any system in which colored lights are used.

"The Conference have concluded that the systems of signaling by pyrotechnic lights which have been brought to their notice are too expensive for general use.

"The Conference have had before them 'A supplementary code of limited scope to convey information of special importance to passing vessels,' which has been prepared by a committee of the British Board of Trade and has been presented by the British Government to the various powers for their consideration.

"The Conference, after careful consideration, recommend the adoption, for optional use, of that supplementary code, with the following change: To strike out signal P. G., 'Beware of derelict dangerous to navigation,' and substitute in its place N. P., 'I want assistance. Remain by me.'

"The Conference decided upon the following fog-signals, to be allotted to pilots and to vessels seeking pilots:

"For vessels requiring pilots—a prolonged blast followed by a short blast, ———— —

"For pilots wishing to offer their services—a short blast followed by a long blast, — ————

"And the Conference recommend that they be inserted in the International Code Book under the Pilot-Signals.

"While considering the subject of signals to convey information of special importance to passing vessels, the decision of the Conference, in adding to the signals now in use, consisting of short and long blasts, and the favor in which such signals seem to be held, and the convenience which an extended use of such signals would be to mariners, have led the Conference to consider the benefits which might accrue from the more general use of the Morse system now in use by the navies of various powers.

"Up to the present time no better system seems to have been devised for signaling purposes; it is one which can be used under all circumstances; it is readily acquired by young persons of ordinary ability, and is already taught on some training-ships. If its use were encouraged it might lead to the study of the code by more young men qualifying as officers of the merchant marine, or as signal men, and thus come into more general use.

"Such studies are beneficial in developing the intellectual activity of seamen, and every accomplishment of the kind acquired and made necessary by the requirements of the service helps to develop the morale of the sailor.

"To thus encourage the use of the system, the Conference suggest that the complete alphabet of the Morse Code be inserted in the International Code Book for optional use."

The United States delegates recommend the adoption of these conclusions, and that when uniform signals for transmitting information between stranded vessels and the shore are adopted, they be inserted in the Revised International Code Book to be published by the Hydrographic Office, Navy Department. It is also recommended that the "Supplementary code of limited scope to convey information of special importance to passing vessels," and the "Uniform signals for transmitting information between stranded vessels and the shore" be printed in the official log-book.

GENERAL DIVISION 9.

Warnings of approaching storms.

(*a*) The transmission of warnings.

(*b*) The uniformity of signals employed.

Under this general division the Conference approved of the following:

"The Conference understand that the various meteorological offices in Europe are in frequent and intimate communication, and interchange telegraphic information for the purpose of weather forecasting on that side of the Atlantic Ocean; while the meteorological offices of the United States and the Dominion of Canada act in concert on the western side; and also that a similar custom prevails in many eastern countries.

"The preparation of weather forecasts and the transmission of warnings regarding expected storms must, by the very nature of the subject, be dealt with locally; and it is the opinion of the Conference very questionable whether any useful purpose would be gained by the adoption of uniformity of methods,.except so far as the general progress of scientific knowledge indicates the direction of possible improvement; and this, it is hardly necessary to say, is more likely to be secured by work carried on independently rather than under any uniform system.

"Storm-warning signals were first introduced in the interests of the shipping or fishing-vessels lying at anchor in harbor or proposing to put to sea. Lately the same warning-signals have been freely extended to coast stations, with a view to give information regarding the weather to passing vessels. Inasmuch as these may be local or foreign traders the Conference are of opinion that such signals should, as far as possible, be in international agreement.

"The established signals originally in use in Europe are evidently founded on the seaman's knowledge of the 'law of storms,' and, while warning him of an approaching cyclone, indicate whether the northern or southern portion is expected to pass over the district. Experience proves that this was practically sufficient information for the masters of vessels in a neighboring harbor, who would know whether the cyclone was approaching or had passed, but it is scarcely sufficient for coasting vessels, especially those proceeding on a course at right angles to the direction in which the cyclone is moving.

"In the opinion of the Conference it is, therefore, desirable that storm-signals displayed at coast stations should give to passing vessels some further information as to whether storms are approaching or have passed the station; and in reference to this the Conference desire to call attention to the fact that this want has been supplied by the system now in use in the United States. The German system indicates four directions from which a storm is expected, and whether its probable course is to the right or the left.

"In dealing with this matter the Conference have had the advantage of hearing the views of General A. W. Greely, the Chief Signal Officer in charge of the United States Weather Bureau; and he has summarized them in a memorandum contained under cover of a letter dated December 23, 1889, both of which are appended to the Report of Committee No. 3, and to which the Conference desire to draw special attention.

" It will be seen that in this memorandum General Greely has indicated the practical reasons for adopting, in lieu of cone-shaped signals, the use of colored flags for notifying storm warnings on the coasts of the United States, which, it is claimed, can be seen (except in very calm weather) at a greater distance, and by means of which additional information can be given.

" The Conference consider that this subject is of such a technical nature that they are not prepared to express a decided opinion upon it. They however invite the various maritime countries to consider the best practical mode of signaling by day, whether by shapes, colored or black, by flags, or by the two combined, and by night by means of lights, colored or white, arranged to represent distinctive forms.

" Together with the memorandum alluded to General Greely inclosed a copy of ' General Orders No. 29,' dated from the Signal Office, War Department, November 11, 1889, and also a paper of diagrams showing the storm, cautionary, and wind-direction signals in use in the United States.

" In recapitulation, the Conference invite the maritime countries interested to take into consideration the establishment of a uniform system of indicating storm warnings by day and by night, and that such a system should, as far as possible, include signals indicating whether the storm is approaching or has passed the station."

The United States delegates recommend the use for off-shore signals of shapes alone—ball, cylinder, and cone. This conclusion is reached from the actual experience of the seamen of the delegation and from the fact that most foreign nations have adopted shapes for such off-shore signals, flags being of no use in calm weather and with the wind blowing in a direct line between the station and the observer.

Should no conclusion regarding this subject be internationally agreed upon before the meeting of the heads of the Meteorological Offices of Nations, which it is understood will take place in Europe during the coming summer, it can very properly be left for their decision, as well as that portion dealing with the establishment of a uniform system of indicating storm warnings.

GENERAL DIVISION 10.

Reporting, marking, and removing dangerous wrecks or obstructions to navigation.

(a) A uniform method of reporting and marking dangerous wrecks and derelicts.

(b) The division of the labor, cost, and responsibility among the several maritime nations, either by geographical apportionment or otherwise:

Of the removal of dangerous derelicts.

And of searching for doubtful dangers with a view of removing them from the charts,

Under this general division the Conference adopted, as follows:

The paragraphs numbered to be submitted for the consideration of the powers.

"The heading of this division leaves it doubtful whether the Conference are expected to consider measures dealing with dangerous wrecks and obstructions in territorial waters, as well as on the high seas.

"The Conference are of opinion that it is not necessary or desirable to propose international action regarding territorial waters, except the marking of wrecks, which subject is treated under General Division 12."

(a) A uniform method of reporting and marking dangerous wrecks and derelicts.

"Wherever the word 'wreck' is used herein, it is meant to designate '*an abandoned vessel aground*,' and wherever the word 'derelict' is used, it is meant to designate '*a vessel afloat permanently abandoned.*'

"Wrecks are not always to be considered a source of danger to navigation. When lying outside of the fair-ways, as for instance on dangerous sands, or on coral reefs, they may even contribute to the safety of navigation by becoming conspicuous day marks; but when they are lying in a fair-way, in water of not sufficient depth to allow vessels to pass without striking the hull or spars of the wreck, they become a serious danger to navigation.

"Derelicts are always a danger to navigation, as other vessels may run into them without any warning, particularly at night or during thick weather. Since January 1, 1889, five collisions with derelicts are known to have taken place in the North Atlantic Ocean alone, by one of which lives were imperiled.

"Undoubtedly the number of lives and the value of property lost through collision with derelicts at sea has been very considerable, and such losses might be greatly reduced if proper steps were taken to clear the seas of such dangers.

"Other dangerous obstructions (icebergs, newly discovered shoals, reefs, etc.), would seem to be included under the heading of 'General Division 10,' and although not alluded to in paragraph (a) should, in the opinion of the Conference, be discussed here, as they may constitute the most serious of all the dangers dealt with in this division.

"REPORTING DANGEROUS WRECKS AND DERELICTS.

"The danger caused by wrecks and derelicts might be considerably lessened if their exact position were known to the mariner. For obvious reasons it is often most difficult to attain this end completely. Much, however, would be gained if as accurate a report as possible were secured and brought to the notice of mariners without loss of time.

"Regarding the manner in which such reports should be brought to the central office in charge of the distribution of 'Notices to Mariners,' the Conference propose the following resolutions:

"1. That it is advisable to make it the duty of any of the officers, or of the crew of a wreck or derelict, to report, as soon as possible after landing, to the nearest harbor authority, if necessary through their consul, as follows:

"(a) Name of the vessel abandoned.
"(b) Her distinguishing number.

"(c) Name of her home port,·port from which she sailed, and place of destination.

"(d) General description of vessel and her rig.

"(e) Place where abandoned (latitude and longitude as near as possible).

"(f) Weather and current experienced before leaving the vessel, and in case she was a derelict, the direction in which she would most likely drift.

"(g) Whether or not not it is intended to take any steps toward her recovery.

"2. That a similar report should be made to the same authorities, by the master of any vessel sighting a wreck or derelict, and a suitable entry made in the ship's log.

"3. Such reports should be published in "Notices to Mariners," the daily press, and, if necessary, by giving telegraphic information to the ports which it most concerns.

"REPORTING OTHER OBSTRUCTIONS TO NAVIGATION, AS ICEBERGS, NEWLY DISCOVERED SHOALS, REEFS, ETC.

"Regarding the manner in which such reports should be transmitted to the proper authorities, the Conference propose the following resolution:

"4. That it is advisable to make it the duty of every commander or master of a vessel to report the fact that an iceberg or dangerous field ice has been sighted, or a shoal, reef, or other obstruction has been discovered, to the harbor authorities or the hydrographic office of that country to which the port next reached belongs, giving a full description of the obstruction, and all facts that may lead to the determination of its position; for instance, the time elapsed since the last reliable astronomical observation, and the rate of the chronometer. If the obstruction be a shoal or reef, the depth of water actually obtained by sounding on it should be given. Also when land is in sight the position of any off-lying shoal or reef should be determined by compass bearings of fixed objects in view; the error of the compass being stated, with information as to how and when that error was observed. Angles should also be taken between such objects, and a drawing of the coast and the position of the observer be added.

"Regarding the reporting of ice met with in the vicinity of the Newfoundland Banks by signal from a vessel to other vessels, the committee are aware that an 'Ice Code' has been published by a private individual which, according to his own statement, is rather extensively used amongst the steamers employed in the regular trade between New York and the ports of northern Europe.

"This code seems to offer some advantages, but as there was no evidence before the Conference, showing whether its use had been found to be beneficial or otherwise, they were unable to decide whether the introduction of this code or a similar one could be recommended.

"MARKING WRECKS AND DERELICTS.

"As it appears impracticable in most cases for the master and crew of a sunken vessel to mark the wreck in any effective manner, no such obligation should be imposed on them; and it would also be a great burden, aside from the peril of the undertaking, to compel a passing vessel to mark a derelict. Neither does it seem feasible that any national government should assume such a duty; but so far as possible, means should be employed by which derelicts may be recognized at first sight, and with this end in view, the Conference adopted the following resolution:

" 5. That whenever practicable it shall be the duty of the crew before abandoning a vessel (a) to hoist some distinctive signal, as: B C F, ‘abandoned by the crew,’ or C R T G, ‘derelict,’ or a ball, shape, or other similar mark, where it can best be seen, and where it should not be mistaken for any other authorized signal; (b) to let go the sheets and halliards of such sails as are not furled.

"MARKING OTHER OBSTRUCTIONS.

"At present it seems impracticable to mark shoals, reefs, etc., whether they be well known or only newly discovered, with the exception of those lying near the coasts of countries having a maritime commerce, and we consider it unnecessary to press for their being marked in other localities where they can be readily avoided by the exercise of ordinary skill and the usual precautions known to navigators; for this reason the Conference have no proposition to submit beyond the introduction, so far as possible, of a uniform system of buoyage."

(b) *The division of the labor, cost, and responsibility among the several maritime nations, either by geographical apportionment or otherwise : of the removal of dangerous derelicts ; and of searching for doubtful dangers with a view of removing them from the charts.*

"DERELICTS, ETC., ON THE HIGH SEAS.

" A geographical apportionment of the waters of the globe amongst the different maritime nations, in order to divide the labor and cost of removing wrecks and derelicts, or searching for doubtful dangers, can not be recommended for adoption.

" In the open sea, with the exception of a part of the North Atlantic, derelicts and dangerous wrecks are exceedingly rare, and as these parts of the ocean are, comparatively speaking, not much frequented by vessels, the danger accruing from such obstructions is not one to warrant the expenditure of such sums of money as would be necessary to institute a regular service, sufficient to insure their removal from regions of such enormous extent. The news of having sighted a derelict is often a week or more old before it is received by the authorities; a rescuing steamer can often not be on the spot for another week; the position given is in many cases not accurate; and in most parts of the sea the drift of the derelict is exceedingly uncertain. It is, therefore, a most difficult task for a vessel sent out to search for a derelict to find it; and the expense incurred by such expeditions may often be out of all proportion to the small chance of finding and removing one.

"The geographical apportionment of the waters of the oceans might, besides this, easily lead to the supposition that the limits so defined would circumscribe, moreover, the sphere of political interest of the respective governments.

"DERELICTS IN THE NORTH ATLANTIC.

" In the North Atlantic, particularly in that part of it bordering the North American coast, westward of a line drawn from the Bermuda Islands to Cape Race, Newfoundland, derelicts are so frequently met with that they must be considered a serious danger to navigation.

"As in these waters the vessels whose safety is imperiled by their existence are exceedingly numerous, the number of persons on board of them very large, and the value of these ships and their cargoes very great, and as, moreover, the chances for locating derelicts and for determining the direction of their drift are particularly favorable, the Conference propose that the various maritime powers should come to some agreement respecting their removal.

"In case this proposition should be entertained, it is submitted that the respective powers should also come to some understanding regarding the proprietary rights which may still exist, whether in the ship or in her cargo.

"Besides this, it seems desirable to point out that, amongst other matters that will necessarily have to be considered, it would be well to take steps to prevent the destruction of derelicts that might readily have been saved, and to make sure that, in case destruction has been decided upon, no evidence of crime should be destroyed also."

Upon this subject the Conference adopted the following resolution:

"6. That the different maritime powers interested in the navigation of that portion of the North Atlantic Ocean bordering the American coast and situated westward of a line drawn from the Bermuda Islands to Cape Race, Newfoundland, be invited to come to an agreement respecting the removal of derelicts in these waters under due official supervision.

"Regarding wrecks and derelicts in coast waters outside the territorial limits, the Conference submit that the duty of marking, and if necessary, of removing wrecks or such portions of them as obstruct navigation, has already been generally acknowledged by the governments whom it concerns, and therefore no further propositions have to be made in this regard.

"WRECKS AND DERELICTS IN COAST WATERS.

"It has, however, been brought to the notice of the Conference that governments who by treaty have acknowledged the exterritoriality of subjects of other powers and of their property, are sometimes very much hampered by the consideration of private interests in their action regarding the removal of wrecks, even when the value of the wreck and cargo is very small and there is scarcely a possibility that salvage operations can be successfully undertaken. The Conference are, therefore, of opinion that a resolution should be adopted to the following effect: That in such cases the consul or consuls concerned shall not have the right of withholding his or their consent to the destruction of a wreck or parts thereof, if it is shown that the wreck constitutes a danger to passing vessels, and if there is no apparent possibility that it will be removed within a reasonable time by the owners or by the insurance companies interested."

Upon this subject the Conference adopted the following resolution:

"7. That in countries which, by treaty, have acknowledged the exterritoriality of subjects of other powers and their property, the consul or consuls concerned shall be instructed not to withhold his or their consent to the destruction of a wreck or parts thereof, if it is shown that the wreck constitutes a danger to passing vessels, and if there is no apparent possibility that it will be removed within a reasonable time by the owners or the insurance companies interested.

"As to derelicts in coast waters there seems to be little doubt but that private enterprise, in order to secure salvage, will prove sufficient to remove any of them. For this reason it would seem to be unnecessary that any proposition should be made which would interfere with the established custom.

"There was, in the opinion of the Conference, some doubt regarding the meaning of the word "responsibility" used in this heading. They consider, however, that no government would acknowledge any responsibility for the waters under discussion which had not been made the subject of some formal agreement entered into after negotiations by the usual diplomatic methods.

"SEARCHING FOR DOUBTFUL DANGERS WITH A VIEW OF REMOVING THEM FROM THE CHART.

"The greater part of these dangers have been entered on the charts from the reports of single ships, and under the assumption that it is often better to do so rather than have the mariner entirely unwarned; though such reports may have appeared from the very first of doubtful accuracy. In order to make sure that these dangers do not exist, it has been conclusively shown by experience that it is not sufficient to sail across the alleged position, but that it is necessary at the same time to take extensive soundings to prove beyond a doubt that nowhere in the vicinity of the alleged danger anything but deep water is found, and that it is therefore justifiable to remove the danger from the chart. This has become the acknowledged custom of the different hydrographic offices.

"In order, therefore, to make such searches effectual, ships employed for this purpose should be fitted out with deep-sea sounding apparatus. Ordinary war vessels are not usually supplied with such means, but only surveying vessels or vessels fitted out for scientific exploration. Such vessels will, as a matter of course, receive from their respective governments instructions to search for dangers of this kind whenever they find them located in a position near which their special mission will take them. What is, however, most wanted at present are accurate surveys on coasts newly opened to trade and commercial enterprise, in order to detect dangers whose existence is entirely unsuspected. The number of these that are yearly discovered (ninety last year), many by the expensive process of losing a ship, proves incontestably how imperfect are the surveys of the world.

"To divert ships engaged in such surveying work, to scour the ocean in order to verify doubtful reports under international engagements, would be to practically stop the production of improved surveys. Under these circumstances the Conference can not recommend any action in the matter.

"If masters of vessels, when seeing indications of shallow water, would act in accordance with the resolution adopted by the Conference, instead of passing on their course without any examination, or even taking a cast of the lead, the number of these dangers reported as doubtful would be greatly lessened."

The United States delegates recommend the adoption of Resolutions 1, 2, 3, 4, and 5 relating to the duties of masters and mariners, and their enactment into law, and that they be printed for the instruction of such masters and mariners, with other navigation laws, in the official log-book.

It is recommended that correspondence be entered into with the maritime powers referred to, relative to carrying out the provisions of Resolution 6.

It is also earnestly recommended that a steam-vessel of about 800 tons displacement be built which shall be especially fitted for and adapted to the service of taking the ocean in bad weather for the purpose of blowing up or otherwise destroying wrecks and derelicts or bringing them into port. Such vessel to be built under the direction of and attached to the Navy Department, and that particular attention be paid to her strength and to the strength, size, and character of her boats, owing to the fact that the services of such vessel are required, principally, just after a storm, when the seas are still running high and when no ordinary boat could take the sea. Special design in the hull is required on account of being subject to rough weather and heavy seas, and on account of having frequently to tow vessels submerged. For this latter reason extra fittings for towing should be added.

It is recommended that the provisions of Resolution 7 be included in the instructions furnished the diplomatic representatives of the United States.

It is also recommended that a suitable vessel be built and especially fitted for the purpose of searching for *vigias* and other doubtful dangers with a view of removing them from the charts.

GENERAL DIVISION 11.
Notice of dangers to navigation.

NOTICE OF CHANGES IN LIGHTS, BUOYS, AND OTHER DAY AND NIGHT MARKS.

(a) A uniform method of taking bearings, of designating them (whether true or magnetic), and of reporting them.

(b) A uniform method of reporting, indicating, and exchanging information by the several maritime nations, to include the form of notices to mariners.

(c) A uniform method of distributing this information.

Under this general division the Conference approved of the following:

" All notices of changes in lights, beacons, buoys. and other day and night marks require not only to be brought to the notice of the public of that country in whose waters these changes have taken place, but also to all other maritime nations, so that the authorities may be enabled to impart information for the benefit of their own sea-faring population.

"This is usually done by publications to which the generic title of 'Notices to mariners' has been applied. They are either issued whenever occasion demands it, or at regular intervals, with an extra edition when necessary.

"They may further be divided into (a) those published by the department of naval affairs of the different countries, or under its direction by the hydrographer; (b) those published by the authorities, central, provincial, colonial, or local, in charge of the light-houses, beacons, and buoys.

The publications mentioned under (a) are intended for the use of the mariner only, and the Conference do not consider it advisable to insist on any change regarding form or arrangement of 'Notices to mariners.'

"What has been said regarding the publications mentioned under (a) is true, as well regarding those mentioned under (b). These 'Notices to mariners' are mainly intended for internal and local use in each country, and supply information not to mariners only, but to local officials, such as light-house keepers, inspectors of buoys, and others ; and, considering that they are published for very different objects, and to be used by men of very different classes and occupations, the Conference do not consider it feasible to insist upon uniformity in matters of detail."

(a) A uniform method of taking bearings, of designating them (whether true or magnetic) and of reporting them.

"*Taking bearings.*—In all countries, as far as we know, except Italy and Norway, the custom prevails that all bearings in 'Notices to mariners,' and in 'light lists,' in order to locate a danger or to determine the limits of a light-sector, are given from seaward, that is from the danger indicated toward the fixed objects by which its position is determined, or from the outer limit of visibility of a light towards the light-house.

"This mode of taking bearings has the advantage that it is in agreement with the mode in which they are used by the mariner, and the Conference recommend that the resolution in this behalf appended to the report be adopted with a view to this custom being made universal.

"The adoption of a uniform method of designating bearings, whether true or magnetic, offers the advantage that bearings given in the publications of any country can be transferred verbatim to similar publications issued in any other country without the necessity for any alteration or calculation. This is of importance in preparing publications the value of which depends in no small degree on the possibility of issuing them immediately after any changes have been made which require to be notified to mariners.

"All the evidence, however, which has been laid before the Conference, tends unmistakably to the conclusion that it would be inexpedient for any country suddenly to adopt a new system of designating bearings in the place of one which has been sanctioned by the custom of many years, and has become an essential part of the system of navigation generally adopted and taught in the nautical schools of the various countries.

" It has also to be borne in mind, that such a change concerns not only experts and scientific men, who can easily understand and adapt a new system to their requirements, but, in a vast majority of cases, it would affect seamen whose knowledge of matters regarding navigation is inseparably connected with the methods with which they have been familiar all their lives, and to whom any change of the kind indicated would be confusing and dangerous.

" For these reasons the Conference do not propose the adoption of a uniform method of designating bearings by giving them either true or magnetic.

" Uniformity might have been attained in another way, *i. e.*, by giving bearings both true and magnetic. It was shown, however, that the advantages of such a plan would be more than counterbalanced by a large increase in the bulk of the text, and by the possibility of errors amongst seafaring men unaccustomed to any but a single system, and who might mistake one set of bearings for another when read in a hurry.

" Having regard to these difficulties the Conference do not propose to advise any action in this matter in the direction of uniformity beyond recommending that in all ' Notices to Mariners ' and ' Light Lists ' intended for exchange with other nations, whenever true or magnetic bearings are given, the variation shall be inserted.

" It seems that in the majority of maritime nations the custom prevails that all bearings are given in degrees. This has the advantage that if the variation, which is always expressed in degrees, has to be applied in order that the bearings be entered on a chart, or when the variation has to be corrected for time elapsed since the date when it was determined, the result is more accurate than if the bearings were expressed in points.

" On the other hand, it has to be borne in mind that the ' Notices to Mariners ' and ' Light Lists,' which are most universally used, retain the custom of giving bearings in points and fractions thereof.

" After a full discussion of this large and intricate question, the Conference decided to adopt the following resolution :

" That the bearings for cuts of different colored sectors of lights, or of bearings of lights defining a narrow channel, should be expressed in degrees where practicable.

"*Counting the degrees.*—The custom adopted universally in geodesy is that of counting the degrees, from the north to the right (or with the sun) beginning with 0 to 360 degrees. In one country the steering compasses are also so marked ; and directions with reference to the course of the vessel are so expressed. This method offers certain advantages, but it is contrary to the custom of the large majority of mariners, and on this account the Conference propose that the number of degrees used in designating bearings should be counted from north and south to east and west, beginning with 0 and ending with 90 degrees.

" North and south are universally designated by the letters N and S. But east is in some countries designated by the letter O, and west in others also by the same letter—O. In order to make these designations uniform the Conference propose that all countries adopt, for use in the publications under consideration, the letter E to designate east and the letter W to designate west, in uniformity with the rules adopted already for publications of meteorological offices.

" *Designating distances.*—The Conference advise that:

" Distances should be expressed in nautical miles and fractions thereof.

" The word ' cable ' should mean the tenth part of a nautical mile."

(*b*)· *A uniform method of reporting, indicating, and exchanging information by the several maritime nations, to include the form of notices to
mariners.*

"REPORTING DANGERS TO NAVIGATION, CHANGE OF LIGHTS, ETC.

" Reports of dangers discovered should be made as promptly and
accurately as possibly, and should be addressed to the proper authorities. This has been pointed out already under General Division 10.

"INDICATING DANGERS, CHANGES OF LIGHTS, ETC.

" Several countries refer the longitude given in the publications under
consideration to a prime meridian, whose difference from the meridians
of Greenwich or Paris, on which most charts in use by mariners are
constructed, may be unknown to a sailor. In such a case, though he
may have become acquainted with the fact of the discovery of a danger,
the establishment of a light-house, etc., he may be unable to enter such
information with sufficient correctness on his chart.
" The Conference, therefore, propose that in all notices which refer
to any other prime meridian but that of Greenwich or of Paris, the difference in longitude between such meridians should be inserted.
" The visibility of a light is given in different ways. In some countries the number of miles given refer to the visibility of light in clear
weather or in ordinary weather; in others, the visibility refers to a
mean state of the atmosphere, *i. e.*, one which may be expected at that
particular locality in 50 cases out of 100. The Conference had not sufficient evidence before them to decide as to the advantages of the two
plans for general adoption; they, however, consider it desirable to
bring the subject before the Conference in order that the attention of
the different maritime powers should be called to it.
" In some 'Light Lists' the geographical range of a light is given, *i. e.*,
the distance resulting from the height of a light above high water, in
connection with the curvature of the earth, together with or without
the additional distance calculated for an observer supposed to be elevated above the sea at a certain height; in other 'Light Lists' the actual
visibility of a light is given without any regard to the height of the
light or the elevation of the observer; in some publications the lesser
of the two distances is given, and in other cases both together.
" Each of these methods offers some advantage, and it seems inexpedient, at the present moment, to propose uniformity in this respect.
" It appears advisable, however, to adopt a standard height for the
observer wherever the geographical range of a light is given in 'Light
Lists' or in 'Notices.'
" The Conference, therefore, propose that the height of 5 meters be
generally adopted in all countries where the metric system is in use,
and that in other countries, where this is not the case, the height taken
should be 15 feet of the measure of the country. This height seems to
the Conference the best suited to the present requirements of navigation. The difference between these measures is of no practical importance.
" The lights of light-houses are classified at present in 'Orders,' according to the size of the lantern or, if dioptric, according to the diameter of the apparatus, though, in this respect, there exists considerable
difference.

" Since the introduction of the electric lights this classification has become inaccurate, and, from a seaman's point of view, misleading, for under its rules a third order electric light generally is much more powerful than a first order oil or gas light. Uniformity in this respect is desirable, and the Conference, therefore, propose that the several maritime powers interested should be requested to consider the question in order to establish, if possible, a uniform classification of lights on the basis of the power of the light as seen by the mariner. At the same time it would be desirable to bring about a uniform classification as regards their character.

" EXCHANGING INFORMATION BY THE SEVERAL MARITIME NATIONS.

" It has become the custom for the hydrographic offices of the different maritime countries, with few exceptions, to ask for any information regarding their publications (' Notices to Mariners,' ' Light Lists,' ' Charts,' ' Sailing Directions,') by direct application to the hydrographic offices of other countries, and to give such information in the same way.

" It is not easy to see how this information could be so speedily and conveniently given in any other way. But the Conference are not aware that this usage has ever been sanctioned by the proper authorities. They have on this account thought it well to call the attention of the Governments to this fact, and they submit that permission to exchange information regarding these publications direct, without the intervention of the foreign offices, should be granted to all central hydrographic offices in the home countries as well as those in the provinces, colonies, and dominions, and also to those central offices which administer the lighthouses, beacons, and buoys of a country, and which publish such information.

" Some maritime powers are without any special hydrographic department. In such cases it would be well to designate some other office, for instance that of harbor master of their principal ports, who could be addressed if occasion occurs.

" In some countries the ' Notices to Mariners ' are published only in newspapers. It would be well if such notices were sent to the different hydrographic offices of the world.

" Contemplated changes in lights and buoys should be brought to public notice, if convenient, before the date on which such change is proposed to be made.

" The information contained in ' Notices to Mariners ' is now brought to the knowledge of the sea-faring population by sending copies of the same to the different shipping offices and consulates, and to captains of the navy, and to masters of the merchant fleet. The Conference have no evidence before them which points to the fact that the measures taken by each country do not fully satisfy the requirements of those interested.

" The Conference invite the several maritime powers to consider the following resolutions with a view to establishing uniformity in the subjects treated in ' Notices to Mariners ' and ' Light Lists ':

" 1. That all bearings should be given from seaward.

" 2. That the bearings of cuts of different colored sectors of lights or bearings of lights defining a narrow channel should be expressed in degrees where practicable.

" 3. That all bearings expressed in degrees should count from north and south, from 0° to 90° towards east and west.

"4. That in designating bearings the letter E shall designate east, and the letter W shall designate west.

"5. That whenever bearings are given the variation of the compass at the place should be stated.

"6. That distances should be expressed in nautical miles and fractions thereof. The word 'cable' should mean the tenth part of a nautical mile.

"7. That whenever the longitude of a position is given it should be stated which prime meridian is adopted, and if other than that of Greenwich or Paris, the difference of longitude should also be stated.

"8. That in defining the visibility of a light it should be stated whether the distance is for 'clear' or 'mean' state of the weather.

"9. That where the geographical range of a light is given it should be calculated as seen at high water from an observer 15 feet or 5 meters above the sea.

"10. That a uniform classification of lights based on luminous intensity and on the character as seen by the mariner should be adopted.

"11. That the central offices that issue 'Notices to Mariners' or 'Light Lists' should be permitted to correspond direct on such subjects.

"12. That from countries where 'Notices to Mariners' are published only in newspapers copies of such papers should be sent to the various hydrographic offices."

The United States delegates recommend the adoption of these resolutions, and that proper measures be taken to put into effect such as are not now in use or in force.

GENERAL DIVISION 12.

A uniform system of buoys and beacons.

(a) Uniformity in color of buoys.
(b) Uniformity in numbering of buoys.

Under this general division the Conference approved of the following:

"Owing to the absence of a uniformity in buoyage, mariners, up to very recent times, seldom attempted to navigate a district by means of the buoyage unless they were specially well acquainted with the local system. But now that a certain degree of uniformity on a fundamental basis prevails, mariners in general are more induced to navigate their vessel, trusting to the chart of the district; it therefore becomes of greater importance that such uniformity should be extended as far as possible.

"Two principal characters are used for distinguishing buoys and beacons, color and shape.

"The first object to be attained, from an international point of view, is uniformity. For that purpose color is the best means, as applying to all systems of whatever kind, while the shape admits numerous exceptions. The color is also applicable in all countries and with little expense, whereas the immediate adoption of shape would involve changes of several existing systems. Moreover, experience has proved that very many, if not the majority of channels, are now buoyed with sufficient distinctness without resorting to difference of form.

" For these reasons, and while the opinion prevails that at night and in thick weather difference in form is a better means of distinction than difference of color the Conference advise that uniformity in color should be adopted as a general rule, and that the use of shape should remain optional.

" While, in the opinion of some members, the single colors of black and red are not so distinctive in contrast as a single color used in connection with a party-color, experience, gained in many buoyage districts, and particularly where used in conjunction with form, has proved that these dark colors are sufficiently distinctive for the safe navigation of districts where a more complicated system is not necessary. Single-colored buoys are also more readily and cheaply repainted than party-colored buoys. We therefore recommend that the largely used red and black colors should be adopted generally for marking, respectively, the starboard and port sides of single channels.

" Many districts, however, require a more complicated system of buoyage to identify the several neighboring channels one from the other, such as the entrances of rivers with numerous channels like the Thames, the outlying shoals off the coast of the North Sea, the numerous shoals separated from each other by complicated channels such as in the Baltic Sea, etc.

" In some of such districts a party-colored buoy is used with much advantage as a port-hand buoy. In a few—notably in England—a single black color is used as a starboard-hand buoy. Inasmuch as a single black color is in general use as a port-hand buoy in neighboring districts visited by the same shipping, we suggest that the authorities of such countries should be invited to consider the great general advantages to shipping that would result from the adoption of uniformity in color by discontinuing this dangerous custom of using a black color to denote a starboard-hand as well as a port-hand buoy.

" In some countries white is used as a distinctive color, and with advantage when contrasted with a dark background. As this practice can not lead vessels into danger we hesitate to advise that it should be compulsorily interfered with.

" We are of opinion that where form is adopted the two shapes 'Conical' (Nun) and ' Can ' are appropriate for marking the starboard and port sides of a channel, a spar-buoy taking the place of the can in certain cases.

" These forms are practically used in the United States, Germany, Canada, India, and Great Britain. But the various countries are not all in agreement as to which side of the channel is to be marked by a conical buoy and which by a can or spar-buoy.

" It follows that one or more of the countries would necessarily have to re-arrange their system, but, if the work were done gradually, the Conference believe that this could be performed at a minimum of expense in no way comparable with the great advantage that would result to navigation.

" In connection with such a change of system we are informed that an extensive re-arrangement in buoyage was recently carried out by Great Britain, the different shapes being changed from one side of the channels to the other side, the change being brought about without any casualty to navigation.

" As regards top-marks, we recommend that those countries whose buoyage is based on color alone should, whenever top-marks are used to denote sides of a channel, use conical or can-shaped marks on the existing buoys or beacons.

" We are of opinion that the mode of distinguishing buoys from each other by names, numbers, or letters should be left to the decision of the various countries, but that all numbers and letters should be in consecutive order, commencing at the seaward end of the district.

"The Conference are of opinion that districts where the buoyage is so complicated as to have led the authorities to adopt a compass system of marking, such as in the Baltic Sea, can not, with a view to general uniformity, be coupled with the simpler systems found sufficient elsewhere; they therefore hesitate to recommend a fundamental change in such districts. But, after studying the 'Sailing Directions,' and the publication of Mr. S. A. Philipsen, Copenhagen, on 'Beaconage and Buoyage of Different Nations,' which presents graphically the plans adopted by several nations, particularly those interested in the navigation of the Baltic seas, the Conference find that the systems now in use, so far as color and top-marks are concerned, are so similar that they suggest to the countries interested the desirability of the adoption of one uniform system, at least as regards color.

"The Conference understand that the following are the colors and top-marks at present in use in the various districts using the compass system to define the bearing of the mark or buoy from the danger it indicates:

Marks on the *north* side of a shoal—

    Norway.... } ..Black.
    Sweden.... }
    Russia..... }
    Finland ... } ..White.
    Denmark... }

Marks on the *south* side of a shoal—

    Norway........White.
    Sweden.... }
    Russia..... }
    Finland.... } ..Red.
    Denmark... }

Marks on the *east* side of a shoal—

    Norway........Black.
    Sweden........Black, with a white horizontal band.
    Russia..... ...Red with white horizontal bands.
    Finland........Half red and half white horizontal.
    Denmark ......Red.

Marks on the *west* side of a shoal—

    Norway.... } ..White.
    Denmark .. }
    Russia.........White and black horizontal bands.
    Finland........Half white and half red horizontal.
    Sweden........Red.

Marks on a *middle ground*, with fair-way channels on either side—

    Norway........Black and white horizontal bands.
    Finland ... } ..Red and white horizontal bards.
    Denmark .. }
    Russia.........Black.

Top-marks.

On buoys or marks on the *north* side of a shoal—
Norway........Brooms turned downwards.
Russia.........Broom or brooms not systematically arranged.
Finland ....A pole without a top-mark.
Sweden........A ball.

On buoys or marks on the *south* side of a shoal—
Russia ....⎫
Finland ...⎬ ..Broom turned upwards.
Norway ...⎪
Sweden....⎭

On buoys or marks on the *east* side of a shoal—
Norway ....Broom turned downwards.
Finland ....A pole without a top-mark.
Sweden.. .....A ball.
Russia.........Two brooms . { upper one turned upwards.
lower one turned downwards.

On buoys or marks on the *west* side of a shoal—
Norway........Broom turned upwards.
Sweden....⎫ ..Broom turned downwards.
Finland ...⎭
Russia ....Two brooms. { upper one turned downwards.
lower one turned upwards.

On marks on a *middle ground* with fair-way channels on either side—
Norway...⎫ ..A ball
Russia.....⎭
Finland........A cross.

"Owing to the difficulty in choosing a fourth single color, green being universally used to denote a wreck, it practically became necessary, in arranging for a general system, if four distinct modes of coloring are adopted to mark the four cardinal bearings of or from a shoal, to resort to one or more party-colors to be used in conjunction with red, black, and white.

"On the principle of using four colors to mark the four sides of a shoal, the Conference put forward the following scheme, based on the least change that would be necessary in altering the present systems to a uniform plan; and they bring it to the notice of the countries interested, as an example showing that uniformity is attainable if they will agree to consider the subject:

" All shoals, marked on the compass system, to be marked—
" On the *north* side by a single black or white color.
" *South* side by red.
" *East* side by half red and half white combined.
" *West* side by half white and half black combined.

" On rocks in fair-way, with channels on either hand, to be marked black or red, with horizontal bands.

" If such colors were adopted, then the following changes of color would be necessary:

" The marks on the *north* side of a shoal would remain colored black or white as they now are in all countries using the compass system.

" The marks on the *south* side of a shoal would in—
" Norway, have to be changed from white to red.

" The marks on the *east* side of a shoal would in—

" Norway, have to be changed from black to half red and half white.

" Sweden, have to be changed from black and white to half red and half white.

" Denmark, have to be changed from red to half red and half white.

" The marks on the *west* side of a shoal would in—

" Norway .. } have to be changed from white to half white and half
" Denmark. } black.

" Sweden, have to be changed from red to half white and half black.

" Finland, have to be changed from white and red to half white and half black.

" The marks on a rock in Fair-way, with channel on either side, if a white horizontal band is generally adopted, would in Russia have to be changed from black to black or red with white horizontal bands, in agreement with the other countries.

" The Conference invite the various powers interested to consider the following general principles, which they put forward as a basis on which to build up a uniform international buoyage system for districts other than those where the compass system is in use.

" The term starboard-hand shall denote that side of a navigable channel which is on the right hand of the mariner entering from sea-ward ;. the term port-hand shall denote that side which is on the left hand under the same circumstances.

" *Color.*—Buoys defining the starboard-hand shall be painted a single red color. Buoys defining the port-hand shall be painted a single black color, or a party-color. Buoys defining middle grounds shall be painted with horizontal bands.

" *Form.*—Wherever form is used as a distinctive character, buoys defining the starboard-hand shall be conical, and those defining the port-hand shall be can or spar.

" *Top marks.*—Countries where form is not used as a distinctive character for buoys, may adopt, as another distinctive feature for the buoys on either side of a channel, top-marks resembling a cone to be used on the starboard side, or a cylinder on the port side of a channel.

" *Numbers and letters.*—Numbers, letters, and names may be painted on the buoys, but they must never be so large as to interfere with their distinctive coloring.

" Wherever numbers and letters are used they shall be in consecutive order, commencing from seaward.

" *Buoying and marking of wrecks.*—(a) All buoys and the top-sides of vessels used for the marking of wrecks shall be painted green with a suitable white inscription. (b) Where it is practicable, by day one ball shall be exhibited on the side of the vessel nearest the wreck and two placed vertically on the other side; three fixed white lights similarly arranged, but not the ordinary riding light, shall be shown from sun-set to sunrise."

The United States delegates agree with the findings of the Conference with reference to this division, and call attention to the recommendations of the Conference in regard to the principles submitted as a basis on which to build up a uniform international system of buoyage.

GENERAL DIVISION 13.

The establishment of a permanent international maritime commission.

(a) The composition of the commission.

(b) Its powers and authority.

Under this general division the Conference adopted the following:

"The delegates and secretaries of the Conference, were, at the commencement of our proceedings, invited to furnish the proposals, if any, prepared by governments of the several powers taking part in the Conference, or of any private societies or persons, bearing upon the subject in question.

"We have considered whether such a commission could be instituted with a practical result, and in such a manner as to lead to its adoption by the maritime powers.

"However desirable such a result would be, a majority of the Conference do not believe it to be possible to carry it into effect, and are of opinion that it can not be regarded as one of practical feasibility at the present time.

"We have also decided, by a majority of votes, that it is not possible to create an international tribunal to try questions of collisions between subjects of different nationalities.

"In coming to this conclusion we have been guided amongst others by the following considerations:

"An international commission could not be invested with any legislative power. It would be a consulting body only, constituted with the view of preparing universal legislation on maritime matters of international importance. Apart altogether from the difficulties connected with the formation of such a body, the questions as to its domicile, as to who are to be its members, and how and by whom the members are to be compensated for their labors—difficulties which by themselves seem to be entirely unsurmountable for the present—it seems to the Conference that such a consulting body of experts would not serve the purpose for which it is intended to be created, viz, that of facilitating the introduction of reforms in maritime legislation, because the advice given by such a commission would not in any way enable the governments of the maritime nations to dispense with the necessity of considering the subjects laid before them and laying the proposals made to them, if adopted, before the legislative bodies of the different States.

"The consequence of instituting a body like that in question on the contrary would, it appears, be this: that merely another investigation of any scheme proposed with a view to reforming international maritime laws would have to be gone through before the opinions of the governments could be taken, and thus the course of procedure as it is now—by correspondence between the different governments—would be made more complicated instead of being simplified. For these reasons the Conference resolve:

"That for the present the establishment of a permanent international maritime commission is not considered expedient."

The United States delegates agree with the conclusion reached by the Conference.

Under this division the Conference also discussed the following resolution:

"*Resolved*, That the Conference recommend that the advisability of a bureau of maritime information should be considered by the governments of the maritime nations."

The functions proposed for this bureau were to consider and recommend to the various powers for experiment all apparatus and appliances for marine use, such as life-saving appliances, systems of running lights, sound-signals in thick weather, etc.; to collect information regarding maritime matters; to publish the same annually, and to prepare all requisite data for the use of any future Conference that might be called together for the consideration of maritime affairs. This subject was debated at length, and after consideration during an entire day and one session of another day, it was decided not to recommend the establishment of such a bureau by a vote of 12 to 7, viz:

Yeas—Denmark, Hawaii, Japan, Netherlands, Norway, Siam, and United States.

Nays—Austria-Hungary, Belgium, Brazil, Chili, China, Costa Rica, Germany, Great Britain, Honduras, Italy, Russia, and Sweden.

France and Spain did not vote, though present.

It will be seen from this vote that the establishment of such an international bureau is impracticable owing to the non-support of most of the great powers, they having already bureaus of this nature, somewhat similar to the Board of Trade of Great Britain.

In order to provide for the discharge of such functions in this country, and to accomplish other important objects hereinafter stated, the United States delegates recommend that immediate steps be taken for the establishment, with headquarters at Washington, D. C., of a board to have charge and general superintendence of matters relating to merchant vessels and seamen, and that said board be authorized to carry into execution the provisions of all laws relating to merchant vessels and seamen, and merchant shipping generally, that are now in operation or that may be hereafter enacted, other than such as relate to the revenue; said board to be under the Treasury

Department, and composed of the Supervising Inspector-General of Steam-Vessels, the Commissioner of Navigation, the Surgeon-General of the Marine Hospital Service, the General Superintendent of the Life-Saving Service, two officers detailed from the line of the Navy, five experts in matters pertaining to the merchant marine, and an admiralty lawyer—the Secretary of the Treasury to be *ex officio* president of the board, and the chairman of the Committee on Commerce of the Senate and the chairman of the Committee on Merchant Marine and Fisheries of the House of Representatives to be *ex officio* members.

The American delegates are constrained to make this recommendation for the following reasons:

1. The absence of proper laws requiring governmental supervision of the great maritime interests represented in the sailing fleet of the country. While the laws regarding the Government inspection of steam-vessels may be assumed to insure upon them the necessary security of life and property at sea so far as the strength of the vessels, proper equipment, etc., are concerned, no such provisions exist by law with regard to sailing vessels. A totally unseaworthy sailing vessel may put to sea at the risk of all lives and property on board; furthermore, she may be overladen and utterly deficient in the necessary equipment for the safety of her crew and passengers in case of accident, such as boats, life-rafts, life-preservers, pumps, etc., or fire-extinguishing apparatus.

There is, moreover, no legal requirement as to the qualifications of officers of sailing vessels, and no certificate of qualification is required by law of such officers. If the owners or insurers do not require some evidence of competency, any man may obtain command of a sailing vessel, however unfit he may be for the position.

This condition of things exists notwithstanding the fact that the number of sailing vessels belonging to the United States is nearly three times as great as the number of steamers, and the tonnage of sailing craft exceeds that of steamers by more than 300,000 tons. The number of casualties occurring to sailing vessels during the year 1888—the last for which statistics of disasters have been reported—was twice as great as those occurring to steamers, and the number of lives lost on board sailing vessels was three times as many as those lost on board steamers, although the great majority of passengers are carried on board steamers.

2. The delegates are of the opinion that the methods now pursued for ascertaining the qualifications of officers of steam-vessels can be improved, and a higher standard of competency thus secured.

3. Upon many of the important points submitted to the Conference for consideration no international agreement was reached, and this was in many instances due to the fact that the more important maritime nations were already provided with satisfactory laws and rules upon these points; and while there is considerable diversity in these rules among the different nations, no nation was willing to abandon a satisfactory system for the sole purpose of securing uniformity. Principal among these points were the questions of construction and equipment of vessels, qualifications of officers of vessels, and those relating to buoyage—matters in regard to which, except as to buoyage, the United States are far behind other powers. It was the judgment of the Conference that the desired end in each case would be best attained by the independent action of each nation.

It is, therefore, the opinion of the United States delegates that the maritime interests of the country could be best subserved and life and property at sea best protected, by combining in one board as above recommended the several bureaus now charged with the execution of duties relating to the maritime affairs, to which should be added experts selected from the important commercial sections of the country. This would secure unity of action and efficient results in the most economical manner and without loss of energy resulting from separate effort by different bureaus upon the same matters, or the total neglect of other important ones, not now assigned to any special charge. The duties required of these several officers under existing laws could still be administered by them and their present corps of assistants, while the different sections of the country interested would be properly represented.

The United States delegates would further respectfully suggest in submitting this report that the large and growing interests of our merchant marine render it desirable that they should be looked after by a separate department of the Government. The administration of the laws regarding the commerce of the nation, afloat and ashore, and the development of other legislation already demanded, together with that which the growing importance of our national commerce will soon render necessary, will require the best energies of a separate department, of which the board above recommended would constitute an important part.

It is also recommended that Congress appropriate $5,000, to be expended in making exhaustive experiments with fog-signal apparatus, side lights, and mast-head lights similar to those now manufactured and sold in this country, and used on board of the different classes of United States merchant vessels, for the purpose of ascertaining the distance at which such lights can be seen and still retain their distinctive colors under different conditions and circumstances at different angles of heel, and as seen from different parts of the sector of visibility, these experiments to be made by a board of five naval officers, with suitable assistants, and carried out over a measured range with the lights level and heeled, and with the lamps burning for a period of ten hours, with observations taken and tabulated for each hour; and that the Secretary of the Navy be empowered to designate such a board, draw up instructions for their guidance, and have the experiments undertaken. The object is to ascertain just how far the mast-head and side-lights of steamers, and the side lights of ships, schooners, fishing-vessels, and other craft, actually in use in this country, can be seen under different conditions of the atmosphere, and when viewed from the different portions of the arcs over which the lights are required to show.

Similar experiments should be made by the same board as to the distance fog-horns, whistles, and bells, used on the above-mentioned craft, can be heard over clear space, with no obstructions intervening.

This board should be empowered and directed to examine any and all improved patterns of lamps, lanterns, and fog-signal apparatus for use on board ships, which are brought to their notice before a certain date, to be set by the Secretary of the Treasury, and, if such be deemed more serviceable than the articles now in use for similar purposes, they be experimented with, and their range of visibility or audibility, as required above, be ascertained and reported upon.

All of which is respectfully submitted.

S. R. FRANKLIN,

Rear-Admiral, U. S. Navy, President,

W. T. SAMPSON,

Captain, U. S. Navy.

S. I. KIMBALL,

General Superintendent Life-Saving Serice.

JAS. W. NORCROSS,

Master Mariner.

JOHN W. SHACKFORD,

Master Mariner.

WILLIAM W. GOODRICH,

Counsellor at Law.

CLEMENT A. GRISCOM,

President International Navigation Company,

Delegates.

V. L. COTTMAN,

Lieutenant U. S. Navy,

Secretary.

INDEX.